THE COMPLETE ILLUSTRATED ENCYCLOPEDIA OF

# ANIMALS
## OF THE WORLD

# THE COMPLETE ILLUSTRATED ENCYCLOPEDIA OF
# ANIMALS
## OF THE WORLD

### AN EXPERT REFERENCE GUIDE TO 840 AMPHIBIANS, REPTILES AND MAMMALS FROM EVERY CONTINENT

**TOM JACKSON • CONSULTANT: MICHAEL CHINERY**

HERMES
HOUSE

**Publisher:** Joanna Lorenz
**Senior Editor:** Felicity Forster
**Illustrators:** Peter Barrett, Jim Channell,
Julius Csotonyi, Rob Dyke, John Francis,
Rob Highton, Stuart Jackson-Carter,
Paul Jones, Martin Knowelden, Stephen Lings,
The Magic Group, Shane Marsh, Robert
Morton, Richard Orr, Fiona Osbaldstone, Mike
Saunders, Sarah Smith and Ildikó Szegszárdy
**Maps:** Anthony Duke
**Copy Editors:** Alison Bolus, Gerard Cheshire,
Jen Green, Richard Rosenfeld and Steve Setford
**Designer:** Nigel Partridge
**Production Controller:** Pirong Wang

ISBN: 978-1-4351-1837-9

Manufactured in China

4 6 8 10 9 7 5 3

PAGE 1: *Tiger.*
PAGE 2: *Kudu.*
PAGE 3: *Brown bear.*

# CONTENTS

hellbender, greater siren, mudpuppy, three-toed amphiuma, tiger salamander, axolotl,
red-spotted newt, ringed caecilian, California newt, Amazon climbing salamander,
arboreal salamander, black salamander, dusky salamander, seal salamander, ensatina,
long-tailed salamander, slimy salamander, mud salamander, California tiger salamander,
blue-spotted salamander, small-mouthed salamander, marbled salamander, ringed
salamander, Pacific giant salamander

### Frogs and toads 84

Surinam toad, Darwin's frog, South American bullfrog,
four-eyed frog, marine toad, red-eyed tree frog,
strawberry poison-dart frog, paradoxical frog, tailed
frog, golden toad, American toad, crested forest
toad, North American bullfrog, Mexican burrowing
toad, eastern spadefoot toad, Couch's spadefoot toad,
crawfish frog, green frog, red-legged frog, pig frog, eastern
narrow-mouthed toad, Johnson's casque-headed treefrog, northern cricket frog, striped
chorus frog, Pacific treefrog, green treefrog, bird-voiced treefrog, gladiator treefrog

### Turtles and tortoises 98

matamata, alligator snapping turtle, Galápagos tortoise, stinkpot, snapping turtle,
Central American river turtle, painted turtle, wood turtle, giant river turtle, bog turtle,
Blanding's turtle, common map turtle, diamondback terrapin, eastern box turtle,
flattened musk turtle, gopher tortoise

### Lizards 106

rhinoceros iguana, gila monster, green basilisk, green anole, desert horned lizard,
chuckwalla, black and white tegu, ajolote, marine iguana, knight anole, green iguana,
ctenosaur, collared lizard, greater earless lizard, keel-scaled earless lizard, Florida scrub
lizard, eastern fence lizard, leopard lizard, diving lizard, bridled forest gecko, western
banded gecko, Texas banded gecko, tropical house gecko, Mexican beaded lizard,
five-lined skink, black-spotted skink, six-lined racerunner, Sonoran spotted whiptail,
golden tegu, northern caiman lizard, southern alligator lizard, large-scaled forest lizard

### Crocodilians 122

American alligator, black caiman, spectacled caiman, American crocodile,
dwarf caiman, Schneider's dwarf caiman, Cuban crocodile, Morelet's crocodile

# INTRODUCTION

Animals populate every corner of the globe and can be found in an extraordinary array of shapes, sizes and colours; correspondingly, the subject of zoology is absolutely vast. This book concentrates on amphibians, reptiles and mammals, with a discussion about the diversity of life followed by three directories of animal species from around the world.

The book opens with the question, "What is an animal?" From very simple animals such as jellyfish and corals through to complex creatures such as birds and mammals, the first part of the book shows how animal bodies are organized, how they have evolved over time, and how their current forms survive and reproduce. We focus on amphibians, reptiles, placental mammals, monotremes and marsupials, as well as providing information about migration and hibernation, introduced and endangered species, and how ecologists conserve wildlife. Next, we look at the principal habitats, or biomes, in which animals live – oceans, fresh water, tropical forests, temperate forests, boreal forests, grasslands, polar regions, deserts, islands, mountains and human settlements – and how animals are able to survive in such varied environments.

*Above: Islands around the world are home to some of the most unusual animals in nature. For example, lemurs are found only in Madagascar. These animals live in the island's forests. Similar forests elsewhere in the world are populated by monkeys, not lemurs.*

*Below: Snakes are a large group of legless reptiles. Most, like this emerald boa, live in hotter parts of the world, such as rainforests. Many snakes have a venomous bite, while others squeeze the breath out of their prey with their muscular, coiled bodies.*

The three directories take us on a journey across the globe, sampling the many animals that populate every region – first covering the Americas, then Europe and Africa, and finally Asia, Australia and New Zealand. Animals are displayed in related groups, beginning with amphibians such as salamanders, frogs and toads, then reptiles such as tortoises, lizards and crocodiles, and finally mammals such as big cats, hoofed animals and apes.

In South America, the shallow waters of swamps and stream banks are home to the green anaconda. Away from the swamps in the dense jungle, one may encounter the world's largest otter basking by a stream, and the capybara, the biggest rodent, feeding close by. In North America, we look at the brown bear,

*Above: Not all mammals are furry and four-legged. Although dolphins have a few bristly hairs and are related to the land mammals, they never leave the water. Like whales and other sea mammals, a dolphin's limbs look more like a fish's fins than the legs of a land animal.*

*Above: Amphibians, such as this African bullfrog, were the first land animals. They have kept their close links to water, where their ancestors originated. Therefore amphibians are most common in damp places, such as riverbanks, where they can easily keep their bodies moist.*

the largest predator on land, and also a variety of rattlesnakes, armadillos and some tiny snakes that live underground. On the opposite side of the Atlantic Ocean, Africa is home to great beasts such as the rhinoceros and lion, and Europe has a number of rare species such as the chamois and European bison. The Asian continent is renowned for its wild horses and the majestic tiger, while Australia is home to many unusual species – especially marsupials such as the koala, Tasmanian devil and red kangaroo.

Each geographical section of the book is prefaced by an introduction to the ecology and habitats of the region, and the characteristics of its animals. Throughout the directories, there are fact boxes containing distribution maps and summarized information about each animal's habitat, food, size, maturity, breeding, lifespan and conservation status, as well as lists of related animals and their main characteristics and behaviour. Last but not least, a glossary at the back of the book explains key terms.

*Below: Cheetahs live in the open grasslands of Africa. They are the fastest-running animals on Earth and can accelerate as quickly as any sports car. These big cats use their speed to chase down nimble, dodging prey, such as the antelopes that graze on the plains.*

*Below: African elephants are the largest land animals in the world, weighing up to 7.5 tonnes (16,500lb) and living for 70 years. Their trunk functions as a nose, hand, extra foot and signalling device, as well as being a tool for gathering food, siphoning water and digging.*

# UNDERSTANDING ANIMALS

Animals can be defined in terms of their body organization, their place in evolution and their anatomy and key features, and this first part of the book examines how they see, hear, smell and taste, how they find food, how they defend their territories, and how they find mates and care for their offspring. It then examines amphibians, reptiles and placental mammals, describing and illustrating each type's body features and some of their behaviours. There are also discussions about ecology, migration and hibernation, introduced species, endangered species and conserving wildlife. The section then looks at the world's principal life zones or biomes – oceans, fresh water, tropical forests, temperate forests, boreal forests, grasslands, polar regions, deserts, islands and mountains – and how animals have adapted to life there. For example, desert-dwelling animals are frequently only active at night when temperatures are cooler, and many of them do not need to drink liquid because they get all the moisture they need from plants. In contrast, animals from mountainous regions are often specially adapted for climbing and surviving windswept conditions, with sturdy legs and dense coats. The section concludes with an examination of the fastest growing habitat in the world – human settlements – with examples of the opportunistic animals that have learned to thrive in our cities.

*Left: A young zebra and its mother take a drink at a watering hole in eastern Africa. Behind them a family of elephants plods past as they, too, head for the water. Some animals get all the moisture they need to survive from their food, but most need to drink water, so in dryish regions watering holes are often crowded with wildlife.*

# WHAT IS AN ANIMAL?

*More than two million animal species have been described by scientists, and there are probably millions more waiting to be discovered. They live in all corners of the world, and come in a huge range of shapes and sizes. The largest weighs over a hundred tonnes, while the smallest is just a fraction of a millimetre long.*

## Active feeders

The living world is divided into five kingdoms: animals, plants, fungi, protists and monerans, which include bacteria. The protists and monerans are micro-organisms. Each individual is just a single cell, and although they often form large masses or colonies – for example, yoghurt is actually a colony of bacteria – the micro-organisms do not form bodies. The plants, fungi and animals do grow bodies, which are made from millions of cells, all of which work together. These three types of macro-organism, as they are called, tackle the problems of life in different ways.

Plants are the basis of life on Earth, and without them animals would not exist. This is because plants get the energy they need from sunlight (because they do not have to feed actively they are called autotrophes, meaning self-feeders). The green pigments in the plants' leaves trap the energy found in light and convert carbon dioxide and water into glucose, a simple sugar, in a process of food production called photosynthesis. Its by-product is oxygen, which gradually drifts into the atmosphere.

*Below: Anemones are members of the group of cnidarians, like jellyfish. Starfish belong to the group of echinoderms.*

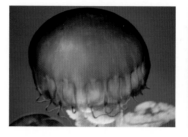

*Above: Jellyfish are very simple animals, related to corals and sea anemones. They catch food by spearing prey with tiny cells called nematocysts.*

*Above: Snails belong to a large group of invertebrates called molluscs. Most live in water, but many snails, such as this giant land snail, survive on land.*

*Above: Crabs, such as this hermit crab, are crustaceans. Other crustaceans include lobsters, prawns and krill. Their forelegs are armed with strong pincers.*

*Above: Spiders, scorpions and mites are arachnids. Many spiders build a sticky silk web to trap prey; others lie hidden and pounce on passing victims.*

Fungi are largely invisible organisms that live in large masses of tiny fibres which run through the soil. They only pop up above the surface in the form of mushrooms and toadstools when they are ready to reproduce. Fungi do not photosynthesize, but they are valuable as decomposers. They grow over the dead bodies of other organisms, such as trees which have fallen to the ground, secreting digestive enzymes that break down the dead body from the outside. They thereby release valuable carbon, nitrogen, phosphorus and other elements which each tree locks up in itself over its lifetime.

Animals, on the other hand, could not be more different. They are active feeders (called heterotrophes or "other-eaters") which collect food from their surroundings. Unlike plants and fungi, animals have bodies that can swim, walk, burrow or fly during at least the early part of their lives.

## Body organization

With the exception of primitive forms, such as sponges, all animal bodies are organized along the same the lines. They process their food in a gut, a tube which passes through the body. In most cases the food enters the gut through an opening in the head, that is, the mouth. Once inside the body, the food is broken down into its constituent parts. The useful parts, such as proteins, fats and sugars – made by plants during photosynthesis – are absorbed into the body. The left-over waste material passes out of the gut through the anus, a hole at the other end of the body.

The useful substances absorbed from the food then need to be transported around the body to where they are needed. This job is done by the animal's circulatory system. The insides of many animals are simply bathed in a liquid containing everything required by the body. However, larger animals, including reptiles, amphibians and mammals, need to pump the useful substances around the body in the blood. The pump is the heart, a strong muscle that keeps the blood circulating through a system of vessels.

The blood carries food for the body and also oxygen, which reacts with the sugar from the food, releasing the energy that is essential for all living things to survive. Animals get their oxygen in a number of ways. Some simply absorb it through their skin, many that live in water extract it using gills, and those that live in air breathe it into their lungs.

Compared with other organisms, animals are more aware of their surroundings and certainly more responsive to them. This is because they have a nervous system which uses sensors to detect what is happening in their

*Left: Apart from bats, birds, such as this bee-eater, are the only flying vertebrates. Their forelimbs have evolved into wings that allow them to perform amazing feats of flight. Feathers are better than hair for keeping the body streamlined for flight.*

environment, such as changes in temperature, the amount of light and various sounds. This information is then transmitted by means of nerves to what could be called the central control. This might just be a dense cluster of nerves, of which the animal might possess several, or it may be a single controlling brain. The brain or nerve cluster then passes the information from the senses to the muscles so that the body can respond appropriately, for example either by running away to avoid being eaten or by attacking its prey.

Mammals, reptiles and amphibians share a similar body plan, having four limbs. They are members of the larger group of tetrapods, to which birds also belong. Almost all possess a visible tail. The brain and most of the sensors are positioned at the front of the body in the head. The vital organs, such as the heart and lungs (or gills), are located in the central thorax (chest area), while the gut and sex organs are found mainly in the abdomen at the rear of the body.

*Above: Fish live in all corners of the world's oceans. They also live in fresh water, where they are found everywhere from submerged caves to mountain lakes.*

*Above: Frogs are the most familiar of the amphibians. Others include salamanders and newts. This frog spends its life in trees, using suckers on its feet to cling to the branches.*

*Above: While a few other lizards can alter the shade of their scales slightly, chameleons can change colour completely. This may help them hide from predators or it may reflect their mood.*

*Above: Mammals, such as this ground squirrel, are the most widespread of vertebrates. They can survive in just about any habitat on Earth.*

# EVOLUTION

*Animals and other forms of life did not just suddenly appear on the Earth. They evolved over billions of years into countless different forms. The mechanism by which they evolved is called natural selection. The process of natural selection was first proposed by British naturalist Charles Darwin.*

Many biologists estimate that there are approximately 30 million species on Earth, but to date only about two million have been discovered and recorded by scientists. So where are the rest? They live in a staggering array of habitats, from the waters of the deep oceans where sperm whales live to the deserts of Mexico, inhabited by the powerful, poisonous, gila monster lizard. The problems faced by animals in these and other habitats on Earth are very different, and so life has evolved in great variety. Each animal needs a body that can cope with its own environment.

## Past evidence

At the turn of the 19th century, geologists began to realise that the world was extremely old. They studied animal fossils – usually the hard remains, such as shells and bones, which are preserved in stone – and measured the age of the exposed layers of rock found in cliffs and canyons. Today we accept that the Earth is about 4.5 billion years old, but in the early 1800s the idea that the world was unimaginably old began to change people's ideas about the origins of life completely.

In addition, naturalists had always known that there was a fantastic variety of animals, but now they realized that many could be grouped into families, as if they were related. By the middle of 19th century, two British biologists had independently formulated an idea that would change the way that people saw themselves and the natural world forever. Charles Darwin and Alfred Wallace thought that the world's different animal species had gradually evolved from extinct relatives, like the ones preserved as fossils.

Darwin was the first to publish his ideas, in 1859. He had formulated them while touring South America where he studied the differences between varieties of finches and giant tortoises on the Galápagos Islands in the Pacific Ocean. Wallace came up with similar ideas about the same time, when studying different animals on the islands of South-east Asia and New Guinea.

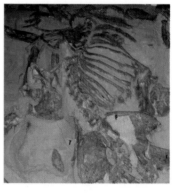

*Above: Scientists know about extinct animals from studying fossils such as these mammoth bones. Fossils are the remains of dead plants or animals that have been turned to stone by natural processes over millions of years.*

## Survival of the fittest

Both came up with the same idea – natural selection. As breeders had known for generations, animals pass on their characteristics to their young. Darwin and Wallace suggested that wild animal species also gradually evolved through natural selection, a similar system to the artificial selection that people were using to breed prize cattle, sheep and pedigree dogs.

The theory of natural selection is often described as the survival of the fittest. This is because animals must compete with each other for limited resources including food, water, shelter and mates. But they are not all equal or exactly similar, and some members of a population of animals will have characteristics which make them "fitter" – better suited to the environment at that time.

The fitter animals will therefore be more successful at finding food and avoiding predators. Consequently, they will probably produce more offspring, many of which will also have the same characteristics as their fit parents. Because of this, the next generation

---

## Jumping animals

Most animals can leap into the air, but thanks to natural selection this simple ability has been harnessed by different animals in different ways. For example, click beetles jump in somersaults to frighten off attackers, while blood-sucking fleas can leap enormous heights to move from host to host.

*Above: The flying frog uses flaps of skin between its toes to glide. This allows these tree-living frogs to leap huge distances between branches.*

*Above: This Thomson's gazelle is pronking, that is, leaping in high arcs to escape a chasing predator. Pronking makes it harder for predators to bring the antelope down.*

will contain more individuals with the "fit" trait. And after many generations, it is possible that the whole population will carry the fit trait, since those without it die out.

## Variation and time

The environment is not fixed, and does not stay the same for long. Volcanoes, diseases and gradual climate changes, for example, alter the conditions which animals have to confront. Natural selection relies on the way in which different individual animals cope with these changes. Those individuals that were once fit may later die out, as others that have a different set of characteristics become more successful in the changed environment.

Darwin did not know it, but parents pass their features on to their young through their genes. During sexual reproduction, the genes of both parents are jumbled up to produce a new individual with a unique set of characteristics. Every so often the genes mutate into a new form, and these mutations are the source of all new variations.

As the process of natural selection continues for millions of years, so groups of animals can change radically, giving rise to a new species. Life is thought to have been evolving for 3.5 billion years. In that time natural selection has produced a staggering number of species, with everything from oak trees to otters and coral to cobras.

A species is a group of organisms that can produce offspring with each other. A new species occurs once animals have changed so much that they are unable to breed with their ancestors. And if the latter no longer exist, then they have become extinct.

New species may gradually arise out of a single group of animals. In fact the original species may be replaced by one or more new species. This can happen when two separate groups of one species are kept apart by an impassable geographical feature, such as an ocean or mountain range. Kept isolated from each other, both groups then evolve in different ways and end up becoming new species.

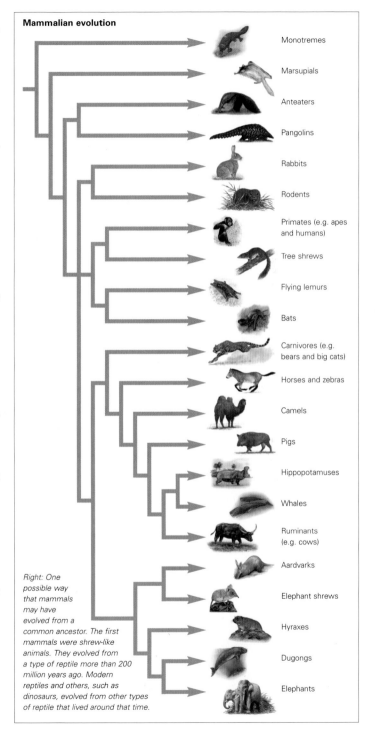

**Mammalian evolution**

Monotremes
Marsupials
Anteaters
Pangolins
Rabbits
Rodents
Primates (e.g. apes and humans)
Tree shrews
Flying lemurs
Bats
Carnivores (e.g. bears and big cats)
Horses and zebras
Camels
Pigs
Hippopotamuses
Whales
Ruminants (e.g. cows)
Aardvarks
Elephant shrews
Hyraxes
Dugongs
Elephants

*Right: One possible way that mammals may have evolved from a common ancestor. The first mammals were shrew-like animals. They evolved from a type of reptile more than 200 million years ago. Modern reptiles and others, such as dinosaurs, evolved from other types of reptile that lived around that time.*

# ANATOMY

*Mammals, reptiles and amphibians (which are vertebrates, as are fish and birds), come in a mind-boggling array of shapes and sizes. However all of them, from whales to bats and frogs to snakes, share a basic body plan, both inside and out.*

Vertebrates are animals with a spine, generally made of bone. Bone, the hard tissues of which contain chalky substances, is also the main component of the rest of the vertebrate skeleton. The bones of the skeleton link together to form a rigid frame to protect organs and give the body its shape, while also allowing it to move. Cartilage, a softer, more flexible but tough tissue is found, for example, at the ends of bones in mobile joints, in the ears and the nose (forming the sides and the partition between the two nostrils). Some fish, including sharks and rays, have skeletons that consist entirely of cartilage.

## Nerves and muscles

Vertebrates also have a spinal cord, a thick bundle of nerves extending from the brain through the spine, and down into the tail. The nerves in the spinal cord are used to control walking and other reflex movements by coordinating blocks of muscle that work together. A vertebrate's skeleton is on the inside, in contrast to many invertebrates, which have an outer skeleton or exoskeleton. The vertebrate skeleton provides a solid structure which the body's muscles pull against. Muscles are blocks of protein that can contract and relax when they get an electrical impulse from a nerve.

## Invertebrates

The majority of animals are invertebrates. They are a much more varied group than the vertebrates and include creatures as varied as shrimps, slugs, butterflies and starfish. Although some squid are thought to reach the size of a small whale, and while octopuses are at least as intelligent as cats and dogs, most invertebrates are much smaller and simpler animals than the vertebrates.

*Below: The most successful invertebrates are the insects, including ants. This soldier army ant is defending workers as they collect food.*

## Reptile bodies

Reptiles have an internal skeleton made from bone and cartilage. Their skin is covered in scales, which are often toughened by a waxy protein called keratin. Turtles are quite different from other reptiles. They have a simpler skull and a shell that is joined to the animal's internal skeleton.

*Below: Crocodiles have a very strong body, designed for life in and around shallow water.*

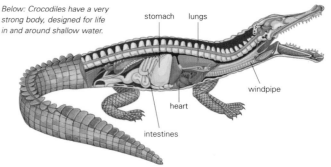

stomach
lungs
windpipe
heart
intestines

*Below: Lizards have a similar body plan to crocodiles, although they are actually not very closely related.*

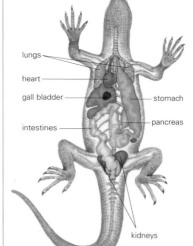

lungs
heart
gall bladder
intestines
stomach
pancreas
kidneys

*Below: Snakes' internal organs are elongated so that they fit into their long, thin body. One of a pair of organs, such as the lungs, is often very small or missing.*

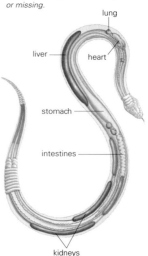

lung
liver
heart
stomach
intestines
kidneys

When on the move, the vertebrate body works like a system of pulleys, pivots and levers. The muscles are the engines of the body, and are attached to bones – the levers – by strong cables called tendons. The joint between two bones forms a pivot, and the muscles work in pairs to move a bone. For example, when an arm is bent at the elbow to raise the forearm, the bicep muscle on the front of the upper arm has to contract. This pulls the forearm up, while the tricep muscle attached to the back of the upper arm remains relaxed. To straighten the arm again, the tricep contracts and the bicep relaxes. If both muscles contract at the same time, they pull against each other, and the arm remains locked in whatever position it is in.

## Vital organs

Muscles are not only attached to the skeleton. The gut – including the stomach and intestines – is surrounded by muscles. These muscles contract in rhythmic waves to push food and waste products through the body. The heart is a muscular organ made of a very strong muscle which keeps on contracting and relaxing, pumping blood around the body. The heart and other vital organs are found in the thorax, that part of the body which lies between the forelimbs. In reptiles and mammals the thorax is kept well protected, the rib cage surrounding the heart, lungs, liver and kidneys.

Vertebrates have a single liver consisting of a number of lobes. The liver has a varied role, making chemicals required by the body and storing food. Most vertebrates also have two kidneys. Their role is to clean the blood of any impurities and toxins, and to remove excess water. The main toxins that have to be removed are compounds containing nitrogen, the by-products of eating protein. Mammal and amphibian kidneys dissolve these toxins in water to make urine. However, since many reptiles live in very dry habitats, they cannot afford to use water to remove waste, and they instead get rid of it as a solid waste similar to bird excrement.

**Mammalian bodies**

Most mammals are four-limbed (exceptions being sea mammals such as whales). All have at least some hair on their bodies, and females produce milk. Mammals live in a wide range of habitats and their bodies are adapted in many ways to survive. Their internal organs vary depending on where they live and what they eat.

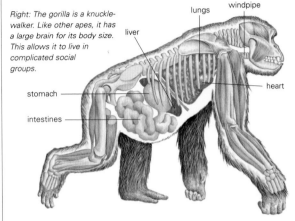

*Right: The gorilla is a knuckle-walker. Like other apes, it has a large brain for its body size. This allows it to live in complicated social groups.*

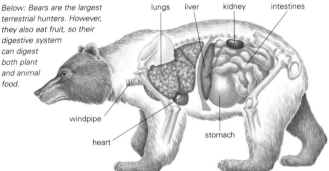

*Below: Bears are the largest terrestrial hunters. However, they also eat fruit, so their digestive system can digest both plant and animal food.*

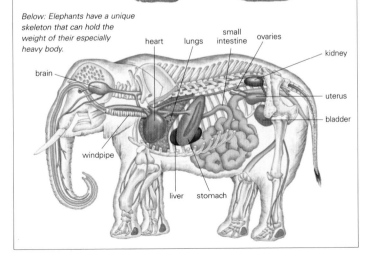

*Below: Elephants have a unique skeleton that can hold the weight of their especially heavy body.*

# SENSES

*To stay alive, animals must find food and shelter, and defend themselves against predators. To achieve these things, they are equipped with an array of senses for monitoring their surroundings. Different species have senses adapted to nocturnal or diurnal (day-active) life.*

An animal's senses are its early-warning system. They alert it to changes in its surroundings – changes which may signal an opportunity to feed or mate, or the need to escape imminent danger. The ability to act quickly and appropriately is made possible because the senses are linked to the brain by a network of nerves which send messages as electric pulses. When the brain receives the information from the senses it coordinates its response.

In many cases, generally in response to something touching the body, the signal from the sensor does not reach the brain before action is taken. Instead, it produces a reflex response which is "hardwired" into the nervous system. For example, when you touch a very hot object, your hand automatically recoils; you don't need to think about it.

All animals have to be sensitive to their environment to survive. Even the simplest animals, such as jellyfish and roundworms, react to changes in their surroundings. Simple animals, however, have only a limited ability to move or defend themselves, and therefore generally have limited senses. Larger animals, such as vertebrates,

have a much more complex array of sense organs. Most vertebrates can hear, see, smell, taste and touch.

## Vision

Invertebrates' eyes are generally designed to detect motion. Vertebrates' eyes, however, are better at forming clear images, often in colour. Vertebrates' eyes are balls of clear jelly which have an inner lining of light-sensitive cells. This lining, called the retina, is made up of one or two types of cell. The rod cells – named after their shape – are very sensitive to all types of light, but are only capable of forming black and white images. Animals which are active at night generally have (and need) only rods in their eyes.

Colour vision is important for just a few animals, such as monkeys, which need, for example, to see the brightest and therefore ripest fruits. Colour images are made by the cone cells – so-named because of their shape – in the retina. There are three types of cone, each of which is sensitive to a particular wavelength of light. Low wavelengths appear as reds, high wavelengths as blues, with green colours being detected in between.

*Above: Frogs have large eyes positioned on the upper side of the head so that the animals can lie mainly submerged in water with just their eyes poking out.*

The light is focused on the retina by a lens to produce a clear image. Muscles change the shape of the lens so that it can focus the light arriving from different distances. While invertebrates may have several eyes, all vertebrates have just two, and they are always positioned on the head. Animals such as rabbits, which are constantly looking out for danger, have eyes on the side of the head to give a wide field of vision. But while they can see in almost all directions, rabbits have difficulty judging distances and speeds. Animals that have eyes pointing forward are better at doing this because each eye's field of vision overlaps with the other. This binocular vision helps hunting animals and others, such as tree-living primates, to judge distances more accurately.

Eyes can also detect radiation in a small band of wavelengths, and some animals detect radiation that is invisible to our eyes. Flying insects and birds can see ultraviolet light, which extends the range of their colour vision. At the other end of the spectrum many snakes can detect radiation with a lower wavelength. They sense infrared, or heat, through pits on the face which enables them to track their warm-blooded prey in pitch darkness.

*Below: This slow loris is nocturnal, that is, night-active. It has very large eyes that collect as much light as possible so that it can see in the gloom of the night.*

*Below: Like other hunters, a seal has eyes positioned on the front of its head. Forward-looking eyes are useful for judging distances, making it easier to chase down prey.*

## Hearing

An animal's brain interprets waves of pressure travelling through the air, and detected by the ears, as sound. Many animals do not hear these waves with ears but detect them in other ways instead. For example, although snakes can hear, they are much more sensitive to vibrations through the lower jaw, travelling through the ground. Long facial whiskers sported by many mammals, from cats to dugongs, are very sensitive touch receptors. They can be so sensitive that they will even respond to currents in the air.

In many ways, hearing is a sensitive extension of the sense of touch. The ears of amphibians, lizards and mammals have an eardrum which is sensitive to tiny changes in pressure. An eardrum is a thin membrane of skin which vibrates as the air waves hit it. A tiny bone (or in the case of mammals, three bones) attached to the drum transmit the vibrations to a shell-shaped structure called a cochlea. The cochlea is filled with a liquid which picks up the vibrations. As the liquid moves inside the cochlea, tiny hair-like structures lining it wave back and forth. Nerves stimulated by this wave motion send the information to the brain, which interprets it as sound.

A mammal's ear is divided into three sections. The cochlea forms the inner ear and the middle ear consists of the bones between the cochlea and eardrum. The outer ear is the tube joining the outside world and the

auricle – the fleshy structure on the side of the head that collects the sound waves – to the middle ear. Amphibians and reptiles do not possess auricles. Instead their eardrums are either on the side of the head – easily visible on many frogs and lizards – or under the skin, as in snakes.

## Smell and taste

Smell and taste are so closely related as to form a single sense. Snakes and lizards, for example, taste the air with their forked tongues. However, it is perhaps the most complex sense. Noses, tongues and other smelling

*Above: Snakes have a forked tongue that they use to taste the air. The tips of the fork are slotted into an organ in the roof of the mouth. This organ is linked to the nose, and chemicals picked up by the tongue are identified with great sensitivity.*

organs are lined with sensitive cells which can analyze a huge range of chemicals that float in the air or exist in food. Animals such as dogs, which rely on their sense of smell, have long noses packed with odour-sensitive cells. Monkeys, of the other hand, are less reliant on a sense of smell, and consequently have short noses capable only of detecting stronger odours.

*Below: Hares have very large outer ears which they use like satellite dishes to pick up sound waves. They can rotate each ear separately to detect sound from all directions.*

*Below: Lizards do not have outer ears at all. Their hearing organs are contained inside the head and joined to the outside world through an eardrum membrane.*

*Below: Wolves have an excellent sense of smell and taste. They communicate with pack members and rival packs by smell, as part of a complex set of social behaviours.*

# SURVIVAL

*In order to stay alive, animals must not only find enough food, but also avoid becoming a predator's meal. To achieve this, animals have evolved many strategies to feed on a wide range of foods, and an array of weapons and defensive tactics to keep safe.*

An animal must keep feeding in order to replace the energy used in staying alive. Substances in the food, such as sugars, are burned by the body, and the subsequent release of energy is used to heat the body and power its movements. Food is also essential for growth. Although most growth takes place during the early period of an animal's life, it never really stops because injuries need to heal and worn-out tissues need replacing. Some animals continue growing throughout life. Proteins in the food are the main building blocks of living bodies.

## Plant food

Some animals will eat just about anything, while others are much more fussy. As a group, vertebrates get their energy from a wide range of sources – everything from shellfish and wood to honey and blood. Animals are often classified according to how they feed, forming several large groups filled with many otherwise unrelated animals.

Animals that eat plants are generally grouped together as herbivores. But this term is not very descriptive because there is such a wide range of plant foods. Animals that eat grass are known as grazers. However, this term can also apply to any animal which eats any plant that covers the ground

*Above: Bison are grazers. They eat grass and plants that grow close to the ground. Because their food is all around them, grazers spend a long time out in the open. They feed together in large herds, since there is safety in numbers.*

in large amounts, such as seaweed or sedge. Typical grazers include bison and wildebeest but some, such as the marine iguana or gelada baboon, are not so typical. Animals such as giraffes or antelopes, which pick off the tastiest leaves, buds and fruit from bushes and trees, are called browsers. Other browsing animals include many monkeys, but some monkeys eat only leaves (the folivores) or fruit (the frugivores).

Many monkeys have a much broader diet, eating everything from insects to the sap which seeps out from the bark of tropical trees. Animals that eat both plant and animal foods are called omnivores. Bears are omnivorous, as are humans, but the most catholic of tastes belong to scavenging animals, such as rats and other rodents, which eat anything they can get their teeth into. Omnivores in general, and scavengers in particular, are very curious animals. They will investigate anything that looks or smells like food, and if it also tastes like food, then it probably is.

## A taste for flesh

The term carnivore is often applied to any animal that eats flesh, but it is more correctly used to refer to an order of mammals which includes cats, dogs, bears and many smaller animals, such as weasels and mongooses. These animals are the kings of killing, armed with razor-sharp claws and powerful jaws crammed full of dagger-like teeth. They use their strength and speed to overpower their prey, either by running them down or taking them by surprise with an ambush.

*Below: Zebras are browsers, not grazers. They will eat some grass but also pick tastier leaves, buds and fruit off trees and shrubs. They often live in herds to stay safe from attack.*

*Below: Lions are unusual cats because they live together in prides. The members of the pride cooperate to catch food. They hunt as a team and share the food between them.*

Above: African elephants have few predators. Younger elephants are at risk of leopard attacks, and the adults defend them by trumpeting, stamping and flapping their large ears. If that fails, they will charge.

However, land-dwelling carnivores are not the only expert killers. The largest meat-eater is the orca, or killer whale, which is at least three times the size of the brown bear, the largest killer on land.

While snakes are much smaller in comparison, they are just as deadly, if not more so. They kill in one of two ways, either suffocating their prey by wrapping their coils tightly around them, or by injecting them with a poison through their fangs.

**Arms race**
Ironically, the same weapons used by predators are often used by their prey to defend themselves. For example, several species of frog, toad and salamander secrete poisons on to their skin. In some cases, such as the poison-dart frog, this poison is enough to kill any predator that tries to eat it, thus making sure that the killer won't repeat its performance. More often, though, a predator finds that its meal tastes horrible and remembers not to eat another one again. To remind the predators to keep away, many poisonous amphibians are brightly

coloured, which ensures that they are easily recognized.

Many predators rely on stealth to catch their prey, and staying hidden is part of the plan. A camouflaged coat, such as a tiger's stripes, helps animals blend into their surroundings. Many species also use this technique to ensure that they do not get eaten. Most freeze when danger approaches, and then scurry to safety as quickly as possible. Chameleons have taken camouflage to an even more sophisticated level as they can change the colour of their scaly skins, which helps them to blend in with their surrounding environment.

Plant-eating animals that live in the open cannot hide from predators that are armed with sharp teeth and claws. And the plant-eaters cannot rely on similar weapons to defend themselves. They are outgunned

*Right: Chameleons have skin cells that can be opened and closed to make their skin colour change.*

because they do not possess sharp, pointed teeth but flattened ones to grind up their plant food. The best chance they have of avoiding danger is to run away. Animals such as antelopes or deer consequently have long, hoofed feet that lengthen their legs considerably; they are, in fact, standing on their toenails. These long legs allow them to run faster and leap high into the air to escape an attacker's jaws.

Animals that do not flee must stand and fight. Most large herbivores are armed with horns or antlers. Although used chiefly for display, the horns are the last line of defence when cornered.

# REPRODUCTION

*All animals share the urge to produce offspring which will survive after the parents die. The process of heredity is determined by genes, through which characteristics are passed from parents to offspring. Reproduction presents several problems, and animals have adopted different strategies for tackling them.*

Animals have two main goals: to find food and a mate. To achieve these goals, they must survive everything that the environment throws at them, from extremes of the weather, such as floods and droughts, to hungry predators. They have to find sufficient supplies of food, and on top of that locate a mate before their competitors. If they find sufficient food but fail to produce any offspring, their struggle for survival will have been wasted.

## One parent or two?

There are two ways in which an animal can reproduce, asexually or sexually. Animals that are produced by asexual reproduction, or parthenogenesis, have only one parent, a mother. The offspring are identical to their mother and to each other. Sexual reproduction involves two parents of the opposite sex. The offspring are hybrids of the two parents, with a mixture of their parents' characteristics.

The offspring inherit their parents' traits through their genes. Genes can be defined in various ways. One simple definition is that they are the unit of inheritance – a single inherited

*Below: Crocodiles bury their eggs in a nest. The temperature of the nest determines the sex of the young reptiles. Hot nests produce more males than cool ones. Crocodile mothers are very gentle when it comes to raising young.*

*Above: Many male frogs croak by pumping air into an expandable throat sac. The croak is intended to attract females. The deeper the croak, the more attractive it is. However, some males lurk silently and mate with females as they approach the croaking males.*

*Above: In deer and many other grazing animals, the males fight each other for the right to mate with the females in the herd. The deer with the largest antlers often wins without fighting, and real fights only break out if two males appear equally well-endowed.*

characteristic which cannot be subdivided any further. Genes are also segments of DNA (deoxyribonucleic acid), a complex chemical that forms long chains. It is found at the heart of every living cell. Each link in the DNA chain forms part of a code that controls how an animal's body develops and survives. And every cell in the body contains a full set of DNA which could be used to build a whole new body.

Animals produced through sexual reproduction receive half their DNA, or half their genes, from each parent. The male parent provides half the supply of genes, contained in a sperm. Each sperm's only role is to find its

way to, and fertilize, an egg, its female equivalent. Besides containing the other half of the DNA, the egg also holds a supply of food for the offspring as it develops into a new individual. Animals created through parthenogenesis get all their genes from their mother, and all of them are therefore the same sex – female.

## Pros and cons

All mammals reproduce sexually, as do most reptiles and amphibians. However, there are a substantial number of reptiles and amphibians, especially lizards, which reproduce by parthenogenesis. There are benefits and disadvantages to both types of reproduction. Parthenogenesis is quick and convenient. The mother does not need to find a mate, and can devote all of her energy to producing huge numbers of young. This strategy is ideal for populating as yet unexploited territory. However, being identical, these animals are very vulnerable to attack. If, for example, one is killed by a disease or outwitted by a predator, it is very likely that they will all suffer the same fate. Consequently, whole communities of animals produced through parthenogenesis can be wiped out.

Sexual animals, on the other hand, are much more varied. Each one is unique, formed by a mixture of genes from both parents. This variation means that a group of animals produced by sexual reproduction is more likely to triumph over adversity than a group of asexual ones. However, sexual reproduction takes up a great deal of time and effort.

### Attracting mates
Since females produce only a limited number of eggs, they are keen to make sure that they are fertilized by a male with good genes. If a male is fit and healthy, this is a sign that he has good genes. Good genes will ensure that the offspring will be able to compete with other animals for food and mates of their own. Because the females have the final say in agreeing to mate, the

Above: Lions live in prides, in which one or two males father all the children. When a new adult takes control of the pride, he kills the cubs of his deposed rival so that the pride's females will be ready to mate with him sooner.

Below: Rhinoceroses are generally solitary animals, but offspring stay with their mother for at least a year while they grow big enough to look after themselves.

males have to put a lot of effort into getting noticed. Many are brightly coloured, make loud noises, and they are often larger than the females. In many species the males even compete with each other for the right to display to the females. Winning that right is a good sign that they have the best genes.

### Parental care
The amount of care that the offspring receive from their parents varies considerably. There is a necessary trade-off between the amount of useful care parents can give to each offspring, the number of offspring they can produce and how regularly they can breed. Mammals invest heavily in parental care, suckling their young after giving birth, while most young amphibians or reptiles never meet their parents at all.

By suckling, mammals ensure that their young grow to a size where they

Above: Gibbons are highly intelligent animals. Parents rear their offspring intensively while the young learn to survive the complexities and dangers of the rainforest. Many gibbons form strong male–female pair bonds that last throughout their lives.

can look after themselves. Generally, the young stay with the mother until it is time for her to give birth to the next litter – at least one or two months. However, in many species, including humans, the young stay with their parents for many years.

Other types of animals pursue the opposite strategy, producing large numbers of young that are left to fend for themselves. The vast majority in each batch of eggs – consisting of hundreds or even thousands – die before reaching adulthood, and many never even hatch. The survival rates, for example of frogs, are very low.

Animals that live in complicated societies, such as elephants, apes and humans, tend to produce a single offspring every few years. The parents direct their energies into protecting and rearing the young, giving them a good chance of survival. Animals which live for a only a short time, such as mice, rabbits, and reptiles and amphibians in general, need to reproduce quickly to make the most of their short lives. They produce high numbers of young, and do not waste time on anything more than the bare minimum of parental care. If successful, these animals can reproduce at an alarming pace.

# CLASSIFICATION

*Scientists classify all living things into categories. Members of each category share features with each other – traits that set them apart from other animals. Over the years, a tree of categories and subcategories has been pieced together, showing how all living things seem to be related to each other.*

Taxonomy, the scientific discipline of categorizing organisms, aims to classify and order the millions of animals on Earth so that we can better understand them and their relationship to each other. The Greek philosopher Aristotle was among the first people to do this for animals in the 4th century BC. In the 18th century, Swedish naturalist Carolus Linnaeus formulated the system that we use today.

By the end of the 17th century, naturalists had noticed that many animals seemed to have several close relatives that resembled one another. For example lions, lynxes and domestic cats all seemed more similar to each other than they did to dogs or horses. However, all of these animals shared common features that they did not share with frogs, slugs or wasps.

Linnaeus devised a way of classifying these observations. The system he set up – known as the Linnaean system – orders animals in a hierarchy of divisions. From the largest division to the smallest, this system is as follows: kingdom, phylum, class, order, family, genus, species.

Each species is given a two-word scientific name, derived from Latin and Greek. For example, *Panthera leo* is the scientific name of the lion. The first word is the genus name, while the second is the species name. Therefore *Panthera leo* means the "*leo*" species in the genus "*Panthera*". This system of two-word classification is known as binomial nomenclature.

*Above: Like the tiger, the lion* (Panthera leo) *belongs to the cat family,* Felidae. *This is divided into two main groups, the big and small cats. The group of small cats includes cougars, bobcats and domestic cats.*

*Below: The tiger* (Panthera tigris) *belongs to the genus* Panthera, *the big cats, to which lions also belong. All cats are members of the larger order of* Carnivora (carnivores) *within the class of* Mammalia (mammals).

Lions, lynxes and other genera of cats belong to the *Felidae* family. The *Felidae* are included in the order *Carnivora*, along with dogs and other similar predators. The *Carnivora*, in turn, belong to the class *Mammalia*, which also includes horses and all other mammals.

Mammals belong to the phylum *Chordata*, the major group which contains all vertebrates, including reptiles, amphibians, birds, fish and some other small animals called tunicates and lancelets. In their turn, *Chordata* belong to the kingdom *Animalia*, comprising around 31 living phyla, including *Mollusca*, which contains the slugs, and *Arthropoda*, which contains wasps and other insects.

Although we still use Linnaean grouping, modern taxonomy is worked out in very different ways from the ones Linnaeus used. Linnaeus and others after him classified animals by their outward appearance. Although they were generally correct when it came

## Close relations

Cheetahs, caracals and ocelots all belong to the cat family *Felidae*, which also includes lions, tigers, wildcats, lynxes and jaguars. Within this family there are two groups: big and small cats. These can generally be distinguished by their size, with a few exceptions.

For example, the cheetah is often classed as a big cat, but it is actually smaller than the cougar, a small cat. One of the main differences between the two groups is that big cats can roar but not purr continuously, while small cats are able to purr but not roar.

*Above: The cheetah (Acinonyx jubatus) differs from all other cats in possessing retractable claws without sheaths. This species is classed in a group of its own, but is often included within the group of big cats.*

*Above: The caracal (Caracal caracal) is included in the group of small cats, (subfamily Felinae), but most scientists place it in a genus of its own, Caracal, rather than in the main genus, Felis.*

*Above: The ocelot (Felis pardalis) is a medium-sized member of the Felis or small cat genus. Like many cats, this species has evolved a spotted coat to provide camouflage – unfortunately attractive to fashion designers.*

## Distant relations

All vertebrates (backboned animals) including birds, reptiles and mammals such as seals and dolphins, are thought to have evolved from common fish ancestors that swam in the oceans some 400 million years ago. Later, one group of fish developed

limb-like organs and came on to the land, where they slowly evolved into amphibians and later reptiles, which in turn gave rise to mammals. Later, seals and dolphins returned to the oceans and their limbs evolved into paddle-like flippers.

*Above: Fish are an ancient group of aquatic animals that mainly propel themselves by thrashing their vertically aligned caudal fin, or tail, and steer using their fins.*

*Above: In seals, the four limbs have evolved into flippers that make highly effective paddles in water but are less useful on land, where seals are ungainly in their movements.*

*Above: Whales and dolphins never come on land, and their hind limbs have all but disappeared. They resemble fish but the tail is horizontally – not vertically – aligned.*

to the large divisions, this method was not foolproof. For example, some early scientists believed that whales and dolphins, with their fins and streamlined bodies, were types of fish and not mammals at all. Today, accurate

classification of the various genera is achieved through a field of study called cladistics. This uses genetic analysis to check how animals are related by evolutionary change. So animals are grouped according to how they evolved,

with each division sharing a common ancestor somewhere in the past. As the classification of living organims improves, so does our understanding of the evolution of life on Earth and our place within this process.

# AMPHIBIANS

*Amphibians are the link between fish and land animals. One in eight of all vertebrate animals are amphibians. This group includes frogs, toads and newts as well as rarer types, such as giant sirens, hellbenders and worm-like caecilians. Amphibians are equally at home in water and on land.*

Amphibians live on every continent except for Antarctica. None can survive in salt water, although a few species live close to the sea in the brackish water at river mouths. Being cold-blooded – their body temperature is always about the same as the temperature of their surroundings – most amphibians are found in the warmer regions of the world.

Unlike other land vertebrates, amphibians spend the early part of their lives in a different form from that of the adults. As they grow, the young gradually metamorphose into the adult body. Having a larval form means that the adults and their offspring live and feed in different places. In general the larvae are aquatic, while the adults spend most of their time on land.

The adults are hunters, feeding on other animals, while the young are generally plant eaters, filtering tiny plants from the water or grazing on aquatic plants which line the bottom of ponds and rivers.

*Below: Amphibians must lay their eggs near a source of water. In most cases, such as this frog spawn, the eggs are laid straight into a pond or swamp. The tadpoles develop inside the jelly-like egg and then hatch out after the food supply in the egg's yolk runs out.*

*Above: Amphibians begin life looking very different from the adult form. Most of the time these larval forms, such as this frog tadpole, live in water as they slowly develop into the adult form, growing legs and lungs so that they can survive on land.*

## Life changing

Most amphibians hatch from eggs laid in water or, in a few cases, in moist soil or nests made of hardened mucus. Once hatched, the young amphibians, or larvae, live as completely aquatic animals. Those born on land wriggle to the nearest pool of water or drop from their nest into a river.

The larvae of frogs and toads are called tadpoles. Like the young of salamanders – a group that includes all other amphibians except caecilians – tadpoles do not have any legs at first. They swim using a long tail that has a fish-like fin extending along its length. As they grow, the larvae sprout legs. In general the back legs begin to grow first, followed by the front pair. Adult frogs do not have tails, and after the first few months a tadpole's tail begins to be reabsorbed into the body – it does not just fall away.

All adult salamanders keep their tails, and those species that spend their entire lives in water often retain the fin along the tail, along with other parts, such as external gills, a feature that is more commonly seen in the larval stage.

## Body form

Amphibian larvae hatch with external gills but, as they grow, many (including all frogs and the many salamanders which live on land) develop internal gills. In most land-living species these internal gills are eventually replaced by lungs. Amphibians are also able to absorb oxygen directly through the skin, especially through the thin and moist tissues inside the mouth. A large number of land-living salamanders get all their oxygen in this way because they do not have lungs.

All adult frogs and toads return to the water to breed and lay their eggs, which are often deposited in a jelly-like mass called frog spawn. Several types of salamander do not lay eggs, and instead the females keep the fertilized eggs inside their bodies. The larvae develop inside the eggs, fed by a supply of rich yolk, and do not hatch until they have reached adult form.

*Above: After the first few weeks, a tadpole acquires tiny back legs. As the legs grow, the long tail is gradually reabsorbed into the body. The front legs appear after the back ones have formed.*

## Adult form

Most adult amphibians have four limbs, with four digits on the front pair and five on the rear. Unlike other land-living animals, such as reptiles or mammals, their skin is naked and soft. Frogs' skin is smooth and moist, while toads generally have a warty appearance.

The skins of many salamanders are brightly coloured, with patterns that often change throughout the year. Colour change prior to the mating season signals the salamander's readiness to mate. Many frogs also have bright skin colours. Although their skin shades can change considerably in different light levels, these colours are generally not mating signals to fellow frogs. Instead they are warnings to predators that the frog's skin is laced with deadly poison. While toads tend to be drab in colour, many also secrete toxic chemicals to keep predators away. These substances are often stored in swollen warts which burst when the toad is attacked.

*Below: Adult frogs may live in water or on land. Aquatic ones have webbed feet, while those on land have powerful legs for jumping and climbing. All frogs must return to a source of water to mate.*

### Forever young

Salamanders which have changed into adults, but which have not yet reached adult size, are called efts. The time it takes for an amphibian to grow from a newly hatched larva to an adult varies considerably, and the chief factor is the temperature of the water in which it is developing. Most frogs and toads develop in shallow waters, warmed by the summer sun, and they generally reach adulthood within three to four months. However, salamanders, especially the largest ones, can take much longer, and at the northern and southern limits of their geographical spread some salamanders stay as larvae for many years. It appears that the trigger for the change into adult form is linked to the temperature, and in cold climates this change happens only every few years. In fact it may not happen during a salamander's lifetime, and consequently several species have evolved the ability to develop sexual organs even when they still look like larvae.

*Below: Marbled salamanders are unusual in that the females lay their eggs on dry land and coil themselves around them to keep them as moist as possible. They stay like this until the seasonal rains fall. The water stimulates the eggs to hatch.*

# REPTILES

*Reptiles include lizards, snakes, alligators, crocodiles, turtles and tortoises, as well as now-extinct creatures such as dinosaurs and the ancestors of birds. Crocodiles have roamed the Earth for 200 million years and are still highly successful hunters.*

Reptiles are a large and diverse group of animals containing about 6,500 species. Many of these animals look very different from each other and live in a large number of habitats, from the deep ocean to the scorching desert. Despite their great diversity, all reptiles share certain characteristics.

Most reptiles lay eggs, but these are different from those of an amphibian because they have a hard, thin shell rather than a soft, jelly-like one. This protects the developing young inside and, more importantly, stops them from drying out. Shelled eggs were an evolutionary breakthrough because they meant that adult reptiles did not have to return to the water to breed. Their waterproof eggs could be laid anywhere, even in the driest places. Reptiles were also the first group of land-living animals to develop into an adult form inside the egg. They did not emerge as under-developed larvae like the young of most amphibians.

*Below: Alligators and other crocodilians are an ancient group of reptiles that have no close living relatives. They are archosaurs, a group of reptiles that included the dinosaurs. Other living reptiles belong to a different group.*

Released from their ties to water, the reptiles developed unique ways of retaining moisture. Their skins are covered by hardened plates or scales to stop water being lost. The scales are also coated with the protein keratin, the same substance used to make fingernails and hair.

All reptiles breathe using lungs; if they were to absorb air through the skin it would involve too much water loss. Like amphibians, reptiles are cold-blooded and cannot heat their bodies from within as mammals can. Consequently, reptiles are commonly found in warm climates.

## Ancient killers

Being such a diverse group, reptiles share few defining characteristics besides their shelled eggs, scaly skin and lungs. They broadly divide into four orders. The first contains the crocodiles, and includes alligators and caimans; these are contemporaries of the dinosaurs, both groups being related to a common ancestor.

In fact today's crocodiles have changed little since the age when dinosaurs ruled the world over 200 million years

*Above: Turtles and their relatives, such as these giant tortoises, are unusual reptiles. Not only do they have bony shells fused around their bodies, but they also have skulls that are quite different from other reptiles. Turtles are also unusual because many of them live in the ocean, while most reptiles live on land.*

ago. Unlike the dinosaurs, which disappeared 65 million years ago, the crocodiles are still going strong. Technically speaking, the dinosaurs never actually died out; their direct descendents, the birds, are still thriving. Although birds are now grouped separately from reptiles, scientists know that they all evolved from ancestors which lived about 400 million years ago. Mammals, on the other hand, broke away from this group about 300 million years ago.

*Above: Most reptiles, including this tree boa, lay eggs. The young hatch looking like small versions of the adults. However, several snakes and lizards give birth to live young, which emerge from their mother fully formed.*

## Distant relatives

The second reptile order includes turtles, terrapins and tortoises. These are only distantly related to other reptiles, and it shows. Turtles are also the oldest group of reptiles, evolving their bony shells and clumsy bodies before crocodiles, dinosaurs or any other living reptile group existed. Although turtles evolved on land, many have since returned to water. However, they still breathe air, and all must return to land to lay their eggs.

The third group of reptiles is the largest. Collectively called the squamates, this group includes snakes and lizards.

Snakes, with their legless bodies and formidable reputations, are perhaps the most familiar reptiles. They evolved from animals that did have legs, and many retain tiny vestiges of legs. The squamates include other legless members such as the amphisbaenians (or worm lizards) and slow worms. Both of these groups are more closely related to lizards than snakes, despite looking more like the latter. Lizards are not a simple group of reptiles, and many biologists refer to them as several different groups, including the skinks, monitors, geckos and iguanas.

*Below: Lizards, such as this iguana, are the largest group of reptiles. Most are hunters that live in hot parts of the world, and they are especially successful in dry areas where other types of animal are not so common.*

The squamates are so diverse in their lifestyles and body forms that it is hard to find factors which they have in common. One feature not found in other reptile orders is the Jacobson's organ. It is positioned in the roof of the mouth and is closely associated with the nose. All snakes and most lizards use this organ to "taste" the air and detect prey. The long forked tongue of most of these animals flicks out into the air, picking up tiny particles on its moist surface. Once back inside the mouth, each fork slots into the Jacobson's organ which then analyzes the substances.

The fourth and final order of reptiles is very small: the tuataras. These include just a few species, all of which are very rare indeed, clinging to life on islands off the mainland of New Zealand. To most people a tuatara looks like a large iguana. However, scientists believe that it is only a distant relative of lizards and other squamates because it has an odd-shaped skull and no eardrums.

> **Tuatara**
> Despite their differences from lizards and other squamates, tuataras do share one feature with lizards: the so-called third eye. This light-sensitive gland inside the head can detect light penetrating the thin skull. Both types of reptile use the third eye to regulate their exposure to the sun and so regulate their body temperature throughout the year.
>
> *Below: The tuatara is a living fossil, living on just a few islands around New Zealand. It looks like a lizard, but its skull and skeleton show that it is the last member of another ancient group of reptiles.*
>
>

# PLACENTAL MAMMALS

*Mammals are the most familiar of all vertebrates. This is because not only are human beings mammals, but also most domestic animals and pets belong in this category. Placental mammals are also more widespread than other types of animal, being found in all parts of the world.*

Mammals are grouped together because they share a number of characteristics. However, these common features do not come close to describing the huge diversity within the mammal class. For example, the largest animal that has ever existed on Earth – the blue whale – is a mammal, and so this monster of the deep shares several crucial traits with even the smallest mammals, such as the tiniest of shrews. Other mammals include elephants and moles, monkeys and hippopotamuses, and bats and camels. To add to this great diversity, mammals live in more places on Earth than any other group of animals, from the frozen ice fields of the Arctic to the humid treetops of the Amazon rainforest, and even under the sandy soil of African deserts.

Above: With their thick white fur and powerful clawed paws, polar bears are very well adapted to life on the pack ice. However, they are not so different from other types of bear. The adaptability of the basic body plan is what makes mammals so successful.

### Mammal bodies

The most obvious mammalian feature is hair. All mammals have hair made of keratin protein and, in most cases, it forms a thick coat of fur, though many mammals are relatively naked, not least humans. Unlike reptiles and amphibians, all mammals are warm-blooded, which means that they can keep their body temperature at a constant level. While this requires quite a lot of energy, it means that mammals are not totally dependent on the temperature of their surroundings. In places where other vertebrates would be frozen solid, mammals can survive by seeking out food and keeping themselves warm. Many mammals, including humans, can also cool their bodies using sweat. The water secreted on the skin cools the body efficiently, but it does mean that these animals need to drink more replacement water than do other groups.

Incidentally, the name mammal comes from the mammary glands. These glands are the means by which all female mammals provide milk (or liquid food) to their developing young. The young suck the milk through teats or nipples for the first few weeks or months of life.

### Reproduction

Mammals reproduce in a number of ways. Monotremes, such as the duck-billed platypus, lay eggs, but all other mammals give birth to their young. Marsupials, a relatively small group of animals which includes kangaroos, give birth to very undeveloped young which then continue to grow inside a fold or pouch on the mother's skin.

Below: Although they are often mistaken for fish, dolphins are mammals: they breathe air and suckle their young. However, life under water requires flippers and fins, not legs.

*Above: Elephants are the largest land mammals in the world. They are most closely related to rabbit-like hyraxes and walrus-like dugongs and manatees.*

*Above: Plenty of mammals can glide, but only bats join birds and insects in true flight. A bat wing is made from skin that is stretched between long finger bones.*

The majority of mammals, called the placental mammals or eutherians, do not give birth to their young until they are fully formed and resemble the adults. The developing young, or foetuses, grow inside a womb or uterus where they are fed by the mother through a placenta. This large organ allows the young to stay inside the mother for a lot longer than in most other animals. It forms the interface between the mother's blood supply and that of the developing foetus, where oxygen and food pass from the parent to her offspring. The placenta is attached to the foetus by means of an umbilical cord which withers and drops off soon after the birth.

## Widespread range

Mammals are found in a wider variety of habitats than any other group of animals. While mammals all breathe air with their

*Right: One factor that makes mammals unique is that the females have mammary glands. These glands produce milk for the young animals to drink, as this fallow deer fawn is doing. The milk is a mixture of fat, protein and sugars.*

lungs, this has not prevented many from making their homes in water. In many ways the streamlined bodies of whales and dolphins, for example, resemble those of sharks and other large fish. However, they are very much mammals, breathing air through a large nostril or blowhole in the top of the head, but their body hair has been reduced to just a few thick bristles.

At the other end of the spectrum, some mammals even fly. Bats darting through the gloom of a summer evening may appear to be small birds, but they too are mammals with furry bodies and wings made from stretched skin instead of feathers. Although most other mammals have a more conventional body plan, with four legs and tail, they too have evolved to survive in a startling range of habitats. They have achieved this not just by adapting their bodies but by changing their behaviour. In general, mammals have larger brains than reptiles and amphibians, and this allows them to understand their environment more fully. Many mammals, such as monkeys and dogs, survive by living in complex social groups in which individuals cooperate with each other when hunting for food, protecting the group from danger and even finding mates.

# MONOTREMES AND MARSUPIALS

*Not all mammals begin their lives as foetuses growing inside a uterus within their mother. Monotremes and marsupials develop in other ways. Monotremes are the only mammals to lay eggs like birds or lizards, while marsupials raise their young inside pouches on the outside of their bodies.*

## Egg-laying mammals

Monotremes are a group of just three mammal species which still lay their young inside eggs: two species of echidna, short and long-nosed, (also called spiny anteaters), and the odd-looking duck-billed platypus. Although monotremes are hairy and feed their young with milk, they are distant relatives of other mammals.

Monotremes lay two or three very tiny spherical eggs which have a much softer shell than those of birds or many reptiles. And unlike other mammals, monotremes do not have a birth canal. Instead, their eggs travel through the same body opening as the urine and faeces. A single multi-purpose body opening like this is called a cloaca (Latin for drain), and is a feature that monotremes share with birds and reptiles. In fact, the name monotreme means one-holed animal.

The young of monotremes stay in the egg for only a matter of days before hatching out, and then they continue their development while being nursed by their mother. Nursing

*Above: Monotremes, such as this echidna, are in the minority compared to other mammals. They lay eggs, more like a bird or a reptile, rather than give birth to their young. However, the monotremes are mammals because they feed their young on a supply of milk.*

echidnas keep their young in a pouch on their underside, while platypus young spend their early days in an underground nest. While all other mammals have teats for delivering milk, the monotremes do not possess this adaptation. Instead, the mother secretes the fatty liquid on her fur and the young then lap it up.

Monotremes hatch out in a very undeveloped state. They are hairless, blind, barely 1cm (⅓in) long and have just blunt buds for limbs. The young are dependent on their mother's milk for a long time – six months in the case of echidnas. Although they are a tiny group compared to other mammal orders, the monotremes are highly adapted to their habitats and are quite amazing mammals.

## Life in a pouch

Although their 270 species make the marsupials a much larger group than the monotremes, they are still very much the minority compared to the

*Below: Kangaroos are the most familiar marsupial mammals. Like most marsupials, the young grow inside a pouch on the mother's belly, where they are fed on milk from a nipple. Some other marsupials do not have such a developed pouch.*

### Monotreme features

Monotremes were living nearly 200 million years ago, long before any other types of mammal existed. However, this does not mean that animals similar to monotremes were the ancestors of all modern mammals. Further, today's monotremes (which live only in Australasia) are by no means primitive. In fact they have some highly developed features which are not found in any other mammal group. For example, male platypuses sport a venomous spur behind the knee which they use when defending themselves and fighting each other.

*Below: Because of its strange appearance, the duck-billed platypus was thought to be a fake when specimens were first displayed. However, it is a very well-adapted underwater hunter, using its bill to detect the electric fields produced by its prey's muscles.*

*Above: Most marsupials live in Australia where there are few large predators. The koala is adapted to living in trees and eating leaves, and has evolved features that are seen in other animals who live in a similar way, for example grasping hands and a long, fermenting digestive system.*

4,000 or so species of placental mammals that inhabit every corner of the world. Marsupials are found only in Australia and the islands of New Guinea, and a few species live in the Americas.

Marsupials are much more closely related to placental mammals than monotremes. Biologists believe that marsupials evolved first in the Americas and then spread to Australia via Antarctica, in the days when the three continents were joined together. Once Australia became an island, its marsupials remained the dominant mammals, while placental mammals began to take over from them elsewhere in the world.

The placental mammals have a single uterus connected to both ovaries by oviducts, while marsupials have two much smaller uteruses, each connected to a single ovary. The uterus of a placental mammal can swell up as the foetus grows. However, those of a marsupial cannot, which means that the young have to be born much earlier.

Like a newly hatched monotreme, the tiny marsupial baby is hairless and blind, and has stubby forelegs. After two or three weeks in the uterus, the baby makes its way out through a birth canal that grows especially for this journey. Once outside, the baby battles through its mother's fur to her nipples.

Many marsupials have their nipples inside a pouch or marsupium. Once inside, the baby latches on to the nipple which swells inside its mouth to create a very firm connection. The larger marsupials, such as red kangaroos, spend several months inside the pouch and may later be joined by younger siblings. The mother's milk supply is tailored for each of her young, with each baby getting the right amount of fats and proteins for its age. A baby marsupial that is old enough to leave the pouch is called a joey. Joeys often return to their mother's pouch to sleep or feed for several months more before becoming completely independent.

*Right:*
*Tasmanian devils used to be found right across Australia. Now they only survive on the southern island of Tasmania. Many other marsupial species have suffered due to the activities of humans and their domestic animals.*

# ECOLOGY

*Ecology is the study of how groups of organisms interact with members of their own species, other organisms and the environment. All types of animals live in a community of interdependent organisms called an ecosystem, in which they have their own particular role.*

The natural world is filled with a wealth of opportunities for animals to feed and breed. Every animal species has evolved to take advantage of a certain set of these opportunities, called a niche. A niche is not just a physical place but also a lifestyle exploited by that single species. For example, even though they live in the same rainforest habitat, sloths and tapirs occupy very different niches.

To understand how different organisms interrelate, ecologists combine all the niches in an area into a community, called an ecosystem. Ecosystems do not really exist because it is impossible to know where one ends and another begins, but the system is a useful tool when learning more about the natural world.

## Food chains

One way of understanding how an ecosystem works is to follow the food chains within it. A food chain is made up of a series of organisms that prey on each other. Each habitat is filled with them, and since they often merge into and converge from each other, they are often combined into food webs.

*Below: Nature creates some incredible alliances. The American badger, for example, goes on hunting trips with a coyote. The coyote sniffs out the prey, and the badger digs it out of its burrow for both of them to eat.*

Ecologists use food chains to see how energy and nutrients flow through natural communities. Food chains always begin with plants. Plants are the only organisms on Earth that do not need to feed, deriving their energy from sunlight, whereas all other organisms, including animals, get theirs from food. At the next level up the food chain come the plant-eaters. They eat the plants, and extract the sugar and other useful substances made by them. And, like the plants, they use these substances to power their bodies and stay alive. The predators occupy the next level up, and they eat the bodies of the plant-eating animals.

At each stage of the food chain, energy is lost, mainly as heat given out by the animals' bodies. Because of this, less energy is available at each level up the food chain. This means that in a healthy ecosystem there are always fewer predators than prey, and always more plants than plant-eaters.

## Nutrient cycles

A very simple food chain would be as follows: grass, wildebeest and lion. However, the reality of most ecosystems is much more complex, with many more layers, including certain animals that eat both plants and animals. Every food chain ends with a top predator, in our example, the lion. Nothing preys on the lion, at least when it is alive, but once it dies the food chain continues as insects, fungi and other decomposers feed on the carcass. Eventually nothing is left of the lion's body. All the energy stored in it is removed by the decomposers, and the chemicals which made up its body have returned to the environment as carbon dioxide gas, water and minerals in the soil. And these are the very same substances needed by a growing plant. The cycle is complete.

*Above: Nothing is wasted in nature. The dung beetle uses the droppings of larger grazing animals as a supply of food for its developing young. Since the beetles clear away all the dung, the soil is not damaged by it, the grass continues to grow, and the grazers have plenty of food.*

## Living together

As food chains show, the lives of different animals in an ecosystem are closely related. If all the plants died for some reason, it would not just be the plant-eaters that would go hungry. As all of them began to die, the predators would starve too. Only the decomposers might appear to benefit. Put another way, the other species living alongside an animal are just as integral to that animal's environment as the weather and landscape. This is yet another way of saying that animal species have not evolved isolated from each another.

The result is that as predators have evolved new ways of catching their prey, the prey has had to evolve new ways of escaping. On many occasions this process of co-evolution has created symbiotic relationships between two different species. For example, honeyguide birds lead badgers to bees' nests.

Some niches are very simple, and the animals that occupy them live simple, solitary lives. Others, especially those occupied by mammals, are much more complex and require members of a species to live closely together. These aggregations of animals may be simple herds or more structured social groups.

## Food chain

Food chains show how the energy needed for life passes through an ecosystem. The energy originates in the Sun. This makes plants grow, which are then eaten by animals. The plant-eating animals then become meals themselves.

*Below: This food chain shows what animals eat in a temperate country, such as Britain. Herbivores eat only plants, while carnivores eat mainly other animals. Animals that eat both plants and animals are omnivores – for example, humans.*

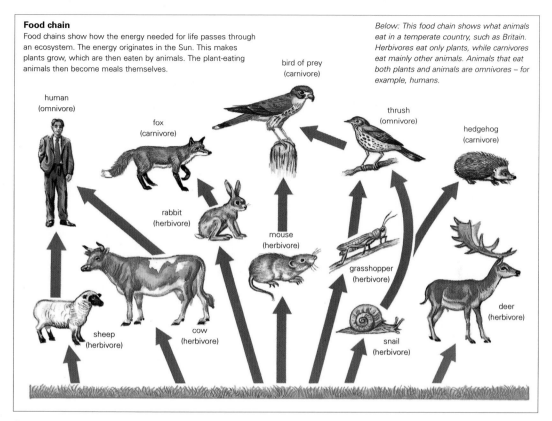

human
(omnivore)

fox
(carnivore)

bird of prey
(carnivore)

thrush
(omnivore)

hedgehog
(carnivore)

rabbit
(herbivore)

mouse
(herbivore)

grasshopper
(herbivore)

deer
(herbivore)

sheep
(herbivore)

cow
(herbivore)

snail
(herbivore)

## Group living

A herd, flock or shoal is a group of animals which gathers together for safety. Each member operates as an individual, but is physically safest in the centre of the group, the danger of attack being greatest on the edge. Herd members do not actively communicate dangers to each other. When one is startled by something and bolts, the rest will probably follow.

Members of a social group, on the other hand, work together to find food, raise their young and defend themselves. Many mammals, for example apes, monkeys, dogs, dolphins and elephants, form social groups, and these groups exist in many forms. At one end of the spectrum are highly ordered societies, such as lion prides and baboon troops, which are often controlled by one dominant male, the other members often having their own ranking in a strict hierarchical structure. At the other end of the spectrum are leaderless gangs of animals, such as squirrel monkeys, which merge and split with no real guiding purpose.

There are many advantages of living in social groups, with members finding more food and being warned of danger, for example. However, in many societies only a handful of high-ranking members are allowed to breed. In these cases, the groups are held together by a complex fusion of family ties in which brothers and sisters help to raise nephews and nieces. Politics also plays its cohesive part, with members forming and breaking alliances in order to rise to the top.

*Below: Meerkats live in family groups called bands. They need to live together because they live in a dry habitat where they must cooperate to find food, raise young and avoid being eaten by predators.*

# MIGRATION AND HIBERNATION

*Migration and hibernation are two ways in which animals cope with the changing seasons and fluctuations in the supply of food. By hibernating, they sleep through periods of bad weather when food is hard to find, and by migrating, they reach places where food is more readily available.*

Everywhere on Earth, the climate changes throughout the year with the cycle of seasons. In some places these changes are hardly noticeable from month to month, while in others each new season brings extremes of weather from blistering hot summers to freezing winters, or torrential rains followed by drought.

## Change of lifestyle

In temperate regions, such as Europe, the year is generally divided into four seasons. Other regions experience a different annual cycle of changes. For example, tropical regions do not really have fluctuating temperatures, but many areas do experience periods of relative dryness and at least one period of heavier rains each year. By contrast, in the far north, the change between the short summer and long winter is so quick that, in effect, there are only two seasons.

### Hibernating heart rate

The hibernating animal's heart rate slows to just a few beats per minute. It breathes more slowly and its body temperature drops to just a few degrees above the surrounding air temperature.

*Below: The bodies of true hibernators, such as the dormouse, shut down almost completely during hibernation. Other hibernators, such as bears, may be out of sight for most of the winter, but they do not become completely dormant and their temperature does not fall drastically.*

*Above: Reptiles that live in cooler parts of the world – rattlesnakes, for example – spend a long time lying dormant. They do not hibernate like mammals, but because they are cold-blooded and do not need lots of energy to function, they can go for long periods without food.*

Animals must, of course, react to these changes if they are to survive the harshest weather and make the most of clement conditions. Monkeys, for example, build up a mental map of their patch of forest so that they know where the fresh leaves will be after the rains, and where to find the hardier forest fruits during a drought. Wolves living in chilly northern forests hunt together in packs during the cold winter, working together to kill animals which are much larger than they are. However, when the summer arrives they tend to forage alone, picking off the many smaller animals, such as rodents and rabbits, which appear when the snow melts.

## Hibernation

The reason the wolves find these smaller animals in the summer is that they suddenly emerge having passed the winter in cosy burrows or nests. This behaviour is commonly called hibernating, but there is a distinction between true hibernation and simply being inactive over winter.

Animals such as bears and tree squirrels are not true hibernators. Although they generally sleep for long periods during the coldest parts of winter, hunkered down in a den or drey, they do not enter the deep, unconscious state of hibernation. Unable to feed while asleep, these animals rely on their bodily reserves of fat to stay alive. However, they often wake up during breaks in the harshest weather and venture outside to urinate or snatch a meal. Because tree squirrels have smaller fat reserves than bears, they frequently visit caches (stores) of food which they filled in the autumn.

On the other hand, the true hibernators, such as dormice or woodchucks, do not stir at all over winter. They rely completely on their reserves of fat to stay alive, and to save energy their metabolism slows to a fraction of its normal pace.

Only warm-blooded animals hibernate because they are the main types of animals which can survive in places where hibernation is necessary. However, rattlesnakes often pass the winter in rocky crevices and burrows. Reptiles and amphibians which live in very hot and dry places have their own form of hibernation, called aestivation.

They become dormant when their habitat becomes too dry. Most bury themselves in moist sand or under rocks, only becoming active again when rain brings the habitat back to life. Some aestivating frogs even grow a skin cocoon which traps moisture and keeps their bodies moist while they wait for the rains to return.

## Migration

Another way of coping with bad conditions is to migrate. Migrations are not just random wanderings, but involve following a set route each year. In general they are two-way trips, with animals returning to where they started once conditions back home become favourable again.

All sorts of animals migrate, from insects to whales, and there are many reasons for doing so. Most migrators are looking for supplies of food, or for a safe place to rear their young. For example, once their home territory becomes too crowded, young lemmings stampede over wide areas looking for new places to live, sometimes dying in the process. Herds of reindeer leave the barren tundra as winter approaches, and head for the relative warmth of the forest. Mountain goats act in a similar way: having spent the summer grazing in high alpine meadows, they descend below the treeline when winter snow begins to cover their pastures.

Other migrations are on a much grander scale, and in some cases an animal's whole life can be a continual migration. Wildebeest travel in huge

*Above: Whales make the longest migrations of all mammals. They move from their warm breeding grounds near the equator to feeding areas in cooler waters near the poles.*

herds across southern Africa in search of fresh pastures. They follow age-old routes but may take a detour if grass is growing in unusual places. Among the greatest migrants are the giant whales, which travel thousands of miles from their breeding grounds in the tropics to their feeding grounds near the poles. The cool waters around the poles teem with plankton food, while the warmer tropical waters are a better place for giving birth.

## Day length

How do animals know that it is time to hibernate or migrate? The answer lies in the changing number of hours of daylight as the seasons change.

All animals are sensitive to daylight, and use it to set their body clocks or circadian rhythms. These rhythms

*Above: Bats spend long periods hibernating. They mate before winter, and the females store the sperm inside their body, only releasing it on the eggs as spring approaches.*

affect all bodily processes, including the build-up to the breeding season. The hibernators begin to put on weight or store food as the days shorten, and many migrants start to get restless before setting off on their journey. However, not all migrations are controlled by the number of hours of daylight. Some migrators, such as wildebeest and lemmings, move because of other environmental factors, such as the lack of food caused by drought or overcrowding.

*Below: The migrations of enormous herds of wildebeest across the huge grasslands of Africa is one of the natural wonders of the world. These large antelopes travel in search of watering holes and new areas of fresh grass. The migrations do not follow the same route each year, but the herds generally do stay on tried and tested trails.*

# INTRODUCED SPECIES

*Centuries ago, as people started exploring and conquering new lands, many animals travelled with them.
In fact, that's the only way many animals could travel such long distances, often crossing seas. Many
introduced species then thrived in their new habitats, often at the expense of the native wildlife.*

Perhaps one of the first introduced animals was the dingo. This Australian dog is now regarded as a species in its own right, but it was introduced to the region by the Aboriginals. These migrants had domesticated the ancestors of the dingo, probably from grey wolves, many years before.

Dingoes were one of the first placental mammals to come to Australia, which had previously been populated by marsupial mammals. In a chain of events that has been repeated many times since, the introduced dingoes became feral (living as wild animals), and were soon competing with native hunters for food. Not only did the introduced mammals begin to take over from the marsupial predators, such as Tasmanian devils and marsupial wolves, but they also wiped out many smaller marsupials which were unable to defend themselves against these ferocious foreign hunters. In fact, many more of the native Australian marsupials

*Below: Dingoes are wild dogs that live in Australia. However, they did not evolve there; no large placental mammals did. They are actually the relatives of pet dogs that travelled with the first people to reach Australia.*

have now become extinct, or are in danger of doing so, though not just dingoes are responsible. As European settlers have arrived over the last couple of centuries, they have also introduced many new animals, including cats.

## Domestic animals

Looking around the European countryside, you would be forgiven for thinking that cows, sheep and other farm animals are naturally occurring species. In fact, all come from distant parts of the world. Over the centuries, livestock animals have been selectively bred to develop desirable characteristics, such as lean meat or high milk production. Despite this, they can be traced back to ancestral species.

For example, goats – a domestic breed of an Asian ibex – were introduced to North Africa about 3,000 years ago. These goats, with their voracious appetites, did well feeding on dry scrubland. In fact they did too well, and had soon stripped the plants, turning even more of North Africa into desert. Similarly, horses introduced to the Americas by European settlers had

**Cows and sheep**
European cows are believed to be descendants of a now-extinct species of oxen called the auroch, while modern sheep are descended from the mouflon. From their beginnings in the Middle East, new breeds were introduced to all corners of the world, where they had a huge effect on the native animals and wildlife.

*Above: Cattle have been bred to look and behave very differently from their wild ancestors. Few breeds have horns, and they are generally docile animals. Some breeds produce a good supply of milk, while others are bred for their meat.*

*Below: Sheep were among the first domestic animals. They are kept for their meat and sometimes milk, which is used for cheese. The thick coat or fleece that kept their ancestors warm on mountain slopes is now used to make woollen garments.*

*Above: While the ancestors of domestic horses have become extinct, horses have become wild in several parts of the world. Perhaps the most celebrated of these feral horses are the mustangs, which run free in the wild American West, after escaping from early European settlers.*

a marked effect on that continent. Native people, as well as the settlers, began to use them to hunt bison on the plains, which eventually gave way to cattle. Groups of the introduced horses escaped from captivity and began to live wild. The feral American horses were called mustangs.

### Rodent invaders

While many animals were introduced to new areas on purpose as livestock or pets, other animals hitched a lift. For example, some animals were more or less stowaways on ships, but only those that could fend for themselves at their new destination were successfully introduced. These species tended to be generalist feeders, and none was more successful than rodents, such as mice and rats. In fact the house mouse is the second most widespread mammal of all,

after humans. It lives almost everywhere that people do, except in the icy polar regions, although it is very likely that rodents did reach these places but then failed to thrive in the cold.

The black rat – also known as the ship rat – has spread right around the world from Asia over the last 2,000 years. On several occasions it has brought diseases with it, including bubonic plague, or the Black Death, which has killed millions of people. Another prolific travelling rodent is the brown rat which is thought to have

spread from Europe, and now exists everywhere except the poles.

Rodents are so successful because they will eat almost anything and can reproduce at a prolific rate. These two characteristics have meant that mice and rats have become pests wherever they breed.

*Below: With their sharp and ever-growing teeth, rodents are very adaptable animals. Mice and rats have spread alongside humans, and wherever people go, these little gnawing beasts soon become established, breeding very quickly and spreading into new areas.*

# ENDANGERED SPECIES

*Many animals are threatened with extinction because they cannot survive in a world which is constantly being changed by human intervention. Many species have already become extinct, and if people do nothing to save them, a great many more will follow.*

Surprising though it may sound, there is nothing unusual in extinctions, for they are an important part of the natural world. As the climate and landscape have changed in a given area over millions of years, the animals that live there have also changed. And as a new species evolves, so another is forced out of its habitat and becomes extinct. All that remains, if we are lucky, are a few fossilized bones – a record in stone.

## Mass extinction?

Biologists estimate that there are at least several million species alive today, and possibly as many as 30 million. Whatever the figure, there are probably more species on Earth right now than at any other time. Therefore, because of the habitat destruction caused by people, more species are becoming extinct or are being threatened with extinction than ever before.

Geologists and biologists know that every now and then there are mass extinctions, in which great

*Below: Okapis are rare mammals whose closest living relatives are giraffes, despite the zebra-stripes on their hindquarters and forelegs. They live in the forest of the Congo in central Africa. This forest has been ravaged by war and deforestation, and okapis and other forest-dwellers are now very rare.*

*Above: Leatherback turtles are the largest turtles in the world – even larger than the better-known giant tortoises. They are becoming rare because of the decline in untouched beaches on which to lay their eggs. Fewer leatherbacks are being born, and even fewer reach adulthood.*

numbers of the world's animals die out forever. For example, it is widely believed that the dinosaurs and many other reptiles were wiped out after a meteorite smashed into Mexico 65 million years ago. But the questions are now: are we witnessing the natural world's latest mass extinction? And are humans the cause?

Most of the world's animal species are insects – especially beetles – and other invertebrates. It is likely that many of these species, especially those living in tropical forests, are becoming extinct. However, since scientists may never have had a chance to describe many of them, nobody knows the true number.

## Life list

With vertebrate animals, it is a different story. Because there are only a few thousand species of animals with backbones, most of which have been recognized for hundreds of years, we know a great deal more about the plight of each species. Many species, for example mice, dogs and horses, thrive in a world dominated by people. However, a great many more species have suffered as people have destroyed their habitats, either deliberately or by upsetting the balance of nature by introducing species from other parts of the world.

The International Union for the Conservation of Nature and Natural Resources (IUCN) produces a Red List of animals which are in danger of extinction. There are currently about 5,500 animals listed in a number of categories, including extinct in the wild, endangered and vulnerable. Nearly one quarter of all mammals are

included on the list, and about four per cent of reptiles and three of amphibians. However, while the status of all mammals has been assessed by the IUCN, only a fraction of reptiles and amphibians has been as thoroughly checked, and it is very likely that many more species are much closer to extinction than was previously thought.

*Below: Golden lion tamarins are small monkeys that have been saved from extinction by extensive captive breeding programmes in zoos around the world. An area of the monkey's forest habitat in Brazil is now being protected, and captive-bred monkeys are being reintroduced to the wild.*

*Above: Gorillas are endangered because their forest habitats are being destroyed. They are not able to thrive anywhere else. Also, these great apes are hunted for meat. Although illegal, the bush-meat trade is highly profitable, but soon there may be no gorillas left.*

## Wiped out

As the forests of Europe and China were cleared over the past thousand years, forest animals had increasingly fewer places to live. And as they inevitably came into increasingly close contact with people, wild animals, such as boars, bears and wolves, became persecuted and were eventually wiped out in many areas.

*Above: Pandas live in bamboo forests and do not breed very often or eagerly. They were once on the verge of extinction, however the latest technology – from artificial insemination to test-tube baby pandas – is increasing the numbers of these popular mammals.*

As the world's human population soared in the 20th century, a similar process took place elsewhere. Another major habitat being destroyed was, and still is, the tropical rainforest. The number of species living in these areas is much higher than elsewhere, and a proportionately huge number of species are finding it harder to survive.

Although few animals on the Red List have actually become extinct, the situation is becoming graver for most species. The monkeys and apes of the tropical rainforests are among the worst affected, with nearly one in four species being very close to extinction. This is because rainforests are complicated places, and many primate species there have evolved a specialized lifestyle, for example feeding on fruit in the tallest trees. These species are very badly affected by sudden changes in their environment, for example when a logging team cuts down all the tall trees leaving, just the shorter ones behind.

# CONSERVING WILDLIFE

*With so many species facing extinction, conservationists have their work cut out. Conservationists try to protect habitats and provide safe places for threatened animals to thrive, but the activities of ordinary people can often also have an adverse effect on the future of natural habitats.*

People give many reasons why wildlife should be conserved. Some argue that if all the forests were cleared and the oceans polluted, the delicate balance of nature would be so ruined that Earth would not be able to support any life, including humans. Others suggest that if vulnerable species were allowed to die, the natural world would not be sufficiently diverse to cope with future changes in the environment. Another reason to save diversity is that we have not yet fully recorded it. Also, there are undoubtedly many as yet unknown species – especially of plants – which could be useful to humankind, for example in the field of medicine. But perhaps the strongest argument for the conservation of wildlife is that it would be totally irresponsible to let it disappear.

## Habitat protection

Whatever the reasons, the best way to protect species in danger of being wiped out is to protect their habitats so that the complex communities of

plants and animals can continue to live. However, with the human population growing so rapidly, people are often forced to choose between promoting their own interests and protecting wildlife. Of course, people invariably put themselves first, which means that the conservationists have to employ a range of techniques in order to save wildlife.

In many countries it has now become illegal to hunt certain endangered animals, or to trade in any products made from their bodies. Whales, gorillas and elephants are protected in this way. Many governments and charitable organizations have also set up wildlife reserves, where the animals stand a good chance of thriving. The oldest

*Below: One of the main causes of deforestation is people clearing the trees and burning them to make way for farmland. The ash makes good soil for a few years, but eventually the nutrients needed by the crops run out and so the farmers often begin to clear more forest.*

*Above: If logging is done properly, it can make enough money to pay to protect the rest of the rainforest. Only selected trees are cut down and they are removed without damaging younger growth. Forests can be used to grow crops, such as coffee and nuts, without cutting down all the trees.*

protected areas are in North America and Europe, where it is illegal to ruin areas of forest wilderness and wetland. Consequently, these places have become wildlife havens. Other protected areas include semi-natural landscapes which double as beauty spots and tourist attractions. Although these areas often have to be extensively altered and managed to meet the needs of the visitors, most still support wildlife communities.

In the developing world, wildlife refuges are a newer phenomenon. Huge areas of Africa's savannahs are protected and populated with many amazing animals. However, the enormous size of these parks makes it very hard to protect the animals, especially elephants and rhinoceroses, from poachers.

## Reintroduction

Large areas of tropical forests are now protected in countries such as Brazil and Costa Rica, but often conservation efforts come too late because many animals have either become rare or are completely absent after years of human

## Zoo animals

Once zoos were places where exotic animals were merely put on display. Such establishments were increasingly regarded as cruel. Today, the world's best zoos are an integral part of conservation. Several animals, which are classified as extinct in the wild, can only be found in zoos where they are being bred. These breeding programmes are heavily controlled to make sure that closely related animals do not breed with each other. Later, individual animals may be sent around the world to mate in different zoos to avoid in-breeding.

*Below: Many of the world's rarest species, such as the red panda, are kept in zoos, partly so that people can see them, since they are too rare to be spotted in the wild. Some people are opposed to animals being put on display for this reason.*

damage. However, several conservation programmes have reintroduced animals bred in zoos into the wild.

To reintroduce a group of zoo-bred animals successfully into the wild, conservationists need to know how the animal fits into the habitat and interacts with the other animals living there. In addition, for example when trying to reintroduce orang-utans to the forests of Borneo, people have to teach the young animals how to find food and fend for themselves.

*Below: Breeding centres are an important way of increasing the number of rare animals. Most, such as this giant panda centre in China, are in the natural habitat. If the animals kept there are treated properly, they should be able to fend for themselves when released back into the wild.*

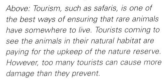

*Above: Tourism, such as safaris, is one of the best ways of ensuring that rare animals have somewhere to live. Tourists coming to see the animals in their natural habitat are paying for the upkeep of the nature reserve. However, too many tourists can cause more damage than they prevent.*

## Understanding habitats

A full understanding of how animals live in the wild is also vitally important when conservationists are working in a habitat that has been damaged by human activity. For example, in areas of rainforest which are being heavily logged, the trees are often divided into isolated islands of growth surrounded by cleared ground. This altered habitat is no good for monkeys, which need large areas of forest to swing through throughout the year. The solution is to plant strips of forest to connect the islands of untouched habitat, creating a continuous mass again.

Another example of beneficial human intervention involves protecting rare frogs in the process of migrating to a breeding pond. If their migration necessitates crossing a busy road, it is likely that many of them will be run over. Conservationists now dig little tunnels under the roads so that the frogs can travel in safety. Similar protection schemes have been set up for hedgehogs and ducks, to allow them safe passageways.

# BIOMES

*The Earth is not a uniform place but has a complex patchwork of habitats covering its surface from the equator to the poles. Biologists have simplified this patchwork by dividing it into zones called biomes, each of which has a particular climate and a distinct community of animals.*

The places where animal communities live can be radically different. So, for example, vipers slither along the tops of sand dunes in the middle of the Sahara Desert while sperm whales live hundreds of metres down in the gloomy, ice-cold depths of the ocean. The environmental conditions determine what kind of animals and plants are able to survive there.

## Climate control

The world's habitats are generally divided into 11 biomes: oceans, freshwater rivers and wetlands, tropical forests, temperate forests, boreal forests, tropical grasslands or savannahs, temperate grasslands or prairies, tundra, polar ice caps, deserts and mountains.

The overriding factor that determines whether a piece of land belongs to one biome or another is its climate – chiefly the rainfall and

temperature. Understanding the climate of a place is a complicated business because the factors involved – including rainfall, temperature and light levels – vary from day to night and throughout the year. The latitude is probably the best place to start. In general terms, regions close to the equator, at a latitude of 0°, are hot. The coldest places are the poles, with a latitude of 90°. The territory in between generally cools as you travel to higher latitudes.

However, other factors also affect climate. For example, during the hot days of summer, the land at certain latitudes warms up more quickly than the ocean. Six months later, in the depths of winter, the land cools down more quickly than the ocean. This means that the oceans and the areas of land bordering them tend to enjoy a mild climate with smaller fluctuations

of temperature each year, while the interiors of large continental landmasses experience very hot summers and extremely chilly winters.

## Animal communities

Other geographical factors – ocean currents, mountains and depressions in the Earth's surface – also have a major influence on climate and biomes. The climate defines which plants can grow in any particular spot and how quickly. And since the plants form the basis of all food webs and ecosystems, each biome has a particular community of animals which have evolved to exploit the plant life.

*Below: This map shows how the world can be divided into biomes. The climate of a region has the greatest effect on the sorts of plants and animals that can survive there. Some animals may live across an entire biome, while others are found only in particular habitats.*

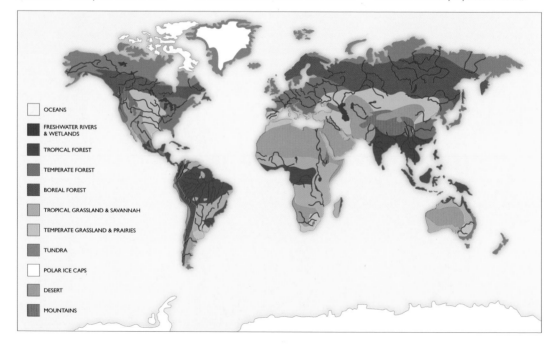

- OCEANS
- FRESHWATER RIVERS & WETLANDS
- TROPICAL FOREST
- TEMPERATE FOREST
- BOREAL FOREST
- TROPICAL GRASSLAND & SAVANNAH
- TEMPERATE GRASSLAND & PRAIRIES
- TUNDRA
- POLAR ICE CAPS
- DESERT
- MOUNTAINS

## Biomes and ear size

Closely related animals that live in different biomes have different features that help them function under different conditions. For example, foxes live in similar ways across the world. However, the Arctic fox, which lives in cold polar areas, has very small outer ears. The red fox that lives in the mild temperate biome of Europe has medium-sized ears, while the bat-eared fox and other species that live in hot areas have very large ears. Ear size is linked to the control of body heat. The small size of the Arctic fox's ears prevents heat wastage, while the large ears of the bat-eared fox are useful for radiating away unwanted heat, helping the animal keep cool. The red fox's ears are a compromise: large enough to hear very clearly, but small enough to conserve heat in the winter.

Arctic fox

Red fox

Bat-eared fox

Rainfall has a major influence on biomes. It is generally heaviest in tropical regions, resulting in lush rainforests. In colder regions, rainfall may be almost as high but it results in a different type of forest. In areas with less rain, deserts or grasslands appear.

The animals in different biomes face the same challenges: finding enough food and water, and finding a mate to raise offspring. However, the different conditions in each biome mean that the animals have to meet these challenges in very different ways.

In all biomes, the animal communities have a similar structure. Grazers and other plant-eating animals survive by eating any plants which have evolved to make the most of the climatic conditions. These grazers are, in turn, preyed upon by a series of hunters. In the most productive biomes, such as forests, many of these hunting animals might be hunted in turn by larger, fiercer predators.

However, the plant-eaters of grasslands, such as bison and antelopes, live a very different life from their counterparts in tropical forests, such as monkeys and tapirs. Similarly, ocean hunters, such as mighty orcas (killer whales), have a body adapted to swimming at great speed through the water; the predators in a boreal forest, such as wolves, have very different bodies for covering long distances quickly and bringing down animals more than twice their size. One of the main purposes of biology is to understand how communities of plants and animals have evolved to survive in the world's different biomes.

## Grassland animals

Grasslands are unusual habitats because food is everywhere. While animals that live in other biomes must seek out and defend a source of food, grazing animals are surrounded by it, and no single animal can control it. Instead of competing for food, they compete for mates, and many grazers are big and tough fighters. Grass and other plant foods are not very nutritious, so animals have to eat a lot of them. Therefore many of them, such as bison and elephants, are big. Being large also helps defence against predators. Grassland predators such as lions tend to hunt in groups so that they can work together to bring down powerful animals.

Bison

Elephant

Lion

# OCEANS

*The oceans cover nearly three-quarters of the Earth's surface and create by far the largest and most complex biome. They contain the world's largest and smallest animals, from tiny zooplankton to the mighty blue whale. Between these two extremes, the oceans contain an incredible wealth of life.*

The oceans are not a simple biome because they consist of countless habitats, including everything from colourful coral reefs to mysterious, deep-sea hydrothermal vents. The depth of the ocean obviously has a marked effect on the conditions. Depth can range from just a few centimetres along the coast to about 11km (6.75 miles), the deepest ocean point in the Mariana Trench, near the Pacific island of Guam. The first few 100m (330ft) or so below the surface is called the photic zone, where the water is bathed in sunlight during the day. This upper layer is the limit of plant growth in the ocean because below this depth the light fades, unable to penetrate any deeper, and plants rely on light to make their food.

As on land, many ocean animals graze on plants, which means that they have to live in the photic zone. Ocean plants tend to be simple algae, known as phytoplankton, which float in the current. These plants do not have complicated body structures, and many

Marine iguanas can be found along rocky coastlines. They can stay underwater for over an hour.

Sea otters do not need land to survive. When sleeping, they wrap themselves in kelp.

Common seals have large, sensitive eyes which help them to see underwater.

Dugongs have specially shaped mouths with overhanging upper lips for cropping sea grasses.

are just single cells. Consequently, many of the ocean plant-eaters are also tiny floating organisms, known collectively as zooplankton. Zooplankton – largely shrimp-like crustaceans – is a very important part of the ocean food chain, being the main food for toothless baleen whales. These ocean giants filter out the zooplankton from gulps of sea water.

Deeper down, in the dark depths, life continues without plants. Despite conditions being too dark for plants, most deep-sea animals still get their energy from them indirectly by feeding on marine "snow". This consists of the waste products and dead bodies of the organisms higher up.

These food chains provide the basis of animal life in the ocean, feeding many types of larger vertebrate animals including fish, turtles and sea mammals.

While fish evolved in the sea, the sea-living reptiles, such as turtles and sea snakes, and the sea mammals, such as seals and whales, actually evolved from animals which once lived on land. A great deal of this evolution must have taken place in shallow coastal waters, and while whales and dolphins have become completely independent of land, other sea mammals and most reptiles must return to land at some point during the year to breed.

Seals and sea lions make their homes in coastal waters where the ocean meets the land. These shallow waters are very different from the dark abyss of the deep ocean. Coral reefs, sometimes described as the rainforests of the ocean because they support so much life, are a feature of coastal waters in the tropics. In shallow seas, tall kelps and other kinds of seaweed can grow into thick underwater forests, providing habitats for a whole range of animals, such as sea otters.

*Orcas, also known as killer whales, live throughout the world's oceans. They are expert hunters.*

*White-beaked dolphins live in coastal waters. They are famed for leaping and somersaulting.*

*In autumn, northern right whales migrate from cold northern waters to warmer areas in the south.*

*Humpback whales live in deep waters, spending the summer in cold waters near the poles.*

# FRESH WATER

*Only three per cent of the world's water is fresh, but experts estimate that this covers a total of over 100,000sq km (38,610sq miles), including the polar icecaps. The rivers, lakes and wetlands supplied by fresh water are some of the best places to see wildlife. But where does fresh water come from?*

The Earth's atmosphere is a huge water pump that transfers water from the oceans to the land. The heat from the sun makes water evaporate from the surface of the ocean, and the water vapour produced becomes part of the atmosphere. The warm water vapour in the air may then cool down for various reasons. As it cools, the vapour begins to turn back into a liquid, forming tiny droplets on the surface of particles of dust carried in the wind. These moist dust particles gather to form the clouds that often obscure clear skies. If the air cools even more, the amount of water condensing in cloud becomes too much for it to hold, and the water falls to the surface as rain.

Since most of the Earth's surface is covered by oceans, most of the rain falls back into the sea. However, some falls on to land where it forms rivers, lakes and waterlogged ground, such as swamps and marshes, known collectively as wetlands. Mountain ranges receive high rainfall because they force the moist air to rise up

Beavers dam rivers to make pools by cutting logs with their teeth and floating them into position.

Capybaras live in herds on the banks of rivers and in swampy areas, using water as a refuge.

Otters hunt along river banks. They are good swimmers but will stray away from water to find food.

Green anacondas spend much of their time in shallow water, waiting for their prey to drink.

over them and cool. The rain then flows down the mountainsides in torrents and waterfalls. Down on the lowlands, these fast-flowing streams join together to make larger, deeper rivers which move more slowly across the landscape. Nearly all the fresh water falling on land eventually makes its way back to the oceans via rivers. Some fresh water does seep into rocks under the ground, but it reappears as springs which feed yet more rivers.

All the rivers in the world combined contain just a fraction of the Earth's water, though some of them form huge freshwater systems. The largest river system is in the Amazon Basin. This South American network of rivers contains more water than the Nile, Mississippi and Yangtze rivers together, and hosts many thousands of animal and plant species.

Rain water and other forms of precipitation provide fresh water. When water evaporates from the oceans, the salt is left behind and only the water molecules rise into the atmosphere. Although fresh water acquires small amounts of dissolved salts as it flows over rocks on its journey to the sea, it is much less salty than sea water, and this has a marked effect on the animals that live in it. While sea water is saltier than the body fluids of animals, fresh water is less salty, which means that water tends to flow into the animal from outside. If the animal does not frequently get rid of some moisture, it will become swollen, and its body fluids will be too diluted to work efficiently.

Freshwater fish and amphibians tackle this problem by urinating all their excess water. Semi-aquatic animals, such as otters and anacondas, rely on their skin to act as a barrier to the influx of water.

*Amazon river dolphins inhabit slow-moving river waters. They use sounds to find their prey.*

*Hippopotamuses keep cool in water, with only their nostrils, eyes and ears above the surface.*

*Nile crocodiles are excellent at fishing, herding fish into shallow waters before catching them.*

*Gharials inhabit quiet backwaters. Their flattened tail and webbed feet are well adapted for swimming.*

# TROPICAL FORESTS

*Tropical forests are the oldest and most complex forests on Earth. They contain a greater variety of animal species than anywhere else on land, from the great apes, such as gorillas and orang-utans, and big cats, such as tigers and leopards, to tiny frogs and pencil-thin snakes.*

The lush, steamy jungles of tropical forest grow in a band around the Earth's equator. These forests are packed with wildlife, more so than any other biome. The total number of animal species living in tropical forests is unknown because most have never been identified, but it probably adds up to several million. The majority of these species are insects, such as beetles and bugs, but tropical forests also contain the greatest diversity of vertebrate animals. Unfortunately, large tracts of these forests are now under threat from human activities such as logging.

Tropical forests are among the wettest places on Earth. Most receive about 2.5m (8ft) of rain every year, while forests that grow on ocean islands often receive over 6m (19½ft). The tropics receive so much rain because near the equator the sun is always high in the sky, keeping temperatures elevated. Consequently, a great deal of water evaporates from the oceans and rises into the sky here. The water vapour cools as it rises and

Emerald tree boas have leaf-green camouflage which helps keep them safe from birds of prey.

Brazilian tapirs live in woodland habitats with a source of water. They are excellent swimmers.

Brown capuchins are highly adaptable, living in dense jungle trees and also in towns and cities.

Ocelots are agile climbers, often hunting in trees. They sleep in shady thickets and hunt at night.

condenses into vast rain clouds. Generally towards the end of the day, these clouds release their load of water.

Rainfall defines the two main types of tropical forest – rainforest and monsoon forest. Rainforests grow in places where rainfall is heavy all year round, although there are often drier spells throughout the year. The main areas of rainforest are South America's Amazon Basin, the African Congo and South-east Asia. Monsoon forests grow in tropical areas where most rain falls during an annual wet season. The largest monsoon forests are found in India, Australia and along the coast of Brazil.

With so much water and warmth, plants grow larger and more quickly than just about anywhere else on land. Most trees reach at least 50m (165ft) tall and form a dense network of branches, or canopy, high above the ground. The canopy is so thick in places that underneath it is very gloomy and humid. Taller trees poke their crowns out above the canopy. The tallest of these emergent trees grow over 100m (330ft) high.

Tropical forest plants grow more thickly than elsewhere, too. Some plants, known as air plants or epiphytes, do not grow in the ground

but attach themselves on to the trunks or branches of larger plants. Within this complex framework of plant life, there are countless places for all types of animal to thrive. For example, amphibians need to live in water during the early stages of their life. And with so much rain falling, tropical forests are rarely short of water. Some epiphytes have bowl-shaped leaves to catch the rain, and several amphibian species use these aerial ponds as breeding sites. Down on the ground some frogs and salamanders just lay their eggs in damp soil, which is wet enough for their young to develop in.

*Okapi live in dense tropical forests, communicating with vocalizations and mutual grooming.*

*Tigers' orange and black striped coat helps them to blend in with dense forest undergrowth.*

*Asian elephants use their trunk to forage for grass, foliage, fruit, branches, twigs and tree bark.*

*Orang-utans live in trees, moving slowly from branch to branch. They sleep in nests high in the canopy.*

# TEMPERATE FORESTS

*Before the rise of agriculture, temperate forests covered most of Europe, the eastern part of North America and China. Today, however, nearly all of these wild woodlands have been replaced by meadows and farmland. After tropical forests, temperate forests contain the greatest diversity of animal life on land.*

Temperate forests grow in mild regions that receive a lot of rain but do not get too hot or cold. The largest temperate forests are in the northern hemisphere, in a belt north of subtropical regions.

The main difference between the temperate forests and other forest biomes is that most temperate trees are deciduous, dropping their leaves in the autumn, and growing new ones in spring. Although there are a few deciduous trees, such as paper birch, growing in the southern zones of northern boreal forests, there are many more evergreen conifers.

The reason why temperate forests lose their leaves is to save energy during the winter. Because it is rarely very bright over winter, the leaves would not be able to photosynthesize food from sunlight. And because the cold and frosts would damage the redundant leaves during winter, it is best that they are dropped. As autumn progresses, the leaves' valuable green pigments, which trap the sun's energy, withdraw back into the tree. Then, as the

Striped skunks forage under thick vegetation at night. They produce a foul spray when threatened.

Grey squirrels make nests, or dreys, from twigs and leaves among woodland tree branches.

Porcupines rest in hollow trees by day and spend the night looking for food, using their sensitive nose.

Common toads often live in dry areas. They have a thick skin that prevents them from drying out.

green disappears, so the less important red and brown pigments are revealed, giving the forest its autumn colours.

As with a few other land biomes, temperate forests are poorly represented in the southern hemisphere, with only a few patches in South Africa and Australia, because there is very little southern land with an appropriate climate. One exception is New Zealand, which once had many areas of temperate forest. However, the forests of this isolated region are very different from the huge forests which grow in the north. Instead of the broad-leaved flowering trees, such as

oak, ash and maple that are common in most temperate forests, many New Zealand forests are dominated by tree-sized ferns and other plants which were common many millions of years ago.

The temperate forests that grow in slightly warmer and drier regions, such as California, the Mediterranean and South Africa, are not deciduous. They are populated with evergreen trees with toughened leaves that keep the moisture in with a coating of oily resin. Perhaps the most spectacular forests in this biome are the temperate rainforests found on the coast of British Columbia, Canada. Due to the unusual climate,

the forests receive more rain than most tropical rainforests, which is one reason why the redwood, the world's largest tree, flourishes here.

During winter, with the leaves fallen, temperate forests become desolate places with little food available. Larger animals may migrate to warmer, more productive areas to spend the winter, or scratch out a living while depending on their body fat reserves. Smaller animals, such as dormice and ground squirrels, hibernate to save energy until the spring, while others, such as most tree-living squirrels, rely on food caches that they built up in the autumn.

*Grass snakes are able to hunt on land and in the water. They need to bask in the sun to keep warm.*

*Fallow deer inhabit woodlands with clearings, where they eat grass, foliage, berries and fungi.*

*Wombats dig out extensive forest burrows and make nests inside using either leaves or bark.*

*Koalas live in eucalyptus trees. They have long intestines to help them digest fibrous leaves.*

# BOREAL FORESTS

*Boreal forest, or taiga as it is also known, grows in the icy conditions of the far north. This biome is dominated by conifers, which are the only trees that can survive the harsh conditions. Boreal forests form the largest swathes of continuous forest and cover about ten percent of the Earth's land.*

Boreal forest gets its name from the Greek god of the north wind, Boreas. The name is apt because this type of forest only grows in the northern hemisphere – not because the climatic conditions for boreal forest do not exist in the southern hemisphere, but because there is little land down there where such forests can grow. The

alternative name, taiga, is a Russian word meaning marshy pine forest. This name is also apt because boreal forests often grow around moss-filled bogs, the actual bogs being too wet for tree growth.

Boreal forests grow in huge unbroken swathes in Siberia and Canada, and are also found in Scandinavia, Alaska

and northern Japan. A few small patches have survived in Scotland, but most natural conifer forests were cut down many years ago. These parts of the far north enjoy a short summer with very long days and a long, cold winter when the sun only rises for a few hours. Winter temperatures regularly plunge to –25°C (–13°F).

Brown bears live a solitary life in the forest but may gather in groups when hunting for salmon.

Pine martens have large eyes to compensate for low light levels in northern conifer forests.

Grey wolves live in conifer forests, in packs with strict hierarchies. They hunt by scent and hearing.

Moose plod through forests and marshes, browsing on a variety of leaves, mosses and lichens.

Compared to other forests, boreal ones are very simple because they contain far fewer species; in fact, almost all the trees in these forests are conifers. Because of the cold and dark, boreal forests appear frozen in time for much of the year as the wildlife endures the cold, waiting for the intense activity of the short summer growing season. Even the summer is too cold for nearly all cold-blooded animals, such as amphibians and reptiles. Rattlesnakes do survive in the southern fringes of the Canadian forest, but amphibians are uncommon. Mammals such as marmots and bears

hibernate during the coldest months of the year. Incredibly, wood frogs endure the winter frozen inside river ice, becoming active again after the thaw.

Mammals that do not hibernate often adopt a very different lifestyle to survive the winter months. For example, herds of reindeer migrate into the forests, only heading back to the barren tundra in summer. Small rodents, such as mice or shrews, construct tunnels in the snow during winter, and moose survive by eating strips of bark.

Because their growth is so slow and intermittent, boreal forests are

relatively free of animals compared to other forests. However, many of the animals that do live there are much larger than their relatives living farther south. For example, the moose is the world's largest deer and wolverines are the size of a dog, much larger than most mustelids.

The reason for this is that larger animals need to eat less food per unit of weight than smaller ones. They lose heat more slowly, and do not have to burn food at a such a high rate. Scientists have noticed that even animals of the same species tend to be bigger if they are living further north.

Wolverines prefer remote areas, far away from humans. Females give birth in rocky dens.

Red squirrels live alone, high up in conifer trees. In winter they are able to survive on caches of food.

Eurasian lynxes have furred feet that give them a good grip as well as warmth on frozen ground.

Sables build dens on the forest floor. When weather is extreme, they store their prey in the dens.

# GRASSLANDS

*Although a lot of wild countryside is covered in different grasses – not to mention the many acres of garden lawns – little of it is true grassland. If left alone, these habitats would eventually become thick woodland. True grasslands, from prairies to the savannah, have very few trees but contain many creatures.*

Grasslands appear in areas where there is some rain, but not enough to support the growth of large numbers of trees. These conditions exist on all continents, and consequently grasslands come in many forms, growing in both tropical and more temperate regions.

The world's grasslands also have many different names. The temperate grasslands of North America are called prairies, in South America they are known as the pampas, and in Europe and Asia they are the steppes. The tropical grasslands of east Africa and Australia are called savannah, and in southern Africa they are the veldt.

Temperate grasslands tend to be located in so-called rain shadows. For example, the North American prairies are in the rain shadow of the Rocky Mountains. A rain shadow is an area which rarely gets rain because the wind bringing it must first travel over a range of mountains. As the wind rises up it cools and releases the rainwater on the windward side. The wind then whistles down the leeward

American bison move about the grassland continuously, eating a variety of grasses and rushes.

Pronghorns live in large herds. They have excellent eyesight, with almost 360-degree vision.

Black mambas live in permanent savannah lairs, actively hunting small mammals and birds.

Cheetahs are the fastest land animals in the world, hunting a range of hoofed grassland animals.

side carrying much less water. If the wind is very dry, then that area becomes a desert. However, the wind often carries enough moisture to let grasses grow.

The main plant food in grasslands is, of course, grass. Grass is an unusual type of plant because its growing points are near to the ground rather than at the tip of the stem, as with most other plants. This means that it can keep growing despite having its juicy blades eaten by grazing animals.

Grazing animals are commonly found in grasslands, as are the browsers which pick the leaves and fruit of small shrubs which often grow in the area. With few places to hide in the wide-open spaces, grazing animals group together into herds for safety. Fortunately, grass and other plant foods are virtually omnipresent, which means that members of these herds only need to compete when it comes to choosing a mate. This has led them, especially the males, to evolve elaborate weapons and display structures, such as horns or tusks. Grazing animals are large anyway because they have to survive on huge meals of tough grass which is low in nutrition, while the pressure to compete with each other has made them even larger.

Without trees to hide in, smaller animals, such as ground squirrels and marmots, take refuge under the ground in burrow complexes. Many, such as moles and mole rats, have adapted to a totally subterranean lifestyle.

Much of the world's temperate grasslands have been turned into farmland for growing cereal crops and raising livestock. Cereals, such as wheat and rye, are actually domestic breeds of grass which would naturally grow in these regions anyway.

Most of the animals once found on grasslands have suffered badly because of the rise of agriculture.

*Zebras' black and white stripes help them to blend in with natural patterns of light and shade.*

*Black rhinoceroses enjoy mud baths in wallowing sites, which help to keep their skin healthy.*

*Saigas are nomadic, migrating south to warmer climes and better feeding grounds in autumn.*

*Kangaroos have a specialized digestion process than allows them to break down dry grass.*

# POLAR REGIONS

*Despite being freezing cold and largely covered with ice, polar regions can be characterized as deserts. Although there is solid water almost everywhere, the few plants and animals which do live there often have great difficulty in obtaining liquid water, just like the wildlife in scorching deserts.*

The polar regions – the Arctic in the north and Antarctic in the south – begin at 66° North and 66° South. These positions on the globe are marked as the Arctic and Antarctic Circles. Within these imaginary circles, something very strange happens on at least one day every summer: the sun does not set. Similarly, for at least a single 24 hours in winter, it does not rise. The wildlife of the Arctic is not similar to that around the Antarctic. This is not just because they are at opposite ends of the world, but also because the geography of the two areas is very different. The Antarctic is dominated by Antarctica, a mountainous landmass which is a significantly sized continent, larger than Australia. Meanwhile the Arctic has the Arctic Ocean – the world's smallest ocean – at its centre.

The wildernesses of ice and rock in the Antarctic are the coldest places on Earth, and are too inhospitable for any completely terrestrial animals. Antarctic animals, such as seals,

Snowshoe hares shelter in shallow depressions called forms, which they dig out of soil or snow.

Lemmings construct tunnel systems under the snow. This protects them from predators.

Reindeer have broad, flat hooves which help them to walk over soft ground and deep snow.

Polar bears cover vast distances in search of food, swimming across water and coming far inland.

penguins and whales, rely on the sea for their survival. No reptiles or amphibians survive there, and even warm-blooded animals leave in winter, with the exception of the hardy emperor penguin.

In the Arctic, seals, whales and other sea life also thrive, while the lands and islands of the Arctic Ocean provide a home for many animals dependent on land, such as muskoxen and reindeer. Animals such as polar bears spend their time on the thick shelves of sea ice which extend from the frozen coastlines for much of the year.

While Antarctica is almost entirely covered in snow and ice, the ground in lands around the Arctic circle is mainly ice-free during the summer and so has periods of frenzied growth and breeding. North of the boreal forests it is too cold and dark for trees to grow, and treeless tundra takes over. Plants – mainly tough grass and sedges, mosses and lichens (not actually plants but a symbiotic relationship between fungi and tiny algae) must be able to survive the long and desolate winters. When the summer – which generally lasts little more than six weeks – arrives, they must be ready to reproduce.

While the summer sun thaws the snow and ice, it never heats the soil for more than a few centimetres below the surface. The deep layer of soil remains frozen and is called permafrost. It forms a solid barrier which prevents the melt waters from seeping away. The trapped water forms shallow pools and bogs, which are a haven for insects.

Billions of insects, which spent the winter underground as inactive pupae, emerge from hiding in the spring. They swarm across the tundra, mating and laying eggs in the water as they race against time to produce the next generation before winter arrives again.

*Walruses spend most of their life in water. They have a thick coat of blubber to help keep them warm.*

*Harp seals congregate in huge numbers to give birth on ice floes. Pups have very thick fur.*

*Adult beluga whales are almost completely white, helping them to hide among ice floes.*

*Narwhals use a sophisticated system of ultrasonic clicks to find food in coastal Arctic waters.*

# DESERTS

*Deserts make up the largest terrestrial biome, covering about one-fifth of the world's dry land.*
*The popular image of a desert is a parched wilderness with towering sand dunes and no sign of life.*
*However, deserts can also be very cold places and most contain a surprising amount of wildlife.*

A desert forms wherever less than 25cm (10in) of rain falls in a year. Areas that get less than about 40cm (16in) of rain per year are semi-deserts. The largest desert is the Sahara in North Africa, which covers about the same area as the United States. Other desert regions are found in the south-western USA, southern Africa, Australia, central Asia, South America and China.

Desert life is tough. The wildlife has to contend with lack of water and also survive extremes of temperature. With little or no cloud cover for most of the year, land temperatures rocket during the day to over 40°C (104°F) but can plunge to near freezing at night.

Desert plants are the basis for all life in this biome, being the food for grazing animals. Some plants have to extend enormously long underground roots to collect enough water to live. For example, the roots of mesquite trees in the Sonoran Desert of Mexico grow down over 80m (262ft) to reach water. Other plants, such as cacti and

*Gila monsters are active at night. During the day they shelter in rocky crevices or burrows.*

*Desert kangaroo rats live where there are wind-blown sand-dunes. They never need to drink water.*

*Camels can endure very hot, dry conditions. They can survive for long periods without drinking.*

*Arabian oryxes range over vast areas to obtain food. They are able to detect areas of rainfall.*

other succulents, store water inside their fleshy stems and leaves, and have a thick, waxy covering to stop the water from evaporating.

Deserts are not completely dry, of course, because rain does eventually arrive. True to the extremes of a desert, rainstorms are so violent that they often cause devastating flash floods which gush down temporary rivers, known as wadis or arroyos. Then the desert plants bloom and breed for a few short weeks before withering and waiting for the next supply of water.

Many desert animals, such as blind snakes and several types of frog, follow a similar pattern. They only come to the surface during and after the rains, preferring to stay moist underground during the hot and dry parts of the year. Desert frogs prevent themselves from drying out by growing a thin, fluid-filled skin bag around their bodies.

Even the more active desert animals remain hidden during the day, sheltering from the scorching sun among rocks or in burrows. When night falls, plant-eaters, such as the addax and ass, begin to pick at the dried leaves, fruit and twigs of scrawny desert plants, while smaller jerboas and ground squirrels collect seeds and insects.

Other insect-eaters include geckoes and other lizards. Many have wide, webbed feet to help them walk across the loose sand and burrow into it when danger approaches. Larger meat-eaters include vipers, which patrol in search of small rodents, and jackals, which scavenge for the carcasses of dead animals.

Most of these animals never drink liquid water. They get all the moisture they need from their food. Camels' humps store fat, which keeps them alive when there is no food. Lizards and several desert rodents store fat in their tails, while other desert animals build up food stores in their burrows.

Fennec foxes have large ears filled with blood vessels, which are used to radiate body heat away.

Addaxes rarely drink, obtaining most of the moisture they need from the plants they eat.

Thorny devils have spiny defences to protect them when they are catching ants in the open desert.

Dingos are successful predators in times of drought, able to catch rabbits, rodents and marsupials.

# ISLANDS

*Because they have been isolated from the rest of the world for so long, islands tend to contain species which have evolved independently of their relatives on the mainland. Consequently, islands are good place to observe the process of natural selection at work.*

Islands do not really constitute a biome because they exist in all parts of the world and come in all sorts of shapes and sizes. For example, Greenland, the world's largest island, is a place of vast ice fields edged with tundra. Most islands lie in warmer climes and are little more than rocks or reefs poking a few centimetres above the surrounding surf.

Small islands and coasts generally are unusual places to live because they are regularly transformed by tides washing in and out. While life in a desert or on an icy mountain may have its challenges, coastal plants and animals must cope with being immersed in salt water twice a day and then being dried by the sun and wind.

While island edges are a haven for coastal wildlife, many of the animals found inland are rather unusual. This is because islands are populated by animals which were there before the land became an island, or by those which have flown or swum from the mainland. On continents, an animal that is successful in a particular habitat

Galápagos giant tortoises have saddle-shaped shells so they can reach up to leaves on tall plants.

Malagasy leaf-nosed snakes blend perfectly into the background of their Madagascan habitat.

Fossas are the largest carnivores in Madagascar, preying on lemurs, rodents, birds and frogs.

Ruffed lemurs live in eastern Madagascar, using scent markings to signal their home territory.

will eventually spread across the land until it lives in all areas where that habitat is found. For example, brown bears live in conifer forests across the world. They did not evolve in all these places at the same time but spread out from a single location. But because brown bears and many other continental animals cannot get to islands, their place is filled by the animals that were originally there.

An excellent example of this is in New Zealand, an isolated group of islands in the south Pacific. Before people arrived on these islands about 1,000 years ago, there were only two species of mammal in the region. Both were bats descended from individuals which must have flown the 2,400km (1,500 miles) from Australia. Interestingly, these New Zealand bats have evolved to become ground-feeders, living a life more similar to that of a mouse than their winged relatives. New Zealand is also home to the tuataras, a tiny group of reptiles which are distantly related to lizards and snakes.

Madagascar is another well known example of an island with unique wildlife. It is the fourth largest island in the world, and home to the lemurs – relatives of the monkeys and apes.

A third example is the Galápagos Islands, 1,610km (1,000 miles) off the coast of Ecuador in the Pacific Ocean. These islands contain a couple of extremely unusual reptiles: the marine iguana, which is one of the few lizards to feed in salt water (it grazes on seaweed) and the extraordinary Galápagos giant tortoise. These huge reptiles, which are thought to live for at least 100 years, are now highly endangered. The different shell shapes of the tortoises on each of the Galápagos Islands helped Charles Darwin to formulate his theory of evolution.

*Komodo dragons are a species of giant lizard that have evolved on a group of Indonesian islands.*

*Tarsiers are nocturnal primates, living in the thick forest habitats of Sumatra and Borneo.*

*Echidnas are unusual Australian mammals – they lay eggs into a pouch on their abdomen.*

*Tuataras, often described as living fossils, can only be found on the coastal islands of New Zealand.*

# MOUNTAINS

*Mountains form an unusual biome because they encapsulate a number of climate zones within a small geographical area. This variation defines the lives of the inhabitants. Some animals are highly evolved for mountain life; others have extended their lowland ranges into high altitudes.*

A mountainside is like several biomes stacked on top of one another. As the mountain rises out of the surrounding lowlands, the air temperature, wind speed, light levels, water supply and, on the highest peaks, even the amount of oxygen begin to change. Most of the largest mountain ranges, such as the Himalayas of Asia, the Alps of Europe and the Rockies of North America, rise out of temperate or boreal biomes. Therefore the foothills of these ranges are generally covered in temperate forest or woodland. As the altitude increases, the weather conditions become colder and harsher and the trees of the temperate forest find it increasingly hard to grow. They eventually become smaller and more gnarled, and then conifer trees take over. Like their relatives in boreal forests, mountain conifers are better at surviving in colder conditions than broad-leaved trees.

As the journey up the mountain continues, the conditions get worse. Rain that falls on the mountain runs

Mountain goats have strong, sturdy legs and hooves to allow them to negotiate steep slopes.

Cougars ambush their prey from high vantage points. At night they shelter in caves and thickets.

Pikas collect piles of grass and leaves, which dry to make alpine hay. They shelter in areas of scree.

Vicuñas have specialized blood cells with a high oxygen affinity, allowing them to live at altitude.

through or over the surface before joining a torrential mountain stream and being carried swiftly down. With all the water sluicing rapidly down the mountain, territory nearer the top has less water for the plants to draw on, and eventually there is not enough moisture in the soil for trees to grow. The point where conditions become just too tough for even conifer trees to grow is called the timberline.

Above the timberline, small, hardy alpine plants grow in regions which resemble a cold desert. Alpine plants share features with desert species because they, too, must hang on to

any water they can get before it is evaporated by the strong mountain wind. At even higher altitudes, as in the polar regions, plant life eventually gives way to snow and ice at the snowline. From here upwards very little plant life survives and animals are infrequent visitors, except for the birds of prey soaring on the thermals of warmer air high above the peaks.

The story is different in tropical regions. Here the mountain slopes are clothed in so-called cloud forests which are similar to other tropical forests, but with shorter trees and a thinner canopy. In the humid tropics, these

mountain forests are often shrouded in cloud, and this extra moisture makes them ideal places for epiphytes (plants which grow on other plants rather than in the ground).

Many mountain forests have subspecies which are distinct from lowland populations, but they are still fundamentally the same species. However, many mountain species are specially adapted to living on steep slopes. A large proportion of these are small animals, such as rock hyraxes. Large species, such as mountain goats, are sure-footed animals that can move safely around rocky slopes.

*Rock hyraxes have rubber-like soles on their feet, enabling them to climb steep surfaces with ease.*

*Giant pandas have strong teeth to help them digest the bamboo that grows at high altitudes.*

*Yaks have stocky bodies and long, woolly fur to help them cope with cold mountain conditions.*

*Markhors have thick white and grey coats and shaggy manes to keep them warm in the mountains.*

# HUMAN SETTLEMENTS

*The fastest growing habitats are those made by humans, which are generally expanding at the expense of natural ones. Fortunately, many animals (as well as pets) do thrive with people. Animals that feed on a wide range of foods are the most successful species in human settlements.*

Human beings have a huge effect on their environment. Since the dawn of agriculture, people have been clearing natural landscapes to make way for their livestock and crops. Agriculture began in the Middle East 14,000 years ago, and is now so extensive that nearly all the world's grasslands and temperate forests have been replaced by fields. More recently, tropical and boreal forests have also been cut back to make room for agriculture. In evolutionary terms, this change has been very fast, and the natural world is reeling in shock, unable to respond to the changes quickly enough.

### Building cities

Several thousand years ago, people began to learn how to farm more efficiently, and farmers began to produce more than they could consume themselves. With a surplus of food, farmers began to trade it for other items. In the fertile river valleys of the Middle East, India and China, agricultural communities were so successful that the first cities grew up. Uniquely among mammals, some members of these large human communities did not find any of their own food. Instead, they bought what they needed with other products.

But while agriculture creates a habitat that mirrors the grassland in some ways, cities were a brand new type of habitat. In 1500, the world population was about 500 million. Only 500 years later, this figure had increased 12-fold, topping six billion in 2000. By this time there were over 200 cities containing over one million

Above: Red foxes are very adaptable animals. They have become very common in suburban and more built-up areas, where they make their homes in gardens and wasteland, and feed on rubbish.

Below: Barbary macaques on Gibraltar are the only monkeys living in Europe. They were introduced to the rock by the Romans, and those that survive there rely on being fed by tourists or stealing food from people's homes.

*Above: Raccoons are generalist feeders that have found rich pickings in human settlements. They use their climbing and digging abilities to get at food wherever it may be.*

people each. Huge sprawling urban centres, such as Mexico City and Tokyo, now contain more than 25 million people each – and, of course, also millions of animals.

## Opportunists

Although changes to the environment caused by humans are happening at a lightning pace, many animals have made the most of the opportunity presented. The destruction of natural habitats has had a terrible effect on those animals which live in particular places. For example, leaf-eating monkeys cannot survive without trees bearing plentiful leaves. However, animals which make the most of any feeding opportunity can survive anywhere, including cities. These so-called generalist feeders have thrived alongside humans for many thousands of years. The most familiar generalists are rodents such as mice and rats. They are typical generalist feeders because they will investigate anything for its food potential and are not fussy about what they eat. Other generalists are monkeys, such as macaques, vervets and capuchins, which are a common sight in many tropical cities. Here and elsewhere, suburban areas packed with gardens are the perfect environment for many other adaptable animals, such as squirrels, racoons and foxes.

Although some people enjoy sharing their cities with wildlife, others regard wild creatures in cities as dirty and dangerous. Several diseases, such as typhus and plague, are associated with rats and other city animals. These animals are so successful that their populations have to be controlled. On the whole, however, as cities mature, their wildlife communities stabilize into a sustainable ecosystem, just as they do in the wild.

## Prized pets

Another group of animals live in our cities – pets. People have kept pets for thousands of years. Typical pets, such as cats and dogs, are not generalist feeders and rely on their owners to provide food and shelter. Unlike scavenging city animals, pets live in partnership with people and have done well out of this relationship in which almost every facet of their lives, including their reproduction, is often controlled. Without their human masters, many of these species would now be close to extinction.

*Below: The domestic cat is a very popular pet. Like most wild cats, domestic ones are solitary animals and spend their time patrolling their territory looking for mates and rivals.*

*Below: Domestic guinea pigs, or cavies, are related to wild forms that live in South America. Selective breeding has resulted in individuals that have long, colourful fur.*

*Below: Perhaps the most popular pet reptiles are tortoises, which can live for many years if properly looked after. Trade in tortoises is heavily controlled to protect wild populations.*

# DIRECTORY
# OF ANIMALS

The world has five main landmasses – the Americas, Antarctica, Australia, Africa and Eurasia, this last one being the largest of them all. This section of the book focuses on the most significant amphibians, reptiles and mammals that live in each of these continents, such as the alligators and bears of the Americas, Africa's elephants and gorillas, the koalas and kangaroos of Australia and the pandas and pythons of Asia. The animal species are organized into a number of related groups: salamanders, frogs and toads, turtles and tortoises, lizards, crocodilians, snakes, cats, dogs, bears, small carnivores, raccoons, rodents, rabbits, bats, armadillos, marsupials, insectivores, apes, monkeys, hoofed animals, seals, dolphins and whales. Each entry is accompanied by a fact box containing a map that shows where the animal lives, and details about the animal's distribution, habitat, food, size, maturity, breeding, life span and conservation status. This last category gives a broad indication of each species' population size, as recorded by the International Union for the Conservation of Nature and Natural Resources (IUCN). At one end of the scale a species might be described as common or lower risk, then vulnerable, threatened, endangered or critically endangered. In addition to the main animal entries, the directory also contains lists of related animals, with short summaries indicating their distribution, main characteristics and behaviour.

*Left: A herd of springboks rest on an African grassland. These wild grasslands host the largest populations of grazing beasts on Earth. The springboks are known for "pronking" – leaping high into the air – when predators attack.*

# ANIMALS OF THE AMERICAS

North and South America stretch from the barren ice fields of the Arctic to the stormy coast of Cape Horn, which twists into the Southern Ocean. A huge number of different animals make their home in the Americas because the continents support a wide range of habitats. These include the humid forests of the Amazon – the world's largest jungle; the searing Atacama Desert – the world's driest place; and the rolling plains of the American wild west. The Americas are home to many of the world's record-breaking animals. The world's largest deer, the moose, is a common resident of the conifer forests of Canada and the northern United States. The largest land carnivore, the Kodiak bear, is found on Alaska's Kodiak Island. The world's largest rodent, the capybara, lives in the Amazon rainforest, and the largest snake in the world, the green anaconda, is found in the wetlands across tropical South America.

*Above from left: Caribou, grizzly bear, double-crested basilisk.*

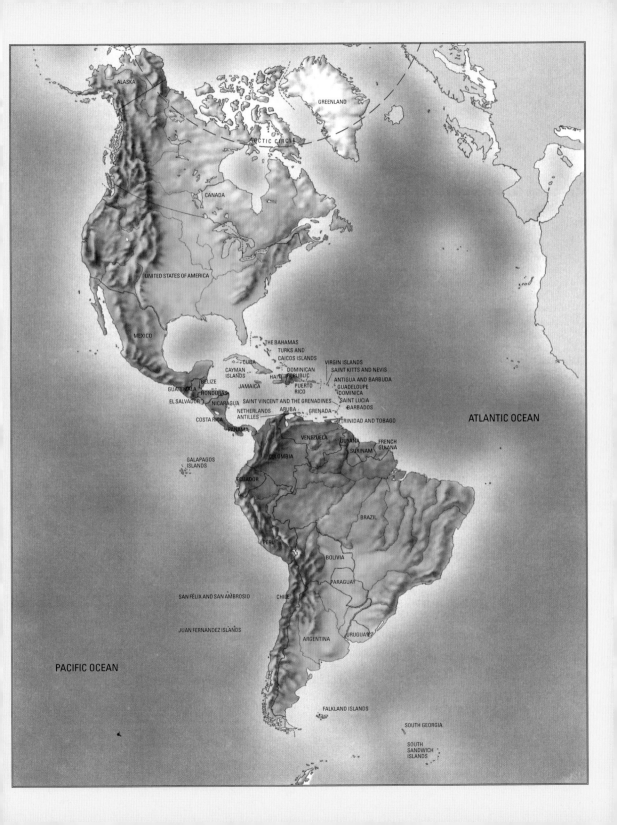

# SALAMANDERS

*Salamanders and newts are amphibians with tails. All of them have legs, although a few species have lost a pair or have vestigial limbs. Like all amphibians, salamanders need a certain amount of water to reproduce. Some species are completely aquatic, while others live entirely on land. Many species are truly amphibious, spending the early part of their lives in water and living both on land and in water as adults.*

## Hellbender

*Cryptobranchus alleganiensis*

Hellbenders are among the largest salamanders in the Americas and one of three giant salamanders in the world. These monstrous and heavy set amphibians spend their entire lives on the beds of rivers and streams.

Hellbenders are nocturnal and spend the day sheltering under rocks. At night the animals become more active, but generally lurk in crevices while waiting for prey. Giant salamanders lose their gills as they change from larvae into adults. They absorb most of their oxygen through their wrinkly skin but will sometimes rise to the surface to take gulps of air into their small lungs.

Hellbenders breed in late summer. A male digs a hole under a rock and will only allow females that are still carrying eggs into his hole. Several females may lay their eggs in a single male's hole before he fertilizes them with a cloud of sperm. The male guards them for three months until the young hatch out.

*Hellbenders have a dark, wrinkled skin that secretes toxic slime. These salamanders do not have gills, and the wrinkles in their skin increase the surface area of their bodies so that they can absorb more oxygen directly from the water.*

**Distribution**: Eastern North America.
**Habitat**: Rivers and streams.
**Food**: Crayfishes, worms, insects, fish and snails.
**Size**: 30–74cm (12–29in).
**Maturity**: 2–3 years.
**Breeding**: 450 eggs laid in late summer.
**Life span**: 50 years.
**Status**: Unknown.

## Greater siren

*Siren lacertina*

The greater siren lives in the mud on the bottom of slow-flowing creeks and in swamps. Most salamanders change considerably as they mature into adults, but the adult body of a siren, with its external gills, long tail and single pair of legs, is very similar to the larval form. Greater sirens spend the day resting on the bottom. At night they drag themselves through the mud with their small legs or swim, with an S-shaped motion, through the murky water. These salamanders do not have teeth, but suck their prey through tough, horny lips.

Greater sirens sometimes live in seasonal pools, which dry up in the summer. The salamanders survive these droughts by burying themselves in the moist sediment and coating their bodies with slimy mucus. Breeding takes place at night, under mud. It is thought that females lay single eggs on water plants and males follow the females around, fertilizing each egg soon after it is laid.

*The greater siren has a very long body with feathery gills behind its head and a single pair of legs. The body is mottled to help the salamander hide on the river bed. The greater siren propels itself through the water, twisting its body into S-shaped curves.*

**Distribution**: Eastern parts of the United States.
**Habitat**: Swamps, streams and lakes.
**Food**: Crayfishes, worms and snails.
**Size**: 50–90cm (19.5–36in).
**Maturity**: Unknown.
**Breeding**: Eggs laid in spring.
**Life span**: 25 years.
**Status**: Unknown.

# Mudpuppy

*Necatrus maculosus*

**Distribution**: Eastern United States.
**Habitat**: Muddy ponds, lakes and streams.
**Food**: Aquatic insects, crayfishes and fish.
**Size**: 29–49cm (11.5–19in).
**Maturity**: 4–6 years.
**Breeding**: Mating occurs in autumn; eggs laid in spring.
**Life span**: Unknown.
**Status**: Common.

Mudpuppies and waterdogs, their close relatives, get their names from the myth that they bark like dogs when handled.

Mudpuppies spend their whole lives underwater. They do not change a great deal when they metamorphose from larvae into adults, retaining their gills for breathing and their long tail for swimming. The gills vary in size depending on how much oxygen there is dissolved in the water. They are very large in stagnant pools, where there is not very much oxygen available, and smaller in faster-running streams.

Mudpuppies mate in the late autumn or early winter. The eggs are fertilized inside the female's body, but they are not laid until spring. Before laying, the female makes a nest in a hollow under a rock or log on the bed of a shallow stream. The eggs have a gelatinous coating and stick together in layers.

*Mudpuppies have a long, mottled body with two pairs of legs and a laterally flattened tail. There is a pair of feathery gills behind the head, but mudpuppies also have small lungs.*

---

**Cave salamander** (*Eurycea lucifuga*): 8–16cm (3–6in)
Cave salamanders are pale orange with black spots on their back. They live in the mouths of caves in the Midwest region of the United States. Cave salamanders have a long, grasping tail, which they use for clinging to the rocky cave walls. Lacking lungs, they absorb oxygen from the air through their skin and through the lining of their mouth. Their skin must be kept moist for oxygen-absorption to occur, so they can only live in damp areas while on land, and have long periods of inactivity when conditions are unfavourable.

**Olympic torrent salamander**
(*Rhyacotriton olympicus*): 9–12cm (3.5–4.75in)
The Olympic torrent salamander is one of four salamanders found in the rocky watercourses of the Pacific North-west in North America. This species lives in crystal-clear streams that tumble down mountainsides. The water is so rich in oxygen that the adult salamanders have only tiny lungs because they can easily get enough oxygen through their skins.

**Coastal giant salamander** (*Dicamptodon tenebrosus*): 17–34cm (6.5–13.5in)
Coastal giant salamanders are the largest land-living salamanders in the world. They have brown skin, mottled with black, which helps them to blend in with the floor of their woodland homes. They secrete foul-tasting chemicals through their skin as a defence when attacked by predators.

# Three-toed amphiuma

*Amphiuma tridactylum*

With their slimy, cylindrical bodies, amphiumas are also called Congo eels. This is misleading because they are amphibians, not eels (which are fish), and they live in North America, not the African Congo.

Three-toed amphiumas are the longest salamanders in the Americas, although large hellbenders are probably heavier. Adult amphiumas have neither lungs nor gills. They have to take in oxygen directly through their skin. Three-toed amphiumas spend most of their lives in water, foraging at night and sheltering in streambed burrows during the day. However, during periods of heavy rainfall, the salamanders may make brief trips across areas of damp ground.

Three-toed amphiumas begin to mate in late winter. The females rub their snouts on males they want to attract. During mating males and females wrap around each other, while sperm is transferred into the female's body. The females guard their strings of eggs by coiling their bodies around them until they hatch, about 20 weeks later. By then, the water level may have dropped, so the larvae often have to wriggle over land to reach the water.

**Distribution**: Southern United States.
**Habitat**: Swamps and ponds.
**Food**: Worms and crayfishes.
**Size**: 0.5–1.1m (1.5–3.5ft).
**Maturity**: Not known.
**Breeding**: 200 eggs laid in spring.
**Life span**: Unknown.
**Status**: Common.

*Three-toed amphiumas have a very long, cylindrical body with a laterally flattened tail. They have two pairs of tiny legs, each with three toes. The legs are too small to be of use for locomotion.*

## Tiger salamander

*Ambystoma tigrinum*

Tiger salamanders are found in grassland, forest and marshy habitats. The adults spend much of the year underground. They usually dig their own burrows, sometimes down to a depth of more than 60cm (24in). The burrows not only provide them with the humidity levels they need, but also shelter them from the extremes of temperature on the surface. Tiger salamanders start life in pools of water. While larvae, they have external gills and a fin down the middle of their tails. They feed on aquatic insects and even on other tiger salamander larvae. The larvae may stay in the water for several years before metamorphosing into the adult body form. The gills are then absorbed into the body, the tail fin is lost, and the skin becomes tougher and more resistant to desiccation. Metamorphosis is thought to be catalyzed by the warming of the water during summer. Warm water can absorb more oxygen than cold water, which may trigger the change. However, the warming of the water may also suggest to the animal that the pool is in danger of drying up, indicating that it ought to leave.

The metamorphosed salamander now looks like an adult, but it is still smaller than the mature animal. This subadult form is called an eft. The eft crawls out of the water and begins to forage on the leaf-strewn floor. It catches insects and other animals with flicks of its sticky tongue, and then shakes them to death before chewing them up. After hibernating in burrows, mature adults make mass migrations in springtime to pools and mate over a period of two or three days.

*Tiger salamanders may be dark green or grey with black markings, or yellow with black markings. Some specimens have yellow and black stripes, which make them even more reminiscent of their namesake.*

**Distribution**: Central and south-eastern North America.
**Habitat**: Woodland.
**Food**: Worms and insects.
**Size**: 18–30cm (7–12in).
**Maturity**: Unknown.
**Breeding**: Migrate to breeding pools in spring.
**Life span**: 20 years.
**Status**: Common.

## Axolotl

*Ambystoma mexicanum*

Axolotls are related to tiger salamanders and other species that spend their adult lives on land. However, axolotls never go through the change from the aquatic larval stage to the more robust, terrestrial adult form. Consequently, they spend their whole lives in water.

Adult axolotls look almost identical to the larval stage. They have four legs – which are too small for walking on land – feathery gills behind their head and a long, finned tail used for swimming. Like the larvae, the adults feed on aquatic insects and other invertebrates, such as worms. The only major difference between the two forms is that the adults have sexual organs, enabling sperm to be transferred from male to female during mating.

Axolotls do not metamorphose because their thyroid glands cannot produce the hormone necessary to bring about the change. When biologists injected captive axolotls with this hormone they found that the animals changed into a land-living form similar to that seen in other species. Because they cannot naturally get out of the water, axolotls are confined to their aquatic habitat. They live in a single lake system in Mexico and are therefore vulnerable to pollution and exploitation, and are becoming increasingly rare.

**Distribution**: Lake Xochimilco, Mexico.
**Habitat**: Water.
**Food**: Aquatic insects.
**Size**: 10–20cm (4–8in).
**Maturity**: Unknown.
**Breeding**: Unknown.
**Life span**: 25 years.
**Status**: Vulnerable.

*In the wild, most axolotls are black, but several colour variants have been bred in captivity. In fact, there are more axolotls in captivity around the world than in the wild.*

**Long-toed salamander**
(*Ambystoma macrodactylum croceum*): 10–17cm (4–6.5in)
The long-toed salamander is found in the Pacific North-west, from northern Canada to British Columbia. It is a member of the mole salamander group, which includes tiger salamanders and axolotls. These amphibians are called mole salamanders because many, such as the long-toed salamander, live in burrows below damp ground. In spring, they breed in ponds.

**Cayenne caecilian** (*Typhlonectes compressicauda*): 30–60cm (12–24in)
The Cayenne caecilian lives in the tributaries and lakes of the Amazon River basin system. Its long, dark body resembles that of an eel at first glance, but, like other caecilians, it has well-defined rings around its body. This species is completely aquatic: its tail is flattened into a paddle shape, and a small fin runs along the top of the body. Female Cayenne caecilians carry their developing eggs inside their bodies. Then they give birth to live young, which look like miniature adults.

# Red-spotted newt

*Notophthalmus viridescens*

**Distribution**: Eastern United States.
**Habitat**: Damp land and fresh water.
**Food**: Tadpoles, insects, slugs, worms and other small invertebrates.
**Size**: 6.5–11.5cm (2.5–4.5in).
**Maturity**: 1–4 years.
**Breeding**: In water in spring.
**Life span**: Unknown.
**Status**: Common.

Red-spotted newts, also known as eastern newts, have a very complex life cycle. Their lives begin in water, where they hatch out from eggs as aquatic larvae. The larvae then develop into land-living juveniles called efts. The eft stage has the body form of a normal adult salamander, with four legs and a long, grasping tail. However, it is unable to breed.

The eft spends up to four years living out of water in damp woodland and grassland. Red-spotted newts must return to ponds and streams to become mature. When they return to water, the maturing red-spotted newts actually redevelop many larval features, such as a deep tail – ideal for swimming – and a thinner skin, used for absorbing oxygen directly from the water.

The adults breed during spring and early summer in bodies of fresh water. They then leave the water and return to a life on land. Many newts return to the same ponds to breed each year. They may navigate by storing maps of their surroundings in their memory, or by using either the Earth's magnetic field or polarized light from the Sun.

*Red-spotted newts are named after the red and black markings along their back. During the juvenile or eft stage, the newts are bright orange, but when they eventually reach maturity, they turn green with yellow undersides.*

**Distribution**: North-eastern South America.
**Habitat**: Tropical forest.
**Food**: Worms and insects.
**Size**: 20–40cm (8–15.5in).
**Maturity**: Unknown.
**Breeding**: Rainy season.
**Life span**: 10 years.
**Status**: Common.

*Ringed caecilians have blue, scaly bands around the body. Like all caecilians, ringed caecilians have a retractable tentacle on each side of the head, near to their nostrils.*

# Ringed caecilian

*Siphonops annulatus*

Caecilians are amphibians, but they belong to a separate group entirely from salamanders, newts, frogs and toads. All caecilians lack legs and resemble large worms. The ringed caecilian burrows through the soil of steamy tropical forests, wriggling its body in waves to push its way forward. It breathes using only one properly developed lung.

Ringed caecilians eat anything they come across while on the move, providing it is small enough. They use their head like a trowel to probe areas of soil, and use their tentacles to pick up the scent of prey. The tentacles are closely linked to the nose, and detect chemicals in the soil. They can also detect the movements and faint electric currents produced by the muscles of prey animals.

Ringed caecilians mate when the soil is at its most damp, during the rainy seasons. The female's eggs are fertilized by the male when they are still inside her body. She lays the eggs in the soil. Unlike many species of caecilian, which have an aquatic larval stage, young ringed caecilians hatch looking like miniature adults.

## California newt

*Taricha torosa*

These newts are found only in the state of California. There are two main populations. The larger group lives in the coastal region, ranging from San Diego in the south to Mendocino County north of San Francisco. The second population lives on the western slopes of the Sierra Nevada mountains in the north-west of the state. California newts are mostly found in slow-flowing streams, lakes and ponds surrounded by forests of oak or evergreen conifers. Those in the Sierra Nevada occupy more swiftly flowing waterways.

The females lay their eggs between December and May. The eggs are deposited on aquatic plants or among leaf litter that has settled on the bottom of a waterway. The larvae, which are just 1cm (0.4in) long, live underwater until at least the autumn, or until the following spring in colder areas. Once the larvae reach the right size, they transform into the land-living adult form. These terrestrial newts return to water to breed.

*This species has warty skin that is reddish-brown on the upper side and dark yellow underneath. The eyes are larger than those of most newts. Breeding males develop smooth skin and become fatter.*

**Distribution**: Coastal region of California and Sierra Nevada mountains.
**Habitat**: Streams, lakes and ponds in hill and mountain forests, grasslands and chaparral.
**Food**: Invertebrates.
**Size**: 12.5–20cm (5–8in).
**Maturity**: 1–2 years.
**Breeding**: 20 eggs laid underwater in spherical masses in winter or spring
**Life span**: Unknown.
**Status**: Common.

## Amazon climbing salamander

*Bolitoglossa altamazonica*

Amazon climbing salamanders live in the shrubs and bushes that carpet the floor of lowland rainforests in the northern Amazon Basin of Brazil. These amphibians spend their whole lives off the ground. They are most often seen on the wide leaves of low-growing bushes, and also on the long leaves of large epiphytes, including bromeliads. (Epiphytes are plants that grow perched on trees and other larger plants.) The salamanders are rarely seen higher than 2m (6.5ft) above the forest floor.

Amazon climbing salamanders are nocturnal animals. They forage for small insects that move up into the trees when night falls. During the daytime, these small salamanders curl up underneath a large leaf, or in leaf debris trapped amid the branches.

Comparatively little is documented about the breeding habits of this species, although it is known to reproduce all year round. The females lay small clutches of large eggs in moist nooks and crannies at the base of leaves or among branches. The young do not hatch as aquatic larvae, since there is no standing water for them to live in. Instead, the young salamanders emerge in the full adult form.

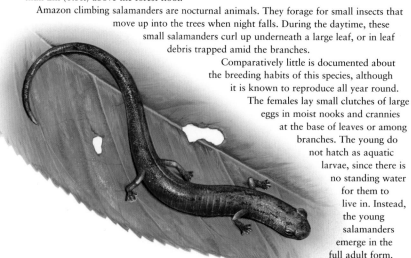

**Distribution**: Northern Amazon Basin.
**Habitat**: Bushes.
**Food**: Insects.
**Size**: 7.5–9cm (3–3.5in).
**Maturity**: 1 year.
**Breeding**: No larval stage.
**Life span**: Unknown.
**Status**: Common.

*These climbing salamanders have grey-brown skin, webbed feet and a constriction at the base of their tail. The tail is a little longer than the combined head and body length. Bolitoglossa salamanders wave their tail and arch their back when threatened.*

# Arboreal salamander

*Aneides lugubris*

**Distribution**: Coastal mountains of California and Baja California.
**Habitat**: Woodlands.
**Food**: Insects.
**Size**: 11–18.5cm (4.25–7.25in).
**Maturity**: 1 year.
**Breeding**: 10–30 eggs laid in summer; hatching is in autumn.
**Life span**: Unknown.
**Status**: Common.

As their name suggests, arboreal salamanders live in trees, especially yellow pines and black oaks. While climbing through the branches, they grip with wide pads on the tips of their toes. Their long prehensile tail can be wrapped around branches to give extra stability.

Arboreal salamanders are lungless salamanders. Lacking lungs, they breathe through their skin, especially the thin and moist areas inside the mouth. As a result, these salamanders are only able to get a limited amount of oxygen into their bodies, restricting the size to which they can grow. This is one of the larger species.

Female arboreal salamanders lay their eggs on rotting wood or in moist leaf litter. There is no larval stage, and the young emerge as miniature, fully formed salamanders about three months later.

*Like most lungless salamanders, this climbing species spends its whole life on land. However, its grey-brown skin must be kept moist because, being a lungless salamander, this is where oxygen passes from the air into the amphibian's blood.*

**Bassler's slender caecilian** (*Oscaecilia bassleri*): 90cm (36in)
With its narrow, grey body this amphibian is often mistaken for a giant earthworm. It does not burrow into soil, but moves through thick leaf litter on the floor of its rainforest habitat. Bassler's slender caecilian lives in the north-west of the Amazon Basin in Ecuador, Peru and Colombia. The head can be differentiated from the tail because it is slightly paler than the rest of the body. It has a shovel-shaped snout with white nostrils. The eyes are covered in bone and are not visible. Little is known about this species' reproductive behaviour. It does not seem to have an aquatic phase in its life cycle, and it probably gives birth to live young rather than laying eggs.

**Desert slender salamander** (*Batrachoseps aridus*): 5.5–9.5cm (2.25–3.75in)
This rare, thin-bodied lungless salamander is only found in two canyons in the Mojave Desert, California. It survives the arid desert conditions by making use of water that seeps from the canyons' limestone. It shelters from the heat under loose limestone rocks.

**Green salamander** (*Aneides aeneus*): 8–14cm (3–5.5in)
This lungless species is closely related to black and arboreal salamanders. It is native to the Appalachian Mountains in the eastern United States, where it inhabits damp woodlands. The upper body is black with green patches. The green salamander spends the daytime in moist crevices, emerging at night to climb tree trunks in search of ants, beetles and other insect prey.

# Black salamander

*Aneides flavipunctatus*

Black salamanders are lungless salamanders that live almost exclusively in California, although a few are found in the far south of Oregon. Their range encompasses the low Coastal Range mountains of the West Coast, but they rarely occur above 600m (2,000ft).

In southern parts of their range, black salamanders are most common in moist areas of evergreen or deciduous forest, while in the north, they inhabit open grassy environments. Along the California and Oregon border, these salamanders are usually found in moss-covered rock slides.

Grasslands are drier than woodlands, so grassland-dwelling salamanders aestivate in summer to protect themselves against heat and drought. Aestivation is a similar dormant state to hibernation. A black salamander may aestivate in an burrow for six or seven months.

**Distribution**: United States, from Northern California to southern edge of Oregon.
**Habitat**: Forests and prairies.
**Food**: Insects.
**Size**: 10–16.5cm (4–6.5in).
**Maturity**: Unknown.
**Breeding**: Eggs laid in summer; hatching is in autumn.
**Life span**: Unknown.
**Status**: Common.

*This species is black all over, with a frosted colouring on its upper surface and a paler underside. Black salamanders are buck-toothed, with their upper teeth sticking out over their lower jaw.*

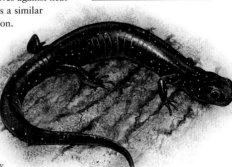

## Dusky salamander

*Desmognathus fuscus*

*The brownish back of the adult dusky salamander is covered in darker blotches, which sometimes join to form ragged stripes. The young salamanders have yellow or red spots on the back. The hind legs of this species are sturdier than the front legs, and the tail is laterally compressed.*

This species is the most common of the dusky salamanders. Its range covers much of the eastern United States, from New England and the eastern Great Lakes to the Mississippi Delta. It does not live along the southern Atlantic coast, and is almost unheard of in Florida, where its place is taken by the southern dusky salamander, a close relative.

In the northern parts of its range, the dusky salamander inhabits creeks and rocky pools. In more southerly parts, it is usually found in swampy areas. Being largely nocturnal, this salamander spends daylight hours under debris or in a burrow. It feeds on a variety of invertebrates, and may occasionally eat other salamanders and their larvae.

The female lays her eggs between June and September, depositing a single cluster of up to 40 eggs in a moist location near water, perhaps under a rock or in a hole in the bank of a stream. The aquatic larvae hatch about two to three months later. The rate at which the eggs and larvae develop depends on temperature, and takes longer in colder regions.

**Distribution**: Eastern United States, from New Brunswick to Louisiana.
**Habitat**: Rocky creeks running through woodlands.
**Food**: Insect larvae, woodlice and worms.
**Size**: 6.5–14cm (2.5–5.5in).
**Maturity**: 3–4 years.
**Breeding**: Up to 40 eggs laid in mid- to late summer; hatching takes 6–13 weeks.
**Life span**: Unknown.
**Status**: Common.

## Seal salamander

*Desmognathus monticola*

*This average-sized salamander has a laterally compressed tail and a stout body. It is light brown or grey on the upper surface, often with dark blotches surrounded by pale borders. The underside is paler, and there is an obvious transition between the two. Juveniles have a similar background coloration, but with four pairs of orange-brown spots along the back.*

This salamander always remains close to water, and as it rests beside a stream it resembles a seal basking on a rocky shore. A shy, nocturnal animal, the seal salamander scurries beneath rocks or dives into stream-side burrows when disturbed. Most of the time it stays under cover, lying in wait for passing insect prey, particularly ants and beetles. When an insect wanders within range, the salamander pounces. It may also eat other salamanders. This species is one of the lungless salamanders, in which respiration occurs through the skin and the lining of the mouth.

In the breeding season, males will attack and bite rivals that try to interrupt their courtship of the females. A female seal salamander lays her eggs between June and October. Each egg is attached individually to the underside of a submerged rock or in a cavity in a rotten log. The salamander always lays in a damp area where water seeps out of the soil or runs off the ground into streams after rain storms. The female guards the eggs until they hatch in the autumn, and the larvae live in the stream water. They are about 2cm (0.8in) long when

**Distribution**: United States, in Appalachian Mountains and uplands of Pennsylvania and Alabama.
**Habitat**: Mountain streams.
**Food**: Insects, especially ants and beetles; occasionally other salamanders.
**Size**: 7.5–15cm (3–6in).
**Maturity**: 1–2 years
**Breeding**: 10–40 eggs laid in mid- to late summer; hatching is in autumn
**Life span**: Unknown.
**Status**: Common.

they emerge from the egg. Once they reach a length of 4–5cm (1.5–2in), the larvae transform into juveniles. The larval stage of this species usually last for nine to ten months.

# Ensatina

*Ensatina eschscholtzii*

**Distribution**: West coast of North America, from British Columbia to Baja California.
**Habitat**: Woodland, mountain forest and scrubland.
**Food**: Spiders, grasshoppers and springtails.
**Size**: 7.5–15cm (3–6in).
**Maturity**: 2–4 years.
**Breeding**: Eggs laid in late spring hatch 4–5 months later.
**Life span**: 15 years.
**Status**: Common.

This lungless species is found along the Pacific coast of North America, in a variety of habitats and climate types. In the north of the range, which experiences high rainfall, ensatinas occupy fir and maple forests. Along the coast, between the ocean and the Coastal Range mountains, the salamanders live in forests of redwoods and oaks, and, in the south, dry areas of bush known as chaparral. There is also a population in the cedar forests that grow on the slopes of the Sierra Nevada mountains in central California.

The ensatina is most often seen after rains. At the height of summer, it retreats to a damp burrow or log crevice to avoid the heat and dry conditions. It does the same in winter to avoid the cold weather. When threatened, this salamander becomes stiff and arches its tail and head toward each other. If a predator takes hold of the tail, the salamander can shed the grasped portion and make its escape. It has no tadpole stage.

The ensatina is the only five-toed salamander possessing a tail with a constricted base. In males, the tail is longer than the body. This species has a variety of colours on its upper surface, from red-brown to yellow and black. There are also spots and blobs in cream, yellow or orange. The belly is white or pink.

**Pygmy salamander** (*Desmognathus wrighti*): 3.5–5cm (1.5–2in)
This small, nocturnal salamander spends the day under rocks or in leaf litter. It lives in fir and spruce forests at the southern end of the Appalachian Mountains in eastern North America. Pygmy salamanders are most active after rain, when they emerge to forage for insects. They may also climb up tree trunks in search of food. In spring and autumn, a small clutch of eggs is laid at the end of a single stalk and left dangling from a rock over running water. The female guards the eggs. There is no aquatic larval stage, and the young hatch in miniature adult form.

**Mountain dusky salamander** (*Desmognathus ochropaeus*): 7–11cm (2.75–4.25in)
The mountain dusky salamander is found in the north-eastern United States, west of the Hudson River and south to the northern tip of Georgia. Much of its range is mountainous. It is found in large numbers close to springs, especially at lower altitudes. Higher up, where it is cooler and damper, this species is less dependent on standing water, and often inhabits conifer forests. Its diet consists of flies, beetles and mites.

**Imitator salamander** (*Desmognathus imitator*): 7–10cm (2.75–4in)
This rare salamander lives in the Great Smoky Mountains along the Tennessee–North Carolina border. It has the same coloration as either the mountain dusky salamander or the Appalachian woodland salamander. It is such a good mimic that only laboratory analysis of its DNA could prove that it was in fact a separate species.

# Long-tailed salamander

*Eurycea longicauda*

The long-tailed salamander lives in damp environments close to streams and flooded areas. It is found throughout most of the eastern United States, from the Arkansas Valley (a major western tributary of the mighty Mississippi River) to the Atlantic Coast. Like many species in this part of the world, it does not spread into Florida, where the climate and habitat are very different to conditions in the rest of eastern North America.

Long-tailed salamanders are nocturnal animals. They are most active on damp nights, when they patrol the forest floor looking for invertebrates such as insects and springtails. Eggs are laid in crevices close to pools and streams. The larvae hatch about two months later. After living in water for three to seven months, they transform into the juvenile form, which resembles the adult.

**Distribution**: New York state to northern Florida and western Mississippi Valley.
**Habitat**: Streams and swamps.
**Food**: Small insects.
**Size**: 10–20cm (4–8in).
**Maturity**: 2 years.
**Breeding**: Eggs are laid between late autumn and spring.
**Life span**: Unknown
**Status**: Common.

Only a handful of other lungless salamanders grow to a larger size than this species, and none of them is as widespread. Despite being long, this salamander's tail rarely measures more than the combined length of its head and body.

## Slimy salamander

*Plethodon glutinosus*

Slimy salamanders live in ravines and flooded woodlands (bayous) in the southern part of their range. Much of their habitat is filled with mountains, and this species is found from sea level to 1,700m (5,600ft). The slimy salamander gets its name from the fact that it secretes a sticky substance on to its shiny black skin. If this salamander is touched, the slime is extremely difficult to remove from the fingers.

Slimy salamanders are nocturnal and spend the day hidden under flat rocks and rotting logs. They emerge on most nights to search for insects on the forest floor. In the south of their range, it is warm and wet enough for this species to be active all year round. In the north, the salamanders spend the coldest part of the winter and the driest periods of summer under cover. These territorial salamanders can become aggressive to competitors from both their own and other species.

Breeding takes place in spring and autumn in the north, when it is wet enough. In the south of the range, the salamanders lay their eggs in summer. The male develops breeding colours, with his chin, feet and spots turning first pink and then red. Prior to mating, he performs an elaborate courtship dance. About 25 eggs are laid in a nest under leaves or a log and guarded by the female. There is no aquatic larval stage, and the young that emerge from the eggs a few months later are miniature versions of the adults.

*The slimy salamander has black skin, covered by a liberal sprinkling of silver-white or brass-coloured specks, or both. The underside is generally lighter than the back.*

**Distribution**: Eastern United States, from New York south through much of the eastern seaboard to northern Florida and the Gulf coast, and west to parts of Oklahoma and Texas.
**Habitat**: Swamps and stream sides.
**Food**: Insects, especially ants and beetles, and earthworms and other invertebrates.
**Size**: 11.5–20.5cm (4.5–8in).
**Maturity**: 3 years.
**Breeding**: 25 eggs laid; hatching takes 3 months.
**Life span**: Unknown.
**Status**: Common.

## Mud salamander

*Pseudotriton montanus*

This North American amphibian is aptly named, since the adults are found in mud and swampy ground. Although relatively common in such habitats, these secretive salamanders are rarely seen, since they burrow into the mud and may hide in moist places such as under sphagnum moss, rocks or logs. They may even retreat into crayfish holes to escape predators. Their diet consists mainly of invertebrates, although they have been known to eat other salamanders. Mud salamanders are native to the United States, occurring at sea level on the coastal plain between the Appalachian Mountains and the Atlantic Ocean.

Breeding takes place in autumn or early winter, when the female lays about 100 eggs. The aquatic larvae that hatch in late winter breathe underwater using gills. The larvae live in the silt or plant debris that builds up on the bottom of streams. After a year or two in the water, the larvae transform into a lungless, air-breathing form which then goes on to develop the adult coloration. In males this takes about a year, while females continue to mature for two or three years after leaving the water.

*The coloration of this stout, short-tailed salamander varies throughout its range. Young salamanders have bright pink or red skin with black spots, with a red or yellow underside. As the salamanders age, the background fades to a brownish colour, and older individuals develop red-brown spots.*

**Distribution**: Eastern United States, from the Appalachian Mountains to the Atlantic coast.
**Habitat**: Muddy streams and swamps.
**Food**: Beetles, spiders, mites and other small invertebrates.
**Size**: 7.5–19.5cm (3–7.75in).
**Maturity**: 3–5 years.
**Breeding**: Eggs are laid in autumn or early winter and attached to the substrate or to submerged objects such as roots or leaves; hatching is in late winter.
**Life span**: Unknown.
**Status**: Common.

**Zigzag salamander** (*Plethodon dorsalis*):
6.5–11cm (2.5–4.25in)
Named after the jagged stripe running from its
neck to its tail, this small, slender lungless
salamander lives in two populations: the smallest
is found in the Ozark hills of Arkansas; the larger
group extends from central Indiana to northern
Alabama and Georgia. This species occurs in
rocky areas such as ravines, scree and caves.
The eggs are laid in spring and lie dormant over
the dry summer in an underground retreat, before
hatching into efts during autumn. As with most
lungless species, there is no aquatic phase.

**Red salamander** (*Pseudotriton ruber*): 10–18cm
(4–7in)
This robust lungless species is red when young,
but turns orange or purple with age. It lives near
springs in the eastern United States, from the
western slopes of the Appalachians to the coast
of New Jersey and the Gulf of Mexico. It does
not reach the southern Atlantic coast. Females
lay up to 100 eggs in an underground nest in
autumn. The larvae hatch in early winter and
make their way to the water. They change into
adults after after about two or three years.

**Four-toed salamander** (*Hemidactylium
scutatum*): 5–10cm (2–4in)
This species has four toes on its hind feet and a
constriction at the base of its tail. It occurs right
across the Mississippi Basin, from the Great
Lakes to the Gulf coast. Adults live under stones
in boggy areas within forests. Like many
salamanders, this species will break off its tail
when attacked. The lost tail quickly grows back.

# California tiger salamander

*Ambystoma californiense*

The California tiger salamander is a mole
salamander, so-called because many of them
are burrowers. Their stout bodies, strong
legs and blunt heads allow them to dig
efficiently. Mole salamanders also have
lungs in their adult form, which makes it
easier for them to breathe in the confines
of an underground burrow.

This species lives on the slopes of the
Coastal Range mountains in south
California, where it can be found under
plant debris or in soft soil near to ponds
in grasslands and woodlands. It feeds on
worms, insects and other invertebrates.

Breeding takes place in puddles and
temporary bodies of water in January and
early February, when heavy rains reach
California. The jelly-covered eggs
are laid singly on plants, and the
aquatic larvae hatch out
soon after and
burrow into
wet ground.
The larvae
breathe using gills,
and feed on various
invertebrates such as
water snails and tadpoles. They transform
into the adult form after four months.

**Distribution**: West of the
Sierra Nevada in south
California.
**Habitat**: Burrows near
streams and ponds.
**Food**: Invertebrates.
**Size**: 15–21.5cm (6–8.5in).
**Maturity**: 1–2 years.
**Breeding**: Eggs laid in rainy
season during January.
**Life span**: Unknown.
**Status**: Common.

*Despite their names, few of
the tiger salamanders have
stripes. The upper body of this
species is black, with a few
cream or yellow spots. The belly
is grey and also often spotted.
The snout is rounded and the
eyes are relatively small.*

# Blue-spotted salamander

*Ambystoma laterale*

**Distribution**: Great Lakes
region, St Lawrence River
Valley and New England.
**Habitat**: Forest.
**Food**: Invertebrates.
**Size**: 7.5–13cm (3–5in).
**Maturity**: Unknown.
**Breeding**: Up to 200 eggs
laid underwater between
March and April.
**Life span**: Unknown.
**Status**: Common.

This species is found around the Great Lakes and north through Quebec to the south of
Hudson Bay. The range also follows the St Lawrence River valley to the Atlantic coast and
the Canadian Maritime provinces. Blue-spotted salamanders are also found in New England
and as far south as New Jersey.
They inhabit deciduous forests. The
adults stay under cover in winter to
avoid the freezing temperatures. As
a mole salamander, this species is a
skilled burrower.

In spring, the salamanders
gather at breeding ponds and
mate in the water. The eggs are
laid singly or in small masses at
the bottom of the pond. The larvae
change into adult form in late summer.

When alarmed, a blue-spotted salamander
holds its tail over its body. If a predator attacks
this part of the body, it gets a mouthful of a
noxious fluid released by glands on the tail.

*Blue-spotted salamanders have been interbred
with Jefferson salamanders, which live in a
similar habitat to the south. These crosses
produce new female-only species. Blue-
spotted males can mate with these
female hybrids; their sperm does
not result in fertilization, but it
stimulates egg development.*

## Small-mouthed salamander

*Ambystoma texanum*

Small-mouthed salamanders live in much of the Mississippi Basin, from Ohio in the north to Louisiana on the Gulf of Mexico. To the west, the salamanders range into Texas and Kansas. This species is often found alongside marbled and spotted salamanders. They live in pine woodlands and low-lying deciduous forests, generally near to streams and springs. In the west of their range, they are found in drier prairies, where they make use of temporary ponds.

Being a mole salamander, this species spends a lot of its time hiding in burrows. Breeding takes place during late winter and spring in flooded ditches and other bodies of standing water. The females lay about 700 eggs close to the water's edge. They are laid in small clusters attached to sticks, blades of grass on under rocks. The larvae are 1.3cm (0.5in) when they hatch. They spend a few months living in water before transforming into an air-breathing form when they are about 4cm (1.5in).

**Distribution**: Ohio to Texas.
**Habitat**: Forests and prairies near ponds and streams.
**Food**: Invertebrates.
**Size**: 11.5–18cm (4.5–7in).
**Maturity**: 1 year.
**Breeding**: 700 eggs laid in late winter and spring.
**Life span**: Unknown.
**Status**: Common.

*The small-mouthed salamander has a very small head and a correspondingly small mouth. It is dark brown or black on its back, with grey-blue or yellow mottled patches, although on some individuals these patches are absent. The belly is black and covered with tiny flecks.*

## Marbled salamander

*Ambystoma opacum*

**Distribution**: Eastern United States, except Florida and New England.
**Habitat**: Woodland.
**Food**: Invertebrates.
**Size**: 9–12.5cm (3.5–5in).
**Maturity**: 1–2 years.
**Breeding**: 50–200 eggs laid in autumn or winter.
**Life span**: Unknown.
**Status**: Common.

Marbled salamanders occupy a large range that covers most of the eastern United States. They are found from Massachusetts and the shore of Lake Erie in the north to the Florida panhandle and the Gulf of Mexico in the south. They live in woodlands and are especially common in lowland swamps, but they also live at higher altitudes, where the ground is drier and better drained.

The only time that marbled salamanders come together is during the breeding season. The breeding strategy relies on the rains that arrive in autumn and winter. In the north of their range, breeding occurs during the autumn to avoid the freezing winter conditions. In the south, the eggs are laid in early winter, which is wet but not too cold. The female lays up to 200 eggs in a nest made inside a small hollow. She wraps her body around the eggs and waits for the rains. After heavy rain, the hollow fills with water, allowing the eggs to hatch.

*This species is so-named because the silvery-white bands that cross the black skin on its back look like seams of marble or quartz. Young marbled salamanders have brown or grey skin.*

**Dwarf waterdog** (*Necturus punctatus*): 11.5–19cm (4.5–7.5in)
The smallest of the waterdogs, this species has narrow gills behind the head, and a short tail that is used for swimming. Waterdogs and their close relative the mudpuppy remain in the aquatic larval form throughout their lives, retaining their gills and paddle-like bodies even after reaching sexual maturity. Dwarf waterdogs live on the coastal plain of the eastern United Sates, between Virginia and Georgia. They are found in muddy streams with slow-moving water, and are also common in irrigation ditches.

**One-toed amphiuma** (*Amphiuma pholeter*): 21–33cm (8.25–13in)
This rarely seen, eel-like salamander has four tiny, largely functionless legs, each possessing just a single toe. The one-toed amphiuma lives in the Florida panhandle, from the Gulf coast to southern Georgia. It spends almost all of its time at the bottom of muddy ponds and streams, where the long body is ideal for squirming through the soft sediment.

**Lesser siren** (*Siren intermedia*): 18–70cm (7–27.5in)
The lesser siren occurs from the Atlantic coast coast of Virginia to eastern Texas and northern Mexico, and northward up the Mississippi Valley to Michigan. It is found in swamps, ponds and other shallow bodies of water. The diet of the lesser siren is made up of invertebrates and the tadpoles of other amphibians. Like other sirens, this species has two forelegs but no hind legs. It makes clicking noises and yelps when captured.

## Ringed salamander

*Ambystoma annulatum*

**Distribution**: Central Missouri to western Arkansas and eastern Oklahoma.
**Habitat**: Damp forests.
**Food**: Invertebrates such as insects, worms and snails.
**Size**: 14–23.5cm (5.5–9.25in).
**Maturity**: 1–2 years.
**Breeding**: Over 100 eggs laid underwater in clusters of 10–20 during autumn.
**Life span**: Unknown.
**Status**: Common.

Ringed salamanders live on the Ozark Plateau and in the Ouachita Mountains, the only significant highlands in North America between the Rockies and Appalachians. They are found in the damp forests and clearings of this region. Apart from during the breeding season, ringed salamanders are solitary and rarely seen above ground. They are most active during wet weather. Their diet probably consists of insects and other invertebrates that move through the leaf litter on the forest floor.

The autumn rainfall in the area is high, and numerous temporary pools form in the forests. Ringed salamanders breed in the water, after which the females lay small clusters of eggs on submerged plants. The larvae hatch in October and spend the winter in the water, where they feed on insect larvae and other small invertebrates. They change into the air-breathing form and emerge from the water during early summer.

*This very long mole salamander has a slender body and a small head. It has a brown or black upper body and a grey belly. The body and tail of the salamander are circled by yellow bands – hence its common name.*

## Pacific giant salamander

*Dicamptodon ensatus*

**Distribution**: Coast of southern British Columbia to central California and the Rockies of Idaho and Montana.
**Habitat**: Rivers, streams, lakes and ponds, and surrounding forests.
**Food**: Large insects, mice, amphibians and small snakes.
**Size**: 18–30cm (7–12in).
**Maturity**: 2–3 years.
**Breeding**: Both terrestrial and aquatic forms can breed. Females lay 85–200 eggs underwater singly and in clumps.
**Life span**: Unknown.
**Status**: Rare.

The Pacific giant salamander inhabits the many rivers that flow into the Pacific ocean along the US and Canadian coasts. In central California, in the south of its range, the rivers are smaller and more seasonal. Further north, a wetter climate along the coastal mountains makes the rivers larger. Pacific giant salamanders are found in the lower reaches of the huge Columbia River and its tributaries, including the Willamette of western Oregon. A smaller population survives far from the ocean, in the mountain streams of the Rockies in Idaho.

Giant Pacific salamanders spend more time in water than most mole salamanders. They lay their eggs on submerged wood or rocks. In colder places, the weather may not get warm enough to stimulate the change from aquatic larvae to air-breathing, land-living adults, even though they become sexually mature. Their offspring, however, may transform into land-living adults if the conditions are suitable. Transformed animals forage on the forest floor on rainy nights.

*The Pacific giant salamander, one of the world's largest land-living salamanders, has large eyes and a laterally compressed tail. The salamander's coloration typically consists of dark marbling on a brown background. In some parts of this species' range – generally the cooler regions – the salamanders never transform into land-living adults but retain their larval features, including the gills.*

# FROGS AND TOADS

*Frogs and toads form the largest group of amphibians, called Anura. Toads are better adapted to terrestrial habitats with thicker, warty skin to avoid desiccation, while frogs have thin, smooth skin that needs to be kept moist. Most species follow similar life cycles. Tailed larvae called tadpoles hatch from eggs called spawn and develop in water before sprouting legs, losing their tails and emerging on to land.*

## Surinam toad

*Pipa pipa*

Surinam toads spend their whole lives in water. The toads' fingers have a star of highly sensitive tentacles at their tips, which they use to feel for prey on the muddy bottoms of turbid ponds streams and ponds. They also have sense organs along their sides that can detect water movements caused by other animals. The eyes are located on the top of the head so the toads can spot danger approaching from above the surface.

These toads mate during the wettest time of the year. A male grabs a female around the waist and the couple spin around in the water several times. The female releases her eggs and the male uses his hind feet to sweep them into the space between her back and his belly. His sperm fertilizes the eggs, which then embed themselves on the mother's back. The eggs develop into tiny toadlets after three or four months.

*Surinam toads have flattened bodies with triangular heads and large, webbed hind feet. Their forefeet have sensitive fingers for feeling around in murky waters. A female may carry up to 100 fertilized eggs on her back.*

**Distribution**: Amazon Basin and northern South America.
**Habitat**: Muddy water.
**Food**: Small fish and aquatic invertebrates.
**Size**: 5–20cm (2–8in).
**Maturity**: Unknown.
**Breeding**: Rainy season.
**Life span**: Unknown.
**Status**: Common.

## Darwin's frog

*Rhinoderma darwinii*

*Darwin's frogs have small, slender bodies with pointed snouts and long fingers. The upper body is green or brown, the underside dark brown or black. The long digits on the hind feet are webbed. There are spur-like skin extensions on the rear legs – hence the alternative name of cowboy frog.*

Darwin's frogs live in the steamy mountain forests of the Andes in Chile and Argentina. Despite their natural habitat being damp and lush, Darwin's frogs do not have the aquatic stage that typifies the amphibian life cycle. Most frogs, toads and other amphibians spend at least part of their lives – generally the larval stage – living in water, but Darwin's frogs do not need this truly aquatic form because of their unusual breeding system. The frogs breed at all times of the year. The male first attracts the female with a bell-like call. The female lays around 20 eggs in a suitably moist spot, and the male fertilizes the eggs and guards them for about 25 days until they hatch into tadpoles. He then scoops the tadpoles into his mouth. Males of a species related to Darwin's frogs carry the tadpoles to the nearest body of water, but male Darwin's frogs keep the tadpoles in their mouths until they develop into froglets. The tadpoles develop in their father's vocal pouch for another 50 days before climbing out and becoming independent.

**Distribution**: Southern Andes, in southern Chile and Argentina.
**Habitat**: Shallow cold streams in mountain forests.
**Food**: Insects.
**Size**: 2.5–3cm (1–1.25in).
**Maturity**: Unknown.
**Breeding**: All year.
**Life span**: Unknown.
**Status**: Common.

# South American bullfrog

*Leptodactylus pentadactylus*

**Distribution**: Central and northern South America, from Costa Rica to Brazil.
**Habitat**: Tropical forest near water.
**Food**: Insects and other invertebrates.
**Size**: 8–22cm (3.25–8.5in).
**Maturity**: Unknown.
**Breeding**: Rainy season.
**Life span**: Unknown.
**Status**: Common, although these frogs are hunted by humans in some areas and their hind legs eaten.

South American bullfrogs are not closely related to the bullfrogs of North America. They all have powerful bodies and large external eardrums, but the similarity ends there. The South American bullfrog is, in fact, more closely related to the horned frogs, which have pointed protuberances of skin above their eyes.

The South American bullfrog is mainly nocturnal. It shelters under logs or in burrows by day and during periods when it is too dry to move around. The bullfrog reportedly lets out a piercing scream when picked up. This is probably intended to startle predators so that they drop the frog in fright, giving it a chance to make its escape.

South American bullfrogs breed in the wet season when the forest streams and ponds are swelled by the rains. The males whip up mucus into a blob of foam, using their hind legs, and attach it to a branch over a body of water. The females then choose a male's foam nest in which to lay their eggs. The tadpoles hatch out and fall into the water below.

*The South American bullfrog is a large, robust, aggressive animal with long limbs and widely spaced toes without webbing. Male South American bullfrogs defend territories at the edges of ponds. They have a sharp, black spine on each forethumb. During the mating season, they use these spines as weapons in fights with rival males over females.*

---

**Greenhouse frog** (*Eleutherodactylus planirostris*): 2–4cm (0.75–1.5in)
One of the world's smallest frogs, this nocturnal species lives in Florida and on several Caribbean islands, including Cuba. It inhabits damp forests and woodland, where it uses suction discs on its fingers and toes to cling to smooth bark, large leaves or, on occasion, greenhouse glass. It prefers wet weather, and is often seen foraging on lawns that are watered by sprinkler systems.

**Amazon harlequin toad** (*Atelopus pulcher*): 4cm (1.5in)
There are 65 species of harlequin toad in South America, most of them outside of the Amazon Basin. The Amazon harlequin has been found in the rainforests of Peru, but it is unclear whether its range spreads across the rest of the basin. This species has orange areas on its inner thighs and the soles its feet, which are exposed when the toad stretches its limbs. They are probably flashed to startle would-be predators.

**Mexican treefrog** (*Smilisca baudinii*): 5.1–9cm (2–3.5in)
This large frog of eastern Mexico and southern Texas occurs in a variety of colours, from light green to grey and yellow. Like other treefrogs, it has sucker-like toe-pads to give it a firm grip as it moves over branches or leaves. Unusually for a treefrog, this species is found in canyons and other dry environments in the north of its range. Further south, it lives in humid forests.

## Four-eyed frog

*Physalaemus nattereri*

Four-eyed, or false-eyed, frogs inhabit tropical forests near the Atlantic coast of South America. The adults spend their lives foraging on land. They breed after heavy rains have created ponds and puddles for the tadpoles to develop in. The male four-eyed frog, like his South American bullfrog counterpart, whips up a nest of foamy mucus near to water. The female's eggs hatch into tadpoles, which wriggle or drop the short distance into the water.

While most frogs rely on poisons or alarm calls to ward off predators, four-eyed frogs have a different strategy. When threatened, they inflate their bodies so that they appear to be much larger. They then turn around and point their rump at the attacker. The eyespots on the rump convince the attacker that it is looking at the face of a much larger, and potentially dangerous, animal. The frogs also secrete a foul-smelling fluid from a gland in their groin.

**Distribution**: Southern Brazil and northern Argentina.
**Habitat**: Coastal forest.
**Food**: Insects.
**Size**: 3–4cm (1.25–1.5in).
**Maturity**: Not known.
**Breeding**: Rainy season.
**Life span**: Unknown.
**Status**: Unknown.

*Four-eyed frogs are so-named because of the two black eyespots on their rumps.*

## Marine toad

*Bufo marinus*

Marine toads are the largest toads in the world. They have several other common names, including giant toads and cane toads, their Australian name. Marine toads occur naturally from the southern United States through Mexico to Chile. They were introduced to Queensland, Australia, in the 1930s to help control the pest beetles that were infesting sugar cane crops. However, the toads did not like living amongst the cane plants because there were few places to shelter during the day. Consequently, the toads spread out over the countryside, where they ate not beetle pests but small reptiles and mammals, some of which are now rare because of their predation. Today the toads are a serious pest in Australia.

Marine toads are extremely adaptable. They live a wide range of habitats, eating just about anything they can get into their mouths, from small rodents, reptiles and birds to invertebrates such as snails, centipedes, cockroaches, grasshoppers, ants and beetles. They protect themselves against attack using the toxin glands on their backs, which ooze a fluid that can kill many animals that ingest it. In small amounts, the toxin causes humans to hallucinate.

Female cane toads produce several thousand eggs each year. They lay them in long strings, wrapped around water plants. The eggs are then fertilized by the males.

*Female marine toads are larger than the males. Both sexes have warty glands on their backs that squirt a milky toxin when squeezed.*

**Distribution**: Southern North America and Central and South America, from Texas to Chile; now introduced to other areas, including eastern Australia.
**Habitat**: Most land habitats, often near pools and swamps.
**Food**: Insects (particularly beetles), snakes, lizards and small mammals.
**Size**: 5–23cm (2–9in).
**Maturity**: 1 year.
**Breeding**: 2 clutches of between 8,000 and 35,000 eggs produced each year. Eggs hatch into tadpoles that become adult in 45–55 days.
**Life span**: 40 years.
**Status**: Common.

## Red-eyed tree frog

*Agalychnis callidryas*

*Red-eyed tree frogs have long toes with rounded suction discs at their tips. Their bodies have a bright green upper side. These colourful frogs have blue and white stripes on their flanks and yellow and red legs. The family of tree frogs, about 600 species strong, is found on all the continents except Antarctica.*

Red-eyed tree frogs live in the rainforests of Central America. Their long legs allow them to reach for branches and spread their body weight over a wide area when climbing through flimsy foliage. The discs on the tips of each toe act as suction cups, so the frogs can cling to flat surfaces, such as leaves.

Red-eyed tree frogs are nocturnal. Their large eyes gather as much light as possible so the frogs can see even on the darkest nights. During the day, the frogs rest on leaves. They tuck their brightly coloured legs under their bodies so only their camouflaged, leaf-green upper sides are showing.

At breeding time, males gather on a branch above a pond and call to the females with clicking sounds. When a female arrives, a male climbs on to her back and she carries him down to the water. She takes in water and climbs back to the branch again, where she lays eggs on a leaf. The male fertilizes the eggs and they are then abandoned. After hatching, the tadpoles fall into the water below.

**Distribution**: From north-eastern Mexico along the Caribbean coast of Central America to Panama.
**Habitat**: Tropical forests in the vicinity of streams.
**Food**: Insects, including flies crickets, grasshoppers and moths; sometimes small frogs.
**Size**: 4–7cm (1.5–2.75in).
**Maturity**: Unknown.
**Breeding**: Eggs laid in summer.
**Life span**: Unknown.
**Status**: Common.

# Strawberry poison-dart frog

*Dendrobates pumilio*

**Distribution**: Southern Central America.
**Habitat**: Tropical forest.
**Food**: Ants, termites, beetles and other small leaf-litter arthropods.
**Size**: 2–2.5cm (0.75–1in).
**Maturity**: Unknown.
**Breeding**: Rainy season; clutches of 3–5 eggs laid in a jelly-like mass that keeps them moist.
**Life span**: Unknown.
**Status**: Common.

Many frogs and toads secrete toxic chemicals on to their skins. Most are harmless to humans, but many make predators sick after they eat the frogs. However, the strawberry poison-dart frog and other closely related species have much more potent toxins. A single lick is enough to kill most predators.

The frogs earn their name from the fact that their skins are used by forest people to make poison for hunting darts. The toxins of some frogs are so strong that a single skin can produce enough poison to tip 50 darts. Hunters use them to kill monkeys and other forest animals.

The strawberry poison-dart frog is not always red. During the breeding season, males often change colour to brown, blue or green. Although these frogs rarely climb trees when foraging, the females will scale tree trunks to lay their eggs in holes filled with water. The males then fertilize the eggs.

*Strawberry poison-dart frogs have bright red bodies with blue on their hind legs. These bright colours serve as a warning to predators that their skins are covered in a poison so deadly that just one lick is generally fatal. The family contains around 120 species.*

**Reticulated glass frog** (*Centrolenella valerioi*): 2–5cm (0.75–2in)
This species of glass frog lives in mountain rainforests in South and Central America. It lives in the trees and is an expert climber, having slender legs with suction discs on its toes for clinging to the flat surfaces of leaves. Glass frogs get their common name from their translucent skin, through which the major bones and blood vessels are visible.

**Blue poison-dart frog** (*Dendrobates azureus*): 4.5cm (1.75in)
This arboreal frog, one of the larger poison-dart species, has a bright blue body with black spots and bars on its back. The potency of the poison in the skin, which gives this and similar frogs their common name, depends on the frog's diet. This species eats ants. Red ants contain formic acid, which the frog uses to make powerful toxins.

**Pasco poison-dart frog** (*Dendrobates lamasi*): 1.5cm (0.5in)
The tiny Pasco poison-dart frog of eastern Peru divides its time between the rainforest floor and moss-covered tree trunks and branches. This species has five green or yellow stripes along its black back. Females lay their eggs in the small pools that form among the leaves of bromeliad plants, which grow on trees and other plants, often high above the ground. The tadpoles develop into frogs while swimming in these suspended pools.

# Paradoxical frog

*Pseudis paradoxa*

The paradoxical frog is aptly named. Most other frogs are considerably larger than their tadpoles. However, adult paradoxical frogs are smaller than their fully grown tadpoles, hence the paradox. Young paradoxical frogs stay in their larval tadpole stage for much longer than other species. They grow to 25cm (10in) long – four or five times the size of an adult. As they metamorphose into adults, the frogs therefore shrink in size, mainly by absorbing their tails back into their bodies.

Adult paradoxical frogs have bodies that are well adapted to a life in water. Their powerful hind limbs are webbed and are used as the main means of propulsion. Like many other aquatic frogs, this species has long fingers that are good for delving into the muddy beds of lakes and ponds. They stir up the mud to disturb prey animals and catch them in their mouths. The female lays her eggs in a floating foam nest, before the male fertilizes them.

*Paradoxical frogs have slimy bodies and a dark green and brown coloration. They have very long hind legs with webbed feet. Their forefeet have two long toes.*

**Distribution**: Central and eastern South America.
**Habitat**: Fresh water.
**Food**: Aquatic invertebrates.
**Size**: 5–7cm (2–2.75in).
**Maturity**: Unknown.
**Breeding**: Rainy season.
**Life span**: Unknown.
**Status**: Common.

## Tailed frog

*Ascaphus truei*

Tailed frogs live in the clear mountain streams of the Cascade Range in the north-western United States and southern Canada. These frogs often stray from the water into damp forests, and are especially common on land during periods of damp weather.

Tailed frogs have a head with rounded a snout. The males have a short, tail-like extension, which is actually a flexible organ used to deliver sperm to a female's eggs while they are still inside her body. This is an adaptation to ensure fertilization, where releasing sperm and eggs into the fast-flowing water would be unlikely to succeed. After mating, the females lay short strings of eggs on the downstream side of rocks. The tadpoles develop into adults slowly, taking up to four years in colder parts of their range. They use their mouth as a sucker to cling on to rocks so that they are not swept away by the current. Tailed frogs will attempt to eat anything solid that comes within reach. Their diet generally consists of plant matter and the aquatic larvae of insects and other invertebrates. They will bite into human flesh given the opportunity.

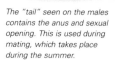

*The "tail" seen on the males contains the anus and sexual opening. This is used during mating, which takes place during the summer.*

**Distribution**: Pacific coast of North America, from southern British Columbia in Canada to northern California in the United States and the northern Great Basin.
**Habitat**: Cold mountain streams up to the treeline.
**Food**: Algae and aquatic invertebrates.
**Size**: 4cm (1.5in).
**Maturity**: 3 years.
**Breeding**: Strings of eggs laid in fast-flowing streams between May and September.
**Life span**: Unknown.
**Status**: Common.

## Golden toad

*Bufo periglenes*

The golden toad is probably extinct in the wild – its tiny population is thought to have been wiped out by drought. It was last reported in 1991, although there continue to be unverified sightings, so it is possible that a small number of golden toads still survive and may one day repopulate their range. Golden toads have always been very rare. They were known to live only in a small area of cloud forest in the mountains of Costa Rica. Their habitat was protected until 1991, and is still being preserved in case the toads make a recovery.

Golden toads are explosive breeders, meaning they reproduce in huge numbers when conditions are right. The toads gather in huge crowds around temporary pools of water that form during the rains. The male to female ratio is about 8:1, and several males may cluster around each female, forming "toad balls." Competition between males is fierce, and males will try to interrupt mating pairs. Mating itself can be prolonged: one pair was recorded locked in an embrace for 25 hours. The females deposit between 200 and 400 large eggs at a time, and the tadpoles take five weeks to metamorphose into adults.

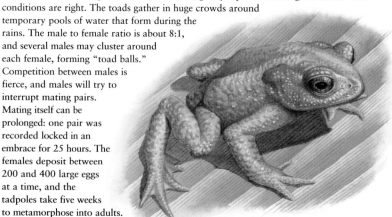

**Distribution**: Northern Costa Rica.
**Habitat**: Cloud forest.
**Food**: Invertebrates.
**Size**: 4–5cm (1.5–2in).
**Maturity**: 5 weeks.
**Breeding**: Eggs laid between April and June.
**Life span**: Unknown.
**Status**: Extinct in the wild.

*Only the male golden toads are in fact bright gold or orange in colour. Females, which are slightly larger, are black with scarlet blotches edged with yellow. Developing toads do not display this sexual colour difference. It is only possible to distinguish their sex when the toads reach maturity.*

# American toad

*Bufo americanus*

American toads are found in most parts of eastern North America, from Hudson Bay to the Carolinas. Some American toads survive in irrigated areas of the western United States, where it is too dry for them to live naturally. They are also widespread from California to Washington.

This species is similar to its European cousin, the common toad, in that it has a brownish, wart-covered body. American toads are most active at night, especially in warm and humid weather. They eat mainly insects, slugs and worms.

The toads catch their prey by flicking out their sticky tongue, which grabs food and drags it back into the mouth. The tadpoles graze on water plants.

American toads breed in spring, when the days lengthen and the temperature rises. These normally solitary animals congregate in large numbers to mate. The females lay thousands of eggs in the water, forming a huge string of eggs up 20m (66ft) long.

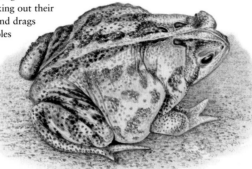

**Distribution**: United States and eastern Canada.
**Habitat**: Ponds.
**Food**: Insects and slugs.
**Size**: 5–9cm (2–3.5in).
**Maturity**: 2 years.
**Breeding**: Eggs laid in spring.
**Life span**: 10 years.
**Status**: Common.

*This toad has relatively short legs compared to its stout body. Like many toads, it has warts on its head and back. The warts squirt a toxic milky liquid into the mouth of any attacker that tries to bite the toad.*

---

**Oak toad** (*Bufo quercicus*): 1.9–3.3cm (0.75–1.25in)
This is the smallest toad in North America. It is found in the extreme south-east of the United States. Its range covers the whole of Florida, including the Keys, and extends up the east coast to southern Virginia, as well as along the Gulf coast to Louisiana and eastern Texas. It occupies oak woodlands that grow on sandy soils, where it hunts for insects during the day. Oak toads have a white stripe down their back, and the males have a dark throat. The males produce a high-pitched whistle to attract mates. Breeding takes place in summer after thunderstorms. The storms swell streams and produce temporary pools in which the toads lay their eggs.

**Canadian toad** (*Bufo hemiophrys*): 5–8.5cm (2–3.25in)
This large species has crests on its head that connect between the eyes to form a ridge. The body is greenish-brown with hints of red. The warts, which are characteristic of toads, are pale brown. This species lives in the Great Plains region of North America, specifically the southern Canadian provinces of Alberta, Manitoba and Saskatchewan. A small population exists in North Dakota and Montana. The range does not extend to the extreme north of the plains region, where it is too cold for the toads, nor to the extreme south, where conditions are too dry. Canadian toads are nocturnal. When threatened, they seek refuge in water; if that is not available, they dig into soft soil using spade-like appendages on their hind feet.

# Crested forest toad

*Bufo margaritifer*

This species occurs in most forest habitats across northern South America. Crested forest toads live in both primary and secondary forests. A primary forest is a pristine habitat that has been undisturbed for many years. Increasingly, however, the forests of South America are becoming secondary forests, where the communities of trees and other large plants are disturbed regularly, mainly by human activities. Such disturbance increases the amount of small, fast-growing shrubs in the forest.

Crested forest toads are most commonly seen at night, often in clearings and gaps between trees, as they perch on a wide leaf or flimsy branch a few feet off the ground. Breeding occurs all year around, with males calling to females from the banks of watercourses. The females lay large egg clutches in quiet streams and pools.

**Distribution**: Northern South America.
**Habitat**: Forest.
**Food**: Insects and other invertebrates.
**Size**: 7cm (2.75in).
**Maturity**: Unknown.
**Breeding**: Up to 2,000 eggs laid in forest pools.
**Life span**: Unknown.
**Status**: Common.

*This species has two large crests on either side of its head. The crests vary in size across what many scientist believe is a number of separate, but as yet undescribed, species.*

## North American bullfrog

*Rana catesbeiana*

The North American bullfrog is the largest frog in North America. It is found from Nova Scotia on the Atlantic coast of Canada south to central Florida and into Mexico. From the east coast it ranges west as far as the Great Plains and Rocky Mountains. It seldom strays far from a pond or other source of water. North American bullfrogs have also been introduced to areas west of the Rockies, such as California and Colorado. Here, they generally survive in cultivated areas that are irrigated by rivers and groundwater.

The North American bullfrog has a reputation for having a large appetite, and will consume almost any animal that it can overpower. It lives in lakes, ponds and slow-flowing streams. During the summer breeding season, the males defend their territories by wrestling with their rivals. They attract females by voicing deep croaks. The female bullfrog deposits a foaming mass of eggs in water, and the eggs are then fertilized by one or more males.

*This large green frog is perhaps most recognizable from the large external eardrums on either side of its head, which in the males are bigger than the eyes. At dusk and during summer, American bullfrogs give a deep call that sounds like "jugoram."*

**Distribution**: Atlantic coast of North America west to Rocky Mountains and south to Mexico.
**Habitat**: Ponds and lakes.
**Food**: Snakes, worms, fish, insects, crayfish, tadpoles, turtles, frogs and small mammals.
**Size**: 9–20cm (3.5–8in).
**Maturity**: 3 years.
**Breeding**: Up to 20,000 eggs laid in early summer; hatching occurs after about 4 days.
**Life span**: 16 years.
**Status**: Common.

## Mexican burrowing toad

*Rhinophrynus dorsalis*

*The Mexican burrowing toad has a unique, egg-shaped body – ideal for wriggling through soft soil – and a small, pointed head with a calloused snout. The body is dark brown to near black, with a mid-dorsal red to dark orange stripe and similar coloured patterning on the flanks. Females of this species tend to be substantially larger than males.*

Mexican burrowing toads are found from southern Texas to Costa Rica, in areas with soft, sandy soils that are easy to burrow into. The frogs have smooth, moist skin with a red or yellow line running along their back.

Mexican burrowing toads eat insects and other invertebrates. They are especially fond of termites, which they lick up with their tongues. These toads spend most of their time underground to avoid drying out, and only coming to the surface after heavy rain. The smooth skin and pointed body makes it easier for the toads to shimmy through the soil, propelled by the powerful rear legs. The hind feet have a thick arc of skin supported by very long toes, making them very effective digging tools. To deter predators, a threatened toad swells its body by swallowing air. In this inflated state, the toad is difficult to extract from its burrow.

These toads breed in the temporary pools that form after heavy rains at the start of the wet season. The tadpoles are filter-feeders, straining tiny, floating plants and animals from the water. They take up to three months to transform into adults.

**Distribution:** Extreme southern Texas and Mexico through Central America as far south as Costa Rica.
**Habitat**: Soil in savannah and seasonally dry forests.
**Food**: Termites and other insects.
**Size**: 6–8cm (2.5–3.25in).
**Maturity**: 3 months.
**Breeding**: Several thousand eggs laid in the rainy season, either individually or in small groups; the fertilized eggs sink to the bottom and hatch within a few days.
**Life span**: Unknown.
**Status**: Common.

# Eastern spadefoot toad

*Scaphiopus holbrookii*

**Distribution**: Eastern United States.
**Habitat**: Areas of loose soil in a range of habitats.
**Food**: Worms and insects.
**Size**: 4.4–8.25cm (1.75–3.25in).
**Maturity**: 8 weeks.
**Breeding**: Eggs laid in summer.
**Life span**: Unknown.
**Status**: Common.

Eastern spadefoot toads live in two main populations in eastern North America. The smaller population lives in eastern Texas and the western Mississippi Valley, and extends to north-eastern Mexico. The larger population lives to the east of the Mississippi and covers most of the south-eastern United States, reaching as far north as Ohio and Massachusetts. The toads are absent from the higher areas of the Appalachian Mountains, which cut through their range.

Both populations of these toads prefer areas with loose, sandy soil. These toads are found in a range of habitats, from forests to dry scrublands. Eastern spadefoot toads are nocturnal. By day, they remain hidden in burrows. They emerge on damp nights to hunt for worms and insects. Breeding takes place when heavy summer rainfall creates temporary pools. Females are attracted to the pools by the grunting calls of the males. After mating, the females lay their eggs on underwater vegetation.

*Eastern spadefoot toads are so named for the spade-shaped structure on each hind foot with which they dig burrows in loose, sandy soil.*

**Plains spadefoot toad** (*Scaphiopus bombifrons*): 3.8–6.3cm (1.5–2.5in)
The plains spadefoot toad lives to the north of Couch's spadefoot. It is found from northern Mexico to the southern edge of Canada, including the prairies and semi-deserts of the Great Plains region in western North America. This nocturnal toad is rarely seen above ground when it is not raining. It hunts for beetles, ants, earthworms and other invertebrates. When startled, the toad burrows backwards into the soil with its spade-like feet. As a defence, the warts on its back can secrete an unpleasant liquid that smells of garlic.

**Plains leopard frog** (*Rana blairi*): 5.1–11.1cm (2–4.25in)
This is another species that survives on the arid grasslands of the Great Plains, where it inhabits the region's few streams and ponds. It is most common on the eastern plains of Indiana and Nebraska, where rainfall is higher. The frog's skin is greenish-brown, with dark spots on yellow ridges across the back. Plains leopard frogs hunt at night for insects along the water's edge.

**Colombian horned frog** (*Ceratophrys calcarata*): 6.5cm (2.5in)
Occupying a range of habitats in northern South America, this frog is found from Colombia and Venezuela to northern Peru. Females are brown with pale patches; males are similar but smaller, and they have horn-like projections on their upper eyelids. Like other horned frogs, this species has a huge head. Colombian horned frogs feed on insects and small lizards. They have a powerful bite, which is often used against rivals.

# Couch's spadefoot toad

*Scaphiopus couchii*

This toad occurs in the extreme south of California, Arizona and New Mexico, as well as in much of western Texas and northern Mexico. Like other spadefoot toads, this species lives in burrows dug in soft soil. Couch's spadefoot toad is most commonly found in dry grassland and areas covered by mesquite shrubs.

Couch's spadefoot toads use their burrows to avoid the high temperatures of their arid habitat. In the warmest part of the year, the toads dig a deep burrow and stay dormant until rainy weather arrives, spending up to 10 months underground. During the rainy season, the toads emerge on the surface on cool nights to hunt for insects. Males attract females by calling from temporary pools of rainwater. A male will grab hold of a receptive female and fertilize her eggs as she lays them in the water.

**Distribution**: South-western United States, California and northern Mexico.
**Habitat**: Soil of grasslands.
**Food**: Insects.
**Size**: 5.6–8.8cm (2.25–3.5in).
**Maturity**: 40 days.
**Breeding**: Eggs laid in summer.
**Life span**: Unknown.
**Status**: Common.

*Like other spadefoot toads, this species digs burrows using the spade-like structures on the underside of its hind feet. The toad's skin is covered in tiny tubercles.*

## Crawfish frog

*Rana areolata*

**Distribution**: South-eastern United States, from coast of Carolinas to Gulf of Mexico and river valleys farther west.
**Habitat**: Meadows and woodlands.
**Food**: Insects, crayfish, amphibians and reptiles.
**Size**: 5.7–11.4cm (2.25–4.5in).
**Maturity**: 3 years.
**Breeding**: Up to 7,000 eggs laid in spring; hatching takes about 12 days.
**Life span**: Unknown.

This species is found in areas of North America with large floodplains and many wetlands, where it feeds on crayfish (crawfish), insects, reptiles and other frogs. There are two separate populations. One follows the upper Mississippi Valley from south of the confluence with the Arkansas River up the Mississippi to Iowa, from where it extends west to the Missouri River. The range also reaches into the watershed of the Ohio and Tennessee Rivers. The second population ranges from the Atlantic coastal plain of the Carolinas to the coast of the Gulf of Mexico.

Crawfish frogs may spend much of the year underground, waiting for the right conditions for breeding. They do not dig their own burrows, but occupy tunnels abandoned by other animals, including those of crayfish and small mammals. During the spring rains, crawfish frogs emerge from their tunnels and arrive beside the swelling waterways in large numbers. The males attract mates with their snore-like calls.

*This frog has a stout body and short, strong legs. On the back and sides it is brownish or greyish in colour with darker spots, while the belly is white and the undersides of the legs and groin are yellowish. These frogs can move swiftly on land, but in the water they tend to be rather slow swimmers.*

## Green frog

*Rana clamitans*

This frog is found in the marshes of the maritime provinces of Canada in the north and east. From here, it ranges south to the swamps of northern Florida and the mountain lakes of Oklahoma. Older adults lead relatively sedentary lives, but younger frogs often disperse through damp woodlands and meadows during periods of heavy rain. If a young frog is caught away from water as a dry period approaches, it may survive if it buries itself in moist soil until the rains return. Those that reach suitable bodies of standing water spend the summer feeding on insects and other invertebrates, both in the water and along the banks. In periods of cold weather, the frogs submerge themselves in the leaf litter and sediment at the bottom of a pond or stream. Like leopard frogs and bullfrogs, startled green frogs often emit a loud, high-pitched yelp as they leap away.

Breeding occurs in late spring, when males attract females with their twanging calls. Some males, however, stay silent and mate with females as they approach calling males. Each female lays up to 7,000 eggs, which float on the water's surface or hang from aquatic plants. The eggs hatch in about a week, and the tadpoles are usually green and speckled with black, often with a yellow belly. Some tadpoles change into adults before winter, but many hibernate and delay the transformation until spring. In fact, it can take up to 22 months for metamorphosis to occur.

**Distribution**: Eastern North America to Oklahoma, Florida and Eastern Canada.
**Habitat**: Swamps, ponds, lakes and rivers.
**Food**: Insects, slugs and crayfish.
**Size**: 5.4–12.5cm (2.25–4.75in).
**Maturity**: 2 years.
**Breeding**: Eggs laid in late spring.
**Life span**: 10 years.
**Status**: Common.

*Although most members of this species are green or brown, a few rare individuals are blue. Males also have a bright yellow patch on the throat.*

**Amazonian rain frog** (*Eleutherodactylus altamazonicus*): 3cm (1.25in)
Amazonian rain frogs live in the shrubs and large herbaceous plants that grow on rainforest floors. These tiny frogs are found in Ecuador and Peru in the west and across the Amazon Basin to southern Brazil. This species is largely brown with white speckles. It is most active at night, when it feeds on tiny insects. The males, which are slightly larger than the females, attract mates with a soft clicking call.

**Forest chirping frog** (*Adenomera hylaedactyla*): 2.5cm (1in)
The forest chirping frog has a sharp nose and a plump-looking fawn body with a dark V or X between the eyes. It inhabits the rainforests of Peru, Ecuador, Colombia and Brazil, where it is found in the thick leaf litter on forest floor. The diet comprises insects, spiders, millipedes and other small invertebrates. This frog is named for the chirping calls the males use to attract mates. Females lay eggs in a foam nest. The tadpoles only emerge from the nest once they have lost their tail and grown into miniature froglets.

**Sharp-nosed jungle frog** (*Leptodactylus bolivianus*): 10cm (4in)
This species has long hind legs and a pointed nose, giving it an elongated look. Sharp-nosed jungle frogs live in open areas beside ponds or in forest clearings, often near human settlements. They live in the upper Amazon in Peru and Bolivia. Males attract females with a single "whop" call. The female encloses the eggs in a floating foam nest. Each nest contains several hundred eggs.

# Red-legged frog

*Rana aurora*

**Distribution**: West coast of the United States.
**Habitat**: Rivers and ponds.
**Food**: Small mammals, invertebrates and other amphibians.
**Size**: 5.1–13.6cm (2–5.25in).
**Maturity**: 4 years.
**Breeding**: Eggs laid in spring.
**Life span**: 15 years.
**Status**: Threatened.

This species inhabits the ponds and streams of the coastal mountains that run along the west coast of North America. The northern tip of the range is Vancouver Island in British Columbia. The range then extends south all the way to Mexico's Baja California. Red-legged frogs are seldom found far from water, preferring deep and slow-moving stretches with thick vegetation. They may wander into damp forests in search of food such as insects and, occasionally, small mammals and frogs.

Red-legged frogs live alone. They are generally most active during the day, although those in California are primarily nocturnal. This may reflect the fact that the California frogs have different predators, including wading birds, which are a threat during daylight.

*Female red-legged frogs grow to a larger size than males. Only the hind legs are red. Male red-legged frogs in the south of the range have a pair of vocal sacs, which swell when the frogs croak. Males in the north lack these sacs.*

# Pig frog

*Rana grylio*

*This frog is often called a bullfrog by people in southern US states, due to the large external eardrum on either side of its head. Females continue growing after the males have stopped, and may eventually reach a larger size.*

The highly aquatic pig frog prefers to live in streams and ponds with thick vegetation, especially bladderworts, water lilies and saw grass. Pig frogs occur throughout Florida and as far north as the swamplands of southern Georgia. The range also extends west along the Gulf of Mexico to the Mississippi Delta and the barrier islands of the Texas coast.

Pig frogs are named after their mating call, which sounds like the grunt of a pig. During the breeding season, choruses of males create a roaring barrage of sound as they float in the water. After mating, the female attaches several thousand eggs to the stems of pickerel weed and other plants. Pig frogs hunt at night. They feed on insect larvae and small crustaceans that live underwater.

**Distribution**: South-eastern United States.
**Habitat**: Rivers and lakes.
**Food**: Insects and crustaceans.
**Size**: 8–16.2cm (3.25–6.5in).
**Maturity**: 2 years.
**Breeding**: Eggs laid in summer.
**Life span**: Unknown.
**Status**: Common.

## Eastern narrow-mouthed toad

*Gastrophryne carolinensis*

**Distribution**: South-eastern United States, from eastern Texas to the Florida peninsula (including the Keys) and north to Oklahoma and Maryland.
**Habitat**: Ponds and ditches.
**Food**: Ants, termites, beetles and other insects.
**Size**: 2.2–3.8cm (1–1.5in).
**Maturity**: 30 days to metamorphosis.
**Breeding**: Mating, which is brought on by the rains, occurs between March and September. Up to 800 eggs are laid in floating clusters.
**Life span**: Unknown.
**Status**: Common.

The eastern narrow-mouthed toad lives in a variety of different habitats across the south-east of the United States. The toad is most commonly seen in areas with plenty of moisture and places to hide. This species is a good burrower – its narrow shoulders enable it to wriggle easily into soft earth. The toad will also seek refuge under logs and amongst leaf litter.

Eastern narrow-mouthed toads are nocturnal hunters. They prey on beetles, termites, ants and other ground-dwelling insects. They are especially fond of ants, and several toads may be seen feeding at a single anthill. Since these toads do not have teeth, the ants are licked up by the tongue. The toads have a flap of skin running behind each eye. These fold forward when the toad is feeding to protect the eyes from attack by their insect prey.

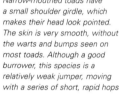

*Narrow-mouthed toads have a small shoulder girdle, which makes their head look pointed. The skin is very smooth, without the warts and bumps seen on most toads. Although a good burrower, this species is a relatively weak jumper, moving with a series of short, rapid hops.*

## Johnson's casque-headed treefrog

*Hemiphractus johnsoni*

Although Johnson's casque-headed treefrog is rarely seen and is known only from about 20 specimens, it has been recorded across a huge swathe of South America. It is possible that within this range the frog exists in severely fragmented populations. Some experts believe that Johnson's casque-headed treefrog is actually a number of closely related species, particularly those populations in Brazil. The main habitat of this frog is the dense rainforest that covers the low-lying Amazon Basin, but it also survives at altitudes of up to 2,000m (6,500ft) in forests on the slopes of the Andes in Colombia, Ecuador, Peru and northern Bolivia. The frog is thought to divide its time between the branches and the forest floor.

This species does not lay eggs in water or enclose them in a nest. Instead, the female holds about a dozen eggs in a pouch on her back. The eggs develop through the tadpole phase inside the pouch, and then emerge as fully formed froglets.

Johnson's casque-headed frog hunts for insects and other invertebrates, plus smaller frogs and the occasional lizard. When disturbed, the frog attempts to ward off attackers by gaping its large mouth as wide as possible and snapping at anything that comes near.

**Distribution**: Western Andes and Amazon Basin.
**Habitat**: Rainforest.
**Food**: Insects.
**Size**: 5.3–7.7cm (2–3in).
**Maturity**: Unknown.
**Breeding**: Eggs develop in dorsal pouch.
**Life span**: Unknown.
**Status**: Unknown.

*When seen from above, this frog's head is triangular, due to two pointed sections, or casques, behind each eye. The females of this species tend to be larger than the males.*

## Northern cricket frog

*Acris crepitans*

The northern cricket frog is found across much of the United States. Its most northerly extent is to Michigan south of the Great Lakes. The range extends west to Nebraska and south to Texas. In the east, the range covers the Deep South (except most of Florida) and extends northward along the Atlantic coastal plain to southern New England. Northern cricket frogs live close to ponds and streams where plenty of cover is provided by aquatic plants. They are often seen basking on sunny banks to raise their body temperature. These frogs cannot climb, but they can make large leaps of up to 1m (3ft). They are diurnal (day-active) hunters, seeking out mosquitos and other damp-loving insects.

Large numbers of northern cricket frogs gather at ponds in the breeding season. However, many of these frogs do not survive long enough to become sexually mature, and the species is now classed as vulnerable due to the loss of its habitat. The frog's range covers some of the most intensively farmed land on Earth, and much of the standing water that the frogs need to survive is channelled and collected to drain and irrigate fields.

**Distribution**: Eastern and central north America.
**Habitat**: Ponds and streams.
**Food**: Insects.
**Size**: 1.6–3.8cm (0.5–1.5in).
**Maturity**: 1 year.
**Breeding**: Eggs laid in summer.
**Life span**: 1 year.
**Status**: Vulnerable.

*This species is closely related to treefrogs, although it lives on the ground. It has webbed hind feet rather than long, suckered toes like the treefrogs. There is a dark triangular mark on the head.*

---

**Southern cricket frog** (*Acris gryllus*): 1.6–3.2cm (0.5–1.25in)
This treefrog lives in swamps, marshes and streams. Its range covers the south of the United States and overlaps with that of the northern cricket frog, but only this species occurs in the Florida peninsula. Cricket frogs are strong jumpers – hence the comparison to crickets and grasshoppers. During the day they feed on insect prey, hiding in waterside vegetation and ambushing victims as they pass.

**Lowland burrowing treefrog** (*Pternohyla fodiens*): 2.5–6cm (1–2.5in)
Although it is related to frogs that live in trees, this species makes its home underground in the deserts of western Mexico and southern Arizona. The frog shelters from the daytime heat in burrows, where conditions are cooler and more humid than the surface. It only emerges on cool nights. Like many burrowing frogs, this species has a spade-like tubercle (projection) on its hind feet. It may use its large, bony head to plug the burrow entrance, preventing predators from entering and making it difficult for them to pull the frog out.

**Spring peeper** (*Hyla crucifer*): 2–3.5cm (0.75–1.25in)
This insect-eating species ranges from southern Canada and New England to Texas; it is absent from the swamplands of southern Georgia and Florida. Spring peepers are related to treefrogs and can climb well, although they are most often seen on river banks or in damp leaf litter. They are named after the high-pitched whistling calls that the males make to attract females in spring.

## Striped chorus frog

*Pseudacris triseriata*

This species, sometimes simply called the chorus frog, is another "treefrog" that does not live in trees. Chorus frogs live further north than most American frogs, with a range that extends into the far north of Canada, reaching the Great Bear Lake and the often icy upper reaches of the Mackenzie River. Their range also encompasses much of central North America, as well as the Deep South of the United States, where the climate is much warmer and more humid.

Chorus frogs feed on a range of invertebrates, depending on their location. They are nocturnal and spend the day hiding under logs or in the burrows of larger animals. In the north of their range, they hibernate in these hideaways for several months of the year. However, on rare occasions they may emerge and begin to call before all the winter snow has melted.

**Distribution**: Central North America.
**Habitat**: Marshes and meadows.
**Food**: Insects and spiders.
**Size**: 1.9–3.8cm (0.75–1.5in).
**Maturity**: 1 year.
**Breeding**: Eggs laid in early summer.
**Life span**: 5 years.
**Status**: Common.

*The three pale stripes running down the back of this frog are the source of its common name. Males have a yellow vocal sac that expands as the animal makes its calls.*

## Pacific treefrog

*Hyla regilla*

*This variably coloured species has a dark stripe that runs from the nostril to the shoulder. The frog's rough skin can change colour. Such changes are triggered by the prevailing temperature and humidity, rather than being actively controlled by the frog itself. Female Pacific treefrogs are slightly larger than males.*

The Pacific treefrog occurs in the Pacific North-west region of North America. The northern limit of its range is southern British Columbia and Vancouver Island. From here, the frogs range along the Pacific coast and through the coastal mountains to Mexico's Baja California. They are found inland as far as Montana and Nevada.

Pacific treefrogs usually live on the ground. They occupy a wide range of habitats, and are most often found near ponds, springs and streams. They prefer rocky areas, where there are plenty of damp nooks and crannies in which to hide.

Pacific treefrogs are generally solitary, but they may assemble in large numbers during the breeding season. At night, the males repeat their two-toned "kreck-ek" mating call to attract females and tell other males to stay out of their territory.

As tadpoles, the frogs eat aquatic plant material such as algae. The adult frogs are carnivores. They catch flying insects with their tongue, which they flick out at high speed. The tongue is coated with a sticky substance that helps the frogs to grab prey.

**Distribution**: Western North America, from southern Canada and United States to Baja California, Mexico.
**Habitat**: Close to water.
**Food**: Insects.
**Size**: 1.9–5cm (0.75–2in).
**Maturity**: 1 year.
**Breeding**: Mating season in spring. Female lays a mass of 10–70 eggs, which either floats or is attached to vegetation; eggs hatch within 3–4 weeks.
**Life span**: Unknown.
**Status**: Common.

## Green treefrog

*Hyla cinerea*

*This species has rough, bright green skin and a dark spot under each eye. There are bright yellow patches on the inner thighs. The skin becomes greyer during cold weather, and males turn yellow during the breeding season. The long legs and large, adhesive pads at the end of the toes are adaptations to an arboreal existence. These small frogs can leap about 3m (10ft), and they are able to hang on to leaves and other surfaces by just one toe.*

Green treefrogs live along the edges of swampy ponds and in marshes. They are often found at ground level, but also climb into the tall shrubs and trees that grow beside the water. This species is found across south-eastern North America, from Delaware to Florida and Texas. The range also extends north up the Mississippi River Valley to the southern tip of Indiana.

Green treefrogs spend the day lurking under the cover of plants. They give away their presence by their clanking, bell-like calls. During periods of high humidity, many frogs may call together, creating a loud chorus. The rise in humidity is often a prelude to rain, and consequently to mating. The green treefrog is often nicknamed the "rain frog", since it begins to call just before wet weather arrives.

However, not all the males call in these mating choruses. Some "satellite" males remain silent and attempt to intercept and mate with females attracted by the bellowing choruses.

By night, the frogs hunt for insects. They are often seen near houses, where they feed on insects attracted by the light.

**Distribution**: Eastern United States.
**Habitat**: Swamps and river banks.
**Food**: Insects.
**Size**: 3.2–6.4cm (1.25–2.5in).
**Maturity**: Unknown.
**Breeding**: Mating season is between March and September, but later in the Deep South. The female lays up to 400 eggs in small packets or films in shallow water at or near the surface, attached to floating vegetation; hatching occurs within a week.
**Life span**: Unknown.
**Status**: Common.

# Bird-voiced treefrog

*Hyla avivoca*

**Distribution**: Southern Mississippi Valley, south-eastern United States.
**Habitat**: Swamps.
**Food**: Insects.
**Size**: 2.8–5.1cm (1–2in).
**Maturity**: Unknown.
**Breeding**: A total of about 500 eggs laid in late summer.
**Life span**: Unknown.
**Status**: Common.

The bird-voiced treefrog has one of the most melodic calls of any American frog. The males produce whistles while perched on waterside shrubs. Bird-voiced treefrogs live in the wooded swamps that are common along the coasts of the Gulf of Mexico. The range extends north following the wetlands created by the seasonal flooding of the Mississippi.

Bird-voiced treefrogs hunt at night. They prey on spiders and small insects that live in trees and shrubs. These treefrogs only come down to the ground during the breeding season, which begins in June. The males climb to a prominent perch, perhaps up to 1.5m (5ft) above the ground, to make their mating calls. They then clamber down to mate with the females that approach. The females lay packets of 6–15 eggs in shallow water. The eggs hatch after a few days, and the tadpoles transform into frogs in about a month.

*Like many treefrogs, this species has bright patches on the inner surfaces of its long legs. When the frog is resting, these patches are hidden, but they flash into view when the frog stretches. It is thought that they are used to startle predators.*

---

**Barking treefrog** (*Hyla gratiosa*): 5–7cm (2–2.75in)
This plump frog is found in the south-east of the United States, along the coastal plain from Virginia to the Gulf coast of Louisiana and the northern half of Florida. This treefrog rarely comes down to the ground. Like other treefrogs, it has sucker-like toe pads to help it grip smooth surfaces. In the summer breeding season, males gather beside permanent bodies of water and give loud, bell-like calls to attract females.

**Clown treefrog/giraffe treefrog** (*Hyla leucophyllata*): 3cm (1.25in)
This species lives in forests in the Amazon Basin. It has two common names because it exists in two colour phases, possibly more. At all times the frog has orange fingers and toes, which are also webbed. During the "clown" phase, the back is purplish-brown, with golden patterns on the snout. The "giraffe" phase is characterized by reticulations like those of a giraffe. These frogs lay their eggs on leaves overhanging water, and the tadpoles fall into the water when they hatch.

**Flat-headed bromeliad treefrog** (*Osteocephalus planiceps*): 5cm (2in)
Bromeliad treefrogs are a group of small frogs, some of which breed in the tiny ponds that form when rain water collects amid the leaves of bromeliads. These epiphyte plants often grow on trees many metres above the ground. This particular species of bromeliad frog, which is found across the Amazon, is flat in appearance. It sometimes lays its eggs in bromeliad ponds, but also uses standing water on the ground.

# Gladiator treefrog

*Hyla boans*

Gladiators are among the largest treefrogs. They live across the Amazon Basin, where they are most often found along the banks of the many small rivers and streams that flow through the dense rainforests. Gladiator treefrogs are named after their impressive physique and because males often wrestle with each other to protect their nesting sites.

Reproductive activity is most common during periods of low atmospheric pressure, which herald heavy rains. The males call for mates with a hollow booming note while perching in riverside trees. They use the spurs on their heels to dig a nest in a muddy riverbank. The nest hollow is positioned just below the surface of the water, so that it is kept filled with a pool of water by the rain-swelled waterway. The female deposits her eggs in the nest. After hatching, the gladiator tadpoles disperse into the main waterway.

**Distribution**: South America, throughout the Amazon Basin.
**Habitat**: River banks.
**Food**: Insects.
**Size**: 12.5 (5in).
**Maturity**: 1 year.
**Breeding**: Up to 3,000 eggs laid in rainy season.
**Life span**: Unknown.
**Status**: Common.

*This large treefrog has olive skin with dark blotches. During periods of inactivity, the frog becomes darker. This is a swimming treefrog, so the feet have suction discs on their toes for gripping branches, and webs between the toes to help them swim.*

# TURTLES AND TORTOISES

*Turtles and tortoises have lived on Earth for over 200 million years. They belong to a group of reptiles that have existed since the dinosaurs roamed the Earth. Their soft bodies are protected by shells called carapaces. There is no major difference between turtles and tortoises, however turtles (and terrapins) live in water, while tortoises tend to live on land.*

## Matamata

*Chelus fimbriatus*

**Distribution**: Amazon Basin and northern South America; also on Trinidad.
**Habitat**: Beds of rivers and streams.
**Food**: Fish.
**Size**: 30–45cm (12–17.5in).
**Maturity**: Not known.
**Breeding**: 20–30 eggs laid.
**Life span**: 40 years.
**Status**: Common.

Matamatas live on the bottom of tropical lakes and rivers. They take breaths by poking their long snouts out of the water, so they can remain hidden below the water at all times. Their knobbly shells are often turned green and red by algae growing on them, helping them blend with rocky river beds. Matamatas wait in ambush for prey to swim near. They have small eyes, set on the sides of their flattened heads, which are useless for hunting in the murky waters, but the turtles are sensitive to the water currents created by prey close by. The flaps of skin on their long necks aid their camouflage, and may also act as lures to attract fish. When the fish come within range matamatas strike with great speed. They suck the unsuspecting fish into their wide mouths. The suction is caused by a rapid opening of the mouth, creating an area of low pressure inside. Matamatas have also been observed walking along river beds, herding fish into shallow water where they can be sucked up more easily.

*Matamatas are unusual-looking turtles. They have triangular heads with long flexible snouts, which are used as snorkels to breathe air from above the surface.*

## Alligator snapping turtle

*Macroclemys temminckii*

The alligator snapping turtle is the largest freshwater turtle. During the day it is mainly an ambush hunter, lying half-buried in mud on the river bed. While waiting for prey to approach, this turtle holds its large mouth open. The turtle's tongue has a small projection on it, which becomes pink when engorged with blood. The turtle wiggles this fleshy protuberance as a lure to attract prey. Fish and other animals investigate the lure, assuming it is a worm in the mud. As the prey swims into a turtle's mouth, the jaws snap shut. Small prey are swallowed whole, while the sharp, horny beak makes light work of larger prey, which may even be another species of turtle. The largest prey are held in the jaws, while the alligator snapping turtle uses its forefeet to tear it apart.

Male alligator snapping turtles spend their whole lives in muddy rivers and lakes. Females, however, climb on to land in spring to lay eggs in holes dug into mud or sand.

*Alligator snapping turtles have a tough carapace covered in pointed, triangular knobbles. They have a large head with a sharp, horny beak.*

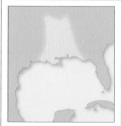

**Distribution**: South-eastern United States, in the lower Mississippi River Valley.
**Habitat**: Beds of lakes and slow-flowing rivers.
**Food**: Fish and turtles.
**Size**: 40–80cm (15.5–31.5in).
**Maturity**: Not known.
**Breeding**: 10–50 eggs buried in mud.
**Life span**: 70 years.
**Status**: Vulnerable.

# Galápagos tortoise

*Geochelone elephantopus*

Galápagos tortoises are the largest of all the testudines (tortoises and turtles). They are found only on the islands of the Galápagos Archipelago in the equatorial Pacific, off the coast of Ecuador. In general, the shell folds around the body like a saddle. However, the different subspecies located on various islands in the group have varying shell shapes. The general saddle shape allows the forefeet and neck to move more freely than in most tortoises.

Galápagos tortoises are plant-eaters. They use their long necks to reach up to bushes and shrubs, foraging for leaves with their toothless jaws. They also eat grass and even cacti. Their giant size is probably due to this diet. The Galápagos Islands are arid places and plants are not widely available. Plant food contains only small amounts of energy, and larger animals use energy more efficiently than small ones.

For most of the year, the tortoises live in small herds. During the breeding season, however, males defend territories. The dominant males are the ones that can lift their heads higher than the other males. They hector passing females into mating with them. The females dig nest chambers and lay large, spherical eggs.

**Distribution**: Galápagos Islands in the eastern Pacific.
**Habitat**: Varied, depending on the island, from moist forest to arid land.
**Food**: Plants.
**Size**: 1–1.4m (3.25–4.5ft).
**Maturity**: Unknown.
**Breeding**: Several large eggs.
**Life span**: Over 100 years.
**Status**: Vulnerable in general; some subspecies are endangered.

*These giant tortoises have different shell shapes depending on the island they live on in the Galápagos Archipelago. Charles Darwin cited these shell differences to support his theory of natural selection.*

---

**Green turtle** (*Chelonia mydas*): 1–1.2m (3.25–4ft)
This rare, endangered species has flipper-like legs and a smooth carapace. Green turtles only visit land to lay their eggs. They gather to mate off deserted, sandy beaches across the world, including the Americas. The females then emerge to lay their eggs in holes dug in the sand with their flippers. Green turtles eat sponges, jellyfish, sponges and molluscs.

**Hawksbill turtle** (*Eretmochelys imbricata*): 87cm (34.25in)
Hawksbills are found in the warm, tropical waters of the Atlantic and the Pacific. They lay eggs on beaches on North America's eastern coast. Adults live in fairly shallow, rocky waters or near reefs, diving down up to 20m (60ft) to feed on crustaceans, molluscs, and sponges. The young remain near the surface and eat floating seaweed. This species is endangered.

**Loggerhead turtle** (*Caretta caretta*): 0.7–2.1m (2.3–7ft)
Loggerheads are found in all the world's oceans, except the coldest polar waters. The large, chunky head houses powerful jaws capable of crushing hard-shelled prey such as crabs and lobsters. Loggerheads breed every second year, laying their eggs on sandy beaches. They are vulnerable.

# Stinkpot

*Sternotherus odoratus*

Stinkpots are so-named because they release a nasty smelling musk from glands beneath their shells. This smell is meant to ward off predators, but the stinkpot will also give a painful bite if the musk does not do its job.

Stinkpots spend their lives in slow-flowing, shallow streams and muddy ponds and lakes. Their shells often have mats of microscopic algae growing on them. Stinkpots feed both during the day and at night. They use the barbels on their chins to sense the movements of prey buried in the muddy stream beds. Like many other musk turtles, stinkpots have a toughened "shelf" attached to their upper jaws. The turtles uses this shelf to crush the shells of water snails and other prey.

Female stinkpots leave the water to lay their elongated eggs. They make nests under mats of decaying plant matter or under the stumps of trees. Stinkpots lay the smallest eggs of all turtles – only 1.5 × 2.5cm (0.5 × 1in).

*Stinkpots have smooth, streamlined shells suitable for living in running water. They have sensitive fleshy projections, called barbels, on their chins.*

**Distribution**: South-eastern United States.
**Habitat**: Shallow, muddy water.
**Food**: Insects, molluscs, plants and carrion.
**Size**: 8–13cm (3.25–5in).
**Maturity**: Unknown.
**Breeding**: Eggs laid under tree stumps.
**Life span**: 54 years.
**Status**: Common.

## Snapping turtle

*Chelydra serpentina*

The snapping turtle lives in the rivers and swamps of eastern North America. It prefers fresh-water habitats, but it also occurs in brackish environments, where salt water mixes with fresh water in estuaries and coastal marshes.

Snapping turtles are almost completely aquatic, although they will move across land in search of a new place to live should their home range become too crowded. These highly solitary turtles ensure that no other turtle encroaches into their feeding territory. They ambush their prey, burying themselves in mud on the river bottom and then cutting the heads off their victims using their sharp beaks. They also eat plants and carrion.

The only time a snapper will tolerate another individual's presence is during the mating season, between April and November. The male positions himself on the female's back during mating, clinging to her shell with his claws. Between 20 and 30 eggs are laid in a hole in sandy soil, hatching between 9 and 18 weeks later in autumn or winter.

*The shells of snapping turtles range in colour from light brown to black. The tail has a serrated keel, while the legs and neck are covered in points called tubercles.*

**Distribution**: Central and eastern North America, from southern Alberta and Nova Scotia in Canada to Texas and the Gulf of Mexico.
**Habitat**: Rivers and tidal swamps.
**Food**: Fish, birds, amphibians and small mammals.
**Size**: 20–45cm (7.75–17.75in).
**Maturity**: Not known.
**Breeding**: 20–30 eggs laid in a hole in spring.
**Life span**: 30 years.
**Status**: Lower risk.

## Central American river turtle

*Dermatemys mawii*

This large, drab-coloured species is the sole surviving member of a turtle family that dates back more than 65 million years to the Cretaceous Period. Central American river turtles (also known as Mesoamerican river turtles) live in a range of habitats throughout northern Central America. They thrive wherever there is sufficient food, which is primarily aquatic plants such as river grass. They feed below the waterline, and often eat fruits that have fallen into the water. Among the most aquatic of all turtles, they spend much of their time submerged, only occasionally rising to the surface to breathe. Consequently, they move rather awkwardly on land. When submerged, oxygen from the water is absorbed through the thin skin of the throat.

Among the most aquatic of all turtles, Central American river turtles live in all types of water, from deep and clear streams to shallow, muddy marshes. They are most common in lakes and large rivers. They are sometimes also found with barnacles on their shells, which suggests that this species is also able to survive in salty water, perhaps in the tidal region of a river mouth.

The female turtle lays up to 20 eggs just above the water level in a muddy river bank during the flood season. Unlike their plant-eating parents, the young turtles are carnivores, eating molluscs and crustaceans, and perhaps also fish.

**Distribution**: Southern Mexico (excluding the Yucatan Peninsula) to Guatemala and Honduras.
**Habitat**: Lakes and swamps.
**Food**: River grass.
**Size**: 65cm (25.5in).
**Maturity**: Not known.
**Breeding**: 6–20 eggs laid during rainy season.
**Life span**: 30 years.
**Status**: Endangered.

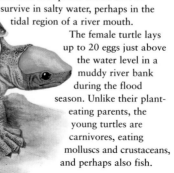

*Adult Mesoamerican river turtles have broad, smooth, streamlined shells that sometimes resemble leather. Younger turtles have a ridge along the centre line above the spine, but this gradually disappears as they get older.*

# Painted turtle

*Chrysemys picta*

**Distribution**: Central North America, from southern Canada to Mexico.
**Habitat**: Muddy freshwater.
**Food**: Plants, fish, insects and crustaceans.
**Size**: 15–25cm (6–9.75in).
**Maturity**: 3–10 years.
**Breeding**: Eggs laid in late spring and early summer.
**Life span**: 40 years.
**Status**: Common.

Painted turtles live in fresh water from British Columbia and much of southern Canada to Georgia and northern Mexico. The turtles sleep on muddy river beds at night, and during the daytime feed on leaves, fruits and a range of animal prey. Between feeding periods, large numbers of painted turtles can be seen basking in the sun, often perched on logs. The sun helps to keep parasites such as leeches at bay. If disturbed, the turtles dive into the water and take refuge in the mud or under a submerged object.

Males mature much earlier than female painted turtles. Mating takes place in late spring and early summer after the turtles emerge from hibernation. Eggs are buried in sandy soil in an open area that is exposed to a lot of sun. Each female lays about ten soft-shelled eggs. The young turtles are independent as soon as they hatch.

*Painted turtles are so-called because of their smooth, brightly coloured shells. They have black, olive or brown shells with red, black and yellow markings along the edges. Female painted turtles tend to be larger than the males.*

---

**Pond slider** (*Chrysemys scripta*): 12.5–29cm (5–11.5in)
This large pond turtle is found in lowland areas of south-eastern North America, from south of the Great Lakes to West Virginia and south to the Gulf coast, Texas and New Mexico. Pond sliders live in quiet habitats such as slow-flowing streams with plenty of mud and basking sites. If disturbed, they quickly slide into the water. Young turtles eat small animals such as snails, tadpoles, and crayfish; adults mainly browse on duckweed and water lilies. During courtship, the male rattles his claws on the female's head. If she is receptive, she sinks to the bottom, where mating takes place.

**Big-headed river turtle** (*Peltocephalus dumerilianus*): 63cm (24.75in)
This species has a large head, a sharply pointed nose and a high-domed shell with a keel along the spine. The head holds powerful jaws, which are used to catch and kill fish and other prey. The turtle lives in the western Amazon Basin, in black-water regions. These are areas of permanently flooded forest where the water is clear but dyed dark brown by tannins leached from submerged leaves.

**Amazon mud turtle** (*Kinosternon scorpioides*): 9–27cm (3.75–10.5in)
Amazon (or scorpion) mud turtles inhabit shallow water from Mexico to Paraguay. In rainy conditions, when the rivers rise considerably, Amazon mud turtles leave the water and roam through the forest. They often take up residence in a new area when the waters recede. Those stranded far from water as a period of dry weather begins bury themselves until the rains return.

# Wood turtle

*Clemmys insculpta*

Wood turtles have a fragmented range across eastern North America. They live in running water, from small streams to the mighty St Lawrence River. Although they prefer watercourses with rocky bottoms, they are also found in woodlands and meadows far from water. (Females seem to be less water dependent than males.)

Wood turtles feed both in the water and on land. Being omnivores, they eat a range of foods, from leaves and fallen fruits to slugs, tadpoles and fungi. They cannot catch fast-moving, warm-blooded animals, such as small birds and mammals, but they will eat carrion if the chance arises. The turtles drive earthworms, a favourite food, to the surface by thumping their plastron (lower shell) on the ground. Taking the thumping to be vibrations caused by heavy rain, the worms rise to the surface to avoid drowning – only to be eaten by the turtles.

*The shells of wood turtles have a low keel along the spine. The scutes, or plates, that make up the shell have well-defined "growth rings".*

**Distribution**: From eastern Canada to New England and the Midwest in the United States.
**Habitat**: Running water.
**Food**: Plants, fruits, fungi, snails, slugs, tadpoles and worms.
**Size**: 14–25cm (5.5–7.5in)
**Maturity**: 14–20 years
**Breeding**: Eggs laid in nests in May and June.
**Life span**: Unknown.
**Status**: Vulnerable.

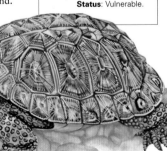

# Giant river turtle

*Podocnemis expansa*

The giant river turtle is found in large rivers throughout the Amazon Basin, where it is often seen floating near the surface. The adult females are significantly larger than the males, often twice as large. Like many reptiles, this species never stops growing, although the growth rate slows considerably after the onset of maturity, which is triggered by size. The speed at which the young turtles develop is influenced by the amount food available and other conditions, including temperature. As a result, maturity occurs at different ages, depending on how long the turtles take to reach the required size.

Breeding takes place at the start of the dry season, with the turtles crowding into the narrow river channels as the waters recede. After mating in the water, the females spend several weeks basking for up to six hours per day, presumably to hasten egg development. They then lay between 50 and 180 eggs at night in a hole dug in the shore or on an exposed sandbar. These turtles often nest in groups, and nesting sites may become so overcrowded that several females may use the same nesting hole. Incubation of the eggs takes 45–65 days, but the baby turtles may remain longer in the nest, until the rains begin, when they emerge and begin to move down toward the flooded river.

**Distribution**: Amazon Basin.
**Habitat**: Large rivers.
**Food**: Plants, fish, insects and crustaceans.
**Size**: 61–107cm (24–42in).
**Maturity**: Females 61cm (24in); males 20cm (7.75in).
**Breeding**: Up to 180 eggs laid in holes in dry season.
**Life span**: Unknown.
**Status**: Endangered.

*This is the largest turtle species in the Amazon Basin, capable of weighing more than 90kg (200lb). The giant river turtle has a smooth, gently domed shell that is grey-brown. This species has facial markings when young, but these fade with age.*

# Bog turtle

*Clemmys muhlenbergii*

Bog turtles are distributed patchily across the eastern United States. A northern population lives from New York and Massachusetts to northern Maryland, while a southern population can be found in the mountains of Virginia and North Carolina. There are also smaller populations in western Pennsylvania and along the southern shore of Lake Ontario.

The bog turtle's distribution is limited because it is restricted to a very specific habitat – shallow wetlands with water that is slow-flowing yet not choked by aquatic vegetation. Habitats like this tend to support dozens of different water-plant species. Human interference often reduces the number of plants in the habitat, or introduces new species that become rampant and make the area unsuitable for bog turtles. As a result, bog turtles are increasingly endangered. Bog turtles are popular as pets, but collecting wild bog turtles is now banned. Individuals bred in captivity fetch high prices, and this continues to fuel illegal collecting. Bog turtles are only active during the warmer parts of the day. They emerge from their nocturnal shelters and bask for a while before foraging. These turtles hibernate through winter, and they may also aestivate during the driest months of the year (July and August).

**Distribution**: Eastern United States.
**Habitat**: Wetlands.
**Food**: Invertebrates, seeds, fruits and leaves.
**Size**: 7.9–11.4cm (3–5in).
**Maturity**: 10 years.
**Breeding**: Up to 6 eggs laid yearly in shallow nests in June.
**Life span**: 40 years.
**Status**: Endangered.

*This species is the smallest of the pond turtles. Younger individuals have obvious growth rings, or annuli, on their scutes. By the time a turtle reaches maturity, these marks have been smoothed away.*

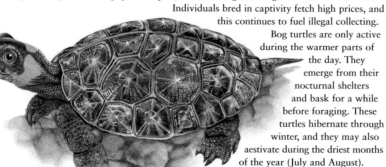

# Blanding's turtle

*Emydoidea blandingii*

**Distribution**: Primarily Great Lakes region of North America.
**Habitat**: Shallow ponds and marshes.
**Food**: Crustaceans, frogs, fish, plants, snails and insects.
**Size**: 15–27.5cm (6–10.75in).
**Maturity**: 14–20 years.
**Breeding**: 6–21 eggs laid in June.
**Life span**: 40 years.
**Status**: Lower risk.

Blanding's turtle has a fragmented range, with the main population being found around the Great Lakes, from southern Ontario across to Minnesota and Illinois. It is also found as far west as Nebraska, and a third population exists to the east in New Hampshire, Massachusetts and south-eastern New York.

Blanding's turtles prefer shallow and slow-flowing watercourses that are filled with weeds and have a muddy bottom. They lie in wait for prey, such as crustaceans, fish, frogs and even leeches, and lunge forward by extending their long neck and grabbing the food in their mouths.

These turtles hibernate on the bottom between October and April. However, they can sometimes be seen moving around during this time, even under ice. During the breeding season, females may travel up to 1.2km (0.75 mile) away from their wetland homes to lay their eggs in sandy soil, usually at night. The hatchlings emerge 55–75 days later.

*The notch on the upper jaw of Blanding's turtle makes it look as if it has a permanent smile on its face. Somewhat similar to a box turtle, this species also has hinge on its plastron (lower shell). Blanding's turtles often bask in the sun on sandbanks or logs.*

---

**Common toad-headed turtle** (*Phrynops nasutus*): 30cm (11.75in)
The common toad-headed turtle is a large, highly aquatic turtle that inhabits the cochas (oxbows) and swamps of Amazonian Brazil, Ecuador and Colombia. The turtle's body is a uniform green-grey colour, perhaps a little lighter on the plastron. This long-necked, meat-eating species hunts for water snails and small fish.

**Western twist-necked turtle** (*Platemys platycephala*): 15cm (6in)
The western is the only twist-necked turtle to live in the Amazon. Its name comes from the way the neck folds as the turtle pulls its head under its shell. Unlike other similar species, this turtle is often found far from water during the rainy season. Western twist-necked turtles are mainly carnivorous, but they also eat some plant matter.

**Cooter** (*Chrysemys floridana*): 19–40cm (7.5–15.75in)
Cooters live in the coastal plain of eastern North America, from the Gulf of Mexico in the south, across Florida and north to Virginia. The shell is brown with yellow stripes, bars and doughnut shapes. Males have longer claws than females, especially on the forefeet, which they use to stroke females during courtship rituals. Cooters live in large ponds, lakes, sluggish rivers and canals, where they can be seen basking in huge numbers, often alongside their close relatives river cooters and Florida red-bellied turtles. Breeding takes place in late May and early July. Female cooters lay two or more clutches of eggs in small holes.

# Common map turtle

*Graptemys geographica*

Common map turtles occur from southern Quebec and Vermont past the Great Lakes to Wisconsin. The range extends south over the Appalachians to Alabama and west to the plains of Kansas and Arkansas. These turtles live at the bottom of large bodies of water with abundant aquatic vegetation. They prefer environments with plenty of partially submerged debris, such as logs and fallen trees, on which they can bask.

Map turtles hibernate in much of their range, hiding away under submerged logs during the coldest weather. However, some map turtles move across land to new locations in winter. When warmer weather returns, the turtles hunt both day and night. On sunny days they can be seek basking, but they slide into the safety of the water when danger approaches.

**Distribution**: Southern Canada to Georgia.
**Habitat**: Ponds, rivers and lakes.
**Food**: Snails, clams, crayfish and plants.
**Size**: 9–26cm; (3.5–10.25in).
**Maturity**: Not known.
**Breeding**: Up to 20 eggs laid in nests during early summer.
**Life span**: Unknown.
**Status**: Common.

*The turtle's shell has markings resembling contour lines or a map of a river system. There is a yellow spot behind each eye, and yellow stripes on the turtle's neck, head and legs.*

# Diamondback terrapin

*Malaclemys terrapin*

*Diamondback terrapins are named after the pattern of growth rings that appear on the pyramidal scutes (plates) that make up the carapace. They use their ridged, beak-like jaws to crush the bodies of their prey. Males may only be half the size of females.*

Diamondback terrapins range from southern Texas and the Gulf of Mexico, where they are most common, around Florida and up to southern New England. They inhabit the brackish water of the salt-marshes, estuaries and tidal lagoons that form behind barrier islands, being most abundant in heavily reeded areas. While these terrapins can cope with saline conditions, they still need access to fresh drinking water.

Diamondbacks feed on a range of animal life in the tidal zone, including marine snails, clams and crabs. When not feeding, the terrapins may be seen basking on exposed sandbars or walking across mudflats between feeding sites. They avoid danger by running into water, where they are much more agile and better able to hide than on land.

**Distribution**: Eastern coast of United States.
**Habitat**: Estuaries and lagoons.
**Food**: Snails, crustaceans, fish and insects.
**Size**: 14–23cm (5.5–9in).
**Maturity**: 7 years.
**Breeding**: About 10 eggs (maximum 18) laid in sand during late spring and early summer.
**Life span**: Unknown.
**Status**: Common.

# Eastern box turtle

*Terrapene carolina*

*The keeled, high-domed shell of this species has variable markings throughout its range. As in other box turtles, the lower shell (plastron) is hinged, enabling the turtle to close the shell almost completely when its head, tail and legs are withdrawn inside. Shut in a near-impregnable "box" of horny plates, the turtle is safe from most predators. Male eastern box turtles tend to be slightly larger than the females.*

The Eastern box turtle occurs only in North America, where it ranges from Texas in the south to Michigan in the north, and across the Appalachians to the Atlantic coast. (A western box turtle species lives in the central United States.)

Eastern box turtles are seldom found far from streams and ponds, but often forage in woodland and damp meadows. The diet of these omnivorous reptiles includes several plants and mushrooms that are poisonous to humans, and many people have died after eating poisoned box turtle meat. The turtles' feeding behaviour is influenced by temperature. In midsummer, box turtles are most active in the morning and afternoons. During the hottest part of the day they crawl under logs or into burrows to keep cool. In the spring and autumn, the weather is mild enough for the turtles to feed all day long. In the northern part of their range, box turtles hibernate in burrows in the river bed during winter.

Many eastern box turtle populations have been reduced by the destruction of their habitat for urban development or agriculture. Collection of wild turtles for the pet trade also threatens their future.

**Distribution:** Eastern United States, from Texas in the south to Michigan in the north, and eastward across the Appalachians to the Atlantic coast.
**Habitat**: Woodlands, meadows and marshes.
**Food**: Snails, insects, worms, roots, amphibians, snakes, birds' eggs and fruit; turtles become more herbivorous with age.
**Size**: 10–21.5cm (4–8.5in).
**Maturity**: 5–7 years.
**Breeding**: Usually 4–5 eggs (maximum 11) laid from May to July in sandy or loamy soil; 2–3 (maximum 6) clutches may be laid per year.
**Life span**: 100 years.
**Status**: Lower risk.

## Flattened musk turtle

*Sternotherus depressus*

**Distribution**: Black Warrior River in Alabama.
**Habitat**: Rocky river bed.
**Food**: Snails and mussels.
**Size**: 7.5–10cm (3–4in).
**Maturity**: 4–6 years.
**Breeding**: Normally 2 eggs laid in a riverbank hole twice a year.
**Life span**: Unknown.
**Status**: Vulnerable.

The flattened musk turtle is a very rare species, restricted to a single river system in northern Alabama. It is now limited to the upper reaches of the river by a dam. It lives in the clear shallow streams that feed the main river. Avoiding muddy areas, it prefers to move around on rocky or sandy bottoms.

The flattened musk turtle feeds on invertebrates such as clams, snails, insects, crayfish and arachnids. There appears to be a correlation between light levels, feeding behaviour and the age of turtles: the adult turtles tend to feed at night, juveniles feed in twilight and hatchlings hunt during the daytime.

This species is thought to hibernate during the winter, but it is not known how it does this. Like other musk turtles, it probably buries itself in sand or hides under logs and rocks to avoid the coldest weather.

*In common with all musk turtles, this species has two glands under the edge of its shell that produce a bad-smelling liquid to deter predators. It has a wider and more flattened carapace than other species in the musk turtle group, which enables it to squeeze between rocks on the river bed.*

**Red-footed tortoise** (*Chelonoides carbonaria*): 45cm (17.75in)
The red-footed tortoise has a black, highly domed shell with the centre of each scute in orange. The head and the front of the forelegs have orange or red scales. Red-footed tortoises live on the edges of rain forests, where trees give way to grassland. This habitat type is found across South America. Most of the tortoise's diet is made up of plant material, but it will occasionally eat insects and other small animals. Breeding takes place all year round. The males attract a mate by making a clucking noise. The females produce a clutch of about 10 eggs that hatch after four months.

**Desert tortoise** (*Gopherus agassizii*): 15–36cm (6–14.25in)
Found in the deserts of the western United States, from southern Utah to California and northern Mexico, this species is most abundant in California, where there are about 80 individuals per square kilometre (200 per square mile). Like other land-living turtles, it has unwebbed feet. The flattened forelegs are used for digging burrows, while the sturdy, rounded hind legs push the body forward through soft earth. Desert tortoises eat low-growing grasses and herbs. They are slow moving, and are most commonly seen out of their burrows in the early morning. In the hottest part of the year, they spend the daytime below ground, emerging at night to feed. To initiate mating, the male hisses and butts the female. The eggs are laid in a deep hole. The shells of desert tortoises stay soft for the first few years. This species has been collected in large numbers for the pet trade, and is now endangered.

## Gopher tortoise

*Gopherus polyphemus*

This tortoise occurs in the southern United States, including Florida. It lives in sandy areas where the water table never reaches the surface but still supports scrub and woodland. Longleaf pine forests are its preferred habitat.

Gopher tortoises are skilled diggers. They make a long burrow ending in a chamber, up to 3m (10ft) beneath the surface, where temperature and humidity are fairly constant. The tunnel leading to it can be about 12m (40ft) long. The tortoises retreat to their burrows during hot, dry periods. They may share their burrows with small mammals, snakes, toads and even burrowing owls.

On cool days, gopher tortoises bask at the entrance to their burrows to warm up before heading off to feed on grasses and herbs. They mate in spring and nest in early summer, laying their eggs in a shallow pit.

*Gopher tortoises use their short, flattened forelegs for burrowing. The hind feet are smaller than the forefeet.*

**Distribution**: Southeastern United States.
**Habitat**: Sand dunes.
**Food**: Grasses and herbs, occasionally berries.
**Size**: 10–24cm (4–15in)
**Maturity**: 16 to 21 years.
**Breeding**: Several clutches of 2–7 eggs laid in early summer.
**Life span**: 40–100 years.
**Status**: Vulnerable.

# LIZARDS

*Lizards are reptiles, belonging to the same group as snakes. They are found all over the world except for Antarctica, especially in places that are too hot or dry for mammals to thrive. The main group of American lizards are the iguanas, which include the basilisks and anoles. More widespread lizards, such as geckos and skinks, are also found in the Americas, especially South America.*

## Rhinoceros iguana

*Cyclura cornuta*

**Distribution**: Island of Hispaniola and other Caribbean islands.
**Habitat**: Forest.
**Food**: Leaves and fruit.
**Size**: 1–1.2m (3.25–4ft).
**Maturity**: Not known.
**Breeding**: 2–20 eggs laid in a burrow.
**Life span**: Unknown.
**Status**: Vulnerable.

These large grey iguanas live on the island of Hispaniola – divided into the countries of Haiti and the Dominican Republic – as well as a few smaller islands in the Caribbean Sea. They are most active during the day and often bask in the sun to warm up their bodies. They walk slowly through the forest, browsing on leaves and fruit. Their teeth are very sharp and are ideal for cutting through tough leaves and other plant materials.

*The rhinoceros iguana gets its name from the toughened scales on its snout that resemble small horns. Males have larger "horns" than females.*

When threatened, rhinoceros iguanas will run away at high speed. They can only achieve these speeds over short distances. If cornered, they will give a painful bite and thrash their tails, which are armoured with spiky scales.

Male rhinoceros iguanas maintain a hierarchy based on the size of their throat flaps, or dewlaps. The males frequently contest this social structure during the short summer breeding season. The top-ranked males control access to females. They attract females with elaborate displays involving bobs of their heads, press-ups and showing off their dewlaps. Females lay up to 20 eggs in burrows and guard them until they hatch three months later.

## Gila monster

*Heloderma suspectum*

Gila monsters are one of only two poisonous lizards in the world. They produce venom in salivary glands in their lower jaws. The venom flows by capillary action along grooves in their teeth, giving the lizard a poisonous bite. The venom acts on the prey animal's nervous system, preventing the heart and lungs from working. For a healthy human, a bite from a gila monster will be very painful but not life-threatening.

Gila monsters are most active at night. They shelter from the heat of the day in rocky crevices or burrows abandoned by mammals. However, in northern parts of their range, the lizards are completely inactive for several months during the winter. Inactive individuals rely on fat stored in their tails to keep them alive when they cannot feed.

Gila monsters mate in springtime, and their copulation can last for over an hour. The eggs develop inside the females for about ten weeks. They then bury the eggs in areas that are often bathed in sunlight. The eggs incubate for up to ten months.

*Gila monsters have long, robust bodies with short legs. Their bodies are covered in rounded, bead-like scales. Most of them are dark but some have blotches of pink, yellow or orange.*

**Distribution**: South-west United States and northern Mexico.
**Habitat**: Desert.
**Food**: Small mammals and eggs.
**Size**: 35–50cm (14–19.5in).
**Maturity**: Unknown.
**Breeding**: Eggs laid in summer.
**Life span**: 20 years.
**Status**: Vulnerable.

# Green basilisk

*Basiliscus plumifrons*

**Distribution**: Central America.
**Habitat**: Forest.
**Food**: Insects, small mammals, smaller lizards, plus fruits and some flowers.
**Size**: 60–75cm (23.5–29.5in).
**Maturity**: Unknown.
**Breeding**: 20 eggs per year.
**Life span**: 10 years.
**Status**: Common.

Green basilisks spend most of their time in trees. They have long fingers and toes that help them grasp branches as they scuttle about looking for food. However, they prefer to stay in trees that are close to water. When threatened by predators, such as birds of prey, the lizards dive into the water below. The crests on their backs and tails are used to propel the reptiles through the water to safety. Basilisks will also shimmy into soft sand to avoid a predator. They can close their nostrils to keep sand out. On land, they run at high speed on their hind legs. They do not have to stop running when they reach water, because their hind feet have scaly fringes that spread their bodyweight, enabling them to sprint over the water's surface. This adaptive ability has earned them (along with other related species) the nickname of "Jesus Christ lizards".

Male basilisks control their territories very aggressively, chasing any other males away. A successful male will control an area that contains a number of females. He has sole mating rights to this harem.

*Green basilisks are also known as plumed basilisks because they have crests on the backs of their heads, down their back and along their long tails.*

---

## Giant amphisbaenian

(*Amphisbaena alba*): 75cm (29.5in)
This is one of the world's largest amphisbaenians, or worm lizards. These are legless, burrowing reptiles lacking obvious eyes. They form a distinct group from snakes and legless lizards, such as slow-worms and glass snakes. The giant amphisbaenian is found throughout the Amazon Basin, typically among the roots of trees, where it preys on earthworms and insect larvae, such as beetle grubs. The body is pale brown, with little patterning on it. The scales form distinct rings around the body.

## Florida worm lizard (*Rhineura floridana*): 18–40cm (7–15.5in)

Most American amphisbaenians live in the soils of tropical Central and South America. The Florida worm lizard is the only one to occur north of Mexico, being found in central Florida, where it lives in the sandy soils of pine woodlands. Florida worm lizards are pink with rings of scales, and resemble large earthworms. In fact, this reptile species hunts for earthworms as well as termites and other subterranean prey. Florida worm lizards sometimes come to the surface after heavy rains, when the sandy soil is saturated.

# Green anole

*Anolis carolinensis*

Green anoles live in trees. Their long, thin legs are well adapted for leaping from branch to branch and perching on all but the flimsiest of branches. Thanks to the pads on the tips of their fingers and toes, anoles can grip on to just about any surface, including the fronds of palm trees.

Green anoles rest in dense cover at night. When not foraging in daylight, the lizards bask in the sun, generally on vertical surfaces, such as tree trunks or walls. Anoles can change their body colour, although not to the same extent as chameleons. For example, they may darken their normally bright skin when resting in the shade so as not to attract attention.

Although both sexes have dewlaps, only the males use them for communication. They extend them to signal to rival males and mates. A male begins courtship by bobbing his head and displaying his dewlap to a female. He then walks towards her with his legs straightened. If she is receptive to his advances, she allows him to position his body next to hers. He then grasps the back of her neck with his mouth and holds her tail with his hind legs as they copulate. The female lays one egg at a time under moist leaf litter.

**Distribution**: South-eastern United States.
**Habitat**: Woodland and shrubbery.
**Food**: Insects.
**Size**: 12–20cm (4.75–8in).
**Maturity**: Unknown.
**Breeding**: Single eggs laid throughout breeding season.
**Life span**: Unknown.
**Status**: Common.

*Both male and female green anoles have pink dewlaps – fans of skin beneath their throats. The lizards have very long tails – nearly twice the length of the rest of their bodies – and their elongated fingers and toes are tipped with pads.*

## Desert horned lizard

*Phrynosoma platyrhinos*

These small reptiles are sometimes referred to as horned toads, because of their rounded bodies. Despite living in dry areas, much of the desert horned lizard's range can get cold, especially at night. Its round body helps it to warm up quickly in the morning sunshine. The lizard can eat huge quantities of ants, which it licks up with its long tongue.

The many spikes on this lizard's body serve two functions. They help to break up the profile of the lizard so that it can blend in with the rocky terrain, and if the lizard is spotted by a sharp-eyed predator, the tough spikes make it a difficult and potentially painful meal to swallow. Armed with these weapons, a horned lizard will not run when danger approaches. Instead, it will freeze to avoid giving its position away and rely on its camouflage to hide it. If this defensive strategy fails and it is scooped into the mouth of a predator, such as a coyote, the reptile has one final weapon. The horned lizard can ooze blood from membranes that haemorrhage around its eyeballs. The blood mixes with a foul-tasting chemical, causing the predator to release its grip on the lizard.

**Distribution**: South-western United States.
**Habitat**: Rocky desert.
**Food**: Ants.
**Size**: 7.5–13.5cm (3–5.25in).
**Maturity**: Unknown.
**Breeding**: Eggs laid in spring.
**Life span**: Unknown.
**Status**: Common.

*The desert horned lizard has three pointed scales that form horns pointing backwards from the rear of its head. There are smaller spikes on its back and along the tail.*

## Chuckwalla

*Sauromalus obesus*

Chuckwallas live in the Mojave Desert, one of the driest and hottest places in North America. Like all other living reptiles, chuckwallas are cold-blooded or exothermic. Their bodies do not make any heat of their own apart from that generated by muscle movement. The lizards rely on sunlight and the temperature of the air around them to warm up enough for daily activity. Chuckwallas only become fully active when their body temperature exceeds 38°C (100°F). The temperature of the Mojave Desert regularly exceeds this, but in other areas of their range, chuckwallas remain inside their rocky dens until the weather gets warm enough.

Chuckwallas are herbivores. They search through the rock-strewn desert for hardy plants that can survive the scorching conditions. With only a limited food supply, female chuckwallas may not be able to reproduce every year. Some females save energy by skipping a breeding season.

Chuckwallas have an unusual defence strategy. When they are under attack by a bird of prey or coyote, they scuttle into a tight crevice between rocks and inflate their lungs. These reptiles have loose folds of skin around their throats and flanks which allow their bodies to swell up to a considerable size. This makes it difficult for a predator to extract the lizard from its hiding place.

**Distribution**: California, Arizona and northern Mexico.
**Habitat**: Desert.
**Food**: Fruit, leaves and flowers.
**Size**: 28–42cm (11–16.5in).
**Maturity**: Unknown.
**Breeding**: Females breed every 1–2 years.
**Life span**: Unknown.
**Status**: Common.

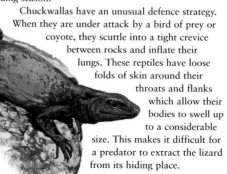

*Chuckwallas have powerful limbs and thick tails. The males have completely black heads, while the females have yellow and orange patches on black.*

# Black and white tegu

*Tupinambis merianae*

The black and white tegu is the only tegu to be common outside the Amazon and similar jungle habitats. It is larger than its forest-living relatives and lives in the tall grasses of the pampas and open woodlands. Tegus hunt on the ground during the day. They patrol on four legs, but may rise up on to their hind feet to scare off threats or sprint away from predators. Adults have powerful jaws which are used for crushing prey. The large jaw muscles are especially noticeable in the males, where they appear as jowels. As with other tegu species, these lizards supplement their meat diet with plant food.

Tegus spend cold nights in burrows. During the winter, they stay in these burrows for many days, and breeding takes place after the rains. Females create an intricate nest constructed of two chambers, the lower one containing between 10 and 30 eggs, which are surrounded by dried leaves. The heat produced by the leaves as they compost keeps the eggs warm. The female then builds a chamber above the eggs, where she sits guard for about 70 days.

*Black and white tegus vary in colour depending on their habitat. Tegus that live in drier grasslands are paler than those that live in damper woodlands.*

**Distribution**: Southern Brazil to eastern Argentina.
**Habitat**: Open woodlands and pampas.
**Food**: Insects, rodents, snails, lizards and fruits.
**Size**: 1.2m (4ft).
**Maturity**: 2 years.
**Breeding**: 30 eggs each year.
**Life span**: Unknown.
**Status**: Common.

---

**Pink tailed skink** (*Eumeces lagunensis*): 16–20cm (6.25–8in)
This skink lives in Baja California. When young, the lizard's long tail is bright pink, but it fades with age. The bright tail probably serves as a diversion to predators, which are more likely to strike at the brightly coloured tail than the camouflaged head. Many lizards can live without their tails, and skinks have special bones in their tails that are designed to break when the tail is attacked. In most cases, a lost tail will grow back again in a matter of weeks.

**Middle American night lizard** (*Lepidophyma flavimaculatum*): 7–12cm (2.75–4.75in)
Female Middle American night lizards produce young without having to mate – parthenogenetically. Some populations of these lizards contain no males at all. The lizards do not lay eggs, but keep them inside their bodies until they hatch. The young are then born live from the mother.

**Crocodile skink** (*Tribolonotus gracilis*): 15–20cm (6–8in)
This armoured lizard lives on the island of Hispaniola in the Caribbean. Its triangular head is protected by a bony shield and it has four rows of scaly spines running along its back and tail, making it look somewhat like a crocodile. Crocodile skinks live in pairs or threesomes, consisting of a male and one or two females. The females lay single eggs in leaf litter.

# Ajolote

*Bipes biporus*

Despite their appearance, ajolotes are not snakes or lizards, but members of a small group of reptiles called amphisbaenians, or worm lizards. These reptiles spend their whole lives burrowing through soft soil, feeding on subterranean prey.

The ajolote is also called the mole lizard or "little lizard with ears". Early observers must have mistaken the ajolote's tiny but powerful forelimbs for ears. This is an easy mistake to make, since the forelegs are very close to the head. Ajolotes use their clawed forefeet to dig tunnels. They also wriggle through the soil, using their blunt heads to push earth aside.

Unlike other amphisbaenians, ajolotes sometimes come to the surface, generally after heavy rains. Above ground they are ambush hunters, lying in wait for lizards and other small animals. They use their forelimbs to haul their long bodies across the ground to grab their prey, which they generally drag underground to be eaten in safety.

**Distribution**: Baja California.
**Habitat**: Burrows.
**Food**: Worms and insects.
**Size**: 17–24cm (6.75–9.5in).
**Maturity**: Unknown.
**Breeding**: Lays eggs.
**Life span**: 1–2 years.
**Status**: Common.

*Ajolotes have long bodies with scales arranged in rings. They are unique among worm lizards because they still have forelimbs.*

# Marine iguana

*Amblyrhynchus cristatus*

Marine iguanas live on the coastline of the Galápagos Islands in the Pacific Ocean. These volcanic islands, which were made famous by Charles Darwin's use of their fauna to explain his theory of evolution, have never been attached to the mainland. Along with the Galápagos land iguana and the famous giant tortoises, the marine iguanas are the only four-legged land animals on the islands. The iguanas are thought to have floated to the islands on fallen trees.

Marine iguanas dive into the ocean to feed on the seaweed that grows on submerged rocks. Large adults can stay underwater for over an hour at a time. They spend the rest of the day basking in the sun on the rocky shoreline. They need to keep warm when on land because they rapidly lose heat when they enter the water, since the islands are surrounded by cold ocean currents. Marine iguanas may gather in crowds containing thousands of individuals. When they bask, they expel excess salt from their bodies through glands in the nose. As a result, the faces of marine iguanas are often covered in a spray of white salt crystals.

*Although there is some variation in skin colour between marine iguanas that live on different Galápagos islands, they are generally black when wet and greyer after basking in the sun. A ridge of triangular scales runs down the back. Young marine iguanas have a pale stripe along their back.*

**Distribution**: Galápagos Islands.
**Habitat**: Rocky shores.
**Food**: Seaweed.
**Size**: 50–100cm (19.5–39.5in).
**Maturity**: Unknown.
**Breeding**: 2–3 eggs laid in autumn in holes in the sand.
**Life span**: Unknown.
**Status**: Endangered.

# Knight anole

*Anolis equestris*

Knight anoles are found at the top of large trees in Cuba. They have been introduced to southern Florida, where they are common in the Miami-Dade and Palm Beach areas.

This diurnal species searches for beetle grubs and adult insects such as grasshoppers, cockroaches and moths. It also eats spiders and smaller lizards. When the lizard spots a predatory tree snake, it adopts a defensive stance, turning to the side and extending the throat fan, while raising the crest of spines along the back. The lizard then gapes its mouth at the predator.

Rival males display a similar behaviour when confronting one another, except that the throat fan is pulled in and out several times, and the anole stands tall on its four legs. The scales also turn a brighter green. If fighting commences, the males rush forward with gaping mouths and bite at their opponent's limbs or mouth.

**Distribution**: Cuba.
**Habitat**: Trees.
**Food**: Grubs, grasshoppers, moths and spiders.
**Size**: 32–50cm (12.5–19.5in).
**Maturity**: Unknown.
**Breeding**: Eggs laid during summer.
**Life span**: Unknown.
**Status**: Common.

*The knight anole is the largest of the anole lizards. The tail is compressed and the head is wedge-shaped. The body is covered by small scales that can change from bright green to grey-brown. The males have a pink throat fan that extends when they become excited.*

**Brown basilisk** (*Basiliscus vittatus*): 60cm (24in)
Basilisks are often called Jesus Christ lizards, because of their habit of running over the surface of water to escape predators. Brown basilisks live in Central America and northern Colombia, and are now wild in Florida after escaping from captivity. They are most common in Guatemala, where they are found beside almost all bodies of standing water. These lizards are largely brown, with yellow stripes along their sides. Males have a crest projecting from the back of the head, and another along the back. Females have a hood around the back of the head, as well as a crest on the back, which is smaller than that of the males. Brown basilisks live in thick vegetation beside water. They feed on insects and fruits.

**Land iguana** (*Conolophus subcristatus*): 120cm (48in)
A close relative of the marine iguana, this large lizard occurs only on the Galápagos Islands. Biologists believe that this species diverged from the common ancestor of marine iguanas about 10 million years ago. Marine iguanas use the ocean to keep cool, but land iguanas seek refuge from the midday sun in burrows. They eat the cacti that grow on the arid volcanic islands.

**Forest dragon** (*Enyalioides laticeps*): 30cm (12in)
This species lives in the Amazon Basin. Forest dragons are largely arboreal, but they rarely climb far above the ground. Like many lizards, they gape when confronting a threat. It is believed that exposing the bright pink lining of the mouth helps the lizard to startle or scare off predators.

# Green iguana

*Iguana iguana*

The common green iguana occurs throughout Central and South America, from central Mexico to Paraguay. It also lives on many of the Caribbean islands and some islands off the Pacific coast of South America. This species has been introduced to Hawaii and Florida, where it has escaped from captivity and now lives wild.

Green iguanas live high up in trees. Older iguanas tend to live higher up than younger ones. This may be because the young cannot compete with the older iguanas for good basking sites near the top of the canopy, and so are forced to look for patches of sunlight that break through the tree cover lower down. These iguanas prefer to be close to water. They are good swimmers and will leap into the water to escape danger.

Green iguanas eat leaves and some insects. Like all vertebrates, the lizards do not have the correct digestive juices to break down tough plant food. Instead, they have a soupy mixture of bacteria in their colon that digests the plant fibres for them.

*Although adult members of this species are largely green, young green iguanas often also have brown bands. The colour of the lizard changes with temperature and humidity. The skin becomes darker during cold weather to absorb more heat. In hot periods, the skin turns paler to reflect the heat. The crest and dewlap are better developed in males than females. The long, whip-like tail is not only used for swimming, but also acts as a defensive weapon that can lash out at adversaries. These lizards will also bite when cornered, although they prefer to flee rather than fight.*

**Distribution**: Central and South America.
**Habitat**: Trees.
**Food**: Plants.
**Size**: 1.75m (5.75ft).
**Maturity**: 4 years.
**Breeding**: About 50 eggs laid in dry season.
**Life span**: 20 years.
**Status**: Common.

# Ctenosaur

*Ctenosaura similis*

**Distribution**: Mexico and Central America.
**Habitat**: Rocky areas.
**Food**: Plants and small animals.
**Size**: 91cm (36in).
**Maturity**: 4 years.
**Breeding**: Up to 25 eggs laid in a burrow.
**Life span**: 60.
**Status**: Common.

*A male ctenosaur has a spiny crest along the back and a dewlap. When the animal becomes excited, these are raised to make it look larger, with the aim of deterring rivals and other threats.*

Ctenosaurs are found throughout Central America, from northern Mexico to Panama, and also on some of the small islands off the Panamanian coast. Ctenosaurs live in rocky areas, where they spend a lot of the time basking in the sun or digging hollows and burrows to escape the extreme heat. Their skin is dark so that they can absorb the sun's heat quickly to warm up their bodies in the morning.

Ctenosaurs live in large colonies, and individuals spend a lot of time defending territories from their neighbours. The male's crest and dewlap are used for this purpose as well as for attracting females during the breeding season. The dewlap can be extended by a bone in the throat. The ctenosaurs can also change the colour of their scales to ward off rivals, but fights are still common. These involve bites and scratches. Large males secure larger territories encompassing the areas of a number of females; consequently, they breed more. Courtship displays are complex. The male initiates the courtship, but it only proceeds if the female responds in the correct way. After mating, the female digs a burrow and lays her eggs inside. She guards the burrow for a while to stop other females nesting in the same place. When the young ctenosaurs hatch they spend about a week digging their way out of the nest.

## Collared lizard

*Crotaphytus collaris*

This medium-sized iguana is found across the central region of North America, from the western banks of the Mississippi River in Arkansas and Missouri to northern Mexico and Nevada. It lives in rocky areas with only a thin covering of vegetation. Such places tend to be quite dry and hot.

Collared lizards are often seen during the hottest parts of the day. They bask on boulders to warm their bodies in the sunlight. When warmed up, they forage on the ground for insects and other small invertebrates, as well as any smaller lizards they come across. Collared lizards will eat plant material, including flowers and berries, if they cannot find other sources of food.

At night and during cold periods, collared lizards retreat to the relative warmth of a burrow dug under a large rock. They lay their eggs in similar holes.

The adults can be aggressive when threatened, and if cornered they will sometimes bite opponents much larger than themselves. However, escape is always preferred to combat, and the lizards usually run off at high speed on their hind legs, using their tails as a counterbalance.

*This species is named after the black-and-white collar around its neck. The rest of the body is generally olive green, with pale yellow spots and stripes, although colour and pattern can vary markedly. The adult males have blue throats. The collard lizard is stocky-bodied, with a chunky head and large eyes and powerful jaws. The strong hind legs make the lizard a good climber and a fast runner. The long tail aids balance when moving through branches or swiftly across ground.*

**Distribution**: Central North America.
**Habitat**: Rocky areas.
**Food**: Insects and smaller lizards.
**Size**: 35cm (14in).
**Maturity**: Unknown.
**Breeding**: About 5 eggs laid in summer.
**Life span**: Unknown.
**Status**: Common.

## Greater earless lizard

*Cophosaurus texanus*

The greater earless lizard is a desert species. It inhabits the dry rock fields of northern Mexico and parts of Texas, New Mexico and Arizona. This lizard lives and hunts on the ground, but may climb up cliffs in some parts of its range. In such places, the young lizards are often found higher up than their older counterparts.

Like other lizards and reptiles, greater earless lizards are cold-blooded, or more correctly ectothermic. This means that their body temperature is controlled using an external source of heat – in this case, sunlight. Before they can hunt, the lizards must spend the early part of the day basking in sunshine to warm up their muscles. They search for prey in the warmest part of the day, running across rocks and along the ground in pursuit of insects. On cloudy days, the lizards do not get warm enough to hunt and are very lethargic.

*Although the ears of many lizards are not easy to see, most species have small ear openings on the sides of their heads. This species, as its name suggests, lacks such openings, although the lizard can still hear using its inner ear.*

**Distribution**: Northern Mexico and the southern United States.
**Habitat**: Deserts and other rocky areas.
**Food**: Insects, especially beetles and grasshoppers.
**Size**: 7–18cm (2.75–7in).
**Maturity**: 1 year.
**Breeding**: Clutches of about 5 eggs laid monthly from March to August, up to a total of about 25.
**Life span**: 2 years.
**Status**: Common.

# Keel-scaled earless lizard

*Holbrookia propinqua*

These unusual lizards live in southern Texas and along the north-eastern coast of Mexico. They live in sand dunes and on the region's long beaches. Keel-scaled earless lizards are well adapted to life both on and under the sand. They have very long legs for their size, allowing them to run quickly across exposed areas of dune and so avoid predators. Their blotchy scales give them further protection, making the lizards hard to spot among the knotted dune grasses. Lacking external ears, they can burrow easily into the loose sand, which they do at night in order to stay warm. During the day, these earless lizards bask in the sun before hunting down sand-dwelling insects. They are largely solitary animals and avoid other lizards, which they ward off with displays of aggression that resemble press-ups.

*The tiny scales of this earless lizard have ridges, or keels, along them. The lizard has up to six dark spots or streaks along the belly. Females carrying eggs turn yellow-green.*

**Distribution**: Texas and Mexico.
**Habitat**: Dry areas.
**Food**: Insects.
**Size**: 11–15cm (4.5–6in).
**Maturity**: Unknown.
**Breeding**: Eggs laid in early summer.
**Life span**: Unknown.
**Status**: Common.

---

**Texas horned lizard** (*Phrynosoma cornutum*): 7cm (2.75in)
This species ranges from Kansas to northern Mexico. It lives in barren sandy areas that are too dry for most plants to grow. The Texas horned lizard is a diurnal hunter. It must spend the early part of the day basking to get its body warm enough to forage. As the cool of night approaches, the lizard retreats to the relative warmth of a burrow. It does not dig its own burrow, but takes over one that has been abandoned by another animal. Texas horned lizards are often based close to a nest of harvester ants, their preferred food. They have broad but flattened bodies, which gives them a passing resemblance to a large toad or frog (hence their nickname, the Texas horned toad). The "horns" are spines on the back of the head. Similar spines skirt the body.

**Common monkey lizard** (*Polychrus marmoratus*): 35cm (14in)
This large lizard has a very long, slender tail, which may be twice as long as its body. The lizard often wraps the tip of this long appendage around a branch, just like many New World monkeys do with their flexible, prehensile tails. The monkey lizard lives in the western Amazon. It is generally olive brown, but may take on a bright green colour.

**Amazon thornytail** (*Tropidurus flaviceps*): 19cm (7.5in)
This arboreal lizard, which lives in the north-western Amazon, gets its name from the large ridges, or keels, on its tail. Other thornytails in the Amazon are green, but this species is predominantly grey, with a white collar around the neck. This large lizard feeds on ants.

# Florida scrub lizard

*Sceloporus woodi*

*This species has rough, overlapping scales. Males are slightly smaller than the females, with a blue patch on each side of the throat.*

This member of the iguana family occurs in four small ranges in central and southern Florida. The largest population lives among the sand dunes of Florida's eastern coast. Elsewhere, the lizard is found inland in pine forests that grow in sandy soils.

Florida scrub lizards lie in wait for prey such as ants, beetles and spiders to walk past, then strike with a rapid lunge. Scrub lizards spend a long time basking at the edges of woodlands or in other exposed areas. They often crowd together into basking sites, which results in frequent conflicts between males. As they warm up, the males bob their heads up and down at an increasing rate. Larger, dominant males bob their heads at smaller males, which then flee the area. A more evenly matched rival will turn sideways and compress his body so that he looks larger. This also has the effect of showing off the blue patch on the throat. Males also bob to attract females. Unreceptive females hop away sideways.

**Distribution**: South-eastern United States, restricted to Florida.
**Habitat**: Sandy areas, including pine, oak and rosemary scrub.
**Food**: Insects, spiders and other small arthropods.
**Size**: 9–14cm (3.5–5.5in).
**Maturity**: 1 year.
**Breeding**: 2–8 eggs laid in clutches of 4, with about 3 clutches per season in early summer.
**Life span**: Unknown.
**Status**: Common.

## Eastern fence lizard

*Sceloporus undulatus*

The eastern fence lizard is so-named because it prefers to bask in a raised, sunny location, such as on top of a fence. It may also be spotted sunbathing on fallen logs, grassy dunes and open prairies, and in sunny woodland clearings. This lizard is perhaps most often seen on tree trunks, with its head pointing upwards so that it can run up into the branches if threatened.

This species occurs from Delaware on the east coast of the United States to northern Mexico. The range covers most of the southern states (except southern Florida) and extends to Utah and Arizona in the west. Eastern fence lizards are also found in Kansas and Missouri.

Fence lizards are diurnal. However, unlike many lizards that become most active at the hottest times of the day, this species heads for the shade. At night the lizards retreat to burrows and other hidden shelters. Eastern fence lizards hibernate through the winter and breed soon after emerging in spring.

*This species is seen with various colourings, ranging from brown to grey. Often individuals have spots or streaks, and a dark band along the back of the thighs. Males have blue patches on the throat and belly. The scales are strongly keeled, each scale having a prominent spine.*

**Distribution**: From Delaware west to Utah and south into north-central Mexico, including most of the south-eastern United States.
**Habitat:** Woodland and prairie.
**Food**: Insects, snails and other invertebrates.
**Size**: 9–19cm (3.5–7.5in).
**Maturity**: 1 year.
**Breeding**: Several clutches of up to 12 eggs each laid in summer.
**Life span**: Unknown.
**Status**: Common.

## Leopard lizard

*Gambelia wislizenii*

*Like the coat of a leopard, the skin of this long, slender lizard is covered in dark patches. Most leopard lizards are grey-brown, but they become darker in cold conditions. Females carrying eggs have orange spots and stripes. This species often takes up residence in rodent burrows, but it is perfectly capable of digging its own burrows when necessary. It occasionally climbs into bushes.*

The leopard lizard lives in the region between the Rocky Mountains and the smaller coastal ranges closer to the west coast of North America. Many parts of its range are at high altitude and can be very cold, especially in the north around Idaho and Wyoming. Conditions are also very dry, because few of the rain clouds that come in from the ocean make it over the coastal mountains. Consequently, much of the leopard lizard's range is desert – especially in the south around the US–Mexico border. There are few plants in this habitat, and the soil is loose and sandy.

Leopard lizards are active during the day. Once warmed up, they are very agile hunters, and are often seen dashing from bush to bush as they actively search for insects and spiders. They also hunt by ambushing their prey, lying hidden beneath a shady bush and leaping out when prey approaches. They will eat small lizards too, and even members of their own species on rare occasions. When threatened, the leopard lizard hisses and may bite.

**Distribution**: North America, including California, Nevada and Utah to extreme western Texas and south to northern Mexico.
**Habitat**: Sandy and gravely areas.
**Food**: Mostly insects and spiders, but also other lizards and occasionally small rodents and plant matter.
**Size**: 22–39cm (8.5–15.5in).
**Maturity**: Unknown.
**Breeding**: Female lays 5–6 eggs in early summer, and sometimes again in late summer; hatching takes about 5–6 weeks.
**Life span**: Unknown.
**Status**: Common.

# Diving lizard

*Uranoscodon superciliosus*

**Distribution**: Northern South America, in the eastern and northern Amazon region.
**Habitat**: Swampy forest.
**Food**: Invertebrates.
**Size**: 45cm (18in).
**Maturity**: Unknown.
**Breeding**: Up to 10 eggs laid.
**Life span**: Unknown.
**Status**: Common.

Despite being the sole member of its genus, this species is far from rare. It is found across the northern and eastern Amazon Basin, where it is often seen diving from branches into streams and rivers. This behaviour is largely an escape tactic but, being good swimmers, diving lizards do habitually enter the water to move through the forest. Unusually for lizards, they can also swim well underwater. Furthermore, like basilisks they are able to run on water for short distances.

Diving lizards hunt in trees overhanging water, feeding on arboreal insects and similar invertebrates. Their dark colouring helps to camouflage them as they bask on tree trunks and branches. When danger threatens, they will remain motionless, but if the threat comes comes too close, they plunge into the water and seek refuge beneath submerged debris.

*The diving lizard has a slender body and a long tail. The long legs and toes enable it to move swiftly on land and with great agility through shrubs and trees. The skin is brownish-grey, and there is a crest that runs along the back. In some individuals the back also has golden flecks.*

**Fringe-toed lizard** (*Uma notata*): 12.7–23cm (5–9in)
The comb-like fringes on this lizard's toes help it to walk over fine sand in the deserts of southern California, Arizona and northern Mexico. The fringes act like snowshoes and spread the lizard's weight, preventing its feet from sinking in the shifting sand. When alarmed, the fringe-toad lizard uses a swimming motion to bury itself in the sand. It also heads underground to avoid the worst of the sun's heat and, on rarer occasions, any cold snaps. The lizard's upper jaw overhangs the lower jaw to keep sand out of the mouth. It also has valves to close the nostrils, flaps over the ears and overlapping eyelids.

**Mediterranean gecko** (*Hemidactyus turcicus*): 10–12.5cm (4–5in)
Native to North Africa, southern Europe, the Middle East and India, this lizard was introduced to Texas and southern Florida, and it is now the most conspicuous gecko in North America. This nocturnal species has pads on its toes that help it to grip on to very flat surfaces, such as leaves, smooth tree trunks, walls and ceilings. The male geckos produce tiny squeaks during fights.

**Reef gecko** (*Sphaerodactylus notatus*): 4.5–6.3cm (1.75–2.5in)
Reef geckos live in the Florida Keys, an archipelago of islands at the state's southern tip. They also live along the southern coast of the mainland. Reef geckos prefer thick mangrove forest, and they are also common in gardens. This species is the smallest North American lizard. It is diurnal and hunts for insects in leaf litter.

# Bridled forest gecko

*Gonatodes humeralis*

This small lizard inhabits tropical forest across northern South America, from Bolivia and Brazil in the south to Colombia and the island of Trinidad in the north. Although most geckos are nocturnal hunters, this species is diurnal. By night, the bridled forest gecko sleeps on a large leaf or clinging to a stem.

The bridled forest gecko is most often seen on the edges of forests and in clearings. It has also been known to stray into human houses. Unlike many geckos, especially those in Europe, Africa and Asia, the bridled forest gecko does not have toe pads. (These are used to cling to smooth surfaces, even windows.) As a result, this species is not so well adapted to life among humans as many of its relatives.

Female bridled forest geckos lay single eggs at irregular intervals throughout the year. The eggs have a hard shell, and the young hatch looking like adults in miniature.

**Distribution**: Northern South America.
**Habitat**: Rainforest.
**Food**: Insects.
**Size**: 6–8cm (2.5–3.25in).
**Maturity**: Unknown.
**Breeding**: Several eggs laid singly throughout the year.
**Life span**: Unknown.
**Status**: Common.

*Female bridled forest geckos are grey with dark spots, while the males occur in a range of colours, including olive bodies with red and blue spots. The "bridle" is a pale band that runs from each eye around the back of the head.*

## Western banded gecko

*Coleonyx variegatus*

The western banded gecko is found in southern California, Arizona and northern Mexico, including half of the Baja peninsula. This slender-limbed, flexible-bodied lizard occupies rocky and sandy habitats such as the walls and beds of canyons. Agile and quick-footed, the Western banded gecko is active at night, when it forages for insects and spiders. Its days are spent sheltering in rocky crevices or rodent burrows.

The western banded gecko holds its tail in the air, rather like a cat, as it stalks insects and spiders. When trapped, this lizard makes high-pitched squeaks and, like many other geckos, it may shed its tail when attacked. There is a constriction at the base of the tail where the break occurs. The tail keeps moving for a short while after separation from the body. This behaviour is meant to confuse the predator, which may focus on the tail while the gecko makes its escape. The tail quickly regrows.

**Distribution**: South-western United States to northern Mexico, including California, Arizona, and Baja California.
**Habitat**: Rocky deserts, also arid grassland and chaparral.
**Food**: Insects and spiders.
**Size**: 12–15cm (4.75–6in).
**Maturity**: Unknown.
**Breeding**: 3 clutches of 2 eggs laid in summer.
**Life span**: Unknown.
**Status**: Common.

*As well as the dark brown or black bands across the tan back, Western banded geckos can be identified by their moveable, protruding eyelids. The bands are most prominent in juveniles, and fade as the lizards get older.*

## Texas banded gecko

*Coleonyx brevis*

Texas banded geckos live in Texas, northern Mexico and parts of New Mexico. They are mainly found west of the Pecos River, in the so-called Trans-Pecos region. These geckos live in dry, rocky areas. They dig burrows in the sandy soil underneath flat rocks.

Texas banded geckos are nocturnal hunters. They feed on insects and spiders, which they stalk on the ground. Being cold-blooded, they have only a short time when their body is sufficiently warm enough to enable them to forage. They begin hunting at dusk, and generally finish about four hours later, by which time it is too cold for them to continue. The geckos find prey by tasting the air and ground to detect chemicals produced by nearby insects. They also locate prey by sight.

If the gecko is threatened by a predator, it turns around and waggles its tail at its attacker. When the predator strikes at the tail, the tail breaks away from the body, enabling the lizard to flee. The tail regrows, as it does in other tail-shedding species.

**Distribution**: Texas, New Mexico and Mexico.
**Habitat**: Rocky areas.
**Food**: Insects.
**Size**: 10–12cm (4–4.75in).
**Maturity**: Unknown.
**Breeding**: 2 clutches of eggs laid in late spring and early summer.
**Life span**: Unknown.
**Status**: Common.

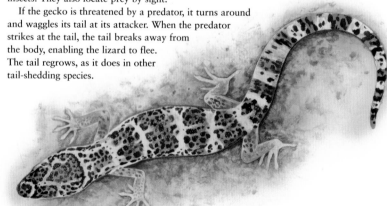

*Female Texas banded geckos are larger than males. As the lizards get older, the solid bands across the back break up into spots and blotches. In banded gecko species, the males have a pair of thorn-like spurs at the base of the tail.*

# Tropical house gecko

*Hemidactylus mabouia*

**Distribution**: Amazon and southern Florida (introduced from Africa).
**Habitat**: Tree trunks and houses.
**Food**: Insects.
**Size**: 10cm (4in).
**Maturity**: 1 year.
**Breeding**: Several clutches of 2 eggs laid throughout year.
**Life span**: Unknown.
**Status**: Common.

*The tropical house gecko is one of many found in Africa, Asia and Europe. The wide pads on its toes help it to cling to tree trunks and other vertical surfaces.*

The tropical house gecko has been introduced to the Amazon from Africa by human migrations. In the wild, these geckos flourish in the forests of Brazil and other Amazonian countries. However, as their name suggests, they have also become common in many settlements, including the largest South American cities.

House geckos are nocturnal hunters. They have very wide toe pads, which have scales arranged in tiny folds across the bottom. These folds give the toes a firm grip, even on extremely flat surfaces. House geckos often rest on tree trunks and walls in a head-down position, so that they are ready to escape to the safety of the forest floor (or another hiding place) should danger approach.

By day, tropical house geckos sleep on a leaf or in a sheltered nook. Their skin is darker at these times, but grows lighter when they forage for food. It has been observed that geckos hunting on white-washed walls become very pale in response to the white background.

---

**Turnip-tailed gecko** (*Thecadactylus rapicaudus*): 15–20cm (6–8in)
This gecko, the sole member of its genus, is the largest in South and Central America. It ranges from southern Mexico to southern Brazil and Bolivia. This gecko's name refers to the fact that when its tail is lost during an attack by a predator, it regrows in a rounded, turnip-like shape. Turnip-tailed geckos are largely forest-dwellers, but they often appear around rural settlements. Like many other geckos, they climb using retractable claws.

**Amazon pygmy gecko** (*Pseudogonatodes guianensis*): 5cm (2in)
This pygmy gecko is found across the Amazon Basin, being especially common in the Peruvian section. Its tail is about the same length as the body. If the tail is shed during an attack, the new tail does not reach the full length of the original. The Amazon pygmy gecko's small size makes it hard to spot, so it is likely that its numbers have been underestimated. Most geckos are nocturnal, but pygmy geckos are active by day, foraging on the forest floor for insects and other invertebrates. They lack the large toe pads of many larger species.

**Coal skink** (*Eumeces anthracinus*): 13–17.8cm (5–7in)
There are several disjointed populations of these diurnal lizards in central and eastern North America, the largest being in Oklahoma and Kansas. Other populations are found in the Mississippi Delta region, the Appalachians, Florida and Georgia. Coal skinks prefer damp areas with loose stones and leaf litter among which they can forage. They dive into water to avoid predators.

# Mexican beaded lizard

*Heloderma horridum*

Mexican beaded lizards are the only close relatives of the gila monster. They are able to survive in deserts, just like the gila monster, but they also thrive in a number of other habitats. Their range extends from central Mexico to Guatemala and most of northern Central America. In the north of this range, beaded lizards live in rock-strewn semi-deserts. However, further south, where there is enough rainfall for trees and shrubs to grow, the lizards inhabit forests. Despite their large size, Mexican beaded lizards are accomplished climbers and are often seen high on ledges on the sides of canyons.

Mexican beaded lizards are hunters, preying on small vertebrates such as bird chicks, mice and smaller lizards. They also raid bird and reptile nests to eat the eggs. Most prey is swallowed whole. These lizards are venomous, and their bites become infected with bacteria from the lizard's saliva.

**Distribution**: Mexico and Central America.
**Habitat**: Semi-desert and woodland.
**Food**: Small mammals, birds, lizards, insects and eggs.
**Size**: 75–90cm (29.5–35.5in).
**Maturity**: Unknown.
**Breeding**: Up to a dozen eggs laid in early summer.
**Life span**: Unknown.
**Status**: Vulnerable.

*Male Mexican beaded lizards are slightly larger than females. The species is named for its rounded, bead-like scales. Adults are black or brown, with yellow spots on the back and tail. The plump tail is a store of fat, which is used to keep the lizard alive when food becomes scarce.*

## Five-lined skink

*Eumeces fasciatus*

The five-lined skink ranges across eastern North America, from southern Quebec and Ontario just north of the Great Lakes to southern New England. The range extends south, covering most the eastern United States and Midwest to eastern Texas, however this species is not found in Florida. Five-lined skinks occupy a range of habitats within their extensive range. They prefer damp areas such as woodlands and meadows, but avoid areas that are prone to flooding or becoming too water-logged.

These lizards also require prominent basking sites, preferably rocky outcrops or tree stumps. They forage on the ground for insects and other invertebrates. They also eat small frogs, snails, baby mice and smaller lizards.

Male five-lined skinks are territorial and will not allow another adult male to come near. They advertise their ownership of an area using chemical markers, and also by displaying their brightly coloured bodies and tails.

**Distribution**: Eastern North America.
**Habitat**: Woodland.
**Food**: Insects, spiders and other invertebrates.
**Size**: 12.5–21.5cm (4.75–8.5in).
**Maturity**: 3 years.
**Breeding**: About 15 eggs laid in summer.
**Life span**: 6 years.
**Status**: Common.

*This skink is named after the yellow stripes that run along its back. The stripes become lighter as the lizard ages.*

**Mole skink** (*Eumeces egregius*): 8.9–16.5cm (3.5–6.5in)
The mole skink is found in southern Georgia, south-eastern Alabama and most of Florida (including the Keys but not the Everglades). This lizard is a good tunneller. It digs to find soil-dwelling prey such as insect larvae and spiders. The mole skink prefers areas with sandy soil in which it can dig with ease. Most of this soil is found on the coastal plain. Inland, the lizard is more restricted to lowland areas where sand gathers.

**Broad-headed skink** (*Eumeces laticeps*): 16.5–32.4cm (6.5–12.75in)
This skink has a very wide head. It occurs across the central and eastern United States, from Texas in the south to eastern Nebraska and southern Pennsylvania in the north. Broad-headed skinks live mainly in woodland, but also occur in open areas where there is plenty of plant debris or rocks to provide shelter. The young have wide white stripes across their back, which fade with age. Broad-headed skinks are active by day. They are known to hunt for insects high up in the trees, sometimes shaking the nests of paper wasps to dislodge the pupae inside. The wasps' stings cannot penetrate the lizard's thick scales.

**Western skink** (*Eumeces skiltonianus*): 16.5–23.7cm (6.5–9.25in)
The Western skink lives under rocks and in leaf litter in the Great Basin plateau of the western United States, which includes Nevada, Idaho and Oregon. The lizard's range also extends along the west coast to Baja California. The Western skink hunts by day for insects, spiders and earthworms.

## Black-spotted skink

*Mabuya nigropunctata*

*The black-spotted skink has pale and dark stripes along its sides, with dark spots underneath and brown scales above. The scales are smooth and shiny. There is a bluish tinge to the juveniles' scales.*

The black-spotted skink is the only member of the skink family to be found in the Iquitos region of the Amazon Basin, which lies on either side of the Peru–Ecuador border and contains many of the Amazon River's major sources. From here, the skink's range extends throughout most of the Amazon watershed.

This species is a good climber, and it is sometimes found clambering through forest trees, especially when searching for a sunlit spot on which to bask. The black markings on its skin help it to absorb the sun's warmth more quickly.

Despite their tree-climbing abilities, black-spotted skinks are mainly terrestrial in habit. They hunt small invertebrates among the leaf litter of the forest floor, and may sometimes be seen foraging on village garbage tips. This species is viviparous, meaning that it gives birth to live young rather than laying eggs.

**Distribution**: Amazon Basin, including parts of Brazil, French Guiana, Venezuela, Peru, Ecuador and Bolivia.
**Habitat**: Forest.
**Food**: Insects, arachnids and other invertebrates.
**Size**: 17–23cm (6.75–9in).
**Maturity**: Unknown.
**Breeding**: Up to 8 young born in each litter, with 1 litter born per year.
**Life span**: Unknown.
**Status**: Common.

## Six-lined racerunner

*Cnemidophorus sexlineatus*

This species is often just called the racerunner. The name is derived from this wary lizard's habit of running for cover whenever a person approaches. The racerunner lives across the lowland areas of south-eastern and central United States, from the east coast to the eastern foothills of the Rocky Mountains. It prefers to live in dry areas where sandy soil prevents thick vegetation from covering the ground. The lizard scurries around hunting for insects, snails and other soft-bodied invertebrates. It is almost never seen climbing trees.

Racerunners shelter under flat rocks and in other nooks and crannies. To avoid low temperatures at night and on cold days, they retreat into burrows. They sometimes dig burrows themselves, but they more often occupy burrows abandoned by other animals, especially those of moles. A racerunner's burrow has two entrances, one of which is always blocked up by the lizard when it is inside. In the north of this species' range, the lizards hibernate from autumn until late spring.

**Distribution**: Eastern and central United States.
**Habitat**: Sandy grasslands and woodlands.
**Food**: Insects.
**Size**: 30cm (12in).
**Maturity**: Unknown.
**Breeding**: 4–6 eggs laid in summer.
**Life span**: Unknown.
**Status**: Common.

*Despite their name, six-lined racerunners sometimes have seven pale stripes along the back. The males have green or blue throats, while the females have white throat patches.*

## Sonoran spotted whiptail

*Cnemidophorus sonorae*

The Sonoran spotted whiptail lives in the Sonoran Desert, which extends from north-western Mexico into southern Arizona. The lizard occupies the less arid upland areas in the eastern portion of the desert, where grasslands and woodland can grow.

The whiptail is a close relative of the racerunner, which is also a whiptail. However, there is one crucial difference that sets this lizard apart from other whiptails: there are no males of the species. Female Sonoran spotted whiptails reproduce by parthenogenesis. This is a form of asexual reproduction in which the lizards can produce eggs without mating. The young have exactly the same genes as their mothers. Egg production is stimulated by a ritual between two females that is similar to the courtship seen in sexual species. Asexual reproduction is a very efficient way of reproducing quickly and with the minimum of effort, but without a variety of genes in the population the species is less able to withstand changes in the environment.

**Distribution**: Sonoran desert, from southern Arizona to north-western Mexico.
**Habitat**: Dry grassland, desert scrub and mountain oak woodlands.
**Food**: Insects and other invertebrates, and smaller lizards.
**Size**: 20–28cm (8–11in).
**Maturity**: Unknown.
**Breeding**: 2–3 clutches of 3–4 eggs produced between mid-May and late July by parthenogenesis.
**Life span**: Unknown.
**Status**: Common.

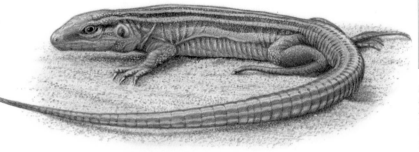

*All Sonoran spotted whiptails are female. They have six pale stripes on their dark, spotted back. The tail is paler than the back, and the belly is cream coloured. These lizards eat mainly insects and other invertebrates, but also prey on smaller lizards. They are most active in the first part of the morning. They rest during the intense midday heat, and resume activity in the afternoon.*

## Golden tegu

*Tupinambis teguixin*

*The tail makes up two-thirds of a golden tegu's total length. The body has a dark background marked with yellow or golden rings. Juveniles are greener than adults, and adult males turn slightly blue.*

The golden tegu is the largest lizard in the Amazon. These heavily built, ground-living hunters prey on all sorts of small animals, including mammals, other reptiles and amphibians, as well as large arthropods. They also supplement their diet with plant food.

Golden tegus are diurnal hunters. They generally walk on four legs but can run at high speeds on their hind legs to escape from danger. Golden tegus retreat into burrows at night and when conditions are too cold for hunting. They occupy a range of habitats across the north of South America, from forest edges and river banks to thick jungle and cultivated fields.

Female golden tegus lay up to a dozen eggs, which apparently lie dormant for a few months before beginning to develop. As a result, the eggs take up to seven months to hatch.

**Distribution**: Amazon and Orinoco Basins in northern South America.
**Habitat**: Forests and cultivated areas.
**Food**: Small mammals, reptiles, amphibians, large arthropods, plants, some bird and caiman eggs and carrion.
**Size**: 95cm (37.5in).
**Maturity**: Unknown.
**Breeding**: Up to 12 eggs laid each year.
**Life span**: Unknown.
**Status**: Common.

## Northern caiman lizard

*Dracaena guianensis*

This lizard leads a similar aquatic life to the crocodile tegu. The two species are not very closely related, but both resemble crocodilians. The caiman lizard is the larger and more robustly built species. It has three rows of spines on its tail and powerful jaws, which it uses to crush the shells of water snails and crustaceans. The northern caiman lizard is an Amazonian species. It is found in areas of flooded forest and in the many rivers and creeks that criss-cross the Amazon Basin. This northern species has a southern relative that lives south of the Amazon in the wetlands of Paraguay.

The northern caiman lizard often basks on the banks of rivers or on a large piece of floating debris. This lizard is a diurnal hunter with a specialized diet of water snails. It has powerful jaws with enlarged sites for muscle attachment and flat, molar-like teeth for crushing snails. The snail flesh is swallowed and indigestible fragments of shell are pushed out of the mouth by the tongue. In the dry season, when snails are less abundant, this lizard may climb trees to feed on eggs and invertebrates.

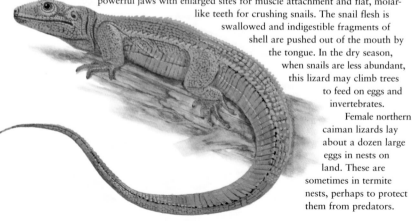

Female northern caiman lizards lay about a dozen large eggs in nests on land. These are sometimes in termite nests, perhaps to protect them from predators.

**Distribution**: Peru and Brazil.
**Habitat**: Flooded forest.
**Food**: Water snails; plus some invertebrates and eggs.
**Size**: 90–120cm (35.5–48in)
**Maturity**: Unknown.
**Breeding**: Up to 12 eggs laid beside a river.
**Life span**: Unknown.
**Status**: Common.

*This species has a large head, which ranges in colour from green to orange. The body varies from olive brown to dark green. The belly is grey. The lizard's common name derives from the knobbly scales on its back, which resemble those of caimans.*

# Southern alligator lizard

*Elgaria multicarinata*

**Distri**bution: West coast of North America.
**Habitat**: Grassland and woodland.
**Food**: Small mammals and insects.
**Size**: 25–43cm (9.75–17in).
**Maturity**: Unknown.
**Breeding**: Females lay 2–3 clutches of about 20 eggs during summer.
**Life span**: Unknown.
**Status**: Common.

The southern alligator lizard belongs to the anguid family. Most anguid lizards live outside of the Americas. They include monitor lizards and the fearsome Komodo dragon. American anguids, such as the alligator lizards, are much smaller than their foreign cousins.

The southern alligator lizard has a patchy range in the mountain woodlands along the west coast of North America. It is most common in California and Baja California, Mexico, but its range also extends north through the Cascade Mountains as far as southern Washington.

The southern alligator lizard is a diurnal hunter that often climbs in bushes, using its prehensile tail to grasp branches. The lizard eats anything it can catch, from small mammals and lizards to insects and other invertebrates.

Females lay more than one clutch of eggs per year during warmer periods. Each clutch contains about 20 eggs.

*The southern alligator lizard has a distinct fold along its side, and dark crossbands on its brown back. The young have lighter bands.*

**Californian legless lizard** (*Anniella pulchra*): 15.2–23.5cm (6–9.25in)
This is one of two lizards in North America. The other is found in the Baja peninsula. Legless lizards look like large worms or snakes. They are most closely related to the anguid lizard group, and should not be confused with amphisbaenians. The Californian species burrows in the soft soils of coastal California up to San Francisco Bay. It hunts for insects in the soil or the leaf litter that builds up in forest habitats. Its flexible legless form and blunt head make it a good tunneller. The California legless lizard is most active at night.

**Granite night lizard** (*Xantusia henshawi*): 10–14.5cm (4–5.5in)
This secretive, nocturnal lizard lives in the rocky deserts of southern California and Mexico's Baja peninsula. Its large, lidless eyes give it good night vision. Night lizards are viviparous, meaning that the young develop inside the females, nurtured by a placenta-like organ. They are born tail first. Most litters contain two young.

**Crocodile tegu** (*Crocodilurus lacertinus*): 60cm (23.5in)
The crocodile tegu has two rows of keel-like spines along its long tail, giving the animal a passing resemblance to a crocodile. The tail makes up about two-thirds of the lizard's overall length. Crocodile tegus frequently move in and out of water, although they also spend time in the trees. They occur right across the Amazon Basin, from the flooded forests of eastern Peru to the wetland region around the mouth of the Amazon River in eastern Brazil.

# Large-scaled forest lizard

*Alopoglossus angulata*

This is one of several forest lizards that live in the Amazon. This particular species is found all over the region, and its range probably extends into surrounding areas as well. It seldom strays far from permanent bodies of water.

The forest lizards are characterized by having no ridges, or keels, on the scales of the head. This species is no exception, although its head scales are somewhat rough. The rest of the body, however, is covered in keeled scales.

Very little is known about the reproductive behaviour of this species, but it is thought that the females lay small clutches of eggs at varying times during the year.

**Distribution**: Amazon Basin.
**Habitat**: Moist forest.
**Food**: Insects.
**Size**: 10–13cm (4–5in).
**Maturity**: Unknown.
**Breeding**: Small clutches laid throughout the year.
**Life span**: Unknown.
**Status**: Common.

*As its name suggests, the body of the large-scaled forest lizard is covered in large, rough scales. Even the lower eyelid has scales, although these are translucent to allow a little light to pass through even when the eyes are shut. (Most lizards, in contrast, have much more transparent scales on the lower eyelid.)*

# CROCODILIANS

*Crocodilians are an ancient group of reptiles. They include crocodiles, alligators, caimans and gharials. They all live in or near water. Most crocodilians in North and South America belong to the alligator and caiman group. In fact only one type of alligator – the Chinese alligator – lives outside of the Americas. American crocodiles tend to be larger than their alligator and caiman cousins, and most are very rare.*

## American alligator

*Alligator mississippiensis*

Young American alligators feed on insects, small fish and frogs. As they get bigger, they begin to take larger prey, such as turtles and water birds. Adults feed on land as well as in water. They are opportunistic feeders, attacking anything that comes within reach. They even leap up to snatch birds perching on low branches.

During cold weather, American alligators become dormant in burrows dug into mud banks. In dry periods, they will travel long distances to find water, sometimes ending up in swimming pools.

After mating, the female makes a mound of vegetation and mud above the high waterline and lays her eggs in a hole in the top. When she hears the hatchlings calling, she breaks open the nest and carries her young to the water. They stay with their mother for about a year.

**Distribution**: South-eastern United States.
**Habitat**: Swamps and rivers.
**Food**: Birds, fish and mammals.
**Size**: 2.8–5m (9.25–16.5ft).
**Maturity**: 5–10 years.
**Breeding**: Eggs laid in nest of mud and vegetation during spring.
**Life span**: 40 years.
**Status**: Common.

*The American alligator has a broad snout. Unlike other crocodilians, the fourth teeth on either side of its lower jaw are not visible, since they fit into sockets in the upper jaw when the mouth closes.*

## Black caiman

*Melanosuchus niger*

Black caimans are the largest alligators in the Americas. Young black caimans rely heavily on aquatic crustaceans for food, especially crabs and crayfish. Adults eat fish, such as catfish and piranhas, and often take large rodents called capybaras that live along the banks of rivers. At night, they may hunt on land, taking advantage of their excellent hearing and sense of sight to track large animals, which may include livestock and even humans.

Breeding takes place during the dry season, presumably to reduce the chance that the eggs become submerged while they incubate. The females build nest mounds that are about 1.5m (5ft) high. The nest mounds are built in a variety of places, some concealed, others in the open. Each female digs a conical hole in her nest and lays 30–65 eggs in the top. They hatch about three months later, at the beginning of the wet season.

**Distribution**: Northern South America.
**Habitat**: Rivers and flooded forests.
**Food**: Fish, capybaras and other aquatic vertebrates.
**Size**: 4–6m (13–19.75ft).
**Maturity**: 5–10 years.
**Breeding**: Eggs laid in nest during dry season.
**Life span**: 40 years.
**Status**: Lower risk.

*As their name suggests, black caimans have dark bodies. They have grey-brown bands on their lower jaws. The young have yellow or white bands on their flanks, which fade as they age.*

# Spectacled caiman

*Caiman crocodilus*

**Distribution**: Central America and northern South America.
**Habitat**: Areas of still water.
**Food**: Fish, wild pigs and water birds.
**Size**: 1.5–2.5m (5–8.25ft).
**Maturity**: 4–7 years.
**Breeding**: Eggs laid in nests during wet season.
**Life span**: 40 years.
**Status**: Common.

Spectacled caimans live in a wide range of habitats from rivers to coastal wetlands. They prefer stiller waters than the black caimans that share parts of their range, and consequently they have taken up residence in many reservoirs.

Spectacled caimans rarely come out of the water, only attacking land animals when they come to the water's edge. They spend the day floating on the surface and hunt mainly at night. During periods of drought, they aestivate – enter a period of dormancy to avoid desiccation – in cool burrows dug deep into mud.

The breeding season coincides with the wet season in May and June. The dominant males get the best territories and attract most females. Females lay eggs in mounds of vegetation that they build on banks or rafts of plants. Several females may lay eggs in a single nest, which they guard together. The young live in large groups called crèches.

*Spectacled caimans are smaller than most crocodilians. They get their name from ridges of bone located on their snouts between their eyes. The ridges appear to join the eyes together, looking similar to the frames of a large pair of spectacles.*

**Orinoco crocodile** (*Crocodylus intermedius*): 4–7m (13.25–23ft)
These crocodiles live in the middle and lower reaches of the Orinoco River, Venezuela, where they prey on fish, birds and land animals. Females lay their eggs in holes dug into sandbars during low-water periods in January and February. The eggs hatch when the rains arrive about 70 days later. A mother will guard her young for up to three years.

**Broad-snouted caiman** (*Caiman latirostris*): 2–3m (6.5–11.5ft)
This medium-sized caiman has an even broader snout than the American alligator. It is found from Bolivia to southern Brazil and northern Argentina, in freshwater habitats and brackish coastal mangroves. Broad-snouted caimans eat aquatic snails, amphibians, small fish and even turtles. The female lays 20–60 eggs in a nest, sometimes on a river island. She guards them for 70 days, then breaks open the nest and carries the hatchlings to water.

**Red caiman** (*Caiman yacare*): 2.5–3m (8.25–9.75ft)
This species lives in the rivers, lakes and wetlands of northern Argentina, Paraguay, southern Brazil and Bolivia. Its alternative name, piranha caiman, refers to the many teeth visible in its mouth. It feeds on water snails, fish and snakes. The female guards her 20–40 eggs, which she lays in an earthen nest.

# American crocodile

*Crocodylus acutus*

American crocodiles live in fresh water, such as rivers and lakes, but will venture out into coastal waters, especially near estuaries and in lagoons, where the water is brackish. The crocodiles cope with the salty water by taking long drinks of fresh water when possible and removing salt from the body through glands on their faces – secreting "crocodile tears" in the process.

Feeding takes place at night, and the crocodiles occasionally come on to land to prey on livestock. They have also been known to attack humans. During periods of drought, the crocodiles burrow into mud and do not feed until the water returns.

Most females lay their eggs in holes dug in the ground, but they may build nest mounds in areas where the soil is likely to become waterlogged and thus chill the incubating eggs. Nesting takes place in the dry season. Between 30 and 60 eggs are laid, which hatch three months later as the rainy season begins. The mother guards her nest until the hatchlings have dispersed.

*The American crocodile's diet consists mainly of fish and other small aquatic animals. Larger individuals may also eat small mammals, birds and turtles. American crocodiles often exceed the size of other crocodilians in North and South America.*

**Distribution**: Southern Florida, Mexico, Central America and northern South America.
**Habitat**: Rivers and brackish water.
**Food**: Fish, turtles and birds.
**Size**: 4–5m (13–16.5ft).
**Maturity**: 5–10 years.
**Breeding**: Eggs laid in dry season.
**Life span**: 40 years.
**Status**: Vulnerable.

## Dwarf caiman

*Paleosuchus palpebrosus*

The dwarf caiman, also known as Cuvier's dwarf caiman, is the smallest of all crocodile species. It lives throughout the Amazon Basin, from the foothills of the Andes in the east to the Atlantic in the west, and from Venezuela in the north to Paraguay in the south. Preferring fast-running, clear water, it is mainly found in rivers, but it also ventures into flooded forests, stagnant pools and swamps.

Dwarf caimans spend the day in burrows or basking in the open, becoming active at night, when they hunt for small animals such as frogs, snails, fish, aquatic mammals and crabs. Their short, curved teeth are particularly good at crushing shellfish. Younger individuals feed on smaller prey, including insects. Like all crocodiles, dwarf caimans have very strong stomach acid, which is capable of dissolving bone. They also swallow small stones (gastroliths) that help to grind the stomach contents into a more digestible paste.

**Distribution**: Amazon Basin.
**Habitat**: Rivers and wetlands.
**Food**: Frogs, shellfish, snails and small fish.
**Size**: 1.2–1.6m (4–5.25ft).
**Maturity**: 10 years.
**Breeding**: Eggs laid in nests in dry season.
**Life span**: 30 years.
**Status**: Lower risk.

Breeding takes place at the end of the dry season, when the males attract mates by roaring in shallow water with the head and tail raised above the surface. Females lay up to 25 eggs in mounds of rotting vegetation. (Well-fed females can lay eggs two or three times a year.) The young hatch after about 90 days, and the female opens the nest when she hears their cries.

*The dwarf caiman has more scutes, or osteoderms, than any other species. The scutes are bony plates that cover the skin and protect the body from damage by debris carried in fast-flowing water.*

## Schneider's dwarf caiman

*Paleosuchus trigonatus*

Schneider's dwarf caiman is the world's second smallest crocodile species. Males can reach more than twice the size of females, but are generally only slightly larger. This caiman prefers colder water than most crocodiles, which is why it is often found in the cooler, fast-flowing water under waterfalls and in rapids.

Schneider's dwarf caimans only gather together for breeding. Mating occurs at the end of the dry season. This ensures that the eggs – of which there are rarely more than 15 in a nest – hatch as the rains arrive, giving the young a better chance of survival. The nests are often built next to termite mounds, so that the heat from the mound helps to incubate the eggs. (This may be to compensate for the reduced incubating effect of the sun's rays in their shady rainforest habitat.) Female dwarf caimans become sexually mature when they reach 1.3 m (4.2ft), which may take between 10 and 20 years. They do not breed every year.

*Schneider's dwarf caiman is also known as the smooth-fronted caiman, because it lacks the characteristic ridge between the eyes seen in other South American crocodiles. Hatchlings emerge from the eggs with a golden patch on their heads – hence the species' alternative name of crowned caiman.*

**Distribution**: Amazon and Orinoco Basins, from Peru in the west to French Guiana in the east, and from Venezuela south to Bahia state in Brazil.
**Habitat**: Fast-flowing water.
**Food**: Fish, birds, lizards and snakes, plus rodents and similar small mammals.
**Size**: 1.4–2m (4.5–7.5ft).
**Maturity**: 10–20 years.
**Breeding**: Eggs laid in nests before rainy season in early summer.
**Life span**: 25 years.
**Status**: Common.

# Cuban crocodile

*Crocodylus rhombifer*

**Distribution**: Northwestern Cuba.
**Habitat**: Freshwater marshes.
**Food**: Fish, turtles and small mammals.
**Size**: Up to 3.5m (11.5ft).
**Maturity**: Not known.
**Breeding**: Eggs laid in holes or under mounds.
**Life span**: Unknown.
**Status**: Endangered.

*The rare Cuban crocodile is of medium size. It has unusually large legs, with keels of sturdy scutes that project from the back of the rear legs.*

This crocodile has the smallest range of any species. It is only found in the Zapata swamp in northwestern Cuba and on Isla de Juventud. It was once found in other parts of the Greater Antilles, such as the Caymans and Bahamas, but is now extinct outside of Cuba. There are probably less than 6,000 Cuban crocodiles in the wild. After years of damage by humans, their swamp habitat has now been protected and hunting is banned. However, a large population is kept in zoos to ensure the species' survival.

Fossil records indicate that millions of years ago Cuban crocodiles preyed on the now-extinct giant ground sloths. Today, they mainly eat fish and turtles, whose shells they crush with their broad back teeth, and also small mammals. They are unusually agile on land, thanks to their strong legs and the reduced webbing on their feet. Using their powerful tails, they can propel themselves out of the water to snatch prey off waterside trees.

Little is known of the breeding behaviour of Cuban crocodiles, but they are reported to both dig nest holes and build mound nests, depending on the availability of suitable material. The normal clutch size is between 30 and 40 eggs. Many eggs and hatchlings are lost to predation by various mammals, reptiles and birds.

# Morelet's crocodile

*Crocodylus moreletii*

**Distribution**: Mexico (Yucatan Peninsula), Belize and northern Guatemala.
**Habitat**: Freshwater swamps and rivers in forests.
**Food**: Lizards, turtles, fish and birds.
**Size**: 2–2.2m (7–7.25ft).
**Maturity**: 8 years.
**Breeding**: 20–45 eggs laid in nest at end of dry season.
**Life span**: 65 years.
**Status**: Endangered.

*This rare North American crocodile has a blunt, alligator-like snout. Morelet's crocodile is similar to the American crocodile, but its skin is darker in colour.*

Morelet's crocodile, also called the Mexican or soft-belly crocodile, lives on the eastern coastal plane of Mexico, ranging south along the Caribbean coast through Belize and also into Guatemala. It inhabits slow-flowing water in swamps and marshy areas, and sometimes in rivers that flow through forests. By day it basks in the sun, or lies submerged with just its eyes, ears and nostrils above the water. Hunting takes place mainly at night. As in all crocodile species, the diet changes with age. Young eat invertebrates, such as insect larvae and small fish, while juveniles feed on snails, small water birds and small mammals. Adults can tackle a range of prey, from turtles and lizards to small domestic animals, even dogs.

At the end of the dry season, the female Morelet's crocodile builds a nest of vegetation up to 3m (10ft) across and 1m (3.25ft) high close to water, occasionally on floating debris in the water itself. She remains nearby until the eggs hatch about 80 days later, and helps the youngsters out of the nest. Males sometimes assist with the early care of hatchlings. In hard times, hatchlings may be cannibalized.

# NON-VENOMOUS SNAKES

*Most snakes do not have a venomous bite and are completely harmless to humans. The largest American snakes – the boas – are non-venomous. They kill by coiling around prey and squeezing until their victims suffocate. Colubrids, typified by the garter snakes, are the largest group of snakes, with 1,700 species found worldwide. Most colubrids are non-venomous, although a few use their saliva to stun their prey.*

## Green anaconda

*Eunectes murinus*

**Distribution**: Northern South America.
**Habitat**: Wetlands and flooded forests.
**Food**: Birds, caimans, deer and capybaras.
**Size**: 6–10m (20–33ft); 250kg (550lb).
**Maturity**: 6 years.
**Breeding**: 4–80 young born from mother.
**Life span**: 25 years.
**Status**: Common.

Green anacondas are the world's heaviest snakes, if not the longest. They are not venomous but kill by constriction, squeezing their prey in coils of their massive bodies.

Green anacondas spend most of their time in shallow water, being most common in open wetlands. Their eyes and nostrils are positioned on top of their heads, so that they can lie hidden underwater with only their heads breaking the surface. Anacondas are ambush predators: they wait for prey to come to the water's edge to drink, then they strike with lightning speed. Their bodies are powerful enough to squeeze the life out of a horse or a fully grown black caiman. Anacondas can kill humans, but only occasionally do so.

Male anacondas have claw-like spurs on their lower bodies, which they use to stimulate females. A single female may be tangled up with several males during mating. Like other boas, anacondas do not lay eggs but give birth to live young.

*Compared to their huge bodies, green anacondas have small heads. Their bodies are covered in smooth olive scales, and they have black ovals on their backs. The males are smaller than the females. The young, born live from the mother, measure about 66cm (26in) at birth.*

## Emerald tree boa

*Corallus caninus*

Emerald tree boas spend their entire lives away from the ground, gripping tree branches with their coils. The snake's bright leaf-green body has flashes of white running across its back that help it to blend in with the forest foliage. This camouflage keeps the snake safe from predatory birds, such as owls and eagles.

Tree boas hang from sturdy branches and wait for small birds to fly by or small mammals to pass beneath them. The snake's eyes have vertical pupils. Just like small cats, this makes them better at sensing the movements of small prey in the gloom of the forest. Tree boas also have heat-sensitive pits on their snouts, which allow them to detect the body heat of prey moving near them. The snake waits, ready to pounce, with its upper body in an S-shape. When a prey animal comes close enough, the tree boa lunges forward and grabs it in its mouth. The snake's backward-curving teeth stop victims from struggling free.

During mating, the male entwines his tail with the female's. The female gives birth to between 3 and 15 young. The young snakes are red or orange for the first year of their lives.

**Distribution**: Northern South America.
**Habitat**: Rainforest.
**Food**: Birds and mammals.
**Size**: 1.5–2m (5–6.5ft).
**Maturity**: Not known.
**Breeding**: Young born live.
**Life span**: 40 years.
**Status**: Common.

*The emerald tree boa has a long, slender body with a prehensile tail that is used for gripping branches. The snake's camouflaged body is reinforced down each side, like a girder, so it is powerful enough to reach across open spaces between branches.*

**Rosy boa** (*Charina trivirgata*): 60–110cm (23.5–43in)
Rosy boas live in the deserts of the south-western United States and northern Mexico. The head is narrow for a boa species, and the body has smooth scales that form red and cream stripes. Rosy boas are nocturnal hunters that burrow under rocks and slither into crevices in search of prey. They mostly hunt on the ground, but occasionally climb into shrubs. They mainly eat small mammals and birds.

**Amazon tree boa** (*Corallus hortulanus*): 1.4–1.8m (4.5–6ft)
This boa occurs throughout the northern and eastern parts of the Amazon Basin. The Amazon tree boa hunts at night for tree frogs and lizards. Its long, slender body spreads its weight, so that the snake can move easily among all but the flimsiest of branches. When resting and digesting a meal, the snake wraps itself into a coil and hangs from a branch.

**Western blind snake** (*Leptotyphlops humilis*): 70–90cm (28–35in)
This small snake has a smooth, shiny, cylindrical body, and rudimentary eyes covered by large scales. It is found around the US–Mexico border, in dry habitats such as deserts, grasslands and canyons, where the soil is loose enough for burrowing. The snake spends the day underground and emerges on warm evenings to forage for ants and termites.

# Kingsnake

*Lampropeltis getulus*

Kingsnakes are constrictors, killing their prey by squeezing them to death. They are very active hunters, slithering into rodent burrows and climbing through bushes to catch their diverse prey. They appear to be immune to the venom of other poisonous snakes, which they include on their menu. Kingsnakes are competent swimmers, and they often patrol riverbanks in search of frogs and small aquatic mammals.

As well as threatening many animals, these non-venomous snakes also have several enemies of their own, from large birds of prey to raccoons and other carnivores. If cornered, a kingsnake will try to bite its attacker. When captured, the snake's final defence is to smear its captor with foul-smelling faeces.

Kingsnakes live in a variety of climates and may be active during the day or night. They hibernate during cold periods, which may last for several months at the northern extent of their range.

The males bite their mates on the backs of their necks to restrain them during mating. About 12 eggs are laid under rotting vegetation.

*Kingsnakes have different coloured bodies in different parts of their range. For example, Mexican kingsnakes are black, while those found in the deserts of Arizona have yellow bodies with black spots.*

**Distribution**: Southern United States and northern Mexico.
**Habitat**: All land habitats.
**Food**: Birds, lizards, frogs and other snakes.
**Size**: 1–2m (3.25–6.5ft).
**Maturity**: Not known.
**Breeding**: Eggs laid in rotting vegetation.
**Life span**: 25 years.
**Status**: Common.

# Texas thread snake

*Leptotyphlops dulcis*

The Texas thread snake, or Texas blind snake as it is also known, spends most of its life burrowing through the ground. Its body is well adapted for this lifestyle, being equipped with smooth scales and a blunt head for shoving earth out of the way.

The snakes feed on worms and other invertebrates that they come across, using their keen sense of smell to locate them. They also tunnel into the nests of ants and termites. When they enter a nest, the snakes begin to release the same chemical pheromones used by the insects themselves. This fools the normally aggressive insects into thinking the snakes belong there. The invading reptiles are free to slither about and feast on insect eggs and larvae. Texas thread snakes will come to the surface at night, especially after heavy rains, when the soil beneath is waterlogged.

After mating, the female lays only a handful of eggs and stays close to them while they incubate, often coiling around them. The thread snake family numbers 80 species in all.

*The long, thin body of the Texas thread snake is covered in smooth, silvery scales. Even the snake's eyes are covered in thin scales.*

**Distribution**: Southern United States and northern Mexico.
**Habitat**: Underground.
**Food**: Insects and spiders.
**Size**: 15–27cm (6–11in).
**Maturity**: Not known.
**Breeding**: Female incubates eggs in coils.
**Life span**: Unknown.
**Status**: Common.

# Boa constrictor

*Boa constrictor*

Boa constrictors are among the commonest large snakes in the Americas. They are found in a number of habitats, from northern Mexico all the way to Argentina. These snakes are equally at home in the branches of rainforest trees, in the grasses of open savannahs and among rocks in a desert. They are also frequently seen in many South American cities.

Boa constrictors hunt through the trees and on the ground for large lizards, small birds and medium-sized mammals. They kill by constriction, rather than with venom (although they will bite if handled). A boa wraps its body in coils around its prey and squeezes so hard that the animal eventually dies of suffocation. Each time the animal exhales, the snake tightens its grip. Boas find their prey using heat-sensitive pits on their face. Their preferred food is bats, which they catch by hanging from a branch or at the mouth of a roosting cave and knocking the bats to the ground as they fly past.

When they do not need to feed, these snake are fairly sedentary, and may remain in the same spot for several days. In colder parts of this species' range, the boas may have periods of inactivity that last for a number of weeks.

*Boa constrictors occur in a range of patterns. Their coloration depends on where they live, but the background is often greyish or tan, with dark-red or brown blotches or saddle-shaped markings. The snake's muscular body is used for gripping branches when climbing and for constricting prey.*

**Distribution**: From northern Mexico through Central and South America to Argentina; also found on the Lesser Antilles and other islands.
**Habitat**: Deserts, savannah and tropical forests.
**Food**: Lizards, small birds, bats, opossums, mongooses, rats and squirrels.
**Size**: 1–3m (3.25–10ft).
**Maturity**: Unknown.
**Breeding**: The female retains her eggs internally until they hatch, and gives birth to 20–50 live young, between 100 and 150 days after mating.
**Life span**: Unknown.
**Status**: Common.

# Rubber boa

*Charina bottae*

This small snake is one of just two boas found in North America, where it lives in damp woodlands and mountain conifer forests in the west of the continent. Rubber boas are burrowers, as well as good swimmers, so they are especially common in sandy areas close to streams. Their small, blunt head and sturdy body help them to force their way through soft soil. Rubber boas are crepuscular, spending the day underground and coming to the surface around dusk or just before dawn.

The prey of rubber boas consists of small mammals, lizards, and birds, which the snakes kill by constriction. These snakes hunt on the ground, but they also use their slender, prehensile tail to climb into shrubs and the lower branches of trees. If danger threatens, a rubber boa will slither under a rock or burrow into sand or leaf litter.

This species does not lay eggs. Instead, the female retains the eggs inside her body until they hatch. When the young emerge, they are miniature versions of the adults. Young rubber boas prey on insects, salamanders, frogs and other small woodland animals.

**Distribution**: British Columbia to Utah and southern California.
**Habitat**: Damp woodland and coniferous forest.
**Food**: Small mammals, birds and lizards.
**Size**: 35.5–84cm (14–33in).
**Maturity**: Unknown.
**Breeding**: 2–8 young born in late summer.
**Life span**: 10 years.
**Status**: Common.

*With a short, rounded snout and an equally blunt tail, this snake looks as if it has two heads. The dark and matt scales on its body give the snake a rubbery appearance and texture.*

## Rainbow boa

*Epicrates cenchria*

Rainbow boas live in tropical forests in parts of Central and South America. They also stray into agricultural areas. This species is closely related to the rare boas that live on the islands of the Caribbean. There are several subspecies of the rainbow boa, many of which have been bred in captivity. The two main wild forms are the Brazilian rainbow boa and the Peruvian rainbow boa, both of which are found in the Amazon Basin.

Rainbow boas hunt for small, warm-blooded animals such as mammals and birds. They hunt in the tree tops using their heat-sensitive pits to locate prey. Like other boas, they squeeze their victims to death. Younger rainbow boas tackle small rodents and nestlings, and they are also more likely to prey on tree frogs and lizards than their elders. At night, when they are most active, rainbow boas often become paler, especially around the flanks.

**Distribution**: Costa Rica to Argentina.
**Habitat**: Tropical forest.
**Food**: Birds, small mammals and large lizards.
**Size**: 1.5–2m (5–6.5ft).
**Maturity**: Unknown.
**Breeding**: 6–20 offspring produced.
**Life span**: Over 15 years.
**Status**: Common.

*Rainbow boas exist in several subspecies. Most have an orange-brown body with dark rings that become paler in the middle. Some subspecies have solid rings.*

---

**Cuban wood snake** (*Tropidophis melanurus*): 80–100cm (31.5–39.5in)
Also called the dusky dwarf boa, this is the only dwarf boa to be found on the Caribbean island of Cuba. It lives both in forests and alongside people. The Cuban wood snake is a welcome neighbour, since it is non-venomous and helps to keep down the numbers of rats and other pest rodents. However, when disturbed its defensive response is less appreciated: the snake rolls itself up into a ball and squirts a foul-smelling slime from its cloaca at the intruder. In the forest it preys on frogs and small snakes as well as rodents. Like other boas, this snake does not lay eggs, giving birth to about eight young at a time.

**Mexican burrowing python** (*Loxocemus bicolor*): 1–1.3m (3.25–4.25ft)
Despite its common name, this snake is no more closely related to the true pythons of Africa, Asia, and Australia than it is to the boas that inhabit North and South America. Like other burrowing snakes, this species has a narrow head and slender body to help it wriggle through loose soil and leaf litter. The Mexican burrowing snake lives in the forests of southern Mexico and much of Central America. It feeds on rodents, lizards and reptile eggs. Unlike boas, but like pythons, this species lays eggs in an underground chamber.

**Red-tailed boa** (*Boa constrictor constrictor*): 2.4m (8ft)
This boa is larger than other forms of the snake. It is named after the dark-red saddles on the rear of its body. The snake's coloration helps it to blend in with fallen leaves on the forest floor.

## Brown snake

*Storeria dekayi*

The brown snake of eastern North and Central America occupies a range of habitats, from highland woods to salt-water marshes – in fact, anywhere with plenty of loose stones or other debris for it to hide beneath.

The brown snake spends most of its time underground. It hibernates through winter, often sharing its nest with other snakes, such as smooth green snakes and garter snakes. Mating takes place in spring, soon after the snakes emerge from their nests. The female produces a pheromone to attract males; a male will taste her with his tongue to check that she is the right species before mating.

**Distribution**: Southern Canada to Honduras.
**Habitat**: Rocky areas, wetlands, woodland and cities.
**Food**: Earthworms and other soft-bodied invertebrates, including slugs and snails.
**Size**: 25–52cm (10–20.5in).
**Maturity**: 2 years.
**Breeding**: 10–20 young born in late summer.
**Life span**: 7 years.
**Status**: Common.

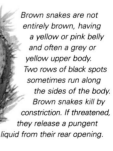

*Brown snakes are not entirely brown, having a yellow or pink belly and often a grey or yellow upper body. Two rows of black spots sometimes run along the sides of the body. Brown snakes kill by constriction. If threatened, they release a pungent liquid from their rear opening.*

## Milksnake

*Lampropeltis triangulum*

Milksnakes range from Colombia and other northern parts of South America to southern Canada. They thrive in a wide range of habitats, including semi-desert and rainforest. They live high up in the Rockies and are also found in edge habitats, such as where farmland meets woodland. The longest milksnakes live in tropical regions. Those that are found in dry or cold areas to the north are barely half the size of their tropical cousins.

Milksnakes are nocturnal hunters, preying upon small rodents and amphibians. During the day, they hide out in leaf litter or under a rotting log, and sometimes in damp garbage. They live and hunt alone, but gather in large groups to hibernate together. Milksnakes mate while in their winter quarters and the females lay their eggs in early summer. They construct nests under rocks, in tree stumps and in other secluded spots.

*Milksnakes are very colourful, with at least 25 different colour variants described so far. Many milksnakes mimic the bold, banded colours of venomous snakes, such as the coral snake, while others have mostly monochrome bodies, usually in tan, black or red. Hatchlings are particularly brightly coloured, but their markings become duller with age.*

**Distribution**: Southern Canada and United States through Central America to Colombia, Ecuador and Venezuela.
**Habitat**: Desert, grassland and forests.
**Food**: Invertebrates, amphibians and small rodents.
**Size**: 0.6–0.9m (2–3ft).
**Maturity**: 3–4 years.
**Breeding**: 15 eggs laid in summer.
**Life span**: 21 years.
**Status**: Common.

## Corn snake

*Elaphe guttata*

Corn snakes range from New Jersey to Florida and across to central Texas. They are most common in the south-eastern United States. These snakes live in woodland and meadows, and they are at also home around rural and suburban settlements.

Corn snakes hunt on the ground, up trees and among rocks. Like other members of the rat snake group, to which they belong, corn snakes have a wide underside that helps them grip onto near vertical surfaces such bark, rubble and even walls. They are not venomous, but when threatened these rattlesnake mimics will waggle their tail and rise up as if to strike. Corn snakes kill their prey – mainly small rodents – by constriction.

This species mates between March and May. Like other snakes, mating is more or less indiscriminate. The females lay eggs in rotting debris by midsummer. The heat produced by the rotting material incubates the eggs, helping them to hatch more quickly. The young corn snakes eat lizards and tree frogs; adults prey on rodents, bats, and birds.

**Distribution**: Eastern United States, from New Jersey to Florida and west into Louisiana and parts of Kentucky.
**Habitat**: Woodland, rocky areas and meadows.
**Food**: Mice, rats, birds and bats.
**Size**: 1–1.8m (3.25–6ft).
**Maturity**: 3 years.
**Breeding**: Between 10 and 30 eggs laid in summer; incubation takes around 60–65 days.
**Life span**: 20 years.
**Status**: Common.

*Corn snakes belong to the rat snake group. Like their relatives, they occur in several colour forms. There are four subspecies, which tend to be more colourful in the south of their range.*

# Common rat snake

*Elaphe obsoleta*

**Distribution**: Eastern United States to Texas and Wisconsin.
**Habitat**: Grassland, forests and suburban areas.
**Food**: Small rodents and birds.
**Size**: 1.2–1.8m (4–6ft).
**Maturity**: Unknown.
**Breeding**: 20 eggs laid in summer.
**Life span**: 20 years.
**Status**: Common.

The common rat snake belongs to a group of three dozen rat snake species, which also includes corn snakes and fox snakes. This particular species is found across the eastern United States, from New England in the north to Texas, Nebraska and Wisconsin in the west. Common rats snakes are most abundant in the warmer parts of their range around the Gulf of Mexico and along the Atlantic coast.

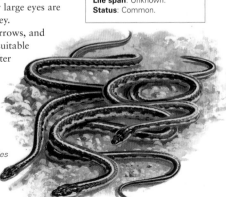

*The common rat snake occurs in three colour forms: almost completely black; yellow with black stripes; and orange with black stripes.*

The common rat snake lives in a variety of habitats, with each of the many subspecies being adapted to a particular habitat type. For example, black rat snakes are found in highland regions, while yellow rat snakes inhabit oak woodlands and human habitations.

Rat snakes do not inject their prey with venom, but kill them by constriction. When threatened, these snakes coil themselves up and rustle dead leaves with their tail to imitate a rattlesnake. They also spread a foul musk with their tail to further discourage any attacker.

**Kirtland's snake** (*Clonophis kirtlandii*): 60cm (23.5in)
This rare snake lives in the Midwest of the United States, being most common in Ohio, Indiana and Illinois. Kirtland's snake is found in marshy areas and flooded fields. Although a water snake, it spends most of its time on dry land. Its diet consists of slugs and earthworms. To escape danger, this snake flattens its body and squeezes under rocks, where it shelters until the threat has passed.

**Regal black-striped snake** (*Coniophanes imperialis*): 30–51cm (12–20in)
This is one of several related species with two thin stripes running from the snout past the eyes and over the head. Black-striped snakes live in the extreme southern tip of Texas and along the Atlantic coast of Mexico and Central America. This species employs a mild venom to subdue prey such as frogs, toads, smaller snakes and mice.

**Amazon egg-eating snake** (*Drepanoides anomalus*): 60cm (24in)
This largely orange, Amazonian snake is most often seen on the edge of forests and in clearings. It mainly feeds on lizards' eggs, which are softer than birds' eggs. Snakes do not have chewing muscles in their jaws, so the eggs must be swallowed whole. Like most snakes, the Amazon egg-eating snake can separate its lower jaw, enabling it to stretch its mouth wide enough to accommodate large food items – sometimes even bigger than the snake's own head.

# Common garter snake

*Thamnophis sirtalis*

This species has one of the widest ranges of any North American snake. At one extreme, the common garter snake lives on the southern shores of Hudson Bay in eastern Canada and survives the long and icy sub-Arctic winters. At the other end of its range, it lives in the humid, subtropical swamps of Florida.

Garter snakes are closely associated with water. They are able swimmers, but search for prey both in and out of water. Garter snakes are active hunters and generally have to pursue their victims. They seek out meals by poking their small heads into nooks and crannies and flushing out prey. The snakes' long bodies allow them to move with great speed, and their large eyes are well suited to tracking fleeing prey.

Garter snakes hibernate in burrows, and many snakes may crowd into a suitable hole. Mating takes place soon after hibernation. In northern regions with short summers, the pressure to mate quickly is very strong, while in the south of the range the snakes have a longer breeding season.

**Distribution**: Southern Canada to Florida.
**Habitat**: Close to water.
**Food**: Worms, fish and amphibians.
**Size**: 65–130cm (25–51in).
**Maturity**: Not known.
**Breeding**: Mate after hibernation.
**Life span**: Unknown.
**Status**: Common.

*Common garter snakes have long bodies and small heads. They are found in a variety of colours, which provide camouflage in different habitats.*

# Rough green snake

*Opheodrys aestivus*

This slender species ranges along the Atlantic coast of North America, from Connecticut to Florida and inland to Kansas and Ohio. Rough green snakes prefer damp areas, including flooded meadows and around the edges of lakes, marshes and streams, and they will occasionally enter the water. They are good climbers and are frequently found several metres above the ground, often in trees and bushes that overhang water, where they are well hidden by their bright green coloration.

Rough green snakes are non-venomous. They do not need to constrict their prey either, since they eat only moths, grasshoppers, caterpillars and other soft-bodied invertebrates, which they simply snatch and swallow. Mating occurs in spring, and in summer the females produce about a dozen elongated, soft-shelled eggs, which are coated in an adhesive gel so that they stick together. The eggs are laid under or in rotting logs and beneath moss or rocks. Several females will often lay their eggs in the same place. The young, which are paler than the adults, hatch from their eggs in August and September.

**Distribution**: Eastern and southern United States.
**Habitat**: Wetlands.
**Food**: Insects and spiders.
**Size**: 71cm (28in).
**Maturity**: 2 years.
**Breeding**: Mates in spring.
**Life span**: Unknown.
**Status**: Common.

*This snake is a vibrant green, with a paler, yellowish underside. The scales are keeled (they have a raised mid-line), a characteristic that differentiates this species from the smooth green snake, its close relative, which is found further north.*

# Racer

*Coluber constrictor*

The racer occurs across southern North America, from the extreme south-west of Canada to Florida. It is also found in parts of Mexico and all the way to Guatemala. This species avoids the driest areas and is absent from large areas of the western United States. There are at least 11 subspecies, all living in distinct ranges with subtle differences in colour.

Racers are often seen basking in sunlit areas such as forest clearings and along hedgerows. Their name suggests that these are fast-moving snakes, but they do not exceed more than 6.5kmh (4mph), which is a fairly average speed for a snake. Because of this, racers never stray far from dense undergrowth, into which they retreat to shelter from danger. If a racer is caught by a predator, the snake will writhe to spread a vile-smelling liquid over its body. Sometimes the writhing is so violent that the snake's tail breaks off, startling or distracting the attacker long enough for the snake to escape.

**Distribution**: Southern British Columbia to Guatemala.
**Habitat**: Grasslands, woodlands and rocky areas.
**Food**: Large insects, frogs, lizards, small snakes, birds and rodents.
**Size**: 86–195cm (34–77in).
**Maturity**: 2–3 years.
**Breeding**: Mating occurs in spring.
**Life span**: 10 years.
**Status**: Common.

Juvenile racers eat insects, spiders, frogs, lizards, small snakes and young rodents. The adult snakes also take bigger animals, including cottontail rabbits, squirrels, turtles and larger snakes. Prey is not constricted, but may be held in a loop or two of the snake's body and pressed to the ground. Large prey are shaken, then chewed with the racer's powerful jaws; smaller food is swallowed alive.

*This species is often called the blue racer, because its dark, shiny scales often have a blue-grey tinge. Jet black, greenish-grey or light brown colorations are also seen. Juvenile racers have brown and red patterns on their bodies, but these fade to grey as the snake gets older.*

# Sharp-tailed snake

*Contia tenuis*

The sharp-tailed snake is a secretive reptile that spends much of its time hidden in burrows or under rocks and logs. It is found mainly in the Sierra Nevada Mountains of western North America. The snake ranges from California (including the mountains of the Coastal Range) through Oregon and Washington state to southern British Columbia.

In the mountains, the sharp-tailed snake occupies a range of habitats. It prefers damp areas that have a large amount of leaf litter and other debris covering the ground. Unusually, it becomes more active in cooler and damper conditions. During the warmer parts of the year, the snake seeks refuge in mammal burrows and under logs. The sharp-tailed snake preys on slugs, and probably also eats snails and small lungless salamanders. Sharp-tailed snakes are most likely to be found after heavy rains, which bring their prey out into the open.

**Distribution**: Western North America.
**Habitat**: Mountains.
**Food**: Slugs.
**Size**: 25–48cm (10–19in).
**Maturity**: Unknown.
**Breeding**: Mating occurs in spring.
**Life span**: Unknown.
**Status**: Locally common.

*The sharp spine on this snake's tail probably helps it to anchor its body when capturing its prey, while its needle-like teeth grip the slugs.*

---

**Mexican hook-nosed snake** (*Ficimia streckeri*): 23–48cm (9–19in)
Identifiable from its a hook-shaped, upturned snout, this snake is found in the southern tip of Texas and in northern Mexico. It inhabits thorn forests in the north of its range and the cloud forests of the Sierra Madre Oriental mountains to the south. The Mexican hook-nosed snake spends most of the time underground, but regularly emerges after heavy rains to feed on spiders and centipedes. It probably lays its eggs in its burrow.

**Night snake** (*Hypsiglena torquata*): 30–66cm (12–26in)
This nocturnal species occurs across the deserts and dry prairies of the south-western United States and northern Mexico. Its range also stretches over the Rockies, into the Great Basin and up to the dry Scablands of the Columbia River Valley of Washington state. Despite its large range, it is rarely encountered. By day, it lies hidden under rocks or in leaf litter, while at night it hunts for frogs and lizards. When the night snake catches prey animals, it holds them using the large teeth at the back of its jaws. The snake's saliva stuns the victims slightly so that they struggle less and are easier to swallow.

**Striped whipsnake** (*Masticophis taeniatus*): 100–180cm (39.5–72in)
Striped whipsnakes live in the deserts and dry woodlands of northern Mexico, western Texas and up to Oregon and Washington, mainly on uplands in the south of their range. These slender, fast-moving snakes eat amphibians, lizards, smaller snakes, birds and eggs. They track down their prey by sight and smell.

# Ring-necked snake

*Diadophis punctatus*

This small North American snake ranges from the maritime provinces of Canada to the Great Lakes, as well as along the coastal plain of the Atlantic seaboard and through the Appalachians to western Texas and northern Mexico. The ring-necked snake is found wherever there are plenty of hiding places.

This species preys on salamanders, frogs, worms and other small animals, plus young snakes of other species. Victims are partially constricted to stop them struggling free, and generally swallowed alive. Active at night, ring-necked snakes spend the day under logs and flat stones. In some places up to 100 snakes will share a refuge.

Mating takes place in spring. The females attract males by releasing pheromones. Eggs are laid in June or July, often in communal nests. The young emerge in August.

**Distribution**: Eastern North America.
**Habitat**: Moist areas.
**Food**: Worms, slugs, lizards, salamanders and newly hatched snakes.
**Size**: 25–76cm (10–30in).
**Maturity**: 2–3 years.
**Breeding**: Eggs laid in summer.
**Life span**: 20 years.
**Status**: Common.

*This snake has a grey or light brown upper body and a yellow or red belly. The ring around the snake's neck may be yellow, cream or orange.*

## Rainbow snake

*Farancia erytrogramma*

The rainbow snake occurs in the south-eastern United States, south and east of the Appalachian Mountains. It is most common in South Carolina and Florida. This species lives near to water, especially on the sandy banks of rivers and streams. It is one of the most aquatic snakes in this part of the world, and is often found among floating plant debris.

Female rainbow snakes lay eggs in July. They make a small dip in the sand and deposit up to 50 eggs, each of which is about 4cm (1.5in) long. The snake stays with her eggs and incubates them for a while before they hatch.

Rainbow snakes are nocturnal hunters that lie in wait in water to ambush their prey. Adult rainbow snakes eat nothing but eels, but younger individuals eat salamanders, small fish, and tadpoles.

The spine at the end of the tail is used in self defence. The spine is pressed into an attacker's flesh, provoking a bite to the tail (the least important part of the reptile's anatomy) instead of a lethal strike at the snake's head.

**Distribution**: Coastal plain of south-eastern United States.
**Habitat**: Sandy areas near water.
**Food**: Eels.
**Size**: 89–167cm (35–66in).
**Maturity**: Unknown.
**Breeding**: Eggs laid in July.
**Life span**: Unknown.
**Status**: Rare.

*This burrowing snake has a cylindrical body with glossy dark scales. There are yellow or red strips along the edges of the belly. The underside is generally red. The spine at the tip of the tail is actually a pointed horny scale.*

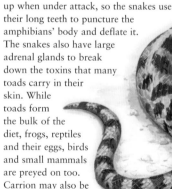

## Western hog-nosed snake

*Heterodon nasicus*

The western hog-nosed snake is found across a swathe of North America, from northern Mexico to southern Canada. It inhabits the Great Plains region between the Mississippi River in the east and the Rocky Mountains in the west. This region is relatively dry, and the hog-nosed snake spends much of its time burrowing through loose, sandy soil, using its snout as a shovel to excavate soil.

Western hog-nosed snakes hibernate between September and March. Mating occurs soon after the snakes emerge in the spring. Females have multiple mates, and initiate the breeding season by moulting their skins and releasing an odour that attracts the males. About a dozen eggs are laid in soil in late summer, and these hatch just before the winter hibernation.

Hog-nosed snakes use their snout to dig up buried toads. Many toads puff themselves up when under attack, so the snakes use their long teeth to puncture the amphibians' body and deflate it. The snakes also have large adrenal glands to break down the toxins that many toads carry in their skin. While toads form the bulk of the diet, frogs, reptiles and their eggs, birds and small mammals are preyed on too. Carrion may also be consumed sometimes.

**Distribution**: Southern Canada to northern Mexico.
**Habitat**: Dry prairies and rocky areas.
**Food**: Mainly toads, plus other small vertebrate prey.
**Size**: 40–100cm (15.5–40in).
**Maturity**: 2 years.
**Breeding**: Eggs laid in summer.
**Life span**: 14 years.
**Status**: Common.

*The snout of this snake is sharply upturned and pointed, so that it resembles a pig's nose. The western hog-nosed snake has three colour forms: brown, grey and tan. These forms closely resemble the eastern and southern hog-nosed species, which also have red forms.*

**Big-headed snail-eating snake** (*Dipsas indica*): 100cm (40in)
As its common name suggests, this species eats snails. It extracts the snail's soft body from the hard shell by first biting the snail's fleshy foot and then hooking its lower jaw inside the shell to draw the snail out. The big-headed snail-eating snake lives in northern South America. It is most often seen in trees and will retreat to high branches when under threat. This species has a larger head than its relatives, and is thought to be able to eat larger snails that most.

**Pine snake** (*Pituophis melanoleucus*): 1.2–2.5m (4–8.25m)
The pine snake is found across western North America, from Mexico to southern Alberta and British Columbia. There is also a smaller population in the eastern United States, ranging from New Jersey to Kentucky and Florida. The pine snake hunts during the day. By night, it rests in the burrow of a tortoise or mammal. Its diet comprises rodents such as gophers – burrowing animals that are common in North America. Consequently, this species is often called the pine-gopher snake.

**Queen snake** (*Regina septemvittata*): 40–93cm (15.5–36.5in)
This brown-green snake lives in rivers and streams across the Midwest and southern US states. It is an excellent swimmer and drops or slips into water to escape danger. Queen snakes eat mainly crayfish. They search rocky stream beds for crayfish that have recently shed an old shell and are still hardening their new one.

# Northern water snake

*Nerodia sipedon*

This species occurs from New England and the Great Lakes through the central United States and south to the Mississippi Delta. Its range also extends down the Atlantic coast as far south as the Carolinas. The snake is found in all freshwater habitats, from swamps to rivers, as well as in the salt marshes of the Outer Banks in North Carolina.

Water snakes are a common sight, since they are active both day and night. They are often observed basking on sand banks and tree stumps, and in other open areas. By night, they may be seen feeding on minnows and other small fish in shallow pools.

Water snakes will bite if cornered, and their saliva contains an anticoagulant. When the saliva enters a bite wound, it prevents the blood from clotting properly, thus weakening the victim.

**Distribution**: New England to Colorado and Louisiana.
**Habitat**: Rivers and wetlands.
**Food**: Small fish, young turtles, salamanders and crustaceans.
**Size**: 56–134cm (22–53in).
**Maturity**: 2–3 years.
**Breeding**: Mating occurs in early summer.
**Life span**: 10 years.
**Status**: Common.

*The body of the northern water snake is patterned in dark grey and reddish brown, with bands crossing behind the neck. When out of water, the pattern often fades as the snake's skin dries.*

# Coachwhip

*Masticophis flagellum*

One of the largest snakes in America, the coachwhip is found across the southern part of the United States and northern Mexico, where it mainly occupies arid habitats. The coachwhip is perhaps the fastest snake in North America, being able to race away over the ground at about 13kmh (8mph). It uses its speed to escape danger, but when foraging, the coachwhip moves slowly so as to not alert its prey, which includes grasshoppers, cicadas and other large insects, as well as lizards, small snakes and rodents. It keeps its head raised off the ground as it hunts, so that it can track prey by smell and sight.

When under threat itself, the coachwhip slithers up trees or into mammal burrows to escape. If cornered, it coils up and vibrates its tail to mimic a venomous rattler. It also bites its attacker repeatedly, often aiming for the face – behaviour that led early observers to believe that the snake killed its prey by whipping them to death.

**Distribution**: Southern United States and northern Mexico.
**Habitat**: Desert, scrubland and open woodland, and rocky areas.
**Food**: Birds, rodents, lizards, other snakes and insects.
**Size**: 90–260cm (35.5–102in).
**Maturity**: Unknown.
**Breeding**: Mating occurs in spring, egg-laying in summer.
**Life span**: 16 years.
**Status**: Lower risk.

*This long, smooth, uniformly brown snake resembles a thick whip. Individuals in the eastern parts of the range, where the soil is less sandy, have darker bodies.*

# VENOMOUS SNAKES

*About 10 per cent of snake species use modified fangs to inject prey with venom. One of the main groups of venomous snakes is the* Viperidae *family – the vipers. There are about 230 viper species worldwide, including the American rattlesnakes and cottonmouths. The world's most venomous snakes, such as taipans, seasnakes and cobras, belong to the* Elapidae. *The most dangerous American elapids are the coral snakes.*

## Sidewinder

*Crotalus cerastes*

Sidewinders are named for their unusual method of locomotion, in which they move sideways across loose ground, such as sand. Many snakes that live in similar habitats also "sidewind". This involves a wave-like undulation of the snake's body, so that only two points are in contact with the ground at any given moment. The snake progresses in a sideways direction across the ground (compared to the orientation of the body), leaving parallel S-shaped tracks in the sand.

Sidewinders are desert rattlesnakes that lie under shrubs and ambush small animal prey at night, using sensory pits below their eyes to detect their victims' body heat. They strike with lightning speed, injecting venom from glands in their upper jaws through their hollow fangs. If the prey escapes a short distance before being overcome, the snake soon locates the corpse with its heat-sensitive pits.

**Distribution**: South-western United States and north-western Mexico.
**Habitat**: Desert.
**Food**: Lizards and rodents.
**Size**: 45–80cm (18–32in).
**Maturity**: Not known.
**Breeding**: Live young born in late summer.
**Life span**: Unknown.
**Status**: Common.

*Sidewinders have wide bodies so that they do not sink into sand. Their tails are tipped with rattles that increase in length as the snakes age. Their heads are flattened and triangular.*

## Western diamondback rattlesnake

*Crotalus atrox*

Western diamondbacks are the largest and most venomous rattlesnakes in North America. The snake's rattle comprises dried segments, or buttons, of skin attached to the tail. The rattle is used to warn predators that the snake gives a poisonous bite. Although it will readily defend itself when cornered, the diamondback would prefer to conserve venom, and enemies, including humans, soon learn to associate the rattle with danger.

Like all rattlesnakes, diamondbacks are not born with a rattle. Instead they begin with just a single button, which soon dries into a tough husk. Each time the snake moults its skin, a new button is left behind by the old skin. The rattle grows in this way until it contains around ten buttons that give the characteristic noise when shaken.

Western diamondbacks have a very potent venom. They kill more people each year than any other North American snake, although this number rarely reaches double figures. The venom can kill even large prey, such as hares, in seconds. Like other rattlesnakes, diamondbacks can sense body heat using sensory pits on their faces.

**Distribution**: Southern United States and northern Mexico.
**Habitat**: Grassland and rocky country.
**Food**: Vertebrate prey including small mammals, birds and lizards.
**Size**: 2m (6.5ft).
**Maturity**: 3–4 years.
**Breeding**: Young born live.
**Life span**: Unknown.
**Status**: Lower risk.

*Diamondbacks are so named because of the brown diamonds, bordered with cream scales, seen along their backs.*

# Western coral snake

*Micruroides euryxanthus*

**Distribution**: South-western United States and northern Mexico.
**Habitat**: Desert.
**Food**: Snakes and lizards.
**Size**: 60–90cm (24–35in).
**Maturity**: 1–2 years.
**Breeding**: Eggs laid in summer.
**Life span**: Unknown.
**Status**: Common.

As they are relatives of cobras and mambas, western coral snakes have a similarly potent venom. Their bright bands warn potential predators that the snakes are very dangerous. The venom will kill most small animals. One in ten humans who leave a bite untreated are overcome by the toxins.

Coral snakes spend much of their time underground. Their thin, cylindrical bodies covered in smooth scales are ideal for this tunnelling lifestyle, and their rounded heads are used for burrowing through soft soil. However, the snakes also venture into the burrows of other animals to seek out resting snakes and lizards, their main source of food. They rarely come to the surface during the day, but may emerge to hunt in the cool of night. Western coral snakes mate in early summer; the females lay eggs about a month later. They are the only venomous snakes in the Americas to lay eggs rather than bear live young.

*The western coral snake, with its brightly banded body, is typical among American coral snakes. Many non-venomous snakes mimic the colours of coral snakes to deter predators.*

---

**Green vine snake** (*Oxybelis fulgidus*): 1.8m (6ft)
This is the largest vine snake in the tropical forests of the Amazon. It is also found throughout Central America and in Mexico. Like all vine snakes, this species is very long and slender, with a sharply pointed nose. The snake's thin green body allows it to move through even the flimsiest of branches unnoticed. The green vine snake sometimes hunts in the trees, but it is usually found in bushes close to the forest floor.

**False coral snake** (*Erythrolamprus aesculapii*): 65–78cm (25.5–31in)
This mildly venomous snake lives in Amazonian South America and Trinidad and Tobago. It mimics the brightly banded colours of highly venomous coral snakes. After one bad experience with a coral snake, a predator learns to avoid all snakes with a similar coloration – including false coral snakes. These snakes even behave like coral snakes when they are attacked, raising and coiling their tail as a warning. False coral snakes use their own mild venom to kill their lizard and snake prey.

**Eyelash pit viper** (*Bothriechis schlegelii*): 45–75cm (17.5–29.5cm)
This small, arboreal pit viper lives in the forests of Central America, as well as in parts of Colombia and Ecuador. It is most active at night, when it preys on tree frogs, lizards and small mammals, detecting prey in the dark using the heat-pits on its face. The snake sometimes hunts during the day, plucking hummingbirds from the air as they feed on flowers. It may also catch nectar-drinking bats at night in the same way. The "eyelashes" of this species are raised scales above the eyes.

# Common mussurana

*Clelia clelia*

Common mussuranas are found across the Amazon Basin and also extend northward into Central America and south to the forests of northern Argentina. They are most commonly spotted in forest clearings and near to swamps. These snakes hunt on the ground but will also swim across rivers.

Mussaranas are mildly venomous. They inject venom into their prey with fangs located at the back of the mouth. These fangs also perform a holding function, keeping prey lodged firmly in the mouth until the venom subdues them. The snakes kill prey by constriction as well. Their diet includes lizards, small mammals and other snakes – many of them venomous. While mussuranas have only a weak venom, they seem to be largely resistant to the stronger venoms of their victims. Mussuranas lay up to 40 eggs in a single clutch, although the clutch size is usually smaller than this.

**Distribution**: Guatemala to Argentina.
**Habitat**: Forests near water.
**Food**: Lizards, snakes, ground birds and small mammals.
**Size**: 1.8–2m (6–6.5ft).
**Maturity**: Unknown.
**Breeding**: Up to 40 eggs laid.
**Life span**: Unknown.
**Status**: Common.

*Mussaranas change colour as they get older. The young snakes are vivid red, while the adults are jet black. As the snake ages, the red changes to brown, then to green and finally to black.*

## Red pipesnake

*Anilius scytale*

This unusual snake is the only member of the *Aniliidae* family. It is included in this section on venomous snakes because its bright stripes convince predators that it is poisonous, however it is actually only mimicking venomous snake species such as the coral snake.

The red pipesnake is found only in the northern half of South America, ranging as far south as Amazonian Peru and southern Brazil. It prefers habitats with rich, moist soil, and uses its cylindrical body to tunnel underground or through deep leaf litter as it hunts subterranean animals, such as rodents and small snakes. Among its chief prey are caecilians and amphisbaenians, or worm lizards, which are common in the tropics of South America. It may also enter the water to find food, and in certain regions eels make up much of its diet.

Being burrowing animals, pipesnakes have small eyes and they are not able to rely on their sense of vision to locate prey. Furthermore, unlike their boa neighbours (and the pythons living elsewhere in the world), they do not have heat-sensitive pits to locate prey. Instead, they rely on their senses of touch and hearing, which are closely linked in snakes, to detect the movements of nearby animals.

**Distribution**: Northern South America.
**Habitat**: Tropical forests.
**Food**: Worm lizards, snakes, rodents and caecilians.
**Size**: 70–110cm (27.5–44in).
**Maturity**: Unknown.
**Breeding**: 3–13 live young.
**Life span**: Unknown.
**Status**: Lower risk.

*Like many other tropical snakes, this species mimics the colours of the highly venomous coral snake. Its bright red and black stripes are rarely seen, however, because the species spends most of its time hidden underground. With dense, solid skull bones, the red pipesnake is well suited to a burrowing lifestyle.*

## Lancehead

*Bothrops atrox*

Lancehead snakes are pit vipers. Like rattlesnakes, they have heat-sensitive pits between the nostrils and eyes. Lanceheads are among the most dangerous snakes in the Americas. Others have more potent venom, but lanceheads are often found living alongside people, feeding on rats and other rodents, so they present more of a hazard. Although they prefer to avoid conflict, when disturbed they bite repeatedly in self defence. Lanceheads are especially common in plantations. In the wild they are found in forests, woodlands and grasslands. In some parts, such as the West Indies, these snakes are called fer-de-lance snakes.

Like many other vipers, male lanceheads tussle with each other over females. The females do not lay eggs but give birth to live young, producing up to 80 babies at a time, although less than half this figure is more usual. The young snakes, which are about 30cm (12in) long, are born with venom glands. Like their parents, they can give a dangerous bite.

Lanceheads ambush their prey. Their camouflaged scales keep them well hidden as they lie in wait. When prey comes near, they strike rapidly and aggressively with their long fangs. Lanceheads are good swimmers, and they may even climb trees to reach their prey.

**Distribution**: Central and northern South America.
**Habitat**: Tropical forests.
**Food**: Small mammals, birds, lizards and smaller snakes.
**Size**: 1–1.5m (3.25–5ft).
**Maturity**: Unknown.
**Breeding**: 10–25 babies born per clutch.
**Life span**: Unknown.
**Status**: Common.

*Lanceheads are named after their arrow-shaped heads, which are typical among vipers. The snake's colouring varies between regions, ranging from grey to brown and green, with "geometric" markings that give effective camouflage. Lanceheads are mainly solitary. Breeding may occur all year round.*

# Copperhead

*Agkistrodon contortrix*

*The copperhead is named after the solid copper of its triangular head. This colour continues along the rest of the body, where it is patterned with brown bands. Young copperheads have a bright yellow tip to the tail, which they use to lure frogs and lizards within striking range.*

Copperheads are also called highland moccasins, being closely related to water moccasins (cottonmouths). Copperheads live across the United States, from Massachusetts to Nebraska in the northwest and Florida and the Big Bend region of the Rio Grande on the Texas–Mexico border.

Copperheads are less aquatic than their close relatives, although they do occasionally enter water. They are most often encountered in rocky areas, especially on hillsides – hence the species' alternative name – but also in lowland regions.

These snakes use heat-sensitive pits on their face to track prey at night. They inject prey animals with a venom that breaks down the victim's blood cells. Although the venom would eventually kill the prey, the snake does not wait for them to die but swallows them as soon as they are sufficiently subdued.

**Distribution**: Eastern United States to western Texas.
**Habitat**: Rocky outcrops in wooded areas.
**Food**: Small rodents, frogs and large insects.
**Size**: 56–135cm (22–53in).
**Maturity**: 2–3 years.
**Breeding**: Mating occurs in spring; about a dozen young are born in autumn.
**Life span**: About 18 years.
**Status**: Common.

**Red-bellied snake** (*Storeria occipitomaculata*): 20–40cm (8–15.5in)
This snake ranges across the whole of the eastern half of the United States, from North Dakota and eastern Texas to southern Florida and Nova Scotia in south-eastern Canada. It is a specialist slug- and snail-hunter. The red-bellied snake lives in damp habitats, such as woodlands and bogs, where its mollusc prey are common. Its westward range is limited by the dry prairies of the Great Plains. The snake hunts by day, locating prey by smell, and is most commonly seen after heavy rainfall. It can reach into a snail's shell with its small head to pull out the soft body, gripping the slimy, struggling prey with its long, backward-curving teeth. This species also has a mild venom that weakens the prey and also reduces the effect of their slimy secretions. Some red-bellied snakes eat only slugs, while others supplement their diet with worms and insect larvae.

**Massasauga** (*Sistrurus catenatus*): 45–100cm (17.5–39.5in)
This massasauga is an unusual rattlesnake that lives along the western side of the Appalachian Mountains, from the Great Lakes to southern Texas. It has nine large scales on its head, a stocky tail and only a small rattle. Massasaugas live in mossy bogs, swamps and woodlands in the north and east of their range. In other areas, they inhabit brushlands and dry grasslands. Massasauga means "great river mouth" in Chippewa, a Native American tongue, reflecting the fact that the snake is often seen in the swamps around river mouths and confluences.

# Cottonmouth

*Agkistrodon piscivorus*

Cottonmouths, or water moccasins, are among the most venomous of all North American snakes. Although they rarely bite people, they are still persecuted and often killed on sight, along with many harmless water snakes, with which they are frequently confused.

These semi-aquatic snakes live in damp habitats near to swamps and streams in the lowland areas of south-eastern United States. The cottonmouth is a nocturnal hunter that catches a wide range of prey, from fish and frogs to baby alligators and small mammals. The snake holds cold-blooded victims in its jaws until the venom takes its effect, but it releases warm-blooded animals after it has delivered a bite. The victim runs away but dies nearby, and the snake locates the body using its sense of smell.

**Distribution**: South-eastern United States, including Florida, North Carolina and the Mississippi Valley and Delta.
**Habitat**: Swamps, streams and other wetlands.
**Food**: Amphibians, fish, birds, reptiles and small mammals.
**Size**: 51–190cm (20–75in).
**Maturity**: 3 years.
**Breeding**: Up to 12 young born in late summer.
**Life span**: Unknown.
**Status**: Common.

*This snake has a striking cotton-white lining to the mouth, which it reveals when it gapes to warn off attackers. Adults are uniformly dark olive or black; juveniles are lighter with a banded patterning.*

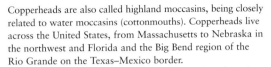

## Timber rattlesnake

*Crotalus horridus*

The range of timber rattlesnakes extends north-east along the Appalachian Mountains to the Adirondacks of New York. Further south, they occur on either side of the mountains to the swampy Atlantic coastal plain between the Carolinas and northern Florida. They are also found across the Mississippi flood plain to eastern Texas and northern Mexico.

In the north and east, timber rattlesnakes live in forested rocky hills. They are often seen coiled on a tree stump waiting for passing prey such as tree squirrels, chipmunks and other rodents. In the south, the snakes are more common in damp meadowlands and swampy areas.

A timber rattlesnake on the lookout for food will remain motionless to avoid being detected by its prey, but it will also freeze when a threat approaches. The attack stance is only adopted at at the last minute, which itself is often enough to surprise the aggressor and deter it from attacking. If the danger persists, the snake raises its head and neck into an S-shape, before striking forward with exposed fangs.

Timber rattlesnakes often gather in large groups to hibernate, sometimes with rat snakes and copperheads. Breeding occurs in spring, when the snakes emerge from their dens. At this time, rival males may tussle with each other, intertwining the rear part of their bodies while they raise the front half and try to push their opponent to the ground. The successful male then mates with the female.

**Distribution**: Eastern United States.
**Habitat**: Forests.
**Food**: Squirrels, mice, chipmunks and small birds.
**Size**: 89–190cm (35–75in).
**Maturity**: 9 years.
**Breeding**: Up to a dozen young born in late summer and autumn.
**Life span**: 30 years.
**Status**: Common.

*In the northern part of their range, timber rattlesnakes are brown, grey and black, while those living further south are pink, tan and yellow. All timber rattlesnakes have black tails. Female timber rattlesnakes only breed every three to four years.*

## Pigmy rattlesnake

*Sistrurus miliarius*

Pigmy rattlesnakes are also called ground rattlers, because they are generally seen slithering along the ground in summer, or sunning themselves in quiet locations. They are rarely found far from a source of water, and they are good swimmers. Pigmy rattlesnakes range from southern Virginia to Oklahoma, and along the coast of the Gulf of Mexico to the Florida Keys.

Pigmy rattlesnakes spend a lot of time underground. However, these nocturnal snakes do not dig themselves but occupy burrows made by small mammals and tortoises. Although they are small, pigmy rattlesnakes often strike when disturbed. Unlike other types of rattler, this species does not rise up into a defensive posture. Instead, it sways its head from side to side before biting. The venom is rarely fatal to humans, but it is powerful enough to cause serious illness – and kill its prey.

Pigmy rattlesnakes hunt small animals such as mice, frogs and other snakes. They also eat insects, spiders, centipedes and newly hatched bird chicks.

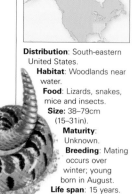

*This is one of the smallest of all rattlesnakes. Its tiny rattle is no louder than a buzzing insect, and cannot be heard from more than a couple of metres away.*

**Distribution**: South-eastern United States.
**Habitat**: Woodlands near water.
**Food**: Lizards, snakes, mice and insects.
**Size**: 38–79cm (15–31in).
**Maturity**: Unknown.
**Breeding**: Mating occurs over winter; young born in August.
**Life span**: 15 years.
**Status**: Common.

# Bushmaster

*Lachesis muta*

This species is the largest venomous snake in the Americas, and also the longest viper in the world. One in every five people bitten by a bushmaster dies, even if they get to hospital in time to be treated with antivenin drugs. This makes the bushmaster one of the deadliest snakes on the planet. Fortunately, it avoids contact with people whenever it can.

Like many other vipers, the bushmaster is an ambush hunter. It lies coiled up in the undergrowth along a trail or at the edge of a clearing, where it waits for small animal prey to wander by. The black-and-tan pattern along its back provides excellent camouflage, and this is another reason why bushmasters are rarely seen. Bushmasters rarely stray from the cover of pristine forests. They are most active at night, being more subdued during daylight. Unlike other vipers in South America, bushmasters lay eggs. Larger females lay more eggs than smaller ones. The female guards the eggs until they hatch.

**Distribution**: Northern South America and Central America.
**Habitat**: Tropical forest and scrubland.
**Food**: Small mammals.
**Size**: 3m (9.75ft).
**Maturity**: About 4 years.
**Breeding**: Up to 20 eggs laid in a burrow.
**Life span**: Up to 20 years.
**Status**: Common.

*The bushmaster is the longest venomous snake in the Americas. The red-brown body is covered in crosses and diamonds, and there are spine-shaped scales on the tail.*

---

**Northern coral snake** (*Micrurus fulvius*): 56–120cm (22–47in)
This is one of two North American species of coral snake. It ranges from North Carolina to Florida and around the Gulf of Mexico to central Mexico. This species is sometimes referred to as the eastern coral snake, to differentiate it from the western coral snake (or Arizona coral snake), which is also found as far north as the United States. Northern coral snakes are found mainly in forests, where they spend most of their time buried in damp soil or in leaf litter. These highly venomous snakes are often mistaken for harmless species that mimic their banded warning patterns.

**Tropical rattlesnake** (*Crotalus durissus*): 1.40m (4.5ft)
This snake, also known as the cascabel, has a greater range than any other rattlesnake. It is found in Mexico and much of Central America. In South America it lives on the edges of the Amazon Basin, from the coastal regions of Colombia and Venezuela to the monsoon forests of eastern Brazil and the scrublands of the Gran Chaco and Mato Grosso in Paraguay and northern Argentina. Tropical rattlesnakes are highly venomous: three-quarters of the people bitten by one of these snakes will die unless they get immediate medical attention. However, an effective antivenin has been developed so the chances of survival are high if treatment is given. Tropical rattlesnakes hunt in darkness, using the heat-sensitive pits on their face to track prey. The females give birth to live young, producing 6–12 offspring at a time.

## Western Amazon coral snake

*Micrurus spixii*

One of the many elapid snakes that live in the Americas, the western Amazon coral snake is a relative of the cobras of Asia and Africa. It is just as deadly as its more famous cousins. In common with all coral snakes, this species advertises that it has dangerous venom by having bright rings round its body. However, as the snake gets older, the black base colour becomes stronger and the red and yellow rings begin to become less vivid.

Western Amazon coral snakes live across the Amazon Basin, from Venezuela to Peru and Bolivia. They inhabit rainforests and can be found resting under logs or other large debris. They are also able to swim.

Their diet consists of other smaller species of snakes and lizards. When threatened, western Amazon coral snakes coil up their body and bury their head under the coils for protection.

**Distribution**: Venezuela to Bolivia.
**Habitat**: Forests.
**Food**: Other snakes and lizards.
**Size**: 1.5m (5ft).
**Maturity**: 2 years.
**Breeding**: Eggs laid in summer.
**Life span**: Unknown.
**Status**: Common.

*The red, black and yellow bands warn that this is a deadly snake. Many non-venomous snakes copy this coloration. In North America the rhyme "red to yellow, kill a fellow; red to black, venom lack" is used to tell true coral snakes apart from their mimics; it does not work in Central or South America, where there are many more coral snake species and mimics.*

# CATS

*Cats belong to the* Felidae *family of mammals. They fall into two main groups. The* Panthera *genus contains the big cats, such as lions and tigers, while* Felis *comprises the small cats, including the domestic cat. The majority of American cats belong to the second group, with the jaguar being the only big cat found on both continents. Most American cats are rarely seen, and some are threatened with extinction.*

## Cougar

*Felis concolor*

*Extremely strong and agile, cougar adults are able to leap more than 5m (16.5ft) into the air. Once they make a kill, their victims are dragged into secluded places and eaten over several days.*

Cougars are also known as pumas, panthers or mountain lions, and have the most widespread distribution of any American species. They live in nearly all habitats, from the mountainsides of the Canadian Rockies to the jungles of the Amazon and the swamps of Florida.

The cougar is the largest of the small cats in America, with males up to 2m (6.5ft) long. They patrol large territories, moving both in the daytime and at night and taking shelter in caves and thickets. Their preferred food is large deer, such as mule deer or elk. They stalk their prey before bringing it down with a bite to the throat, or ambush it from a high vantage point. Cougars live alone, marking their territories with scent and by scraping visual signals in the soil and on trees.

**Distribution**: North, Central and South America from southern Canada to Cape Horn.
**Habitat**: Any terrain with enough cover.
**Food**: Deer, beavers, raccoons and hares.
**Size**: 1–2m (3.25–6.5ft); 60–100kg (132–220lb).
**Maturity**: 3 years.
**Breeding**: Every 2 years; litters of 3 or 4 cubs.
**Life span**: 20 years.
**Status**: Some subspecies endangered.

## Margay

*Felis wiedii*

**Distribution**: Central America and Amazon Basin.
**Habitat**: Tropical forest.
**Food**: Birds, eggs, lizards, frogs, insects and fruit.
**Size**: 46–79cm (18–31in); 2.5–4kg (5.5–8.75lb).
**Maturity**: 1 year.
**Breeding**: Single cub or twins born once a year.
**Life span**: 10 years.
**Status**: Endangered.

Margays are small cats that live in the lush forests of Central and South America. These slender cats spend nearly all of their lives in the tree tops, rarely touching ground. They are active at night, searching through the branches for food, which ranges from small tree-dwelling mammals, such as marmosets, to insects and fruit.

Margays are very acrobatic climbers. They use their long tails to help them balance, and their broad, padded feet give them a good grip on flimsy branches. Margays are unique among cats because they can twist their hind feet right round so they face backwards.

Like most cats, margays live alone, defending large territories from intruders. They do, of course, pair up briefly with mates for breeding, but the males leave the females before litters are born. Breeding takes place throughout the year and most litters have one or perhaps two cubs.

*Margays can climb down tree trunks head-first like squirrels, or hang upside down with the claws on their reversed hind feet embedded in tree bark.*

# Jaguar

*Panthera onca*

*The jaguar is the only big cat in the Americas. It is smaller in length than the cougar, but much bulkier and heavier. Jaguars are usually a tawny yellow with dark rings, but they can also be black.*

Jaguars prefer to live in areas with plenty of water for at least part of the year, although they will stray on to grasslands and into deserts in search of food. They live alone, taking refuge in secluded spots during the day and stalking prey at night. Despite being expert climbers, they hunt on the ground and drag their kills to hideaways before devouring them.

Female jaguars defend smaller territories than males, and a male's territory may overlap those of two or three females. The cats advertise their presence by scenting landmarks with urine or faeces and by scraping marks on tree trunks and rocks. When a female is ready to breed, she will leave her home range and be courted by outside males. Litters usually stay with their mother for about two years.

**Distribution**: South-western United States, Mexico, Central and South America to northern Argentina.
**Habitat**: Forests and swamps.
**Food**: Capybaras, peccaries, caimans and tapirs.
**Size**: 1.1–1.9m (3.5–6.25ft); 36–158kg (80–350lb).
**Maturity**: 3 years.
**Breeding**: Litters of 1–4 cubs born every 2 or 3 years.
**Life span**: 22 years.
**Status**: Lower risk.

---

**Little spotted cat** (*Felis tigrina*): 45–65cm (18–25.5in); 3.5kg (7.75lb)
Tawny coated, with rosette-shaped spots, these cats look similar to, but are smaller than, ocelots and margays. Little spotted cats are rare throughout their range, which extends from the north of Panama southward to northern Argentina. They are found in lowland rainforests and montane cloud forests up to 3,000m (10,000ft), but they may also be seen in drier regions, such as scrub and deciduous forests. Little spotted cats live alone and hunt at night, preying on small mammals, such as rodents, and small birds. In the Brazilian forests, they have also been known to catch small monkeys.

**Northern lynx** (*Felis lynx*): 80–100cm (31.5–39.5in); 5.1–30kg (11.25–66.14lb)
Most of these cats live in Canada, although they spread south into Montana, Idaho and Washington, and there are small populations in New England and Utah. They prefer mature forests with thick undergrowth where they can lurk unseen, but they also venture into open habitats such as tundra. The fur is long, thick and yellow-brown, sometimes with dark spots. The tail is short, with dark rings and a black tip, and the ears are tufted. Lynx hunt at night, finding their food in a defended territory. They stalk prey such as snowshoe hares, rodents and birds, pouncing on their victims when they come within range. They also eat fish. A litter of two or three cubs is produced in early summer. The young are suckled for five months and stay with their mother for a year. The young lynx reach adulthood between the ages of two and three.

# Ocelot

*Felis pardalis*

Ocelots are medium-sized small cats found across most of the American tropics. These agile hunters are most common in the dense jungles of the Amazon Basin, but are also found high on the slopes of the Andes and in the dry shrublands of northern Mexico.

An ocelot's typical day is spent sleeping in the cool of a shady thicket or on a leafy branch, but at night the cat comes out to hunt. Ocelots eat a wide range of animals, including rodents, snakes and even young deer and peccaries if the opportunity arises.

Ocelots are largely solitary animals, although males will maintain social links with a number of females in their local areas. They communicate with quiet mews, which become loud yowls during courtship. In the heart of the tropics, ocelots breed all year round, while at the northern and southern extremes of their range, they tend to mate during the late summer and fall.

*Ocelots used to be hunted for their fur. They are now protected but are still threatened by deforestation.*

**Distribution**: Mexico to northern Argentina.
**Habitat**: Tropical forest.
**Food**: Rodents, rabbits, birds, snakes and fish.
**Size**: 55–100cm (22–40in); 11.5–16kg (25.25–35.25lb).
**Maturity**: 18 months.
**Breeding**: Litters of 2–4 born once a year.
**Life span**: 15 years.
**Status**: Lower risk.

# Bobcat

*Felis rufus*

Bobcats are found throughout North America, except its colder northern fringes. They are especially common in the south-eastern United States, where there is a population of more than one million. Bobcats survive in a range of habitats including forests, semi-deserts, mountains and brush – in fact, anywhere that has plenty of hidden spaces, such as hollow trees, thickets and crevices, in which the cats can make a den.

Bobcat fur varies from brown to tan, often marked with brown or black stripes and spots. In the past, bobcats were widely hunted for their pelts. Although it is still legal to hunt bobcats in some parts of their range, hunting is strictly controlled. Bobcats are solitary animals and most active at night, especially around dawn and dusk. They are good climbers but spend most of their time on the ground, using their exceptional vision, hearing and sense of smell to locate prey in the gloom. Rabbits and hares are favoured prey, but squirrels, chipmunks, rodents and birds are also eaten. In winter, when other prey is scarce, bobcats may hunt deer. Bobcats defend a territory, the size of which depends on the amount of food available in the area. Each cat marks the boundaries of its territory with urine, faeces and oils secreted from an anal gland. A male will control a large territory that overlaps the smaller territories of several females, but he will only interact with them during the mating season, when these normally quiet cats may vocalize with yowling and hissing.

**Distribution**: From southern Canada to southern Mexico.
**Habitat**: Forest, semi-desert, mountains and brushland.
**Food**: Rodents, rabbits, small deer, large ground birds and reptiles.
**Size**: 65–105cm (25.5–41.5in); 4–15 kg (8.75–33lb).
**Maturity**: 8 months.
**Breeding**: Litter of 1–4 babies born once a year.
**Life span**: 12 years.
**Status**: Common.

*Bobcats get their name from their short tails, which are generally only about one-fifth of the animal's overall body length. The tip of the tail and ears are black. Bobcats have hairy tufts on their ears, and sideburn-like tufts the side of the head, which extend from the base of the ears to the jowl.*

# Pampas cat

*Felis colocolo*

*The pampas cat is the most widespread of all South American cats. The colour and patterns of the fur vary greatly across its range. The most conspicuous features are the ears, which are larger and more pointed than those of other American cats of a similar size.*

Pampas cats are native to the pampas grasslands – the South American equivalent of the prairie or steppe – which are found mainly in Argentina, east of the Andes. These cats have also spread south into Argentina's cold and desolate Patagonia region. They are found in the forests of the Andes, too, and can even survive above the tree line. Pampas cats thrive in areas of swamp, but they are equally at home in drier regions, such as the Paraguayan Chaco – an arid shrubland that lies between the pampas and the fringes of the Amazon rainforest. Pampas cats are grey in the high Andes, with reddish stripes and spots. In Argentina, their coats are longer and yellow-brown. Brazilian pampas cats have long hair too, but their fur is also redder. These cats hunt at night for cavies and other small mammals, and also ground-nesting birds, such as tinamous. During the day, pampas cats rest in trees or in hidden dens.

**Distribution**: South America, from Ecuador, Peru and Brazil to southern Argentina.
**Habitat**: Mountains, cloud forest, brushland, woodland and pampas (grassland).
**Food**: Small mammals and ground birds.
**Size**: 57cm (22.5in); 5kg (11lb).
**Maturity**: 2 years.
**Breeding**: Single litter of 2–3 kittens born in summer.
**Life span**: 15 years.
**Status**: Common.

# Jaguarundi

*Felis yagouaroundi*

**Distribution**: Texas to southern Argentina.
**Habitat**: Grassland, shrubland and tropical forest.
**Food**: Small mammals, reptiles, birds, frogs and fish.
**Size**: 77cm (30.5in); 9kg (19.75lbs).
**Maturity**: 2–3 years.
**Breeding**: Single litter of 1–4 cubs born in summer.
**Life span**: 15 years.
**Status**: Common, although rare in North America.

Jaguarundis live in a range of habitats, from arid shrublands and exposed grasslands to steamy jungles and mountain forests up to 3,200m (10,500ft). They are often found near waterways and swamps. With small heads, short legs and long bodies, jaguarundis most resemble the flat-headed cats of South-East Asia. Jaguarundis tend to have unspotted fur, either brownish-grey or reddish in colour. Cubs are sometimes spotted at birth but they lose these markings in their first two years.

In tropical regions, where food is available all year round, jaguarundis may produce two litters per annum. Elsewhere, breeding is confined to summer. When not breeding, they live a secretive and solitary existence. They hunt by day and return to dens at night.

*With their long bodies, dark fur and rounded ears, jaguarundis have a passing resemblance to small mustelid carnivores, such as weasels and otters. This led early zoologists to name them "weasel cats".*

**Kodkod** (*Felis guigna*): 40–50cm (16–20in); 2.2kg (4.75lb)
The kodkod (or guigna) – the smallest cat in the western hemisphere – lives in central and southern Chile and Argentina, in the temperate forests of the low Andes and coastal mountain ranges. Kodkods are arboreal, and typically occur in mature forests with many storeys of growth. Kodkods can survive in agricultural regions and areas of disturbed forest, but they are becoming less common as their primary-forest habitat is destroyed. Kodkods are grey-brown, with several black spots and some black streaks on their head and shoulders. The tail has black rings. Many kodkods are completely black, a condition called melanism. Kodkods hunt at night for tree-living mammals, birds and reptiles. It is possible that kodkods live in social groups, or packs, but very little is known about this. The cats become sexually mature at the age of two.

**Mountain cat** (*Felis jacobita*): 70–75cm (28–30in); 4kg (8.75lb)
Mountain cats, or Andean cats, range from northern Chile and north-western Argentina to southern Peru and Bolivia. They inhabit dry, sparsely vegetated rocky slopes at 3,000–5,000m (9,840–16,400ft). They feed mainly on chinchillas and viscachas, hunting them at night among the rocks and shrubs. Their fur is thick and silver or grey with rust-coloured spots. There are dark stripes on the back, and grey bars on the forelegs and chest. There are brown rings on the thick tail. Mountain cats are often mistaken for pampas cats, but they have a much longer tail, three times the length of the body. The long tail helps the cat to balance as it moves over rocky terrain.

# Geoffroy's cat

*Felis geoffroyi*

Although Geoffroy's cat is sometimes seen in grasslands and savannahs, it prefers denser habitats. It occurs from lowland Amazon rainforests up to 3,500m (11,500ft) in the forests of the high Andes. Being primarily a forest dweller, Geoffroy's cat is an expert climber. It it also a good swimmer, and it often lives close to marshes and swamps.

The male cat controls a home range that encompasses the territories of several females, and he will breed with most of the females in that area. Smaller, weaker males cannot secure a territory, and usually do not reproduce.

This nocturnal cat hunts in the trees, on the ground and in water, taking frogs and fish as well as lizards, birds and small mammals. It will even hang upside down under branches to get at hard-to-reach prey.

**Distribution**: South America; southward from Bolivia and central Brazil to Patagonia.
**Habitat**: Scrubland, forests, open woodland and marshes.
**Food**: Birds, fish, amphibians, reptiles and small mammals.
**Size**: 54cm (21.5in); 4 kg (8.75lb).
**Maturity**: 18 months.
**Breeding**: Single litter of 1–4 cubs born in late summer.
**Life span**: 15 years.
**Status**: Common.

*No larger than a domestic cat, Geoffroy's cat is small for a wild species. The tail is about half the length of the rest of the body. The coat is covered in black spots for camouflage.*

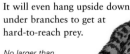

# DOGS

*Domestic dogs belong to the* Canidae *family, which includes wolves (from which they are descended), foxes and jackals. Most types of wild canid live in large family groups called packs. Dog societies are very complex, because the animals must cooperate to survive, especially during winter. The dogs hunt together and take it in turns to care for the young.*

## Maned wolf

*Chrysocyon brachyurus*

The maned wolf lives in areas of swamp and open grassland in central South America, east of the Andes. Its name comes from a dark swathe of hair on its nape and along its spine. The hairs in this mane stand erect when the animal is threatened.

*Maned wolves have fox-like coloration, with a reddish-brown coat of longish fur. These canids are omnivorous, supplementing their diet with fruit.*

Maned wolves form monogamous pairs throughout their lives. Males and females share territory and have dens hidden inside thick vegetation. Most of the time they stay out of each other's way, hunting alone at night. The pair only spend time together during the breeding season at the end of winter. Both parents help to raise the litter, regurgitating food at the den for the young to feed on.

Unlike other wolves, which run down their prey, maned wolves stalk their victims more like foxes. Despite having very long legs, maned wolves are not great runners. Instead, their height allows them to peer over tall grasses in search of prey.

**Distribution**: Central and eastern Brazil, eastern Bolivia, Paraguay, northern Argentina and Uruguay.
**Habitat**: Grassland.
**Food**: Rodents, other small mammals, birds, reptiles, insects, fruit and other vegetable matter.
**Size**: 1.2–1.3m (4–4.25); 20–23kg (44–51lb).
**Maturity**: 1 year.
**Breeding**: Monogamous pairs produce litters of 2–4 cubs.
**Life span**: 10 years.
**Status**: Lower risk.

## Grey wolf

*Canis lupus*

*Grey wolves howl to communicate with pack members over long distances.*

All domestic dogs are descended from grey wolves, which began living alongside humans many thousands of years ago. Grey wolves are the largest dogs in the wild, and they live in packs of about ten individuals. A pack has a strict hierarchy, with a male and female "alpha pair" in charge. The alpha dogs bond for life and are the only members of the pack to breed. The rest of the pack is made up of the alpha pair's offspring.

In summer, pack members often hunt alone for small animals such as beavers or hares, while in winter, the pack hunts together for much larger animals. Grey wolves are strong runners and can travel 200km (125 miles) in one night. They generally detect prey by smell and chase them down, taking turns to take a bite at the faces and flanks of their victims until they collapse from exhaustion.

**Distribution**: Canada and some locations in the United States and Europe, and across most of Asia.
**Habitat**: Tundra, pine forest, desert and grassland.
**Food**: Moose, elk, musk ox and reindeer.
**Size**: 1–1.6m (3.25–5.25ft); 30–80kg (66–175lb).
**Maturity**: 22 months.
**Breeding**: Once per year.
**Life span**: 16 years.
**Status**: Vulnerable.

# Kit fox

*Vulpes macrotis*

**Distribution**: Western United States.
**Habitat**: Desert and scrub.
**Food**: Rodents, pikas, insects and fruit.
**Size**: 38–50cm (15–19.5in); 1.9–2.2kg (4.25–4.75lb).
**Maturity**: 1 year.
**Breeding**: Litters of 4–5 cubs.
**Life span**: 15 years.
**Status**: Vulnerable.

Kit foxes live in the dry desert and scrub areas of the high plateaux and valleys beside the Rocky Mountains in the United States. They generally live in breeding pairs, but social bonds are quite loose and pairs often split. The female does not leave her den – made in a disused burrow – while she is suckling her litter of four or five cubs. During this time she relies on the male for food, which is generally small rodents and rabbits, insects and fruit.

After three or four months, the young are strong enough to travel with their parents to other dens in their territory. A kit fox family's territory overlaps widely with those of other groups in the area. The size of the territory depends on the climate. Desert territories have to be large to supply enough food for the family. The kit fox is very similar in appearance and behaviour to the swift fox (*Vulpes velox*) which lives on the great plains farther east. It is possible that hybridization takes place where the ranges of these two dogs overlap.

*The kit fox's large ears are lined with blood vessels that radiate heat to cool the animal down in hot desert climes.*

**Red wolf** (*Canis rufus*): 100–130cm (39.5–51in); 20–40kg (44–88lb)
Red wolves once roamed over mountains, forests and wetlands across the whole of the south-eastern United States. Today they are critically endangered, and limited to the south-eastern tip of Texas and south-western Louisiana. The red wolf is smaller than its more common northern relative, the grey wolf, with longer legs and ears and shorter fur. It gets its name from the grizzled red hair on its underside; the rest of the fur is dark grey or black. Red wolves live in packs. Only the dominant male and female pair breed. Other pack members help to raise the young and find food. Red wolves hunt mainly at night, often alone. They prey on raccoons, rabbits, pigs, rice rats, nutria, and muskrats. When hunting together, they attack white-tailed deer.

**Swift fox** (*Vulpes velox*): 38–53cm (15–21in) 1.8–3kg (4–6.5lb)
This aptly named fox can run at 50kmh (30mph) when pursuing prey or fleeing predators. Once found from the Great Plains in western Canada to Texas, swift foxes became extinct in Canada in the 1930s. A tiny population has since been reintroduced. Today the largest populations live in Colorado, Kansas, New Mexico and Wyoming. The fox's decline was caused by the loss of its prairie habitat to farming. The swift fox is the smallest North American wild dog, about the size of a house cat. Its fur is light grey or tan, with white areas on the throat and chest; the bushy tail has a black tip. Between two and six pups are produced in a single litter. Adults begin to breed between the ages of one and two.

# Bush dog

*Speothos venaticus*

Bush dogs live in wetlands and flooded forests in highly social packs of about ten dogs. Pack members hunt together, chasing ground birds and rodents. As with other pack-hunting dogs, the victims – which in this case include capybaras, agoutis and rheas – are often much bigger than the dogs themselves. These dogs are believed to be expert swimmers, sometimes diving into water in pursuit of their prey.

Bush dogs are diurnal (active during the day) and keep together by making high-pitched squeaks as they scamper through the dense forest. As night falls, the pack retires to a den in a hollow tree trunk or abandoned burrow. Little is known about the social system within the packs, but it is likely that there is a system of ranking.

Litters of two or three young are produced during the rainy season. The females only become ready to breed when they come into contact with male bush dogs.

**Distribution**: Northern South America, east of the Andes.
**Habitat**: Forests and swampy grasslands.
**Food**: Ground birds and rodents.
**Size**: 57–75cm (22.5–29.5in); 5–7kg (11–15lb).
**Maturity**: 1 year.
**Breeding**: Litter of 2–3 cubs born in rainy season.
**Life span**: 10 years.
**Status**: Vulnerable.

*Bush dogs are unusual members of the dog family, looking more like weasels or mongooses than other dogs.*

## Coyote

*Canis latrans*

Coyotes live throughout North America and Central America, from the humid forests of Panama to the treeless tundra regions of Canada and Alaska. They are most common in the unpopulated desert areas of the south-western United States and northern Mexico.

These dogs look a little like small grey wolves. They are less likely to form packs than wolves, and are typically found alone, in pairs or in small family groups. Coyotes may dig their own den or enlarge the burrow of another animal. They are primarily nocturnal, being most active around dawn and dusk, but they do sometimes hunt during the day. They can reach speeds of up to 64kmh (40mph) when chasing swift jackrabbits and other prey.

These dogs are adaptable opportunistic feeders, and they are able to survive in farmland and suburban regions. They are increasingly coming into conflict with human communities expanding into the desert, which see them as pests.

*Coyote fur varies from grey to yellow. The head and legs may have reddish hair on them. A black line runs along the back. The bushy tail is about half as long as the rest of the body. Coyotes are much smaller than wolves, but significantly larger than foxes.*

**Distribution**: From Canada and the United States through Mexico to Panama.
**Habitat**: Desert, forest and tundra.
**Food**: Small mammals, such as rabbits, ground squirrels and mice, occasionally birds, reptiles and large invertebrates; carrion and some plant matter.
**Size**: 76–100cm (30–39.5in); 8–20kg (17.75–44lb).
**Maturity**: 1 year.
**Breeding**: Single litter of 6 pups born in early summer.
**Life span**: 10–14 years.
**Status**: Common.

## Crab-eating fox

*Dusicyon thous*

The crab-eating fox inhabits woodland and grassland in the highlands around the Amazon Basin, although it is also found on the fringes of the region's lush lowland rainforests. It ranges from Columbia and Venezuela in the north to Paraguay, Uruguay and Argentina in the south.

Crab-eating foxes feed on both coastal and freshwater crabs, but the diet of this omnivorous animal also encompases a wide range of other foods, including small mammals, insects, fruits and carrion. These nocturnal foxes locate crabs in the dark by listening for the rustling they make as they move through thick vegetation.

The foxes live in male-female pairs, and these pairings persist until one partner dies. Although they travel and den in pairs, they hunt alone. The pair will defend a territory, which grows during the dry season as food becomes more scarce. During this time of year, the territories of breeding pairs overlap considerably. Breeding may take place at any time of the year, although it is most common in late summer. The pups are weaned by about 90 days. Both parents share the task of finding food for the young and guarding them until they become independent, which occurs some five to six months after birth.

**Distribution**: South America; highlands around the Amazon Basin.
**Habitat**: Woodland and grassland.
**Food**: Land crabs, small mammals, birds, insects and other invertebrates, fruit and carrion.
**Size**: 60–70cm (23.5–27.5in); 6–7kg (13.25–15.5lb).
**Maturity**: 1 year.
**Breeding**: Single litter of 3–6 pups born in January or February.
**Life span**: 10 years.
**Status**: Common.

*Crab-eating foxes have a bodyform typical of foxes, although their legs are a little shorter than most. The fur is grey to brown, with a pale underside and some red on the face, ears and legs. The tips of the ears, legs and tail are black.*

**Arctic fox** (*Alopex lagopus*): 55cm (21.5in); 4kg (8.75lb)
The Arctic fox inhabits tundra, pine forests and mountain slopes in northern Canada and Alaska. It is also found in Greenland, Iceland, Siberia and Scandinavia. Arctic foxes are scavengers, taking whatever they can find. In summer they feed on small mammals, such as lemmings, but in winter they must diversify their diet to survive, eating invertebrates, berries, carrion, and even the faeces of other animals. While the land is iced over they rely on marine animals, such as sea birds and fish, for their meat. Arctic foxes have two colour forms: those in exposed tundra regions are more or less white all year around, becoming paler in winter; those in less-exposed areas have pale brown fur in summer, which becomes tinged with pale blue in winter.

**Culpaeo** (*Dusicyon culpaeus*): 90cm (35.5in); 10kg (22lbs)
Culpaeos, or coloured foxes, live from Ecuador to Chile, and even extend to Tierra del Fuego in Argentina. They are primarily found west of the Andes, where they live in pampas grasslands and high deciduous forests. The fur is a variety of colours, ranging from red to grey. Culpaeo females live in large sisterhoods that cooperate to raise the young of one dominant female. Males are solitary, but join the group to help care for the young in the breeding season. Pups are born in spring, in litters of about four. At a week old they start to establish a dominance hierarchy by fighting over milk and food. The ranking among the females established at this time lasts into adulthood.

## Hoary zorro

*Dusicyon vetulus*

The hoary zorro lives in the tall-grass pampas and sparsely wooded savannahs of Brazil's Matto Grosso and Minas Gerais regions in the south of the country. It is referred to as the zorro – Spanish for fox – to avoid confusion with the royal, or hoary, fox (*Vulpes cana*) of South-east Asia.

Hoary zorros have short coats of grey and silver hairs. They shelter in burrows deserted by other animals, such as armadillos. These foxes hunt small mammals and birds, but much of their diet consists of insects such as grasshoppers and termites, especially in dry periods. Since the teeth are used for crunching small animals rather than ripping flesh, they are not as sharp as those of other foxes, and the grinding molar teeth are wider. Like many foxes, hoary zorros live in male-female pairs, with both parents raising the young.

*The word "hoary" refers to the white hairs that are mixed in with the fox's grey coat, which produces a grizzled effect.*

**Distribution**: Southern Brazil.
**Habitat**: Pampas and savannah grasslands.
**Food**: Small mammals, birds and insects.
**Size**: 59–64cm (23–25in); 4kg (8.75lb).
**Maturity**: 1 year.
**Breeding**: 2–4 pups produced in autumn.
**Life span**: Unknown
**Status**: Unknown.

## Grey fox

*Vulpes cinereoargenteus*

Grey foxes are found in woodlands and forests, mostly in the southern half of North America. Their range continues down the western side of Central America to northern Colombia and Venezuela. They are not found in the Rockies and other mountain ranges of the western United States and Canada, nor in the highlands of Central America. They are also absent from the Great Plains region.

Male grey foxes are slightly larger than females. A mature fox has only one sexual partner during each breeding season, the timing of which depends on the location. For example, Canadian grey foxes breed in April, while those in the southern United States mate in February. The family group usually stays together until autumn, but the young will occasionally stay with their parents until the following breeding season to help raise the next litter. Grey foxes are unusual for dogs because they climb trees in search of prey such as insects and birds. They also eat fruits.

**Distribution**: Southern Canada to Venezuela.
**Habitat**: Woodland.
**Food**: Rabbits, other small mammals and birds.
**Size**: 80–112cm (31.5–44in); 3.6–6.8kg (8–15lb).
**Maturity**: 1–2 years.
**Breeding**: About 4 pups born in spring.
**Life span**: 8 years.
**Status**: Common.

*Grey foxes have the bushy tail and large ears that typify foxes. The features that distinguish them from other foxes are the grizzled underparts and black tip to the tail.*

# BEARS

*The world's largest land carnivore, the Kodiak bear – a subspecies of brown bear – lives in North America. It is a huge, hairy animal that can grow to 3m (10ft) tall. Despite their immense size and strength, bears are generally not the vicious predators many people think they are. Most eat more plant food than meat, and they are usually shy beasts, preferring to stay away from humans.*

## Polar bear

*Ursus maritimus*

**Distribution**: Arctic Ocean to southern limits of floating ice, and Hudson Bay.
**Habitat**: Ice fields.
**Food**: Seals, reindeer, fish, seabirds and berries.
**Size**: 2–2.5m (6.5–8.25ft); 150–500kg (330–1,100lb).
**Maturity**: 6 years.
**Breeding**: 1–4 cubs born every 2–4 years.
**Life span**: 30 years.
**Status**: Vulnerable.

*Polar bears have proportionally longer necks than other types of bear so that they can lunge after seals and other aquatic prey.*

Polar bears are semi-aquatic animals. They live on the fringes of the vast ice fields that surround the North Pole, where they feed on seals and other marine animals. The bears may cover large distances in search of food, sometimes coming far inland or swimming for several kilometres across open water. Their feet have hairy soles to keep them warm and give them a good grip on the ice. Their forefeet are also very broad, making them good paddles in water.

The bears' snow-white coats help them to blend in with their surroundings and stay hidden from their prey. The staple food of polar bears is the ringed seal. The bears either wait beside holes in the ice for seals to surface, or sneak up on them across the ice. They sometimes dig down into seal dens beneath the surface snow to get at new-born pups.

Polar bears put on a lot of weight in summer because they have less opportunity to feed in winter. They often take shelter from extreme weather in underground dens. Pregnant females sleep inside large dens for long periods during the winter months, before giving birth to their pups in spring. The young stay with their mothers for two years.

## Brown bear

*Ursus arctos*

Brown bears live in many parts of the northern hemisphere, and although they belong to a single species, they look rather different from place to place. For example, the brown bears in Europe and Asia are smaller and darker than their American cousins. In North America, there are two subspecies of brown bear: Kodiaks and grizzlies.

Brown bears make their homes in cold places, such as northern forests, mountains and barren tundra. They feed on a range of fruits, plants and small animals. Only grizzlies regularly attack large animal prey, which may include deer and even smaller black bears.

Brown bears are generally solitary, although they may gather in groups around large food supplies, such as schools of salmon beneath waterfalls. As winter approaches, the bears dig themselves dens for semi-hibernation. Although they sleep during most of the winter, they often come out of the den for short periods between sleeps. Mating takes place in early summer. The female gives birth in spring, and her cubs stay with her for at least two years.

*Brown bears have humps between their powerful shoulders, and longer claws than most other bears.*

**Distribution**: North America, Siberia, Europe and Caucasus Mountains.
**Habitat**: Tundra, alpine meadows and forests.
**Food**: Salmon, grasses, roots, mosses, bulbs, insects, fungi, rodents, deer, mountain sheep and black bears.
**Size**: 1.7–3m (5.5–10ft); 100–700kg (220–1,540lb).
**Maturity**: 6 years.
**Breeding**: 1–4 cubs born every 3–4 years.
**Life span**: 25–30 years.
**Status**: Endangered in some places.

# American black bear

*Ursus americanus*

**Distribution**: Alaska and Canada, and patchily throughout parts of the United States, from New England to Tennessee, Florida, Mississippi and western states. Also in northern Mexico.
**Habitat**: Forests.
**Food**: Fruits, nuts, grass, roots, insects, fish, rodents and carrion.
**Size**: 1.3–1.8m (4.25–6ft); 100–270kg (220–595lb).
**Maturity**: 6 years.
**Breeding**: 1–5 cubs born every 2 years.
**Life span**: 25 years.
**Status**: Lower risk.

American black bears are the smallest bears in North America. They live in the conifer forests of Canada and a few wilderness areas as far south as Mexico. They share these forests with grizzly bears and are sometimes eaten by them. Their main defence against this is to climb trees out of the reach of the less agile grizzly.

Black bears are most active at night. Three-quarters of what they eat is plant matter, with small animals, such as fish and rodents, making up the rest. Like other bears, black bears semi-hibernate through the winter in dens under fallen trees or in burrows. Although they sleep heavily, they often wake through the winter, going on excursions during breaks in the severe winter weather.

Although black bears generally forage for food alone, they will congregate around a large source of food. In general they stay away from each other, especially unknown bears. In the middle of summer, males and females come together for short periods. The male leaves soon after mating and cubs are born at the end of winter, while the mother is still in her winter den. The young stay with their mother until at least two years old, when they are usually driven away by the aggression of males courting their mother.

*American black bears vary in coloration from black to dark or reddish-brown and pale tan. They differ from grizzlies in several respects, including their shorter fur and the lack of a shoulder hump. Black bears also have shorter legs and claws, which makes them far better tree climbers than grizzlies. The size of American black bears depends to some extent on the quality of food available in their locality.*

# Spectacled bear

*Tremarctos ornatus*

**Distribution**: Northern Andes Mountains, including Colombia, Ecuador, Peru, Bolivia and into Chile.
**Habitat**: Tropical mountain forest and alpine grassland.
**Food**: Fruits, epiphytes, bamboo hearts, corn, rodents and insects.
**Size**: 1.2–1.8m (4–6ft); 60–175kg (132–385lb).
**Maturity**: Unknown.
**Breeding**: 2 cubs born every 2–3 years.
**Life span**: 25 years.
**Status**: Vulnerable.

The spectacled bear is the only species of bear in South America. It lives mainly in the lush, high-altitude forests that clothe the slopes of the Andes Mountains from Colombia southward as far as northern Chile.

Spectacled bears are active at night, especially during the twilight hours. During the day they shelter in caves, under tree roots or on tree trunks. They are expert climbers and spend a great deal of time foraging in trees. Once up trees, the bears often build feeding platforms from broken branches. They use these platforms to reach more food.

The spectacled bear eats mainly fruit, and it will travel through the forest collecting ripe fruits. During periods when ripe fruit is unavailable, the bears eat epiphytes – plants that grow on other plants – called bromeliads, feasting on the soft edible hearts of the plants.

Being a tropical species, breeding occurs all year round. Pairs stay together for a few weeks after mating, and the cubs are born seven months later. The cubs stay with their mother for at least two years before being chased away by adult males seeking to mate with their mother.

*Spectacled bears are so-named because of the large white circles or semi-circles of whitish fur around their eyes.*

# SMALL CARNIVORES

*Most small carnivores belong to the* Mustelidae *family. The mustelids are a diverse group, including otters, martens and badgers, which are adapted to aquatic, arboreal and subterranean lifestyles respectively. The world's largest and most successful mustelids live in the Americas, where they are found from the icy north to the humid tropics.*

## Striped skunk

*Mephitis mephitis*

The striped skunk is well known for the foul-smelling spray it produces to ward off attackers. This spray comes out of two tiny apertures inside the anus. The discharge, known as musk, is squirted in spray form or as a directed arc of droplets.

The skunk will only spray when it has exhausted all other defensive tactics. These strategies include arching its back, holding its tail erect and stamping its feet. If these fail, the skunk will twist its body into a U-shape – so that its head and tail are facing the attacker – and release its musk. The musk, which can be smelled by humans over a mile away, causes discomfort to the eyes of an enemy.

Striped skunks are most active at night, foraging for food under the cover of thick vegetation. They spend the day in sheltered places, such as disused burrows. During the winter, skunks hibernate in their dens, staying underground for between two and three months. Mating takes place in springtime. Litters of up to ten young are born in summer.

*The striped skunk is characterized by the broad white stripes that extend from the top of its head to the tip of its tail.*

**Distribution**: North America.
**Habitat**: Woods, grasslands and deserts.
**Food**: Rodents, other small vertebrates, insects, fruits, grains and leaves.
**Size**: 28–30cm (11–12in); 0.7–2.5kg (1.5–5.5lb).
**Maturity**: 1 year.
**Breeding**: 1–10 young born every summer.
**Life span**: 6 years.
**Status**: Common.

## American mink

*Mustela vison*

American mink are small carnivores that live close to water, where they feed on small aquatic animals. They originally came from North America, but were brought to Europe and Asia to be farmed for their fine fur. They have since escaped into the wild and are now a common pest. They are also competition for the similar, but very rare, European mink.

Mink prefer to live in areas with plenty of cover. Their river-bed dens are generally deserted burrows made by other river mammals, but mink will dig their own burrows if necessary. Mink are active at night and dive into water to snatch their prey. They live alone and will defend their own stretches of riverbank against intruders. Two months after mating a litter of up to five young is born in a dry underground nest lined with fur, feathers and leaves. The young begin to fend for themselves in autumn.

*Mink are known for their luxurious fine fur, which is used for clothing. Several domestic varieties of mink have been bred, each with different-coloured fur.*

**Distribution**: North America. Introduced to northern Europe.
**Habitat**: Swamps and near streams and lakes.
**Food**: Small mammals, fish, frogs and crayfish.
**Size**: 33–43cm (13–17in); 0.7–2.3kg (1.5–5lb).
**Maturity**: 1–1.5 years.
**Breeding**: 5 young born in late spring.
**Life span**: 10 years.
**Status**: Common.

# Wolverine

*Gulo gulo*

Wolverines are giant relatives of weasels. As well as being found in the conifer forests of North America, these mustelids occur in northern Europe and Siberia, where they are known as gluttons due to their catholic feeding habits.

Wolverines are generally nocturnal, but will forage by day if they need to. Their diet varies throughout the year. In summer, they feed on small animals, such as rodents and ground-living birds, and readily feast on summer fruits. In winter, when most other carnivores are hibernating, wolverines may tackle bigger prey, such as deer. The wolverines' wide feet act as snowshoes and allow them to walk over deep snow; deer, by contrast, flounder in the snow and find it difficult to escape from the wolverines. Wolverines mate in early summer and the young are born in underground dens the following spring. They leave their mothers in the autumn.

*Wolverines have large heads and heavily built bodies. Their dense coats have hairs of different lengths to prevent winter snow and ice from getting too close to the skin and causing heat loss.*

**Distribution**: Canada, northern United States, Scandinavia and Siberia.
**Habitat**: Tundra and conifer forest.
**Food**: Carrion, eggs, rodents, berries, deer and sheep.
**Size**: 65–105cm (25–41in); 10–32kg (22–70lb).
**Maturity**: 2–3 years.
**Breeding**: Litter of 2–4 born in early spring every 2 years.
**Life span**: 10 years.
**Status**: Vulnerable.

**Eastern spotted skunk** (*Spilogale putorius*): 29cm (11.5in); 600g (21.25oz)
Eastern spotted skunks live throughout the eastern United States. They range as far west as Minnesota and south into Mexico, and are especially common in the mid-western states and the Appalachian Mountains. These skunks prefer woodland or other habitats with plenty of cover, such as areas of tall grass and even rocky regions. They dig burrows, possibly expanding a den abandoned by another animal. Several skunks will occupy each burrow. The eastern spotted skunk has short legs, so its body is held close to the ground. The head is small relative to the body size. This skunk is named after the spots on its head and rear.

**Pygmy spotted skunk** (*Spilogale pygmaea*): 22cm (8.5in); 500g (17.5oz)
The pygmy spotted skunk is restricted to a small area of woodland along Mexico's Pacific coast, where it lives in burrows or in trees. The black coat has white stripes over the back, which break into spots on the rump. Two large scent glands beside the anus spray a cloud of foul-smelling droplets to scare off predators. This is a tactic of last resort: the skunk's initial response to a threat is to lift its tail and make itself appear larger by raising its outer hairs. Then it stands on two legs and marches toward the attacker. Only if this is unsuccessful will it release the spray. Pygmy spotted skunks mate between February and March, and their young are born in May. They hunt at night, preying on smaller mammals, birds and reptiles. They also eat carrion, insects and fruits, and may climb trees to reach birds' eggs.

# American badger

*Taxidea taxus*

American badgers are tough animals that live in the open country in the Great Plains region of North America. They are expert burrowers and use this skill to dig out their preferred foods – rodents, such as prairie dogs and ground squirrels. They rest in their own burrows during the day and emerge to feed at night. During the coldest weeks of the year, American badgers do not hibernate, but they sleep underground for several days at a time.

The badgers may bury some of their food so that they can eat it later, or even dig holes big enough for both themselves and their prey to fit into. American badgers and coyotes are known to hunt together in teams. The coyotes sniff out the buried prey and the badgers dig them out. Both parties then share the food.

Mating occurs in summer and early autumn, and births take place in the following spring. The young leave home after two months.

*American badgers have a white stripe running from the nose along the back. In northern badgers the stripe runs to the shoulders, while on those in the south of the range it runs all the way along the back.*

**Distribution**: Central and southern North America.
**Habitat**: Dry, open country.
**Food**: Rodents, birds, reptiles, scorpions and insects.
**Size**: 40–70cm (16–28in); 4–12kg (9–26.5lb).
**Maturity**: Females 4 months; males 1.3 years.
**Breeding**: 1–5 young born in spring.
**Life span**: 14 years.
**Status**: Lower risk.

## Sea otter

*Enhydra lutris*

Sea otters live in the cold coastal waters around the northern Pacific Rim. They do not need to come on to land to survive, but often do. Unlike other marine mammals, sea otters do not have thick blubber under their skins for insulation. Instead, they rely on a layer of air trapped by their soft fur to insulate them against the cold. Pollution, such as oil in the water, can reduce the fur's ability to trap air, and otters may die of hypothermia as a result.

The otters spend a minute or two at a time underwater, collecting food such as shellfish and urchins. They then float on their backs to feed. They smash the hard shells against stones to get at the soft meat inside, using their chests as tables.

Sea otters are active during the day. At night they wrap themselves in kelp before going to sleep to prevent themselves from floating away. They sometimes put their forepaws over their eyes while sleeping.

Sea otters live alone and only tolerate each other when mating. A male will defend his territory, but fights are unusual, since most disputes are settled by splashing and vocal contests. Breeding occurs all year round. Pups are carried on the female's chest for about two months, when they begin to feed themselves. They are independent by the time they are six months old.

**Distribution**: Northern Pacific coasts from California and Baja, Mexico, to Japan. Sea ice limits their northern range.
**Habitat**: Temperate coastal waters up to 20m (60ft) deep and less than 1.6km (1 mile) from shore.
**Food**: Fish and shellfish, such as sea urchins, abalones, crabs and molluscs.
**Size**: 1–1.2m (3.25–4ft); 15–45kg (33–99lb).
**Maturity**: Females 4 years; males 6 years.
**Breeding**: Single pup every 1–3 years.
**Life span**: 20 years.
**Status**: Threatened.

*Sea otter fur comprises 100,000 hairs per 1sq cm (0.15sq in), making it the densest fur of any mammal. This keeps the animal warm in the cold ocean. The hind feet are webbed and flipper-shaped.*

## Giant otter

*Pteronura brasiliensis*

The giant otter is the largest mustelid in the world, although it is not as heavy as the sea otter. This semi-aquatic mammal inhabits the tropical river basins of South America. It lives in groups of about six, each communicating with chirping sounds. Generally, the group comprises an adult pair and their offspring of various litters. Each group controls its own stretch of stream, preferring those areas with plenty of cover.

The giant otter swims at high speed by waving its tail and body up and down, using its webbed feet to steer. On land it is far less agile, and is often seen sitting grooming itself. Giant otters are diurnal – only active during the day. They catch prey in their mouths and hold it in their forepaws to eat it on the shore. During the dry season, the otter groups are restricted to small areas of water, but when the rains come to flood the forest, the otters can roam over larger areas. Little is known about the mating habits of giant otters, other than that the young stay with their parents for a few years before reaching adulthood.

**Distribution**: Central America and South America from Venezuela to Argentina.
**Habitat**: Slow-moving rivers and creeks in forests and swamps.
**Food**: Fish, fish eggs, crabs, birds and small mammals.
**Size**: 0.8–1.4m (2.5–4.5ft); 22–34kg (48.5–75lb).
**Maturity**: Unknown.
**Breeding**: 1–3 young produced every year.
**Life span**: 15 years.
**Status**: Vulnerable.

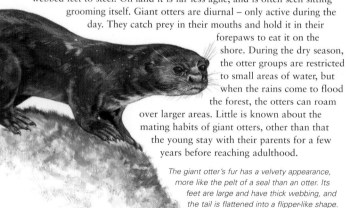

*The giant otter's fur has a velvety appearance, more like the pelt of a seal than an otter. Its feet are large and have thick webbing, and the tail is flattened into a flipper-like shape.*

# North American river otter

*Lutra canadensis*

**Distribution**: Widespread across most of North America.
**Habitat**: Rivers and lakes.
**Food**: Amphibians, fish, crayfish and aquatic insects.
**Size**: 60–110cm (23.5–43in); 3–14kg (6.5–30lb).
**Maturity**: 2–3 years.
**Breeding**: 1–5 young born every year.
**Life span**: 20 years.
**Status**: Lower risk.

North American river otters rarely stray far from the banks of shallow rivers. They live alone or in pairs, but often play with other individuals in the area. This play strengthens social ties. Each of the otters has an individual scent which it uses to mark its territory. River otters communicate with each other through sounds such as whistles, growls, chuckles and screams.

North American river otters are known for their boundless energy, and they must eat frequently. They catch fish in their mouths and detect other prey by feeling with their whiskers along the bottoms of streams. Unlike many other otters which chew their food, the river otter's prey is gulped down immediately.

Mating takes place in March and April. The young are born almost a year later. The females give birth in dens close to the water's edge. They drive the males away soon after the birth of their young, but the dog otters return later to help raise the offspring. The young depart at the age of one year.

*River otters have streamlined bodies with dark fur, thick tails and short legs with webbed feet.*

**Marine otter** (*Lontra felina*): 90cm (35.5in); 4.5kg (10lb)
The marine otter, or sea cat, lives on South America's Pacific coast, from its southern tip to northern Peru. Small populations also exist on the South Atlantic coast of Argentina. This is the smallest of the American river otters, which form a separate genus to the Old World otters and the sea otter. It is the only river otter that lives exclusively in the sea. It occupies exposed rocky coasts, sheltering from rough seas and strong winds in caves and crevices. Marine otters eat fish and shellfish such as crabs and mussels. They sometimes catch birds and small mammals.

**Neotropical river otter** (*Lontra longicaudis*): 36–66cm (14–26in); 5–15kg (11–33lb)
This river otter lives in tropical regions from north-western Mexico to Argentina. It is the most common otter in Mexico. Further south other, larger otters predominate, but this species is more widespread than any of its relatives. It spends the night in a burrow. By day it forages for fish, crustaceans and molluscs. It will also eat insects, reptiles, birds and small mammals.

**Southern river otter** (*Lontra provocax*): 66–110cm (26–43in); 6–9kg (13.25–19.75lb)
Southern river otters live in southern Chile and parts of Argentina, in both marine and fresh water habitats with plenty of vegetation cover. Chilean otters eat mainly fish and crustaceans; those in Argentina eat less fish, but supplement their diets with molluscs and birds. These otters live in family groups, consisting of an adult female and her young. Males are solitary.

# Fisher

*Martes pennanti*

The fisher, or pekan, lives in the thick forests of North America. Despite its name, it feeds on small land animals, such as mice and porcupines. Fishers have no permanent dens, but take shelter in hollow trees, holes in the ground and even abandoned beaver lodges.

They are active during the day and night, and despite being expert climbers, spend most of their foraging time on the ground. When they come across suitable prey animals, they rush forward and kill them with bites to the back of the neck. Larger animals are killed with repeated bites to the face.

Males seek out mates during the spring breeding season and litters are born about ten months later. As with many mustelids, the fertilized eggs do not begin to grow immediately inside the females. Their development is delayed for several months so that they are born at the right time of year. Unusually, births always take place in trees.

**Distribution**: Canada and northern United States.
**Habitat**: Conifer forest.
**Food**: Birds, rodents, carrion.
**Size**: 49–63cm (19–25in); 1.3–3.2kg (2.75–7lb).
**Maturity**: 1–2 years.
**Breeding**: 3 young born every spring.
**Life span**: 10 years.
**Status**: Lower risk.

*Fishers have dark fur that is coarser than that of most mustelids. Nevertheless, they are still hunted by humans for their fur.*

## Black-footed ferret

*Mustela nigripes*

Before the prairies of the North American West were cultivated for farmland and turned into cattle pasture, black-footed ferrets would have been a common sight. The burrows that they and their prey made in the ground formed dangerous obstacles to grazing cattle and farm machinery, so the animals were methodically exterminated by pioneer farmers. Today the ferrets – the only species of ferret native to North America – occur wild in just three places in Montana, South Dakota and Wyoming (all reintroduced populations).

Black-footed ferrets live on and under prairies that have short or medium-length grasses. Each ferret occupies about 40ha (100 acres) of prairie, in which it finds all its food, but a nursing mother needs two or three times this space. Black-footed ferrets take up residence in burrow systems abandoned by prairie dogs, their main food. In places where prairie dogs form large communal "towns", the ferrets may actually live among their prey.

The breeding season is in late spring. The young remain underground for a month after they are born. Mother and young forage together in late summer, generally at night, and by autumn the young begin to drift away. Males take no part in raising the young.

**Distribution:** Historically southern Canada to northern Mexico; today reintroduced populations exist in Montana, South Dakota and Wyoming.
**Habitat**: Prairie.
**Food**: Mainly prairie dogs, along with some mice, ground squirrels and other small animals.
**Size**: 38–60cm (15–23.5in) 645–1,125g (22.75–39.75oz).
**Maturity**: 1 year.
**Breeding**: Single litter of 1–6 young produced in early summer, after a gestation of 35–45 days.
**Life span**: 5 years.
**Status**: Endangered.

*As well as having black feet, these ferrets have a black "mask" over their eyes. The underside of the body is covered in yellowish fur. Male black-footed ferrets are slightly larger than females.*

## Greater grisón

*Galictis vittata*

The greater grisón's range stretches from southern Mexico to Brazil and Bolivia. These animals are found mainly in lowland areas, rarely ascending to more than 1,500m (5,000ft) above sea level. Within its large range, the greater grisón lives in a variety of habitats, from dry savannahs and grasslands to more verdant areas, including rainforests. The grisón makes its home in secluded spots, such as under tree roots or in rock crevices, and it sometimes takes over the abandoned burrows of armadillos.

Like other small carnivores, the grisón has a long, powerful body, with short legs and a short tail. While the bodyform limits the animal to slow running speeds, it does enable it to wriggle into tight spaces, such as the burrows of its prey. The ears are small, so they do not get snagged in tight spots, and the claws are wide and very long for digging and extracting food.

**Distribution**: From Mexico through Central and South America to Brazil and Bolivia.
**Habitat**: Grasslands and rainforest, often near water.
**Food**: Small mammals including chinchillas, viscachas, agoutis and mice; occasionally reptiles, birds and some fruits.
**Size**: 51cm (20in); 2kg (4.5lb).
**Maturity**: 1 year.
**Breeding**: 2–4 young born between March and October
**Life span**: 5 years.
**Status**: Rare.

*Grisóns have more robust bodies than weasels. The greater grisón's most obvious feature is the white stripe across its face and around its ears. This stripe divides the black face from the grey forehead, giving the animal's face a banded appearance. The rest of the body is grizzled grey and black. Greater grisóns may live alone, in pairs or in small groups. These agile predators despatch their prey with a bite to the neck.*

# Stoat

*Mustela erminea*

Although rarely seen, stoats are common in the countryside, where they mainly feed on rodents. The large males will often prey on rabbits, even though rabbits are considerably larger. Stoats are said to mesmerize their prey by dancing around them, before nipping in for the kill. This is not just a rural myth. Stoats have been observed leaping around near rabbits in a seemingly deranged fashion. This curious "dance" seems to have the effect of confusing the rabbits, which just watch the stoat draw slowly closer and closer, until it is too late to escape. The stoats then grasp the prey with their sharp teeth.

In mild climates, stoats have chestnut fur all year round. In colder areas, their coats change to pure white by the time the first snows have fallen. White stoats are known as ermines, and their fur was once prized for its pure colour and soft feel.

*Stoats are distinguished from their smaller cousins, weasels, by having black tips to their tails.*

**Distribution**: Widespread in northern and central Europe, extending into Asia and across northern North America. Introduced to New Zealand.
**Habitat**: Anywhere with enough cover.
**Food**: Mammals up to the size of rabbits.
**Size**: 16–31cm (6.25–12.25in); 140–445g (5–15.75oz).
**Maturity**: 1 year.
**Breeding**: Single litter of 5–12 young.
**Life span**: 10 years.
**Status**: Common.

---

**Colombian weasel** (*Mustela felipei*): 22cm (8.5in); 140g (5oz)
Living in the highlands of Colombia, this is one of only three weasels native to South America. Little is known about the Colombian weasel because only a few specimens have ever been handled, and even fewer observed in the wild. The coat is dark brown or black on top, with a reddish-tan underside. The webbed feet have naked soles, suggesting that the weasel spends a lot of time foraging in mountain waterways.

**Tropical weasel** (*Mustela africana*): 32cm (12.5in); weight unknown
This is another poorly understood species. It has been found in Peru, east of the Andes, and in Brazil it probably ranges across most of the Amazon lowlands. With continued destruction of Amazon rainforests, the tropical weasel is now classed as endangered. The coat is red-brown, becoming lighter on the underside. Like the Colombian weasel, this species has naked feet. Zoologists initially classified the tropical and Colombian weasels in their own genus. Now, however, all weasels are grouped together.

**Lesser grisón** (*Galictis cuja*): 45cm (18in); 1kg (2.2lb)
Lesser grisóns occur across central and southern South America, from southern Peru, Paraguay and central Chile to northern Patagonia in Argentina. They are at home in a range of habitats, including the arid scrubland of Paraguay's Chaco region, as well as moister grasslands and forests. This species closely resembles the greater grisón, having the same banded face. The lesser grisón is found at altitudes up to 4,000m (13,120ft).

# Least weasel

*Mustela nivalis*

Least weasels are common throughout Canada and Alaska. Their North American range extends to the forests of the Carolinas and the prairies of Wyoming. They are also found throughout much of the northern hemisphere, with the exception of most islands and Arabia. Least weasels survive in a wide variety of habitats, but they avoid thick forests, sandy deserts and any exposed spaces.

Least weasels have a very long body, with a long neck and flat head. This allows them to move with ease over broken ground and inside burrows. The size of this weasel varies with its distribution across the globe. The largest least weasels are found in North Africa, while those in North America have the smallest bodies.

Least weasels live alone outside of the breeding season. Males occupy territories that are home to two or more females. They forage for food at all times of the day or night. They watch carefully for movements caused by prey, before launching an attack and dispatching their victims with a bite to the neck.

**Distribution**: Arctic to North Carolina; also found in Northern Asia, Africa and Europe.
**Habitat**: Forest, prairie, farmland and semi-desert.
**Food**: Rodents, eggs, nestlings and lizards.
**Size**: 16–20cm (6.25–8in); 30–55g (1–2oz).
**Maturity**: 8 months.
**Breeding**: Two litters of up to 7 young, born in spring and late summer.
**Life span**: 7 years.
**Status**: Common.

*In summer, the least weasel's brown fur is about 1cm (0.4in) long, but the winter coat is more than double this length. In the far north, the coat also turns white in winter.*

# American marten

*Martes americana*

The American marten lives in the cold northern pine forests of Canada, ranging from Newfoundland in the east to the US state of Alaska in the west. Martens also live in the high-altitude mountain areas of the continental United States, where conditions are similar to the cold north. The fur of the American marten is highly valued, and although the species is not endangered, hunting and the destruction of its conifer-forest habitat have caused a severe decline in numbers in many parts of its range.

American martens spend the day in nooks and crannies in the forest, and move through the trees and along the ground in search of food at night. To compensate for the low light levels, martens have large eyes, and large ears (for a mustelid) that resemble those of a cat. They kill their prey with their long, curved claws and sharp teeth. Their diet includes small mammals, carrion, fruits and insects.

Young martens are born in spring. Animals of breeding age locate each other by scent, releasing a strong odour from their anal glands. They live alone for the rest of the year.

**Distribution**: Canada to northern California and Colorado.
**Habitat**: Pine forests.
**Food**: Small mammals, carrion, fruits and insects.
**Size**: 32–45cm (12.5–18in); 0.3–1.3kg (0.75–2.75lb).
**Maturity**: 2 years.
**Breeding**: Up to 5 kits produced in March or April.
**Life span**: 10 years.
**Status**: Lower risk.

*The American marten has a long, slender body, and large eyes and ears. The fur on the head is light brown or grey, while the legs, tail and upper surface of the body are dark brown or black. The underside is pale yellow or cream.*

# Tayra

*Eira barbara*

This unusual species is found from central Mexico to northern Argentina, and also on the island of Trinidad. It lives in thick forests, from lowland regions to about 2,400m (7,900ft) above sea level. A few tayras are known to live in areas of tall grass.

Tayras forage for food on the ground and also in the trees, where their long tail helps them to balance as they move through the branches. As well as being nimble climbers and agile on the ground, these weasels can also swim well. Tayras are mainly active during the day. They make their nests in hollow trees or logs, grassy thickets, or in the burrows of other animals. Most tayras live alone or in pairs. Sometimes they form small groups of up to four individuals. Members of the group may work together to prey on animals such as large rodents and small deer. When they are being chased by predators, tayras will evade capture by running up trees and leaping from branch to branch.

Tayras can be tamed, and they are sometimes kept as pets. Indigenous people once used them to control rodents pests in homes.

*When fully grown, this large weasel is as big as a medium-sized dog. The short coat varies from grey to black, and the tail is bushy and long. The tayra has a long, robust body, and large hind feet with long claws.*

**Distribution**: From Central Mexico to Bolivia and Argentina; also found on the island of Trinidad.
**Habitat**: Tropical deciduous and evergreen forests,
**Food**: Mainly rodents, but also rabbits, small deer, birds, reptiles, invertebrates, honey and fruits.
**Size**: 100cm (40in); 4–5kg (8.75–11lb).
**Maturity**: 2 years.
**Breeding**: 3 kits born between March and July; however, some authorities claim that breeding is non-seasonal.
**Life span**: Unknown.
**Status**: Lower risk.

## Long-tailed weasel

*Mustela frenata*

This species has the largest range of any American weasel, from southern Canada through the United States and Central America to the lower slopes of the Bolivian Andes.

Long-tailed weasels occupy a range of habitats, from farmland and gardens to woodland. However, they avoid dense forests and desert areas. The weasels are most easily spotted emerging from their burrows, which tend to be inside tree hollows, under rocks and in other secluded spots. They often take over the burrow of one of their prey, enlarging the accommodation if necessary. Long-tailed weasels are good climbers and swimmers. They hunt at night, tracking prey by scent.

The fur is red-brown, with a yellowish underside. In colder regions, where snowfall is common, the weasel develops a white winter coat.

*This weasel's tail is particularly bushy compared with those of other weasels. Apart from this, the form is fairly typical, with short legs, small ears and a long, flexible body.*

**Distribution**: From southern Canada to Bolivia.
**Habitat**: Grassland, shrubland and open woodland.
**Food**: Small rodents, rabbits, birds and reptiles.
**Size**: 20–26cm (8–10in); 80–350g (3–12oz). Males are larger than females.
**Maturity**: 6 months.
**Breeding**: 6 young born in spring.
**Life span**: 5 years.
**Status**: Common.

---

**Western hog-nosed skunk** (*Conepatus mesoleucus*): 55cm (21.5in); 1.9kg (4.25lb)
Western hog-nosed skunks live in the south-western United States and Mexico, from Colorado to the highlands of northern Mexico. This species is most often found on low hills with brush or open woodland, but rarely ventures into exposed territory, such as desert, or more dense habitats, such as forest. The fur is dark brown with a stripe running from the head to the base of the bushy tail. The long snout has a naked patch that gives the species its common name.

**Eastern hog-nosed skunk** (*Conepatus leuconotus*): 75cm (29.5in); 3.25kg (7.25lb)
Less common than its western relative, the eastern hog-nosed skunk is limited to southern Texas and eastern Mexico. It lives in a wide range of habitats, including woodlands, grasslands, cactus forests and thorny brush areas, where it dens in fallen trunks or among rocks. This species is the largest of the North American skunks. It resembles the western hog-nosed skunk, but is about 25 per cent larger. The back stripe is slightly thinner and often does not reach the tail.

**Striped hog-nosed skunk** (*Conepatus semistriatus*): 57cm (22.5in); 1.6kg (3.5lb)
The striped hog-nosed skunk, or Amazonian skunk, ranges from southern Mexico to northern Peru and eastern Brazil. It occupies a variety of habitats duirng the dry season, but in the wet season it spends most of its time in deciduous mountain forests. Like other hog-nosed skunks, it has a bald patch on its snout. Two white stripes run from the nape of the neck along the black back.

## Patagonian weasel

*Lyncodon patagonicus*

The Patagonian weasel ranges from the southern and western parts of Argentina into Chile. It is most commonly found in the pampas – areas of tall grass and few trees in the colder, dryer regions. This weasel has a short, bushy tail and legs that are short even for a mustelid. This accentuates the appearance of the long, slender body.

Most of the animals of the pampas live in burrows or at least depressions in the ground. Patagonian weasels are known to enter burrows to get at their prey, which comprise insects and small burrowing mammals such as rodents and insectivores. The weasel's small ears and short legs are designed to help it move easily through narrow burrows.

Patagonian weasels defend territories. A male weasel will occupy an area that covers the territories of several females. When a female is ready to mate with the male in the area, she produces a signalling odour to attract him.

*The Patagonian weasel's coat comes in a range of colours, from white to brown and black. A white or yellow band runs along the back.*

**Distribution**: Argentina and Chile.
**Habitat**: Pampas and desert.
**Food**: Small burrowing animals.
**Size**: 30–35cm (12–14in); 225g (8oz).
**Maturity**: 1 year.
**Breeding**: Unknown.
**Life span**: Unknown.
**Status**: Common.

# RACCOONS AND RELATIVES

*Raccoons and their relatives belong to a family of mammals called the* Procyonidae. *Procyonids are small opportunistic feeders and scavenging animals. Many live in trees, but the most successful – the raccoons – live mainly on the ground. Most procyonids live in the Americas, where they range from the cold northern forests of Canada to the humid, tropical swamps of the Amazon.*

## Common raccoon

*Procyon lotor*

Raccoons live in woodland areas and rarely stray far from water. They are more active at night than during the day. Periods of rest are spent in dens in tree hollows or other sheltered places. When on the move, raccoons will readily swim across streams and rivers and climb into trees in search of food. They use their touch-sensitive hands to grab prey and then break it into mouth-sized pieces.

Raccoons do not hibernate in warmer parts of their range, although in cooler northern parts they may do so. In fact, they only semi-hibernate, popping out every now and then to feed during breaks in the severest weather.

Males are largely solitary but will tolerate the presence of females living in or near their territories. Mating takes place in spring, and young are born a couple of months later. The young stay with their mothers until the following spring.

*The common raccoon is well known for its black "bandit" mask across the eyes and its tail ringed with black hoops. The animal's footprints look similar to those of a human infant.*

**Distribution**: Southern Canada throughout the United States to Central America.
**Habitat**: Forests and brushland.
**Food**: Crayfish, frogs, fish, nuts, seeds, acorns and berries.
**Size**: 41–60cm (16–23.5in); 2–12kg (4.5–26.5lb).
**Maturity**: 1 year.
**Breeding**: 3 or 4 young born in summer.
**Life span**: 5 years.
**Status**: Common.

## Olingo

*Bassaricyon gabbii*

**Distribution**: Central America to northern South America as far as Brazil.
**Habitat**: Tropical forest.
**Food**: Fruits, insects and small mammals.
**Size**: 35–48cm (14–19in); 0.9–1.5kg (2–3.25lb).
**Maturity**: 21 months.
**Breeding**: Single offspring.
**Life span**: 5 years.
**Status**: Lower risk.

Olingos live in the trees of tropical forests. They are active at night and spend the day in nests of leaves high up inside hollow trees. Equipped with long claws, olingos are expert climbers, and they rarely descend to the ground. They can also jump long distances through the tree tops, using their long tail to keep them balanced.

An olingo's diet comprises mainly fruit, although the animal will seek out insects and small vertebrates, such as lizards, on occasion. Olingos live alone, although they are often found living alongside kinkajous – procyonids that are close relatives – as well as opossums and night monkeys.

Olingos mark objects in their territories with urine, although it is not known whether this is to ward off intruders or to help them navigate in the darkness. Mating takes place all year round. Gestation lasts about ten weeks and generally results in a single offspring.

*Olingos have thick, pinkish fur. These procyonids have long bodies with short limbs and flattened tails.*

# Ring-tailed coati

*Nasua nasua*

**Distribution**: Northern South America as far as Argentina.
**Habitat**: Woodland.
**Food**: Fruits, insects, rodents.
**Size**: 41–67cm (16–26.5in); 3–6kg (6.5–13.25lb).
**Maturity**: 2 years.
**Breeding**: 2–7 young born in rainy season.
**Life span**: 10 years.
**Status**: Common.

Coatis have long muzzles compared to raccoons and other procyonids. They use these to root out food from rocky crevices and from knots in trees. Coatis forage both on the ground and in trees. On the ground they hold their long tails erect, with the tips curled. In trees, coatis' tails are prehensile enough to function as a fifth limb. The tips curl around branches to provide support in more precarious locations.

Ring-tailed coatis are most active during the day. When there is plenty of fruit on the trees, they will eat little else. However, during seasons when fruit is less abundant, they come down to the forest floor to forage for insects and rodents.

Ring-tailed coatis tend to congregate in bands of up to 20 females and young. Adult males live alone and are only allowed into bands during the breeding season, which is the time when there is plenty of fruit available. When fruit is not as easy to find, male coatis may try to eat smaller members of their band, and consequently are expelled by the adult females.

*Like all coatis, this species has a long and pointed muzzle with an articulated tip. Ring-tailed coatis have long, coarse fur, and tails banded with white stripes.*

---

**Cozumel Island raccoon** (*Procyon pygmaeus*):
Length unknown; 3–4kg (6.5–8.75lb)
The world's smallest raccoon, this species is also known as the pygmy raccoon. It lives solely on Cozumel Island off Mexico's Yucatan Peninsula, inhabiting the mangrove swamps that fringe the island's coast. The Cozumel Island raccoon is about one-third of the size of the common raccoon of the American mainland. This raccoon is considered endangered because of its small range and the continued coastal development on Cozumel to cater for tourism. Some zoologists think that the Cozumel Island raccoon is not a distinct species, merely an unusual population of common raccoons introduced to the island by humans in prehistoric times.

**Guadeloupe raccoon** (*Procyon minor*):
Size unknown
Another endangered animal, this raccoon lives on the island of Guadeloupe in the French West Indies. Thought to be of a similar size to the common raccoon, the Guadeloupe raccoon has paler fur than its mainland relative. Like other island raccoons, including *Procyon maynardi* of Nassau in the Bahamas, some zoologists argue that this "species" is merely the remains of an introduced population of common raccoons.

**Tres Marias raccoon** (*Procyon insularis*):
Size unknown
The Tres Marias raccoon is found on Maria Madre Island and Maria Magdalene Island off the western coast of Mexico. Until recently, these raccoons were thought to be a variety of the common raccoon, rather than a separate species.

# Kinkajou

*Potos flavus*

Kinkajous are almost entirely arboreal (tree-living). Thanks to their long claws and prehensile tails, they are very agile climbers. Kinkajous are nocturnal and spend the day in dens inside hollow trees. On the hottest days they emerge from their stifling dens to cool off in the open on branches.

At night, kinkajous race around the trees in search of fruit. After searching through one tree, they will cautiously move to the next before beginning to forage again. They use their long tongue to reach the soft flesh and juices inside the fruit.

Kinkajous tend to return to the same roosting trees each dawn. They travel alone or in breeding pairs. However, groups of kinkajous may form in trees that are heavy with fruit. Kinkajous leave their scent on branches, probably as a signal to potential mates. They also give shrill calls to communicate with partners. Mating takes place all year round, and single offspring are born after four months.

**Distribution**: Mexico to central Brazil.
**Habitat**: Forests.
**Food**: Fruits, insects and small vertebrates.
**Size**: 40–76cm (15.5–30in); 1.4–4.6kg (3–10.25lb).
**Maturity**: 1.5–2.5 years.
**Breeding**: Single offspring.
**Life span**: 15 years.
**Status**: Endangered.

*Kinkajous have soft and woolly fur, with rounded heads and stockier bodies than most of their relatives. They are sometimes mistaken for the African primates known as pottos.*

**Mountain coati** (*Nasuella olivacea*): Head and body 35–45cm (14–18in); 2kg (4.5lb) Mountain coatis closely resemble other coatis, but they tend to be smaller and have shorter tails. They are very rare and live in tropical forests on the slopes of the Andes Mountains in northern South America. They feed on insects, fruits and small vertebrates, which they find in the trees and on the ground.

**Allen's olingo** (*Bassaricyon alleni*): 42–47cm (16.5–18.5in); 1.6kg (3.5lb) Allens's olingo is very similar to the common olingo (*Bassaricyon gabbii*). It lives in a similar range and is about the same size, if not slightly larger. The most distinguishing feature of Allen's olingo is that its tail is bushier than that of the common olingo. This species is a nocturnal forager, moving through the treetops in search of food. Allen's olingo mainly feeds on fruits and insects, but it occasionally eats small arboreal mammals and lizards.

**Other olingos**
While Allen's olingo and the common olingo are not currently considered to be in danger of extinction, the three other olingo species are much more threatened. These three species also live in Central and South America: *Bassaricyon lasius* is found in Costa Rica, *Bassaricyon pauli* lives in the forests of Panama, while *Bassaricyon beddardi* is native to Guyana. This last species is sometimes considered to be a subspecies of Allen's olingo. All are on the endangered list.

# Cacomistle

*Bassariscus sumichrasti*

Sometimes called ringtails (but not to be confused with *Bassariscus astutus*, their close relative) cacomistles have a small, cat-like body and a bushy, black-and-white-striped tail. They range from southern Mexico to Panama. They prefer to live in forested areas, especially in mountainous regions where the ground is broken by rocky outcrops.

Cacomistles seldom stray far from water and are most active at night, foraging mainly for insects, rodents and fruit. Being agile climbers, they move up and down cliffs with ease. As with many other climbing animals, a cacomistle's hind feet can twist around 180 degrees. This allows the animal to climb down trees and rocks headfirst, with the claws on the hind feet clinging to the surface behind them. Breeding can occur all year around, but most young are born in summer.

**Distribution**: From southern Mexico to Panama.
**Habitat**: Rocky areas.
**Food**: Insects, rodents and fruits.
**Size**: 30–42cm (12–16.25in); 0.8–1.3kg (1.75–2.75lb).
**Maturity**: 10 months.
**Breeding**: 1 offspring born in early summer.
**Life span**: 10 years.
**Status**: Vulnerable.

*The feet of cacomistles have naked soles. This helps them to grip on to rocky surfaces and tree branches as they move around their varied habitat.*

# Crab-eating raccoon

*Procyon cancrivorus*

The crab-eating raccoon, or mapache, lives in swamps or by streams across much of South America east of the Andes and north of Patagonia. Southern Costa Rica is the most northerly extent of the raccoon's range. This species has much shorter hair and a more slender body than most of its raccoon cousins.

Although they prefer being close to water, crab-eating raccoons also survive in a range of other habitats, including scrubland and even Amazonian rainforest. They search the water for food at night, detecting prey – crabs, crayfish, fish and worms – with their touch-sensitive paws. Raccoons also have excellent night vision, which not only helps them to locate prey but also makes it easier to spot ripe fruits in the dark.

A male crab-eating raccoon will occupy a territory that encompasses the home ranges of several females. He will control mating access to all these females until a younger, stronger male arrives to take control of the territory.

**Distribution**: Costa Rica to northern Argentina; only found east of the Andes.
**Habitat**: Forests.
**Food**: Crustaceans, worms, fish, frogs, fruits and seeds.
**Size**: 45–90cm (18–35.5in); 2–12kg (4.5–26.5lb).
**Maturity**: 1 year.
**Breeding**: Single litter of 3–4 young born between July and September.
**Life span**: 5 years.
**Status**: Common.

*Crab-eating raccoons are smaller and slimmer than common raccoons, because they lack thick, insulating underfur.*

# Ringtail

*Bassariscus astutus*

*This species is named after its bushy tail, which is ringed with black and white stripes, much like the tails of raccoons. However, ringtails have more agile, cat-like bodies than raccoons. Both the ringtail and the cacomistle, its relative, are largely solitary, and become aggressive towards intruders into their territory. A ringtail scent-marks its territory by regularly urinating at specific sites.*

Ringtails are found from the western United States to southern Mexico. They are most commonly found in highland forests. They prefer rocky areas, such as canyons, but also occupy a range of lowland habitats, including deserts, woodland and shrubland. Although they prefer dry environments, they are also common near rivers, where food is easier to find.

When ready to give birth, females make a den under a boulder or in a hollow tree. The young are suckled for ten weeks, after which the mother has to find food for the young. The father may stay nearby – and be tolerated by the female – and play with his offspring as they grow. The young disperse after about ten months.

Ringtails are most active at night, spending most of their time foraging. They are excellent climbers, and literally search high and low for rodents, squirrels, insects and other small animals. When they finish eating, they groom themselves by licking their fur, wiping their head clean with damp paws. If threatened, their tail bristles and arches over their head, making them look larger.

**Distribution**: From southern Oregon and eastern Kansas in the western United States to southern Mexico, including Baja California.
**Habitat**: Rocky areas, woodland and shrubland, and montane conifer forest.
**Food**: Small mammals, insects, birds, lizards, frogs, nuts and fruits.
**Size**: 30–42cm (12–16.5in); 0.8–1.4kg (1.75–3lb).
**Maturity**: 10 months.
**Breeding**: Single litter of 1–4 young born between April and July
**Life span**: 7 years.
**Status**: Common.

# White-nosed coati

*Nasua narica*

The white-nosed coati is found in a variety of forest types, from rainforest to drier, high-altitude woodland. The silver hairs mixed into the grey-brown fur produce a grizzled look. The snout, which is long and flexible, has a white band near its tip. There are also white spots above and below each eye, and one on each cheek. The long tail, which has black rings, is raised above the body when the animal walks.

White-nosed coatis are most active during the day. They forage for insects on the ground and then retreat to the trees to spend the night. Males live alone, while females form bands of up to 20 individuals. Males under the age of about two are tolerated by the females, but once they approach sexual maturity the males are chased away.

In early spring, the most dominant male in the area is accepted into the female band. He mates with each of the females in a tree, after which they chase him off. Before giving birth, a female will leave the band and build a secluded nest in a tree. After about five weeks, the mother and her young rejoin the band. New bands form when existing ones become too large and split.

**Distribution**: From Arizona to Columbia and Ecuador.
**Habitat**: Forests.
**Food**: Insects.
**Size**: 40–70cm (15.75–27.5in); 3–5kg (6.5–11lb).
**Maturity**: 3 years.
**Breeding**: Up to 7 young born in summer.
**Life span**: 10 years.
**Status**: Common.

*This species has plantigrade feet, meaning that its bodyweight is spread over the whole foot. This provides stability as the coati moves through the trees. (Only a few species are plantigrades, including bears and humans.) The long, semi-prehensile tail aids balancing and climbing.*

# RODENTS

*The Rodentia order is the largest, most widespread and most diverse mammal group. There are more than 2,000 species of rodent, making up almost half of all mammal species. The secret of the rodents' success is their teeth. Their long, chisel-shaped incisors keep growing throughout their lives. These teeth are self-sharpening, enabling rodents to eat almost any food, from wood to meat and even household rubbish.*

## Grey squirrel

*Sciurus carolinensis*

**Distribution**: Eastern North America. Introduced to parts of Europe.
**Habitat**: Woodlands.
**Food**: Nuts, flowers and buds.
**Size**: 38–52cm (15–20.5in); 0.3–0.7kg (0.75–1.5lb).
**Maturity**: 10 months.
**Breeding**: 2 litters born each year with 2–4 young per litter.
**Life span**: 12 years.
**Status**: Common.

Grey squirrels are native to the open woodlands of eastern North America. They have also been introduced into parts of Europe, where they have out-competed the smaller red squirrels for food and breeding sites.

Grey squirrels feed primarily on the nuts and buds of many woodland trees. In summer, when they are most active just after dawn and before dusk, grey squirrels also eat insects. In winter, when most animals of their size are hibernating, grey squirrels spend their days eating stores of food which they buried throughout the previous summer. Grey squirrels may make dens in hollow trees, but are more likely to make nests, or dreys, from twigs and leaves in the boughs of trees.

There are two breeding seasons each year: one beginning in midwinter, the other in midsummer. Males begin to chase females through the trees a few days before they are receptive to mating. When females are ready, their vulvas become pink and engorged. Litters of three are born six weeks later.

*Grey squirrels have, as their name suggests, greyish fur, although many individuals have reddish patches. Their tails, which have many white hairs, are bushier than those of most other squirrels.*

## Woodchuck

*Marmota monax*

*Woodchucks are the largest squirrels in North America. These stocky-bodied rodents are well adapted to burrowing, with short, legs and curved claws.*

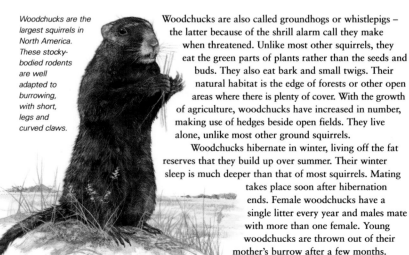

Woodchucks are also called groundhogs or whistlepigs – the latter because of the shrill alarm call they make when threatened. Unlike most other squirrels, they eat the green parts of plants rather than the seeds and buds. They also eat bark and small twigs. Their natural habitat is the edge of forests or other open areas where there is plenty of cover. With the growth of agriculture, woodchucks have increased in number, making use of hedges beside open fields. They live alone, unlike most other ground squirrels.

Woodchucks hibernate in winter, living off the fat reserves that they build up over summer. Their winter sleep is much deeper than that of most squirrels. Mating takes place soon after hibernation ends. Female woodchucks have a single litter every year and males mate with more than one female. Young woodchucks are thrown out of their mother's burrow after a few months.

**Distribution**: Southern Canada southward through eastern North America.
**Habitat**: Woodland or open areas that have plenty of ground cover.
**Food**: Plant leaves and stems.
**Size**: 45–65cm (17.5–25.5in); 2–5kg (4.5–11lb).
**Maturity**: 2 years.
**Breeding**: 3–5 young born in May.
**Life span**: 6 years.
**Status**: Common.

# Northern pocket gopher

*Thomomys talpoides*

*Northern pocket gophers have robust, tubular bodies with short legs. Their forefeet have long claws and their tails are naked at the tip. Male gophers are much larger than females.*

Pocket gophers spend a great deal of their time burrowing. They feed on the underground parts of plants, such as roots, tubers and bulbs. The gophers access their food by digging temporary feeding tunnels out and up from deeper and more permanent galleries, located 1–3m (3.25–10ft) underground.

Gophers keep their burrow entrances blocked with earth most of the time, and rarely appear above ground during the day. At night they may move around on the surface.

Gophers carry food in pouches inside their cheeks to storage or feeding sites in their burrow systems. They do not drink water, and so get all of their liquid from plant juices.

Only during the mating season will a male be allowed into a female's burrow. Litters are born just 18 days after mating, which generally takes place in summer.

**Distribution**: Western North America from Canada to Mexico.
**Habitat**: Burrows under desert, prairie and forest.
**Food**: Roots, bulbs and leaves.
**Size**: 11–30cm (4.5–12in); 50–500g (1.75–17.75oz).
**Maturity**: 1 year.
**Breeding**: 1–10 young born in summer.
**Life span**: 2 years.
**Status**: Common.

**Hoary marmot** (*Marmota caligata*): 45–57cm (18–22.5in); 3.6–9.1kg (8–20lb)
This species occurs in the northern Pacific region of North America, from Idaho and Washington to Alaska. It inhabits the pine forests typical of cold climates and high mountains, and also the alpine meadows that bloom above the tree line in summer. It is called hoary because of the white hairs that grizzle its black fur, giving it a silver-grey appearance. Like other ground squirrels, the hoary marmot is an expert digger, using the long, robust claws on its forefeet for excavation. It hibernates through winter in large burrows.

**Yellow-bellied marmot** (*Marmota flaviventris*): 34.5–48cm (13.5–19in); 1.5–5kg (3.3–11lb)
These marmots occur in western North America, from south-western Canada to the US–Mexico border, typically in meadows, prairies and around forest edges. Their underside is lined with yellow fur, and there are yellow speckles on the neck. Yellow-bellied marmots live in extensive burrows, in groups comprising an adult male and two or three females. Hibernation burrows are dug several metres down to avoid ground frost. The diet consists of fruits, seeds and some insects.

**Plains pocket gopher** (*Geomys bursarius*): 19–36cm (7.5–14in); 300–450g (10.5–16oz)
This brown, burrowing animal lives on the plains between the Mississippi River and the Rocky Mountains, from Texas and north-eastern Mexico to the Canadian border. Common in open habitats, it also occurs in sparsely wooded areas where tree roots do not dominate the soil. It prefers deep sandy soils supporting plants that produce storage tubers and roots – the gopher's main food.

# American beaver

*Castor canadensis*

Beavers are among the largest of all rodents. Family groups of beavers live in large nests, called lodges, in or near forest streams or small lakes. Beavers eat wood and other tough plant foods, which have to be soaked in water before being eaten.

They use their large front teeth to gnaw through the base of small trees. Sections of these logs are transported back to the lodge via a system of canals dug into the forest. If necessary, beavers will also dam a stream with debris to make a pool deep enough to store their food. A beaver colony may maintain a dam for several generations. The lodge has underwater entrances so beavers can swim out to their food supply even when the pool is frozen.

**Distribution**: North America.
**Habitat**: Streams and small lakes.
**Food**: Wood, leaves, roots and bark.
**Size**: 60–80cm (23.5–31.5in); 12–25kg (26.5–55lb).
**Maturity**: 1.5–2 years.
**Breeding**: 2–4 young born each spring.
**Life span**: 24 years.
**Status**: Locally common.

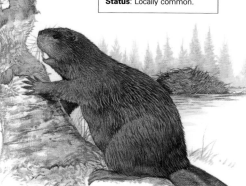

*A beaver has webbed hind feet, a flattened tail for swimming and large front teeth for gnawing through wood. Its fur is coated with oil to keep it waterproof.*

# Alaska marmot

*Marmota broweri*

Alaska marmots are found only in small areas of the Brooks Mountains in northern Alaska, where they live amid rock slides and on boulder-strewn slopes. The marmots occupy the spaces formed under the rocks, burrowing into the permafrost with their strong foreclaws to make a living area. The plants that grow on the broken, rocky ground resemble those of tundra and alpine areas, and they provide the marmots with most of their food.

Alaska marmots are social animals living in colonies of up to 50 individuals. The colony shares and maintains a tunnel system, although each marmot has its own den. Within a few metres of each den is an observation post, where a marmot can keep a lookout for predators such as wolverines and bears. Members of the colony take turns to keep watch. The larger the colony, the less time each animal has to spend on sentry duty, and the more time it can devote to sunbathing, feeding and grooming. When danger is spotted, sentries let out a warning call and the colony disappears below ground.

**Distribution**: Brooks Mountains of northern Alaska.
**Habitat**: Scree, rocky outcrops and boulder fields.
**Food**: Grasses, forbs, fruits, seeds, legumes and occasionally insects.
**Size**: 54–65cm (21.5–25.5in); 2.5–4kg (5.5–8.75lb).
**Maturity**: 2 years.
**Breeding**: Single litter of 3–8 young born in spring, after a gestation period of about 5 weeks.
**Life span**: 14 years.
**Status**: Common.

*The Alaska marmot has thick, coarse hair, which makes its heavyset body appear even more rounded. It is adapted to a burrowing lifestyle, with powerful legs and strong, sharp claws for digging. Its body weight varies during the year, since it has to build up substantial fat reserves in summer to see it through hibernation, when it loses one-fifth of its bodyweight.*

# Southern flying squirrel

*Glaucomys volans*

Southern flying squirrels inhabit woodlands, and their range extends from Quebec in eastern North America to Honduras in Central America. Their bodies resemble those of other squirrels, except that they have loose folds of skin that run along their sides and attach to their elongated arms and legs. When the limbs are outstretched, these skin folds are pulled tight to form wing-like membranes.

The flying squirrel cannot actually fly, since the lift force created by the flaps of skin is not enough to keep the animal aloft. It can, however, glide down from tall tree tops to lower branches or to the ground. The squirrel uses its flattened tail as a rudder during glides. For example, when it is time to land, the tail is lifted, altering the animal's centre of gravity and tilting the body upward. This causes the skin membrane to act as a brake, slowing the squirrel for a safe landing. Once on the ground, the squirrel scurries around to the other side of the tree to avoid predators that may have spotted the glide. To get back up the tree, it climbs in conventional squirrel fashion. Flying squirrels are nocturnal. As a result, they have large eyes that enable them to see well enough in the dark to perform complex and risky gliding manoeuvres.

**Distribution**: South-eastern Canada to Central America.
**Habitat**: Woodland.
**Food**: Nuts, seeds, fruit, insects, leaf buds, bark, young birds, young mice and fungi.
**Size**: 21–26cm (8.25–10.25in); 50–180g (1.75–6.5oz).
**Maturity**: 1 year.
**Breeding**: 2–3 young born twice a year, in spring and autumn.
**Life span**: Up to 10 years.
**Status**: Common.

*The fur-covered flap of skin between a flying squirrel's fore and hind legs is called the gliding membrane. It extends along the side of the body from the ankle to the wrist, and tightens when the animal spreads its limbs during a "flight".*

# Black-tailed prairie dog

*Cynomys ludovicianus*

**Distribution**: From south-western Canada to north-eastern Mexico.
**Habitat**: Grassland.
**Food**: Grasses and forbs.
**Size**: 28–33cm (11–13in); 0.7–1.4kg (1.5–3lb).
**Maturity**: 2 years.
**Breeding**: 3–6 young born in early spring.
**Life span**: 5 years.
**Status**: Low risk.

This species of prairie dog inhabits the great prairies that roll south from south-western Canada to north-eastern Mexico. Black-tailed prairie dogs live in large colonies that excavate extensive communal burrows called towns. In frontier times, one huge town in west Texas was estimated to contain 400 million prairie dogs. Today, these rodents are much rarer. They have been exterminated in many places, partly because they devour cereal crops, and partly because grazing livestock injure themselves in the prairie dogs' burrow holes.

Prairie dogs are the most social of all ground squirrels. Each town is divided into smaller neighbourhoods, or coteries. Females stay in the coterie they were born in, forming a band of sisters and female cousins. However, young males set up home in the surrounding coteries. Generally there is one adult male per coterie, although brothers sometimes occupy a particularly large coterie.

*This rodent is actually a type of ground squirrel, but it is referred to as a prairie "dog" because of its barking call. Black-tailed prairie dogs moult twice a year. After each moult, their hairs are a slightly different mixture of colours, ranging from red and yellow to silver and black. The tail has a black tip.*

---

**Olympic marmot** (*Marmota olympus*): 46–53 cm (18–21in); 3–9kg (6.5–19.75lb)
Olympic marmots live on the rock-strewn alpine meadows of the Olympic Peninsula, Washington State, in the north-west of the United States. They live in groups of a about a dozen, made up of an adult male plus two or three females and their offspring. Females produce litters every two years. The marmots forage throughout their territory by day for seeds, fruits and insects. At dusk they follow scent trails back to their burrows.

**Northern flying squirrel** (*Glaucomys sabrinus*): 27–34cm (10.5–13.5in); 75–180g (2.5–5oz)
The northern flying squirrel is smaller than its southern relative, but it has the same gliding membrane for swooping between trees. It occurs from Alaska down North America's Pacific coast to California. Inland it is found in the Rockies, the Appalachians, across the Great Lakes and New England, and as far south as the Sierra Nevada of Mexico. This species inhabits a variety of woodland, from the pine-clad peaks of the sub-Arctic to the lowland deciduous forests of the Midwest. It eats nuts, fungi, fruits and lichens.

**White-tailed prairie dog** (*Cynomys leucurus*): 34–37cm (13.5–14.5in); weight unknown
Slightly larger than the black-tailed prairie dog, this rodent lives in the grasslands of the western United States. It does not live in such large social groups as its black-tailed cousin. White-tailed prairie dogs hibernate from late summer to spring, and breed as soon as they emerge from their winter burrows.

# Mountain beaver

*Aplodontia rufa*

The main populations of mountain beavers are found in two mountain ranges, one extending from southern British Columbia to northern California, and the other from California to western Nevada. Although these forest-dwelling rodents can be found right up to the tree line at 2,200m (7,200ft), they are more common at lower levels. They prefer to be near a source of water, and they also need areas of deep soil in which they can dig their burrows. The burrows are often located under fallen logs.

Mountain beavers live solitary lives and rarely stray more than a few metres from their burrows. They rely on their senses of smell and touch to orientate themselves. Their diet consists of very tough plant food, and they have to digest it twice in order to get all the nutrients out of it. This involves eating pellets of faeces.

*Despite their name, these animals are not true beavers, and they do not dig canals, fell trees or build dams.*

**Distribution**: British Columbia to California and Nevada.
**Habitat**: Forest and alpine meadows.
**Food**: Forbs, grasses and ferns.
**Size**: 30–46cm (12–18in); 0.8–1.5kg (1.75–3.25lb).
**Maturity**: 1 year.
**Breeding**: 2–3 young born in spring.
**Life span**: 5–10 years.
**Status**: Lower risk.

# American red squirrel

*Tamiasciurus hudsonicus*

American red squirrels live in a range of forest habitats, from the pine forests of Canada's cold northern regions to the deciduous woodlands that grow further south as far as Arizona. Although the squirrel's name suggests that it has red hairs, in reality the fur changes colour throughout the year, ranging from a dark brown to ginger. The belly is covered in much paler fur. Each eye has a white ring around it.

Red squirrels live alone. They forage for food during the day and do not hibernate, although they become less active in the coldest regions during winter, when they survive on caches of food. They make their homes in tree hollows and similar small hideaways, including the abandoned holes of woodpeckers. In areas prone to severe frosts, red squirrels den in underground burrows to escape from the freezing temperatures.

During the breeding season, females are receptive to males for just one day. After mating, the male and female separate, and the female cares for the young on her own. Red squirrels eat a wide range of foods. Their diet largely consists of vegetable matter, but they will also feed on eggs, young birds and small mammals when the opportunity arises.

*The tail of the American red squirrel is less bushy than those of related species, and it is more than half the length of the body. The squirrel's coat varies in colour, depending on the time of year.*

**Distribution**: North America, including Canada, New England, the Appalachian Mountains and northern Rockies.
**Habitat**: Forest.
**Food**: Seeds, fruits, nuts, bark, buds, shed antlers, small animals.
**Size**: 16–23cm (6.25–9); 140–250g (5–8.25oz).
**Maturity**: 1 year.
**Breeding**: Up to 8 young born in late winter. In warmer climates there are two breeding seasons, in the late winter and mid-summer.
**Life span**: 7 years.
**Status**: Common

# White-tailed antelope squirrel

*Ammospermophilus leucurus*

White-tailed antelope squirrels inhabit the deserts of the south-western United States and Mexico's Baja California peninsula, and the arid scrub and grasslands of the Great Basin of the north-western United States. They prefer areas with sandy or gravel soils that can be dug into easily. The squirrels burrow into the loose soil to avoid the most intense heat of the day. They also enlarge the abandoned dens of other burrowing desert rodents, such as those of kangaroo rats.

White-tailed antelope squirrels are solitary for most of the year. They forage at dawn and in the late afternoon to avoid the worst of the heat. They retreat to shaded areas to eat, carrying food in their cheek pouches. At the height of summer, when it is especially hot, the squirrels lie underground, pressing their underside to the cool floor of the burrow. In the northern part of their range, winter temperatures often plummet to below freezing. In these situations, the squirrels huddle together in small groups to conserve their body heat.

**Distribution**: South-western North America, from Oregon to New Mexico and Baja California, Mexico.
**Habitat**: Deserts and scrublands.
**Food**: Leaves, seeds, plant stems, roots and fruits, as well as some insects and carrion.
**Size**: 18–24cm (7.4–9.4in); 96–117g (3.4–4oz).
**Maturity**: 1 year.
**Breeding**: Up to 10 young born in spring.
**Life span**: Unknown.
**Status**: Common.

*The body of the white-tailed antelope squirrel is typical of ground squirrels, although the legs are slightly longer than in most species. The underside of the tail is white. This surface may reflect sunlight when the tail is held over the body.*

**Cliff chipmunk** (*Tamias dorsalis*): 21–25cm
(8.5–10in); 61–74 g (2.15–2.6oz)
The cliff chipmunk is found in south-western
United States and northern Mexico. It lives near
cliffs in high desert hills covered by scrub, and
makes dens under rocks. This solitary species is
grey with dark stripes on the back. By day, the
cliff chipmunk forages over a wide area, defending
a relatively large territory for such a small animal.
It searches for seeds, acorns and juniper berries.
Up to six young are produced in spring.

**Eastern fox squirrel** (*Sciurus niger*): 45–70cm
(18–27.5in); 0.7–1.2kg (1.5–2.5lb)
The eastern fox squirrel is an average-sized, tree-
dwelling squirrel. Its back is usually covered in
yellow-orange fur, but many individuals are
completely black. In winter, the squirrel's ears
grow tufts. This squirrel ranges from eastern
Canada through the eastern and central United
States and into northern Mexico. It is found in all
forest types, but does best in those with a variety
of tree species. This diurnal, largely solitary species
eats a range of foods, from nuts, fruits and buds
to insects, young birds and even dead fish.

**Variegated squirrel** (*Sciurus variegatoides*):
22–34cm (8.5–13.5in); 430–900g (15.25–32.75oz)
Variegated squirrels range from Chiapas in
southern Mexico to Panama. They live in all types
of tropical forest, from moist evergreen forests to
drier deciduous or monsoon forests. The coats of
variegated squirrels display a variety of bands and
other patterns. These solitary animals spend most
of their time up in the branches. They eat mainly
plant matter such as nuts, fruits and flowers.

## Grey-collared chipmunk

*Tamias cinereicollis*

Grey-collared chipmunks are not a widespread
species, although they are common within
their range in the south-western United
States. Their preferred habitat is relatively dry
mountain conifer forest, where they are rarely
found below 1,950m (6,400 ft). However,
grey-coloured chipmunks have also adapted
to living in suburban areas at lower altitudes,
following the recent rapid expansion of
human settlements in the region. Here, the
chipmunks are often found living under
patios and in the foundations of buildings.

Grey-collared chipmunks are diurnal,
being most active in the cool of the morning
and evening. They live alone in burrows. In
winter, they spend long periods underground
to avoid the worst of the weather. They mate
soon after emerging from their burrows in
spring, and breed again in autumn before
preparing for hibernation.

*Grey-collared chipmunks, so called because of
the distinctive colour bands on their body, have
dextrous hands and unusually protruding
incisors. They hold food in their hands
and remove any unwanted
material with their teeth, before
pushing the
food into a
cheek pouch.*

**Distribution**: Arizona and
New Mexico.
**Habitat**: Mountain conifer
forests.
**Food**: Nuts, berries, seeds
and insects.
**Size**: 8–16cm (3.1–6.3in);
55–70g (2–2.5oz).
**Maturity**: 1 year.
**Breeding**: Litters of 2–5 born
in spring and autumn.
**Life span**:
3 years.
**Status**:
Common.

## Eastern chipmunk

*Tamias striatus*

These rodents are found in eastern North America. They
live in woodland and bushy habitats, feeding on nuts, seeds,
mushrooms and fruits during the daytime. These solitary
animals retire to burrows at night. The burrows are only
just below the surface, but their tunnels may extend for
several metres. The burrow entrances are hidden (the
excavated earth is scattered), and they are often
located in secluded areas to avoid discovery by
predators such as foxes, snakes and birds of prey.

Eastern chipmunks forage for food in a small
territory around the burrow. They chase away any
intruders looking for food in that area. These chipmunks
sleep through the winter in their burrows, waking regularly
to feed on caches of food made during the autumn.

Chipmunks are named after the "chip chip"
noises they frequently make, and often
gather in groups to "sing" to each other.
These noises and other vocalizations are
used by chipmunks in communication.

*Eastern chipmunks are larger than
most chipmunks. Their most
obvious feature is the pouched
cheeks located inside their
mouths. These
pouches are used
to store food.*

**Distribution**: Eastern North
America, from Quebec and
Ontario to Iowa and Illinois
**Habitat**: Woodland.
**Food**: Nuts, seeds,
mushrooms and fruits.
**Size**: 13–19cm (5.25–7.5in);
70–140g (2.5–5oz).
**Maturity**: 1 year.
**Breeding**: About 4 young are
produced in early spring, and
again in summer.
**Life span**: 1 year.
**Status**:
Common.

## North American porcupine

*Erethizon dorsatum*

North American porcupines are nocturnal animals that spend most of the night looking for food on the ground. However, they occasionally climb slowly into trees to find food. They cannot see very well, but have sensitive noses for detecting danger.

During the daytime, porcupines rest in hollow trees, caves or disused burrows. They regularly move from den to den throughout the year. They do not hibernate and keep feeding throughout the winter, but they will stay in their den during periods of harsh weather.

Porcupines live solitary lives, but do not defend territories, although they may attempt to drive away other porcupines from trees laden with food. When cornered by predators, porcupines turn their backs on their attackers and thrash around with their spiky tails. If the barbed quills penetrate the attacker's skin, they detach from the porcupine and work their way into the assailant's body.

In early winter, males seek out females and shower them with urine before mating. The males are chased away by the females after mating. They give birth to their litters in summer.

*Porcupines have sharp, barbed quills (thickened hairs) on their rumps and short tails. In New World porcupines the quills are set individually in the skin; in Old World species they are grouped into clusters.*

**Distribution**: North America, including Alaska and Canada, south to northern Mexico.
**Habitat**: Forest and brush.
**Food**: Wood, bark and needles in winter; buds, roots, seeds and leaves in summer.
**Size**: 64–80cm (25–31.5in); 3.5–7kg (7.75–15.5lb).
**Maturity**: 2.5 years.
**Breeding**: Single young born in summer.
**Life span**: 18 years.
**Status**: Common.

## Capybara

*Hydrochaerus hydrochaeris*

Capybaras are the largest rodents in the world. They live in herds of about 20 individuals, feeding by day on the banks of rivers and in swampy areas. These grazing herbivores use their incisors to clip the grasses off at ground level. Although they are well suited to being in water, with eyes and nostrils high on the head and webbed hind feet, capybaras do not feed for long periods in water. They tend to use water as a refuge from predators and as a means of keeping cool on hot days. If startled, capybaras gallop into water and may swim to the safety of floating plants. When they surface, only their eyes and nostrils are visible.

Capybaras do not make permanent dens, but sleep in waterside thickets. Each herd contains several adults of both sexes plus their offspring, all conforming to a hierarchy. A single male leads the herd. Only he can mate with the females in the herd. Fights often break out between the other males as they attempt to improve their rank.

Capybaras can breed all year round, but mating is most common at the start of the rainy season. Usually females give birth to one litter, but two may be produced if conditions are favourable. The young are well developed at birth, and soon able to follow their mother and eat grass. They are weaned after about four months.

**Distribution**: Central America to Uruguay.
**Habitat**: Thickly vegetated areas around fresh water.
**Food**: Grass, grains, melons and squashes.
**Size**: 1–1.3m (3.25–4.25ft); 27–79kg (59–174lb).
**Maturity**: 15 months.
**Breeding**: Single litter of 5 young born at any time of year.
**Life span**: 10 years.
**Status**: Common.

*Capybaras have bodies similar to guinea pigs, except that they are much bigger and more heavyset. The males possess large sebaceous (oil) glands on their short rounded snouts.*

# Pygmy mouse

*Baiomys taylori*

Pygmy mice are the smallest rodents in the Americas, little more than the size of a person's thumb. They live in areas where plants, logs and rocks provide them with plenty of cover. The mice create networks of runs through undergrowth and under rocks, leaving piles of droppings at junctions. These may act as signposts or be signals to other mice in their network. Pygmy mice are most active at dawn and dusk, but will also feed throughout the day.

At night they sleep in nests made from plants and twigs. They do not live in groups as such, but will tolerate the presence of other mice close by. Pygmy mice can breed at a young age. Females can become pregnant after just a month of life. They breed throughout the year, often producing several litters per year. Both parents care for the young, which are born in nests inside shallow dips dug into the ground or in secluded cavities under logs or rocks.

*The pygmy mouse's ears are smaller and rounder than those of most mice. It has black and brown hairs on its back with lighter red and brown fur underneath.*

**Distribution**: South-western United States to central Mexico.
**Habitat**: Dry scrub.
**Food**: Stems, leaves, insects and seeds.
**Size**: 5–8cm (2–3.25in); 7–8g (0.2–0.3oz).
**Maturity**: Females 28 days; males 80 days.
**Breeding**: Several litters of 1–5 young each year.
**Life span**: 2 years.
**Status**: Common.

---

**Prehensile-tailed porcupine** (*Coendou prehensilis*): 30–60cm (12–23.5in); 0.9–5kg (2–11lb)
Primarily a forest dweller, this porcupine is found from Venezuela to southern Brazil and the foothills of the Bolivian Andes, and also on the Caribbean island of Trinidad. It occurs in lowland and coastal areas, and up to 2,500m (8,200ft). Prehensile-tailed porcupines eat plants, especially tender leaves, stems and flowers. They gnaw at the young wood under bark, and sometimes raid commercial fruit crops. After spending the day resting in trees they forage in darkness, winding their tail around branches for extra support when moving through the trees. The porcupines rely on their sharp quills to ward off predators, but they may try to frighten aggressors away by stamping their feet. If all else fails, they curl up into a ball to protect themselves from attack.

**Bahamian hutia** (*Geocapromys ingrahami*): 20–60cm (8–23.5in); 5kg (11lb)
This unusual rodent lives in the Bahamas; subspecies are found on other Caribbean islands and on the Venezuelan mainland. Bahamian hutias live in forested habitats, spending time both on the ground and in trees. They are mainly vegetarian, eating eat bark, nuts, leaves and fruits. The body is rat-like in form, although the species is more closely related to cavies and coypus.

**Southern mountain cavy** (*Microcavia australis*): 22cm (8.5in); 275g (9.75oz)
This species, a relative of domestic guinea pigs, is found in Argentina, southern Chile and southern Bolivia, where it lives in dry brush habitats. It is rarely seen, since it moves through runs hidden among the thick vegetation. Where the cover is less thick, southern mountain cavies dig burrows. They feed during the day, climbing in shrubs to get at the most tender leaves.

# Guinea pig

*Cavia aperea*

Guinea pigs, or cavies as they are also known, are most active in the twilight hours – around dawn and dusk. At these times, most predators are less active because their eyes cannot cope with the rapidly changing light levels. Guinea pigs are found in a wide range of habitats and altitudes, even living high up in the Andes Mountains.

Guinea pigs generally rest underground or in thickets. They may dig their own burrows, but are more likely to take over holes made by other animals. When on the move, these rodents follow well-trodden paths to areas where food is available.

Guinea pigs live in small groups of fewer than ten individuals. Many groups may crowd around a large supply of food, forming a temporary mass of rodents. The groups have hierarchies, with single males and females ruling over the others. Contenders for the top positions in the group may fight each other to the death. Breeding takes place throughout the year.

**Distribution**: Colombia to Argentina, excluding the Amazon Basin.
**Habitat**: Grassland, swamp and rocky areas.
**Food**: Plants.
**Size**: 20–40cm (8–15.5in); 0.5–1.5kg (1–3.25lb).
**Maturity**: 3 months.
**Breeding**: Up to 5 litters per year.
**Life span**: 8 years.
**Status**: Common.

*Although domestic guinea pigs often have long, soft coats of many colours and patterns, wild specimens have shorter and coarser fur, generally made up of grey, brown and black hairs.*

# Mara

*Dolichotis patagonum*

Maras are the largest members of the cavy family, which includes the wild ancestors of domestic guinea pigs. They live in the pampas grasslands of Argentina. Maras graze out in the open during the day on most types of plant, although they prefer the young shoots of grasses and leafy, low-growing herbs. At night, they shelter in burrows, which they dig themselves using the sharp claws on their forefeet.

Adults pair off as they reach maturity, and stay with their mates for life. Living in pairs helps the maras to avoid danger in their open grassland habitat, where pampas cats, large birds of prey and other predators are always on the look out for a meal. As a pair moves around grazing, the maras take turns to keep watch while their partner feeds. When danger is spotted, they gallop to safety on their long legs, reaching speeds of up to 45kmh (28mph).

*Maras do not look like typical rodents. Their long legs make them resemble a small hoofed animal, such as a deer. This appearance is reinforced by the animal's square snout and large, pointed ears.*

**Distribution**: Central and southern Argentina.
**Habitat**: Open pampas grassland and dry scrub.
**Food**: Grass and herbs.
**Size**: 73–80cm (29–32in); 8–16kg (18–36lb).
**Maturity**: 6 months.
**Breeding**: Litters of up to 3 young born two or three times a year.
**Life span**: 15 years.
**Status**: Lower risk.

---

**Northern viscacha** (*Lagidium peruanum*): 30–45cm (12–18in); 0.9–1.6kg (2–3.5lb)
While these animals resemble rabbits, with long pointed ears and large hind feet, they are actually relatives of chinchillas. Living high up the Peruvian Andes, they occupy dry rocky areas that exist between the tree line and the snow line. Viscachas live in large colonies of up to 80 individuals. They survive by eating the grasses, lichens and mosses that grow in the harsh alpine conditions.

**Green acouchi** (*Myoprocta acouchy*): 32cm (12.5in); weight unknown
These relatively large, long-legged rodents are related to agoutis. The fur is often greenish, but it can also be red or grey. Green acouchis live in the forests of the Amazon Basin and the surrounding highlands. They are most active by day, and bury food to be used in times of drought. They eat fruits, nuts, succulents and roots, and may be pests in cassava and peanut plantations.

**Social tuco-tuco** (*Ctenomys sociabilis*): 18–24cm (7–9.5in); 180g (6.5oz)
This grassland species of southern Argentina occurs between the Andes Mountains and the Patagonian Desert. Social tuco-tucos feed on the grasses and sedges that grow around their burrow entrances. These rodents live in colonies containing many small family groups. Each group comprises several closely related females. During the breeding season, a male is accepted into the group's den and allowed to breed with the females. He is then chased away, and moves to another group elsewhere in the colony.

# Chinchilla

*Chinchilla lanigera*

The chinchilla's dense coat helps it to survive on the bleak, windswept Andean mountain slopes. In the past, chinchillas were hunted for their striking blue-grey fur in an unsustainable fashion. As a result, wild chinchillas, which once ranged across the High Andes from Peru and Bolivia to Chile, are now only found in the mountains of northern Chile. Today, chinchillas are a protected species. They are bred in captivity for their fur (and make good pets), although wild animals are still occasionally hunted illegally.

Chinchillas shelter in rock crevices by day. They eat alpine plants, and do most of their feeding in the gloom of dawn and dusk. They may form colonies of up to 100 individuals. On sunny days, colony members can be seen sunbathing at the entrances to their dens.

*Chinchilla fur is thick and soft, with about 60 hairs growing out of each follicle. Coats made from chinchilla fur were once highly valued. Hunting wild chinchillas for their fur is now illegal.*

**Distribution**: Northern Chile.
**Habitat**: Arid mountain slopes.
**Food**: Grass, seeds, insects and birds' eggs.
**Size**: 22–38cm (8.5–15in); 500–800g (17.75–28.25oz).
**Maturity**: 8 months.
**Breeding**: Litters of 2–3 young born in spring and summer.
**Life span**: 10 years.
**Status**: Vulnerable.

## Brazilian agouti

*Dasyprocta leporina*

Brazilian agoutis are found throughout Brazil and the surrounding South American countries, from dense rainforests to suburban back gardens. They prefer areas with plenty of cover, and are most common close to bodies of water.

Brazilian agoutis are cautious creatures. They are rarely seen out in the open, preferring to move slowly but surely through undergrowth. They are primarily diurnal, although they do feed on bright moonlit nights. Their diet consists mainly of seeds and fruit. When they sense danger, the agoutis dash away on their long, powerful legs. These animals pair up for life. They travel in small groups made up of the breeding pair and their offspring. The young, which can run within an hour of birth, remain with their parents until they are five or six months old. Males are more likely to leave the family group than females. These lone males are often forced to set up home in unsuitable open territory, where they are more likely to be picked off by ocelots and other predators.

**Distribution**: Northern South America, east of the Andes.
**Habitat**: Areas with plenty of cover, mainly forests.
**Food**: Seeds, fruits, leaves and insects.
**Size**: 41–62cm (16–24.5in); 3–6kg (6.5–13.25lb).
**Maturity**: 1 year.
**Breeding**: Litters of up to 3 pups born twice a year.
**Life span**: 15 years.
**Status**: Common

*Brazilian agoutis are also known as red-rumped agoutis because of the red patch on their hind quarters. Their relatively long legs make them look different from most other rodents. They often squat on their back legs, like squirrels, when feeding.*

## Coypu

*Myocastor coypus*

Coypus, or nutrias, live in wetland habitats from southern Brazil and Bolivia to Tierra del Fuego at the southern tip of South America. They have very large, orange-tinged incisors. These are always visible, since the mouth closes behind them in order to keep out water when the animal is swimming.

Coypus are nocturnal feeders, foraging for food both in and out of the water. These small, largely herbivorous rodents eat aquatic plants, but they will occasionally take freshwater molluscs such as mussels and water snails. They are able to remain submerged for up to 10 minutes. When not feeding, the coypus sunbathe and groom each other on platforms of floating vegetation. They may shelter in the burrow of another animal or dig their own burrow, which can be a simple tunnel or a complex system of chambers and passages.

Coypus live in groups of a single adult male, several females (often related to each other) and up to a dozen of their young. Females may produce their single litter at any time of year, and the males play no part in raising the young. Females tend to stay with their family group, while young males disperse.

**Distribution**: Southern South America, east of the Andes; introduced to the Mississippi Delta.
**Habitat**: Marshes; river and lake banks.
**Food**: Water plants and freshwater molluscs.
**Size**: 47–58cm (18.5–23in); 5–10kg (11–22lb).
**Maturity**: 6 months.
**Breeding**: Single litter of about 6 young born at any time of year.
**Life span**: 6 years.
**Status**: Lower risk.

*Coypus look like large water rats, with soft, thick underfur covered by longer, well-oiled hairs. The hind feet are webbed to help with swimming and moving through boggy ground. The unwebbed forefeet are used for holding food.*

# Brown lemming

*Lemmus sibiricus*

Contrary to popular belief, lemmings do not commit suicide. During favourable years, the lemmings' ability to reproduce very quickly leads to population explosions of amazing proportions. As the population size goes up, space becomes more and more difficult to find, and young are pushed away from the best habitat, down the mountains and into the valleys. Lemmings are good swimmers when they have to be, but they have their limits. During dispersal, young lemmings often try to cross large bodies of water that are beyond their swimming capabilities, drowning in the process. It is this behaviour that gave rise to the misconception that they kill themselves.

In summer, lemmings spend much of their time underground in burrows, but when the ground starts to freeze in autumn, they cannot dig through the ground and are forced to forage on the surface. They do not hibernate in the harsh winter, but tunnel under the snow in search of food. The tunnels keep them out of sight from predators such as snowy owls, which are heavily reliant on lemmings as a source of food.

**Distribution**: Arctic mainland and islands of northern Canada, Alaska and Siberia.
**Habitat**: Arctic tundra grassland and sub-Arctic tundra above the treeline.
**Food**: Mosses, grasses and sedges.
**Size**: 13–18cm (5–7in); 50–140g (2–4.75oz).
**Maturity**: 5–6 weeks.
**Breeding**: These prolific breeders may produce as many as 8 litters per year, each of up to 12 young; gestation is about 3 weeks.
**Life span**: Less than 2 years.
**Status**: Common.

*Unlike other lemming species, the brown lemming does not change the colour of its winter coat.*

# Southern bog lemming

*Synaptomys cooperi*

*With their dark, thick hair, bog lemmings look almost round. However, their bodies are small and they are no more robust than other lemmings or voles. They have powerful jaws and the long, orange-coloured incisors typical of rodents, which are kept sharp by frequent gnawing. The fur is grey-grizzled by silver hairs mixed in with the darker ones. Female southern bog lemmings have six nipples, while in northern bog lemmings, their closest relatives, the females have eight.*

Southern bog lemmings live in the eastern region of North America, from Labrador to Ontario and Kansas to North Carolina. They are most often found in bogs, generally sphagnum bogs, so-called because of the large amounts of thick sphagnum moss that dominate the habitat. However, these lemmings are also found in less water-logged areas, such as pine forests and cultivated fields.

Southern bog lemmings may be active by day or night, but they are largely nocturnal. They eat a wide range of plant foods. By gnawing through the base of the stems, they fell tall plants so that they can eat the tender leaves, shoots and fruits growing higher up. Bog lemmings construct tunnels and subsurface runways, or utilize those made by other small mammals. They use dried grass and sedge to build concealed nests in clumps of grass, or under tree stumps and sphagnum mounds.

Bog lemmings breed up to three times a year, although in northern areas more than once is probably unlikely.

**Distribution**: Eastern North America.
**Habitat**: Bogs and wet grasslands.
**Food**: Grasses, moss, sedges, fruits, mushrooms and roots.
**Size**: 11–14cm (4.25–5.5 inches); 20–50g (0.75–1.75oz).
**Maturity**: 5 weeks.
**Breeding**: Litters of 1–8 young (average 3) are produced 2–3 times a year; most young are born between April and September.
**Life span**: 2 years.
**Status**: Common.

# Muskrat

*Ondatra zibethicus*

**Distribution**: Northern
Canada and Alaska to Gulf
of Mexico.
**Habitat**: Swamps and other
wetlands.
**Food**: Water plants.
**Size**: 22–33cm (8.5–13in);
0.7–1.8kg (1.5–4lb).
**Maturity**: 7 months.
**Breeding**: 6 young born in
summer.
**Life span**: 3 years.
**Status**: Common.

Muskrats live in most of
Canada and the United
States, excluding the
high Arctic region. At
the beginning of the last
century, muskrats were
introduced to Eurasia, and
they have thrived in parts
of Scandinavia and northern
Russia, as well as in warmer parts of Siberia.

Muskrats live in large family groups along riverbanks and
in marshes, particularly where there is plenty of bankside
vegetation to provide shelter. They dig burrows into the
banks, which they access through underwater entrances.
When living in more open wetlands, they make domed nests
from grass. Muskrats are largely nocturnal, but crepuscular
(active at dawn and dusk) as well.

In the south of their range, muskrats breed at all times
of the year. In the northern areas, the long winters limit the
breeding season to the summer.

*Muskrats are semi-aquatic
animals, spending time both in
and out of water. Their fur is oily
to make it waterproof, and the
hind feet are webbed. These
rodents use their scaly tails
for steering while swimming.
Muskrats eat water plants and
small aquatic animals, including
mussels and crayfish.*

**Round-tailed muskrat** (*Neofiber alleni*):
38–54cm (15–21.5in); weight unknown
The round-tailed muskrat, or Florida water rat,
occurs from southern Georgia and across Florida,
including the islands off the Florida coast. It is
smaller than other muskrats, which also have
more flattened tails. Round-tailed muskrats live
in swamps, lakes and other wetland areas. They
build a dome-shaped lodge from felled vegetation,
with a grass-lined chamber inside. Round-tailed
muskrats are declining as their habitat is lost to
development along Florida's coast.

**Black rat** (*Rattus rattus*): 16–22cm (6.25–8.5in);
70–300g (2.5–10.5oz)
Originally from India, this rat is found wherever
humans have settled, including throughout the
Americas. It even survives in Arctic settlements,
but no sustainable population exists in Antarctica.
Adaptability is the secret of the black rat's success.
Its medium-sized body makes it a good climber,
jumper, swimmer and runner. Its long teeth allow
it to tackle almost any food, and its intelligence
means that it can investigate new areas quickly
and remember the location of food sources.

**Brown rat** (*Rattus norvegicus*): 20–30cm
(8–12in); 275–575g (9.75–20.25oz)
The brown rat, or Norway rat, has spread from
its native forest habitat in China and is now
common on all continents except Antarctica.
Brown rats share the characteristics that make
its relative the black rat a success. A female
brown rat can produce 60 offspring in one year if
conditions are right, illustrating just how quickly
these rodents can take over a new habitat.

# Hairy-tailed bolo mouse

*Bolomys lasiurus*

Hairy-tailed bolo mice occur throughout
central South America, from Bolivia and
Brazil to northern Argentina. They live in dry
grasslands and savannahs, and sometimes
around the edges of forests. More than four-
fifths of their diet is made up of grass seeds.
The rest consists of leaves and insects. The
mice become especially dependent on insects
after the savannahs have been swept by fires
at the end of the dry season.

Hairy-tailed bolo mice are most active
during the daytime. They produce extensive
burrow systems with several entrances, giving
easy access to the safety of the burrow when
predators approach. Male mice occupy a large
territory that includes the home ranges of
several females. They prevent rival males from
entering the territory. Most mating occurs in
the rainy season.

**Distribution**: Central South
America.
**Habitat**: Savannah.
**Food**: Seeds, leaves and
insects.
**Size**: 18cm (7in); 35g (1.25oz).
**Maturity**: Unknown.
**Breeding**: 3–6 young per
litter; most litters produced in
wet season (January–March),
although breeding occurs all
year round.
**Life span**: Unknown.
**Status**: Common.

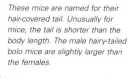

*These mice are named for their
hair-covered tail. Unusually for
mice, the tail is shorter than the
body length. The male hairy-tailed
bolo mice are slightly larger than
the females.*

## Meadow jumping mouse

*Zapus hudsonius*

*Meadow jumping mice have enormously long tails – up to 16.5cm (6.5in) or more – that are much longer than their body length. They also have large hind feet, up to 3.5cm (1.4in) long, with which they propel themselves forward in great bounds. The fur on the back is greyish-brown, the flanks are yellowish-brown, and the underside is whitish. The tail lacks the white tip seen on woodland jumping mice. The meadow jumping mouse is the only mammal species with 18 teeth. Females are sometimes larger than males.*

Meadow jumping mice live across the northern part of North America, from the Atlantic coast of the United States to the Great Plains east of the Rocky Mountains. These mice are also found as far south as New Mexico. Meadow jumping mice live in any area with a layer of undergrowth in which they can move around unnoticed. Despite their name, they do live in woodlands, but prefer the more open habitat of grasslands.

Meadow jumping mice live solitary lives. They are most active during the night, and make their way through the dense undergrowth by following the runways made in the grass by voles. They can hop a considerable distance, up to 15cm (6in) in one bound. These mice can also climb trees, swim across streams and dig into the ground. They forage for food over a wide area, resting in nests made of grass during the day. Their diet consists mainly of seeds, but insects are important in spring. In winter, they hibernate in deep underground burrows. They begin breeding soon after emerging in spring.

**Distribution**: Northern North America, from southern Alaska to Labrador and northern Georgia; isolated populations occur in the mountains of Arizona and New Mexico.
**Habitat**: Moist grasslands.
**Food**: Seeds, berries, fruits and insects.
**Size**: 7.5–11cm (3–4.3in); 12–30g (0.5–1oz).
**Maturity**: 2 months.
**Breeding**: 2–3 litters of 5 or 6 young born in spring and summer; gestation is about 18 days.
**Life span**: 1 year.
**Status**: Common.

## Woodland jumping mouse

*Napaeozapus insignis*

Woodland jumping mice live in the north-eastern region of North America, from central Canada to Labrador, and to the Appalachian Mountains of the United States. They live in forests, being most common in the pine forests that grow at higher latitudes and on high mountains. In the southern part of their range, many of the forests have been reduced in size by agriculture, so these mice are only found in the small patches that remain.

*Like the meadow jumping mouse, the woodland jumping mouse has a long tail, which can measure up to 16cm (6.3in) long. The fur is arranged in three coloured bands. The underside is pale, almost white. The sides of the body are pale brown, with long, black guard hairs. The upper surface has a wide, dark brown stripe from the head to the base of the tail. Females are slightly larger than males, and mice in the northern parts of the range tend to be about 12 per cent larger than individuals from southern parts.*

Woodland jumping mice are nocturnal, but often come out to feed on cloudy days. They dig their own burrows and build grass-lined nests inside. When out foraging, the mice cover the entrances to their burrows with vegetation.

This species hibernates underground for at least six months of the year, during which time it may lose more than one-third of its bodyweight.

When the mice awake, they breed immediately. In warmer parts of their range, the mice may produce two litters if warm weather persists for long enough. The young are weaned when they are about five weeks old.

**Distribution**: North-eastern North America, from south-eastern Manitoba to Labrador and Pennsylvania and south along the Appalachians to northern Georgia.
**Habitat**: Pine and mixed forests.
**Food**: Fruits, seeds, fungi and insects.
**Size**: 8–10cm (3–4in); 17–35g (0.5–1.25oz).
**Maturity**: 8 months
**Breeding**: 1–2 litters of 2–7 young produced in summer; gestation is 23–29 days.
**Life span**: 3 years.
**Status**: Common.

# Giant pocket gopher

*Orthogeomys grandis*

**Distribution**: Central America and Mexico
**Habitat**: Burrows under forests.
**Food**: Roots, turnips, tubers, nuts and seeds.
**Size**: 22–28cm (8.5–11in); 830g (29.25oz).
**Maturity**: 3 months.
**Breeding**: Up to 10 young born in a single litter at any time of year.
**Life span**: 2 years.
**Status**: Common.

Giant pocket gophers are found in Mexico and Central America. They spend most of their time in tunnels that they excavate under forests and farmland. Their body is adapted for moving through burrows in soft ground. Flaps close their ears to keep out dirt, while the eyelids seal the eyes and thick tears wash away any soil from the eye's surface. As the gophers use their teeth to cut through soil, the mouth closes behind the teeth, so they do not swallow earth.

Giant pocket gophers dig two kinds of tunnel. Long, winding tunnels just below the surface are used to find food. Deeper tunnel networks are used to make dens, where young are born and food is stored. Large mounds of earth mark the entrances to these tunnels. The entrances are generally sealed so that flood water and predators, such as snakes, cannot get in. Pocket gophers are named after the fur-lined pockets on the outside of their cheeks, which these rodents use for transporting food. The pockets can be turned inside-out for cleaning.

*The gopher's body is covered in sensitive whiskers that can detect vibrations made by other gophers moving through tunnels. The naked tail is also highly sensitive to touch, and is used to feel objects in the dark. When the tunnels get too hot, excess body heat is released through the tail.*

---

**Pale kangaroo mouse** (*Microdipodops pallidus*):
6.5–7.5cm (2.5–3in); 10–17g (0.25–0.5oz)
Pale kangaroo mice are found in western Nevada and the dry regions of eastern California. They prefer dry shrublands and semi-deserts with sandy or gravel soils, often digging their burrows at the base of shrubs. The kangaroo mouse moves by hopping on its long hind feet, using its tail for balance. The soles of the hind feet are covered in hairs that make them much wider, preventing the mouse from sinking in soft sand. This species has long, silky, tan-coloured fur. Pale kangaroo mice eat mainly seeds, nibbling off the hard husks with their front teeth and carrying the food back to their burrows inside cheek pouches. They feed at night and live alone.

**Bristle-spined rat** (*Chaetomys subspinosus*):
42cm (16.5in); 1.3kg (2.75lb)
These rodents are sometimes called three-spined porcupines. They live in northern and central Brazil, where they occupy both bushlands and forest habitats. Unlike true porcupines, the hairs of bristle-spined rats are more like stiff bristles than sharp quills. These bristles cover the head, neck and forelimbs of the rodent. The tail is long and scaly. Bristle-spined rats are slow-moving animals that jump and climb through trees looking for food, which is mostly made up of fruits and nuts. The rats are nocturnal, sleeping in tree hollows or rock crevices. Bristle-spined rats are found only in small areas of Brazil. Their habitats are gradually being destroyed by logging, agriculture and industry, and this species is now classified as vulnerable.

## Desert kangaroo rat

*Dipodomys deserti*

Desert kangaroo rats live in arid regions of the south-western United States and Mexico, where there is very little vegetation. They inhabit some of the hottest and driest places on Earth, including Death Valley in California. They are also found on desert peaks up to about 1,700m (5,600ft). Desert kangaroo rats only survive where there are wind-blown sand-dunes. These sand-dunes contain enough food for the rats, including old plants covered by sand and seeds blown into the dune by the wind. The rats do not need to drink water, because they get all the water they need from the plants they eat.

Desert kangaroo rats dig complex burrows inside the sand-dunes. The burrows have a central nest chamber and several side spaces for storing food. These solitary rodents only emerge at night, and so avoid the heat of the day. With reduced front limbs, they leap around on their long back legs like kangaroos. The tail may be up to 21cm (8.5in) long.

**Distribution**: South-western North America.
**Habitat**: Sand-dunes.
**Food**: Seeds and dried leaves.
**Size**: 12–16cm (5–6.5in); 95–135g (3.3–4.7oz).
**Maturity**: 2 months.
**Breeding**: 2–3 litters of up to 6 young born January–July.
**Life span**: 5 years.
**Status**: Common.

*This species stores seeds and other foods inside its fur-lined cheek pockets. Male desert kangaroo rats are slightly larger than females. Curiously, desert kangaroo rats have thicker hair than species of kangaroo rat that live in cooler regions.*

## Red tree vole

*Arborimus longicaudus*

Red tree voles live in well-established forests. Most of the forests in their range, which stretches from northern California to southern Washington, are populated with fir and spruce trees. They also prefer areas that get a lot of rain. The voles spend almost their entire lives up trees. Only the males regularly come to the ground, where they den in burrows at the foot of trees. The females build their nests among the branches at all heights, from the lowest branches to the very tops of trees.

Apart from mothers raising young, red tree voles are solitary animals. However, they sometimes live in loose clusters or colonies, in which individuals avoid interaction with each other but gather together in one tree or stand of trees. These voles are nocturnal. They collect needles (predominantly those of the Douglas fir) and bring them back to their nests, then feed on their store of needles during the day. They obtain the water they need from the needles and the dew that forms on them. At night they are cautious creatures. If they are disturbed, the voles will leap to lower branches and head down to the ground, where they hide in the undergrowth.

*These small rodents have fur that ranges from ginger to cinnamon. The females tend to be larger than the males. Red tree voles only have claws on four of their five digits. The first digit has a nail instead. They nest high up in fir trees.*

**Distribution**: Pacific North-west region of United States; west of the Cascade Mountains, from southern Washington to northern Carolina.
**Habitat**: Conifer forests.
**Food**: Conifer needles.
**Size**: 9.5–11cm (3.75–4.3in); 25–50g (1–1.75oz).
**Maturity**: 2 months.
**Breeding**: 3 litters of up to 3 young born mainly in spring and summer.
**Life span**: 2 years.
**Status**: Common.

## Western heather vole

*Phenacomys intermedius*

*The colour of this heather vole's long, soft fur varies across its range, but it is largely greyish brown, with a slightly lighter underside. There are sometimes orange hairs growing on the ears. At 2.5–4cm (1–1.6in), the short tail is only about as long as the hind feet. The heather vole so closely resembles another species, the meadow vole, that the two can sometimes only be identified by examining their skull characteristics and teeth.*

The western heather vole occurs across the western United States as far south as New Mexico. In Canada, the range extends to the Yukon and eastward to the Atlantic coast of Labrador. As its name suggests, this vole lives in highland meadows and more exposed alpine tundras, where heather is common. However, this species is also found in alpine and northern lowland forests, where conifers such as aspen and spruce predominate.

Unusually for a small species living in such a northerly range, heather voles do not hibernate and are active all year round. During the summer, they construct an underground burrow with an entrance hidden by fallen leaves. In winter, the voles cannot dig into the frozen ground. Instead they make nests in the snow, generally underneath a shrub or log for added protection from the elements. The voles keep warm by lining their snow holes with moss, lichens and twigs.

These voles are solitary except during the breeding season, when males fight with each other and females with young become aggressive toward intruders.

**Distribution**: Western United States, as far south as New Mexico, and across Canada, from the Yukon to Labrador.
**Habitat**: Highland meadows, spruce, pine and aspen forests.
**Food**: Bark, buds, heathers, twigs, seeds, berries, lichens and fungi.
**Size**: 9–12cm (3.5–4.8in); 30–50g (1–1.75oz).
**Maturity**: 6 weeks.
**Breeding**: Up to 3 litters of about 4 young each are produced in summer; gestation is 19–24 days.
**Life span**: 1 year.
**Status**: Common.

# Azara's grass mouse

*Akodon azarae*

**Distribution**: Central and southern South America.
**Habitat**: Undergrowth.
**Food**: Leaves, fruits, insects and seeds.
**Size**: 7.5–15cm (3–6in); 10–45g (0.25–1.5oz).
**Maturity**: 2 months.
**Breeding**: 2 litters of 3–4 young produced in summer.
**Life span**: 1 year.
**Status**: Lower risk.

Azara's grass mouse lives in the tall-grass pampas of central Argentina and southern Brazil. It is also found in Bolivia, Paraguay and Uruguay. These mice dig their burrows in the undergrowth close to habitat boundaries, where thick vegetation gives way to more open terrain. Here, they can return to the safety of the plant cover after foraging in the open. This sort of habitat is common in artificial landscapes such as gardens and along roadsides. In winter, this species is also often found in flooded lowland areas. However, at warmer times of year the mice head for high ground.

Azara's grass mice live in groups made up of both males and females. Mice born in autumn will survive for about a year, but those born in spring are unlikely to last more than eight months, because many adult mice struggle to find shelter during winter.

*The tail of Azara's grass mouse can be up to 10cm (4in) long. Being a small mammal, it can fluctuate in weight easily. It is heaviest in spring, but may be half this weight by the autumn.*

**House mouse** (*Mus musculus*): 6.5–9.5cm (2.5–3.75in); 12–25g (0.5–1oz)
From its original range, which stretched from the Mediterranean Sea to China, the house mouse has now spread around the world, making its home wherever humans live. The key to its success is its ability to make use of whatever food sources people provide. Today, house mice are considered to be a major pest, causing billions of dollars' worth of damage to food stores worldwide every year. They also damage buildings, woodwork, furniture and clothing, and are known to carry various diseases, including typhus and salmonella. However, house mice are virtually unrivalled in their capacity to adapt to new surroundings. Their generalist habits, rapid breeding rate and talent for slipping into places unnoticed has enabled them to become possibly the most numerous mammal species in the world today.

**Mexican volcano mouse** (*Neotomodon alstoni*): 10–13cm (4–5in); 40–60g (1.5–2oz)
The Mexican volcano mouse inhabits the volcanic mountains of central Mexico, where it is found in pine forests between 2,600m and 4,600m (8,500–15,000ft). These forests differ from conifer habitats found further north because they have a layer of grass beneath the trees. Mexican volcano mice live in burrows under the rocks that stud the grass. These opportunistic feeders eat seeds, insects, leaves and many other foods. Young are produced between June and September, with about three mice in each litter. The young mice are ready to breed themselves after about five months, which is a slow maturation for a mouse species. Observations also suggest that these mice live for a long time, perhaps up to five years.

# Bushy-tailed woodrat

*Neotoma cinerea*

**Distribution**: Western North America, from Arctic Canada to Arizona.
**Habitat**: From woodland to desert.
**Food**: Insects, bark, fruits and succulent plants.
**Size**: 13–29cm (5–11.5in); 170–580g (6–20.5oz).
**Maturity**: Not known.
**Breeding**: 3 litters of up to 6 young born in spring and summer.
**Life span**: 1 year.
**Status**: Common.

Bushy-tailed woodrats have a huge range. They can be found from the dry scrub of northern Arizona and New Mexico to the icy forests at the edge of the Arctic in Canada. No other woodrat lives in such cold environments as this species. Within this range, bushy-tailed woodrats occupy a number of habitats, including near-desert and dense pine forest. As odd as this may sound, the woodrat has similar problems to overcome in both environments, since both deserts and frozen forests have little running water. Woodrats are most common in mountainous regions.

Like all woodrats, this species builds middens, where the rodent deposits its waste nest material and faeces, which are solidified with calcium carbonate and calcium oxalate crystals from the woodrat's urine. Many generations of woodrat will use the same midden, and nests may even be made within it.

*Male bushy-tailed woodrats are nearly twice as heavy as females. Woodrats that live in cooler, more northerly parts of the range tend to be larger than those that live in warmer areas to the south. The tail of this species can reach about 25cm (10in) in length.*

# RABBITS

*Rabbits, hares and pikas belong to the mammal order Lagomorpha. Most of the lagomorphs that live in the Americas are found north of Mexico. Unlike their cousins in Europe, most American rabbits do not dig burrows. Like hares, they generally shelter above ground. The only rabbit to dig its own burrow is the pygmy rabbit, which is also the smallest rabbit in the world.*

## Pika

*Ochotona princeps*

The pikas of North America live in areas of scree – fragments of eroded rock found beneath cliffs or mountain slopes. They shelter under the rocks and feed on patches of vegetation that grow amongst the scree. Pikas may forage at all times of the day or night, but most activity takes place in the early mornings or evenings.

During the winter, pikas survive by eating "ladders" of grass and leaves that they have collected during the late summer. These ladders are piles made in sunny places, so that the plants desiccate into alpine hay. Like most of their rabbit relatives, pikas eat their primary droppings so that their tough food is digested twice, in order to extract all of the nutrients.

Adult pikas live alone and defend territories during the winter. In spring, males expand their territories to include those of neighbouring females. Most females produce two litters during each summer. When preparing for winter, the females chase their mates back to their own territories and expel their mature offspring.

*Pikas are small relatives of rabbits. They do not have tails, and their rounded bodies are covered in soft red and grey fur. Unlike those of a rabbit, a pika's hind legs are about the same length as its forelegs.*

**Distribution**: South-western Canada and western United States.
**Habitat**: Broken, rocky country and scree.
**Food**: Grass, sedge, weeds and leaves.
**Size**: 12–30cm (4.75–12in); 110–180g (4–6.25oz).
**Maturity**: 3 months.
**Breeding**: 2 litters of 2–4 young born during summer.
**Life span**: 7 years.
**Status**: Common.

## Snowshoe hare

*Lepus americanus*

Like most hares, snowshoe hares do not dig burrows. Instead they shelter in shallow depressions called forms, which they scrape in soil or snow. Snowshoe hares are generally nocturnal, and rest in secluded forms or under logs during the day. When dusk arrives, the hares follow systems of runways through the dense forest undergrowth to feeding sites. They maintain these runways by biting away branches that block the way and compacting the winter snow.

In summer, the hares nibble on grasses and other green plant material. They survive the long winter by supplementing their diet with buds, twigs and bark. Over several years, the overall population of snowshoe hares can rise and fall dramatically. At the low points there may be only two animals per square kilometre. At the peak there may be as many as 1,300 in the same area.

Snowshoe hares are more social than other hares. During the spring breeding season, the male hares compete with each other to establish hierarchies and gain access to mates. Conflicts often result in boxing fights – hence "mad March hares".

**Distribution**: Alaska, Canada and northern United States.
**Habitat**: Conifer forest.
**Food**: Grass, leaves, buds and bark.
**Size**: 40–70cm (15.5–27.5in); 1.35–7kg (2.75–15.5lb).
**Maturity**: 1 year.
**Breeding**: 4 litters of 2–4 young produced per year.
**Life span**: 5 years.
**Status**: Common.

*In summer, the snowshoe hare's fur is a rusty or greyish-brown, but in areas with heavy winter snow the fur is white as a camouflage against predators.*

# Eastern cottontail

*Sylvilagus floridanus*

Eastern cottontail rabbits do not dig burrows, although they may shelter in disused ones dug by other animals. Generally they shelter in thickets or forms – shallow depressions made in tall grass or scraped in the ground. Cottontails forage at night, grazing mainly on grasses, but also nibbling small shrubs. Unlike hares, which rely on their speed to outrun predators, cottontails freeze when under threat, blending into their surroundings. If they have to run, they follow zigzag paths, attempting to shake off their pursuers.

In warmer parts of their range cottontails breed all year round, but farther north breeding is restricted to summer. Males fight to establish hierarchies, with top males getting their choice of mates. A pregnant female digs a shallow hole, which is deeper at one end than the other. She lines the nest with grass and fur from her belly. Once she has given birth, she crouches over the shallow end and her young crawl up from the warm deep end to suckle.

**Distribution**: Eastern Canada and United States to Venezuela.
**Habitat**: Farmland, forest, desert, swamp and prairie.
**Food**: Grass, leaves, twigs and bark.
**Size**: 21–47cm (8.5–18.5in); 0.8–1.5kg (1.75–3.25lb).
**Maturity**: 80 days.
**Breeding**: 3–7 litters per year, each of up to 12 young.
**Life span**: 5 years.
**Status**: Common.

*Female cottontails are larger than the males. The name "cottontail" is derived from their short, rounded tails, which have white fur on their underside. Their upper bodies are covered in grey, brown and reddish hairs.*

**Pygmy rabbit** (*Brachylagus idahoensis*): 21–27cm (8.5–10.5in); 200–450g (7–16oz) These rabbits live on an arid plateau in the north-west of the United States. Pygmy rabbits are related to cottontails, but they are about half the size. They dig burrows under thickets of sagebrush – the only North American rabbit to do so – and move through a network of runways above ground. They eat the sagebrush, and are most active at dawn and dusk.

**Swamp rabbit** (*Sylvilagus aquaticus*): 45–55cm (18–21.5in); 1.5–2.5kg (3.25–5.5lb) Swamp rabbits live in the wetlands along the Mississippi Delta and other rivers in the southern United States. Unlike most rabbits, the males and females of this species are about the same size. Swamp rabbits build nests of dead plants and fur at ground level. They maintain territories by calling to intruders and marking their areas with scent. They breed all year round. Female swamp rabbits may produce up to 40 young per year.

**Collared pika** (*Ochotona collaris*): 18–20cm (7–8in); 130g (4.5oz) Collared pikas inhabit the cold mountains of central and southern Alaska and also north-western Canada, where they are found in scree and other rocky areas above the tree line. There is a greyish "collar" around the neck and shoulders. These diurnal animals feed on herbs and grasses, and make hay piles to eat during winter. Collared pikas produce about three young in each litter.

# Jackrabbit

*Lepus californicus*

Jackrabbits are actually a type of hare and so share many of the hare's characteristics, from long ears to large, hairy hind feet. Jackrabbits live in dry areas with only sparse plant cover. This has benefited the species in the past. Overgrazing of the land by cattle in the arid south-west of the United States and Mexico has created an ideal habitat for jackrabbits.

Unlike other hares, jackrabbits make use of burrows. They do not dig their own, but they modify underground shelters made by tortoises. Jackrabbits feed on grasses and herbaceous plants, which also supply them with nearly all the water they need.

**Distribution**: South-western United States to northern Mexico.
**Habitat**: Dry grasslands.
**Food**: Grass.
**Size**: 40–70cm (15.5–27.5in); 1.3–7kg (2.75–15.5lb).
**Maturity**: 1 year.
**Breeding**: 3–4 litters of 1–6 young each year.
**Life span**: 5 years.
**Status**: Common.

*Female jackrabbits are larger than males. They have grey fur with reddish and brown flecks. Their undersides are paler, and their tails and the tips of their huge ears are black. Like other hares, male jackrabbits indulge in frenzied fights during the breeding season.*

# Arctic hare

*Lepus arcticus*

*The winter coat of the Arctic hare is white, with black tips to the ears. In summer, the fur is a variety of colours, depending on where the hare lives. In the tundra, for example, the hares are blue-grey. The long claws are used for digging in ice and snow.*

Arctic hares live in northern North America, from Labrador and Newfoundland in the south to the Mackenzie River Delta in northern Canada. They also live on the many islands of the Canadian Arctic province of Nunavut. The hares occupy both lowland an upland regions. In the far north, both these landscapes are covered by tundra, where the vegetation is mostly small, ice-resistant plants such as mosses and hardy grasses. The hares make their homes in areas of broken ground, where rocks provide some shelter. In summer, larger plants grow in these sheltered spots, and in winter they do not freeze as deeply as exposed areas.

Arctic hares are most active at dawn and dusk. They forage on their own, but sometimes form loose colonies of up to 300 animals, probably to give some protection against Arctic foxes, polar bears and other predators.

**Distribution**: Northern Canada and Greenland.
**Habitat**: Tundra.
**Food**: Mosses, lichens, leaves, berries, roots and carrion.
**Size**: 40–76cm (15.5–30); 1.2–5kg (2.5–11lb).
**Maturity**: 1 year.
**Breeding**: Mating occurs in April and May; single litter of up to 5 young born in summer.
**Life span**: 5 years.
**Status**: Common.

**Alaskan hare** (*Lepus othus*): 50–70cm (19.5–27.5in); 2–5kg (4.5–11lb)
Alaskan hares live in northern and western Alaska. Some reports also place them across the Bering Straits in eastern Siberia. This species is most often found on tundra and barren mountain slopes, and rarely in lowland areas. Alaskan hares produce just one litter each year. Although this is less than other hares, it is no mean feat in the harsh conditions of their sub-Arctic home. They mate in spring and up to eight young are born two months later. These hares are active at dawn and dusk. Their main foods are leaves, shoots, bark and roots, plus grasses in summer.

**Antelope jackrabbit** (*Lepus alleni*): 48–63cm (19–25in); 2–5kg (4.5–11lb)
This jackrabbit lives in southern Arizona and along the Pacific coast of northern Mexico. It occupies highland areas in the Sonoran Desert, and is especially common on mesas – the steep-sided tables of rock that project from the ground in this region. There is no breeding season, and female antelope rabbits produce several litters per year, each of about three young. Antelope jackrabbits are nocturnal. They do not hide in burrows during the day, but rely on their high-speed running to escape from predators.

**Tehuantepec jackrabbit** (*Lepus flavigularis*): Size unknown
These nocturnal jackrabbits are found only on the northern coast of the Gulf of Tehuantepec in southern Mexico. Tehuantepec jackrabbits live in the forests that grow on sand dunes surrounding salt-water lagoons.

# White-sided jackrabbit

*Lepus callotis*

White-sided jackrabbits occur from southern New Mexico into central Mexico. They live in the high plateaux that are common in this region. These uplands are covered by dry grasslands, with a few shrubs also growing.

White-sided jackrabbits are crepuscular, (active at dawn and dusk), but they are also at large on cloudy days and bright, moonlit nights. They tend to occur in male-female pairs, and this pair bonding is most evident during the breeding season.

When threatened by a coyote or another predator, this hare initially leaps straight up in the air and extends its hind legs to flash its white sides. This behaviour is meant to startle the attacker and give the jackrabbit a chance to flee. If successful, the hare makes its escape with high bounds, propelled by its long hind feet.

**Distribution**: New Mexico and north-western Mexico.
**Habitat**: Grassy plateaux.
**Food**: Grasses and sedge.
**Size**: 43–60cm (17–23.5) 2–3kg (4.5–6.5lb).
**Maturity**: 2 years.
**Breeding**: 2–3 young born in spring or summer.
**Life span**: 5 years.
**Status**: Lower risk.

*Female white-sided jackrabbits are slightly larger than males. In winter, the white areas of fur darken into a dull grey. The black line down the lower part of the back also fades at this time of year.*

# Black jackrabbit

*Lepus insularis*

Black jackrabbits occur only on the volcanic island of Espiritu Santo in the Gulf of California, off western Mexico. The island has rocky hills and steep-sided valleys, but little running water; consequently, only desert shrubs and cacti survive there, along with some grasses.

Black jackrabbits are solitary animals. They do not dig burrows into the rocky volcanic soil, but take shelter in shallow hollows, often scraped out under the shade of a bush.

By day, the jackrabbits are very easy to spot moving around against the pale background of the islands' vegetation and rocky slopes, making them vulnerable to predatory birds such as American kestrels and caracaras. They are therefore most active during the night, when they can move more freely under the cover of darkness.

Black jackrabbits feed almost exclusively on grasses. However, at the driest time of year, when green vegetation is most scarce, these hares survive by gnawing bark. They obtain all the water they need from their plant food.

*Black jackrabbits usually have a few white hairs on the tops of their otherwise black heads. The dark fur extends down the back and the rest of the body is covered with glossy brown fur, which is grizzled with long cinnamon guard hairs. The soles of the feet have heavy padding. As in other hare species, female black jackrabbits tend to be larger than the males.*

**Distribution**: Restricted to Espiritu Santo Island in the Gulf of California off western Mexico.
**Habitat**: Steep valleys with shrubs and cacti.
**Food**: Mainly grasses, plus some bark.
**Size**: 57cm (22.5in); 1.5kg (3.25lb).
**Maturity**: 1 year.
**Breeding**: Up to 3 litters of 2–4 young from January to July; gestation is 41–43 days.
**Life span**: 5 years.
**Status**: Near threatened.

# Mountain hare

*Lepus timidus*

**Distribution**: Northern hemisphere, from Alaska, northern Canada and Greenland to northern Europe and eastern Siberia.
**Habitat**: Tundra, forest and moorland.
**Food**: Leaves, twigs, lichen, grass and heather.
**Size**: 43–61cm (17–24); 2–6kg (4.5–13lb).
**Maturity**: 1 year.
**Breeding**: Breeding season is from end of January to September. Litters of 1–6 young produced twice a year (sometimes more) in spring and summer; gestation varies from 47 to 54 days.
**Life span**: 5 years.
**Status**: Common.

Mountain hares, often regarded as a subspecies of Arctic hare, are found at northern latitudes across the globe, from Alaska, northern Canada and Greenland to Scandinavia, northern Russia and Siberia. Small populations also live in Japan, Ireland, Scotland and even the European Alps. They inhabit tundra, conifer forest and moorland in highland regions. In winter, the hares usually move to the shelter of the forest.

These hares are nocturnal, resting by day in a form (a depression dug into the ground). They do not dig their own burrows, but often take over the burrows of other animals when they need to shelter their young. When not on the move, mountain hares "hook" before resting. This involves making a final jump to the side so that predators cannot follow the hare's tracks.

Mountain hares are mainly solitary, but in severe weather or at sites where food is plentiful they may congregate in large groups of up to 70. In the breeding season, several males will compete for access to a single female. If a male approaches an unreceptive female too closely, he may be aggressively rebuffed, with the female rising up on her hind legs and batting at him with her paws, claws extended. If the male persists, a longer fight may ensue, with both hares "boxing" and biting at each other.

*These hares moult twice a year. During the winter moult, from October to December, their fur becomes grey or even white, but the animals become brown again in the spring.*

## Desert cottontail

*Sylvilagus audubonii*

Despite their name, desert cottontails do not just live in desert habitats, but are also found in grasslands and woodlands. They range from Montana in the north to central Mexico in the south, and from altitudes of 1,800m (5,900ft) in the Rocky Mountains of the east to the Pacific coast in the west.

Desert cottontails tend to live alone and avoid interacting with one another. Males rarely tolerate another male near them, but females are sometimes seen gathering in an area with plenty of food without coming into conflict. In general, however, a single rabbit occupies a territory of about 3 hectares (8 acres). Most feeding takes place in early morning and at dusk. As the heat of the day increases, the cottontails spend as much time as possible under cover. When startled, this rabbit will either freeze or run. If it bolts, it follows a zig-zag path to evade pursuers.

Breeding occurs between December and late summer. The female digs a shallow nest hole in the ground and lines it with fur and grass. They young cottontails leave the nest when they are about two weeks old.

**Distribution**: Western North America.
**Habitat**: Deserts, prairie and woodland.
**Food**: Grass.
**Size**: 38cm (15in); 840–990g (29.5–35oz).
**Maturity**: 3 months.
**Breeding**: Litters of 3 young produced in spring and summer; gestation is 28 days.
**Life span**: 5 years.
**Status**: Common.

*Female desert cottontails are slightly larger than their male counterparts. Both sexes have the characteristic short, white tail that earns this species and its relatives the name cottontail.*

## Brush rabbit

*Sylvilagus bachmani*

Brush rabbits are found along the Pacific coast of the United States, from the south side of the Columbia River Valley along the northern border of Oregon to the deserts of southern California. Their range does not penetrate far inland, only reaching the eastern side of the Cascade and Sierra Nevada ranges.

As their name implies, these rabbits are found living in brush habitats, which are particularly common in the deserts of California. The rabbits stay hidden among the low plants, and are rarely spotted in open country. They feed in large groups but do not have strong social interactions. Grasses comprise the bulk of the diet, but other plant foods may be eaten according to the season, including clover, leaves, forbs, berries and scrubs.

Like many rabbits and hares, brush rabbits are most active in the twilight of dawn and dusk. The rest of the time they lurk in the safety of the brush, digging simple burrows and tunnel networks, or forming runways through the thick vegetation. When a brush rabbit senses danger, it thumps the ground rapidly with its feet to warn other rabbits in the area. It is able to sit still for long periods of time to avoid detection by predators. If chased, it can reach speeds of 12–15 kmh (20–25mph) as it flees, constantly changing direction to wrong foot the pursuing animal. Brush rabbits may even climb trees and scrubs to put themselves out of an attacker's reach.

**Distribution**: Western United States, from Oregon to southern California.
**Habitat**: Brushy cover.
**Food**: Grass and berries.
**Size**: 28–37cm (11–14.5in); 0.7kg (1.5lb).
**Maturity**: 6 months.
**Breeding**: 3 litters of 2–4 young produced from late winter to late summer; gestation is about 27 days.
**Life span**: 5 years.
**Status**: Endangered.

*This rabbit belongs to the same genus as cottontails. However, unlike many of its fluffy-tailed relatives, the brush rabbit's tail is small and dark on top. Compared to other cottontails, brush rabbits are also quite small. Females are usually slightly larger than males.*

# Volcano rabbit

*Romerolagus diazi*

This rabbit species is found only on the slopes of two volcanic mountain ranges in central Mexico. These mountains harbour an unusual habitat known as zacaton. This is a dry, high-altitude pine woodland where clumps of grass grow under the trees. Volcano rabbits live in small colonies in rocky areas of the zacaton, feeding on tender herbs and grasses. They shelter in burrows by day and follow networks of runways through tall grasses when feeding at night. Up to five rabbits share each burrow. The burrows are several metres long and about 40cm (15in) under the surface. The volcanic soil is dark and very rocky.

Volcano rabbits are most active at dawn and dusk. They forage in large groups, like pikas. They also communicate with a series of squeaks and other high-pitched calls. This species breeds mainly in summer. Young are born six weeks after mating.

*The volcano rabbit is an unusual rabbit species, and resembles pikas in many ways. It is the only member of its genus, and is one of the smallest of all rabbits, with short ears, short legs and no visible tail. The dark fur on the back and flanks has yellowish hairs mixed in. The underside is a light grey.*

**Distribution**: Mountains in central Mexico.
**Habitat**: Pine forest with grass undergrowth.
**Food**: Grass.
**Size**: 27–31cm (10.25–12.5in); 370–600g (13–21.25oz).
**Maturity**: 1 year.
**Breeding**: Litters of 1–3 young produced at any time, but mostly in summer; gestation is 38–40 days.
**Life span**: 5 years.
**Status**: Endangered.

---

**Mountain cottontail** (*Sylvilagus nuttallii*): 35–39cm (14–15.5in); 0.7–1.2kg (1.5–2.5lb)
This species lives in the woodland and brush that grows on hill and mountain slopes in the western United States, and also on exposed rocky mountainsides. Mountain cottontails forage at dawn and dusk, usually near running water. They eat grasses, sagebrush and juniper. These rabbits live alone, because otherwise the competition for food would be too great. They are active all year around, and breed in summer. If frightened, a mountain cottontail will run back on itself in a semicircle to confuse its attacker.

**New England cottontail** (*Sylvilagus transitionalis*): 38–42cm (15–16.5in) 1.4kg (3lb)
Also known as the wood rabbit, the New England cottontail lives along the eastern coast of the United States, from Maine to Alabama. Its main habitat is dense deciduous forest, where it often lives alongside eastern cottontails. This species eats plant stems and leaves, but individuals in colder areas are forced to rely on twigs and bark in winter. The coat is pinkish-buff, with a patch of black between the ears. These rabbits generally take over the burrows abandoned by other animals, since they are not able to dig their own.

**Tapeti** (*Sylvilagus brasiliensis*): 35cm (14in); 0.7–1kg (1.5–2.2lb)
The tapeti, or forest rabbit, ranges from southern Mexico to northern Argentina. It lives around the edges of the Amazon Basin. As well as tropical forest, this species also inhabits scrublands such as the Chaco of Paraguay. The tapeti is nocturnal and feeds on low-growing forest plants.

# Marsh rabbit

*Sylvilagus palustris*

Marsh rabbits are cottontail rabbits that live throughout the south-eastern United States, from Virginia to the tip of Florida. This region is characterized by wetlands, especially around the Mississippi Delta. Marsh rabbits live in these swamps and bogs, and also near deeper and faster-running bodies of water.

These rabbits build platforms of rushes and other aquatic vegetation to hold their dens. Marsh rabbits swim regularly, and will also hide from danger in water. They never stray far from solid ground, since they are often forced to take cover in the thick undergrowth that grows along the banks.

Despite their semi-aquatic lifestyle, marsh rabbits forage on land at night for bark and leaves. They eat their hard pellets to extract as much goodness as possible from their tough food. Marsh rabbits are solitary, but when it is time to mate the males organize themselves into a hierarchy by fighting each other.

*Compared to other cottontails and hares, marsh rabbits have short, rounded ears.*

**Distribution**: South-eastern United States.
**Habitat**: Swamps and waterways.
**Food**: Bark and leaves.
**Size**: 35–45cm (14–18in); 1–2kg (2.2–4.75lb).
**Maturity**: 1 year.
**Breeding**: 6 litters of 2–8 young produced spring and summer; gestation is 30–37 days.
**Life span**: 5 years.
**Status**: Endangered.

# BATS

*Bats are grouped together in the* Chiroptera *order of mammals. They are the only mammals that can truly fly. Their wings are made from thin membranes of skin stretched between elongated arms and legs. Most bats are active at night and "see" the world through sound. They emit high-pitched calls and interpret the echoes that bounce back to build up pictures of their surroundings.*

## Common vampire bat

*Desmodus rotundus*

Within their range, vampire bats are found in most types of habitat where there are large animals to feed upon, and they have become common in areas where livestock is being raised. They feed on the blood of animals such as cattle and donkeys and sometimes domestic poultry.

They begin to feed soon after nightfall, flying silently from their roosts in caves and hollow trees. Vampire bats will travel several kilometres to find blood. Once they locate suitable host animals, they lick the target area – usually on the neck or leg – and bite off hairs or feathers to clear a patch of skin. Then the bat cuts away a circle of skin with its long teeth and laps up the blood flowing from the wound.

Vampire bats swallow about 20ml (7fl oz) of blood each day. They return to their roosts to digest their food during the day. Roosts may contain as many as 2,000 bats. Single males mate with small groups of females. They need to guard them, however, because they are often usurped by other males. Births of single young take place in spring or autumn.

*Vampire bats have dark upper bodies with grey undersides. Their upper front teeth are very long and pointed, and their limbs are adapted for walking along the ground.*

**Distribution**: Mexico to Uruguay.
**Habitat**: Caves, hollow trees and disused buildings.
**Food**: Blood.
**Size**: 7–9cm (2.75–3.5in); 15–50g (0.5–1.75oz).
**Maturity**: 10 months.
**Breeding**: Single birth in spring or autumn.
**Life span**: 10 years.
**Status**: Common.

## Tent-building bat

*Uroderma bilobatum*

*Tent-building bats have four white stripes on their faces, with pointed "nose leaves." Up to 20 females may share a tent.*

Tent-building bats live in areas with enough palm or banana trees for them to roost in. They make tents from the broad fronds by nibbling through the central, supportive ribs so that the fronds flop down over them. The tents shelter the bats from the sun and wind while they sleep during the day. The fronds eventually die and fall off the trees because their vascular systems have been damaged by the bats. Consequently, the bats build themselves new shelters every two or three months.

Tent-building bats mainly eat fruit, which they chew up, drinking the juice. They also alight on flowers to grab insects, and will eat any nectar and pollen available. Males roost alone or in small groups, while females rest in groups of 20 or more. Breeding takes place at all times of the year. Nursing mothers leave their single young in their tents while they go on their nightly foraging trips.

**Distribution**: Southern Mexico and northern South America to Brazil.
**Habitat**: Palm or banana forests.
**Food**: Fruit, pollen, nectar and insects.
**Size**: 5.5–7.5cm (2.25–3in); 13–21g (0.5–0.7oz).
**Maturity**: Unknown.
**Breeding**: Single young born throughout the year.
**Life span**: Unknown.
**Status**: Common.

# Velvety free-tailed bat

*Molossus ater*

Velvety free-tailed bats are nocturnal insect-eaters, tracking their prey by echolocation. Echolocation is a system in which the bats bounce chirps of ultrasound off objects and listen to the echoes to build an image of their surroundings.

Velvety free-tailed bats live in damp forests, but will venture out into more open country to find food. They roost by day in tree hollows, in rock overhangs or under palm fronds. At dusk, the bats set off in search of food, which they store in pouches inside their cheeks. When the pouches are full, the free-tailed bats return to their roosts to digest their food.

These bats sometimes use their mobile tails as feelers by crawling backwards along the ground, waggling their tails from side to side. With wings adapted for twisting and turning in pursuit of prey, free-tailed bats are not very good at taking off from the ground. Instead, they take to the wing by climbing up trees and dropping into the air.

*Velvety free-tailed bats are so-named because of their soft fur and because, unlike most bats, they do not have membranes of skin joined to the sides of their tails.*

**Distribution**: Northern Mexico to Argentina in South America.
**Habitat**: Forests and open woodland.
**Food**: Insects.
**Size**: 5–9.5cm (2–3.75in); 10–30g (0.3–1oz).
**Maturity**: 1 year.
**Breeding**: Single offspring produced once or twice per year.
**Life span**: Unknown.
**Status**: Common.

---

**Ghost bat** (*Diclidurus albus*): 5–8cm (2–3.25in); 20–35g (0.7–1.25oz)
This species of bat ranges from southern Mexico to Peru and northern Brazil. Ghost bats have white or grey fur and are found in tropical forests, seldom far from running water. They roost by day under large palm leaves, and pursue moths and other insects by night. Ghost bats live largely solitary lives, but do congregate at roosts, especially during the breeding season in late summer.

**Fishing bulldog bat** (*Noctilio leporinus*): 10–13cm (4–5in); 60–80g (2–2.75oz)
The males of this species of bat, which lives in Central America, have bright orange fur, while the females are dull grey or brown. They have pointed muzzles with heavily folded lips and long hind legs with well-developed claws. These claws are used for catching fish. Fishing bulldog bats hunt over ocean surf as well as lakes and rivers. They even follow flocks of pelicans and snatch small fish disturbed by the birds.

**Peter's disc-winged bat** (*Thyroptera discifera*): 3.5–5cm (1.5–2in); 40–60g (1.5–2oz)
Also known as the New World sucker-footed bat, this species ranges from Nicaragua to Peru and northern Brazil. Its name refers to the suction cups located on short stalks on the soles of its forefeet. The bats use these suckers to hang from smooth leaves in their rainforest habitat. Unusually for bats, which generally hang upside down, sucker-footed bats roost upright.

# Pallid bat

*Antrozous pallidus*

Pallid bats prefer to live in areas with plenty of rocky outcrops, in dry scrubland or forest terrain in western North America. They roost in caves and hollow trees during the day and do not emerge until well after dark. They go on two foraging trips each night, returning to their roosts in between to digest their food. They hunt for food on the wing, frequently descending to about 2m (6.5ft) above the ground before taking a long glide over the terrain. This behaviour is suited to locating slow-moving and ground-based prey, such as beetles and crickets.

Some pallid bats may migrate from cooler parts of their range to warmer areas in winter. Others hibernate during the coldest months. Pallid bats live in large social groups. They call to one another as they return to the roosts after feeding, and communicate as they jostle for position inside their roosting sites. During the summer, males live in male-only roosts. Mating takes place in autumn, soon after that year's young have dispersed from their mothers' roosts. Births, usually of twins, take place in summer.

*Pallid bats have cream to yellow fur, with whitish patches on their underside. Their ears are very large in proportion to their head.*

**Distribution**: Western North America from British Colombia to Mexico.
**Habitat**: Forests and arid scrubland.
**Food**: Insects, spiders and lizards.
**Size**: 6–8.5cm (2.5–3.25in); 17–28g (0.6–1oz).
**Maturity**: 1 year.
**Breeding**: Twins born in summer.
**Life span**: 9 years.
**Status**: Vulnerable.

**Mexican free-tailed bat** (*Tadarida brasiliensis*):
Length 6–7cm (3.5–4in); 12.3g (0.4oz)
This species ranges from southern Texas and
Mexico through Central America to Brazil. The
largest colony is found in Braken Cave near San
Antonio, Texas, with an estimated 20 million bats
occupying this single roost during summer. This is
the largest known gathering of mammals. Several
other caves in the region host more than 1 million
bats. The fact that so many bats can fly through
narrow caves in such huge numbers is testament
to the accuracy of their echolocation sonar.
Mexican free-tailed bats eat small flying insects
such as mosquitoes and other flies.

**Broad-eared bat** (*Nyctinomops laticaudatus*):
5–9cm (3.5–5.5in); weight unknown
A relative of the free-tailed bats, this species has
long jaws and nostrils that end in small tubes.
Broad-eared bats live in the tropical parts of
Central and South America, mainly in lowland
forests. They roost in human dwellings and
caves, as well as on cliffs, and they feed on
flying beetles. Unusually for bats of this size,
some of the calls they make are so low pitched
that they are audible to humans. The species is
threatened, but not high risk.

**Big free-tailed bat** (*Nyctinomops macrotis*):
12–16cm (4.75–6.25in); 22–30g (0.8–1oz)
The big free-tailed bat has a huge range,
stretching from northern British Columbia and
South Carolina to the whole of South America.
Big free-tailed bats live in rugged habitats where
there are plenty of rocky crevices for roosting in.
They mainly feed on large moths.

# Thumbless bat

*Furipterus horrens*

Thumbless bats range from Costa Rica to
Peru and Brazil, including the island of
Trinidad. These bats generally roost in caves
or hollow trees. They hunt at night near
rivers and streams, where they fly 1–5m
(3.25–16.5ft) above the ground, plucking
moths and other insects from the air. Like
nearly all small bats, thumbless bats use
echolocation to find their prey. This involves
making short, high-pitched chirrup calls
(too high for the human ear to detect) and
moving the ears from side to side to scan
the night sky for echoes bouncing
back off large flying
insects. The ears can
be moved independently
if necessary.

Thumbless bats live in
colonies numbering up to
300 individuals. While
roosting, the bats in a colony
will sometimes form smaller
subgroups, each made up of
about 20 individuals.

**Distribution**: Central America
and northern South America,
plus Trinidad.
**Habitat**: Caves in forests.
**Food**: Insects.
**Size**: 4cm (1.5in); 3g (0.1oz).
**Maturity**: 1 year.
**Breeding**: Unknown.
**Life span**: Unknown.
**Status**: Lower risk.

*The thumbless bat is so called
because it lacks a thumb claw (most
bats have claws sticking out of the
leading edge of the wing). The long
fur on the head covers the mouth.*

# Dwarf bonneted bat

*Eumops bonariensis*

Dwarf bonneted bats live in the Veracruz region of Mexico
and spread south through Central America and northern
South America to Paraguay and Uruguay. A few can be
found further south in eastern Argentina. They inhabit
deciduous tropical forests and thorn scrub in lowland areas.

These bats roost in hollow trees and under the roofs
of forest dwellings. They are a common house bat in the
southern portion of their range. They hunt at night using
echolocation to sense their surroundings and
catch insects such as beetles and moths on
the wing. Many of the prey insects are fast
flyers, so the bats need to be quick in the
chase. Their long wings and ability to
shorten their tail membrane allow them to
achieve higher flight speeds than many species.
Dwarf bonneted bats can fly at 65kmh (40mph)
when flying alone; when flying in groups,
they can reach speeds of around 95kmh
(60mph), because there is less drag.

*This is the smallest of the eight
bonneted bat species. The hair
is pale at the base and white
at the tip. The hair is long for a
bat, reaching up to 5mm (0.2in).
Bonneted bats have smaller eyes
than most other types of bat.*

**Distribution**: From Mexico
through Central America to
Uruguay and Paraguay in
South America.
**Habitat**: Dry forest.
**Food**: Beetles, moths
and other insects.
**Size**: 5–7cm
(2–2.75in); 7–13g
(0.2–0.5oz).
**Maturity**: 1 year.
**Breeding**: 1 young born
in summer.
**Life span**: Unknown.
**Status**: Common.

# Western bonneted bat

*Eumops perotis*

The western bonneted bat, also known as the mastiff bat, occurs in small patches across its range, which stretches from Nevada in the western United Sates and south through Texas and Arizona into central Mexico. The bat is also found on the Caribbean islands of Cuba.

The broken pattern of distribution reflects the bat's need for habitats with steep cliffs, on the side of which the bat roosts. The cliffs must be sheer or overhanging so that, when it is time to hunt, the bat can simply let go of its foothold and drop into the air. It freefalls to gain sufficient airspeed before using its wings. This species is unable to get airborne from the ground.

Beneath the cliffs, western bonneted bats hunt in a variety of open habitats, including desert, scrub and even dry woodlands. They spend several hours each night foraging for flying insects. Unusually for bats, this species hunts in cold weather, only becoming inactive when temperatures reach 5°C (41°F).

*The western bonneted bat has large, linked ears that stand high above the head and project forward beyond the end of the snout. If this species finds itself on the ground, it must climb a tree or other object to gain the 5m (16.5ft) or so in height that it needs to launch itself into the air again.*

**Distribution**: Southern California, Nevada, New Mexico and Texas; also Mexico and Cuba.
**Habitat**: Cliffs.
**Food**: Insects.
**Size**: 8cm (3.25in); 57g (2oz).
**Maturity**: 1 year.
**Breeding**: 1 young born in summer.
**Life span**: Unknown.
**Status**: Common.

# Pocketed free-tailed bat

*Nyctinomops femorosaccus*

The pocketed free-tailed bat lives in the region either side of the US–Mexico border. It is most commonly found in desert habitats, where it feeds on flying insects. It eats a range of prey, including moths, crickets, flying ants and lacewings. Many of its prey are pests that feed on crops, and the bat's presence is encouraged by local farmers.

The pocketed free-tailed bat is a swift, high-flying species that is most active in the hours just after dusk and just before dawn. It uses echolocation to find its way around and locate insect prey. It prefers small moths, but will also take crickets, beetles, flying ants, stinkbugs, froghoppers, and lacewings. The bat's ears are joined together, so they move as a single unit when detecting echoes. Prey is usually caught on the wing.

Small colonies of pocketed free-tailed bats, usually fewer than 100 bats, roost in caves and on rugged cliffs, tall rocky outcrops and buildings. Like western bonneted bats, they must drop for a few metres before they achieve the airspeed necessary to stay aloft in powered flight. As well as emitting echolocation calls, this species often makes high-pitched chattering social calls, especially in the first few minutes of flight and while roosting. Pocketed free-tailed bats can frequently be observed flying swiftly over ponds and other watercourses, making audible whistling and fluttering sounds with their wings. To drink, these bats will impact with the water's surface while in flight and scoop up a mouthful of water.

**Distribution**: Southern California, south-eastern New Mexico, western Texas and Michoacán state, Mexico.
**Habitat**: Deserts.
**Food**: Insects.
**Size**: 11cm (4.25in); 12g (0.4oz).
**Maturity**: 1 year.
**Breeding**: 1 young born in June or July.
**Life span**: Unknown.
**Status**: Common.

*Being a free-tailed bat, this species has a tail that extends beyond the skin membrane which forms the wing and other flight surfaces. The "pockets" referred to in the bat's common name are produced by folds in the skin that joins the legs to the arms.*

## Ghost-faced bat

*Mormoops megalophylla*

This species lives in Arizona and Texas in the north and south, through Mexico and Central America to Peru in the west and Venezuela in the east. It typically roosts in caves and smaller nooks and crannies, and often makes its home in artificial structures, such as tunnels and mines. It does not roost in buildings very often because they tend to be too dry. The bats prefer places with a high humidity to stop their wings from drying out too much.

Ghost-faced bats eat large insects such as moths. Little is known about how they catch their prey. It is likely that they take them on the wing, but they may also swoop down and snatch them off the ground.

During the day, ghost-faced bats roost in vast colonies numbering up to half a million individuals. A colony of this size needs an enormous roosting space, since each bat prefers to have about 15cm (6in) between itself and its neighbours. In winter, it is likely that bats in cooler areas migrate toward the warmer regions near the tropics.

*The ears of this medium-sized, reddish-brown or dark brown bat are joined along their inner edges. Together they can be twisted to point in a variety of directions when scanning for sonar echoes from small prey. The ghost-faced bat has relatively small eyes, and its lips are wrinkled into a funnel-like shape. Conspicuous leaf-like flaps of skin protrude from the bat's chin, giving rise this species' other common names: leaf-chinned bat and old man bat.*

**Distribution**: From Arizona and Texas in the United States through Central America to Peru and Venezuela in South America.
**Habitat**: Desert.
**Food**: Large-bodied moths and other large insects.
**Size**: 6.5cm (2.5in); 13–19g (0.5–0.7oz).
**Maturity**: 1 year.
**Breeding**: 1 offspring produced in May or June.
**Life span**: Unknown.
**Status**: Common.

## Mexican funnel-eared bat

*Natalus stramineus*

Mexican funnel-eared bats are found in the tropical region of the Americas on either side of the equator. The northern limit of their range is the Sonoran desert in north-western Mexico, while the southern extent is eastern Brazil. These bats also live on several Caribbean islands, including the Lesser Antilles, Hispaniola (Haiti and the Dominican Republic) and Jamaica.

Mexican funnel-eared bats prefer a deciduous forest habitat, and tend to be absent from the lush tropical forests that grow in equatorial lowlands and on the sides of mountains. The bats roost in colonies of up to 300 individuals, which is relatively small by bat standards.

Mexican funnel-eared bats are most active in the first few hours after sunset. They hunt small flying insects at night, typically in the understorey – the layer of shrubs and small trees that grows near to the ground in forests. These swift, agile flyers twist and turn in flight to avoid the foliage as they pursue their prey. Between hunts, the bats rest in trees for a short while. They return to the roost before dawn.

The sexes appear to separate when the young are born, forming maternity colonies in which the females care for their offspring. The baby bats are comparatively large, often weighing more than 50 per cent of the adult mass.

*This small bat is so called because of its large, funnel-shaped ears. Both sexes have a moustache, and the adult males have a gland on the forehead. Biologists are uncertain what this gland is for. This species is slim bodied with long, slender wings, legs and tail.*

**Distribution**: From north-eastern Mexico patchily through Central America to eastern Brazil; also found on Caribbean islands, including Hispaniola, Jamaica and the Lesser Antilles.
**Habitat**: Dry deciduous and semi-deciduous forest; occasionally evergreen forest.
**Food**: Small flying insects.
**Size**: 3.8–4.6cm (1.5–1.75in); 3–6g (0.1–0.2oz).
**Maturity**: 1 year.
**Breeding**: 1 young, usually born at the end of the dry season; gestation probably lasts 8–10 months.
**Life span**: 20 years.
**Status**: Common.

## Lesser bulldog bat

*Noctilio albiventris*

Like most American bats, the lesser bulldog bat is limited to the tropics. It ranges from southern Mexico to eastern Brazil and the northern tip of Argentina. While this species has been spotted in a range of habitats, it is most common in forests, and never strays far from running water. Lesser bulldog bats roost in tree hollows, thick bushes and in the roofs of houses. They often share roosts with mastiff bats.

Lesser bulldog bats often hunt in small groups of 8–15 bats. Each bat has a personalized echolocation call, which helps it to identify the echoes produced by its own high-frequency clicks. It is uncertain whether the bats make use of the echoes of other bats to help them orientate themselves. A more likely scenario is that hunting in groups increases the chance of finding food. The bats eat insects that fly over water, plucking them out of the air. If the insects drop to the water's surface, the bats scoop them up in their mouths or grab them by trailing their hind claws through the water.

*Male bulldog bats are bright red, while the females are dull brown. These bats have very pointed snouts, but no nose leaf. The tail protrudes beyond the tail membrane. Roosting groups of lesser bulldog bats consist of a single male with multiple females. These social groups of bats remain intact throughout the whole year.*

**Distribution**: Southern Mexico through Central America to northern Argentina and Peru.
**Habitat**: Forests, near running water.
**Food**: Insects.
**Size**: 5.7–8.5cm (2.25–3.25in); 18–44g (0.6–1.5oz).
**Maturity**: 1 year.
**Breeding**: 1 young born in April or May.
**Life span**: 10–12 years.
**Status**: Common.

---

**Big bonneted bat** (*Eumops dabbenei*): 16.5cm (6.5in); 76g (2.75oz)
This insect-eating South American species occurs east of the Andes, from Colombia to northern Argentina, but is absent from Amazonia. Big bonneted bats roost in tree holes and buildings near forests. It is likely that these rare bats are becoming endangered by habitat degradation. The males have a large throat sac, which swells up in the mating season and fills with a pheromone that attracts females. Most females produce a single pup each year, although twins occasionally occur. A few females produce two litters annually.

**Parnell's moustached bat** (*Pteronotus parnellii*): 7.3–10cm (2.75–4in); 10–20g (0.3–0.7oz)
Parnell's moustached bat occurs from southern Mexico to northern Brazil. It lives on the edge of forests and is found in both lowland and mountain habitats. The bat's name derives from the hairs sticking out from its muzzle. At night it hunts moths and flying beetles, flying low and hugging the terrain. By day it roosts in caves.

**Gervais's funnel-eared bat** (*Natalus lepidus*): 35–55cm (13–21.5in); 5–10g (0.2–0.3oz)
Native to lowland forests in the Bahamas and Cuba, Gervais's funnel-eared bats roost in large caves and mines, forming colonies of several hundred bats. The inner surface of the large, funnel-shaped ears is greatly curved and almost covers the eyes. The males have a gland on their forehead, the function of which is unclear. In the mating season, the bats roost in single-sex colonies. These insect eaters take insects on the wing over shrubs and low-growing vegetation.

## Greater bulldog bat

*Noctilio leporinus*

The greater bulldog bat shares its range with its smaller relative, the lesser bulldog bat. Also like its relative, this species hunts over water, such as rivers, lakes and even among the waves breaking along the coast. However, it is not primarily an insect eater, preferring fish, crustaceans and other water animals. The bat hunts by making low, zig-zagging flights over the water, using its sonar system to detect disturbances on the surface. It drags its hind feet, which are equipped with long claws, through the water in an attempt to hook fish. Such behaviour can net fish up to 10cm (4in) long. This hunting technique probably evolved from a method of catching insects on the water's surface, similar to that used by the lesser bulldog bat. A successful bat eats its meal on the wing. This species stores any uneaten fish in pouches inside its elastic cheeks.

**Distribution**: Southern Mexico to northern Argentina and south-eastern Brazil; also found on the Greater and Lesser Antilles, as well as the Bahamas.
**Habitat**: Near water and coasts.
**Food**: Fish.
**Size**: 10–13cm (4–5.25in); 60–78g (2–2.75oz).
**Maturity**: 1 year.
**Breeding**: 1 young born in January.
**Life span**: Unknown.
**Status**: Common.

*Male greater bulldog bats are slightly larger than females. They have red or orange fur, while females are grey or brown. These bats get their name from the fold of skin between the lips and nostrils, which gives them a bulldog-like appearance.*

## Antillean fruit-eating bat

*Brachyphylla cavernarum*

The upper body has yellow or ivory hairs with golden brown tips, while the underside is brown. The small nose leaf has a V-shaped groove. The tail is completely surrounded by the wing membrane.

This species is found on the Caribbean island chain known as the Lesser Antilles. Its range extends south along the chain to Barbados and St Vincent. It is also found further west, on the larger island of Puerto Rico. Antillean fruit-eating bats roost in caves and, increasingly, in artificial structures. They hunt and forage at night in the dense forests that grow on parts of these islands.

As well as insects, these bats will also feed on fruit, pollen, nectar and flowers. Their main source of energy is nectar, a sugary liquid produced by flowers. In return for the nectar, the flowers use the bats to transfer pollen grains from flower to flower as they feed. This form of pollination is more commonly performed by insects. Flowers that are pollinated by bats open at night, not by day. Since bats cannot see very well, the flowers do not need to be brightly coloured. Adult Antillean fruit-eating bats are often aggressive while feeding, hitting, biting and scratching one other.

Colonies of Antillean fruit-eating bats contain 2,000–3,000 individuals. Maternity colonies form during the mating season, and mainly comprise females and their young, with few males and non-breeding females.

**Distribution**: Puerto Rico and the Lesser Antilles south to St Vincent and Barbados.
**Habitat**: Forests.
**Food**: Fruits, pollen, nectar, flowers and insects.
**Size**: 6.5–12cm (2.5–4.75); 45g (1.5oz).
**Maturity**: 1 year.
**Breeding**: 1 young, usually born May–June; gestation is about 4 months. In good years, a second young may be produced later in the year.
**Life span**: Unknown.
**Status**: Lower risk.

## Hairy-legged vampire bat

*Diphylla ecaudata*

Hairy-legged vampire bats live in tropical America, from southern Texas to Peru and Brazil south of the equator. They live in a range of habitats, including deserts and grasslands, but are most commonly seen in forests.

By day, hairy-legged vampire bats roost out of sight in caves, mines and hollow trees. However, the roosts are very small, containing only about 12 individuals. The bats tend to spread out when roosting, rather than huddling together as other species do.

At night, these blood-sucking bats seek out warm-blooded animals using heat sensors on their noses. Their favoured hosts are birds, but the bats will also suck the blood of large mammals. First they select an area of the skin that has plenty of blood vessels near the surface. Then they lick the skin and bite, making a small wound. The bat's saliva contains an anti-clotting substance, and the bat laps up the blood that flows from the wound. Most of the bats' victims are unaware that they have been bitten.

These vampires have smaller bodies and ears than other species of vampire bat. The incisors are longer than the canine teeth, a highly unusual arrangement. The incisors are used to draw blood from prey. These social bats regularly groom each other, and a bat may even regurgitate blood to feed a fellow bat with which it has a strong bond.

**Distribution**: Tropical regions, from southern Texas in the United States through Central America to eastern Peru and southern Brazil in South America.
**Habitat**: Typically forests, but also grassland and deserts.
**Food**: Blood of birds, including domestic chickens, and occasionally livestock.
**Size**: 8.5cm (3.5in); 30–40g (1–1.5oz).
**Maturity**: 9 months.
**Breeding**: 1–2 young born at any time of the year; gestation is 6–8 months.
**Life span**: Unknown.
**Status**: Common.

# Geoffroy's tailless bat

*Anoura geoffroyi*

**Distribution**: Central Mexico to central South America.
**Habitat**: Rainforests and savannah.
**Food**: Insects, fruit, nectar, and pollen.
**Size**: Length unknown; 15g (0.5oz).
**Maturity**: 1 year.
**Breeding**: 1 young born in November or December.
**Life span**: 10 years.
**Status**: Common.

Geoffroy's tailless bats are found across Central America and northern South America, and on the islands of Trinidad and Grenada. They roost in caves or similar humid spaces, and are equally at home in tropical rainforest and savannah, where they fly between the distantly spaced trees.

This species is an agile flyer, and can even hover for short periods. Without a tail, the bat does not suffer from high drag forces. Colonies usually consist of small, same-sex groups that tend to occupy the same roosting site throughout their lives.

Geoffroy's tailless bat eats nectar and pollen. It also snaps up any insects that happen to be feeding on the flowers or the surrounding leaves. As well as using echolocation like other small bats, this species uses its sense of smell to locate suitable flowers. Smell is also important for communicating with other bats in the roost, such as mates and young.

*This species lacks a tail completely. Females appear to have longer wings than males. This makes the females very powerful flyers, and allows them to carry their young on flights until the pup is able to fly on its own.*

**Cuban fruit-eating bat** (*Brachyphylla nana*):
Length unknown; 45g (1.5oz)
A close relative of the Antillean fruit-eating bat, this species is found on different Caribbean islands, including Cuba, Grand Cayman and Hispaniola. Cuban fruit-eating bats roost in deep, humid caves in colonies containing several thousand individuals. Some of the islands in their range possess no suitable caves, so the bats roost wherever they can, generally in smaller groups. These bats sniff out ripe fruits and blooming flowers to feed on nectar and pollen.

**Seba's short-tailed bat** (*Carollia perspicillata*):
Length unknown; 25g (0.9oz)
Seba's short-tailed bats are found from southern Mexico to Bolivia and south-east Brazil. They are commonly found in evergreen and dry forests, generally in lowland areas. These fruit-eaters roost in groups of up to 100 in tree hollows or small caves. In dry periods, when food is scarce, the bats enter a state of torpor – an inactive state similar to hibernation – during which their energy consumption falls by about 99 per cent.

**White-winged vampire bat** (*Diaemus youngi*):
8.5cm (3.25in); 35–45g (1.25–1.5oz)
This blood-drinking bat occurs throughout tropical South America in forests, plantations and farmland. It is the only bat species to have 22 teeth. (Other vampires have fewer teeth, but most bats have more.) The white-winged vampire lives for up to nine years in the wild – several years longer than most species. Like other vampires, it probably crawls along the ground to creep up on its victims, such as domestic chickens and turkeys.

# Mexican long-tongued bat

*Choeronycteris mexicana*

The Mexican long-tongued bat has a large range, which extends from the southern United States through to Colombia and other northern areas of South America. It is most common in Mexico, where it occupies dry habitats such as deserts and alpine scrublands. They roost most often in caves and rocky crevices, but can also be found hanging from the cliffs of desert canyons. In Mexico, this bat has adapted to built-up environments, where it occupies abandoned buildings.

Mexican long-tongued bats eat fruits and pollen, and probably some insects. However, their main source of food is nectar, especially from the flowers of cactus and agave plants, which open their large blooms at night. The bats are important pollinators of these plants, since they transfer pollen from plant to plant while feeding. The bats migrate south in the winter to follow the flowering pattern of the plants.

**Distribution**: Mexico to northern South America.
**Habitat**: Deserts, mountains, rivers and scrublands.
**Food**: Fruits, pollen, and nectar.
**Size**: 8.5cm (3.25in); 25g (0.9oz).
**Maturity**: 1 year.
**Breeding**: 1 young born in later spring and summer.
**Life span**: Unknown.
**Status**: Lower risk.

*This bat's large eyes help it to seek out nectar-producing flowers. It uses its long tongue, which can extend to one-third of the body length, to lick the sweet liquid from the heart of the flower.*

# Southern long-nosed bat

*Leptonycteris curasoae*

The southern long-nosed bat lives in the Sonoran desert, which stretches from the south-western region of the United States to central Mexico. It can also be found in arid areas further south in Mexico. In some parts of its range, the bats inhabit mountain woodlands. By day, the southern long-nosed bat roosts in caves in large numbers, and it occasionally takes up residence in abandoned mines. Roosts may contain tens of thousands of individuals, but despite such vast gatherings, the members of this species do not cooperate with each other.

After dark, the bats can often be seen around flowering cacti, from which they obtain pollen and nectar. They also eat the pulp of cactus fruits. A single bat may visit up to 100 cacti per night, and make a round trip of 30km (18 miles). The cacti tend to flower earlier in the south, so the bats migrate slowly from south to north through their range following blooming patterns. Although cacti are the main food source, the bats will also feed on other plants, including agave and bindweed. Some plants are only pollinated by this species of bat.

*This southern long-nosed bat uses its long tongue, which is the same length as its body, to lick nectar and pollen out of large flowers. Unlike most blooms, the flowers on which bats feed open at night.*

**Distribution**: South-western United States and Mexico.
**Habitat**: Desert, arid grassland, scrubland, tropical dry forest and mountain woodland.
**Food**: Nectar and pollen.
**Size**: 8cm (3.25in); 23g (0.8oz).
**Maturity**: 1 year.
**Breeding**: 1 pup born in December and January; gestation is probably about 5 months.
**Life span**: Unknown.
**Status**: Vulnerable.

# Banana bat

*Musonycteris harrisoni*

These bats are found in banana groves along the Pacific coast of Mexico, west of the Isthmus of Tehuantepec in the south of country. They are found from sea level to 1,700m (5,600ft). Within this small range, banana bats are restricted to dry deciduous forests and thorny shrubland. The species was first described feeding in a banana grove, hence its common name.

Banana bats feed on nectar and pollen, often from banana plants, but not exclusively. Like many flower-feeding bats, they migrate over small distances to find freshly flowering plants. While feeding on nectar at a flower, they may also suck up any insects that they find there. Pollen from the flower clings to the bats' fur, and they swallow this as they lick their fur during grooming.

Young banana bats are cared for by their mothers only. They develop rapidly and are weaned and able to fly within a few weeks. Raccoons, snakes, ringtails, and small cats prey on roosting banana bats, while hawks and owls may catch them when they emerge to feed at dusk.

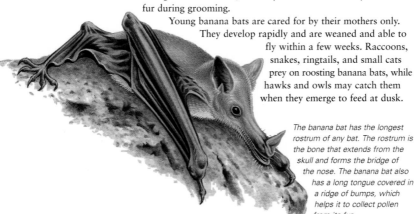

*The banana bat has the longest rostrum of any bat. The rostrum is the bone that extends from the skull and forms the bridge of the nose. The banana bat also has a long tongue covered in a ridge of bumps, which helps it to collect pollen from its fur.*

**Distribution**: Pacific coast of Mexico, in the states of Jalisco, Colima, Guerrero, Mexico, Michoacán and Morelos.
**Habitat**: Thorn scrub and dry forest.
**Food**: Nectar, pollen and insects.
**Size**: 7–8cm (2.75–3.25); weight unknown.
**Maturity**: 1 year.
**Breeding**: 1 pup born in late summer.
**Life span**: Unknown.
**Status**: The bat's restricted range and the loss of its habitat due to human activity have led to this species' classification as vulnerable.

# Big-eared woolly bat

*Chrotopterus auritus*

**Distribution**: Southern Mexico to Paraguay and northern Argentina.
**Habitat**: Lowland forests near streams.
**Food**: Small mammals, reptiles and amphibians; insects and fruit.
**Size**: 13.5cm (5.25in); 200g (7oz).
**Maturity**: 1 year.
**Breeding**: 1 young born in July.
**Life span**: Unknown.
**Status**: Lower risk.

Big-eared woolly bats range from southern Mexico to Paraguay and northern Argentina. They populate lowland forests and cloud forests that grow on the sides of tropical mountains. The bats roost in small groups of only about five individuals. Each bat will regularly move to a new roost.

This large species is unusual in that it preys on vertebrates as well as insects. It also eats a small amount of fruit. Although the big-eared woolly bat uses echolocation to sense its surroundings, it does not rely on this system to locate prey. Instead, it uses its sensitive ears to listen for noises made by prey animals such as mice, birds, lizards, and even smaller bat species. The bat kills its prey by biting it around the head and neck. It then eats the dead animal head first. Some small animals are carried back to the roost to be eaten during the day.

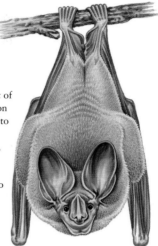

*This is one of the largest of the insect-eating bats – only the fruit bats, or flying foxes, are larger. The big-eared woolly bat can be identified by its large nose leaf, tiny tail and white wingtips.*

---

**Mexican long-nosed bat** (*Leptonycteris nivalis*): 7–9cm (2.75–3.5in); 18–30g (0.6–1oz)
This bat ranges from the southern United States to Guatemala and Honduras. It is most often found on mountain slopes where alpine scrub and pine woodlands grow. The bat's diet consists mainly of pollen and nectar from agave flowers, and the occasional insect, although it also feeds on cacti, berries and fruits. Agave flowers open just once, on a single night, and then perish. Consequently, the Mexican long-nosed bat must migrate to follow the blooming of its prime food source. The species is classed as endangered, because its habitat is diminishing and the agave plants it feeds on are becoming harder to find.

**Thomas's nectar bat** (*Lonchophylla thomasi*): 4.5–6cm (1.75–2.5); 6–14g (0.2–0.5oz)
Thomas's nectar bat is found in Panama and from Peru in western South America to the Brazilian Amazon in the east. It lives in lowland forests, especially near streams and larger watercourses. This bat roosts in caves and hollow trees, usually in small groups. Being a nectar and pollen feeder, it is equipped with a long snout to probe into flowers, and a bumpy tongue for licking up pollen.

**Tomes's sword-nosed bat** (*Lonchorhina aurita*): 5.3–6.7cm (2–2.5); 10–16g (0.3–0.6oz)
Named after the shape of its nose leaf, this forest bat lives in southern Mexico and Central America, and ranges south to Peru and Brazil. It feeds on insects, using its prominent nose leaf to direct echolocation calls and its large ears to detect the echoes returning from its prey.

# Long-legged bat

*Macrophyllum macrophyllum*

The long-legged bat is found throughout northern and central South America. Its range also stretches north through the eastern part of Central America to southern Mexico. The southern limit is the northeastern tip of Argentina. The long-legged bat occupies a variety of habitats. It is generally found close to ponds and lakes in all types of forest. It roosts alone or in small groups in hollow trees and, increasingly, in artificial structures, including in drainage tunnels and under bridges.

These bats feed on small insects that live on the surface of water or flutter close to it. The bats have a large nose leaf (a fleshy flap on the face), which is used to direct their echolocation calls to locate prey more precisely. A large tail membrane spans the long legs and toes. The bats use this membrane to skim insects off the water's surface and scoop them into their jaws.

**Distribution**: Eastern Central America and South America.
**Habitat**: Forests near water.
**Food**: Aquatic insects.
**Size**: 8–10cm (3.25–4in); 7–11g (0.2–0.4oz).
**Maturity**: 1 year.
**Breeding**: 1 pup born at all times of year.
**Life span**: 500 days.
**Status**: Common.

*As well as long legs and large hind feet, this species has a long tail surrounded by a membrane of skin joining the two back legs. This membrane is covered with dotted lines that each end in a bump on the trailing edge. The fur is sooty-brown above and paler below. On the wing, long-legged bats have a fluttering flight, rather like a butterfly.*

## Striped hairy-nosed bat

*Mimon crenulatum*

This bat has a patchy range that includes southern Mexico, the island of Trinidad and most of tropical South America east of the Andes. It is found in lowland forests, where it is most often seen flying near streams. It also frequents the pools that form in bromeliad plants, which grow on the sides of trees. These pools are used for reproduction by the bat's insect prey. As well as insects, the striped hairy-nosed bat also feeds on spiders and small lizards. Prey is often snatched from the surface of leaves.

Striped hairy-nosed bats roost in hollow trees and logs. The roosts contain small family groups of about four bats. Like many other bat species, the striped hairy-nosed bat uses scent to communicate in roosts, and most roosting sites are obvious by the strong smell coming from them. Comparatively little is known about this species' breeding habits. It is thought that the bats form monogamous pairs that reproduce and forage together. The single offspring, which is born at the beginning of the wet season, is nursed by its mother for approximately nine months.

*The young of this species are dark brown-red. As they get older, their fur becomes yellow, orange and red, and a pale line develops along the spine.*

**Distribution**: Southern Mexico, Panama, Trinidad and northern South America.
**Habitat**: Near streams in rainforests.
**Food**: Insects, spiders and other arthropods, plus small reptiles.
**Size**: 5–7.5cm (2–3in); 12–13g (0.4–0.5oz).
**Maturity**: 1 year.
**Breeding**: 1 pup born between December and July.
**Life span**: 20 years.
**Status**: Common.

## Spectral bat

*Vampyrum spectrum*

As the bat's scientific name suggests, this species was once thought to feed on the blood of other animals. The spectral bat is now known to be one of the many "false vampires", being a meat-eater rather than a blood-drinker. It is a powerful hunter that preys on other bats, small rodents, including mice and rats, and also birds, such as parakeets, orioles and wrens. The bat locates prey more by smell than by sight or echolocation. It stealthily creeps up on its victim – it is surprisingly agile on all fours – before pouncing or dropping down a short distance on to the animal and killing it with a bite from its sharp teeth. Fruits and insects may also form part of the spectral bat's diet.

The spectral bat lives in forests in the northern parts of South America and Central America, as far north as southern Mexico. It seldom strays far from water. The bat roosts in hollow trees in small family groups. Each group consists of a breeding pair, their latest offspring and two or three of the offspring from the year before.

Spectral bats form monogamous breeding pairs, possibly for life. Both parents take part in the rearing of the single young, licking their offspring incessantly and foraging for food to bring back to the roost. The adults feed morsels of chewed animal flesh to the young bat when it is being weaned. While roosting, the male spectral bat may wrap his huge wings around both the mother and their offspring.

*This is the largest species of bat in the Americas. It has an average wingspan of about 90cm (35.5in), but in larger individuals this can be as much as 1m (3.3ft). The bat has large ears and a large nose leaf, but no tail. The short, fine fur is reddish-brown above and slightly paler below.*

**Distribution**: From southern Mexico through Central America to Peru, Bolivia and central Brazil; also found on Trinidad.
**Habitat**: Near rivers and swampy areas.
**Food**: Birds and bats, as well as rodents such as mice and rats; possibly some fruit and insects.
**Size**: 12.5–13.5cm (5–5.25in); 170–180g (6–6.5oz).
**Maturity**: 1–2 years.
**Breeding**: 1 pup probably born at the beginning of the wet season, mainly between May and July.
**Life span**: 5 years.
**Status**: Lower risk.

# Wrinkle-faced bat

*Centurio senex*

**Distribution**: From Mexico through Central America to northern South America; also found on Trinidad.
**Habitat**: Dense forest.
**Food**: Fruits.
**Size**: 5.3–7cm (2–2.75in); 13–28g (0.5–1oz).
**Maturity**: 1 year.
**Breeding**: 1 pup born between February and August.
**Life span**: Unknown.
**Status**: Common.

Even for a bat, this species has a very wrinkled and ugly face. It has a very small nose but large eyes compared to other bats. Its favoured food is overripe fruits that are beginning to liquefy, especially mangoes and bananas. The bat sucks the sweet juices directly from the fruit. This may explain the strange facial features, which help the bat to make a strong seal around the fruit as it sucks. The fruit juice is filtered through extensions on the lips and gums, which remove unwanted mush. The bat's wrinkled face enables the cheeks to be greatly distended, and the bats use this extra cheek space to store fruit pulp so that they can eat it when they return to the roost.

The wrinkle-faced bat lives in dense forested areas of Central and South America, where fruits are most abundant. It roosts during the day in pairs or trios under the leaves of large trees.

*The folds of naked skin around the bat's face are the source of its common name. There is also a "beard" of white fur surrounding the lower face.*

---

**California leaf-nosed bat** (*Macrotus californicus*): 8–9cm (3.5–3.75in); 8–17g (0.3–0.6oz)
This species has short wings, large ears and eyes, and a large nose leaf. The nose leaf is a fleshy projection on the snout that acts like a megaphone, amplifying and directing the bat's echolocation calls. Leaf-nosed bats often hunt fast-moving insects – the hardest prey to track accurately. The California leaf-nosed bat is no exception, feeding on ground-dwelling insects, such as grasshoppers and cicadas. It often hovers in the air before striking. These bats live in northern Mexico, southern California, Nevada and Arizona.

**Greater spear-nosed bat** (*Phyllostomus hastatus*): 10–13cm (4–5in); weight unknown
Ranging from Honduras to Peru and Paraguay, the greater spear-nosed bat occurs near streams in both forests and more open habitats. This species has a long, spear-shaped nose leaf, and a V-shaped groove in its lower lip. Males have a large throat sac, which is probably a gland that produces pheromones in the summer mating season. Spear-nosed bats sleep in hollow trees, termite nests and caves, roosting in groups of up to 100. They mainly eat mice, lizards and other small vertebrates, plus pollen and fruits.

**Fringe-lipped bat** (*Trachops cirrhosus*): 7–10cm (3–4in); 32g (1oz)
Named after the bumps on its lips and muzzle, this omnivorous species lives in tropical Central and South America. Its habitat is lowland rainforest, and it roosts in hollow trees, caves and artificial structures such as culverts.

# Ipanema bat

*Pygoderma bilabiatum*

This species is found in the tropical region of South America, from northern Argentina in the south to Bolivia in the west and Surinam in the north. Ipanema bats are found mainly in tropical forests, where they roost in trees. They have increasingly begun to colonize human dwellings as people encroach into the forest. Their range includes the Ipanema neighbourhood of Rio de Janeiro, where they are commonly found feeding on garden fruit trees.

Analysis of the stomach contents of these bats has revealed that they eat almost no fibrous plant material, such as leaves, seeds or stalks, but only energy-packed fruits. The fruits are probably only eaten once they are very ripe, by which time the fruit tissues are beginning to break down, so the bat can absorb their nutrients more quickly. Ipanema bats may also eat pollen and nectar.

**Distribution**: Tropical regions of South America.
**Habitat**: Tropical forest.
**Food**: Fruits, probably also pollen and nectar.
**Size**: 6–8.5cm (2.5–3.25in); 27.5g (1oz).
**Maturity**: 1–2 years.
**Breeding**: 1 offspring born in the wet season.
**Life span**: Unknown.
**Status**: Common.

*The Ipanema bat has dark brown fur on its back and grey hairs on its chest. There are also white patches on each shoulder. This bat has no tail, merely a membrane of skin that connects the legs.*

## Spix's disc-winged bat

*Thyroptera tricolor*

Spix's disc-winged bat lives in tropical parts of the Americas, wherever dense rainforests and other jungles grow. The bat's range extends from southern Mexico through Central America to the lower fringes of the Amazon Basin in southern Brazil. This is one of just two species of disc-winged bats. The other – Peter's disc-winged bat – lives in the same area. Disc-winged bats have suction cups on their thumbs and ankles, enabling them to cling to the surfaces of smooth leaves. The cups are controlled by tiny muscles, which can expand the cups to reduce the pressure of the air trapped inside. The difference between the air pressure outside and inside the cup is what holds the bat in place. A single cup can carry the bat's entire weight.

Spix's disc-winged bats roost inside the leaves of *Heliconia* trees. When young, these leaves are curled up, providing a sheltered hideaway where the bats roost head-up during the daytime, with usually one or two bats per leaf, but sometimes as many as eight. Unlike most bats, this species roosts in a head-up position.

*Spix's disc-winged bat has red fur on its back and pale cream hairs underneath. Instead of a nose leaf, the bat has wart-like bumps on its snout.*

**Distribution**: From southern Mexico through Central America to south-eastern Brazil.
**Habitat**: Tropical forests.
**Food**: Mainly insects, especially beetles and flies, plus jumping spiders and other invertebrates.
**Size**: 2.7–3.8cm (1–1.5in); 4–5g (0.1–0.2oz).
**Maturity**: 1 year.
**Breeding**: 1 pup born twice a year.
**Life span**: Unknown.
**Status**: Common.

## Big brown bat

*Eptesicus fuscus*

The big brown bat, which hibernates in winter, is one of the largest bats of North America. It is a common resident of artificial structures, and can even be found in the heart of cities. Its natural habitat, however, is heavy forest. The nature of these forests changes considerably across this species' range. In the southern limit, at the northern tip of South America, the forests are dense jungles. Moving north, deciduous forests take over from jungles, especially in the eastern United States. At the northern limit, along the southern fringe of Canada, deciduous trees give way to conifers.

*Female big brown bats are slightly larger than males. These bats have 32 sharp teeth inside their large, powerful jaws, which can deliver a painful bite when the bats are handled. The teeth are used to crush the tough outer skeletons of the bats' insect prey. Big brown bats can only feed during the warmer months when their insect prey are active. They eat as much as they can to lay down enough fat reserves to see them through the winter, when their body weight can fall by as much as one-third.*

During summer, when the female bats rear their young, the sexes roost separately. This is a common feature of hibernating bat species. The sexes come together to mate at the end of summer, before forming large, mixed-sex winter roosts. The development of the young is delayed over the winter. The embryos begin to grow in spring, and pups are born in summer. The young bats are able to fly within three to four weeks.

**Distribution**: Southern Canada to Panama and the northern tip of South America; also found in West Indies.
**Habitat**: Heavy forest; often found in urban areas.
**Food**: Insects, especially beetles, plus moths, flies, wasps, flying ants, lacewing flies, and dragonflies.
**Size**: 11–13cm (4.25–5in); 50g (1.75oz).
**Maturity**: 1 year.
**Breeding**: 1–2 offspring born in June and July.
**Life span**: 19 years.
**Status**: Common.

**Jamaican fruit-eating bat** (*Artibeus jamaicensis*): c.10cm (4in); 30–50g (1–2oz)
This species ranges from Mexico to Bolivia and Brazil. It is also found on the Lesser and Greater Antilles island chains. The bat is not restricted to one habitat. It is often seen hunting in open areas. Roosting sites include houses, hollow trees and caves. In forested parts of its range, the bat roosts under "leaf tents", which it creates by nibbling through the central vein of a large leaf so that the leaf bends in the middle. This species roosts in harems of as many as 14 females with just one male. Its diet consists mainly of fruit, including bananas, avocados and figs, but it will also eat nectar, pollen and petals, as well as any insects that it finds on flowers.

**Little white-shouldered bat** (*Ametrida centurio*): 3.5–4.7cm (1.5–1.75in); 7.8–12.6g (0.3–0.4oz)
The little white-shouldered bat is found in Central America and northern South America. It lives in rainforests, and is most often seen flying near running water. The female is 50 per cent heavier than the male. This size difference resulted in the bat's initial classification as two species. Both sexes have pale shoulder patches, and males have fleshy pads under their eyes. The diet probably consists of fruit and some insects.

**Visored bat** (*Sphaeronycteris toxophyllum*): 5.7cm (2.25in); 17g (0.6oz)
These tailless, fruit-eating Amazonian bats live in forest clearings. They get their name from a roll of loose skin under the chin, which can be rolled over the face. The also have fleshy, horn-shaped nose leafs, which are longer on the males.

# Spotted bat

*Euderma maculatum*

Spotted bats occur in small areas of a large range that extends from northern Mexico to British Columbia in south-western Canada. They live in many habitats, including the marshes of the southern United States and the dry hill forests in the south-west.

These bats use low-frequency echolocation calls, some of which are audible to humans as clicks. The low frequency means that the calls only form clear echoes on bigger objects, and consequently they give a relatively basic representation of the bats' surroundings. Because of this, spotted bats only catch large insects such as moths, and they prefer to occupy open habitats where there is plenty of space between obstacles. In densely forested areas, the bats would have difficulty avoiding branches in their flight path. Spotted bats are still expert hunters in the right environment. They have been recorded catching prey every 45 seconds, and are known to hunt for at least four hours each night.

*This species gets its name from the three white spots on its shoulders and rump. The rest of the back is covered by black fur.*

**Distribution**: British Columbia to northern Mexico.
**Habitat**: Dry, open forests and marshlands.
**Food**: Flying insects, especially large moths.
**Size**: 12.6cm (5in); 16–20g (0.6–0.7oz).
**Maturity**: 1 year.
**Breeding**: 1 young born in June.
**Life span**: Unknown.
**Status**: Unknown.

# Allen's big-eared bat

*Idionycteris phyllotis*

**Distribution**: South-western United States and central Mexico.
**Habitat**: Mountain pine forests.
**Food**: Insects, especially moths.
**Size**: 10–12cm (4–4.75oz); 8–16g (0.3–0.6oz).
**Maturity**: 1 year.
**Breeding**: Single pup born in summer.
**Life span**: Unknown.
**Status**: Vulnerable.

These rare bats occupy the pine and oak forests that grow on the dry mountainsides of the south-western United States and central Mexico. The bats need to roost near springs or water holes, so that they can easily replace the moisture they lose through the surface of their wings while roosting. This is important, since most of the roosting sites in their habitat are dry places, compared to the humid surroundings adopted by the majority of bats. Big-eared bats roost in small colonies under overhanging cliffs or in crevices between boulders. The sexes separate during the summer, with the females forming maternity groups, and the males possibly remaining solitary.

Allen's big-eared bats are agile flyers and flit through the tight spaces of their rocky habitats. They often hover before swooping down on moths and other insect prey as they rest on the ground. These bats are useful predators of insect pests that threaten crops. Some people also use the bats' droppings as fertilizer.

*Allen's big-eared bat is most notable for its large ears, which are up to 4.5cm (1.75in) long. Lappets – hanging fringes of skin – extend from the base of the ears and over the forehead.*

# Red bat

*Lasiurus borealis*

*The hairs of this bat's red coat are white at the tips, giving the bat a frosted, grizzled appearance. The coloration of the coat helps to camouflage the bat in sycamore, oaks, elm, and box elder trees, which prove popular roosting sites. The rear part of the skin membrane is covered in fur to help keep the bat warm.*

Red bats range across the Americas, from southern Canada to Chile and Argentina. They are commonly found living alongside humans in rural and suburban areas. Red bats hang in trees during the daytime, often by one foot, and are easily mistaken for dead leaves. In colder parts of their range, they may hibernate in hollow trees or migrate south for the winter.

Red bats are fast flyers, with a medium-sized body and long wings. The head is small, and the jaws are equipped with 32 small, sharp teeth. These insect-hunting bats catch their prey on the wing, and they are often seen feeding in brightly lit areas that attract a wide range of insects. The bats fly through the swarming insects, selecting a target 5m (16.5ft) away. They strike every 30 seconds, and catch about half of their intended victims.

The red bat is one of the few bat species that is regularly preyed on in flight. Since red bats often fly around lights, they make easy targets for owls. Opossums, snakes and racoons also prey on them as they roost in buildings and other structures.

**Distribution**: From southern Canada through Central America to Chile and Argentina.
**Habitat**: Suburban and rural areas.
**Food**: Insects.
**Size**: 9.3–11.7cm (3.7–4.5in); 7–13g (0.2–0.5oz).
**Maturity**: 1 year.
**Breeding**: Mating is in August and September; litter of 2–3 (maximum 4) pups born in summer.
**Life span**: Unknown.
**Status**: Common.

# South-western myotis

*Myotis auriculus*

*These bats have distinctive long, brown ears. Their brown fur lacks the glossiness seen on many other species. The south-western myotis lives in the same area as many of its close relatives. It is easy to identify, because the trailing edge of its tail membrane has no hairs. South-western myotis are able to hover and pluck insect prey from surfaces. They are believed to make seasonal migrations and hibernate in parts of their range.*

Several species of small brown bat share the common name myotis. The group is also known as the mouse-eared bats. South-western myotis occur throughout Mexico and north to New Mexico and Arizona. They live in dry woodlands and desert scrublands. In high-altitude areas, they inhabit chaparral – forests of small trees. These bats are most common in rocky areas where there is a supply of water. They roost on cliffs, in sheltered rock crevices or in rotting trees.

South-western myotis, particularly females, concentrate their hunting along watercourses. They specialize in catching moths and other flying insects that are 3–4cm (1.25–1.5in) long. Moths are taken in flight or snatched up while resting. Foraging trips are alternated with rest periods, when the bats can digest their food. The bats need to drink large amounts of water to wash away the toxic nitrogen waste produced by digesting their high-protein diet, and also to replace water lost from their bodies by evaporation in their arid habitats.

**Distribution**: South-western United States to southern Mexico.
**Habitat**: Dry woodlands and desert.
**Food**: Insects, particularly moths.
**Size**: 27cm (10.5in); 5–8g (0.2–0.3oz).
**Maturity**: 1 year.
**Breeding**: Mating probably occurs in autumn; 1 pup, usually born in June or July, but later in southern parts of range (timing of births shows considerable geographic variation).
**Life span**: 3 years.
**Status**: Common.

# Evening bat

*Nycticeius humeralis*

**Distribution**: North America, from the Great Lakes Basin south to Texas and Florida.
**Habitat**: Forest and near rivers.
**Food**: Insects.
**Size**: 8.6–10.5cm (3.5–4.25in); 6–14g (0.2–0.5oz).
**Maturity**: 1 year.
**Breeding**: 2 pups born in summer.
**Life span**: 2 years.
**Status**: Common

The name evening bat is given to a great many bats belonging to the *Vespertilionidae* family. Their alternative name of vesper bats was acquired because many species would roost in dark church belfries and be seen flying off to hunt while vespers, the evening service, was being conducted. This particular evening bat is found across eastern North America, from the Great Lakes to Texas and Florida. It may live in churches and other buildings, but its natural roosting site is in the hollow of a rotting tree. It forms harems comprising one male roosting with up to 20 females.

This species is medium-sized and dark brown. Like all vesper bats, it lacks a nose leaf. Evening bats catch flying insects, such as beetles, flies and moths. They appear to hunt high up during twilight hours, gradually descending as it gets darker. This may be a defence against owls. In the north of their range, the bats migrate southward in autumn.

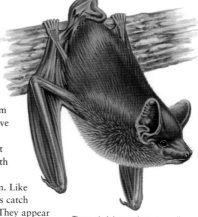

*These dark brown bats never live in caves, even in winter. Instead, they are found in hollow trees, under loose bark and in buildings.*

**California myotis** (*Myotis californicus*): 7–9.4cm (2.75–3.75in); 3.3–5.4g (0.1–0.2oz)
This species has one of the most northerly ranges of all the North American bats. The California myotis is found in south-eastern Alaska and stretches south along the Pacific region of Canada and the United States to southern Mexico. It lives in a range of habitats, from the semi-deserts of the southern parts of its range to the damp coastal forests further north. In open lowland areas, this little bat has pale fur. Higher up, where it lives in forests, the coat is darker. In summer, California myotis roost in small groups, but during winter they form larger colonies in deep caves and other places to avoid the worst of the cold weather. Amazingly, these bats can still fly at temperatures below freezing. They are insect eaters, catching prey on the wing as they make swooping flights.

**Little brown bat** (*Myotis lucifugus*): 8.5cm (3.5in); 7–13g (0.2–0.5oz)
This Myotis species lives all over North America, from Alaska to northern Mexico. Little brown bats often inhabit houses, spending the summer roosting in lofts. They feed in open areas and woodlands, and also over water, catching gnats, beetles, wasps and other small insects. These nocturnal bats are most active a few hours after dusk and just before dawn. In winter they head for humid caves or mines. One pup is born between May and July, which the mother keeps beneath a wing while she is roosting. The pup starts to fly and is weaned at about four weeks old. The mother distinguishes her own offspring from the other pups by its scent and call.

# Western pipistrelle

*Pipistrellus hesperus*

Pipistrelles form another large group of vesper bats. This species lives in the western United States and most of Mexico, where it is most commonly found in dry, rocky habitats. In summer, these bats roost by day in crevices and buildings, but during winter they seek out more secluded, damp hideaways, often ending up in caves and mines.

Western pipistrelles eat a range of insect prey. They search for an insect swarm and then spend the night feeding, consuming up to one-fifth of their body weight in insects. Being small, this bat must eat large quantities of food to survive. (In general, large animals need to eat a smaller proportion of their body weight to stay alive. This is because they lose heat more slowly, and so expend less energy keeping their bodies warm.) Consequently, the western pipistrelle must hibernate, including in the warmer parts of its range, because it cannot tolerate any period when food is even slightly scarce.

**Distribution**: From southern Mexico, including Baja peninsula, to Texas and California in the United States.
**Habitat**: Canyons, cliffs and rocky areas.
**Food**: Insects.
**Size**: 6.6–7.3cm (2.5–2.75in); 3–6g (0.1–0.2oz).
**Maturity**: 1 year.
**Breeding**: 1 pup born in June or July.
**Life span**: Unknown.
**Status**: Common.

*These bats are small compared to other species found in the region. They have distinctive black and leathery skin on their face, ears and wing membranes. Females are slightly larger than males.*

# ARMADILLOS AND RELATIVES

*Armadillos, anteaters and sloths belong to a group of mammals called the* Xenarthra *(formerly named* Edentata, *meaning toothless). Most xenarths live in South and Central America. Only one, the long-nosed armadillo, lives as far north as Texas. These animals are taxonomically related to one another but do not share evident common physical characteristics, except for unique bones that strengthen their spines.*

## Giant armadillo

*Priodontes maximus*

*Like all armadillos, the giant armadillo has bands of bony plates running from side to side across its body to serve as armour. These plates are covered in leathery skin, and a few thick hairs stick out from between them.*

The giant armadillo is the largest of all armadillos. It is nocturnal and shelters by day in burrows dug with the mighty claws on its forefeet. Most of the burrows are dug into the side of termite mounds. Giant armadillos also dig to get at their prey. They typically excavate termite mounds and ant nests, but they also dig out worms, subterranean spiders and occasionally snakes.

Unlike many other armadillos, giant armadillos cannot curl up completely to protect their soft undersides with their armoured upper bodies. Instead, these giants rely on their considerable size to deter predators. If they are attacked, giant armadillos try to dig themselves out of trouble. Armadillos live alone. They breed all year round, and mate when they chance upon the opposite sex during their travels. One or two young are born in a large burrow after a four-month gestation.

**Distribution**: Venezuela to northern Argentina.
**Habitat**: Dense forest and grassland near water.
**Food**: Termites, ants, spiders and other insects, worms, snakes and carrion.
**Size**: 0.7–1m (2.25–3.25ft); 60kg (132lb).
**Maturity**: 1 year.
**Breeding**: 1–2 young born throughout the year.
**Life span**: 15 years.
**Status**: Vulnerable.

## Long-nosed armadillo

*Dasypus novemcinctus*

**Distribution**: Southern United States to northern Argentina.
**Habitat**: Shaded areas.
**Food**: Arthropods, reptiles, amphibians, fruit and roots.
**Size**: 24–57cm (9.5–22.5in); 1–10kg (2.2–22lb).
**Maturity**: 1 year.
**Breeding**: 4 young born in spring.
**Life span**: 15 years.
**Status**: Common.

Long-nosed armadillos are found in a wide range of habitats, but always require plenty of cover. In the warmer parts of their range they feed at night. In colder areas they may be active during the day, especially in winter. These armadillos build large nests at the ends of their long burrows. The nests are filled with dried grasses. In areas with plenty of plant cover, long-nosed armadillos may also build their nests above ground.

Long-nosed armadillos search for their animal prey by poking their long noses into crevices and under logs. They also eat fallen fruit and roots. When threatened, the animals waddle to their burrows as fast as possible. If cornered, they will curl up.

Long-nosed armadillos forage alone, but they may share their burrows with several other individuals, all of the same sex. The breeding season is in late summer. Litters of identical, same-sex quadruplets are born in the spring.

*The long-nosed armadillo is also called the nine-banded armadillo because it typically has that number of plate bands along its back, although specimens can possess either eight or ten bands.*

# Three-toed sloth

*Bradypus tridactylus*

**Distribution**: Eastern Brazil.
**Habitat**: Coastal forest.
**Food**: Young leaves, twigs and buds.
**Size**: 41–70cm (16–27.5in); 2.25–5.5kg (5–12lb).
**Maturity**: 3.5 years.
**Breeding**: Single young born throughout the year.
**Life span**: 20 years.
**Status**: Endangered.

Three-toed sloths spend most of their lives hanging upside down from trees. They are very inactive creatures, but they do climb down to the ground once or twice a week to excrete or move to other trees.

Three-toed sloths feed by pulling on flimsy branches with their forelegs, to bring them close to their mouths. They spend long periods waiting for their tough food to digest. Because they are so inactive, sloths have a lower body temperature than other mammals – sometimes as low as 24°C (75°F). Their fur is sometimes tinged with green because algae are growing in it. The sloths may absorb some of the algal nutrients through their skin, and the green colour helps to camouflage them among branches and leaves.

Sloths have very simple societies. They live alone and females only produce offspring every two years. Mating can occur throughout the year though, with both partners still hanging upside down. Mothers give birth in this position too, and the young cling to the hair on their mothers' breasts.

*Unlike other mammals, three-toed sloths have long, grey hairs that point downwards when the animals are hanging upside down from tree branches. This ensures that rainwater runs off the fur easily. The sloths climb using their strong, hook-like claws.*

---

**Pichi** (*Zaedyus pichiy*): 26–34cm (10–13.5in); 1–2kg (2.2–4.5lb)
The pichi is a small armadillo that lives on the grasslands of southern Argentina and in the alpine meadows of the Chilean Andes. Its armoured head, body and tail have long hairs growing out from behind each plate. When threatened, a pichi withdraws its legs under its body so that the serrated edges of its armour dig into the ground. It uses this technique to anchor itself in its burrow. Pichis probably hibernate in colder parts of their range. Between one and three young may be born at any time of the year. This species eats carrion, small insects and worms.

**Silky anteater** (*Cyclopes didactylus*): 18–20cm (7–8in); 375–410g (13.25–14.5oz)
The silky anteater is found in forests from southern Mexico to Bolivia and Brazil. It lives in ceiba trees, which have large seed pods filled with silky fibres. The seed pods provide the perfect camouflage for the anteater, since the animal's silky fur blends in with the tree's shiny pods, making it almost invisible – even to sharp-eyed predators such as harpy eagles and owls. The anteater rarely leaves the safety of its tree. It rests during the day in a tree-hollow nest; by night, the silky anteater moves slowly through the branches eating ants, termites, beetles and other tree-dwelling insects. In one day, a silky anteater can consume as many as 8,000 ants, which it licks up with its long, sticky tongue. When threatened, this species stands on its back legs and steadies itself by grasping a branch with its prehensile tail. This posture frees up the clawed forelimbs for fighting off predators.

# Giant anteater

*Myrmecophaga tridactyla*

Giant anteaters live wherever there are large ant nests or termite mounds in abundance. They use their powerful claws to rip the colonies apart, then they use their sticky tongues to lick up the insects and their eggs and larvae. A single giant anteater can eat over 30,000 ants or termites in one day.

Despite being powerful diggers, giant anteaters shelter in thickets, not burrows, because of their awkward shape. They spend most of their time alone searching for food, with their long noses close to the ground. While on the move, they curl their forelimbs under their bodies so that they are actually walking on the backs of their forefeet and their claws do not hinder them.

Females often come into contact with one another, but males keep their distance. Breeding can take place all year.

**Distribution**: Belize to northern Argentina.
**Habitat**: Grasslands, forests and swamps.
**Food**: Ants, termites and beetle larvae.
**Size**: 1–1.2m (3.25–4ft); 18–39kg (39.75–86lb).
**Maturity**: 2.5–4 years.
**Breeding**: Single young born throughout the year.
**Life span**: 25 years.
**Status**: Vulnerable.

*Giant anteaters have powerful digging claws on their forelimbs and incredibly long tongues – often over 60cm (24in) – inside their snouts. They have white stripes along their flanks and a long, bushy tail.*

# Six-banded armadillo

*Euphractus sexcinctus*

Six-banded armadillos live in the savannahs of South America. They are active by day, unlike most other armadillos. They prefer arid areas, where it is easier to dig burrows in the dry soil, although some are found in wetter, often muddy areas. These armadillos are omnivores, meaning they eat all types of food. They dig for tubers and roots, and forage for the fruits of succulent plants and palm nuts. Although plant foods make up the majority of their diet, the armadillos will also eat ants and termites, along with other insects and carrion. They even kill small vertebrates, including mice or lizards. Without any proper biting or chewing teeth, eating flesh is difficult for the armadillos. They solve this problem by standing on the dead body and ripping off the meat with their jaws.

Six-banded armadillos mark their burrow and other key features in their territory with a smelly liquid produced by a scent gland under the base of the tail.

**Distribution**: South America east of the Andes, Brazil to northern Argentina.
**Habitat**: Dry savannahs.
**Food**: Fruits, tubers, palm nuts and insects.
**Size**: 40cm (15.5in); 5kg (11lb).
**Maturity**: 1 year.
**Breeding**: 1–3 young born throughout the year.
**Life span**: 8–12 years.
**Status**: Common.

*This species is also called the yellow armadillo because of the pale tone of its armour. It has between six and eight moveable bands on its back.*

---

**Pink fairy armadillo** (*Chlamyphorus truncatus*):
8–10cm (3–4in); 80–100g (2.75–3.5oz)
The smallest of all the armadillo species, this animal lives on sandy plains in Argentina, where it is known as the pichiciego. Burrows are usually dug close to ant nests and termite mounds, which are the pink fairy armadillo's main sources of food. It also eats snails, worms and roots. This solitary, nocturnal species remains underground during the daytime. If it rains, the armadillo evacuates its burrow to avoid drowning.

**Chacoan fairy armadillo** (*Chlamyphorus retusus*): 14–17.5cm (5.5–7in); 1kg (2.2lb)
Slightly larger than the pink fairy armadillo, this species shares many of the same characteristics. It lives in the Gran Chaco scrub region of central South America. Chacoan fairy armadillos are expert burrowers and are seldom spotted above ground, because they quickly bury themselves when alarmed. Once underground, the animal's rear is protected by a circular plate of armour, which presents an effective shield to any predator that tries to dig out the armadillo. Like other armadillos, this species is omnivorous.

**Andean hairy armadillo** (*Chaetophractus nationi*):
22–40cm (8.5–15.5in); 0.75–1kg (1–2.25lb)
This armadillo is found in Bolivia and Chile, on the grasslands of Andean slopes up to 3,500m (11,500ft). Thick hairs stick out between its scales, and the legs and underside are also hairy. In summer, the Andean hairy armadillo is nocturnal in habit, sheltering from the daytime heat in the cool of its burrow. However, during winter it reverses its behaviour, foraging by day and keeping warm in its burrow at night.

# Southern three-banded armadillo

*Tolypeutes matacus*

An inhabitant of South American grasslands, this species ranges from central Argentina northward into Paraguay and southern Brazil, and to Bolivia in the west. Southern three-banded armadillos are sometimes found in marshes or other boggy areas. As a general rule, these habitats are seldom far from drier habitats such as savannahs or forests. The armadillos make dens inside old ant nests.

When threatened, the armadillo can roll itself into a ball. The only unprotected area is between the head and tail section. If a curious predator tries to poke its paw into this space, the armadillo clamps the intruder between its armour plates.

This species eats mainly ants and termites. It uses its powerful forelegs and strong claws to excavate ant nests and termite mounds or lever off tree bark. Then it licks up insects with its long, sticky tongue.

**Distribution**: South America.
**Habitat**: Grasslands and marshes.
**Food**: Ants and termites.
**Size**: 30cm (12in); 1.4–1.6kg (3–3.5lb).
**Maturity**: 9–12 months.
**Breeding**: Single young born between November and January.
**Life span**: 8–12 years.
**Status**: Common.

*This species and the Brazilian three-banded armadillo can roll up into an armoured ball for protection against attack. Contrary to popular belief, this is an unusual behaviour – no other armadillos can roll themselves up so completely.*

# Large hairy armadillo

*Chaetophractus villosus*

*Armadillo means "little armoured one" in Spanish. The armour is made of plates of bone covered in a layer of horny skin. The plates are joined together by flexible skin, so they form a tough but supple covering. Unlike most other armadillos, this species has long, thick hairs.*

**Distribution**: Central South America, from northern Paraguay and southern Bolivia to central Argentina.
**Habitat**: Semi-desert.
**Food**: Insects, invertebrates, small vertebrates, plants and carrion. Plant matter makes up about half of its diet during winter, much less at other times of year.
**Size**: 22–40cm (8.5–15.5in); 2kg (4.5lb).
**Maturity**: 9 months.
**Breeding**: Litter of 2 young born once or twice per year.
**Life span**: 30 years.
**Status**: Common.

This species is found in northern Paraguay and southern Bolivia. It also ranges south into central Argentina. This part of South America is called the Gran Chaco – a dry, sandy region of unique but inhospitable scrubland. Although the area gets enough rain for grasslands and savannahs to grow, much of the soil's water is lost by evaporation due to the high winds and baking sun. Large hairy armadillos escape from the heat by burrowing into the ground, since it is considerably cooler just below the surface. The loose sand makes it easy for armadillos to dig deep holes in a short time, so this is also the main method of avoiding attack by predators. Once in the hole, an armadillo relies on its armoured back to protect it from further danger.

Large hairy armadillos are omnivores. They forage at night for insects, other invertebrates and the occasional small mammal or lizard. They also eat plant food and carrion. They have been known to dig underneath large carcasses to feast on the maggots and grubs growing inside the rotting flesh.

# Northern naked-tailed armadillo

*Cabassous centralis*

**Distribution**: South America, from northern Argentina to Colombia and Venezuela; Central America, from Panama to southern Mexico.
**Habitat**: Grasslands and woodlands.
**Food**: Insects, mainly ants and termites; rarely bird eggs, earthworms, and small reptiles and amphibians.
**Size**: 30–50cm (12–20in); 2–3kg (4.5–6.5lb).
**Maturity**: Unknown, probably about 1 year.
**Breeding**: Single babies.
**Life span**: 8–12 years.
**Status**: Common.

This species has a large range that extends from northern Argentina through Central America, reaching as far north as southern Mexico. It is most commonly found in grasslands and woodlands, wherever there is enough thick undergrowth to hide from predators. The armadillo digs its own burrow, often in the side of an embankment.

Northern naked-tailed armadillos are solitary creatures, like most armadillos. They do sometimes gather in small groups in areas with a good supply of food. However, in these situations they are tolerating the presence of others rather than grouping together for a reason. They are active at night, and never leave their burrows before sunset.

This species has a diet made up almost exclusively of insects, which it apparently locates by scent. The armadillos dig up beetle grubs and excavate termite and ant nests, and then use their long tongue to extract the small insects from their tunnels. The sickle-like claw on each front foot is used to cut through roots to reach the insect prey. Sometimes the armadillos completely bury themselves with soil while digging for food.

*The protective armour so characteristic of these animals is not found on the tail of this armadillo – a feature it shares with three other species. It is also known as the eleven-banded armadillo.*

**Southern tamandua** (*Tamandua tetradactyla*): 53–88cm (21–34.5in); 2–7kg (4.5–15.5lb)
Superficially very similar to its northern relative, the southern tamandua lives in South America, from Trinidad and Venezuela to northern Argentina. In the south of its range, it has a "vest" pattern to its black and blonde coat, which resembles that of the northern tamandua. In the northern part of the range, the fur is of a single colour, ranging from black to blonde and brown. These animals are mainly arboreal, using their long claws to grip tree bark as they climb. On the ground, they walk on the sides of their feet, because the claws would stick into the soles if they walked flat-footed. When cornered, a tamandua uses its claws as weapons. It stands on its hind legs with its back against a tree trunk and stretches out its powerful forelegs. In this position it can deliver slashing blows to any predator that approaches.

**Brown-throated three-toed sloth** (*Bradypus variegatus*): 55–60cm (21.5–24in); 3.5–4.5kg (7.5–10lb)
This species lives in the tropical forests of Central and South America, mainly east of the Andes. It feeds on the foliage of cecropia trees. The sloth's legs are designed to allow the animal to hang from trees; as a result, it is severely disadvantaged on the ground, since its legs are too weak to carry its body weight. In common with other three-toed sloths, this species has three more neck vertebrae than other mammals. These extra bones enable sloths to turn their heads through 270 degrees. Male brown-throated sloths have yellow or orange patches on their backs.

## Northern tamandua

*Tamandua mexicana*

Sometimes called lesser anteaters, tamanduas have a long snout with a tiny mouth, and long, curved claws. They use their claws and prehensile tails to climb through the branches of trees in search of food. They do forage and rest on the ground, but out of the trees they are more clumsy and vulnerable to attack.

Like other anteaters, tamanduas lack teeth, so they grind up their insect food using a muscular stomach sac called a gizzard. The gizzard also contains little pebbles and pieces of grit that are swallowed along with the ants. These hard objects help to break down the food into a digestible paste.

Tamanduas are traditionally known as stinkers of the forest, thanks to the foul-smelling secretions from their anal gland, which they use to mark territories. They also communicate with hisses.

*A V-shaped marking down the back of the neck makes this species look as though it is wearing a vest – hence its alternative name of vested anteater.*

**Distribution**: Central and South America.
**Habitat**: Rainforest, drier forests and grasslands.
**Food**: Termites and ants.
**Size**: 47–77cm (18.5–30.5in); 2–7kg (4.5–15.5lb).
**Maturity**: 1 year.
**Breeding**: Single young born in spring.
**Life span**: 9 years.
**Status**: Common.

## Maned three-toed sloth

*Bradypus torquatus*

This rare species is found only in what remains of the coastal forests of eastern Brazil. Like so many species from this mixed habitat of deciduous and evergreen trees, it is being endangered by deforestation. Although renowned for being slow moving, these sloths occupy a surprisingly large territory, moving through the rainforest along lianas that grow between the crowns of the trees.

The long, thick fur makes it hard for these sloths to regulate their temperature internally. When they are cold, the animals climb up to the highest branches to sunbathe. To cool off, they move down inside the crown of the tree to find a shady spot.

The maned sloth is a leaf eater. Leaves are not very nutritious, so sloths must spend long periods eating and digesting their food. Consequently, they move very slowly to conserve energy. Their metabolic rate is about half that of other similar-sized mammals.

*The long, grey mane of fur on the neck often has traces of green in it. This colour is produced by blue-green algae, a plant-like form of bacteria. The maned sloth has three claws on each foot.*

**Distribution**: Eastern coast of Brazil, South America.
**Habitat**: Coastal forest.
**Food**: Leaves, twigs and buds.
**Size**: 55–60cm (21.5–24in); 3.5–4.5kg (7.5–10lb).
**Maturity**: 3 years.
**Breeding**: Single young born once a year.
**Life span**: 12 years.
**Status**: Endangered.

# Southern two-toed sloth

*Choloepus didactylus*

*While three-toed sloths have very short tails, two toed sloths have no tail at all. Their front feet have two toes while their hind feet have three. All the toes have long, curved claws, which the animal hooks over branches. The sloths move with a hand-over-hand action.*

Southern two-toed sloths live in the rainforests of northern South America as far south as Peru and Amazonian Brazil. They spend almost their entire lives hanging in the crowns of tall trees. They occasionally climb down to the ground, either to empty their bowels or to move to a tree that contains more food.

On the ground they are very awkward, and have to drag themselves along. Their body is adapted to life hanging upside down in trees. Everything takes place upside down, including feeding, mating and giving birth.

When resting, the sloths hang in a ball that looks like a wasp nest, termite nest or branch stump. Southern two-toed sloths live alone, only ever interacting during mating or with young. However, several two-toed sloths may feed in a large tree. These animals eat leaves, twigs and fruits. Because they lack sharp biting teeth, the sloths have hard lips that cut through leaves and twigs. The back teeth grind the hard food. These teeth are continually worn down and grow throughout the animal's life.

**Distribution**: South America east of the Andes, from eastern Venezuela and the Guianas south into northern Brazil and the upper Amazon Basin of Ecuador and Peru.
**Habitat**: Rainforests.
**Food**: Leaves, berries, twigs and fruits.
**Size**: 54–74cm (21.5–29in); 4–8.5kg (8.75–18.75lb).
**Maturity**: 4–5 years.
**Breeding**: Single offspring born every year.
**Life span**: 12 years.
**Status**: Vulnerable.

# Hoffmann's two-toed sloth

*Choloepus hoffmanni*

**Distribution**: Central America and northern South America. There are two distinct populations: the first extends from Nicaragua to Venezuela, the second ranges from Peru to southwestern Brazil and central Bolivia.
**Habitat**: Tropical forests.
**Food**: Leaves, twigs and fruit.
**Size**: 54–90cm (21.5–36in); 4–8.5kg (8.75–18.75lb).
**Maturity**: 4 years.
**Breeding**: Single young born approximately every 18 months.
**Life span**: 12 years.
**Status**: Unknown.

Hoffmann's two-toed sloths live in the rainforests of northern South America as far south as Brazil and Bolivia, and into Central America as far north as Nicaragua. Unlike their three-toed cousins, they have only two digits on each forefoot, but their hind feet have three. Like other sloths, this species lives a slow, nocturnal life, hanging from high branches.

When feeding, Hoffmann's two-toed sloth uses its long arms to pull branches within reach of the mouth. Its diet consists of leaves, fruit and twigs, which do not provide the sloth with large amounts of nutrients or energy. Consequently, it cannot rely on summoning the energy to run from danger. Instead, it hides by staying perfectly still during the day. As in all the sloths, the hair shafts of this species have a long groove that collects blue-green algae, which makes the hairs appear green. The green hair adds to a motionless sloth's camouflage, helping it to blend in with the foliage. If the camouflage fails to prevent attack from harpy eagles, jaguars, or other predators, the sloth may fight back with its claws.

It has been suggested that the sloth may also gain nutrients from the algae, obtained either by absorption through the skin or by licking the hair.

*The sloth's shaggy coat is made up of two types of fur. The short underfur is covered by long, thick guard hairs. The hairs vary in colour from dark brown to pale yellow, although the fur also has green tinges produced by bacteria living on the hairs.*

# MARSUPIALS

*Marsupials are a group of mammals that brood their young in pouches on their bellies, rather than in wombs like placental mammals. The overwhelming majority of marsupials are found in Australia and New Guinea, but several species live in the Americas. However, fossil evidence has led zoologists to conclude that marsupials first evolved in South America, and subsequently spread to Australasia.*

## Water opossum

*Chironectes minimus*

*Water opossums have short waterproof coats with a grey and black pattern. Their hind feet are webbed, and both sexes have pouches opening to the rear.*

Water opossums, or yapoks, live beside bodies of fresh water in tropical forests. They make dens in burrows in the banks of streams or lakes, with entrances just above water level. Unusually, both sexes have pouches. A female can close her pouch using a ring of muscles to keep her developing young dry while she is underwater. A male's pouch is always open and he uses it to protect his scrotum while in water or when moving quickly through forest.

Water opossums are superb swimmers, using their hind feet to propel themselves through the water. However, they also forage on land or in trees. They spend the night in their dens, but may rest in bundles of leaves in secluded places on the forest floor between daytime feeding forays. Most births take place between December and January. After their birth, the young opossums spend a few more weeks in the pouch until they are fully developed.

**Distribution**: Central and South America from southern Mexico to Belize and Argentina.
**Habitat**: Fresh-water streams and lakes.
**Food**: Crayfish, shrimp, fish, fruit and water plants.
**Size**: 27–40cm (10.5–15.5in); 600–800g (21.25–28.25oz).
**Maturity**: Unknown.
**Breeding**: 2–5 young born in summer.
**Life span**: 3 years.
**Status**: Lower risk.

## Virginia opossum

*Didelphis virginiana*

**Distribution**: United States, Central America and northern South America.
**Habitat**: Moist woodlands or thick brush in swamps.
**Food**: Plants, carrion, small vertebrates and invertebrates.
**Size**: 33–50cm (13–19.5in); 2–5.5kg (4.5–12.25lb).
**Maturity**: 6–8 months.
**Breeding**: 2 litters per year.
**Life span**: 3 years.
**Status**: Lower risk.

Virginia opossums generally live in forested areas that receive plenty of rain. However, the species is very adaptable and is making its home in new places across North America. Many survive in more open country beside streams or in swamps, while others make their homes in people's sheds and barns.

Virginia opossums are most active at night. By day they rest in nests of leaves and grass, hidden away in crevices, hollow trees and sometimes in burrows. By night, the marsupials hunt for food. They are good climbers, using their prehensile tails to cling to branches.

Virginia opossums do not hibernate, but they do put on fat as the days shorten with the approach of autumn. They rely on this fat to keep them going during the periods of harshest winter weather, when they cannot get out to feed. In the very coldest parts of their range, these marsupials sometimes suffer frostbite on their naked tails and thin ears.

Mating takes place in both late winter and spring. The young are only 1cm (0.4in) long and underdeveloped at birth. Over 20 are born, but the mother can only suckle 13 at once, so the weaker offspring die.

*Virginia opossums have white faces, often with darker streaks. Their bodies are covered in shaggy coats of long grey and white hairs, but their tails are almost naked.*

# White-eared opossum

*Didelphis albiventris*

**Distribution**: South America.
**Habitat**: Most habitats.
**Food**: Invertebrates, fruits and seeds.
**Size**: 30–50cm (12–20in); 0.4–1.3kg (1–2.75lb).
**Maturity**: 9 months.
**Breeding**: Up to 6 young born in litters produced twice each year.
**Life span**: 3 years.
**Status**: Common.

These highly adaptable marsupials live throughout South America east of the Andes, occupying all habitats that contain enough food. Although they avoid deserts and drier areas, they can survive in a range of temperatures and humidity, including in the mountains of Patagonia and on open areas such as pampas. However, white-eared opossums are most common in deciduous forest. They can survive such diverse habitats because they are generalist feeders. Their diet includes invertebrates, fruits, seeds and small mammals and reptiles. In some parts of their range, the opossums even eat highly venomous pit vipers.

White-eared opossums are nocturnal creatures, sleeping in tree hollows and other hidden spots by day, and foraging at night. They live alone and will not tolerate the presence of another opossum. Males are particularly aggressive, except towards females that are ready to mate. It is possible that individuals form alliances with each other and organize themselves into a loose hierarchy.

*Male white-eared opossums are larger than females. Their bodies are rat-like, although they are not related to these rodents. The females have a pouch on their underside, in which the young are carried.*

**Central American woolly opossum** (*Caluromys derbianus*): Length unknown; 200–400g (7–14oz) With a range extending from central Mexico to western Colombia and northern Ecuador, this species occupies lowland rainforests and similar tropical forests that grow in upland areas. This is the largest of the woolly opossums, which are named after their long, dense fur. It has a black stripe from the top of the head to the tip of the snout. The long, prehensile tail has a naked tip to help grip branches. The opposable thumb, or hallux, on the paws is clawless to avoid damaging the foot pad. This species eats a range of foods, including seeds, fruits and insects.

**Southern opossum** (*Didelphis marsupialis*): 26–45cm (10–17.5in); 0.6–2.4kg (1.25–5.25lb) The southern opossum is a close relative of the Virginia opossum of North America, but it is found further south, ranging from eastern Mexico to north-eastern Argentina. Like other opossums, it is a generalist feeder that occupies a variety of habitats. Southern opossums are typically forest-dwellers, but they also venture into cultivated areas such as coffee plantations. Southern opossums are often seen in urban and suburban areas, where they eat garbage.

**Agile gracile mouse opossum** (*Gracilinanus agilis*): 11–14cm (4.25–5.5in); weight unknown This tiny marsupial lives in Peru, Brazil and northern Argentina. It lives in forests, where it forages and nests alone. It does not dig its own burrow, but occupies a nest abandoned by another animal. Its prehensile tail and opposable big toe help to make it an excellent climber.

# Big-eared opossum

*Didelphis aurita*

This opossum lives along the Atlantic coast of Brazil and extends inland to Paraguay and northern Argentina. It is found in the unique Atlantic rainforests that grow in this region, as well as in other types of forest that clothe the highlands further inland. Many of these habitats, especially the Atlantic rainforest, are under grave threat. However, this adaptable opossum seems to be largely unaffected by deforestation and human settlement. Being a generalist feeder, it can survive just as well by rooting through rubbish tips as it can by eating fruits and insects deep in the forest. The big-eared opossum also eats other mammals, small birds and fish.

This opossum is nocturnal and lives alone. It looks for food on the ground or by climbing through undergrowth and the lower branches of forest trees. In flooded parts of its range, it spends long periods living in trees.

*This species has a distinctive black line that runs down the middle of the forehead. The large ears are hairless. The long, prehensile tail has long black and white fur at the base.*

**Distribution**: Eastern South America.
**Habitat**: Coastal forest.
**Food**: Insects and fruit.
**Size**: 31–39cm (12–15.5in); 0.7–1.9kg (1.5–4.25lb).
**Maturity**: 6 months.
**Breeding**: 2–3 litters of up to 7 offspring each, born at all times of the year.
**Life span**: 2 years.
**Status**: Lower risk.

# Black-shouldered opossum

*Caluromysiops irrupta*

**Distribution**: Andes Mountains.
**Habitat**: Humid forest.
**Food**: Fruit and nectar.
**Size**: 25–30cm (10–12); 2–5kg (4.4–11lb).
**Maturity**: Unknown.
**Breeding**: Several young in each litter.
**Life span**: Unknown.
**Status**: Common.

This opossum lives in the misty forests that grow along the Andes Mountains of South America. It is more arboreal than many of its relatives and rarely comes to the ground, since it mates, feeds and gives birth in the trees. Its eats mainly fruits, but relies on nectar in the dry season, when fruits are less common.

Black-shouldered opossums are solitary, only coming into contact with other members of the species to breed. Mating takes place at all times of the year. As in other marsupial species, the mother lacks a uterus and cannot carry her young for long, so they are born in an underdeveloped state. The mother guides her young to the pouch by licking a path through the fur from the birth canal. Once in the pouch, the young remain attached to a teat for three or four months.

*The black-shouldered opossum's tail is a little longer than the rest of its body. The two black lines on the upper body run from the forefeet and join together at the shoulders, then they divide again and run along either side of the back all the way to the hind feet.*

**Mexican mouse opossum** (*Marmosa mexicana*): 24–43cm (9.5–17in); 20–140g (0.7–5oz)
Mexican mouse opossums are found in Central America, from Panama to southern Mexico. They live in dry monsoon forests, which receive most of their rain during a specific wet season. The opossums live in the lower branches of the trees and rarely venture down to the ground. This species is one of the few marsupials that does not have a pouch. Female marsupials lack a uterus where the embryos can develop. As a result, newborn marsupials are often very undeveloped before being born, after which they seek refuge in their mother's external pouch until they are more fully grown. However, mouse opossums are small enough to reach a relatively advanced stage of development before being born, after which they travel on their mother's back. As many as 13 young are born in each litter, although many of them die before reaching maturity.

**Red-legged short-tailed opossum**
(*Monodelphis brevicaudata*): 16cm (6.25in); 67–95g (2.25–3.25oz)
This species ranges from northern South America to Bolivia and southern Brazil, occupying forests and dense shrublands. Unusually for an American marsupial, its tail is non-prehensile and shorter than rest of its body. The red-legged short-tailed opossum is a solitary forager, being most active by day. It spends most of its time on the ground, although it will also hunt in trees. Cockroaches and grasshoppers are the opossum's favourite foods, supplemented by fruits and seeds.

# Lutrine opossum

*Lutreolina crassicaudata*

The word lutrine in this species' common name means "like an otter", referring to the fact that this opossum is a regular swimmer and is often found near water. It is even at home in flooded forests. Not only is its behaviour lutrine, but it also has a body shape resembling that of a small carnivore, such as an otter or weasel.

Lutrine opossums are also known as thick-tailed opossums. They live in two populations. The larger group occurs in Bolivia, east of the Andes, and in Brazil. The smaller population is found in forests north of the Amazon Basin, from the Guianas to northern Colombia. Lutrine opossums also occur on the pampas of northern Argentina.

These animals are more social than other opossum species, although most live alone. They are active at night, when they climb or swim in search of food. Their varied diet is made up largely of small mammals, birds, fish and insects, but they also eat crabs and other aquatic invertebrates, as well as fruits.

*These hunting marsupials have small ears, a long, slender body, short, stout legs and a long, thick tail. The tail, which can measure about 30cm (12in) long, is not as prehensile as that of other opossums.*

**Distribution**: Eastern Bolivia, southern Brazil and northern Argentina; also in Guyana, Venezuela and Colombia.
**Habitat**: Grassland and flooded woodland.
**Food**: Small mammals, birds, reptiles, fish, insects and aquatic invertebrates.
**Size**: 20–40cm (8–15.5in); 500g–1kg (1.25–2.25lb).
**Maturity**: Unknown.
**Breeding**: 2 litters of about 10 offspring produced in spring and summer.
**Life span**: 3 years.
**Status**: Common.

# Grey slender mouse opossum

*Marmosops incanus*

**Distribution**: Eastern Brazil.
**Habitat**: Humid forest.
**Food**: Insect.
**Size**: 24–43cm (9.5–17in);
20–140g (0.75–5oz).
**Maturity**: 6 months.
**Breeding**: Litters born from
September to December.
**Life span**: 1–1.5 years.
**Status**: Unknown.

*These small opossums have a
mouse-like body. In the more
southerly parts of its range, the
fur is considerably longer in winter
than in summer. Males may be
much larger than females.*

This is another marsupial species that lives in the forests that grow along Brazil's Atlantic
coast. It is also found on a few of the islands that exist along this stretch of coastline.
The grey slender mouse opossum is most common in the damp forests of lowland areas,
although it also occurs in the drier monsoon and gallery forests that grow further inland.

Grey slender mouse opossums feed almost exclusively on insects, especially beetles and
grasshoppers. They are scansorial animals, which means that they are highly curious and
will climb over all parts of their environment, exploring every nook and cranny for feeding
opportunities. They are just as at home in the trees as they are on the ground, and they
frequently move between the two.

The grey slender mouse opossum has a short life
cycle. Breeding takes place between September
and December, after which all the males
die, so that none are left
alive by February. The
females give birth and
then die themselves
in May. The young are
helpless at birth but
develop rapidly. By
August the young
born that year have
reached maturity, and
are ready to mate in the
forthcoming breeding season.

# Brown four-eyed opossum

*Metachirus nudicaudatus*

**Distribution**: Nicaragua to
eastern South America.
**Habitat**: Forest and brush.
**Food**: Primarily fruits, but
also insects, amphibians,
reptiles, molluscs, birds,
eggs, and small mammals.
**Size**: 19–31cm (7.5–12.25in);
0.8kg (1.75lb).
**Maturity**: Unknown.
**Breeding**: Litters of up to 9
young; young are born at all
times of year, and each
female may produce several
litters annually.
**Life span**: 3 years.
**Status**: Common.

This species ranges from Nicaragua in Central America to
Paraguay and northern Argentina in South America. Brown
four-eyed opossums are found in dense lowland forests,
where they move between the branches and the forest floor.
They also live in more open brushlands, including the Gran
Chaco of Paraguay and Argentina. In this habitat they
remain hidden in thick undergrowth.

Brown four-eyed opossums are
nocturnal. They always remain in
their nests until after dark. The
nests are round formations of
leaves and twigs that are generally
built among tree branches or under
rocks and logs. These opossums appear to be
very curious foragers. They do not occupy a
distinct territory, but travel far and wide in
search of food. Brown four-eyed opossums
regularly move to new areas in
search of better food supplies.
Their diet is made up mainly of
fruits, but they are also known to
eat a range of other foods, from
insects to eggs and lizards. They
are sometimes said to damage fruit crops.

*The white spots over this
opossum's eyes are the source
of its unusual common name.
The short, dense, silky fur is
brown on the back and sides,
with traces of black on the rump.
The tail measures 19–39cm
(7.5–15.3in). Females weigh about
one-third less
than males.*

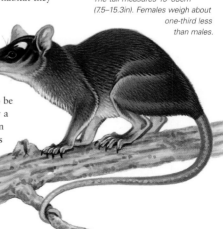

# INSECTIVORES

*Insectivores, or insect-eaters, belong to the* Insectivora *order of mammals. The first mammals to develop their young in uteruses belonged to this group, and most insectivores still resemble these small, primitive animals. However, insectivores have evolved to live in a wide range of niches, including subterranean, terrestrial, aquatic and arboreal habitats.*

## Giant mole shrew

*Blarina brevicauda*

Giant mole shrews live in most land habitats within their range, but they are hard to spot. They use their strong forepaws and flexible snouts to dig deep burrows in soft earth and, when on the surface, they scurry out of sight beneath mats of leaves or snow. However, they do climb into trees in search of food on occasion.

These small mammals feed at all times of the day and night. They rest in nests of grass and leaves made inside their tunnels or in nooks and crannies on the surface. Giant mole shrews will eat plant food, but they also hunt for small prey, such as snails, mice and insects. Their saliva contains a venom that paralyzes prey animals. In the mating season, which takes place between spring and autumn, they expand their territories so that they overlap with those of the opposite sex.

**Distribution**: Central Canada to south-eastern United States.
**Habitat**: All land habitats.
**Food**: Insects, small vertebrates, seeds and shoots.
**Size**: 12–14cm (5–5.5in); 15–30g (0.5–1oz).
**Maturity**: 6 weeks.
**Breeding**: Litters of 5–7 young born throughout the summer.
**Life span**: 2 years.
**Status**: Common.

*Giant mole shrews have stout bodies with long, pointed snouts covered in sensitive whiskers. Their eyes are very small because they spend most of the time underground, and their ears are hidden under thick coats of grey hairs.*

## Star-nosed mole

*Condylura cristata*

**Distribution**: Eastern Canada to south-eastern United States.
**Habitat**: Muddy soil near water.
**Food**: Aquatic insects, fish, worms and crustaceans.
**Size**: 10–12cm (4–5in); 40–85g (1.5–3oz).
**Maturity**: 10 months.
**Breeding**: 2–7 young born in summer.
**Life span**: Unknown.
**Status**: Endangered.

Star-nosed moles live in waterlogged soil. They dig networks of tunnels in the soil, which generally reach down as far as the water table. They push the mud and soil out of the entrances of the tunnels, making molehills in the process. The moles construct nests at the ends of tunnels, which are lined with dry grass.

Star-nosed moles are expert swimmers. They search for food at the bottom of streams and pools, using their sensitive snouts to feel their way and detect prey. In winter, star-nosed moles use tunnels with underwater entrances to get into ponds that are iced over. They feed in water both in the daytime and at night, but they are only really active above ground during the hours of darkness.

Most births take place in early summer. The young already have the star of rays on their snouts. Breeding pairs of males and females may stay together throughout the winter and breed again the following year.

*Star-nosed moles have unusual fleshy rays that radiate from each nostril. These are sensitive feelers that the moles use in the darkness below ground. The moles' dark, dense fur is coated with water-repelling oils.*

# Hispaniolan solenodon

*Solenodon paradoxus*

**Distribution**: Hispaniola.
**Habitat**: Woodland and bushy areas.
**Food**: Insects.
**Size**: 28–33cm (11–13cm); 0.6–1kg (1.25–2.2lb).
**Maturity**: Unknown.
**Breeding**: 2 litters of up to 3 offspring born at all times of year.
**Life span**: 11 years.
**Status**: Endangered.

This highly unusual species of mammal lives on Hispaniola, a large Caribbean island in the Greater Antilles. The island is divided into Haiti and the Dominican Republic. Most solenodons are found in the north of the island, in wooded and brush areas. By day the solenodons shelter in extensive tunnel systems that they excavate themselves. They will also rest in tree hollows and caves. As night falls, the solenodons leave their dens to look for insects, other invertebrates and fruits. Their main foods are millipedes, beetles, grasshoppers, snails and worms.

Solenodons forage by sniffing out prey with their long snout. The Hispaniolan solenodon's snout is unique among mammals, because it is connected to the skull by a ball-and-socket joint, which makes it extremely flexible. As it forages, the animal uses its clawed feet to overturn stones and rip off bark to expose insects.

*Looking like a huge shrew, this rare species uses its large forelegs for digging tunnel networks. All the feet have long claws. The Hispaniolan solenodon has 40 teeth for cutting up insect prey. Some of these teeth can inject venomous saliva when the animal bites its victims.*

**Cuban solenodon** (*Solenodon cubanus*): 28–39cm (11–15.5in); 1kg (2.2lb)
The lesser known of the two solenodon species, the Cuban solenodon is found in eastern Cuba, where it occupies caves and hollows in wet mountain forests. Cuban solenodons live in small family groups, probably made up of a mother and her assorted offspring. Although these solenodons do not have a joint inside their snout like their Hispaniolan relatives, the snout is still extremely flexible. They are believed to have toxic saliva, which is delivered into wounds when the animal bites an attacker. There is no evidence that this venom is used in hunting. The females carry their young while they are still attached to their teats (most insectivores and other mammals carry young in their mouth or on their back). This species has more catholic tastes than the Hispaniolan solenodon: as well as insects, it eats small reptiles, roots and leaves.

**Elliot's short-tailed shrew** (*Blarina hylophaga*): 9.2–12cm (3.6–4.75in); 15g (0.5oz)
Elliot's short-tailed shrew lives in the Midwest region of the United States. It inhabits forests and grasslands, and has adapted to life in the huge wheat and corn fields that cover its range. It requires soft soil for burrowing through and is common close to the banks of rivers, where the damp earth is looser than in drier areas. However, the shrew never takes to the water. It is a skilled climber and forages for insects and plant food all year round. It does not hibernate and generally survives for no more than a year. It relies on stores of food laid down in autumn to get it through the winter.

## Southern short-tailed shrew

*Blarina carolinensis*

This species ranges from southern Illinois to Florida. It prefers to live in damp habitats with well-drained soil for burrowing. It is especially common in woodlands, where the roots of trees create good conditions for digging tunnels.

The southern short-tailed shrew is the smallest in its genus, with members of the species having as few as 36 chromosomes, while their larger relatives, the giant mole shrews, have between 48 and 50.

Southern short-tailed shrews are nocturnal. Even when active, they are often hidden away in tunnels and runways among leaf litter and grass. They are most likely to be seen just after rainfall. The rain water trickles though the soil, flooding lower levels, and this forces insects and worms that are living underground up to the surface, where the shrews are ready and waiting. The shrews also supplement their diet with berries.

Young shrews are born blind and helpless, and are cared for in a nest of grass and other dry vegetation under a log, stump or underground.

**Distribution**: South-eastern North America.
**Habitat**: Moist woodlands.
**Food**: Insects and worms.
**Size**: 7.5–10.5cm (2.9–4.1in); 15–30g (0.5–1oz).
**Maturity**: 12 weeks.
**Breeding**: Several litters produced in summer.
**Life span**: 1 year.
**Status**: Common.

*This is the smallest of the short-tailed shrews. Its fur is almost a completely uniform grey, which becomes slightly paler in summer. As with most shrews, this species has a long flexible nose for probing through loose soil.*

## Least shrew

*Cryptotis parva*

Least shrews live south of the Great Lakes across the eastern United States. They also occur through eastern Mexico to northern Nicaragua in Central America. Within this vast area the shrews occupy a variety of habitats. In northern parts of the range, least shrews are found in grasslands, meadows or areas covered in a thick layer of brush. Further south, where it is generally drier, these shrews are more common in the vegetation that grows along the banks of streams and lakes.

Least shrews move through the plant cover in tunnels called runways, which connect their nests together. The nests are constructed underground in burrows dug by the shrews, and then lined with leaves. Least shrews will also take over and extend burrows made by other animals. Rather unusually for shrews, this species is relatively social. The nests are shared, and more than 30 shrews have been found living together in a single nest.

Least shrews are almost exclusively flesh eaters. They have been seen to open up the abdomens of insects such as grasshoppers to eat only the most nutritious internal organs.

**Distribution**: From eastern United States south to northern Nicaragua in Central America.
**Habitat**: Grass and brush.
**Food**: Insects, worms, slugs and snails, plus some plant matter.
**Size**: 5–8cm (2–3in); 4–6.5g (0.1–0.2oz).
**Maturity**: 5 weeks.
**Breeding**: Several litters of about 5 young produced in summer.
**Life span**: 1.5 years.
**Status**: Common.

*This mammal has black fur on its back and white fur on its underside. In summer, the upper fur often pales slightly to brown. The milk teeth of young shrews fall out while the animals are still in the womb.*

## Desert shrew

*Notiosorex crawfordi*

The desert shrew ranges across the arid south-west of the United States. It is also found in the drier areas parts of Mexico. Although it can survive in desert conditions, this shrew can also be found in a range of other habitats, including marshland.

The desert shrew preys mainly on invertebrates such as worms, spiders and insects, but it also eats lizards, birds and small mammals such as mice. The shrew must consume three-quarters of its own body weight in food each day to survive. (This is actually a relatively small amount for a shrew.) In the driest parts of its range, the desert shrew can survive on the water it gets from its food. However, it is most often found close to a supply of drinking water.

Desert shrews hunt at night, restricting themselves to areas with thick brush to avoid owls and other predators. They rest in the burrow of another animal during daylight hours. In the hottest part of the day, the shrews enter a torpor – an inactive state similar to hibernation. In this state, they use only a fraction of the energy that they would do when normally active. The female makes a crude nest from hair, grass and other vegetation. The blind, hairless young develop rapidly and may accompany their mother for a short period before they disperse.

**Distribution**: South-western United States, from California to Texas and Colorado; also Baja California and northern and central Mexico.
**Habitat**: Deserts, semi-arid grasslands, chaparral, woodland and marshland.
**Food**: Invetebrates such as insects, spiders and worms; also lizards, small mammals and young birds.
**Size**: 5–6cm (2–2.5in); 4.5–8g (0.2–0.3oz).
**Maturity**: 2 months.
**Breeding**: 1–2 litters of 3–5 young born each year.
**Life span**: Unknown.
**Status**: Common.

*The desert shrew's tail is at least half as long as its small body. Desert shrews are often found living in garbage dumps around human settlements.*

# Arctic shrew

*Sorex arcticus*

**Distribution**: Northern North America.
**Habitat**: In forests near fresh water.
**Food**: Invertebrates.
**Size**: 6–7cm (2.5–2.75in); 5–13g (0.2–0.5oz).
**Maturity**: 2 years.
**Breeding**: Up to 9 young born in one litter in April or May.
**Life span**: Unknown.
**Status**: Common.

This species ranges south from Canada's North-west and Yukon Territories to Minnesota in the US Midwest and east to Nova Scotia on the Atlantic coast of Canada. It is most often spotted near to supplies of fresh water. Its preferred habitats are forests growing on boggy ground, which are populated with trees such as wet spruce and tamarack. Such marshy woodland is alive with invertebrates, providing the shrew with an excellent supply of food throughout the year.

Like most shrews and other small, warm-blooded animals, the Arctic shrew must eat huge quantities of food to supply its body with the energy it needs to survive. This is especially true in the colder northern parts of this species' range, where it will die if it goes without food for more than two hours. Consequently, Arctic shrews will eat virtually anything. Most of their diet is made up of invertebrates, mainly insects such as beetles and their larvae, but they also eat earthworms, spiders, snails, seeds and leaves.

*The distinctive three-coloured fur makes the Arctic shrew easy to identify. There is a black band running along the back from nose to tail. The sides are brown, and the underside is grey.*

---

**Giant Mexican shrew** (*Megasorex gigas*): 8–9cm (3.25–3.5in); 10–12g (0.3–0.4oz)
Although members of this species are consistently large, they are not by any means the largest of the shrews. They get their "giant" moniker from the fact that they are the last surviving member of the *Megasorex* genus, which once contained truly giant shrews. Giant Mexican shrews live in tropical forests and grasslands in western Mexico. They find worms, grubs and other invertebrate prey by rooting through loose soil and leaf litter with their pointed snout.

**Gaspé shrew** (*Sorex gaspensis*): 9.5–12.5cm (3.75–5in); 2.2–4.3g (0.1oz)
This shrew is found on the Gaspé Peninsula of eastern Quebec, and in two small ranges in New Brunswick and on Cape Breton Island in Nova Scotia. Gaspé shrews live in mountain conifer forests, where they forage among the leaf litter or mosses that grow on the forest floor. They are grey all over, with a very narrow snout. Their diet comprises mainly grubs, maggots and spiders, but they also eat worms, snails, slugs and plant matter.

**Masked shrew** (*Sorex cinereus*): 7cm (2.75in); 2.5–4g (0.1oz)
This is North America's most widespread shrew, ranging across Canada and Alaska and much of the northern United States. Masked shrews occupy a range of habitats, wherever there is adequate ground cover. They are most commonly found in wet areas, such as near to streams or in marshes. Among American mammals, only the pygmy shrew is smaller than this species.

# Long-tailed shrew

*Sorex dispar*

The long-tailed shrew is found as far north as Nova Scotia in eastern Canada. From there it ranges south to Tennessee and North Carolina in the southern United States. This shrew can survive in a range of forest types, although most of the forests within its range are cool and damp. The long-tailed shrew is especially abundant in mountain forests, on ranges such as the Appalachians and Adirondacks. It makes its dens in cool rock crevices and under boulders and scree.

Long-tailed shrews forage for food both day and night. They do not hibernate. Like most shrews, they lead a solitary life and chase away any shrew that comes near. A long-tailed shrew must eat twice its body weight in food every day to stay alive. The diet consists of insects, spiders, centipedes and other invertebrates, as well as plant foods such as seeds.

**Distribution**: Eastern North America.
**Habitat**: Damp forest.
**Food**: Invertebrates and plants.
**Size**: 4.6–10cm (1.75–4in); 4–6g (0.1–0.2oz).
**Maturity**: 4 months.
**Breeding**: Several litters of about 5 young produced between April and August.
**Life span**: 2 years.
**Status**: Common.

*Long-tailed shrews are often mistaken for smoky shrews, but long-tailed shrews tend to be more slender and have a longer tail.*

# Pygmy shrew

*Sorex hoyi*

*Because of its small size, the pygmy shrew is able to occupy a range of microhabitats, such as moss, leaf litter, root systems, rotting stumps and the burrows of larger animals. It can even travel in the tunnels of large beetles. The coat of the pygmy shrew varies from grey-brown in winter to grey in summer; the underparts are light grey.*

Although this is the smallest American mammal, it is by no means the smallest mammal in the world. The white-toothed shrews living in the so-called Old World – Europe, Africa and Asia – are almost half the weight of this species, and the hog-nosed bat of Thailand is equally small, at about half the weight of a penny coin or a dime.

Pygmy shrews occupy a wide range of habitats, but they are sparsely distributed and often hard to locate. They feed on small invertebrates such as ants and spiders, and will also eat carrion if the opportunity arises. These tiny creatures live life at a feverish pace. They forage in short bursts of just a few minutes and then rest for a similar amount of time. They nose through soil and leaf litter in search of prey, and often venture into the tunnels of larger animals to look for food. When threatened, pygmy shrews release a musky odour from glands on their sides. This smell not only deters the attacker, but also alerts any shrews nearby to the potential danger.

**Distribution**: From Alaska and eastern Canada to the Rockies and Appalachian Mountains in the United States.
**Habitat**: Forest, swamp and grassland.
**Food**: Insects.
**Size**: 5–6cm (2–2.5in); 2–4g (0.1oz).
**Maturity**: 1.5 years.
**Breeding**: One litter of about 5 young born in summer, about 18 days after mating.
**Life span**: Unknown.
**Status**: Common.

# Water shrew

*Sorex palustris*

**Distribution**: Northern North America.
**Habitat**: Near streams and other fresh-water habitats.
**Food**: Insects.
**Size**: 8cm (3in); 8–18g (0.3–0.6oz).
**Maturity**: 1 year.
**Breeding**: 2–3 litters of 3–10 young produced in spring and summer.
**Life span**: 18 months.
**Status**: Common.

One of the most aquatic of all shrews, this species occurs throughout Alaska and Canada. It extends south into high, mountainous regions of the United States, most notably along the Rockies, where climatic conditions are similar to those found further north. This shrew is often found in or close to water. It also lives in damp conifer forests.

Water shrews live alone and are known to hunt for insects. Most of their prey are the aquatic youngsters of insects such as crane flies and caddis flies. While under water, the shrews detect the movements of prey using whiskers on their snouts. They grab the food with their forefeet or mouth. In captivity, water shrews have been seen feeding once every ten minutes. In the wild, they will die if they go without food for about three hours.

*Males of this large shrew species tend to be longer than females. The thick fur traps a layer of air around the body to keep the animal warm while diving in cold water.*

**Montane shrew** (*Sorex monticolus*): 6–8cm (2.5–3in); 5.9–7.2g (0.2–0.25oz)
This solitary species, also called the dusky shrew, occurs from northern Alaska southward to New Mexico, and from the west coast to Manitoba in the east. It occurs in a variety of habitats, including tundra in the far north, prairies in drier parts of the range and also mountain forests. All these habitats have some ground vegetation in which the shrews can hide from predators. Montane shrews feed on insect larvae, spiders, earthworms and occasionally small salamanders. They also eat non-animal foods such as seeds and mushrooms.

**American shrew mole** (*Neurotrichus gibbsii*): 7–9cm (2.75–3.5in); 8–14.5g (0.3–0.5oz)
The smallest American mole, this species is the size of a large shrew. Shrew moles range from northern California to southern British Colombia. They tunnel in soft, deep peaty soils, especially those formed by the highly fertile rainforests of North America's northern Pacific coast. They must eat about one-and-a-half times their body weight in insects and worms each day to survive.

**Townsend's mole** (*Scapanus townsendii*): 18–24cm (7–9.5in); 100–170g (3.5–6oz)
Confined to a small range between the Cascade Mountains and the Pacific coast of California, Oregon and Washington, Townsend's mole is the largest mole in North America. This species lives in lowland areas with deep, loamy soil. The mole preys on earthworms and insect larvae by patrolling their territories through a permanent network of tunnels.

## Eastern mole

*Scalopus aquaticus*

**Distribution**: Eastern and central United States and southern Canada.
**Habitat**: Fields, meadows and open woodland.
**Food**: Earthworms, insects and roots.
**Size**: 11–17cm (4.25–6.75in); 32–140g (1.25–5oz).
**Maturity**: 1 year.
**Breeding**: One litter of 2–5 young produced per year; the breeding season is from March to April in most of the range, but begins in January in the south.
**Life span**: 3 years.
**Status**: Common.

The eastern mole ranges from Wyoming and South Dakota in the north and west to Texas and Florida in the south and New England in the east. There is also a smaller, isolated population in Mexico. This mole needs to dig its burrows in soil that is relatively free of large roots and rocks, so it avoids thick forest and stony ground, preferring areas of moist sandy or loamy soils. When it burrows, the mole thrusts its front limbs forward, then pulls them outward and back to force the loose dirt out of the way.

Most of the eastern mole's diet consists of earthworms, although it will eat adult and larval insects as well as roots. Being a large insectivore, the mole needs to consume just a quarter of its bodyweight in food each day – far less than smaller insectivore species. Eastern moles find their food using their sense of smell and by detecting vibrations in the floor and walls of their tunnels made by the movements of prey. Although the ears are covered by a layer of skin to keep earth out, the moles are still able to hear. The eyes are light-sensitive, even though they cannot form images, so the moles can at least tell when they break the surface.

*The size of this species varies according to geographical location. The largest moles live in the north-east, in areas such as New England, while the smallest individuals are generally found in the south-west, notably Texas.*

## Hairy-tailed mole

*Parascalops breweri*

**Distribution**: Eastern Canada to the Appalachians.
**Habitat**: Forests and meadows.
**Food**: Insects and worms.
**Size**: 11.5–14cm (4.5–5.5in); 40–85g (1.5–3oz).
**Maturity**: 10 months.
**Breeding**: One litter of 4–5 young produced in summer.
**Life span**: 3 years.
**Status**: Unknown.

*This mole differs from other mole species by having a much shorter snout and a hairy tail. It also lacks the protuberances on the snout used by many species to detect the movements of prey.*

The hairy-tailed mole ranges from southern Quebec and Ontario to central Ohio and western North Carolina. It lives in open woodland and meadows. In the south of its range, it occurs at high altitudes in the Appalachian Mountains, which have a colder and wetter climate than lowland areas.

Hairy-tailed moles are most active during the day, when they tunnel under the ground in search of food. They may also move around at night, sometimes emerging from their tunnels to forage on the surface. In winter, each mole occupies its own network of tunnels and will close up any links with the tunnels of other moles. However, during summer the males, females and young all share a network of tunnels.

Having mated in the spring breeding season, the female builds an underground nest out of a ball of dry vegetation approximately 25cm (10in) below the surface. Gestation is about four to six weeks. The newborn young remain in the nest for up to a month, by which time they have been weaned on to solid food.

# NEW WORLD MONKEYS

*Most New World monkeys are found in South America, but some species live as far north as southern Mexico. There are 30 species of New World monkey, including howler monkeys and capuchins. The features that differentiate New World Monkeys from species living in Africa and Asia are their flattened noses, which have broadly spaced nostrils, and their prehensile tails, which they use like a fifth limb.*

## Brown capuchin

*Cebus apella*

*Like some other capuchin species, brown capuchins have a cap of dark hair on the top of their heads, with thick tufts or "horns" above the ears.*

Capuchins are sometimes called ring-tails. This is because they often curl the tip of their semi-prehensile tail into a ring. Capuchins are among the most intelligent and adaptable of all monkeys. They are found in a wide range of habitats, from dense jungles to towns and cities. Some even live on the seashore, where they collect crabs. Capuchins sometimes break open hard nuts by pounding them with stones – an example of animals using tools. This species lives in troops of about 12 monkeys. Most troops have a single adult male, who fathers all the children. The monkeys chatter and squeak a great deal, telling each other of their location and warning of danger. Since they lack a set breeding season, capuchin mothers may give birth to their single babies at any time of the year. Each young capuchin initially clings to its mother's chest, then rides on her back until it becomes more independent.

**Distribution**: From Colombia to Paraguay.
**Habitat**: Rainforest.
**Food**: Fruit, nuts, flowers, bark, gums, insects and eggs.
**Size**: 30–56cm (12–22in); 1.1–3.3kg (2.5–7.25lb).
**Maturity**: Females 4 years; males 8 years.
**Breeding**: Single young born throughout the year.
**Life span**: 30 years.
**Status**: Lower risk.

## Squirrel monkey

*Saimiri boliviensis*

Squirrel monkeys live in many types of forest. They spend most of their time in trees, rarely coming down to the ground. However, some populations of squirrel monkeys have made their homes in areas cleared of trees for agriculture. These monkeys tend to live close to streams for reasons of safety. Squirrel monkeys form complex social groups, or troops, which are larger than those of any other monkey species in the Americas. In pristine rainforests, the troops can number up to 300 individuals.

Males do not help in raising the young and during the mating season (the dry part of the year) they establish hierarchies by fighting each other. Only dominant males get to mate with the females. Soon after giving birth to their single offspring, the new mothers chase away the breeding males, which reform their bachelor subgroups. Adolescent males, too old to stay with their mothers, eventually join these subgroups, having fought their way in.

*Squirrel monkeys have black, hairless snouts and helmets of dark fur around their pale faces. Their ears are covered in pale fur. The rest of the body is more brightly coloured, in hues of pale yellow and red, and the mobile tail has a black tip. The body is slender in shape. Squirrel monkeys travel through the forest on all four legs.*

**Distribution**: Central America to Upper Amazon Basin.
**Habitat**: Tropical forest, close to streams.
**Food**: Fruit, nuts, flowers, leaves, gums, insects and small vertebrates.
**Size**: 26–36cm (10–14in); 0.75–1.1kg (1.65–2.4lb).
**Maturity**: Females 3 years; males 5 years.
**Breeding**: Single young born from June–August.
**Life span**: 20 years.
**Status**: Lower risk.

# Black-handed spider monkey

*Ateles geoffroyi*

Spider monkeys are the most agile of the American primates, not least because their long prehensile tails function as a fifth limb. The animals can pick up food or hold on to branches with their tails. It is not unusual to see one of these monkeys hanging from its tail alone.

Spider monkey troops live high up in forest canopies, and almost never visit the ground. They are most active early in the morning, spending the rest of the day relaxing and digesting tough plant food.

Troops usually contain about 30 individuals, with equal numbers of males and females. However, larger groups of more than 100 have been reported. The males in the troops defend large territories by regularly patrolling the perimeters, while females and young tend to stay close to the centre.

Males tend to stay in the troops they were born into, while females move to other troops in the area. Breeding occurs all year round. Spider monkeys reportedly have a unique defensive strategy: when potential predators approach – including humans – the monkeys drop heavy branches on top of them.

*Spider monkeys have very long, prehensile tails and similarly long legs, hence their name. This allows them to be extremely agile in the treetops.*

**Distribution**: Mexico to Colombia.
**Habitat**: Tropical forest.
**Food**: Fruit, seeds, buds, leaves, insects and eggs.
**Size**: 38–63cm (15–25in); 6–8kg (13.25–17.5lb).
**Maturity**: 4–5 years.
**Breeding**: Single young born throughout the year.
**Life span**: 30 years.
**Status**: Vulnerable.

---

**Black-bearded saki** (*Chiropotes satanas*): 40–51cm (16–20in); 2–4kg (4.5–8.75lb)
The black-bearded saki has a long, thick beard on its elongated chin. Its head, beard and tail are black, while its shoulders, back, hands and feet are reddish-brown to black. This species lives in Guyana, Venezuela and Brazil north of the Amazon. The black-bearded saki eats fruit, the seeds of unripe fruit, leaves, flowers and a few insects. It lives in troops of up to 30 individuals. The monkey's tail is non-prehensile, but the animal is capable of a very strong grip with its hands and feet. It often hangs by a single limb while foraging high in the trees.

**White-nosed bearded saki** (*Chiropotes albinasus*): 38–42cm (15–16.5in); 2–3kg (4.5–6.5lb)
This species lives south of the Amazon River in central Brazil. The white-nosed bearded saki inhabits a range of forests, and is mainly found in the emergent layer, where tall trees poke out above the upper forest canopy. This bearded saki is diurnal and rests in the boughs of trees at night. To avoid being attacked by predators, it never sleeps in the same place for two consecutive nights. The body is covered by black hair, except for the nose and upper lip, which have white fur. When a mature female is ready to mate, her vulva becomes bright red as a signal to males. Matings usually take place in December and June, with the female producing a single young each year. White-nosed bearded sakis live in large troops of up to 30 monkeys. They communicate with whistles and chirps.

# Common woolly monkey

*Lagothrix lagotricha*

Common, or Humboldt's, woolly monkeys are among the largest of all New World monkeys. (Only the muriqui, or woolly spider monkey, is appreciably bigger.) These monkeys live in high forests on the slopes of the Andes Mountains and Mato Grosso in Brazil. They spend much of their time at the top of the tallest trees, which protrude from the forest canopy. On the ground, they may walk on their hind legs, using their heavy tails to keep them upright. They are diurnal animals and eat mainly fruit and insects, but they can survive on leaves and seeds if necessary.

Common woolly monkeys live in groups of about eight individuals. They communicate using a range of facial expressions and calls. Males, which are heavier than females, often display their long canine teeth with wide yawns to warn off rivals.

*The fur is thick and black, and the body is very heavyset compared to other tree-dwelling monkeys. Older monkeys grow a fringe of long hair on the backs of their arms and legs.*

**Distribution**: Northern South America.
**Habitat**: Tropical forest.
**Food**: Fruits, leaves, seeds and insects.
**Size**: 40–70cm (16–28in); 5–10kg (11–22lb).
**Maturity**: 5–8 years.
**Breeding**: 1 young produced every 2 years.
**Life span**: Unknown.
**Status**: Vulnerable.

# Red howler monkey

*Alouatta seniculus*

Howlers are large monkeys that live in the trees of tropical forests. They are known for the roaring howls that fill South American forests. The monkeys have very wide jaws, which allow them to open their mouths wide and make such loud calls.

Howler monkeys roar first thing in the morning before setting off to look for food. Although they eat fruits, such as figs, when they are available, howler monkeys rely for long periods on just leaves. Few other monkeys have such an unvaried, indigestible diet. After a rest in the middle of the day, the monkeys feed some more before travelling back to their sleeping trees while howling to each other again.

Howler monkey troops contain about eight or nine individuals. Larger troops form when there are more fruits available. Males compete with each other to join troops, and the victors may kill the young of the males they depose. The howling call is thought to be a mechanism for locating nearby troops. These monkeys breed all year round. The young ride on their mothers' backs for up to a year. Both males and females leave their mothers' troops when they are sexually mature and join others.

**Distribution**: Northern South America.
**Habitat**: Rainforest and mangroves.
**Food**: Leaves and figs.
**Size**: 55–92cm (21.5–36in); 4–10kg (8.75–22lb).
**Maturity**: 4–5 years.
**Breeding**: Single young born throughout the year.
**Life span**: 20 years.
**Status**: Endangered.

*Howler monkeys typically have reddish-brown hair, although some have a more yellowish or dusky coloration. Their strong prehensile tails have naked patches on their undersides to help them grip branches. The males are larger than the females and generally have darker hair. The loud calls of these monkeys, especially by the males, are made possible by a specialized larynx in the throat, which amplifies the sound.*

# White-faced saki

*Pithecia pithecia*

**Distribution**: Northern South America from Venezuela to north-eastern Brazil.
**Habitat**: Tropical forest.
**Food**: Fruit, honey, leaves, mice, bats and birds.
**Size**: 30–70cm (12–27.5in); 0.7–1.7kg (1.5–3.75lb).
**Maturity**: 2–3 years.
**Breeding**: Single young born in the dry season, which remains with its parents until it is mature.
**Life span**: 14 years.
**Status**: Common.

White-faced sakis live high up in trees. They feed during the daytime and almost never come down to the ground. Although they do occasionally leap from tree to tree, sakis are not the most agile of monkeys. They climb down trunks backwards and generally run along thick branches on all fours. Sometimes, however, sakis have been seen walking on their hind legs with their arms held above their heads.

A lot of the saki's diet consists of vegetable matter and fruit. However, these monkeys do also catch small vertebrate animals, such as birds and bats. The sakis rip their victims apart with their hands before skinning and eating the pieces of flesh. The monkeys have sharp teeth that are useful for biting into forest fruits and slicing up meat.

A saki group is based around a pair of breeding adults. The rest of the group, which may contain up to five individuals, will generally be the chief pair's offspring of different ages. The breeding pair produces a single baby once a year. Most births occur in the dry season at the end of the year.

*Only male white-faced sakis have the white faces after which they are named. The females have black or dark brown faces. Most saki monkeys have broad, round faces with hooded eyebrows.*

# Southern night monkey

*Aotus nigriceps*

Night monkeys, which are also known as douroucoulis, are the only nocturnal monkeys in the world. These rare monkeys live in most types of forest, except those close to water. Biologists used to think there was a single species, but it is now known that there are several living across South America.

The large eyes of these monkeys collect enough light for them to see in the gloom. Night monkeys can only see in monochrome (black and white), but this still allows them to run and jump through the trees even on the darkest nights. By day, they rest in nests made from dry leaves and twigs.

Night monkeys live in family groups, with one adult pair and two or three of their young. Family members warn each other of approaching danger, such as tree snakes or birds of prey, with long "wook" alarm calls. The monkeys have loose sacs of skin under their chins, which they inflate to amplify these calls. At night the monkeys rely on scent as well as calls to communicate with other monkeys and with nearby groups. The scent comes from their urine, and also from glands on their chests, which the monkeys rub against branches.

*Night monkeys have large eyes which give them good night vision. Their thick, woolly fur gives them a rounded appearance, and their tails, which are not prehensile, are thickened and furry at their tips.*

**Distribution**: Central and South America from Panama southward to Brazil, but patchily distributed.
**Habitat**: Forests.
**Food**: Fruit, nuts, leaves, bark, flowers, gums, insects and small vertebrates.
**Size**: 24–37cm (9.5–14.5in); 0.6–1kg (1.25–2.2lb).
**Maturity**: 2 years.
**Breeding**: Single young born throughout the year.
**Life span**: 18 years.
**Status**: Vulnerable.

---

**Northern night monkey** (*Aotus trivirgatus*): 24–47cm (9.5–18.5in); 0.8–1.3kg (1.75–2.75lb)
Northern night monkeys have a brown or grey back and a pale red underside. Like their close relatives, the southern night monkeys, they are nocturnal. (The niche of feeding at night is taken by lemurs, bushbabies and other non-monkey primates in Africa and Asia.) Northern night monkeys range from southern Panama to northern Argentina, and from the Andes to the Atlantic coast. They live in lowland rainforests and mountain cloud forests, moving slowly from tree to tree as they feed on fruit and insects. They have the best-developed sense of smell of all the New World monkeys. Individuals hoot into the darkness to attract mates. Night monkeys form monogamous pairs. A single young or twins are born in January. The males do more than the females to raise the young. The young stay with their parents for several months after weaning, forming a small family group.

**Black uakari** (*Cacajao melanocephalus*): 30–50cm (12–19.5in); 2.4–4kg (5.25–8.75lb)
This more common relative of the bald uakari lives east of the Japura River up to the Negro and Branco Rivers (all tributaries of the Amazon). It lives in flooded forests as well as highland forests. There is black fur on its head and back, but the tail is paler, even yellow in some individuals. Black uakaris eat mainly seeds, which they collect when the fruits are still on the trees. They climb down to the ground to feed on fallen nuts if other food is scarce.

# Bald uakari

*Cacajao calvus*

Uakaris only live in tropical rainforests that are flooded or filled with many slow-flowing streams, and consequently they are very rare. They are active during the day, running on all fours through the tops of large trees. They mainly feed on fruit, but will also eat leaves, insects and small vertebrates. Although they are quite agile, uakaris rarely jump from branch to branch. They almost never come down to the ground.

Uakaris live in large troops of 10–30 individuals. In areas where forests have not been damaged by human activity, groups of over 100 have been reported. Uakari troops often get mixed in with those of other monkeys, such as squirrel monkeys, during daytime feeding forays.

Each troop has a hierarchical structure, which is maintained by fighting among both sexes. The dominant males control access to females in a troop during the breeding season. Females give birth to a single young every two years.

**Distribution**: Upper Amazon from Peru to Colombia.
**Habitat**: Beside rivers in flooded forests.
**Food**: Fruit, leaves and insects.
**Size**: 51–70cm (20–27.75in); 3.5–4kg (7.75–8.75lb).
**Maturity**: Females 3 years, males 6 years.
**Breeding**: Single young born in summer every 2 years.
**Life span**: 20 years.
**Status**: Endangered.

*Bald uakaris have hairless, red faces fringed with shaggy fur, hence their name. The long fur on the body is pale but looks reddish-brown, and a few have white fur. Their clubbed tails are proportionally shorter than those of other New World monkeys.*

## Muriqui

*Brachyteles arachnoides*

The muriqui, or woolly spider monkey, is the largest New World monkey. This extremely rare monkey lives in the coastal forests of south-eastern Brazil. These forests contain a mixture of deciduous and evergreen trees. They have been heavily deforested as land is cleared for agriculture and settlement, and now few areas of forest are large enough to support populations of the muriqui. Despite the decline of their natural habitat, muriquis are adaptable enough to survive in all but the most damaged forests. For example, although they prefer to live almost exclusively in the canopy layer, they will readily troop across open ground to reach isolated pockets of forest.

Little is known about muriqui society. The animals are thought to live in promiscuous groups, where all adults mate freely with each other. Females seem to have more control over mating times than males. With females holding dominant positions, it is they who leave the groups of their birth to join neighbouring ones. The males stay in the same group for their whole lives.

Muriquis eat leaves, flowers and seeds, but fruit is their preferred food. In fact, if a group of muriquis find a rich source of unripe fruit, they may wait for days, feeding on leaves, until the fruit becomes edible. Muriquis are occasionally preyed on by jaguars, ocelots and harpy eagles, and they are hunted by humans for their meat.

**Distribution**: South-east Brazil.
**Habitat**: Coastal forest.
**Food**: Fruit, leaves, flowers and seeds.
**Size**: 45–65cm (18–26in); 12–15kg (26.5–33lb).
**Maturity**: 6–11 years.
**Breeding**: Single young born every 2–3 years.
**Life span**: 12–25 years.
**Status**: Critically endangered.

*Like most New World monkeys, this species has a long prehensile tail, which can grip branches. As it swings through the trees, the muriqui hangs from its fingers. Its thumbs are very small and almost useless. The coat is a greyish-gold, and the face a sooty-black. Both males and females have a pot-bellied appearance.*

## White-bellied spider monkey

*Ateles belzebuth*

The white-bellied spider monkey lives in Colombia, Venezuela, Peru, and Ecuador, and ranges into Brazil along the northern fringes of the Amazon Basin. It lives in the rainforests that grow in the region's lowlands. It is rarely found in forest more than a few hundred metres above sea level.

The white-bellied spider monkey lives in groups of between 20 and 40 individuals. There are generally three adult females for every male group member. (The other males live in small male-only groups and wait for an opportunity to join a mixed troop.) Each female will mate with one or all of the males in the group in quick succession, generally on the same day.

The monkeys forage during the day. They are able to hang from branches by their highly prehensile tails and pick fruits and other foods with their free hands. These little monkeys move around the forest by using their forelimbs to swing from branch to branch.

*This species has very long arms and legs, which are longer than its body. The prehensile tail is used for picking up food and holding branches.*

**Distribution**: North-eastern Amazon Basin.
**Habitat**: Rainforests.
**Food**: Fruit, leaves, seeds and dead wood.
**Size**: 34–59cm (13.5–23in); 5.9–10.4kg (13–23lb).
**Maturity**: 4–5 years.
**Breeding**: Single offspring produced every 2–4 years.
**Life span**: 30–40 years.
**Status**: Endangered.

# Dusky titi monkey

*Callicebus moloch*

*Dusky titi monkeys exhibit a variety of fur colours, ranging from grey to red to gold. Their tails are long and bushy, but not prehensile. When resting, a pair of monkeys will entwine their tails together.*

Dusky titi monkeys occur in most forested parts of Brazil around the Amazon Basin, reaching into Colombia and Venezuela, around the headwaters of the Orinoco River. They tend to live in the lower trees near riverbanks, often climbing down to the shrub plants near the ground to feed on fruit, leaves, birds' eggs, and invertebrates. In periods of drought, these monkeys survive by eating figs, which are among the few forest fruits that are abundant in the dry season. As night falls, dusky titis climb higher into the trees to escape predators. This species lives in family groups, each of which is dominated by a single adult pair. A baby titi monkey is quite large, so the male carries it for most of the time, only giving it to the female for suckling. This ensures that a higher percentage of the young survive than if the females were to raise them alone.

**Distribution:** Central Brazil to Colombia and Venezuela.
**Habitat:** Rainforest.
**Food:** Fruits, insects, leaves, eggs and rodents.
**Size:** 24–61cm (9.5–24in); 0.5–0.75kg (1–1.75lb).
**Maturity:** 3 years.
**Breeding:** 1 young born between December and April.
**Life span:** 12–25 years.
**Status:** Common.

**Brown-headed spider monkey** (*Ateles fusciceps*):
40–60cm (15.5–24in); 9kg (19.75lb)
These spider monkeys live in the rainforests of Central America and the northern tip of South America. They occupy the upper branches of trees, often hanging by their prehensile tail as they forage. Their favoured foods are fruits and leaves, but they will also eat nuts, insects and even birds' eggs. The fur is shaggy, and different subspecies display a variety of colour forms. Brown-headed spider monkeys lack thumbs, enabling them to grip surfaces more firmly while climbing. They move by swinging from branch to branch or by walking along thicker branches on all fours. These monkeys are expert jumpers, being able to leap across gaps of about 9m (30ft). They live in groups of about 20 individuals. Group members rarely all gather in one place, but move around a home range in smaller subgroups.

**Black spider monkey** (*Ateles paniscus*):
49–58cm (19–23in); 7–9kg (15.5–19.75lb)
Black spider monkeys inhabit lowland rainforest in Central and South America, and extend farther south than brown-headed spider monkeys. The males are among the largest American primates. Black spider monkeys have long black hair, and their faces vary from pink to black. Like other spider monkeys, they lack thumbs and have long arms and flexible shoulder joints – all adaptations for an arboreal existence. Black spider monkeys live in groups of about 20 adults, with three females for every male. The males, which mate with several females, co-operate to prevent males from other groups from having access to the females.

# Masked titi

*Callicebus personatus*

Masked titis inhabit the mixed forests that grow along the Atlantic coast of Brazil south of the mouth of the Amazon. They prefer forests with a broken canopy, where enough light reaches the ground for a thick understorey (undergrowth layer) to grow. Masked titis live in widely distributed groups, with only a few monkeys occupying large areas of forest. The destruction of coastal forests has meant that the populations of this species are now small, isolated and increasingly vulnerable.

Like other titi species, masked titis form monogamous pairs that mate for life. The male does the bulk of the carrying once the single young is produced, and he is responsible for nearly all of the parental care after weaning. Young masked titis stay with their parents for at least a couple of years, helping to raise their younger siblings.

**Distribution:** Atlantic coast of Brazil.
**Habitat:** Coastal forests.
**Food:** Fruit, insects, birds' eggs and mice.
**Size:** 31–42cm (12–16.5in); 0.97–1.65kg (2.2–3.75lb).
**Maturity:** Unknown.
**Breeding:** Single young born between August and October.
**Life span:** 20 years.
**Status:** Vulnerable.

*There are five subspecies of masked titi, each with a differently coloured coat. Most have black foreheads and sideburn-like tufts around their dark faces. Their bodies have a range of grey or yellow-orange fur. The tail is not prehensile.*

**Central American squirrel monkey** (*Saimiri oerstedii*): 22–30cm (8.5–12in); 0.5–1.1kg (1–2.5lb)
Found along the Pacific coast of Panama and Costa Rica, this species occurs in a variety of habitats, from rainforest to mangrove swamps and thickets. Like other squirrel monkeys, it has a slender body and a long, prehensile tail. The predominantly yellow fur is slightly paler on the underside, and there is a black crown on the head. Central American squirrel monkeys travel in small troops. They occasionally gather in larger groups, when monkeys may move between troops.

**White-fronted capuchin** (*Cebus albifrons*): 33–44cm (13–17.5in); 1.1–3.3kg (2.5–7.25lb)
Superficially similar to the white-faced capuchin, this monkey is found to the south of its relative. The ranges of the two species may overlap in northern Colombia and Ecuador, but the white-fronted capuchin is more likely to be found at lower altitudes in well-developed rainforest. This capuchin eats mainly fruit, along with insects and other arthropods. Troops contain 15–35 members, and are dominated by a single breeding pair.

**Black howler monkey** (*Alouatta caraya*): 51–67cm (20–26.5in); 4–10kg (8.75–22lb)
This monkey lives in the forests of central South America, from northern Argentina to southern Brazil and eastern Bolivia. It inhabits either flooded gallery forests beside rivers or dry deciduous forests that grow in patches close to savannahs. Like other howlers, this species is a folivore – a leaf eater. Black howler monkeys live in family groups with a few more females than males. Male offspring are chased away as they mature.

# Monk saki

*Pithecia monachus*

These monkeys are found in north-western Brazil, Colombia, Ecuador and Peru. Because they live at the very tops of rainforest trees, they are very difficult to study. Like the majority of New World monkeys, monk sakis are most active during the day. They leap from tree to tree in search of fruits, which they cut up with their long canine teeth before eating them.

Monk sakis live in small family groups of about four or five. Each group contains an adult breeding pair and their offspring of varying ages. A newborn saki clings to its mother's belly. As it grows larger, it rides on her back, until it is able to move around independently. Members of the family communicate using calls, mainly to let each other know where they are. At night, several families will sleep together in the same tree.

*Saki monkeys have very thick tails for their relatively small bodies. The tail is not prehensile and is used for balance. There is a gap between the second and third digit on both the front and rear feet.*

**Distribution**: Northern South America.
**Habitat**: Forest.
**Food**: Fruit, seeds, nuts and insects.
**Size**: 30–50cm (12–19.5in); 1–2kg (2.2–4.5lb).
**Maturity**: Unknown.
**Breeding**: 1 young born every year.
**Life span**: 12–25 years.
**Status**: Lower risk.

# White-faced capuchin

*Cebus capucinus*

*These monkeys are characterized by white fur around the face, as well as on the chest and upper arms. Unlike most New World monkeys, the thumb is opposable and is used to hold a range of foods.*

The white-faced, or white-throated, capuchin ranges from Honduras in Central America and south to the Pacific coast of Colombia. It occupies well-developed rainforests with dense canopies and little undergrowth. This intelligent and adaptable species also lives in mangroves and drier, more open forests.

Capuchins have a cap of dark hair on the head that resembles the hood, or capuche, worn by friars. The tail is slightly prehensile, but it is not the "fifth limb" of certain New World monkeys. The tail is carried coiled up – hence the nickname ringtail. White-faced capuchins live in troops of about 12 individuals. The females in a group are all related, but the males are drawn from different troops. Upon maturity, males are driven away by older males and presumably join other troops. A troop splits if it grows too large for its territory. The two new, smaller groups are able to locate food more easily.

**Distribution**: Northern Colombia and Central America.
**Habitat**: Montane forest.
**Food**: Fruits, nuts, insects, rodents, lizards, frogs, birds and shellfish.
**Size**: 33–51cm (13–20in); 1.1–3.3kg (2.5–7.25lb).
**Maturity**: 4–8 years.
**Breeding**: 1 offspring born every 2 years at any time of year.
**Life span**: 12–25 years.
**Status**: Common.

# Weeping capuchin

*Cebus olivaceus*

**Distribution**: South America.
**Habitat**: Forests.
**Food**: Fruits, palm, nuts, insects, spiders and small vertebrates.
**Size**: 35–50cm (14–20in); 2.5–2.8kg (5.5–6.25lb).
**Maturity**: 4–7 years.
**Breeding**: 1 young born every 2 years.
**Life span**: 35 years.
**Status**: Common.

*The tail of the weeping capuchin is only semi-prehensile, unlike many other capuchin species, which have more dextrous tails. The tail is often carried with the section near the tip coiled up.*

Weeping capuchins live across the whole of tropical South America east of the Andes Mountains. They are most commonly found in the deciduous llanos forests typical of the drier fringes of the Amazon Basin. Weeping capuchins live in the lower reaches of these forests, and can sometimes even be seen searching for food in the deep leaf litter on the forest floor. When a predator threatens, the capuchins take refuge on high branches.

Weeping capuchins live in large groups of about 20 individuals. There is one dominant male in each troop who mates with all the female members. Other males in the troop may sneak an occasional mating, but this is rare. A female usually gives birth to a single young, which clings to its mother's fur with its hands and feet soon after being born. She nurses the youngster for several months.

These monkeys use their dextrous hands to manipulate a wide range of foods. Weeping capuchins appear to use a certain species of millipede to repel unwanted biting insects. They squash the millipedes against their skin, releasing a toxin from the crushed bodies that keeps insects away.

# Mantled howler monkey

*Alouatta palliata*

One of the few primate species to live as far north as Mexico, this species also lives along the eastern side of Central America and in northern Colombia and Ecuador. Mantled howler monkeys live in both lowland rainforests and upland montane forests. They eat mainly leaves and fruit, preferring young leaves that have lower levels of indigestible tannins in them. In the dry season, they supplement their diet with flowers. Fruits are more common in the wet season. The monkeys move slowly through the forest; their energies are devoted to consuming large amounts of food.

Mantled howler monkeys live in groups of 10–20 individuals. There are generally three or four females for every male in the group. These males tend to be at least 6 years old. Younger males live alone or in small groups that contain no females. As in other howler monkey species, the males make loud, persistent calls, which can be heard for up to 3km (1.86 miles). Females initiate mating by wiggling their tongue at a male. He responds in the same way and mating follows soon afterwards.

*Mantled howler monkeys have yellow or brown saddle-shaped patches on their back, and long hairs along their flanks. Both sexes possess a beard, with the males having longer facial hair. The males also have a conspicuous white scrotum.*

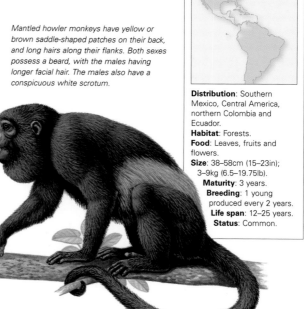

**Distribution**: Southern Mexico, Central America, northern Colombia and Ecuador.
**Habitat**: Forests.
**Food**: Leaves, fruits and flowers.
**Size**: 38–58cm (15–23in); 3–9kg (6.5–19.75lb).
**Maturity**: 3 years.
**Breeding**: 1 young produced every 2 years.
**Life span**: 12–25 years.
**Status**: Common.

# MARMOSETS AND TAMARINS

*Marmosets and tamarins are small, lightweight, swift-moving monkeys that live in South and Central America. Marmosets are among the smallest of all primates. They do not look like other monkeys, having short arms and legs similar to those of small tree-living mammals such as squirrels. Furthermore, they have claws on their fingertips, whereas other monkeys have fingernails.*

## Pygmy marmoset

*Cebuella pygmaea*

**Distribution**: Upper Amazon Basin.
**Habitat**: Rainforest.
**Food**: Fruit, buds, insects and sap.
**Size**: 11–15cm (4.5–6in); 100–140g (3.5–5oz).
**Maturity**: 1.5–2 years.
**Breeding**: 1–3 young born throughout the year.
**Life span**: 10 years.
**Status**: Common.

Pygmy marmosets are the smallest monkeys in the world. They live in the low plants that grow beneath tall trees in tropical forests. They clamber among the thick vegetation in search of food throughout the day, being most active in the cooler hours at the beginning and end of each day.

Pygmy marmosets eat fruit, flower buds and insects, but their preferred food is the sweet, sticky sap from certain trees. Their lower canine teeth are specially shaped for gouging holes in tree bark, causing the sap to leak out from the wood beneath. A tree used by a group of pygmy marmosets will be covered in wounds where the animals have repeatedly bitten through the bark.

Like all monkeys, pygmy marmosets live in complex societies. They live in family groups, with two parents and eight or nine offspring. Families sleep together, huddled on branches. Breeding pairs may mate at any time, but most produce small litters – usually twins – in December or June.

*Pygmy marmosets have grey-brown fur and tails ringed with red-brown stripes. Their tails are prehensile and can be wrapped around branches. They move cautiously through the tree tops to avoid attack by large birds of prey.*

## Golden lion tamarin

*Leontopithecus rosalia*

The golden lion tamarin lives in the forests along Brazil's south-eastern coast. These forests are similar to the rainforests in the north-west of the Amazon Basin, but the trees in the coastal forests are not as tall. The tamarins live in an incredibly dense and humid environment, where leaves block out much of the sunlight, and where vines and other climbing plants fill the spaces under the crowns of trees.

Golden lion tamarins live in groups of about eight. Each group has a single breeding pair. The other members of the group help to rear the young. All group members share food and bond together by grooming each other's fur. The males groom the females more often than the females do the males. The tamarins are diurnal, sleeping throughout the night and often having a nap at midday. They eat fruit, flowers and various small animals, as well as nectar. Golden lion tamarins use their hands to collect and manipulate food. For example, they use their long fingers to extract insects from under bark.

*The golden lion tamarin is named after the golden mane around its small head, which gives it the appearance of a tiny lion. The back is covered in long, silky fur which varies from pale gold to a rich reddish gold. Unlike many primates, this monkey has claws instead of fingernails. It moves through the trees by walking, running and leaping from branch to branch.*

**Distribution**: South-east Brazil.
**Habitat**: Tropical forest.
**Food**: Insects, snails, lizards, eggs and fruit.
**Size**: 34–40cm (14–16in); 630–710g (22–25oz).
**Maturity**: 1.5–2 years.
**Breeding**: 2 litters of twins born in September and March.
**Life span**: 15 years.
**Status**: Endangered.

# Cotton-top tamarin

*Saguinus oedipus*

Cotton-top tamarins have an unusual breeding system. They live in groups of up to 20 adults, but only one pair breeds. The other adults in the group act as helpers. Most of the helpers are younger individuals. Their assistance reduces the infant mortality of this species to levels lower than those of all mammals, apart from humans. Although they appear to lose out by not breeding from an early age, the helpers gain valuable experience by assisting the older breeding pair. When the helpers come to breed themselves, they are likely to be more successful. The helpers form small subgroups that move in and out of the breeding pair's home range. The home range is marked using scent.

About half of the diet of these tamarins is made up of insects. The rest comprises fruits and the sweet gums that exude from tree trunks. Nature reserves have been set up to conserve the species.

*Cotton-top tamarins have a crest of white hair that runs from the forehead to the nape of the neck. The rump and inner thighs are red-orange. These coloured surfaces may be used to flash signals to other tamarins through dense foliage.*

**Distribution**: North-west Colombia.
**Habitat**: Tropical rainforest.
**Food**: Insects.
**Size**: 19–21cm (7.5–8.25in); 260–380g (9.25–13.5oz).
**Maturity**: 1.5–2 years.
**Breeding**: 2 litters of twins born at all times of the year.
**Life span**: 15 years.
**Status**: Endangered.

**Saddlebacked tamarin** (*Saguinus fuscicollis*): 19–30cm (7.5–12in); 260–380g (9.25–13.5oz) This species occurs in Panama, Bolivia, Brazil, Colombia and Peru. Saddlebacks are most often seen near the edge of the rainforest, where the canopy is less developed and where there is more undergrowth. They have a black-and-white pattern on their faces, and a red-brown coat. Saddleback groups contain a single adult female and two adult males. The female mates with both males and they all share the task of rearing the young. Older offspring help to care for the youngest litter. Saddlebacks eat insects and fruits, and lick tree gums and sap to obtain minerals.

**Black-faced lion tamarin** (*Leontopithecus caissara*): 30.5cm (12in); 600g (21.25oz) Discovered in 1990, this critically endangered species lives in about 17,000 hectares (42,000 acres) of forest in south-eastern Brazil. The face, mane and tail have black hair, while the hair on the rest of the body is deep gold. These diurnal monkeys move in groups of up to 10 animals with a dominant monogamous breeding pair. They eat mainly fruit and some invertebrates.

**Golden-rumped lion tamarin** (*Leontopithecus chrysopygus*): 20–33cm (8–14in); 300–700g (10.5–24.75oz) The golden-rumped lion tamarin is another critically endangered species, with under 1,000 surviving in two small pockets of forest in Brazil. Long, black hair covers most of the body, but the thighs, buttocks and tail are golden. These tamarins live in family groups that forage by day. Like most tamarins, they eat insects and fruits.

# Emperor tamarin

*Saguinus imperator*

Emperor tamarins are found in the forests of south-eastern Peru, north-western Bolivia, and vast sweeps of northern Brazil. Many of the forests within this range are regularly flooded, and the tamarins most commonly occur in forests with dry ground. They inhabit all levels of the forest, foraging by day. Being relatively small monkeys, they are able to reach food at the end of the flimsiest of branches, beyond the reach of larger species.

As in other tamarin species, the male washes the young after birth, and he helps to carry them around until they are about two months old.

Emperor tamarins are more widely distributed than most tamarins, which tend to live in small pockets of forest. Consequently, this species is one of the few that is not currently threatened with extinction.

**Distribution**: Northern Brazil, south-eastern Peru and north-western Bolivia
**Habitat**: Tropical rainforest.
**Food**: Fruits, insects and sap.
**Size**: 22–26.5cm (8.5–10.5in); 300–400g (10.5–14oz).
**Maturity**: 16–20 months.
**Breeding**: Up to 2 litters of twins, produced at any time of year.
**Life span**: 15 years.
**Status**: Lower risk.

*The emperor tamarin is one of the largest of the tamarins, although most lion tamarins are larger. Emperor tamarins have a crown of silver and brown hair, and a long white moustache that reaches the chest.*

## White-tufted-ear marmoset

*Callithrix jacchus*

White-tufted-ear marmosets live on the edges of tropical forests in north-eastern Brazil. The species is also known as the common marmoset. However, the destruction of their forest habitat means that they are less common than they once were.

These marmosets are diurnal and live in small troops of up to 12 monkeys. Within each troop a female teams up with two or more males to form a breeding group. The female mates with all of these males. All the breeding males help the female to carry the young and find food for them. It is thought that the babies need multiple "fathers" to help them survive, because the babies are too heavy for just the mother to carry. The other members of the troop are the offspring of the adults, and these also help to raise the young. Only one female in each troop breeds at a given time.

White-tufted-ear marmosets feed mainly on tree sap and other exudates (such as gums and resins). Exudates are such an abundant resource that the marmosets can live in relatively high-density populations. Insects are another important food, and the diet also includes fruits, nectar, flowers, spiders, and sometimes birds' eggs, lizards and frogs. In addition, these marmosets have learned to exploit the food potential of plantations that grow near the forest edge.

**Distribution**: Eastern Brazil.
**Habitat**: Edge of forests.
**Food**: Sap, nectar, insects, spiders, fruit and flowers.
**Size**: 12–15cm (4.75–6in); 300–360g (10.5–12.75oz).
**Maturity**: 2 years.
**Breeding**: Twins born at all times of the year.
**Life span**: 10 years.
**Status**: Lower risk.

*This marmoset is easily recognized by the white tufts on its ears and the white patch on the otherwise brown forehead. It also has stripes on its back and tail. In common with most marmosets, the tail is a little longer than the body.*

## Goeldi's monkey

*Callimico goeldii*

*Goeldi's monkey is unique among marmosets and tamarins, having six molar teeth on either side of its jaws (other marmosets have four). A cape of long hair hangs from the neck and shoulders. There are pale rings near the base of the tail and buff markings on the back of the neck. Juveniles lack the rings and the mane, and often the neck markings.*

This rare, unusual monkey of northern South America forms a separate group within the marmoset and tamarin family. It lives in a range of forest habitats, preferring areas with a broken canopy where light filters through to the forest floor so that undergrowth can grow. This species is also often found in bamboo glades. It spends most of its time at low levels in the forest, less than 5m (16.5ft) above the ground. However, it will climb higher into the trees to reach ripe fruit.

Goeldi's monkeys live in troops that travel together in search of food. A troop typically covers about 2km (1.24 miles) per day, moving in a roughly circular pattern within their territory, which may cover up to 80 hectares (720 acres). These monkeys sleep together as well, sheltering in a hollow tree or in dense undergrowth. They break up their daytime feeding trips with about three rest periods, during which they sunbathe and groom each other to remove parasites from their fur. Grooming also helps to strengthen social ties within the group. There is little contact between different troops.

Goeldi's monkeys make their way through the forest by climbing trees and then leaping forward. Their diet consists mainly of fruits and insects, but they will occasionally jump down to the ground to catch small vertebrate prey.

**Distribution**: Southern Colombia, eastern Ecuador, eastern Peru, northern Bolivia and western Brazil.
**Habitat**: Broken forest with undergrowth, bamboo glades.
**Food**: In the wet season the diet consists of fruits, insects and small vertebrates such as frogs and snakes; in the dry season they eat fungi.
**Size**: 21–31cm (8.5–12in); 390–860g (13.75–30.25oz).
**Maturity**: 14 months.
**Breeding**: Single offspring produced each time, but females sometimes breed twice per year.
**Life span**: 10 years.
**Status**: Vulnerable.

# Silvery marmoset

*Callithrix argentata*

**Distribution**: Eastern Brazil.
**Habitat**: Rainforest.
**Food**: Tree gum and sap. plus fruits, leaves and insects
**Size**: 22cm (8.5in); 300–400g (11–14oz).
**Maturity**: 2 years.
**Breeding**: Twins born twice each year.
**Life span**: 10 years.
**Status**: Lower risk.

Silky marmosets have an unique jaw shape that ends in a sharp tip, and shorter canines than other marmosets and New World monkeys. This is believed to be an adaptation to feeding on exudates (gums, resins and sap) from trees. With canines and incisors of the same length, the silvery marmoset can gouge holes in tree trunks. It then laps up the sweet exudates that ooze from these holes. Exudates are low in protein, so the marmoset supplements its diet with fruits, leaves and insects.

Silvery marmosets live in rainforests east and south of the Amazon Delta. They are active by day, and rarely descend from the tree tops. They rest in hollow trees or thick tangles of vines. Like other marmosets, they have claws rather than nails, which they use to grip tree trunks while climbing.

*The silvery marmoset is one of the smallest monkeys in the Americas, being about the size of a squirrel. Some silvery marmosets are brown rather than silver. These monkeys have hairless ears and faces, and their alternative name is bare-eared marmosets.*

---

**Geoffroy's tamarin** (*Saguinus geoffroyi*):
20–29cm (8–11.5); 350–500g (12.25–17.6oz)
Geoffroy's tamarin is found in south-eastern Costa Rica, Panama and northern Colombia. This small monkey lives in shrubs and tall grasses, and may even be seen in areas of forest that have burnt down. It has brown and black fur with a white triangular patch on its head. The neck and tail are a dark red-brown. This species lives in groups of up to 20 individuals. It practices a polyandrous mating system, in which each female mates with two or more males. The males will help to carry the young despite being uncertain of their paternity. The group uses scent to mark its territory. Although females are dominant in the group, males are more aggressive toward members of other groups who enter the territory. This species eats insects and fruits as well as lizards, flowers and nectar. Due to habitat destruction, this species is endangered.

**Black-mantled tamarin** (*Saguinus nigricollis*):
22cm (8.5in); 475g (16.75oz)
The black-mantled tamarin is found east of the Andes, from Ecuador to southern Colombia and south to Peru and Brazil. It lives in primary and secondary rainforest. Secondary rainforest grows where primary rainforest has been damaged in some way. It is considerably more dense, with shorter trees but more undergrowth. This species has black fur from the head to midway down the back, after which the fur becomes red. The black-mantled tamarin's diet mainly comprises insects, particularly grasshoppers and crickets. These monkeys also eat fruits, seeds, nectar and tree gums.

# Black-pencilled marmoset

*Callithrix penicillata*

Black-pencilled marmosets are found in the coastal region of Brazil and relatively far inland. They live high up in rainforest trees, and are seldom seen far below the upper canopy. This species is usually found in gallery forest, which grows in narrow strips beside rivers and which is characterized by frequent flooding.

This species forms monogamous pairs that often live with their young. They breed twice a year, and the older offspring assist their parents in raising their younger siblings. Black-pencilled marmosets mark their territory with aromatic secretions produced by glands on their chests and near the anus. This is primarily to deter other species of monkey from feeding in the area. Group members alert each other to danger, using specific cries to warn against different types of predator.

**Distribution**: Brazil.
**Habitat**: Gallery forest.
**Food**: Tree sap.
**Size**: 22.5–28cm (9–11in); 450g (16oz).
**Maturity**: 18 months.
**Breeding**: Twins produced twice a year.
**Life span**: 15 years.
**Status**: Unknown.

*The black-pencilled marmoset has large black tufts behind its ears. The long tail is ringed with black and grey. The tail is used to help the monkey balance as it moves around in the tree tops.*

# HOOFED ANIMALS

*Hoofed animals walk on the tips of their toes. Their hooves are made from the same material as fingernails and claws – keratin. Walking on tiptoes makes their legs very long, and most hoofed animals are fast runners because of this. Hoofed mammals belong to two groups:* Perissodactyla *includes horses, zebras, rhinoceroses and tapirs, while* Artiodactyla *includes pigs, sheep, antelope, deer and cattle.*

## Brazilian tapir

*Tapirus terrestris*

Brazilian tapirs, also known as South American tapirs, spend the day in forests of dense vegetation. At night they emerge into more open country, where they browse on vegetation. They prefer to spend part of the night in water or mud, and are surprisingly agile swimmers given their size. When on land, they walk with their snouts close to the ground. Each night, a tapir will follow one of several well-trodden trails to a favourite watering hole.

Tapirs spend most of their lives alone. They are fairly aggressive towards one another at chance meetings. They alert each other to their presence by giving shrill whistling sounds and marking the ground with their urine. Brazilian tapirs breed all year round, but most mate during the rainy season, which means that their young are born just before the rains begin in the following year.

*Tapirs have rounded bodies that are wider at the back than at the front. This helps them charge through thick vegetation when in danger. They have short hairs on their bodies and narrow manes on their necks. Their noses are long and flexible. Young tapirs have red fur patterned with yellow and white stripes and spots.*

**Distribution**: From Colombia and Venezuela southward to northern Argentina.
**Habitat**: Woodland or dense grassy habitats near water.
**Food**: Water plants, fruit, buds.
**Size**: 1.8–2.5m (6–8.25ft); 180–320kg (396–704lb). Height at shoulder 75–120cm (29.5–47in).
**Maturity**: 3–4 years.
**Breeding**: 1 or 2 young born at start of rainy season.
**Life span**: 35 years.
**Status**: Lower risk.

## Collared peccary

*Pecari tajacu*

Collared peccaries are not directly related to pigs and wild boars. Pigs are native to Europe, Asia and Africa, and were introduced to the Americas by humans. Peccaries do resemble pigs, though, having similar blunt snouts for rooting out tubers and other foods, however peccaries have longer, more slender legs than pigs. Peccaries also eat snakes and small invertebrates. Like many pigs, they appear to be immune to rattlesnake bites.

This species ranges from the south-western United States to northern Argentina. It inhabits grassland and scrubland in the north of its range, but is equally at home in tropical rainforests further south. In many areas, these animals have come to live alongside humans, eating rubbish and food stores. Local people call the collared peccary the javelina because of its small, sharp tusks, which resemble the tips of a spear.

*Collared peccaries get their name from the curve of pale hairs that starts behind the neck and runs under the chin to the other side, thus forming a collar. The tusks in the upper and lower jaw fit together snugly and sharpen each other as the jaw is opened and closed.*

**Distribution**: South-western US to northern Argentina.
**Habitat**: Tropical rainforest and grassland.
**Food**: Roots, bulbs, fungi, fruits, eggs, carrion, small animals.
**Size**: 0.75–1m (2.5–3.25ft); 14–30kg (31–66lb). Height at shoulder 44–50cm (17.25–19.75in).
**Maturity**: 11 months.
**Breeding**: 1–3 young born at all times of year.
**Life span**: 8–10 years.
**Status**: Common.

# Guanaco

*Lama guanicoe*

*Guanacos have long limbs and necks for reaching food in trees and shrubs. They have brown, woolly fur on their upper bodies and necks, while their undersides have white hair.*

Guanacos are considered the wild relatives of domestic llamas and alpacas. They are distant cousins of the camels of Africa and Asia. Like camels, guanacos have adapted to living in dry areas, although their preferred habitat – alpine grassland – is not as hot as the habitats of most camels. Like their domestic relatives, guanacos are fast runners. They have more haemoglobin (oxygen-carrying pigment) in their red blood cells than any other mammal. This allows them to survive at altitude. Guanacos mainly graze on grass, but they also pluck leaves from shrubs. They live in herds of about 15 individuals. Each herd is controlled by one adult male. Once a young guanaco reaches adulthood, it is chased away by the dominant male.

**Distribution**: Southern Peru to Argentina and Chile.
**Habitat**: Dry, open areas.
**Food**: Grass.
**Size**: 1.2–2.5m (4–8.25ft); 100–120kg (220–264lb). Height at shoulder 0.9–1.3m (3–4.25ft).
**Maturity**: Females 2 years; males 4 years.
**Breeding**: Single young born in spring.
**Life span**: 28 years.
**Status**: Vulnerable.

---

**Llama** (*Lama glama*): 1–2m (3.25–6.5ft); 130–155kg (290–340lb). Height at shoulder 0.9–1.3m (3–4.25ft) Llamas are widely distributed along the length of the Andes Mountains, from Ecuador to Chile and Argentina. However, all these animals are kept by people – there are no wild llamas. Llamas appear to be domestic breeds of the guanaco. Llamas are the most common members of the *Lama* genus, which also includes guanacos and alpacas, another domestic breed. Llamas can produce fertile offspring with these other animals, so they are probably all the same species. Llamas exhibit the behaviour of wild guanacos. Males defend a harem of about six females in a small territory. The young, or crias, can walk after their first hour of life. Young males are driven off by their fathers when they mature at about two years old.

**Baird's tapir** (*Tapirus bairdii*): 180–250cm (71–98in); 150–300kg (330–660lbs). Height at shoulder 75–120cm (29.5–47in) This species has a range to the north of the more common Brazilian tapir, occurring from southern Mexico to northern Colombia and Ecuador. Baird's tapirs live in wetland habitats such as swamps and along the banks of streams. These nocturnal animals spend most of their time on solid ground, but take to the water to escape unwanted attention. The barrel-shaped body and short legs make them well-suited to running through thick undergrowth. Baird's tapirs forage with their long, flexible snout close to the ground to sniff out food such as twigs, shoots, leaves, fruits and seeds. Edible objects are picked up by the snout and transferred to the mouth.

# Vicuña

*Vicugna vicugna*

Vicuñas are related to guanacos and camels. They live on high-altitude grasslands in the Andes Mountains of Peru, Bolivia, Argentina and Chile. Vicuñas are seldom found below about 3,500m (11,500ft). At this height, the conditions are cold and dry, so vicuñas never stray far from a source of running water.

The vicuña has teeth more like those of rodents than other hoofed mammals. The lower incisors grow throughout the animal's lifetime. The teeth are constantly being worn away by the tough alpine grasses that make up its diet. Vicuñas are ruminants, which means that they digest their plant food with the help of bacteria in the stomach, and they chew half-digested food, or cud, to help with the digestion process. They are especially adapted to living at high altitude, having a large heart and specialized blood cells.

**Distribution**: Andes Mountains, from southern Peru and western Bolivia to north-western Argentina and northern Chile.
**Habitat**: Alpine grasslands.
**Food**: Grass.
**Size**: 1.25–1.9m (4–6.25ft); 36–65kg (79–143lb). Height at shoulder 0.7–1.1m (2.25–3.5ft).
**Maturity**: 2 years.
**Breeding**: Single calf born during February or March.
**Life span**: 15 years.
**Status**: Vulnerable.

*The tawny-coated vicuña is the smallest member of the camel family. It is just a quarter of the weight of the guanaco but has a similar body form, with a long, slender neck and thin legs.*

## Muskox

*Ovibos moschatus*

Although muskoxen look like large hairy cattle or bison, they are in fact relatives of goats and sheep. These animals live on the windswept tundra within the Arctic Circle. This habitat forms in places that are too cold and dry for trees to grow. There is only enough water to sustain grasses and other hardy plants.

Both sexes of this species have large, hooked horns. Male muskox are larger than females, because they must fight other males to win and defend a harem of females. They butt each other with their horns in contests of strength. During the mating season, the bulls produce a strong, musky odour. Muskoxen live in herds, usually of 15–20 animals but occasionally up to 100 strong. When predators threaten, the herd crowds together, often in a circle or semi-circle, with the calves in the middle. This formation provides a highly effective defence, since adversaries are faced with a wall of horns and risk being gored if they attack.

*The muskox's body is covered in long fur, except the area between lips and nostrils. The fur not only keeps the animal warm, but also protects it against the vast numbers of biting insects that swarm across the tundra during the short summer.*

**Distribution**: Arctic of Canada and Greenland.
**Habitat**: Tundra.
**Food**: Grass, moss and sedge.
**Size**: 1.9–2.3m (6.25–7.5ft); 200–410kg (440–900lb). Height at shoulder 1.2–1.5m (4–5ft).
**Maturity**: 2–3 years.
**Breeding**: 1 young produced every 1–2 years in spring.
**Life span**: 18 years.
**Status**: Common, although extinct in Alaska.

## American bison

*Bison bison*

Although rare, the American bison has been saved from extinction. Once, vast herds of over a million bison grazed the vast prairies of western North America, often making migrations of several thousand kilometres to winter feeding grounds in the south. They were almost wiped out by hunters during the 19th century, when the grasslands were cleared to make way for agriculture. Bison were also widely killed for their skin and meat. Originally, bison also occurred extensively in mountain areas, and also in open forest and woodland.

These large grazing animals have well-developed senses of smell and hearing. They can run at up to 60kmh (37mph) and are also able to swim well, sometimes crossing rivers as wide as 1km (0.6 mile). Bison may often be seen rubbing their shoulders and rumps against boulders and tree trunks, and they enjoy taking mud and dust baths. This behaviour scratches off fly larvae and other parasites that live on their hides.

While bison may occasionally gather in herds of several hundred, they generally move around in small bands made up of a number of females and their offspring, including young bulls. Mature bulls either live alone or move in separate groups from the cows. During the mating season, in late summer, the males join the females. They fight for the females by ramming each other head-on. After mating, a bull guards his mate for several days to prevent other rival males from mating with her.

**Distribution**: Patches of western Canada and central United States.
**Habitat**: Prairie and woodland.
**Food**: Grass.
**Size**: 2.1–3.5m (7–11.5ft); 350–1000kg (770–2200lb). Height at shoulder 1.5–2m (5–6.5ft).
**Maturity**: 1–2 years.
**Breeding**: Single young born in spring every 1 or 2 years.
**Life span**: 40 years.
**Status**: Lower risk.

*Male bison are larger than the females of the species. Both sexes have sharp, curved horns, which stick out from the shaggy, brown hair on their heads.*

# Mountain goat

*Oreamnos americanus*

As their name suggests, these goats live on the sides of steep mountains. They prefer broken, rocky slopes to meadows, and they have strong, sturdy legs and hooves to allow them to negotiate such difficult terrain. Mountain goats are native to the mountains of western North America, from southern Alaska to Montana and Idaho. However, they have also been introduced to mountainous regions further south in the United States.

Mountain goats are grazers, feeding on whatever grows in their precipitous habitats – mainly grasses and similar plants. In winter, when snow covers the higher slopes, mountain goats climb down to lowland feeding grounds. As the snows melt in spring, the goats return to the higher altitudes to feed on the new plant growth. In winter, mountain goats gather in large herds, but these break up in summer into smaller groups. During the breeding season, the males fight to form a hierarchy. They do not butt each other head on, like other goats, but stand side by side and jab each other with their short horns.

**Distribution**: From southern Alaska to Idaho.
**Habitat**: Steep, rocky slopes.
**Food**: Grass, mosses, twigs and lichens.
**Size**: 1.25–1.8m (4–6ft); 46–136kg (100–300lb). Height 0.9–1.2m (3–4ft).
**Maturity**: 2.5 years.
**Breeding**: 1–3 kids born in May or June.
**Life span**: 15 years.
**Status**: Common.

*Mountain goats have stout legs with large, oval hooves. The soles of the hooves are very elastic, which helps them to grip surfaces as they climb up rocky slopes.*

---

**Dall's sheep** (*Ovis dalli*): 1.3–1.8m (4.25–6ft); 46–113kg (100–250lb). Height at shoulder 1m (3.25ft)
This sheep is also called the thinhorn. Compared to its close relative, the bighorn sheep, the horns of this species are much smaller and so thin that they may be near transparent. The horns have growth rings that can be counted to show the animal's age. In the mating season, males fight by clashing horns in a test of strength. The range of Dall's sheep encompasses mountain regions in western Canada and Alaska. Dall's sheep can survive at higher altitudes than other American sheep and goats, and since alpine conditions are in many ways very similar to Arctic ones, this species is also found further north than others.

**White-lipped peccary** (*Tayassu pecari*): 95–135cm (37.5–53in); 27–40kg (60–88lb). Height at shoulder 50–60cm (19.7–23.6in)
White-lipped peccaries live in a similar range to collared peccaries, although they are much smaller. They may form herds of up to 100 individuals as they look for food in the forest.

**Chacoan peccary** (*Catagonus wagneri*): 93–106cm (36.5–42in); 29–49kg (64–108lb). Height at shoulder 50–70cm (19.7–27.5in)
This South American peccary is named after the chaco – the dry thorn and shrubland region that lies mainly in Paraguay. The peccary mainly eats cacti, and it has specialized kidneys for dealing with the high acid content of these plants. It supplements its mineral consumption by visiting salt licks formed by ant nests.

# Bighorn sheep

*Ovis canadensis*

Bighorn sheep are the most common wild sheep in North America. They are excellent climbers and are often found on rocky outcrops or high cliffs. They seek refuge in steep areas from cougars and other predators that are not agile enough to keep up with their sure-footed prey.

Flocks of bighorns can contain up to 100 individuals. They head up to high meadows in summer, then retreat to the valleys when the winter snows come. Male bighorns tend to live in separate groups from the ewes and lambs. The rams have hierarchies based on the size of their horns. Fights are ritualized, with the adversaries butting their horns together. Ewes prefer to mate with rams with large horns and refuse the courtship of others.

**Distribution**: South-western Canada to northern Mexico.
**Habitat**: Alpine meadows and rocky cliffs.
**Food**: Grass and sedge.
**Size**: 1.2–1.8m (4–6ft); 50–125kg (110–275lb). Height at shoulder 0.8–1.1m (2.5–3.5ft).
**Maturity**: 3 years.
**Breeding**: 1–3 young born in spring.
**Life span**: 20 years.
**Status**: Lower risk.

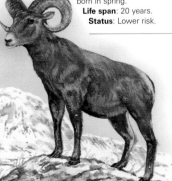

*Bighorns are named after the males' massive spiral horns, which may be up to 1.1m (3.5ft) long. The females have smaller, less curved horns.*

# Moose

*Alces alces*

Moose are the largest deer in the world. They live in the cold conifer forests that cover northern mountains and lowlands. As well as being found in North America, moose live across northern Europe and Siberia, where they are known as elk.

Moose plod through the forests and marshes, browsing on a wide range of leaves, mosses and lichens. They often feed in the shallows of streams and rivers, nibbling on aquatic vegetation. These large deer have even been seen diving underwater to uproot water plants. In summer, they are most active at dawn and dusk. In winter, they are active throughout the day. They paw the snow to reveal buried plants and twigs.

Although moose may gather together to feed, they spend most of the year alone. In the autumn mating season, males fight each other for females. Pregnant females find secluded sites where they can give birth, with thick vegetation to hide the new-born calves. The moose calves are able to stand and walk within two days. They can also swim by the time they are a week old, which is an important survival skill, since taking to water is a good way of escaping some predators. At five weeks they can outrun slower animals such as bears. Mothers will defend their calves aggressively. The calves become independent when they are about a year old.

**Distribution**: Alaska, Canada, northern United States, Siberia and northern Europe. Introduced to New Zealand.
**Habitat**: Marsh and woodland.
**Food**: Leaves, twigs, moss and water plants.
**Size**: 2.4–3.1m (8–10.25ft); 200–825kg (440–1815lb). Height at shoulder 1.4–2.3m (4.5–7.5ft).
**Maturity**: 1 year.
**Breeding**: 1–3 young born in spring.
**Life span**: 27 years.
**Status**: Common.

*Male moose are almost twice the size of females. The males sport huge antlers – nearly 2m (6.5ft) across – and have flaps of skin hanging below their chins, called dewlaps. In fights over females, male moose clash violently, sometimes goring each other with their antlers.*

# White-tailed deer

*Odocoileus virginianus*

White-tailed deer, or Virginia deer as they are called in the United States, prefer areas with tall grasses or shrubs to hide in during the day. When the deer spot predators, they raise their white tails to expose the white patches on their rumps. This serves as a visual warning to other deer that danger is near. If pursued, the deer bound away, reaching 60kmh (37mph).

White-tailed deer live in matriarchies, with each small group being controlled by a single adult female, which is the mother of the rest of the group. The adult males live alone or in small bachelor herds. In the autumn mating season, males mark plants with scent produced by glands on their faces, and urinate in depressions scraped into the ground. The males fight with their antlers – rut – for the right to court females.

*White-tailed deer have brown fur on their upper parts and white undersides. The white fur extends under the tail, which gives the species its name. The males shed their antlers in midwinter and grow new ones in spring.*

**Distribution**: North, Central and South America from southern Canada to Brazil.
**Habitat**: Shrublands and open woodland.
**Food**: Grass, shrubs, twigs, mushrooms, lichens and nuts.
**Size**: 0.8–2.1m (2.5–7ft); 50–200kg (110–484lb). Height at shoulder 0.8–1m (2.5–3.25ft).
**Maturity**: 1 year.
**Breeding**: 1–4 young produced during summer.
**Life span**: 10 years.
**Status**: Common.

# Pronghorn

*Antilocapra americana*

Despite appearances, pronghorns are not true deer. They are the sole members of a separate group of hoofed animals called the *Antilocapridae*. Unlike true deer, pronghorns do not have antlers, but have horns like antelope, although they are forked like those of a deer.

Pronghorns are the fastest land mammals in the Americas. They have been recorded racing along at 72kmh (45mph).

In late autumn, pronghorns gather into large herds of 1,000 or more. They spend the winter in these herds and split into smaller single-sex groups when spring arrives. In October, older males compete for small territories, which they use to attract groups of females. Once females have entered a territory, the resident male will not allow other males near them.

*Pronghorns get their name from the prongs sticking out halfway up their backward-curving horns. Male pronghorns are slightly larger than the females. The males also have black masks on their faces.*

**Distribution**: Southern Canada to northern Mexico.
**Habitat**: Grassland and desert.
**Food**: Grass, leaves and cacti.
**Size**: 1–1.5m (3.25–5ft); 36–70kg (79–154lb). Height at shoulder 0.8–1m (2.5–3.25ft).
**Maturity**: Females 18 months; males 3 years.
**Breeding**: 1–3 young born in spring.
**Life span**: 10 years.
**Status**: Common.

---

**Red brocket deer** (*Mazama americana*): 72–140cm (28.5–55in); 8–25kg (17–55lb). Height at shoulder 67–76cm (26.4–29.9in) Red brocket deer range from eastern Mexico to northern Argentina. They have whorls of hair on their faces and stout bodies covered in reddish-brown hair. The males have simple, spike-like antlers. Red brockets live in woodland and dense forest. They may be active both day and night, feeding on grasses, vines and the new shoots of plants. These shy deer tend to freeze when they spot danger, blending into the thick vegetation.

**Pampas deer** (*Ozotoceros bezoarticus*): 1.1–1.4m (3.5–4.5ft); 25–40kg (55–88lb). Height at shoulder 70–75cm (27.5–29.5in) This species lives on open grasslands – or pampas – in the south-eastern part of South America. It has a dark red or brown coat. Males have forked antlers and glands on their hooves that produce a strong scent. Pampas deer graze on young grass shoots throughout the day. In late summer and autumn the males fight for access to females, and most births occur in the spring.

**Huemul** (*Hippocamelus antisensis*): 1.4–1.65m (4.5–5.5ft); 45–65kg (99–143lb). Height at shoulder 69–77cm (27–33in) Huemuls live in the rugged hill country high in the Andes of Peru, Chile, Bolivia and Argentina. They have coarse coats and black Y-shaped face markings. Huemuls spend the summer grazing on grasses and sedges in high alpine meadows. In winter, they climb down to lower altitudes. Mating takes place in the dry winter season, and fawns are born at the end of the rains.

# Southern pudu

*Pudu pudu*

Southern pudus live in the wet forests on the slopes of southern Andes Mountains. They are the smallest of all deer, being only a little bigger than maras – the long-legged rodents that live in the same region.

Pudus are mainly nocturnal in their behaviour, although they are sometimes spotted feeding during the day. They move through the dense forest slowly, picking off the ripest fruits and most succulent leaves and buds. They try not to draw attention to themselves and stay well hidden as much as possible. If attacked, they run away in zigzag paths and often seek refuge in the branches of trees.

Pudus live alone, patrolling small territories and only occasionally encountering other members of their species. Being so small, pudus can reach maturity much more quickly than other species of deer. They are ready to reproduce at just six months of age. Births take place in the spring, and the year's fawns are ready to take part in the breeding activity that occurs during autumn.

*Southern pudus have grey and brown fur. They have short, thick legs and the males have small spikes for antlers.*

**Distribution**: Southern Chile to south-western Argentina.
**Habitat**: Humid forest.
**Food**: Tree and shrub leaves, vines, bark, fruit and flowers.
**Size**: 60–85cm (23.5–33.5in); 5–14kg (11–30.75lb). Height at shoulder 25–43cm (10–17in).
**Maturity**: 6 months.
**Breeding**: Single young born in spring.
**Life span**: 10 years.
**Status**: Vulnerable.

# Marsh deer

*Blastocerus dichotomus*

*The marsh deer is the largest deer in South America. It has wide feet with an elastic layer of skin between the hooves. This makes the foot webbed, and prevents the heavy deer from sinking into mud and other soft ground. The long, coarse coat is a reddish-brown in summer, turning to a darker brown in winter. There are white rings around the eyes.*

The marsh deer lives in the grasslands that exist along the southern fringe of the Amazon Basin. This habitat begins in southern Peru and Brazil and extends into northern Argentina. The deer once lived in Uruguay, but it is now thought to be extinct there.

Marsh deer browse on a range of plants that grow in waterlogged environments. They inhabit the small areas of swamp and bog that exist all year around. However, many of the grasslands in their range become flooded in the wet season, enabling the deer to disperse over a wider area. They are most active in the half-light of dawn and dusk, although they are sometimes also seen feeding during the day and at night.

Marsh deer generally live alone during floods, but form small groups of about five deer when they gather around water sources in dry periods. Males occupy a home range that covers those of several females. The males rut in October and November to establish their dominance. The ranking established by the rut is maintained throughout the year.

**Distribution**: South America, from southern Peru and Brazil to Paraguay and northern Argentina. Now presumed extinct in Uruguay.
**Habitat**: Marshy areas in grasslands.
**Food**: Grass, leaves and aquatic plants.
**Size**: 1.5–2m (5–6.5ft); 89–125kg (195–275lb). Height at shoulder 1–1.2m (3.25–4ft).
**Maturity**: 2 years.
**Breeding**: Single fawn produced in summer; gestation is about 9 months.
**Life span**: 10 years.
**Status**: Vulnerable.

# Mule deer

*Odocoileus hemionus*

Mule deer are common in the western half of North America. They range from central Mexico all the way to the edge of the Arctic tundra in northern Canada. They occupy all habitats between these points, including desert areas in Nevada, California and Arizona, and around the Great Salt Lake. The deer range eastward to Saskatchewan in the north and Texas in the south. There are also small, isolated populations further east in Iowa and Missouri.

Mule deer are most active at dawn and dusk. They feed mainly on vegetation, plus some fungi and lichens, and they can live almost anywhere where there is sufficient plant growth. Their diet of plant food is relatively poor in nutrients, so it is vital that the deer extract the most from it. To do this, the mule deer ruminate. This involves using stomach bacteria to digest the food for them, and chewing regurgitated food, or cud, to break down as much of the plant fibre as possible.

*Each mule deer has a unique set of markings made up of lines along the tail and pale patches on the rump and throat. These patterns stay the same throughout the deer's life. Female mule deer live in small social groups made up of an adult female and a number of her offspring. Males are either solitary or gather in small groups of unrelated individuals.*

**Distribution**: Western North America, from northern Canada to central Mexico.
**Habitat**: Desert, forest and grassland.
**Food**: Leaves, twigs, grass, moss, fungi and lichen
**Size**: 1.25–1.7m (4–5.5ft); 43–150kg (95–330lb). Height at shoulder 0.8–1.1m (2.5–3.5ft).
**Maturity**: 3–4 years.
**Breeding**: 1–2 fawns born in June or July; gestation is 195–212 days.
**Life span**: 15 years.
**Status**: Common.

# Caribou

*Rangifer tarandus*

The caribou, also known as the reindeer in Europe and Asia, is the only deer species in which both males and females possess antlers. American caribou have mainly brown coats with darker legs, while European and Asian animals are more grey.

Caribou herds are organized into hierarchies based on the size of the animals' bodies and antlers. Most herds make seasonal migrations in pursuit of food. Northern populations often make round trips of more than 5,000km (3,000 miles). During the migration, herds congregate into masses up to half a million strong. Caribou have been domesticated for 3,000 years, and there are huge numbers in northern Siberia.

*The antlers of male caribou can exceed 1m (3.25ft). Caribou hooves are broad and flat – an adaptation for walking on soft ground and deep snow.*

**Distribution**: Alaska, Canada, northern USA, Greenland, Scandinavia, Siberia, Mongolia, and north-eastern China.
**Habitat**: Arctic tundra, boreal forests, mountainous habitats.
**Food**: Plant material (leaves and twigs; especially new growth in spring) and lichens.
**Size**: 1.2–2.2m (4–7.25ft); 60–318kg (130–700lb). Height at shoulder 0.8–1.2m (2.5–4ft).
**Maturity**: 1.5–3.5 years.
**Breeding**: 1 fawn per year.
**Life span**: 15 years.
**Status**: Common.

---

**Grey brocket deer** (*Mazama gouazoupira*): 85–105cm (33.5–41.5in); 17kg (37.5lb). Height at shoulder 30–60cm (12–24in)
Grey brocket deer, or brown brockets, range from southern Central America to northern Argentina and Uruguay. They occupy dry, open habitats such as chaco thorn scrub and savannahs. These deer are slightly smaller than red brocket deer, which are found in the same region but occupy more heavily forested habitats. Grey brocket deer eat fruits in the wet season, but make do with leaves and twigs during the dry season. When water is hard to come by, they feed on cacti and other succulent plants that store water in their flesh. The deer also dig up roots used by plants to store water and nutrients. Male grey brocket deer have small antlers, little more than 10cm (4in) spikes. They breed all year round, and males only need to renew their antlers every couple of years.

**Fallow deer**; introduced (*Dama dama*): Size: 1.3–1.7m (4.25–5.5ft); 40–100kg (88–220lb). Height at shoulder 75–100cm (27.75–39in)
Originally native to the Mediterranean and Middle East, this deer has since been introduced to other continents, including the Americas. Fallow deer are easily identified by their somewhat flattened antlers and spotted summer coats. In some places fallow deer live alone, but in others they form small herds of up to 30 individuals. Breeding behaviour is variable, and may depend on the distribution of food. Males try to attract females with dance-like rituals and bellowing – a rut. Alternatively, they may monopolize females by defending good feeding areas from rival males.

# Wapiti

*Cervus elaphus*

In North America, wapiti are also called elk. Confusingly, in Europe and Asia the name elk is used to describe moose. It is now widely accepted that wapiti are actually an American subspecies of red deer, another large species found in northern Europe and Asia.

Only male wapiti have antlers, which reach up to 1.7m (5.5ft) across, and a shaggy mane around the neck. The males use their antlers during the rut, which takes place in autumn. They fight to establish which males will control the harems of females. Their antlers fall off in winter and regrow in time for the next year's contests.

*Wapiti resemble Old World red deer in many ways, although their coat is more brown, and becomes paler in summer.*

**Distribution**: Canada to New Mexico, as well as northern Africa, Asia and Europe.
**Habitat**: Alpine grasslands, forest edges.
**Food**: Grass, sedge, forbs, twigs and bark.
**Size**: 1.6–2.6m (5.25–8.5ft); 75–450kg (165–990lb). Height at shoulder 1.3–1.5m (4.25–5ft).
**Maturity**: 2 years.
**Breeding**: 1 fawn born in autumn.
**Life span**: 20 years.
**Status**: Common.

# SEALS AND RELATIVES

*Seals, sea lions and walruses are pinnipeds – they belong to the Pinnipedia order of mammals (pinniped means "fin footed"). They are descended from carnivorous, terrestrial ancestors. However, it seems that seals may be only distantly related to sea lions and walruses, despite their similar appearances. Like other sea mammals, pinnipeds have a layer of blubber under their skin, which keeps them warm in cold water.*

## Californian sea lion

*Zalophus californianus*

Californian sea lions spend the year moving up and down the Pacific coast of North America. In autumn and winter, most males move north to feed off the coast of British Columbia. The females and young stray less far from the breeding grounds, and probably head south at this time.

   The sea lions are seldom far from the shore at any time of the year. They generally go on foraging trips at night, although they are often active during the day as well. Each trip can last for several hours.

   During the summer breeding season, the sea lions congregate on flat beaches in the central area of their range. Most choose sandy habitats, but will use open, rocky areas if necessary. The males arrive first and fight each other for control of small territories on the beaches and in the water. They can only hold their territories for a few weeks before having to swim away and feed.

*Californian sea lions have less heavyset bodies than most sea lions because they live in warmer waters. They are fast swimmers, reaching speeds of 40kmh (25mph).*

**Distribution**: Pacific coast of North America and Galápagos Islands.
**Habitat**: Ocean islands and coastline.
**Food**: Fish, squid and seabirds.
**Size**: 1.5–2.5m (5–8.25ft); 200–400kg (440–880lb).
**Maturity**: Females 6 years; males 9 years.
**Breeding**: Single pup born each year.
**Life span**: 20 years.
**Status**: Vulnerable.

## South American sea lion

*Otaria flavescens* or *byronia*

South American sea lions do not travel very far from their breeding sites during the non-breeding season, although they may spend long periods out at sea. These sea lions sometimes feed in groups, especially when they are hunting shoals of fish or squid.

   The breeding season begins at the start of the southern summer. Adults arrive on beaches or flat areas of rock at the beginning of December. Males arrive a few weeks before the females, and defend small patches of the beach. The females give birth to the young they have been carrying since the previous year. After nursing their pups for a few weeks, the females become receptive to mating again. As the number of females increases, males stop controlling territories and begin to defend groups of females. Unsuccessful males without harems of their own gang together on the fringes of the beaches and charge through the females to mate with them.

*Male South American sea lions have dark brown bodies with brown manes on their heads and necks. The females are less heavyset and have paler bodies and no manes.*

**Distribution**: South Pacific and Atlantic waters off the South American coast from northern Peru to Brazil.
**Habitat**: Coastal waters and beaches.
**Food**: Fish, squid and crustaceans.
**Size**: 1.8–2.5m (6–8.25ft); 150–350kg (330–770lb).
**Maturity**: Females 4 years; males 6 years.
**Breeding**: Single pup born in January.
**Life span**: 20 years.
**Status**: Vulnerable

## Walrus

*Odobenus rosmarus*

Walruses live among the ice floes of the Arctic Ocean. These huge sea mammals are well known for their long tusks, which they use to stab opponents during fights. Walruses also use their tusks to "haul out", or pull themselves on to floating ice, and sometimes hook themselves to floes so that they can sleep while still in the water.

Walruses use their whiskered snouts to root out prey and blast away sediment with jets of air squirted from the mouth. They tackle shelled prey by holding them in their lips and sucking out the soft bodies.

Walruses live in large herds, sometimes of many thousands. In winter they feed in areas of thin sea ice, avoiding thick, unbroken ice, which they cannot break through from beneath. In summer, when the ice recedes, they spend more time on land.

*Walruses have long tusks growing out of the upper jaw. Males, which are twice the size of females, also have longer tusks. Their bodies are reddish-brown and sparsely covered in coarse hairs. Males have two air pouches inside the neck, which they use to amplify their mating calls.*

**Distribution**: Coast of Arctic Ocean.
**Habitat**: Pack ice.
**Food**: Worms, shellfish and fish.
**Size**: 2.25–3.5m (7.5–11.5ft); 400–1,700kg (880–3,740lb).
**Maturity**: Females 6 years; males 10 years.
**Breeding**: Single young born once per year.
**Life span**: 40 years.
**Status**: Vulnerable.

---

**Hawaiian monk seal** (*Monachus schauinslandi*): 2.1–2.3m (7–7.5ft); 170–250kg (375–450lb)
This endangered seal lives around small islands in the north-western region of Hawaii and other remote Pacific islands. Hawaiian monk seals hunt flatfish, lobsters, eels, and octopuses. Outside of the breeding season, these seals live alone. The females give birth on sandy beaches in areas controlled by the largest males. They then mate with the male in that area. The offspring from these matings are born the next year.

**Bearded seal** (*Erignathus barbatus*): 2.4m (8ft); 215–360kg (475–790lb)
This large species is found along the Alaskan coast and the edge of the Arctic sea ice, and occasionally as far south as Japan and Scotland. Bearded seals have long white whiskers that stand out against their dark fur. They live in shallow water, feeding on fish, crabs and shrimps.

**West Indian monk seal** (*Monachus tropicalis*): 2.2–2.4m (7.25–8ft); 170kg (375lb)
This species was declared extinct in 1996, the last confirmed sighting being in 1952. The West Indian monk seal once ranged throughout the Caribbean. It was thought to spend much of its time underwater, so it is possible that a small population still survives but is either rarely seen or is mistaken for another species.

## Hooded seal

*Cystophora cristata*

Hooded seals rarely approach land, preferring to spend their whole lives among the ice floes in the cold Arctic Ocean. Apart from during the breeding season, hooded seals live alone. They dive down to depths of more than 180m (590ft) to feed on shoaling fish and bottom-living creatures.

When the breeding season arrives in spring, the seals congregate on wide ice floes. The females take up widely spaced positions on the ice, preparing to give birth to the young conceived the year before. Meanwhile, males compete for access to small groups of females. The victors stay near the females as they nurse their new-born calves, chasing away any intruders while inflating their nasal balloons.

Hooded seal pups are suckled for only four days – the shortest time of any mammal – after which the mothers abandon them.

**Distribution**: Waters around Greenland.
**Habitat**: Drifting ice floes.
**Food**: Octopus, squid, shrimp, mussels and fish.
**Size**: 2–2.7m (6.5–9ft); 145–300kg (320–660lb).
**Maturity**: Females 3 years; males 5 years.
**Breeding**: Single pup born in March.
**Life span**: 30 years.
**Status**: Common.

*Hooded seals are so named because the males possess elastic sacs, or hoods, on the tops of their heads. The hoods are connected to their noses and can be inflated with air to amplify their calls while sparring with rival males. Female seals also have hoods, but their hoods are not inflatable like those of the males.*

## Steller's sea lion

*Eumetopias jubatus*

Steller's sea lions live along the coasts of the northern Pacific Ocean, from Japan to California. They prefer cold coastal water, where they feed on fish, squid and octopus. Between hunts, they rest on rocky shores. Adult males are about twice as large as females. Apart from their size, the main difference between the sexes is that males have huge necks, which are made even chunkier by their manes.

Sexually mature sea lions, including pregnant females, gather at breeding grounds in May. Each male defends an area of shore in the hope of encouraging females to give birth there. Fights between males can be extremely fierce, with the sea lions battering their huge bodies against each other and biting their opponent. The strongest bull is the one with the largest harem of females.

After the pups are born (the result of matings the previous year), he will mate with all the females in his territory. The male is not able to feed during the breeding season, because he is always guarding his harem. This fact, combined with the many injuries that males suffer during fights, means that males usually have considerably shorter lifespans than females.

**Distribution**: Northern Pacific coasts of Canada and the United States to San Miguel Island, California.
**Habitat**: Rocky shores.
**Food**: Fish, octopus, squid, bivalve molluscs and crustaceans, occasionally young fur seals, ringed seals and sea otters.
**Size**: 2.3–2.8m (7.5–9.25); 263–1000kg (580–2204lb).
**Maturity**: 3–7 years.
**Breeding**: Single pup born in summer, usually between late May and early June.
**Life span**: 20 years.
**Status**: Endangered.

*Steller's sea lions are the largest sea lions. Adult males have a distinctive mane that makes them look larger and more impressive, and also provides protection from bites during fights over mates.*

## South American fur seal

*Arctocephalus australis*

This species of fur seal is found on both the Atlantic and Pacific coasts of South America. Its range extends as far north as the rocky shores of Peru on the western side, and to Brazil in the east. It prefers steep shorelines, where boulders provide plenty of shade from the hot sun.

South American fur seals feed on a range of fish, from anchovies to mackerel. They are known to swim up to 200km (125 miles) from the coast to find shoals on which to prey. In shallow waters, mainly near to land, these seals will also feed on crustaceans and bottom-living molluscs, including octopus and shellfish. South American fur seals are themselves preyed on by great white sharks and orcas out at sea, as well as by South American sea lions nearer the shore.

Mating takes place in spring. Large bulls adopt territories along the coast before females arrive to give birth. After the pups are born, a bull mates with all the females in his territory. He drives other males away with threatening displays and calls.

*Male South American fur seals are much larger than the females. Once they reach adulthood, the males have black fur and a golden mane. The females and younger males are greyer. The pups are dark grey or black when born.*

**Distribution**: Pacific and Atlantic coasts of South America, from southern Peru in the west round to southern Brazil in the east
**Habitat**: Rocky shores and islands.
**Food**: Fish, cephalopods, crustaceans, bivalve molluscs, and gastropods.
**Size**: 1.4–1.9m (4.5–6.25ft); 30–200kg (66–440lb).
**Maturity**: 3–7 years.
**Breeding**: Single pup born in summer, usually in November or December.
**Life span**: 30 years.
**Status**: Lower risk.

**Northern elephant seal** (*Mirounga angustirostris*): 3–5m (9.75–16.5ft); 0.6–2.3 tonnes (1,320–5,500lb)
Slightly larger than their southern counterparts, these elephant seals range from the Gulf of Alaska to Baja California. Each year a northern elephant seal will swim about 21,000km (13,000 miles). They migrate north in summer to feed in waters exposed by melting ice. The sexes follow different routes: males move to the far north, beyond the Aleutians, while females head further west into the northern Pacific. The seals come on to land to breed in winter, and again in August to moult their summer coat. They prefer sandy and rocky shores. Males are much larger than females, because they need to compete for access to mates.

**Galápagos fur seal** (*Arctocephalus galapagoensis*): 1.3–1.5m (4.25–5ft); 30–70kg (66–155lb)
This vulnerable species is found only around the Galápagos Islands off the coast of Ecuador. Galápagos fur seals stay close to the islands, and never dive below about 30m (100ft). They spend over a quarter of each day on land – more than any other eared seal (fur seal or sea lion). Their diet consists mainly of fish and squid.

**Grey seal** (*Halichoerus grypus*): 1.8–3m (6–10ft); 150–300kg (330–661lb)
Grey seals live along the coast of Canada's maritime provinces, from Labrador to Nova Scotia. They also range from Iceland to the coast of northern Europe, and into the Baltic Sea. Grey seals eat a range of fish, shellfish and crabs.

# Northern fur seal

*Callorhinus ursinus*

This is the only fur seal in the northern hemisphere. Its well-documented migration takes it from the Bering Sea between Alaska and Siberia, where it spends the summer, to its winter destination of the northern Pacific. Populations are spread down the coasts of the Pacific, reaching Japan to the west and the extreme south of California to the east.

Northern fur seals prefer cold water and spend a lot of time far out at sea. Most of their breeding grounds are on islands in the northern Pacific. As with most seal species, the male northern fur seals arrive at the breeding grounds first and occupy a territory on the shore. The largest bulls take the best locations, usually in the middle of the beach. Females arriving to give birth move into the territory of a male. They seem to choose according to the location of the territory and the number of other females it contains, rather than by the bull's size.

*Male northern fur seals are much larger than females, being up to six times heavier and about 50 per cent longer. While the females tend to be grey, the males' fur is red and black.*

**Distribution**: Coasts of northern Pacific Ocean.
**Habitat**: Rocky beaches.
**Food**: Fish and squid.
**Size**: 1.4–2.1m (4.5–7ft); 50–275kg (110–605lb).
**Maturity**: 3–6 years.
**Breeding**: Single pup born in summer.
**Life span**: 25.
**Status**: Vulnerable.

# Southern elephant seal

*Mirounga leonina*

**Distribution**: Islands around Antarctica.
**Habitat**: Beaches, dunes and rocky shores.
**Food**: Squid, fish and crabs.
**Size**: 2.6–4.5m (8.5–14.75ft); 400–4,000kg (880–8,880lb).
**Maturity**: 5 years.
**Breeding**: 1 pup born in early summer.
**Life span**: 25 years.
**Status**: Common.

Elephant seals live in the waters around Antarctica and come ashore on the region's islands. They are seen as far north as South Georgia in the South Atlantic. Elephant seals feed on fish and squid.

Like northern elephant seals, these huge seals gather on flat beaches to breed in spring. The males arrive first to stake out their territories, and may stay on the beaches for the next two months without feeding. Pregnant females arrive at the breeding ground a few weeks later. A male will try to mate with females as they move up the beach into his territory, even though they have not yet given birth. Mating does occur after the young are born, and during this time a male will battle to keep rivals away from his harem.

However, when males are occupied in fighting, females may move between harems. On a small beach, all the females may be controlled by a single bull, called a beach master.

*Southern elephant seals are the largest animals in the pinniped group, which includes seals, sea lions and walruses. The males, which are up to five times the size of the females, have inflatable, trunk-like noses, with which they amplify their bellowing calls. They do not seem to have any natural predators.*

## Common seal

*Phoca vitulina*

*The common seal's coloration is variable, but it generally consists of a grey or brownish-grey background speckled with darker spots. From a distance, the head of a common seal poking above the waves can closely resemble that of a human. As a result, these seals are sometimes mistaken for swimmers in trouble. This species is also known as the harbour seal, since it is often seen in estuaries and sheltered waters near human habitation.*

The common seal is found along the northern coasts of North America, Europe and Asia, having a very similar range to that of the grey seal. The common seal has a dog-like face, with a more rounded snout than the Roman-style "nose" that typifies the grey seal. It is difficult to make accurate estimates of the size of the common seal population, because this species lives in small, widely distributed groups, and is highly mobile.

Common seals have large, sensitive eyes with specialized retinas, which allow them to see well underwater. However, sometimes the water is too murky for seals to hunt by sight, so they use their long, touch-sensitive whiskers to feel for prey in the gloom. Young seals eat shrimps and bottom-dwelling crustaceans. Older individuals take herring, salmon, anchovies, cod and other fish, as well as octopus. They can dive for up to 10 minutes but average dives last for three minutes.

**Distribution**: Temperate, subarctic and Arctic coastal areas of the North Atlantic and North Pacific oceans.
**Habitat**: Sheltered coastal waters.
**Food**: Fish, cephalopods and crustaceans.
**Size**: 1.2–2m (4–6.5ft); 45–130kg (99–287lb).
**Maturity**: Females 2 years; males 5 years.
**Breeding**: Single pup produced every year.
**Life span**: 26–32 years.
**Status**: Common.

## Leopard seal

*Hydrurga leptonyx*

These predatory seals live all around the Antarctic, where they rest on the pack ice that covers the ocean in winter. Leopard seals are also found on most subantarctic islands, and occasionally further north in the warmer (but still very cold) waters around Tierra del Fuego, Cape Horn and the coast of southern Argentina.

Leopard seals feed on krill, which they filter from the water using their large cheek teeth, and cephalopods. They are also one of the few seal species in which warm-blooded animals make up a significant part of the diet. Penguins and other seals, including crabeaters and fur seals, are actively hunted, and many crabeaters and fur seals carry scars from attacks by leopard seals. Adult penguins are caught in the water, but penguin chicks are snatched on the ice. This species has been known to scavenge the carrion of whales and other seals.

Unlike most other seals, which propel themselves through the water with side-to-side strokes of the hind limbs, leopard seals swim by paddling with their large foreflippers. Apart from during the breeding season, these seals are primarily solitary, although they are seldom far from others of their own species. Leopard seals sometimes congregate in loose groups according to age and maturity. Breeding occurs in summer, apparently in the water, shortly after the birth of that year's pups. The young are born on the shores of the many small islands that surround Antarctica, and also at certain places on the coasts of southern South America and southern Africa. Leopard seal pups are weaned at about four weeks of age. The males take no part in the care of the young.

**Distribution**: Coast of Antarctica.
**Habitat**: Ice and land.
**Food**: Krill and some other seals and penguins.
**Size**: 2.4–3.4m (8–11.25ft); 200–590kg (440–1,300lb).
**Maturity**: 4 years.
**Breeding**: Single pup born in summer.
**Life span**: 25 years.
**Status**: Lower risk.

*Leopard seals have large, sleek bodies, almost reptile-like heads and long canine teeth. Males are generally smaller than females. The coloration is dark grey to near-black on the back, pale on the sides and silver below, with variable amounts of grey spotting.*

# Crabeater seal

*Lobodon carcinophagus*

**Distribution**: Antarctica and surrounding landmasses.
**Habitat**: Pack ice.
**Food**: Krill.
**Size**: 2–2.4m (6.5–8ft); 200–300kg (440–660lb).
**Maturity**: 4 years.
**Breeding**: Single pup born in spring.
**Life span**: 25 years.
**Status**: Common.

Despite its name, the this seal never eats crabs, preferring krill instead. It feeds by swimming open-mouthed through a school of krill, sucking in the small animals from a distance of about 1m (3.25ft). Crabeater seals also eat small fish, which they swallow whole. These seals are capable of diving up to 430m (1,400ft), but the majority of dives are in the first 30m (100ft) or so of water, where they obtain most of their food.

Crabeaters are generally solitary creatures, but sometimes gather in large herds of more than 1,000 individuals. They congregate mainly on the pack ice around Antarctica, although some crabeater herds can be seen on the shores of the extreme tip of South America and other landmasses close to the Southern Ocean.

Pregnant females give birth on the ice in spring. Mating occurs after the pups are weaned at four weeks old.

*The fur of the crabeater seal changes from dark brown to blonde during the course of the year. The winter coat is dark when it grows in autumn, but becomes paler from then on. The pale fur gives the species its alternative common name – the white Antarctic seal.*

---

**Ribbon seal** (*Phoca fasciata*): 1.6m (5.25ft); 70–95kg (155–209lb)
The ribbon seal is found off the coasts of the northern Pacific. The largest populations occur in the Bering Sea, between Alaska and Siberia. Ribbon seals rarely come to land. They raise their pups on the ice floes that extend southward in winter. In summer, they feed voraciously to prepare for the next winter on the ice. This species gets its name from its four ribbon-like stripes. One encircles the neck, another wraps around the body, and the remaining two ring the foreflippers.

**Ringed seal** (*Phoca hispida*): 1.4–1.5m (4.5–5ft); 65–95kg (143–210lb)
Ringed seals are the most common seal inside the Arctic Circle. They spend the winter on and under the thick ice floes that form on the Arctic Ocean. When under the floes, they breathe via air holes that they maintain in the ice. During the long, sunless Arctic winter, ringed seals hunt in the darkness for Arctic cod, using their sensitive whiskers to detect currents caused by these slow-moving fish. In spring, the seals gather in groups on the ice. Females give birth to pups in April, and mating takes place about a month later.

**Weddell seal** (*Leptonychotes weddelli*): 2.5–3.3m (8.25–10.75ft); 400–450kg (880–990lb)
This species lives around Antarctica. It is named after the Weddell Sea, a large bay in the Atlantic coast of Antarctica. Weddell seals are most often found occupying ice floes. They feed at night, hunting for squid and fish, and will even attack prey as large as the Antarctic toothfish, which grows to about 50kg (110lb).

# Harp seal

*Phoca groenlandica*

Harp seals are extremely social animals, congregating in huge numbers to give birth on ice floes in areas along the Arctic coastline.

Their sociability has led ultimately to their decline. The pups have soft, thick fur that is much sought after in some parts of the world. When the pups are gathered in large numbers, they make easy targets for hunters, who club them to death. Extensive hunting by humans reduced the total harp seal population from around 10 million individuals to 2 million by the early 1980s. Once their plight was understood, hunting pressure was reduced and the population is now gradually recovering. It will take a long time for harp seal numbers to reach their previous levels, because this species has a low rate of reproduction. Producing just one pup a year means that the population grows very slowly.

When feeding, adult harp seals may dive to depths of 200m (655ft) in search of herring and cod, which make up the bulk of this species' diet.

**Distribution**: Arctic Ocean.
**Habitat**: Open sea for most of the year.
**Food**: Crustaceans and fish.
**Size**: 1.7–1.9m (5.5–6.25ft); 120–130kg (265–287lb).
**Maturity**: 5 years.
**Breeding**: 1 pup born every year.
**Life span**: 16–30 years.
**Status**: Vulnerable.

*The luxuriant fur of harp seal pups keeps them warm as they grow up on the Arctic icepack. The pups are weaned after 10–12 days and abandoned by their mothers.*

# DOLPHINS AND PORPOISES

*Dolphins are small members of the mammal order* Cetacea, *which also includes the whales. Most dolphins live in the ocean, but a few species are found in the fresh water of large river systems. Porpoises are similar to dolphins, but tend to be smaller and have rounded snouts, rather than long beaks like dolphins. All but one species of porpoise inhabit shallow coastal waters, rather than the open ocean.*

## Amazon river dolphin

*Inia geoffrensis*

**Distribution**: Amazon and Orinoco River Basins.
**Habitat**: Dark, slow-moving river water.
**Food**: Small fish.
**Size**: 1.7–3m (5.5–9.75ft); 60–120kg (132–265lb).
**Maturity**: Unknown.
**Breeding**: Single calf born between April and September.
**Life span**: 30 years.
**Status**: Vulnerable.

Amazon river dolphins live in the wide rivers of the Amazon Basin. During the rainy season, they move into flooded areas of forest and up swollen streams into lakes. They may become isolated in pools when waters recede, but most are able to survive by eating the river fish that are trapped with them.

Dolphins live in small groups. They are thought to defend the areas around them and will stay in an area as long as there is enough food. They breathe at least once a minute, through the nostrils on the top of their head. They dive down to the bottom of rivers to search for food, using their bristled snout to root through mud and weeds.

Like other dolphins, Amazon river dolphins may use echolocation to find their way in the murky river waters. They sometimes feed in the same areas as giant otters. It may be that the hunting behaviour of otters drives fish out of the shallows towards the dolphins.

*When young, Amazon river dolphins have metallic blue and grey upper bodies with silvery bellies. As they age, the dolphins' upper bodies gradually turn pinkish. Their long snouts are covered with sensitive bristles.*

## Vaquita

*Phocoena sinus*

*Most vaquitas have dark grey or black upper bodies, with paler undersides. Like other porpoises, the vaquita has a blunt face. Its triangular dorsal fin is reminiscent of a shark's. Vaquitas live in pods of up to five animals.*

Vaquitas live in the upper area of the Gulf of California, near the mouth of the Colorado River. No other marine mammal has such a small range, and consequently vaquitas are extremely rare and may become extinct.

Vaquitas used to be able to swim up into the mouth of the Colorado. However, in recent years so much water has been removed from the river for irrigation and for supplying cities that the Colorado is little more than a trickle where it reaches the ocean. This has probably changed the composition of the Gulf waters, too. The vaquita population was also affected by the fishing industry in the Gulf. Fishermen drowned many vaquitas in their nets by accident, and their activities have also reduced the amount of fish available for the porpoises to eat.

Biologists know little about the lives of these porpoises. Vaquitas probably spend most of their time alone, locating their prey close to the sea floor using echolocation. Births probably take place all year round.

**Distribution**: Gulf of California in the eastern Pacific.
**Habitat**: Coastal waters and mouth of the Colorado River.
**Food**: Fish and squid.
**Size**: 1.2–2m (4–6.5ft); 45–60kg (99–132lb).
**Maturity**: Unknown.
**Breeding**: Probably 1 calf.
**Life span**: Unknown.
**Status**: Critically endangered.

# Risso's dolphin

*Grampus griseus*

Risso's dolphins live in small groups, called pods or schools, containing about ten individuals. The pods move to warm tropical waters in winter, and head toward the poles in summer. The dolphins are often seen leaping out of the water as the pod members play with one another.

Risso's dolphins feed in deep water. They dive down to catch fast-swimming squid and fish. Like other dolphins, they probably use echolocation to locate their prey in the dark depths. They produce clicking noises that bounce off objects in the water. The dolphins can hear each other's clicks and echoes, and groups may work together to track down shoals of fish or squid. In areas where there is plenty of food, dolphin pods congregate so that thousands of the leaping mammals may be seen together.

**Distribution**: All tropical and temperate seas.
**Habitat**: Deep ocean water.
**Food**: Fish and squid.
**Size**: 3.6–4m (11.75–13ft); 400–450kg (880–990lb).
**Maturity**: Unknown.
**Breeding**: Single young born once per year.
**Life span**: 30 years.
**Status**: Common.

*Risso's dolphins have very blunt faces, lacking the beaks of typical dolphins. They have dark grey bodies, which are often scarred by attacks from other dolphins and large squid. Older dolphins may have so many scars that their bodies look almost white.*

---

### Short-beaked saddleback dolphin

(*Delphinus delphis*): 1.5–2.4m (5–8ft); 70–110kg (154–242lb)
Often called the common dolphin, this species is one of the smallest dolphins. It is common in European waters, but it also swims in coastal areas of the Atlantic and Pacific oceans, including along the shores of the Americas, where it is most often seen in the Gulf of Mexico. Common dolphins prefer to swim in warmer water near the surface. They have many small, curved teeth, with which they snatch herrings and other small, slippery fish. Common dolphins live in small family groups, or pods. Sometimes many pods join together to form vast clans up to 100,000 strong. Most of the time these dolphins swim at about 8kmh (5mph), but their top speed is around 46kmh (29mph).

### Commerson's dolphin

(*Cephalorhynchus commersoni*): 1.4m (4.5ft); 50–85kg (110–187lb)
There are two populations of this dolphin, one in the Indian Ocean, and a larger population along South America's Atlantic coast, from the Straits of Magellan to Rio Negro province in central Argentina. Commerson's dolphins generally live in small pods of about three individuals. Pods may herd together to form temporary assemblies of over 100 dolphins, probably for breeding or feeding purposes. This species eats shrimp, fish, squid and invertebrates that live on the seabed.

# Spectacled porpoise

*Australophocaena dioptrica*

Spectacled porpoises are rarely seen because they spend most of their time far from land. Most often they are spotted when they stray into coastal waters, especially along the Atlantic coast of South America, from Uruguay to Cape Horn and the Falkland Islands. These porpoises are also seen around New Zealand in the south Pacific, and around the Kerguelen Islands in the far south of the Indian Ocean.

Spectacled porpoises dive down into deep water to catch large fish and squid. They tend to feed in cold-water areas, such as in the currents that travel up from the Antarctic. Like most porpoises, they have fewer teeth than dolphins, but each tooth is large and chisel-shaped. This allows the porpoise to catch larger fish than dolphins. In shallower waters, the spectacled porpoise also eats crabs, lobsters and other crustaceans. It is sometimes preyed on by orcas (killer whales).

Spectacled porpoises are mainly solitary, and do not travel in large groups, although two or three individuals are occasionally seen together.

**Distribution**: South Atlantic, Pacific, and Indian oceans.
**Habitat**: Deep ocean.
**Food**: Fish, squid, and crustaceans.
**Size**: 1.8–2m (6–6.5ft); 55–115kg (121–253lb).
**Maturity**: About 5 years.
**Breeding**: Single young born in spring.
**Life span**: 20 years.
**Status**: Data deficient.

*The back of this porpoise is black, while the underside and most of the face is white, except for the black around the eyes, which makes the animal look as though it is wearing spectacles – hence its name.*

## Franciscana

*Pontoporia blainvillei*

This species of river dolphin is also called the La Plata dolphin, after the Rio de la Plata (River Plate), the wide mouth of several rivers that forms the border between Argentina and Uruguay. As river dolphins, franciscanas can survive perfectly well in the fresh river water, although the tides regularly mix it with salt water. The dolphins do not enter any other rivers, but are found along the Atlantic coast as far north as central Brazil and as far south as the Valdez peninsula in Patagonia, southern Argentina.

Known as "white ghosts" by fisherman, franciscanas feed in murky waters churned up by coastal currents and tides. They have long, slender beaks that curve slightly downward. Without being able to see, they probe the bottom with their snouts, feeding on bottom-dwelling fish. Like all dolphins, franciscanas also orientate themselves using echolocation.

These smooth-swimming dolphins rarely roll or splash, and show little of themselves when they surface. On hot days they have been seen "sunbathing" on the sand in the shallows. If danger threatens, franciscanas will remain motionless near the water's surface.

*Franciscanas belong to the river dolphin family. In general, river dolphins look unlike ocean-dwelling dolphins, having smaller fins, many pointed teeth and very long snouts. However, franciscanas may spend their whole lives out at sea, and as a result they look more like oceanic dolphins (although their snout, in relation to body size, is the longest of any dolphin species). The franciscana's body is greyish on top, which sometimes lightens during winter and with also age – in fact, some older dolphins are predominantly white.*

**Distribution**: Mouth of the River Plate and coast of South America.
**Habitat**: Brackish and salt water.
**Food**: Fish.
**Size**: 1.3–1.75m (4.25–5.75ft); 20–61kg (44–134lb).
**Maturity**: 3 years.
**Breeding**: Single young born every two years.
**Life span**: 16 years.
**Status**: Data deficient.

## Tucuxi

*Sotalia fluviatilis*

While franciscanas are river dolphins that are at home in sea water, tucuxis are the opposite – oceanic dolphins that have evolved to live in fresh water as well as in the ocean. Some tucuxis never swim in the sea. They live thousands of miles from the ocean in the headwaters of the Amazon River that flow down the foothills of the Andes in Peru and Colombia. Conversely, some tucuxis spend their whole lives at sea, ranging from the Caribbean coast of Mexico to Argentinian waters. Research suggests that this dolphin exists in two subspecies. Marine tucuxis are larger than riverine tucuxis. They also have a more bluish coloration, to help them blend in with the deep, clear waters of coastal regions.

Tucuxis feed mainly on fish and shrimps. They usually hunt in small groups of two to seven dolphins, although larger groups of up to 20 in fresh water and 50 in the ocean are sometimes seen. The dolphins swim and breathe in synchrony so that they can all attack at the same time when they spot a shoal of fish or other supply of food. Tucuxis sometimes swim upside-down to trap fish against the surface of the water. In fact, individuals often have bare patches on their dorsal fin, where it has been scraped on the river bottom or seabed while swimming inverted.

Tucuxis are energetic swimmers and often leap out of the water, but they are quite timid and tend to keep away from boats.

**Distribution**: Amazon River system, and Atlantic coastline of Central and South America.
**Habitat**: Fresh and salt water.
**Food**: Fish.
**Size**: 1.4–1.9m (4.5–6.25ft); 40–53kg (88–117lb).
**Maturity**: 3 years.
**Breeding**: Single young born in summer every two years.
**Life span**: Unknown.
**Status**: Data deficient.

*Tucuxis are also known as grey dolphins, although their underside is a pale pink. They are small dolphins, especially those that live in the headwaters of rivers. The forehead (melon) is quite rounded, and the longish beak contains 140 teeth.*

# White-beaked dolphin

*Lagenorhynchus albirostris*

**Distribution**: Ranges widely throughout the North Atlantic and Arctic Oceans.
**Habitat**: Coastal waters.
**Food**: Medium-sized fish, squid and crustaceans form the bulk of the diet.
**Size**: 2.3–2.8m (7.5–9.25ft); 180–200kg (397–441lb).
**Maturity**: Unknown.
**Breeding**: 1 calf born every year.
**Life span**: Unknown.
**Status**: Common.

Dolphins are notoriously difficult animals to study because they are very wide-ranging. Consequently, little is known about the habits of this remarkable group compared to most land-living mammals. Like most cetaceans, white-beaked dolphins live in groups known as pods, or schools, which have very complex social structures. Pods are usually made up of 2–20 individuals, but occasionally many pods will come together to form large aggregations containing in excess of 1,000 individuals.

White-beaked dolphins are famed for a behaviour known as breaching, when they leap clear of the water, somersault and splash back down through the waves. They frequently swim alongside small boats and have also been observed playing games underwater, such as chasing seaweed. White-beaked dolphins undertake annual migrations, moving between temperate and subpolar waters as they track and feed on their favoured prey of mackerel and herring.

*The white-beaked dolphin's counter-shaded coloration, with a darker upper side and pale belly, helps to camouflage it from both above and below.*

---

**Black dolphin** (*Cephalorhynchus eutropia*): 1.6m (5.25ft); 50kg (110lb)
This small dolphin lives off the coast of Chile. Mineral-rich currents from Antarctica make the continental shelf here a fertile feeding ground for black dolphins, which feed on fish and sea-floor animals. To help them get at their prey, the dolphins have a relatively flat snout, more like that of a porpoise than the beak-like snout of other dolphins. Black dolphins live in small schools and communicate with clicks. Similar noises are used to locate prey by echolocation.

**Hourglass dolphin** (*Lagenorhynchus cruciger*): 1.6m (5.25ft); 83–100kg (183–220lb)
Hourglass dolphins are found in the colder waters of the southern hemisphere. These shy animals live in small groups and travel huge distances in their lifetime. In general, hourglass dolphins keep to the waters around Antarctica, but they occasionally follow cold-water currents moving north, such as the Humboldt Current that flows along the coast of Chile.

**Short-finned pilot whale** (*Globicephala macrorhynchus*): 6m (19.75ft); 2.1 tonnes (4,630lb)
Sometimes classed as a separate group of toothed whales, pilot whales (and the closely related orcas) are more usually grouped with the dolphins. This species lives in all tropical waters and is often seen in certain bays and other coastal waters that are used as breeding grounds. The name pilot whale refers to the way that pods of these animals – which number up to 20 whales – follow a single individual, or pilot.

---

# Atlantic white-sided dolphin

*Lagenorhynchus acutus*

Atlantic white-sided dolphins are seldom found near shore. They prefer to swim far out to sea in the clear water on the edge of the continental shelf, where the sea floor plunges to the great depths of the mid-ocean. They can dive to about 270m (900ft), and usually hunt at about 40m (130ft) below the surface. These fast, acrobatic swimmers come to the surface for breath every 15–20 seconds.

These dolphins prefer shoaling prey such as herrings, shrimps and even certain squid. They plunge into the shoal, snapping up food with their long snout as they pass through. Like many oceanic dolphins, this species is social, living in small family groups of about six individuals. Although Atlantic white-sided dolphins are rare, they are also reported to mass together far out to sea in clans more than 1,000 strong. Atlantic white-sided dolphins are nomadic – that is, they follow no distinct seasonal migration routes, but simply move throughout their range in search of food.

**Distribution**: Southern Greenland to Massachusetts.
**Habitat**: Cold, open water.
**Food**: Shrimp and small fish.
**Size**: 3m (9.75ft); 180–250kg (397–550lb).
**Maturity**: 12 years.
**Breeding**: 1 calf born every 2–3 years.
**Life span**: 40 years.
**Status**: Common.

*Female Atlantic white-sided dolphins are considerably smaller than the males of the species. These dolphins have a dark grey or black back, pale flanks and a white or cream underside.*

## Bottlenosed dolphin

*Tursiops truncatus*

This is one of the most common and familiar dolphin species. It is found worldwide but often appears along the Atlantic coast of North America, from Cape Hatteras in North Carolina to Argentina, and along the Pacific up to northern California.

Bottlenosed dolphins live in shallow water close to land, and they are generally spotted breaching in large bays. They often enter lagoons and the mouths of large rivers. They do not appear to migrate, but rather make a lifelong journey that may take them to all parts of the world. Since they prefer warmer waters, they tend to move between the Atlantic and Pacific oceans via the Indian ocean.

Bottlenosed dolphins travel at about 20kmh (12mph) and are rarely seen travelling alone. They hunt as a team, corralling shoals of fish and shrimps by circling around them and taking turns to dive through the shoal to snatch mouthfuls of food. These dolphins are known to herd fish on to mudflats and then slide up the shore to seize their prey. Bottlenosed dolphins will also follow shrimp boats to feed off the discarded scraps. Individuals consume around 7kg (15.4lb) per day.

*The bottlenosed is the largest of the beaked dolphins, which are oceanic dolphins with short, stout snouts. Males are much larger than females. This species shows a high degree of intelligence.*

**Distribution**: Tropical and temperate coastal waters worldwide; both Pacific and Atlantic coasts of the Americas, and around Hawaii.
**Habitat**: Warm shallow water and cooler, deeper waters.
**Food**: Fish, squid, shrimp and eels.
**Size**: 1.75–4m (5.7–13ft); 150–400kg (330–880lb).
**Maturity**: 5–12 years.
**Breeding**: Breeding times vary with location. Single calf born every 2–3 years; gestation is about 12 months.
**Life span**: 40 years.
**Status**: Unknown.

## Pacific white-sided dolphin

*Lagenorhynchus obliquidens*

The Pacific white-sided dolphin is found mainly in deep coastal waters, rarely straying more than 160 km (100 miles) from land. It ranges around the northern Pacific Rim, where a narrow continental shelf and steep continental slope create the deep water conditions preferred by this species. The Pacific white-sided dolphin is found from the waters around Hokkaido, the northern island of Japan, and along the Kuril and Aleutian islands to Alaska. It also occurs along the North American west coast as far south as Baja California, Mexico. This friendly, inquisitive species will ride the bow and stern waves of boats, and investigate motionless vessels.

Pacific white-sided dolphins live in small family groups, or pods, of 10–20 individuals. A pod contains a single dominant male who mates with the mature females in the pod. Other males in the pod are unlikely to mate. Several pods often group together, and dolphins probably move between pods during these congregations. Pod members hunt for fish together, with each adult consuming about 9kg (20lb) of fish per day. In British Columbia, pods have been observed seeking out and harassing orcas that feed on local fish shoals.

*These large dolphins have a torpedo-shaped body that allows them to cut through water easily. The body has distinct counter-shading, with black on the upper surface and white below. When swimming with their dorsal fin breaking the water's surface, they look like sharks.*

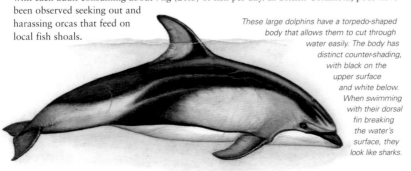

**Distribution**: Continental waters of northern Pacific Ocean; in North America, from the Aleutians Islands and Alaska south to Baja California, Mexico.
**Habitat**: Deep offshore water.
**Food**: Fish, squid and octopus.
**Size**: 1.5–3.1m (5–10ft); 82–124kg (181–273lb).
**Maturity**: 6–8 years.
**Breeding**: Single young born in late summer; gestation is 10–12 months.
**Life span**: 35 years.
**Status**: Common.

# Atlantic spotted dolphin

*Stenella frontalis*

The Atlantic spotted dolphin is found all around the warmer parts of the Atlantic Ocean. Along the North American coast, the species occurs in the waters off Florida and in the Gulf of Mexico. The dolphin rarely moves more than 350km (220 miles) from the coast, and it spends most of its time in shallow water over sand banks, including those in the Bahamas.

Spotted dolphins are very social animals. They live in pods that range in size from just a few individuals to groups of several thousand that mass far out to sea. Within large pods, dolphins of different sexes and stages of maturity are often segregated. The dolphins communicate using high-pitched whistles, clicks, cackles and cries, which are within the range of human hearing. Each individual dolphin has its own unique identifying call.

*Adults of this species have a spotted pattern. These spots are not present at birth, but appear after weaning. The number of spots increases with age.*

Spotted dolphins feed on eels, herrings and other small fish. They often track shoals of prey, swimming above them just below the surface before diving down to attack as a group.

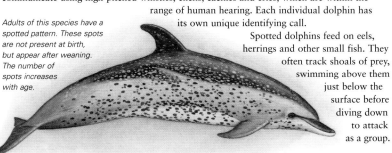

**Distribution**: Warm Atlantic waters.
**Habitat**: Shallow water above continental shelf.
**Food**: Fish.
**Size**: 1.6–2.3m (5.25–7.5ft); 90–110kg (198–242lb).
**Maturity**: 9 years.
**Breeding**: 1 calf born in summer every 2–3 years.
**Life span**: 35 years.
**Status**: Lower risk.

---

**Southern right whale dolphin** (*Lissodelphis peronii*): 1.8–2.3m (6–7.5ft); 60kg (132lb)
This species lives in the southern hemisphere. It is found around the edge of the Southern Ocean surrounding Antarctica. It also swims further north along the cold-water currents that flow from the polar region. The northern limit of the dolphin's range is in the subtropical zones where these cold currents meet warmer water heading south – for example, off the coasts of Chile and Peru, along which the Humboldt Current flows. Like the right whale, this dolphin species is largely black, with white patches on the belly and under the mouth, and it lacks a dorsal fin. The southern right whale dolphin also has a very slender body – unlike its giant namesake, which is known for its enormous girth.

**Striped dolphin** (*Stenella coeruleoalba*): 2.1m (7ft); 90kg (198lb)
Striped dolphins are found in the world's warm seas, including the Caribbean and Gulf of Mexico. They keep to areas where the water temperature is above 20°C (68°F), and they are just as at home in open water as they are in the shallows near the coast. They get their name from the blue stripe that runs along the entire length of the body. There are also black stripes running down to the flippers. Being inshore dolphins, they eat a range of foods, from free-swimming fish to bottom dwelling crabs and octopuses. Striped dolphins are very active swimmers. They also perform an unusual manoeuvre called roto-tailing, in which they leap out of the water in a high arc and spin around their tail.

# Spinner dolphin

*Stenella longirostris*

Spinner dolphins are truly oceanic animals. They roam through all the world's oceans, mainly staying in the warmer regions. They seldom come close to land and are only really seen from ships or around remote islands. Perhaps the best place to see spinner dolphins is from the deck of a fishing ship in the Pacific tuna fisheries off the west coast of South America.

Spinners often track large shoals of yellowfin and skipjack tuna, swimming at the surface several meters above the fish. Tuna fishermen keep an eye out for groups of spinners (and similar dolphins) to lead them to the tuna. As a result, spinner dolphins are often caught and drowned in nets intended for tuna.

Spinners live in pods of about 20 dolphins, but are also reported to gather together in groups of more than 1,000 from time to time. Members of a pod are organized into a dominance hierarchy.

**Distribution**: Tropical waters worldwide.
**Habitat**: Open water.
**Food**: Fish and squid.
**Size**: 1.8–2.1m (6–7ft); 55–75kg (121–165lb).
**Maturity**: 10 years.
**Breeding**: 1 calf born every 2–3 years.
**Life span**: 35 years.
**Status**: Lower risk.

*These dolphins are famous for leaping put of the water and spinning their body round in mid-air. Spinner dolphins that live near to land are slightly different from those that spend their time in deep ocean waters. Biologists have detected at least four subspecies, which have varying coloration and differently shaped dorsal fins.*

# TOOTHED WHALES

*Within the* Cetacea *order (which includes whales, dolphins and porpoises), there are 23 species of toothed whale. These cetaceans are hunting whales, and they include the world's largest predator, the sperm whale. Toothed whales live in family groups called pods. They hunt for food using echolocation – a sonar system that is focused through a fatty mass called the melon, which is located at the front of the head.*

## Sperm whale

*Physeter macrocephalus*

Sperm whales are supremely well adapted to life in the deep oceans. These are the largest hunting predators in the world, with teeth up to 20cm (8in) long and the largest brains of any mammal, weighing over 9kg (20lb). They prefer areas of ocean with cold upwellings at least 1,000m (3,300ft) deep, where squid – their favourite food – are most abundant.

Sperm whales can dive to incredible depths to hunt, occasionally journeying up to 2.5km (1.6 miles) beneath the surface. They are social animals, and they live in groups of between 20 and 40 females, juveniles and young. Sperm whales have been hunted for their oil since the mid-18th century, and after serious population declines between the 1950s and 1980s, this species is now protected.

*The box-like head of the sperm whale contains the spermaceti organ, which is filled with the fine oil so valued by whalers. The purpose of this organ is unclear: it may function as a lens, focusing the sounds that the whale uses to detect its prey, or it may help the whale to control its buoyancy during dives.*

**Distribution**: Ranges throughout oceans and seas worldwide.
**Habitat**: Deep oceans.
**Food**: Mostly squid, including giant deep-sea squid, but also some fish and sharks.
**Size**: 12–20m (40–65ft); 12–70 tonnes (26,500–155,000lb).
**Maturity**: Females 7–13 years; males 25 years.
**Breeding**: 1 calf born every 5–7 years.
**Life span**: 77 years.
**Status**: Vulnerable.

## Narwhal

*Monodon monoceros*

**Distribution**: Parts of the Arctic Ocean near Greenland and the Barents Sea. The range is patchy.
**Habitat**: Coastal Arctic waters.
**Food**: Cuttlefish, fish, crustaceans and squid.
**Size**: 4–5.5m (13–18ft); 800–1,600kg (1,750–3,500lb).
**Maturity**: Females 5–8 years; males 11–13 years.
**Breeding**: Single calf born every 2–3 years.
**Life span**: 50 years.
**Status**: Common.

*The male narwhal's tusk is in fact a greatly elongated front tooth that spirals as it grows from a hole in the whale's lips. Females may possess a short tusk, too. The name narwhal means "corpse whale" in Old Norse, perhaps referring to the deathly hue of their white-blotched, bluish-grey skin.*

Some people believe that the bizarre appearance of the narwhal first gave rise to the legend of the unicorn. The function of the male's long tusk is not fully understood. It may be used as a hunting implement, or as a tool to break up ice and create breathing holes for the whales. However, the most favoured explanation is that the males use their tusks to joust with each other, fighting over access to females during the breeding season.

The narwhal's swollen forehead is known as its melon – a feature shared with dolphins and other toothed whales. The melon serves to focus the ultrasonic clicks that narwhals and other small cetaceans use to navigate and find their food. As in a sophisticated sonar system, the narwhals listen for the high-frequency echoes that rebound off nearby objects. So sensitive is this method of orientation that narwhals can not only distinguish between food and non-food items, but they can also tell the size of an object, how far away it is and how fast it is moving.

# Orca

*Orcinus orca*

*Orcas have black upper bodies and white undersides, with grey patches behind their dorsal fins and white patches above their eyes. They are highly social, travelling and hunting together in pods.*

**Distribution**: Throughout the world's oceans.
**Habitat**: Coastal waters.
**Food**: Seals, dolphins, fish, squid, penguins, crustaceans.
**Size**: 8.5–9.8m (28–32.25ft); 5.5–9 tonnes (12,000–19,800lb).
**Maturity**: Females 6 years; males 12 years.
**Breeding**: Single young born generally in autumn every 3–4 years.
**Life span**: 60–90 years.
**Status**: Lower risk.

Also known as killer whales, orcas are expert hunters, armed with up to 50 large, pointed teeth. Although orcas have been detected 1km (0.6 mile) below the surface, they prefer to hunt in shallow coastal waters.

Orcas typically live in pods of five or six individuals. Generally each pod is run by a large male, although larger groups have several adult males. Females and their young may split off into subgroups. Like other toothed whales and dolphins, orcas produce click sounds that are used for echolocation. The whales also communicate with each other using high-pitched screams and whistles. Orcas have several hunting techniques. They break pack ice from beneath, knocking their prey into the water, or they may rush into shallow water to grab prey from the shore. It is reported that they may crash on to the shore to drive prey into the surf where other members of the pod pick them off. Orcas breed throughout the year, although most mate in the early summer and give birth in the autumn of the following year.

---

**Southern bottlenose whale** (*Hyperoodon planifrons*): 6.5–8m (21–26ft); 6–8 tonnes (13,000–17,500lb)
This species is one of the beaked whales – toothed whales that are like dolphins and pilot whales in many ways, except that they are larger. Bottlenosed whales, as their name suggests, resemble bottlenosed dolphins. Most beaked whales have a bulbous forehead, but bottlenose whales have a flatter head, like oceanic dolphins. However, in common with almost all other beaked whales, this species has only two obvious teeth. These are tusk-like, and in old males they stick out at the front of the mouth. The teeth are used in fights, and older beaked whales bear numerous long scars along their backs caused by bites. The southern bottlenose whale lives in the cold waters of the Southern Hemisphere. It is often found around Cape Horn and the Falkland Islands. This species feeds on squid and fish.

**Pygmy beaked whale** (*Mesoplodon peruvianus*): 3.4 m (11ft); weight unknown
Although a member of the beaked whale family, this cetacean is only a little larger than its dolphin cousins. It is a very rare species and is only found in the warm waters off northern Peru. Pygmy beaked whales are deep-sea hunters that feed on squid and fish. This is one of the latest mammal species to be described. It was only discovered in 1991, and is thought to be the smallest beaked whale. No live member of this species has ever been formally identified, and everything we know about it comes from studying dead specimens.

# Beluga

*Delphinapterus leucas*

Beluga means white in Russian, so these whales are sometimes called white whales. Belugas are also nicknamed sea canaries, because they call to each other with high-pitched trills.

Belugas live in the far north, where daylight is very brief or non-existent much of the year. Some beluga pods, or schools, spend all their time in one area of ocean, such as the Gulf of St Lawrence; others are always on the move. The pods are ruled by large males, and all pods spend their winters away from areas of thick ice. In summer, they enter river estuaries and shallow bays.

Belugas navigate using a well-developed sonar system, which is thought to be controlled by the melon – the large sensory organ on top of the head.

Most calves are born during late summer, and their mothers mate again a year or two later during early summer.

**Distribution**: Arctic to gulfs of Alaska and St Lawrence.
**Habitat**: Deep coastal waters and mouths of large rivers.
**Food**: Fish, squid, octopus, crabs and snails.
**Size**: 3.4–4.6m (11.25–15.25ft); 1.3–1.5 tonnes (2,850–3,300lb).
**Maturity**: Females 5 years; males 8 years.
**Breeding**: Single calf born every 2–3 years.
**Life span**: 25 years.
**Status**: Vulnerable.

*Adult beluga whales are almost completely white, helping them to hide among ice floes. Younger whales begin life with dark bodies, which gradually become yellow and brown before fading to white.*

# OTHER WHALES

*The largest members of the* Cetacea *order are called baleen whales. There are about a dozen species of baleen whale, including humpbacks, right whales and the mighty blue whale. Instead of teeth, these whales have baleen plates – long slats of keratin that form a thick curtain which hangs down from the upper jaw. This keratin curtain sieves krill, plankton and other small food items from sea water.*

## Northern right whale

*Eubalaena glacialis*

These large, slow-swimming whales are often found on the surface, so they were considered just "right" for hunting by whalers – hence the species' common name. The mouth yielded an excellent supply of baleen (whalebone) and the blubber produced a large quantity of oil. The hunting was so relentless that only a few hundred are left in the northern hemisphere.

Each winter, northern right whales migrate from cold northern waters to warmer areas in the south, where the females give birth. In the Atlantic, the whales move from the waters off Nova Scotia and Labrador to Florida. Pacific whales summer in the Bering Sea off Alaska, before heading to wintering grounds on the western coast of Russia.

**Distribution**: Atlantic coastal waters of North America.
**Habitat**: Shallow coastal water.
**Food**: Krill and other zooplankton.
**Size**: 17m (56ft); 55 tonnes (120,000lb).
**Maturity**: 10 years.
**Breeding**: 1 calf born every 3–4 years.
**Life span**: 60 years.
**Status**: Critically endangered.

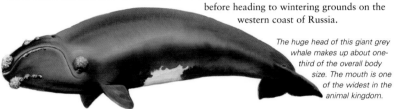

*The huge head of this giant grey whale makes up about one-third of the overall body size. The mouth is one of the widest in the animal kingdom.*

## Humpback whale

*Megaptera novaeangliae*

Humpbacks spend their summers feeding far from shore, in the cold waters near the poles. They feed by taking in huge mouthfuls of sea water. Their baleen plates then strain out any fish or krill from the water. Pairs of humpbacks also corral shoals of fish by blowing curtains of bubbles around them. The fish will not swim through the bubbles, so they crowd together. The whales then rush up from beneath into the mass of fish with their mouths wide open.

As winter approaches, the whales stop feeding and head to warmer, shallow waters near coasts or groups of islands. For example, populations of humpbacks spend the winter near Baja California and the Hawaiian islands. During the winter the whales do not feed; instead they concentrate on reproduction. The males produce songs that they repeat for days on end. The songs probably attract receptive females that are not caring for calves that year, and also help to keep rival males away from each other. Pregnant females stay feeding for longer than the other whales, and arrive in the wintering grounds just in time to give birth.

*Humpback whales are so-called because of the dorsal fin (on the back), which may be swelled into a hump by deposits of fat. Humpbacks have the longest pectoral (arm) fins of any whale species, measuring about one-third of their body length.*

**Distribution**: All oceans.
**Habitat**: Deep ocean water.
**Food**: Small fish and krill.
**Size**: 12.5–15m (41–49.5ft); 30 tonnes (66,000lb).
**Maturity**: 4–5 years.
**Breeding**: Single young born every 2 years.
**Life span**: 70 years.
**Status**: Vulnerable.

# Grey whale

*Eschrichtius robustus*

Grey whales spend their lives
on the move. In autumn
they swim from Arctic
waters down the western
coast of North America,
mating on the way, to spend the winter in bays along
the coast of Mexico. The young that were conceived
during the previous year are born in these bays in late
January and February, and soon after, the whales set off
to spend the summer in the food-rich waters of the Arctic.

A similar migration takes place down the eastern coast of
Asia, but these whales are relatively few in number. Grey whales
spend a good deal of time playing in shallow water during the
winter. They leap out of the water and may become stranded for a
few hours as they wait for the tide to rise. While on the move they
"spyhop", protruding their heads above the surface so that they can look around.

Grey whales are baleen whales that feed on the seabed. They drive their heads
through the sediment to stir up prey. They then suck in the disturbed water and
strain the animals from it. Most feeding takes place in the summer, and whales may
fast for the remaining six months of the year.

**Distribution**: Northern Pacific Rim.
**Habitat**: Shallow coastal water.
**Food**: Amphipods (small crustaceans).
**Size**: 13–15m (43–49.5ft); 20–37 tonnes (44,000–82,000lb).
**Maturity**: Females 17 years; males 19 years.
**Breeding**: Single young born every 2 years.
**Life span**: 70 years.
**Status**: Endangered

*Grey whales do not have dorsal fins, but a series of small humps along their backs. They are often covered in white barnacles.*

**Bowhead whale** (*Balaena mysticetus*): 11–13m (36–42.5ft); 50–60 tonnes (110,000–130,000lb)
Bowhead whales live in the Arctic Ocean. They have huge curved jaws with more baleen plates than any other whale. Adults have black bodies with pale patches on their lower jaws. Bowheads live among ice floes. They feed on tiny floating crustaceans, such as krill and copepods. They can eat 1.8 tonnes (4,000lb) in one day.

**Blue whale** (*Balaenoptera musculus*): 25–30m (82–100ft); 100–160 tonnes (220,000–350,000lb)
The blue whale is the largest animal to have ever existed. It has a blue-grey body, with spots along its back and a pale pleated throat. Blue whales live alone, travelling between subtropical waters and those near the poles. The populations of the northern and southern hemispheres never meet. They eat krill – tiny floating crustaceans – and can gulp down 6 tonnes (13,000lb) of them in a single day. Their pleated throats distend to four times their normal size as the whales take in mouthfuls of krill-laden water.

# West Indian manatee

*Trichechus manatus*

Despite their appearance, manatees are not cetaceans.
Neither are they related to seals (pinnipeds). These
marine mammals belong to the *Sirenia* order, as do
the dugongs – similar animals from South-east Asia.
Sirenians evolved to live in water separately from whales
and seals. In fact, they are believed to be more closely
related to elephants than other sea mammals. Like
elephants, they are vegetarian, not carnivorous.

Manatees live in both salt and fresh water, although
they spend more time in fresh-water habitats. They rarely
stray far from land, and may travel considerable distances
up rivers to sources of warm water during winter.

Manatees feed both during the day and at night.
They use their dextrous lips to pluck leaves from water
hyacinths, sea grasses
and other aquatic
plants. Although
they do not actively
seek them out, the
manatees also eat
the invertebrates,
such as water snails
and insect larvae,
that live on these
plants. The single
young is born
after about a
year's gestation.

**Distribution**: Coast of Florida to Brazil.
**Habitat**: Estuaries and shallow coastal water.
**Food**: Water plants and aquatic invertebrates.
**Size**: 2.5–4.5m (8.25–14.75ft); 500kg (1,100lb).
**Maturity**: 8–10 years.
**Breeding**: Single young born every 2–3 years.
**Life span**: 30 years.
**Status**: Vulnerable.

*Manatees have wrinkled grey-brown skin with a sparse covering of fine hairs. Their fore-flippers have nails on their upper surfaces, while their upper lips, which are very manoeuvrable, have moustaches of thick bristles.*

# ANIMALS OF EUROPE AND AFRICA

Europe and Africa are separated by the Mediterranean Sea, and
although the divide is only a few short miles in some places, the two
continents are very different, both in terms of climate and their animal
life. Europe is not actually a continent at all; it is a large peninsula
stretching from the Ural Mountains to the Atlantic Ocean on the western
side of the huge Asian landmass. Africa also used to be joined to Asia.
It is now cut off entirely by the man-made Suez Canal, but many animals
found in Africa also live in parts of Asia. Europe's wildlife might seem
ordinary compared to many other parts of the world; many of the
animals that once roamed free there, such as lions and bears, are now
extinct or at least very rare. Africa, on the other hand, is well known for
its wildlife. It is home to the largest land animal of all, the African elephant,
as well as the great apes and many other diverse species.

*Above from left: Fire salamanders, mandrill, lion.*

# SALAMANDERS AND RELATIVES

*Of the living amphibians, salamanders and newts are the most similar to ancestral amphibians, known from fossils. Salamanders typically have rougher skin than newts and are better able to survive out of water because they have glands to keep their skins moist. They are also frequently brightly coloured and armed with toxins to repel predators.*

## Olm

*Proteus anguinus*

*Olms have elongated bodies, pinkish skin, external gills and tiny eyes that can only perceive light and shadow. Olms were once more common, but numbers have dropped because of water pollution.*

The olm is the world's largest cave-dwelling vertebrate. It lives in the dark, in bodies of cold, underground water. The olm has dull white, sometimes pinkish skin and three tufted, bright red gills on each side of its neck. Its tail is long and eel-like. The olm's gills are filled with blood, allowing the animal to breathe underwater. Oxygen in the water is transferred to the blood via the surface of the gills. The olm's eyes are reduced to tiny black dots under the skin, leaving it virtually blind. Newly born young can see better than the adults, but their eyes degenerate after a year. The olm has a powerful sense of smell. It can also find food and communicate by detecting weak electric signals emitted by fish and other olms. Olms have tiny legs for the size of their bodies, with only three stumpy toes on their front legs and two on their back legs. Their snouts are broad and help them to burrow into mud to find shellfish.

**Distribution**: Slovenia through to Bosnia-Herzegovina.
**Habitat**: Underground lakes and streams.
**Food**: Freshwater crustaceans.
**Size**: 25–30cm (10–12in).
**Maturity**: Very little information. Thought to be 16–18 years.
**Breeding**: Females normally give birth to 2 larvae. If the water is warm enough up to 80 eggs may be laid instead.
**Life span**: 100 years.
**Status**: Rare.

## Fire salamander

*Salamandra salamandra*

Fire salamanders have poison glands in their skins that are surrounded by special muscles. These are particularly concentrated on their backs. When the muscles contract, they squeeze toxins from the glands. The salamanders can squirt their poison up to 2m (6.5ft). The poison irritates the skin and may affect the nervous systems of any animals that it touches. It can even kill certain predators by paralyzing their lungs, thus stopping them from breathing.

Females are able to store sperm from males for up to two years. They carry 10–40 live young around in their bodies. These are born with their legs well developed, but they still possess larval gills. Some females have been found carrying only four or five young, but these were born fully developed, without gills. By having fewer young, a female is able to provide her offspring with more food. Being so far developed means the young can continue to grow and survive on land, where it is relatively safe.

*The fire salamander has a bright yellow and black pattern that warns all would-be predators that it carries toxins. The underside is dark grey with fewer markings. When adult, females are larger than males.*

**Distribution**: Central and southern Europe, Middle East and north-west Africa.
**Habitat**: Forested, hilly or mountainous country, not far from water.
**Food**: Invertebrates such as slugs, worms, flies, beetles and centipedes.
**Size**: 14–17cm (5.5–6.75in).
**Maturity**: Change into adults 2 or 3 months after birth.
**Breeding**: 10–40 young develop inside female and born after 8 months.
**Life span**: 20 years.
**Status**: Common.

## Alpine salamander

*Salamandra atra*

**Distribution**: Switzerland, Austria, southern Germany, northern Italy, Slovenia and Croatia; separate population in southern Bosnia and northern Albania.
**Habitat**: Mountain woodlands and meadows.
**Food**: Invertebrates.
**Size**: 15cm (6in).
**Maturity**: 2–3 years.
**Breeding**: 2–4 young born live.
**Life span**: 10 years.
**Status**: Common.

The alpine salamander lives in the mountains and meadows of the southern Alps and neighbouring mountain ranges in the southern Balkans. Although it shares a geographical range with the fire salamander, the two species rarely meet. The fire salamander is found at low altitudes, while this species is rarely found below an altitude of about 800m (2,620ft).

Within its range, the salamander can be seen in large numbers. The species is most active at night. It hides by day under stones and logs but may emerge into shady places during daylight hours. Direct sunlight would dry its skin. Alpine salamanders hibernate to avoid colder winter weather. Those that live at high altitudes may stay dormant for eight months.

Alpine salamanders do not lay eggs. Instead the eggs develop inside the female's body and the young hatch while still inside. Once out of the egg, the young eat the wall of their mother's egg chamber. They grow to a third of adult size before being born. In most cases two young are born in each litter.

*Most alpine salamanders are totally black, though the populations that live in northern Italy have a varying amount of pale yellow on their heads, backs and tails. This colour may show as several spots or as a solid band.*

**Corsican fire salamander** (*Salamandra corsica*): 20cm (8in)
This species is similar to the fire salamander found on the European mainland. Like its more common neighbour, it has yellow or orange patches on a black background. However, the Corsican species is plumper and has smaller parotid glands (the lumps behind the eyes). The Corsican fire salamanders live in most habitats and are most common on the slopes of the island's mountains. These mountains are clothed in beech and chestnut woodlands. Females do not lay eggs. During wet periods, the female will give birth to larvae (gilled swimming forms) into shallow pools of stagnant water, where their development continues. During dry periods when there is no standing water, the young will metamorphose inside their mothers into the land-living adult body form before being born.

**Lanza's alpine salamander** (*Salamandra lanzai*): 17cm (6.75in)
This species is a large version of the alpine salamander. However, the adults have a considerably flatter head. It lives at higher altitudes on two mountain ranges, one in western Switzerland and the other in the southern French Alps. It occupies alpine meadows and rock fields, where it searches out slow-moving invertebrates to eat. The flat head enables the salamander to search the rocky crevices that are common in its habitat. It is most active in rainy conditions and emerges into the open by both day and night. At these times it can be seen standing in the open. During dry periods the salamander hides under rocks.

## Luschan's salamander

*Mertensiella luschani*

The Luschan's salamander is the only species of tailed amphibian to live in the south of the Aegean. Its main range is three small islands between Crete and Rhodes, but there are reports of it living on the Turkish coast.

The salamander is most active at night. It may be seen during daylight hours when the weather is wet, but on dry days it lies in shaded nooks, such as under flat stones. Luschan's salamander becomes dormant during the hot summer, when it lies in crevices.

If threatened, Luschan's salamanders rear up on their hind legs and squeak. If attacked, the salamander may drop its tail to buy time for it to escape. The tail quickly re-grows.

The male's spur is used in mating. The male wriggles underneath the female and tickles her cloaca (rear opening) with his spur to stimulate her into mating. The male drops a large sac of sperm, which the female picks up with her cloaca. The eggs hatch inside the mother, and develop for several months before two 7cm (2.75in) young are born fully formed.

**Distribution**: Islands of southern Aegean Sea.
**Habitat**: Dry woodlands and rocky fields.
**Food**: Invertebrates.
**Size**: 14cm (5.5in).
**Maturity**: 2 years.
**Breeding**: 2 young born live.
**Life span**: About 6 years.
**Status**: Common.

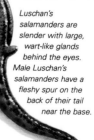

*Luschan's salamanders are slender with large, wart-like glands behind the eyes. Male Luschan's salamanders have a fleshy spur on the back of their tail near the base.*

## Spectacled salamander

*Salamandrina terdigitata*

The spectacled salamander is the only European salamander to have four toes on all four feet. Most others have four on their front feet and five on their back feet. It is found in the mountains of central and southern Italy and has a very particular habitat, living on north-facing slopes in mixed forests that have a thick covering of shrubs. It is often found near to fast-flowing rocky streams.

The spectacled salamander is nocturnal and is most active during spring and autumn. In these warmer periods the salamanders may be seen in the early morning and at dusk. The salamander becomes dormant during extremes of weather. It finds its way deep underground in winter to avoid any frosts that penetrate the upper layers of soil and leaf litter. When it is attacked, the salamander pretends to be dead by rolling on to its back and exposing its bright red underside. Predators are suspicious of dead animals and this is compounded by the startling red colouring.

The females stores sperm from the males, enabling them to produce young as soon as spring arrives, giving them the best chance of survival. They find mates when there is more time later in the year. Mating takes place on land. The male follows the female in a circle as both of them wave their tails in the air.

*Spectacled salamanders have prominent eyes with an orange patch on the top of the head between them. The upper body is black with a ridge running down the spine, while the undersides of the legs and tail are red.*

**Distribution**: Italy.
**Habitat**: North-facing mountain woodlands and forests with clear streams and rocky beds. More common in the west than east.
**Food**: Ground-living invertebrates.
**Size**: 9–11.5cm (3.5–4.5in).
**Maturity**: Able to breed at a length of 7cm (2.75in).
**Breeding**: 30–60 eggs laid in slow-moving water.
**Life span**: 10 years.
**Status**: Common.

## Golden-striped salamander

*Chioglossa lusticanica*

The golden-striped salamander lives in mountainous regions that receive more than 100cm (39.5in) of rain each year. This rain supports thick forests of pine and broad-leaved trees. In the south of its range in central Portugal it reaches altitudes of 1,300m (4,270ft). Mostly it lives lower down, especially in northern and colder areas. The salamander occupies low-growing undergrowth such as moss and is seldom found far from clear rocky streams. It sometimes lives in caves.

In the right conditions, the salamanders occur in large numbers, with a 10m (33ft) stretch of water hosting more than 40 individuals. Golden-striped salamanders are fast-moving and can travel half a mile in one night. This species of salamander is nocturnal. It aestivates (becomes dormant in summer) to avoid the dry conditions. Mating takes place on rocky stream beds. Females lay about 20 eggs in shallow water attached to stones and roots; these hatch after about eight weeks. The larvae live in the water for at least a year before changing into the land-living adult form. Those that live in cold water take up to three years to develop into adults.

*The golden-striped salamander is a long and slender species. The tail may be more than twice as long as the head and body section. A golden stripe runs from behind the head to the tip of the tail. A groove also runs along the centre of this stripe.*

**Distribution**: North-west Spain and northern Portugal as far south as the River Tajo.
**Habitat**: Mountains forests with high rainfall and clear fast-flowing streams surrounded by thick moss.
**Food**: Slow-moving invertebrates caught using long and sticky tongue.
**Size**: 13cm (5in).
**Maturity**: 4 years or at a length of 4 cm (1.5in).
**Breeding**: 12–20 eggs laid in shallow water.
**Life span**: 8 years in the wild and more than 10 years when kept in captivity.
**Status**: Common.

# Great crested newt

*Triturus cristatus cristatus*

**Distribution**: England, Scotland, central Europe from France to Urals, and southern Scandinavia to Alps.
**Habitat**: Spend most of the year in weedy ponds.
**Food**: Small aquatic invertebrates and vertebrates, including other amphibians.
**Size**: 11–16cm (4.5–6.25in).
**Maturity**: Tadpoles change into newts after 8–16 weeks. Reach adult size after 2 years.
**Breeding**: 200–300 eggs laid between April and mid-July.
**Life span**: 27 years.
**Status**: Vulnerable.

During the breeding season, male great crested newts become brightly coloured, particularly on their bellies. They also develop high toothed crests along their backs and white bands along the sides of their tails. The newts hibernate on land during the winter. They return to the water in March, and the males develop their breeding livery two weeks later. Once the breeding season is over, their crests and outer skins are absorbed into their bodies.

Young great crested newts hatch in water as tadpoles. They feed on fish, tadpoles, worms and aquatic insects. The adults feed on larger prey, including newts and frogs. They locate their prey in the mud using smell and sight.

Great crested newts are afforded protection by their skins. If threatened, their skins release a white, creamy fluid, which is an irritant to the eyes, nose and mouth of predators.

*Great crested newts have dark backs, while their bellies are orange or red with large black blotches or spots. The males are more colourful than the females, with tall crests along their backs during the breeding season.*

---

**Pyrenean brook newt** (*Euproctus asper*): 16cm (6.25in)
This species of newt is found only in the Pyrenees and other mountains in northern Spain. It has very rough grey-green skin and the paratoid glands (bumps behind the head) that are common in other species are absent in this newt. Females have a pointed opening to their cloaca (rear opening) and the males have a rounded opening. Females also have yellow stripes and patches on their upper side. This newt lives in cold mountain streams and lakes. It rarely comes out of water by day but in the cool of the night ventures on to the land.

**Corsican brook newt** (*Euproctus montanus*): 13cm (5in)
Apart from the Corsican fire salamander, this is the only other tailed amphibian to live in the mountains of Corsica. It has dull colouring, with a mottled pattern of black and yellow patches. The males have blunt spurs on their hind legs and a cone-shaped swelling at the cloaca (rear opening). It lurks beneath stones in streams or along the bank. This species has small lungs because oxygen is absorbed through the skin.

**Sardinian brook newt** (*Euproctus platycephalus*): 15cm (6in)
The Sardinian brook newt is one of just two tailed amphibians to live on Sardinia, the other being the supramonte cave salamander. Sardianian brook newts exhibit a range of colour patterns on their pale green skin. The main feature is the orange or red stripe along their back. The males have spurs on their hind legs.

# Sharp-ribbed newt

*Pleurodeles waltl*

The sharp-ribbed newt has special rib bones that are able to inject poison into a predator by protruding through pores in its skin. When the poison enters the skin of a predator, it causes a great deal of pain. The newt will also head-butt a predator, exposing glands at the back of its head that exude a toxic fluid. It has similar glands on its tail, which it lashes to release the toxin.

This species lives permanently in water and only leaves if the water level falls. Sharp-ribbed newts breed twice in a year, in early spring and again in midsummer. The males have much longer tails than the females, and during the mating season they develop special pads under their front legs to help grasp the females when transferring their sperm.

**Distribution**: Spain, Portugal and Morocco.
**Habitat**: Entirely aquatic, in standing water such as ponds, lagoons, dams and irrigation systems.
**Food**: Invertebrates, small fish and carrion.
**Size**: 15–30cm (6–12in).
**Maturity**: 4 years.
**Breeding**: Female lays between 100 and 1,000 eggs depending on her size. Breeding takes place twice: once in the spring and again in midsummer.
**Life span**: Unknown.
**Status**: Common.

*The sharp-ribbed newt has a dark brown back. Along its sides it has dark blotches with lines of dull orange circles. These are the pores from which the ribs can protrude from its body. Its belly is generally much paler in colour.*

## Northern crested newt

*Triturus cristatus carnifex*

The northern crested newt, also known as the warty newt, lives across Europe to the north of the Alps. It ranges from Britain (but not Ireland) to the Ukraine. It also lives in southern Scandinavia, where individuals have a solid black underside in place of the orange belly of other members of the species.

Being a newt, this species is more closely associated with water than salamanders. Mating takes place in or close to deep streams. The newt occasionally returns to water outside the breeding season, but it is also common far from water in damp woodlands. Northern crested newts are nocturnal. When it is under threat, the newt plays dead and produces an offensive-smelling white liquid from its skin.

During the breeding season in spring, the males are adorned with crests and gather in groups to display to females. After mating, females lay 200–400 eggs. However, due to a genetic anomaly, only half of these eggs develop. The eggs hatch after three weeks and the larvae live in water for about four months before changing into the adult form. In cold areas, the larvae may never metamorphose, instead living their whole lives in water. They retain the larval body form but grow adult sex organs to allow them to breed. This phenomenon is called neoteny.

**Distribution**: Northern and central Europe. Absent from Ireland and from all but southern Scandinavia. Also occurs in central Asia.
**Habitat**: Broad-leafed woodlands with plenty of pools and streams.
**Food**: Water and land invertebrates as well as fish and other amphibians.
**Size**: 15cm (6in).
**Maturity**: At the age of 3 years or at the length of 12cm (4.75in).
**Breeding**: 300 eggs laid in water. Hatch with 3 weeks.
**Life span**: 8 years.
**Status**: Common.

*Crested newts are named after the jagged ridge that grows from a male newt's back prior to the mating season. Its tail also develops a white stripe. Females lack these crests. The newts' underside is orange with black spots.*

## Alpine newt

*Triturus alpestris*

Despite its name, this species is found in lowland as well as highland regions across much of mainland Europe, from the Atlantic coast to Romania and from Denmark in the north to northern Spain and Greece in the south.

This species of newt is always in or close to water. They prefer cold and clear pools and slow-flowing streams. In southern Europe, the newt is found only at higher altitudes where the water is cold enough. For example, an isolated population lives in the Guadarrama Mountains of central Spain. The alpine newt prefers pools with few plants in them, and therefore is most common above the tree line, sometimes surviving as high as 2,500m (8,200ft). Farther north, where the climate is cooler, water that is cold enough for the newts is located in lowland areas.

Mating takes place in water in spring. At the highest altitudes, the newts may breed only every two years. Females lay about 250 eggs, which hatch between two and four weeks later. The larvae take about three years to mature into adults. In especially cold habitats, the aquatic larvae will never metamorphose, but become sexually mature while still having the swimming body form of larvae.

**Distribution**: Most of central Europe. There are isolated populations in central Spain and southern Italy.
**Habitat**: Ponds and other pools of water.
**Food**: Large invertebrates, tadpoles and fish.
**Size**: 12cm (4.75in).
**Maturity**: 2–4 years.
**Breeding**: 250 eggs laid in spring.
**Life span**: 11 years in the wild and up to 20 years when kept in captivity.
**Status**: Common.

*Alpine newts have grey bodies with black spots on the snout and flanks. The spots extend on to the legs. The underside is solid orange, but there may be spots on the throat. Males grow a smooth crest during the mating season.*

# Common newt

*Triturus vulgaris*

**Distribution**: Northern
Europe and western Asia.
**Habitat**: Damp woodlands,
gardens and fields.
**Food**: Invertebrates.
**Size**: 11cm (4.25in).
**Maturity**: 3 years.
**Breeding**: Up to 300 eggs
laid on water plants.
**Life span**: 7 years.
**Status**: Common.

The common newt, or smooth newt as it is sometimes
called, lives across northern Europe from the British Isles
to Russia and western Asia. It is less reliant on
water than most newts and is seen on the
ground in damp habitats. Like other newts,
however, the common newt must return
to water to breed.

The males develop a large crest
prior to the spring breeding
season. Females are attracted
to males with larger crests. After mating, the female will lay
up to 300 eggs on water plants. The eggs hatch after about
two weeks. The larvae stay close to the bottom of the pool,
which keeps them out of the way of the adults, which are
more common near to the surface. This divide prevents the
two generations competing for food. A larva will
metamorphose into the adult form once it reaches 4cm
(1.5in) long. This might take a year or even longer. In cold
waters the larvae may never take the adult form.

*The common newt exhibits a
variety of colour patterns. The
common form is grey-green skin
on the upper side and an orange
belly with black spots. The male
has large spots on the back and
grows a jagged crest for the
breeding season.*

---

**Marbled newt** (*Triturus marmoratus*):
9–11cm (3.5–4.25in)
The marbled newt is found in south-west
France, Spain and Portugal. It has a green back,
interrupted by black marbling, and a grey belly.
Both males and females develop orange-red
stripes along their backs, from neck to tail. The
females keep this stripe when they return to
water to breed. During this time, the males lose
their red stripes and develop crests, along with
silver bands on their tails. When threatened,
they raise their tails and sway from side to side.

**Danube crested newt** (*Triturus dobrogicus*):
13cm (5in)
The Danube crested newt lives in the vast
wetlands formed by the Danube Delta in
Romania and is also found upstream as far west
as Austria. This newt is red-brown on top with
an orange underbelly speckled with black spots.
It spends long periods in slow-flowing water,
often among thick growths of water plants.
Both adult and larval Danube crested newts
eat invertebrates such as insect larvae.

**Italian crested newt** (*Triturus carnifex*):
15cm (6in)
This crested newt lives in northern Italy. It
resembles the northern crested newt but has
a more orange belly. Adult members of this
species travel far from water outside the
breeding season but must return to water to
reproduce. At high altitudes, where the water
is cold, the aquatic larvae never develop into
the adult form but become neotenous (sexually
mature while retaining the body of larvae).

# Palmate newt

*Triturus helveticus*

The palmate newt lives in western Europe,
from Britain to north-west Spain and
Portugal and Switzerland. This species is
often mistaken for the common newt, but is
generally smaller and has fewer spots on the
belly, which is also a pale yellow rather than
a dark orange. Like the common newt, the
palmate newt is regularly found out of
water but never strays out of moist habitats.

The newts hibernate under logs and
stones from November through to March,
when they return to water to breed. The
males grow a low smooth crest to attract
females and their hind feet become webbed.
After mating, the females lay 290–460 eggs
on aquatic plants. The eggs hatch within
a fortnight. The larvae that emerge have
gills for breathing exclusively underwater.
Once they reach about 3cm (1.25in) long,
their gills are
absorbed into
the body and
they take on the
four-legged adult form
that is capable of surviving
out of water. The adults
breathe with small lungs but they
can also take oxygen from the air
or water in through their damp skin.

**Distribution**: Western
Europe.
**Habitat**: Shallow water and
damp land habitats.
**Food**: Invertebrates.
**Size**: 9cm (3.5in).
**Maturity**: 2 years.
**Breeding**: 400 eggs laid in
water.
**Life span**: 12 years.
**Status**: Common.

*Male palmate newts have
webbed feet, yellow bellies and
thin filaments of skin that extend
5mm (0.25in) from the tips of
their tails. The females are much
duller and lack the tail filaments.*

# Carpathian newt

*Triturus montandoni*

As its name suggests, the Carpathian newt lives in the Carpathian Mountains of Romania, southern Poland and Slovakia. It is a relatively small species, with males being the smaller sex. Montandon's newt, as it is also known, lives in conifer forests that grow mainly above 500m (1,640ft). The maximum altitude the newts survive at is 2,000m (6,560ft). The newts prefer cold and clear streams that are rich in acidic minerals. However, they also inhabit muddier watercourses at lower altitudes.

Montandon's newt occasionally ventures on to land but rarely moves far from the water's edge. The nocturnal amphibians avoid drying out in the sunlight by lurking under stones and fallen leaves and bark.

Breeding takes place in spring. The females lay 30–250 eggs in water. Older females tend to produce more eggs than less-mature individuals. The eggs may hatch in as few as ten days, but in high locations, where the water stays cold all year around, the larvae can take up to a month to emerge. The larvae metamorphose into tiny adult forms when they reach the length of just 1cm (0.4in), which is considerably smaller than the size for other newts. In many places, the larvae stay in the juvenile form through the winter.

**Distribution**: The Carpathian Mountains of eastern Europe, which extend from Romania through Ukraine to western Poland and Slovakia.
**Habitat**: Areas of mountain conifer forests with many ponds and streams.
**Food**: Invertebrates, tadpoles and spawn (eggs).
**Size**: 10cm (4in).
**Maturity**: 3 years.
**Breeding**: Up to 250 eggs laid in later spring.
**Life span**: Unknown.
**Status**: Common.

This small species of newt has three grooves on the head. The upper body is yellow-green with grey mottles, while the underside is yellow or orange and often has small black spots. When ready to breed, the male develops large and more distinctive spots on his upper body.

# Bosca's newt

*Triturus boscai*

Bosca's newts live in ponds and streams in the western part of the Iberian Peninsula. Although this species is often confused with the palmate and common newt species, it is the only newt to be found in this part of the world. Only in the north of its range does this species live alongside similar newts. However, there are some obvious differences between them all. For example, Bosca's newt has a single groove on its snout, while the other two species have three grooves.

Bosca's newts prefer clean, cold and still water, although they also occupy muddier water that is thick with vegetation if that is all that is available. They even survive in animal troughs, caves and brackish lagoons. In warmer spots the newts are completely aquatic and have no reason to leave the water. In damper habitats, however, such as alpine ones, the newts may make forays on to dry land in search of food.

They are most active at night, but during the breeding season the newts are also seen during the day. Female newts lay up to 250 eggs in the water, which hatch within three weeks. The larvae metamorphose into adult forms once they reach 3cm (1.25in) long. This development is delayed in individuals living in cold water. Despite having an adult form, the young newts do not mature sexually for several months.

**Distribution**: Portugal and western and central Spain.
**Habitat**: Clear ponds and streams in both lowland and highland areas. Also lives in brackish lagoons close to the seashore and in underground lakes inside caverns.
**Food**: Land and water invertebrates, tadpoles, frog's spawn and small fish.
**Size**: 10cm (4in).
**Maturity**: 2–4 years.
**Breeding**: 100–250 eggs laid underwater in spring. Eggs hatch within 3 weeks.
**Life span**: 7 years in the wild, longer in captivity.
**Status**: Common.

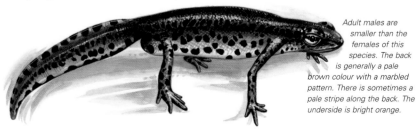

Adult males are smaller than the females of this species. The back is generally a pale brown colour with a marbled pattern. There is sometimes a pale stripe along the back. The underside is bright orange.

# Kirk's caecilian

*Scolecomorphus kirkii*

**Distribution**: Southern Tanzania.
**Habitat**: Soil.
**Food**: Insects and worms.
**Size**: 20–35cm (8–13.75in).
**Maturity**: Unknown.
**Breeding**: Eggs laid underground.
**Life span**: Unknown.
**Status**: Lower risk.

Kirk's caecilian is rarely seen on the surface. It spends its days burrowing through the loose soil of moist savannahs near to Lake Tanganyika and Lake Nyasa. Caecilians are all burrowing amphibians. Like snakes, which also first evolved as burrowers, caecilians have no legs, which helps them to slither through the soil. They move by lifting some of their body off the ground, and pushing back with the parts that remain touching the ground. Grooves around the body, known as annuli, give the animal some purchase on the ground.

Kirk's caecilian has small eyes located on small tentacles. These tentacles can lift the eyes slightly above the head. Little is known about the caecilian's other senses.

When mates do find each other, they copulate underground. The female then lays a clutch of sticky eggs underground. There is no larval stage, as with many amphibians; instead, the young hatch out as small versions of the adults.

*With its apparently segmented body, this bizarre amphibian looks like a giant earthworm. On closer inspection, the head, jaw and teeth show that it is a vertebrate with bones and a spine.*

---

**Ambrosi's cave salamander** (*Speleomantes ambrosii*): 12.5cm (5in)
Like all cave salamanders, this species is a member of a much larger group of salamanders called the lungless salamanders. Most of these species live in the Americas. As their name suggests, lungless salamanders do not breathe using lungs; instead, they absorb all the oxygen they need through their skin. The most active gas-exchange surface is the moist lining of the mouth. Cave salamanders are closely associated with regions of limestone where caves are common. However, they are also found on the surface. Ambrosi's cave salamander lives in southern France and northern Italy. It is nocturnal and often climbs up vegetation to find food.

**Italian cave salamander** (*Speleomantes italicus*): 12.5cm (5in)
The Italian cave salamander is very similar to Ambrosi's cave salamander but lives farther south, in the northern Apennines. It is nocturnal and therefore not often seen. It can exist in large numbers and is most likely to be spotted on a limestone rock.

**Supramontane cave salamander**
(*Speleomantes supramontis*): 13.5cm (5.25in)
The supramontane cave salamander is one of only two salamanders living on the island of Sardinia. This rare salamander lives in the east of the island inland from the Gulf of Orosei. It spends a lot of its time underground in damp caves. When on the surface, the nocturnal salamander does most of its foraging among lush mosses.

# Boulenger's caecilian

*Boulengerula boulengerina*

Boulenger's caecilian lives in the loose soils of the lush and humid forests that clothe the Usambaras Mountains of southern Tanzania. Most caecilians are opportunist feeders: they sit underground and wait for prey to come within their grasp. They will eat almost anything, using a strong bite and two rows of backward-curving teeth to hang on to their prey. Many of the muscles used for swallowing in other amphibians are employed to close the mouth in caecilians, which results in a powerful bite for such a small animal. Boulenger's caecilian, however, is something of a specialist feeder and is seldom far from a source of termites.

Like the other East African caecilians, Boulenger's caecilian lays eggs. Little is known about how Boulenger's caecilians breed. It is thought that the female lays her eggs in an underground chamber and guards them until they hatch.

**Distribution**: South-eastern Tanzania.
**Habitat**: Soil.
**Food**: Termites.
**Size**: 20–28cm (8–11in).
**Maturity**: Unknown.
**Breeding**: Eggs laid in underground chamber.
**Life span**: Unknown.
**Status**: Common.

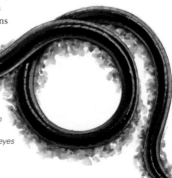

*Boulenger's caecilian is a slender species with a striking blue-grey body with more than 100 rings around it. The throat is pinkish, and the eyes are covered by skin and so rendered useless. Juveniles of this species are pinkish.*

# FROGS AND TOADS

*Throughout the world, there are over 4,000 species of frog and toad – more than ten times the number*
*of salamanders and newts. Frogs are often recognized by their long legs, hopping motion and smooth,*
*often brightly coloured skins. Toads, on the other hand, are often dark brown, warty amphibians that*
*walk rather than hop. However, many frogs and toads are difficult to distinguish from one another.*

## Common toad

*Bufo bufo*

The common toad lives away from water for most of the year. Its thick, loose skin and nocturnal habits help to protect it from drying out. Toads protect themselves with foul-tasting chemicals released by warty glands in their skins. If threatened, the common toad also inflates its body and rises up on its legs, to intimidate predators.

Toads use their sticky tongues to catch ants, their favourite prey. They have a good sense of smell, which helps them to find their way to breeding sites each year. They hibernate until February and March – usually a few weeks later than common frogs.

Rather than laying clumps of spawn, as frogs do, common toads release a strand of spawn that hangs on weeds. In warm weather, tadpoles metamorphose in about eight weeks.

**Distribution**: Europe, north-west Africa, and Asia.
**Habitat**: Woodland, gardens, and fields. In the breeding season, they live in ponds and slow-moving rivers.
**Food**: Insects, spiders, slugs and worms.
**Size**: 8–15cm (3–6in).
**Maturity**: 4 years.
**Breeding**: Lays up to 4,000 eggs.
**Life span**: 40 years.
**Status**: Common.

*Common toads are olive brown and covered in warts. They walk rather than hop like frogs. The males are smaller and have fewer warts than the females, and only the males croak.*

## European common frog

*Rana temporaria*

European common frogs are found in a variety of habitats, including fields and woodland close to water. Their diet is eclectic, including insects, molluscs and worms. Male common frogs have swellings on their first fingers to help them grasp the females when mating. Sometimes two or three males may try to mate with one female. Occasionally she will die in this situation through drowning or being squashed by their combined weight.

Spawning can take place as early as December or January but it is more usual in late February, March or April. Frogs flock to a traditional breeding pond, lake or ditch, where hundreds or thousands may be swimming around. Males emit quiet croaks and can be seen jostling for the best females. While a female is releasing her 1,000–4,000 eggs, the male, directly on top, will spread his sperm over them.

After spawning, the ponds become quiet again, as the frogs leave to live on land. They do so until the autumn, when they hibernate under logs and rocks. When it is very cold, they will rest in the water, usually in amongst thick vegetation.

**Distribution**: Widespread throughout Europe, including Turkey and Russia.
**Habitat**: Live in meadows, gardens and woodland. Breed in puddles, ponds, lakes and canals. Prefer areas of shallow water.
**Food**: Insects, snails, slugs and worms, caught with long, sticky tongues. Tadpoles are herbivorous and feed on algae.
**Size**: 6–10cm (2.5–4in).
**Maturity**: 3 years.
**Breeding**: 1,000–4,000 eggs laid.
**Life span**: 12 years.
**Status**: Common in most of range.

*Common frogs are variable in colour, but generally have a greenish-brown body colour with darker blotches and dark masks on their faces.*

**Marsh frog** (*Rana ridibunda*): Females 7.5–14cm (3–5.5in); males 6.5–10cm (2.5–4in)
The marsh frog lives in the rivers and other waterways that cross the plains of eastern Europe. It also occurs in parts of France, the Rhine Valley and southern England. The species was originally introduced to western Europe by humans. Marsh frogs also live in central Asia. Its loud croaking can be heard from pools during the day and night. When calling, special sacs are inflated and bulge out on either side of the head. The frogs make a number of loud calls to attract mates throughout May and June. It is the largest European frog and usually remains in the water for most of the year.

**Iberian water frog** (*Rana perezi*): 8.5cm (3.25in)
This species of water frog lives in the south of France, Spain and Portugal. It has also been introduced to the Canaries, Balearics and Madeira. The Iberian water frog is seldom out of water. It lives in all types of water, even stagnant and brackish water. It is most often seen by day, sunbathing in warm shallow water. When disturbed the frog ducks into deeper water. The females of this species lay more than 1,000 eggs. The tadpoles have to cope with the temperature of the water rising in the summer and the amount of oxygen in it dropping. Tadpoles in pools that are likely to dry up will metamorphose into adults more quickly than usual so that they can escape on to land. As a result, these newly emerged frogs are much smaller than normal.

# European tree frog

*Hyla arborea*

European tree frogs are bright green frogs. They are able to change colour, and when they first come out from hibernation, in the spring, they are grey-brown. They are good climbers, living in trees throughout Europe. They have suckers on the ends of their toes to help them grasp branches. The green skin helps to keep them hidden among the leaves.

Tree frogs are most active during the night, particularly if it has been raining. They leap around, catching a variety of night-flying flies and moths. In late spring, the males sit by the edges of ponds or on plants overhanging the water, croaking to attract females. When the males call, they inflate vocal sacs, which produce their distinctive sound. When full of air, the sacs are as big as the frogs. The song produced is a mixture of barks and quacks. When a number of males croak together, they can be heard several kilometres away.

*The European tree frog is lime green on top and white underneath. It has a somewhat contorted appearance because the skin on its head is fused to its skull.*

**Distribution**: Europe, below 800m (2,640ft) above sea level.
**Habitat**: Scrub and open woodland with shrubs.
**Food**: Flies and moths.
**Size**: 3–4.5cm (1.25–1.75in).
**Maturity**: Not known.
**Breeding**: 800–1,000 eggs laid in small clumps during late April or May.
**Life span**: 20 years.
**Status**: Vulnerable.

# Midwife toad

*Alytes obstetricans*

**Distribution**: West and south-west Europe.
**Habitat**: Quarries, scree slopes and uncultivated land. Sand dunes and gardens are inhabited in France.
**Food**: Small insects.
**Size**: 5cm (2in).
**Maturity**: 2 years.
**Breeding**: Female lays several batches of 20–60 eggs in strings between April and June, which are carried on the male's back legs. Tadpoles are released into water between 2 and 6 weeks later.
**Life span**: Unknown.
**Status**: Locally common.

The midwife toad looks very similar to the common toad. However, it has vertical pupils instead of horizontal ones, a more pointed snout, and does not have the protective glands behind the head. Midwife toads are night-active and spend the day hidden in crevices in rocks, under logs or in burrows.

In late spring, the males give out short peeping calls to attract females. Mating occurs on land. As the females produce strings of 20–60 eggs, the males catch them with their legs. They then position the strings of spawn between their thighs and waists. The females play no part in looking after the eggs. The eggs remain embedded in a whitish-yellow mass of mucus that keeps them moist.

The male secretes antibiotics over the eggs to protect them from fungus and bacteria. After two to six weeks, the eggs develop into tadpoles. The males travel to ponds where the young release themselves into the water. Some males attract two or more females, and therefore look after a larger number of eggs.

*The midwife toad is dull grey, olive or brown in colour, occasionally with green spots and often with darker markings. The belly is whitish with grey blotches. Females sometimes have red spots running down their flanks. This toad is particularly proficient at leaping.*

## Fire-bellied toad

*Bombina bombina*

Fire-bellied toads are named after the bright red and yellow markings on their undersides; these form a unique pattern, rather like human fingerprints. When adults call, they inflate their throats and show off their bright colours. This species of toad produces a melancholy triple "oop" call, which is sometimes confused with that of a small owl. A chorus of toads can evoke the sound of distant bells.

Fire-bellied toads live across central and eastern Europe. They also occur in Denmark and southern Sweden and appear as far east as Turkey. They live exclusively in lowland habitats, preferring shallow water that is not too clogged with plant growth. This species often makes forays away from the water, especially after rain. In colder areas, the toad hibernates under logs and stones.

In late spring the toad always returns to water to breed. Mating takes place at night, after rain has cooled the water. There is no tadpole stage in this species; instead, tiny baby toads just 1cm (0.4in) long emerge from the eggs after a few weeks. These toadlets are able to survive on land.

*From above, fire-bellied toads are well camouflaged by their dull, mottled colours. They have black or dark brown warty skins, covered in dark spots with green patches on their shoulders and broad, green central lines. By contrast, the bellies are black with bright red or yellow patches.*

**Distribution**: Eastern and central Europe from Denmark and southern Sweden to Russia and Serbia to Turkey.
**Habitat**: Always close to shallow pools, marshes, and streams in lowland areas. Hibernates under logs and flat stones
**Food**: Insects, spiders, slugs and worms.
**Size**: 5cm (2in).
**Maturity**: 1–2 years.
**Breeding**: 150 eggs laid in 5–6 clumps on water plants. Eggs hatch into toadlets.
**Life span**: 20 years.
**Status**: Common.

## Painted frog

*Discoglossus pictus*

The painted frog lives in Mediterranean habitats, including coastal dunes, meadows, vineyards and forests. They like to live in thickets of dense vegetation and are seldom far from shallow water, either still or slow flowing. The frog can also survive in brackish waters (a mixture of sea water and freshwater) in tidal zones.

The frog is probably African in origin. Those on the mainland were probably introduced from the Maghreb (north-west Africa) in prehistoric times. The frogs that live on Mediterranean islands are a separate subspecies. In Sicily, where the species is one of the few frogs on the island, painted frogs are often found in manmade cisterns and watercourses.

Painted frogs breed several times in winter and early spring. The males attract mates with a "rar-rar-rar" call. Females mate with several males, each time laying about 50 eggs. In total each female can lay 5,000 eggs in a year over several breeding periods. The eggs hatch in about a week.

*Despite their colourful name, the painted frogs have a grey-green colour, typical of many European frogs. The name applies to the dark blotches on the back, which are framed by a pale yellow border. Some members of this species also have a pale brown stripe running along the back from the snout to the rump.*

**Distribution**: Sicily, Malta, Gozo, eastern Pyrenees of southern France, Gerona in north-east Spain, and parts of north-west Africa.
**Habitat**: Fields, woodland, sandy areas, and marshes close to hallow water.
**Food**: Catches invertebrates using a disc-shaped tongue.
**Size**: 8cm (3.25in).
**Maturity**: 3–5 years.
**Breeding**: Eggs scattered on lake or river bed.
**Life span**: 10 years.
**Status**: Common.

# Common spadefoot

*Pelobates fuscus*

**Distribution**: Central and eastern Europe from the Baltic to northern Italy and Bulgaria.
**Habitat**: Woodlands, fields and heaths in lowland areas.
**Food**: Invertebrates.
**Size**: 8cm (3.25in).
**Maturity**: 2 years.
**Breeding**: Up to 3,500 eggs laid in long bands.
**Life span**: 10 years.
**Status**: Common.

Spadefoots are a widespread group of frogs. A few species live in Europe and north-west Africa, but most are found in southern Asia and North America. The common spadefoot lives across central and eastern Europe to the edge of Asia, from northern France and Denmark in the west to the Urals and the Aral Sea in the east.

Common spadefoots are active only at night, apart from in the spring breeding season, when they attempt to mate during both night and day. Spadefoots are generally found in areas of sandy soil that are easy to dig through. They dig with their hind feet and use their wide head to barge through loose soil.

The frogs mate in deep pools with thick vegetation growing along the edge. Males attract females with a triple "clock" call. Females lay many hundreds of eggs in strings that can be 1m (3.25ft) long. Tadpoles often spend the winter in the water before developing into the adult form.

*Like all spadefoots, this species has spade-like growths on its hind feet. They are an extension of a foot bone next to the inside toe used for burrowing in soil. The "spade" of common spadefoots is black. The hind feet are also heavily webbed.*

**Iberian frog** (*Rana iberica*): 7cm (2.75in)
The Iberian frog is found only in the western Iberian Peninsula, mostly Portugal and north-western Spain. It is a close relative of the common frog, which is found in the European hinterland to the east. The Iberian species is easily mistaken for this more widespread relative. However, Iberian frogs have extensive webbing on their hind feet, while common frogs do not. Iberian frogs are most common in the mountains and prefer cold, fast-flowing streams that have plenty of shaded areas nearby. In the northern parts of their range, the climate can be cool enough for the frogs to live at lower altitudes. Iberian frogs are active during both the day and night. They breed in the autumn.

**Balkan stream frog** (*Rana graeca*): 8cm (3.25in)
The Balkan stream frog lives across the eastern Balkan Peninsula from Serbia to Greece. It is always found close to or swimming in cold running water and is most common on the middle slopes of mountains, about 1,200m (3,940ft) up. It prefers clear streams without too much vegetation clogging the flow over a rocky bed. By day the frog basks on the bank, only to leap into the water if disturbed. After rain, the frog also makes night-time trips into woodland, but seldom travels far from the water.

**Pyrenean frog** (*Rana pyrenaica*): 5cm (2in)
This species lives in the central region of the Spanish Pyrenees Mountains. It is one of the smallest species of frog in Europe. Pyrenean frogs are good swimmers and live in streams.

# Parsley frog

*Pelodytes punctatus*

Parsley frogs live in a range of habitats in eastern Spain. They are found in swamps and streams but outside the spring breeding season often venture to quite dry habitats. In the south of their range, where the weather is consistently warmer, the frogs live on the slopes of mountains. Farther north, they are limited to lowland habitats.

These frogs are nocturnal. By day they rest under stones and logs and are frequent visitors to caves. During the breeding season, the frogs become more active and can be seen during the day as well.

The frogs' breeding is stimulated by the spring rains. The frogs gather in waters to mate. The females mate several times, and after each mating they wrap strings of up to 350 eggs around stems. In a single season one female may lay up to 1,600 eggs. Tadpoles develop into froglets in late autumn. These young frogs mature the following spring.

**Distribution**: Eastern Spain.
**Habitat**: Swamps, woodlands and meadows.
**Food**: Invertebrates.
**Size**: 5cm (2in).
**Maturity**: 1 year.
**Breeding**: Several strings of eggs twisted around stems.
**Life span**: 15 years.
**Status**: Common.

*This little frog has long legs with very long toes on its hind feet. Its name comes from the bright green spots on its upper back, which resemble sprigs of parsley. Males are slightly smaller and have shorter limbs than females.*

## Natterjack toad

*Bufo calamita*

*The natterjack toad has dark, warty skin like the common toad and a yellow line all the way from the head to the end of the spine. During the breeding season, the males develop purple-violet throats, while the females' throats remain white. Males have large throat sacs, which are used to make loud calls.*

The natterjack toad is found throughout western and central Europe and is the smallest of all the European toads. In northern Europe, including Britain, the toads are restricted to lowland habitats such as heaths and dunes, although they are also often found in broken habitats, such as a quarry. Farther south the toads are able to survive in a wider range of habitats, including the slopes of mountains.

Natterjack toads are nocturnal. They live away from water outside the breeding season and will travel large distances if necessary, using their sense of the Earth's magnetic field as a means of navigating. The toads hibernate under stones and in other sheltered spots during the worst of the winter weather. If alarmed, the toads inflate their bodies and exude an unpleasant-smelling liquid through their skin to scare off predators. The breeding season lasts for most of the spring and summer. Males position themselves in or near to shallow water and attract mates with their croaks. The toads are thought to be Europe's noisiest toads because the male's croaking can be heard up to 3km (2 miles) away. Eggs are laid in ponds. They hatch in about a week.

**Distribution**: Western and central Europe as far east as the Baltic states, Belarus and western Ukraine.
**Habitat**: Meadows, dunes, quarries and woodlands in the north, and also mountains in the south.
**Food**: Invertebrates.
**Size**: 7cm (2.75in).
**Maturity**: 2 years.
**Breeding**: Single and double strings of eggs laid in shallow water. A female can lay 7,000 eggs in one season.
**Life span**: 10 years in the wild; 17 years in captivity.
**Status**: Common.

## Green toad

*Bufo viridis*

*Female green toads are larger than the males. They look similar to the natterjack toad but the females have a more contrasted speckled colouring on their backs. Green toads also generally lack the yellow stripe commonly seen in their western neighbours. The green toads' back legs are also longer than the those of the natterjacks. Green toads hop in a typical frog-like way, while the natterjack crawls on all fours.*

Green toads are an eastern European species. They occur as far west as eastern France and Denmark, but their main range is Russia and on into central Asia. This species is also found on several Mediterranean islands, such as Corsica and Mallorca, and occurs in North Africa. These southern populations are thought to be the result of people introducing (by accident or design) the frogs to these regions in the Bronze Age.

The green toad is nocturnal. It is better able to survive dry conditions than many other toad species and is often found far from water. It is especially common in sandy soils, where it digs itself a burrow to hide out in during the day. Inside the damp burrow, the toad is protected from the dryness and heat. In most parts of the range, the green toad hibernates, seeking refuge in a damp place. It awakes in spring in time for the breeding season. Green toads will lay their eggs in a range of waters, including stagnant and brackish bodies. Eggs hatch within a week of being laid, and the tadpoles metamorphose into the tailless adult form when they reach 1cm (0.4in) in length.

**Distribution**: Eastern and central Europe, western Mediterranean islands, North Africa, Middle East and central Asia.
**Habitat**: Dry habitats, such as sandy and rocky areas. Common close to human settlements.
**Food**: Insects, spiders, worms and slugs.
**Size**: 10cm (4in).
**Maturity**: 3 years.
**Breeding**: Strings of thousands of eggs are laid among water plants.
**Life span**: 10 years.
**Status**: Common.

# Moor frog

*Rana arvalis*

**Distribution**: Scandinavia, central and eastern Europe and northern Asia.
**Habitat**: Moors, bogs, floodplains and tundra.
**Food**: Insects and worms.
**Size**: 8cm (3.25in).
**Maturity**: 2–3 years.
**Breeding**: Up to 4,000 eggs laid in 2–3 clumps.
**Life span**: 10 years.
**Status**: Common.

Moor frogs live in the extreme east of France and Belgium and extend northwards to northern Sweden and Finland and south to the foothills of the Alps. The frog's range extends as far east as the Lake Baikal region in Siberia.

The frog is found at mainly low altitudes and occupies habitats such as moors and bogs. In the south, where the climate is often wet, they occur on mountains. In the north, they live on tundra close to river banks.

Moor frogs have a short breeding season in spring. The frogs gather at pools and mate intensively. Males stay in one location, calling female mates, who come and go. Once mated, the females lay a total of 4,000 eggs in large clumps. Collectively the eggs make up a third of the female's weight. The eggs hatch after a few weeks, or more slowly in cold areas. Tadpoles change into the adult form when they grow to 1cm (0.4in) long.

*Moor frogs are robust frogs with a pointed snout and short legs. When the hind legs are extended, their heels do not reach past the snout. When ready to breed, the males develop a violet colouring (seen here) and grow nuptial pads on their forelimbs for gripping females during mating.*

---

**Italian stream frog** (*Rana italica*): 6cm (2.25in)
This species lives in western Italy and is very similar to the Balkan stream frog. It was classified as a separate species to its eastern neighbour only in 1985. The Italian stream frog is found mainly in mountain habitats, close to fast-flowing streams with rocky bottoms. It may follow these streams to lower altitudes if the water remains clear and free of thick vegetation. The females lay spawn under stones to prevent them being washed away by the current.

**Italian agile frog** (*Rana latastei*): 7.5cm (3in)
This species is found in northern Italy, though it also crosses into southern Switzerland, Slovenia and Croatia. Male Italian agile frogs are smaller than females. The species looks similar to the agile frog but has a pale stripe on the dark background of the throat. Males have pinkish tinges to their throats and legs during the breeding season. Italian agile frogs are a lowland species. They live in woodlands and meadows for most of the year and seek out swampy areas in which to breed.

# Agile frog

*Rana dalmatina*

Agile frogs are found across central Europe as far east as Romania. The range extends south to Turkey and northern Iran. They are absent from northern areas, such as Denmark and the Rhine Valley, and do not occur in Portugal or much of Spain.

When not breeding, agile frogs live in woodlands. Their colouring helps them blend in with the leaves that cover the ground. They hide by day and emerge at dusk to feed. When close to water, the agile frog dives in when danger is near. However, the species is often far from water and instead uses its long legs to bound away from a threat. This behaviour is what gives the species its name.

Agile frogs can be heard during the spring breeding season producing a "quar-quar" call. Choruses gather in still water. The frog prefers to breed in open habitats. Females stick clumps of eggs around twigs in deep water. As the eggs develop, the clumps float to the surface, where the tadpoles hatch after about three weeks. Tadpoles become froglets once they grow to 2cm (0.75in).

**Distribution**: Central Europe.
**Habitat**: Woodlands.
**Food**: Invertebrates.
**Size**: 9cm (3.5in).
**Maturity**: 2–3 years.
**Breeding**: Spawn contains about 1,000 eggs.
**Life span**: 10 years.
**Status**: Common.

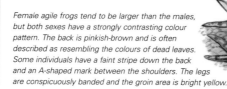

*Female agile frogs tend to be larger than the males, but both sexes have a strongly contrasting colour pattern. The back is pinkish-brown and is often described as resembling the colours of dead leaves. Some individuals have a faint stripe down the back and an A-shaped mark between the shoulders. The legs are conspicuously banded and the groin area is bright yellow.*

# Foam-nesting frog

*Chiromantis xerampelina*

Foam-nesting frogs are found in tropical and subtropical parts of Africa, where they inhabit trees and shrubs of savannahs. When mating, pairs of foam-nesting frogs produce large amounts of foam in which the eggs are laid. The foam masses are attached to branches, overhanging temporary pools of water. The foam stops the eggs from drying out in the hot climate where the frogs live, and females occasionally remoisten it with water.

The tadpoles hatch after two days and survive in the foam as it dries out. After about a week, when the nests become very crowded, the tadpoles drop from the foam into the water below. In most matings, two or three males will be involved with each female. All the males help in beating mucus to produce the foam nests. Male foam-nesting frogs have large testicles to produce copious amounts of sperm. This increases their chances of success in fertilizing the eggs.

Foam-nesting frogs live in areas that reach very high temperatures, and they can be found sitting in direct sunlight. Compared to other types of frogs, they lose very little water from their bodies. The frogs have special skin that turns white in the sunshine. This stops the frogs from heating up and losing water through evaporation. To avoid overheating, they also produce a watery mucus from glands in their waterproof skins.

*The foam-nesting frog is a light-coloured, grainy, pale green frog with light brown lines on its legs and irregular spots across its body. Many individuals are darker with several brown areas on the body.*

**Distribution**: Tropical and southern subtropical parts of Africa, in the south and east of these areas.
**Habitat**: Bushes and trees that grow in dry African grasslands.
**Food**: Large flying insects, such as moths, butterflies, ants, plant bugs and beetles.
**Size**: 6cm (2.5in).
**Maturity**: Not known.
**Breeding**: During the rainy season. Eggs laid in ball of foam on branches. Tadpoles drop into pools.
**Life span**: 2.5 years.
**Status**: Common.

# Bushveld rain frog

*Breviceps adspersus*

*The Bushveld rain frog has a very rounded body. The neck is almost absent completely. It is brown with rows of light yellow or orange patches along its spine and sides. It also has a broad black stripe from each eye to its armpit. Females have a speckled throat, while the throat is black in males.*

The Bushveld rain frog is a rather rotund burrowing frog with a short head and blunt snout. It spends most of its life underground in the soft soils of low hills and grasslands. The frog only comes up to the surface to feed and breed after heavy rains create the right damp conditions. The frog's globular shape makes burrowing through soft sandy soil easier, but it also makes mating difficult. To help the male stay on top of the female, he secretes a sticky substance from glands around his rear. This acts like a glue and binds him to his mate.

The fertilized eggs are laid in an underground chamber. When mating and egg-laying is over, the glue either breaks down or the female sheds her skin to release the male. The tadpoles are unable to feed while underground and have to develop quickly into tailless froglets before they have their first meal.

The males attract female mates by giving short, blurred whistles, which are emitted in a continuous series of single calls. Two or more males may call together in a chorus.

**Distribution**: South Africa and Swaziland, Mozambique, Botswana and Namibia.
**Habitat**: Hot, dry foothills. Dry bushveld, and areas of scrub and grassland, in northern part of southern African range. Breeds in open and closed woodland with sandy soils.
**Food**: Insects.
**Size**: 3–6cm (1.25–2.5in).
**Maturity**: Not known.
**Breeding**: After rains.
**Life span**: Unknown.
**Status**: Common.

**Red-legged pan frog** (*Kassina maculata*):
6.5cm (2.5in)
The red-legged pan frog is grey with black oval spots, outlined with thin, light-coloured lines. The parts of the legs that are less visible, such as the rear and armpits, are bright red with black spots. This species is active at night in the lowlands of eastern Africa, when males congregate to call while floating in the water.

**Trilling reed frog** (*Hyperolius parkeri*):
2.5cm (1in)
This African tree frog is pale lime green in colour with broad, whitish bands on the sides of its body, running from its snout to its tail. It lives in low-lying grasslands in East Africa, where it is active at night. Males send out high-pitched bird-like trills to attract females. The frogs live in trees, reeds and grasses and breed by ponds, where the females lay their 70–110 eggs on vegetation, usually grasses growing over the water. After hatching, the tadpoles drop into the water to complete their development. This is the only African tree frog of which the male is larger than the female.

**Kihansi spray toad** (*Nectophrynoides asperginis*): 1.5cm (0.6in)
This tiny, mustard-yellow toad lives in the forest that grows in the spray of the Kihansi waterfall in southern Tanzania. Surviving in just this tiny habitat, the spray toad is consequently critically endangered. This problem is compounded by the toads' low breeding rates compared to other amphibians. Females do not lay eggs but give birth to a few fully formed toadlets.

# Greater leaf-folding frog

*Afrixalus fornasinii*

Greater leaf-folding frogs inhabit savannah country in eastern and southern Africa. The female lays her eggs on grass overhanging water. She folds the edges over, gluing them together with secretions from a gland on her rear. These leaf nests protect the eggs from predators and from drying out in the sun.

The eggs are pale in colour, lacking pigment. This is common with frogs and toads that lay their eggs in burrows or fold them in leaves. As they are not exposed, the eggs do not need to be coloured or have disruption patterns to camouflage them and help them blend into the surroundings. When the tadpoles have developed, their leaf nests break up and they fall into water, where they continue their development.

**Distribution**: Eastern and southern Africa.
**Habitat**: Grasslands, particularly with large bushes and trees. Also found in coastal lowlands and up to 1,300m (4,260ft) above sea level in Malawi.
**Food**: Eggs and developing larvae of other frogs that breed earlier.
**Size**: 3–4cm (1.25–1.5in).
**Maturity**: Not known.
**Breeding**: 80 pale eggs laid on a grass leaf. The tadpoles hatch and drop into water
**Life span**: Unknown.
**Status**: Common.

*Greater leaf-folding frogs have a dark reddish-brown body colour. They have black warts on their backs and broad silver bands running along their sides from their snouts to their rear. These frogs feed on the spawn and tadpoles of other frogs that breed earlier than they do.*

# Banded rubber frog

*Phrynomerus bifasciatus*

**Distribution**: Southern and East Africa.
**Habitat**: Savannah and scrubland.
**Food**: Ants and other insects.
**Size**: 7.25cm (2.75in)
**Maturity**: Not known.
**Breeding**: Eggs laid in shallow pools of water.
**Life span**: Unknown.
**Status**: Common.

The banded rubber frog is pear-shaped, with shiny smooth skin. It is nocturnal and breeds early in the season in floodwaters. The males issue melodious trills, lasting several seconds, from the banks or on floating vegetation. The eggs are laid in large masses on the water's surface or attached to aquatic plants.

The frog has a bright black and red skin, signalling to predators that it is poisonous. The skin, which becomes paler in bright light, contains toxins that can harm any animal that attempts to eat it. During the dry season the banded rubber frog seeks cover in tree hollows and burrows, away from the heat and dryness. This species is also known as the African snake-necked frog, because it is able to bend its neck much more than typical frogs.

*The banded rubber frog is a shiny black frog with red spots on its legs and thick red-orange bands running from its eyes, right along the sides of its body. The belly is grey with white blotches.*

## African clawed toad

*Xenopus laevis*

Today, chemical tests are used to tell whether women are pregnant. However, African clawed toads were once commonly used in hospitals as pregnancy tests. Pregnant women produce a particular hormone, which is released into their urine. If this hormone is present in the urine when injected into female toads, then the toads spontaneously lay eggs. In nature, the toad's eggs are laid singly and are attached to water plants or rocks.

From the head along the toad's sides there are a few rows of small stitch-like lines. Each line is a little depression containing minute hairs. Currents and vibrations in the water waft these hairs, and so the frog can detect them. This helps to tell the toad where it is and the location of other toads or predators and occasionally of food.

African clawed toads like to hang just below the water surface, waiting for food to swim by.

They are the only South African amphibians to feed and breed in the water for their whole lives. If their pools dry up, they bury themselves in the mud and wait for the rainy season to arrive.

*The African clawed toad is very flat, with small upward-facing eyes. Its skin is very slimy and generally coloured brown, green or grey, with darker spots or blotches on its back. Its belly is a yellowish-white colour. Females are generally larger than males.*

**Distribution**: Southern and Central Africa. The species has been introduced as pets to Britain, Europe and North America. Escaped frogs now live wild in these places.
**Habitat**: Muddy water in permanent pools.
**Food**: Small worms, crustaceans, fly larvae and tadpoles of own species.
**Size**: 6–9cm (2.5–3.5in).
**Maturity**: Females 15–18 months; males 12 months.
**Breeding**: Spawn from August–December.
**Life span**: Over 20 years.
**Status**: Common.

## Cape ghost frog

*Heleophryne purcelli*

Cape ghost frogs live in very fast-flowing mountain streams in the mountains of South Africa. They have well-developed toe pads that act like suckers for clinging to wet rocks in these torrential habitats. Their large hind feet are also heavily webbed, to help them swim against the current. Male Cape ghost frogs also have pads along the insides of their front legs and, prior to the mating season, they develop small spines around the rims of their lower jaws. These modifications help them grasp females and prevent them from being washed away while mating.

The females lay their large eggs under stones or in gravel in shallow backwaters, alongside the main channels of streams. The eggs are protected from the current by a tough capsule of jelly. The tadpoles of ghost frogs are long and flat. They, too, must cling on to rocks to avoid being washed away by the torrents. They attach themselves to smooth rocks

with their large sucker-like mouths. The tadpoles feed on microscopic algae that grow on the surfaces of the rocks. They use their long, muscular tails to swim against the currents for long periods while grazing.

*The Cape ghost frog is a small frog with dull green skin, covered in black-brown spots bordered with yellow. Its eyes are a coppery colour. The body is flatter than those of most frogs.*

**Distribution**: Western South Africa.
**Habitat**: Fast-flowing streams in forested mountain areas. The adults leave the water during damp periods.
**Food**: Tadpoles eat algae while the adult prey on insects and other invertebrates.
**Size**: 3.5–5cm (1.5–2in).
**Maturity**: 2 years.
**Breeding**: Late summer after rain. The rain deepens streams and slows currents.
**Life span**: Unknown.
**Status**: Common.

**Tomato frog** (*Dyscophus antongilii*): 5–10cm (2–4in)
Tomato frogs have orange-red backs, yellowish undersides, green eyes and sometimes black spots on their throats. The females are a brighter red than the males. They live in the lowlands of Madagascar, in swamps and shallow pools. Breeding occurs during the rainy season in stagnant or very slow-moving water. Females lay 1,000–1,500 small black and white eggs on the water's surface. The tadpoles are very quick to hatch and do so only 36 hours later, changing into adults after about 45 days.

**Mountain ghost frog** (*Heleophryne rosei*): 3.5–5cm (1.5–2in)
The mountain ghost frog is extremely rare and restricted to an area only 7–8sq km (1.5sq miles) in size on Table Mountain in South Africa. It has specific breeding requirements and needs areas that have water all year round. The tadpoles take a long time to grow and need at least two seasons before they change into adults.

**African "hairy" frog** (*Trichobatrachus robustus*): 9–13cm (3.5–5in)
The African "hairy" frog lives in western Africa. It gets its name from special hair-like filaments that develop on the male frog's legs and sides. The filaments are full of blood vessels and grow when the frog needs more oxygen to breathe. The species has lungs that are much smaller than the lungs of other frogs of a similar size. This means that when the males become very active as they jostle over females to mate with, they require more oxygen. The filaments act as external lungs, providing them with extra oxygen.

# African bullfrog

*Pyxicephalus adspersus*

To avoid drying up, the African bullfrog can wrap itself in a cocoon. This is made from many layers of dead skin, and looks like plastic film. The frog can survive in this cocoon for two or three months, getting all the moisture it needs by absorbing water from its bladder. When the rains finally arrive, the cocoon softens and splits open. The frog scrambles out and eats the cocoon.

The male guards its eggs and tadpoles in a shallow puddle. Sharp upper teeth and two horny spikes at the tip of the lower jaw help ward off intruders. If the puddle is in danger of drying out, the male digs an escape channel for transferring the tadpoles to water. When the tadpoles develop, they can be aggressive and cannibalistic.

**Distribution**: Tropical areas across central Africa.
**Habitat**: Temporary bodies of water and small lakes in open or bush country.
**Food**: Insects and other invertebrates, reptiles, amphibians, birds and rodents.
**Size**: Up to 20cm (8in); 2kg (4.5lb).
**Maturity**: 1–2 years.
**Breeding**: Female lays up to 4,000 eggs in temporary pools. Tadpoles change into striped froglets but lose their stripes over time.
**Life span**: More than 20 years.
**Status**: Unknown.

*African bullfrogs are generally olive-green, with lighter coloured throats and bellies to help them blend in with their surroundings. Juveniles have obvious stripes, which later fade as the bullfrogs get older.*

# Goliath bullfrog

*Conraua goliath*

Goliath bullfrogs are the largest frogs in the world, and can grow to more than 30cm (12in) in length. They live in only a few rivers in western Africa and are at risk from disappearing altogether because their rainforest home is being cleared for farmland. The species is also collected to be sold as pets.

Adult Goliath bullfrogs eat insects, crustaceans, fish and other frogs. The tadpoles, however, are plant eaters and will only feed on certain species of water plant that are found near rapids.

The Goliath bullfrog is silent, not having a vocal sac in its throat to make any sound. It is a shy species that is hunted by local people, who eat them and keep the thigh bones as good-luck charms.

**Distribution**: Cameroon and Equatorial Guinea.
**Habitat**: Swiftly flowing rivers in dense rainforests.
**Food**: Small freshwater invertebrates, fish and other amphibians. Tadpoles eat plants.
**Size**: 30cm (12in); 3.3kg (7.25lb).
**Maturity**: Unknown.
**Breeding**: Eggs laid in water.
**Life span**: Unknown.
**Status**: Vulnerable.

*The Goliath bullfrog is a very dark coloured frog, mainly a blackish-green. The belly is a lighter pinkish-orange and the eyes are a coppery brown.*

## White-lipped river frog

*Amnirana albolabris*

*Like many of its close relatives found along the western edge of Africa, the white-lipped river frog has a pale stripe along its upper lip. The males have larger eardrums than the females.*

The white-lipped river frog is a widespread and common species. It lives in forests along the coastal strip of West Africa between Sierra Leone and Gabon. Its range also extends inland into the Congo Basin as far east as Uganda. The frog has several common names across this large range, including the Congolo frog and Parker's white-lipped frog.

White-lipped river frogs live in gallery forest – a forest type that grows beside rivers and in flooded areas – and they are also common in deforested areas that have grown a layer of shrubs among the widely spaced trees that remain.

This species belongs to a genus of ten other frogs. All of them have suction discs on their toes, which help them to climb up smooth surfaces such as leaves or tree trunks. However, despite this climbing adaptation, the frogs are classified as belonging to the Ranidae (true frog) family rather than being included with the tree frogs.

**Distribution**: West and Central Africa from Sierra Leone and the Great Lakes of Uganda. Also lives on the island of Bioko.
**Habitat**: Forest rivers, mainly associated with the Niger and Congo River system.
**Food**: Tree-living insects, such as beetles and ants.
**Size**: 10cm (4in).
**Maturity**: Unknown.
**Breeding**: Breeding takes place in water.
**Life span**: Unknown.
**Status**: Common.

## Tropical platanna

*Xenopus muelleri*

The tropical platanna belongs to a small group of seemingly primitive frogs. Most of them live in South America, but a few are found in Africa. They are all highly aquatic species, and the tropical platanna rarely comes out of water. In the dry season, the platannas' pools begin to evaporate and become shallower or may disappear completely. The frogs bury themselves in mud to stay moist during these dry periods.

As well as having long toes and claws, the frog's other unusual features include having no tongue and having lateral-line sense organs, which are more common in fish, such as sharks. These organs are a series of depressions along the frog's flanks that contain minute hairs. These hairs are sensitive to movements in the water and can detect currents produced by the frog's prey. Tropical platannas eat aquatic invertebrates and small river fish. They will also consume their own tadpoles.

Mating takes place underwater. The females lay tiny eggs. Each one is attached to a rock or stem on the river bed. The frogs have ears adapted to hearing mating calls underwater. The tadpoles hatch within a few days. They have flimsy and transparent bodies. The tadpoles are filter feeders. They have only thin tails and do not swim well, so instead they hang with their heads down and filter plankton from the water.

**Distribution**: East Africa from southern Kenya to Mozambique and South Africa. The platanna is also found on Zanzibar and Mafia islands in the Indian Ocean.
**Habitat**: Freshwater.
**Food**: Fish and invertebrates.
**Size**: 9cm (3.5in).
**Maturity**: 1–2 years.
**Breeding**: Tiny eggs deposited in stagnant water attached to stems and rocks on the river bed.
**Life span**: 15 years.
**Status**: Common.

*The tropical platanna is a smooth-skinned frog with long toes on its forelimbs. The hind feet are webbed to help with swimming. Three of the hind toes have claws. It is one of only 30 frog species that have these claws.*

# Marbled snout-burrower

*Hemisus marmoratus*

**Distribution**: Africa south of the Sahara Desert.
**Habitat**: Savannah.
**Food**: Insects.
**Size**: 4cm (1.5in).
**Maturity**: 1 year.
**Breeding**: Eggs laid in underground chamber.
**Life span**: Unknown.
**Status**: Common.

The marbled snout burrower, also known as the pig-nosed frog and mottled shovel-nosed frog, lives across most of Africa south of the Sahara Desert. It is a savannah species and is not found in rainforests, although it does live along the edges of forests near rivers.

The frog survives in open country by digging into loose soil. As their name implies, snout burrowers burrow head first, and they are the only frogs to do so. (Other burrowing frogs use their hind legs to do most of the digging.) By day the marbled snout burrower rests about 15cm (6in) underground. At night it comes up to the surface to feed on insects.

The female digs an egg chamber near to a pond. She lays eggs in the chamber, which are then fertilized by a male. After the tadpoles hatch, the mother carries them to the pond.

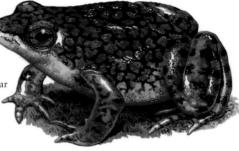

*Snout burrowers are also called shovel-nosed frogs because the small and pointed snout is used for digging. The short forelegs are also used for burrowing. The skin is smooth and covered in a mottled brown pattern, which gives it the look of marble.*

---

**West African live-bearing toad** (*Nimbaphrynoides occidentalis*): 2.5cm (1in)
This small and critically endangered frog is also known as the western Nimba toad because one of the few places in which it survives is the Mount Nimba reserve in Côte d'Ivoire and Guinea. They live in grasses and thickets and lie dormant in rocky crevices during droughts. Females of this species do not lay eggs. Instead the eggs are held inside the body, where the young develop for up to nine months. While inside the mother, the tadpoles are first nourished by the contents of the egg; once that is used up, they are fed by their mother. At birth the young have metamorphosed into tiny toadlets. During the birth, the mother inflates her body with air and uses it to push the toadlets (up to 16 in each litter) out.

**African tree frog** (*Leptopelis modestus*): 4.5cm (1.75in)
The African tree frog lives in two populations. The larger one is located in the forests of Cameroon while the smaller population survives in a pocket of forest in western Kenya. Like all tree frogs, this species has disc-shaped suction pads on the tips of its toes to aid with grip while climbing. The African tree frog is rarely seen and is most easily located by the deep "clack" call that males make to attract females.

**Dwarf-ridged frog** (*Ptychadena taenioscelis*): 2.5–4cm (1–1.5in)
A small savannah frog with a dark band running between each knee under the body. Breeds after rains in temporary pools.

# Sharp-nosed ridge frog

*Ptychadena oxyrhynchus*

The sharp-nosed ridge frog is also known as the rocket frog because of its pointed snout and its ability to make leaps of up to 3m (10ft). It can make such huge jumps thanks to its long hind legs. The frog's leaping is a survival tactic used to escape predators on the open savannah, where there are few places to hide. The species lives across Africa south of the Sahara Desert. In most places the species avoids dense forests, but in East Africa one subspecies lives in mountain forests.

The frogs spend dry periods of the year in or close to rivers. When the rains come, the frogs hop off into open country and prepare to breed. The males position themselves beside a puddle or other temporary pool and attract mates with a short and shrill call. After mating, females lay long strings of eggs on the bottom of the pools. The strings each contain up to 3,500 eggs. These strings slowly break apart, and the eggs float in small groups to the surface, where the tadpoles emerge after a few days.

**Distribution**: Africa south of the Sahara Desert.
**Habitat**: Savannah.
**Food**: Invertebrates.
**Size**: 6cm (2.25in).
**Maturity**: 9 months.
**Breeding**: Eggs laid in temporary pools after rains.
**Life span**: 2 years.
**Status**: Common.

*The sharp-nosed ridge frog is relatively large. The skin is grey-green with brown spots in several rows along the back. The belly is smooth and white, although the groin areas may be yellow.*

## Common squeaker

*Arthroleptis stenodactylus*

*The common squeaker is a plump frog with short legs. The third finger on the forefeet is elongated, especially in males. The body is largely brown, sometimes with a light stripe down the back. There is also a darker swathe of skin curving from behind the eye to the shoulder.*

Common squeakers live among the leaf litter of forests. They are often seen in clearings and appear to be able to survive in many human-influenced habitats. This adaptability is partly due to the fact that this species is not reliant on water to breed. There is no water-based tadpole stage in their development; instead, fully formed froglets that are capable of life on land emerge from the eggs.

These frogs live across much of Central and southern Africa from the coast of Kenya to Angola and South Africa. During the dry season, they lie dormant buried in damp soil. During wet periods, the frogs move around on the forest floor often hidden beneath leaf litter.

The males attract females with a high-pitched call that earns the species its common name. The males hide themselves under leaf litter when calling to make it harder for predators to locate them.

The female buries her eggs in a shallow hole in damp soil most often located under a bush or among tree roots, where the earth is unlikely to dry out. The froglets hatch after a few weeks and dig themselves out once the conditions are damp enough.

**Distribution**: Southern and Central Africa from northern Kenya and Angola to South Africa.
**Habitat**: Forests and forest clearings.
**Food**: Insects, worms and other invertebrates.
**Size**: 4.25cm (1.75in).
**Maturity**: 2 years.
**Breeding**: Froglets grow directly from eggs. There is no tadpole stage.
**Life span**: Unknown.
**Status**: Common.

## Guttural toad

*Bufo gutturalis*

The guttural toad is one of the most common amphibians in southern Africa. It regularly hops into houses and survives in a mixture of habitats, including many manmade ones, ranging from agricultural fields to gardens. It is also a common resident of savannahs, shrublands and wetlands. The toad's range extends as far north as the southern tip of Somalia in the arid region of eastern Africa. However, the species is more common on the western side of the continent from the Democratic Republic of Congo to Namibia and the central region of South Africa. This species of toad is one of the few to be expanding its range. The toad is an insect eater and often snatches flying insects from the air. However, it also feeds on other invertebrates, such as spiders and worms.

The toad is named after its deep "kwaak" call, which is often likened to a snore. The males produce this call to attract mates during periods of rain, when pools begin to fill with fresh water. The toads always lay their eggs in permanent water sources, although many of these pools shrink considerably during the dry season. The females produce eggs in huge numbers because most tadpoles will not survive for long enough to metamorphose into the adult form and leave the water.

*Like other toads, this species is a stocky amphibian with rough, warty skin. Behind the eyes there are bumps called parotid glands, which secrete unpleasant-smelling toxins when the toad is threatened.*

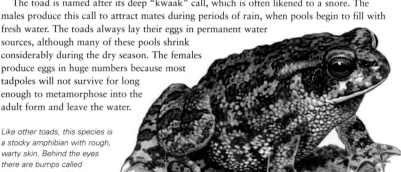

**Distribution**: Across southern Africa from Somalia and Congo in the north to central South Africa.
**Habitat**: Grasslands, thickets, shrublands, marshes, gardens and fields. Not found in tropical forests.
**Food**: Insects and other invertebrates.
**Size**: 10cm (4in).
**Maturity**: 1–2 years.
**Breeding**: Females lay strings containing up to 25,000 eggs in permanent pools of water. The tadpoles hatch out within a few days.
**Life span**: Unknown.
**Status**: Common.

# Woodland toad

*Mertensophryne micranotis*

**Distribution**: Coast of Kenya, Zanzibar and mountains of southern Tanzania.
**Habitat**: Woodland.
**Food**: Invertebrates.
**Size**: 2.5cm (1in).
**Maturity**: 1 year.
**Breeding**: About eight eggs laid in puddles formed in fallen logs and stumps.
**Life span**: Unknown.
**Status**: Common.

The woodland toad lives on the floor of East African forests. East Africa is a dry region and any forests that do grow are associated with microclimates, such as those around mountains and gorges, where enough rain falls to support tree growth. In Kenya, in the north of the range, woodland frogs are found close to the coast. The species also lives on the island of Zanzibar. On the Tanzanian mainland the toad is in the Udzungwa Mountains.

These toads need just a puddle of water in which to lay their eggs. Males call for mates while buried in leaf litter. The females respond to their chirping calls, and after mating the females lay a few eggs in tiny puddles. They have even been known to lay eggs inside a flooded snail's shell or broken coconut. Small pools such as these have limited oxygen, so the tadpoles have small fleshy crowns with a large surface area. They poke these crowns above the surface of the water to absorb oxygen from the air.

*This species has very small, toxin-filled, parotid glands unlike most toad species. The outer toes of the hind feet are also very short, though it is unclear why this is. Males have rough patches on their thumbs to help grip on to females while mating.*

---

**Golden mantella** (*Mantella aurantiaca*): 3cm (1.25in)
This striking frog is found only on the western slopes of Madagascar's spine of mountains. Like most Malagasy species, the golden mantella is vulnerable to extinction due to the loss of its habitat. Many of Madagascar's forests are being cut down for firewood and to make way for farmland. Adult golden mantellas are completely terrestrial and never enter pools of standing water, not even to breed. The frogs mate during the rainy season. The female lays eggs among moist leaf litter on the forest floor. This location is damp enough for the eggs to develop and for tadpoles to hatch out. The young amphibians then rely upon the torrential tropical rain to wash them into the nearest stream or pond, where they can continue their development.

**Senegal kassina** (*Kassina senegalensis*): 4cm (1.5in)
This burrowing frog occurs across sub-Saharan Africa, from Senegal in West Africa to northern Kenya and south to the Cape province of South Africa. The largest individuals in the species live in South Africa, where a few can reach 5cm (2in) long. The Senegal kassina is a striking animal, with its broad brown stripes on a paler, tan background running down its back. The kassina is found mainly in savannah habitats. It spends most of the day underground, emerging on damp nights to eat termites and other insects. The frogs travel to standing water to mate. The males call to females hidden in bankside plants. The females lay eggs underwater.

# Red toad

*Schismaderma carens*

The red toad lives across much of southern Africa, from northern Kenya to the East Cape of South Africa. It is a savannah species and spends most of the year on land. However, like most toads, this species needs water to breed in.

Outside the breeding season, the red toad forages for slugs and insects out in the open. It hunts under the cover of darkness. As day approaches, the toad buries itself in fallen leaves or hides under a stone. As a result of this lifestyle, this species is rarely seen outside the mating season.

The breeding season begins with the rainy season. The males give a low, booming call while floating in deep water. The toads are unfussy about their breeding pools and often gather around dirty water. Females lay up to 20,000 eggs in double strings. Once hatched, the tadpoles crowd the pools and many are eaten before they get the chance to metamorphose into adults.

**Distribution**: Southern Africa.
**Habitat**: Grasslands and woodlands.
**Food**: Invertebrates.
**Size**: 9cm (3.5in).
**Maturity**: 1–2 years.
**Breeding**: 20,000 eggs laid in deep water.
**Life span**: Unknown.
**Status**: Common.

*The red toad gets its name from its rusty-coloured back. This section of its body is demarcated from the pale and mottled flanks by a ridge of warts.*

## Common reed frog

*Hyperolius viridiflavus*

*The common reed frog is found in a vast array of colours and patterns. Each pattern is strongly associated with one location. For example, the frogs in coastal Kenya are cream all over; in Uganda they are green; while in Tanzania they are yellow with dark stripes.*

The common reed frog is found across the tropical region of Africa. It lives in the grasslands and small areas of woodland that make up African savannah. The frogs have small suction discs on all their toes and this makes them able to climb well, even on smooth surfaces such as leaves.

There are currently 28 subspecies of common reed frog that have been described. Many of these subspecies themselves have two or three colour forms. Biologists are currently attempting to work out how each group is related. The frogs are described as a species complex and that may actually turn out to be a collection of different species.

Each colour pattern, or morph, is found at a certain location and there are almost no places where two morphs live alongside each other in the whole of Africa. Instead, individuals that live at the boundary between morphs display a transitional hybrid pattern. To add to the confusion, the colour patterns of individual frogs can become bleached by long exposure to sunlight.

**Distribution**: 28 subspecies live across Africa south of the Sahara Desert. Some biologists suggest that the species is actually comprised of several species, which do not interbreed.
**Habitat**: Savannah, grassland and woodlands.
**Food**: Insects and other invertebrates.
**Size**: 4cm (1.5in).
**Maturity**: Unknown.
**Breeding**: Males call to females with clicks. Females lay 300 eggs in open water.
**Life span**: Unknown.
**Status**: Common.

## Tinker reed frog

*Hyperolius tuberilinguis*

*The tinker reed frog is relatively nondescript with its uniform colouring, which can be anything from pale green to brown. However, it is easily recognizable by its pointed snout, a backward-pointing triangle between the eyes and its toe pads. No other frog in the lowlands of East Africa shares all these features.*

The tinker reed frog lives in the lowlands of eastern Africa from the southern coastal region of Kenya through Mozambique and Malawi to South Africa and Zimbabwe. It is most common in the wooded savannahs in this region, where it breeds in watering holes and temporary pools that are surrounded by thick vegetation.

The males climb up the stems of tall waterside plants to call for mates from a high vantage point. They produce a series of slow clicks to attract mates. After mating, the females lay small white eggs on vegetation that hangs above the water. The eggs are surrounded by a clear, sticky jelly, which keeps them in place. After a few days, the tadpoles emerge from the eggs and drop into the water below.

The tadpoles feed in the pool for several weeks, preying on aquatic insect larvae. Once they grow to a length of 4.5cm (1.75in), they begin to change into the adult form. Paradoxically, the tadpole is longer than the tailless adult form into which it metamorphoses.

**Distribution**: Eastern Africa from Kenya to northern parts of South Africa.
**Habitat**: Savannahs and woodlands.
**Food**: Insect larvae and other invertebrates.
**Size**: 3.5cm (1.5in).
**Maturity**: Unknown.
**Breeding**: Sticky masses of eggs are fixed to plants that hang above the water's surface. When tadpoles emerge they fall into water below to continue their development.
**Life span**: Unknown.
**Status**: Common.

# Natal puddle frog

*Phrynobatrachus natalensis*

**Distribution**: Whole of the south of the Sahara Desert.
**Habitat**: Savannahs.
**Food**: Termites, other insects and spiders.
**Size**: 4cm (1.5in).
**Maturity**: 1–2 years.
**Breeding**: Mat of eggs laid on surface of temporary pool of water.
**Life span**: Unknown.
**Status**: Common.

The Natal puddle frog's name tells two stories. Firstly, the species is indeed found living in the savannahs of South Africa's Natal, but, as one of Africa's most widespread frog species, it also lives in most other parts of the continent as far north as the Sahara. Secondly, the frog does not need permanent flowing water to lay its eggs in; instead, it relies on shallow puddles that form after rains.

Puddle frogs live on the African savannah. In rainy periods most of their diet is made up of termites. In drier times they eat other insects, such as crickets, and spiders. The frogs can be seen by night or day.

They are most active during the rainy season, when males gather beside puddles and call to attract mates with a snore-like call. The female floats her small white eggs on to the surface of the puddle, forming a thin mat.

*The Natal puddle frog exhibits a bewildering number of colour types across the continent. The species can be identified by its pointed snout and short, webbed toes, which, unlike those of many frogs, have fleshy tips.*

---

**Spotted reed frog** (*Hyperolius puncticulatus*): 3cm (1.25in)
This relatively large orange-brown reed frog is named after the large yellow spots fringed with black that appear on its snout and back. The spotted reed frog is a forest species found in East Africa. It spends most of its year among leaf litter and undergrowth on the ground and breeds in temporary pools after heavy rains. The males attract mates by climbing into low vegetation beside the pool and giving out a series of high-pitched clicks. The female lays eggs on leaves that overhang the water so that hatching tadpoles can fall into the pool.

**de Witte's frog** (*Afrana wittei*): 6cm (2.25in)
This small frog lives in three separate populations in the highlands of Ethiopia, Kenya and Uganda, where it is found in marshy areas. These habitats form the watershed of the Nile and are often fed by heavy rains. The frog is active during the day and seldom strays too far from water, where it escapes to when danger approaches. The eggs are laid in the water, where the tadpoles develop only slowly compared to other tropical species.

**Boettger's dainty frog** (*Cacosternum boettgeri*): 2cm (0.75in)
This tiny frog is another highland species. Outside the breeding season it lives in meadows, sheltering by day in burrows abandoned by rodents or in other crevices. In the breeding season, males call for mates from thick vegetation beside marshy pools.

# Ornate frog

*Hildebrandtia ornata*

The ornate frog is a burrowing species. It prefers dry habitats, such as savannahs, but is also seen along forest edges. The frogs avoid hot weather by resting in burrows. They emerge at night or on damp, cloudy days to feed on ground insects.

The frog's breeding season begins as soon as the rains arrive. As the rains replenish the savannah's water holes, the male frogs begin to call for mates with a harsh bellow. The calls come from beside the water, but the frogs are nowhere to be seen. This is because they are calling from underground.

After mating, the eggs are laid in masses of up to 200 eggs that float on the surface of the water. The colour of the tadpoles matches that of the bottom of the pool. This adaptation may make the tadpoles harder to spot and so save them from predators.

**Distribution**: Sub-Saharan Africa.
**Habitat**: Savannah and dry forest.
**Food**: Invertebrates.
**Size**: 7cm (2.75in).
**Maturity**: Unknown.
**Breeding**: Large egg masses laid in marshes.
**Life span**: Unknown.
**Status**: Common.

*This small fat frog has smooth skin and a bright pattern. The back is bright green with black blotches. Dark broken bands run along the sides of the snout and through the eyes. The throat has a pair of marks in the shape of a Y. The hind feet have short toes and are only slightly webbed.*

## Cryptic sand frog

*Tomopterna cryptotis*

*This burrowing frog has a large, spade-like structure on the heel of each hind foot. The back has a mottled pattern of grey, rusty brown and tan blobs. The flanks continue this pattern but with smaller markings. A pale line down the back is sometimes present.*

The cryptic sand frog's colouring helps it to remain hidden against the dry sandy soil of its savannah habitat. (The word "cryptic" is used by biologists to refer to this and other adaptations that help an animal to hide.)

The sand frog is found in most of Africa south of the Sahara Desert. It lives far from running water, relying instead on seasonal rains to produce temporary pools for its tadpoles. For much of the rest of the year the frog lies dormant deep underground. The frog burrows into loose sandy soil to a depth of about 50cm (20in), where the soil remains damp and cool all year round.

When the rains arrive, the sand frogs have no time to waste. A male will find a raised mud bank near a pool to call a mate from. He produces a rapid "bing bing" call that sounds like a telephone ringing. After mating, the female scatters the dark eggs one by one into shallow, muddy water. One female may produce as many 3,000 eggs in a season. The eggs hatch into tadpoles after a few days. The tadpoles metamorphose into froglets after about a month in the water.

**Distribution**: The whole of Africa south of the Sahara Desert.
**Habitat**: Dry grassland areas with rainfall between June and October. Also found in woodlands in a few areas.
**Food**: Termites and beetles.
**Size**: 6cm (2.25in).
**Maturity**: 1 year.
**Breeding**: Eggs laid at night in temporary pools. Tadpoles stay in the water for 30 days.
**Life span**: Unknown.
**Status**: Common.

## Angola river frog

*Afrana angolensis*

The Angola river frog spends most of its time in shallow parts of permanent bodies of water. It has long legs with highly webbed toes, which are used to paddle through the water. The frog does sometimes climb out of a pond or stream either in pursuit of prey or to call for a mate. It prefers to do this at places where the bank is covered by thick vegetation for it to hide among. The river frog cannot survive out of water for long.

Despite its name, the Angola river frog is found across most of the southern half of Africa, from Eritrea and the Democratic Republic of Congo to South Africa. It occurs in most habitats where there are sufficient bodies of water. As long as there is a pond or river, this species is just as happy in the middle of tropical rainforest as it is in an arid grassland.

The Angola river frog hunts in and out of water. It feeds on insects, especially aquatic larvae, and it also preys on smaller frogs. As the breeding season approaches, males develop swollen thumbs with dark areas. These swellings, called nuptial pads, are used to grip on to females during mating. Competition for partners is stiff, so males must hang on tightly to avoid being knocked off by a rival. The males call to females either floating in shallow water or from along the bank. The call is a complex one and ends in a long rattle and croak. After mating, the females lay the eggs in a shallow area of still water.

*The Angola river frog is relatively large. It has an olive back with dark spots. There are heavy folds of skin behind the forelegs on the flanks. The belly is pale with a mottled brown pattern that is strongest at the throat.*

**Distribution**: Much of equatorial and southern Africa, from Eritrea and the Congo in the north to South Africa. Absent from Namibia. The species is likely to be comprised of several separate species.
**Habitat**: Rivers, ponds and permanent bodies of water. Prefers water with thick plant growth on the banks.
**Food**: Large insects and small frogs.
**Size**: 9cm (3.5in).
**Maturity**: Unknown.
**Breeding**: Eggs laid in large numbers in shallow water.
**Life span**: Unknown.
**Status**: Common.

# Bocage's tree frog

*Leptopelis bocagii*

**Distribution**: Most of southern Africa from Ethiopia and the Congo to the Transvaal of South Africa.
**Habitat**: Savannah.
**Food**: Invertebrates.
**Size**: 5cm (2in).
**Maturity**: Unknown.
**Breeding**: Eggs laid in holes.
**Life span**: Unknown.
**Status**: Common.

Bocage's tree frog may never climb a tree in its life. This species has evolved to survive on grasslands, where it exists as a burrower rather than a climber. It is found across southern Africa. It also appears likely that the frogs identified as Bocage's tree frog in fact belong to a number of different species, some of which look indistinguishable. However, evidence suggests that they will breed with only a certain subgroup of frogs. A species is a group of animals that can breed successfully with each other. Since some Bocage's tree frogs will not breed with others, they must by definition belong to a different species, irrespective of the fact that they all look and behave in the same way.

The frogs spend hot periods underground. Breeding begins as heavy rain soaks into the ground. Males take up a position on low vegetation and call with a low "quaak" call. Females lay their eggs in deep holes. The soil around these holes is waterlogged enough for tadpoles to develop quickly into froglets.

*Being a tree frog by name only, this species lacks the round sucker-like pads on the tips of the toes as used by climbing frogs to grip on to flat surfaces. It also lacks webbing between its feet, since it rarely enters water.*

---

**Dwarf bullfrog** (*Pyxicephalus edulis*): 10cm (4in)
Despite being a dwarf, this species is still a large frog compared to most other frogs. Males are a mottled brown while females are a dull grey-green. It lives across Central and southern Africa, from Nigeria and Somalia in the north to South Africa. The dwarf bullfrog is found in a range of habitats from marshy ground to dry savannahs. For many months of each year, the frog lives underground. It conserves water by surrounding itself in a bag-like cocoon of dead skin. During the breeding season, the males position themselves in a flooded thicket and produce a barking call to attract females. The females lay eggs in shallow water. The tadpoles develop very quickly to avoid predation. The dwarf frog is also called the edible bullfrog, and it is hunted by people across Africa for its meat.

**Mababe puddle frog** (*Phrynobatrachus mababiensis*): 2cm (0.75in)
This tiny frog lives in woodlands across eastern and southern Africa. They are very common and often seen in huge numbers as they gather to breed in temporary pools. Males produce a long buzzing sound to attract females. The males stay hidden in leaf litter until a female approaches, at which time there is fierce competition to mate with her. Once the eggs are fertilized, they are floated on to the surface of the water.

**Eastern puddle frog** (*Phrynobatrachus acridoides*): 2cm (0.75in)
A species that lives alongside the Mababe puddle frog. It is distinguished by its pale grey-green skin and its creaking call.

# Yellow-spotted tree frog

*Leptopelis flavomaculatus*

The yellow-spotted tree frogs live in the dry deciduous forests of eastern Africa. Their range runs from the southern coast of Kenya to the Save River in Mozambique and southern Zimbabwe. By contrast, their close relative, *L. vermiculatus*, lives in the damp evergreen forests that grow in this region.

The species is a relatively large tree frog. It has webbed feet and large toe pads. These pads help the frog to grip while climbing.

The frog's forest habitat experiences long periods without rain. The trees drop their leaves during dry periods. The frogs sit out the drought crammed into damp hollows.

When the rains return, the frogs prepare to breed. The males climb up into a tree to a high point 4m (13ft) above the ground to attract females with a "clack" call. They may even call from underground burrows in dangerously exposed locations. The females lay eggs on floating vegetation.

**Distribution**: Eastern region of Africa.
**Habitat**: Forests.
**Food**: Invertebrates.
**Size**: 6cm (2.25in).
**Maturity**: Unknown.
**Breeding**: Eggs laid on floating vegetation.
**Life span**: Unknown.
**Status**: Common.

*Despite their name, many adult yellow-spotted tree frogs are grey-brown in colour. They often have a darker brown triangle between the eyes. Younger frogs tend to be paler, with yellow spots on their backs.*

# TURTLES AND TORTOISES

*Tortoises, terrapins and turtles appeared on Earth around 200 million years ago. Tortoises are the land
form of the three and generally have dome-shaped shells. Terrapins tend to live in fresh water while
turtles live in the sea. Tortoises are most common in warm regions and are therefore uncommon in
northern Europe. However, turtles and terrapins are found right across both Europe and Africa.*

## European pond turtle

*Emys orbicularis*

European pond turtles used to be common in
Britain when the weather warmed after the
last Ice Age, but they disappeared around
5,000 years ago when temperatures fell once
more. Today the species is found across the
rest of Europe, including northern France.
Although the adult turtle can survive the
British climate, it is too cool for the eggs to
hatch successfully. During warm weather,
European pond turtles can be found basking
on exposed rocks. They can be quite shy and if
disturbed will quickly dive back into the water where their
webbed feet allow them to move around rapidly.

Males can mate with females throughout a seven-month
period from March to October, although most activity is seen
during March and April. Two or three months after mating the
females lay 3–16 eggs in burrows. The young turtles hatch in
August and September before the onset of autumn and winter.

*The European pond turtle has
a smooth, oval shell. Younger
individuals have lighter,
sometimes yellowish, spots
and streaks on their shells,
necks and heads. Older
individuals are entirely dark.
They hibernate in winter,
burying themselves in mud.*

**Distribution**: Europe, North
Africa and western Asia.
**Habitat**: Ponds, lakes and
slow-moving streams.
**Food**: Fish, amphibians,
insects, molluscs, young
snakes and small mammals.
**Size**: 18–35cm (7–14in); 5–10kg
(11–22lb). Female larger.
**Maturity**: Females 15 years;
males 12 years.
**Breeding**: Females lay eggs
in soil during June.
**Life span**: Up to 120 years.
**Status**: Common.

## Marsh terrapin

*Pelomedusa subrufa*

The marsh terrapin is one of Africa's most common freshwater reptiles. Also known as the
African helmeted turtle, the marsh terrapin is found in still waters across most of central and
southern Africa. The north-western limit of its range is Ghana, and the species is found all
the way down to South Africa's Cape Province. The terrapin is even found on the island of
Madagascar and across the Red Sea in Yemen.

Marsh terrapins are side-necked turtles, which means that, when threatened, they tuck
their head under the shell to one side. They do not pull it backwards like other species.
Perhaps surprisingly, marsh terrapins are voracious hunters. They eat waterborne insect
larvae, freshwater crabs and other crustaceans, and other shellfish, such as water snails and
mussels. They also catch fish underwater and have even been known to drag birds into the
water when they come to drink.

The breeding season begins in spring. The male
courts the female by following her with his head
on her back. He gives her back legs
regular nips. After mating, the female
buries her eggs in a nest in soft sand.

*The marsh terrapin is small by turtle
standards, but one of the larger terrapin
species. The flat green shell is often
discoloured by mud and slime. The neck is long
and there are two soft sensory tentacles on the chin.*

**Distribution**: Central and
southern Africa, Madagascar
and Yemen.
**Habitat**: Rivers, lakes and
marshes.
**Food**: Insects, crustaceans,
small birds, snails and
worms.
**Size**: 20–32cm (8–12.5in).
**Maturity**: Unknown.
**Breeding**: 30 soft eggs laid
in sand. Hatch after 75 days.
**Life span**: Unknown.
**Status**: Common.

# Leatherback turtle

*Dermochelys coriacea*

The leatherback turtle is the world's largest marine turtle. Its shell has a leathery texture and is semi-rigid; it is made from thousands of individual tiny bony plates connected together. Each plate can move a little, making the shell more flexible than if it were completely solid. The turtles have long front flippers that enable them to swim up to 30km (20 miles) per day.

Leatherback turtles are very unusual reptiles because they are able to generate body heat through the movement of their muscles. The heat is maintained by the turtle's huge size, layers of fat under the skin and also by a long oesophagus, which coils back before reaching the stomach, helping to heat up swallowed food.

The turtles also have special blood vessels that stop heat being lost to cold water. Heat is transferred from arteries entering the flippers to veins carrying blood away from the flippers, keeping the limbs colder than the rest of the body. Mating takes place at sea and the females nest on tropical beaches, where they lay eggs in pits dug into sand.

**Distribution**: Atlantic, Pacific and Indian Oceans.
**Habitat**: Marine water.
**Food**: Jellyfish.
**Size**: 2–3m (6.5–10ft); up to 900kg (1,980lb).
**Maturity**: 30–50 years.
**Breeding**: 80–100 eggs laid on beaches every other year, hatching after 60 days.
**Life span**: Over 50 years.
**Status**: Critically endangered.

*The leatherback turtle has a dark grey or black upper surface with additional spotting. Ridges run from the front end of the shell down to the tail. The span of the flippers is equal to the length of the animal.*

# Loggerhead turtle

*Caretta caretta*

Loggerhead turtles live in all the world's oceans and seas. They avoid the cold polar waters, but have been spotted as far north as Norway and eastern Russia.

Like other large chelonians (turtles and tortoises), loggerheads grow slowly and have a long life. Adults may travel across thousands of kilometres of ocean in a lifetime, although these sea turtles tend to stay in shallow waters close to the shore, and they are often spotted in river mouths and in bays.

Adult loggerheads forage for much of their food on the sea bed, although they can survive perfectly well in very deep waters by hunting for fish. Very young loggerheads cannot dive to the bottom to find food. Instead they foraging near to the surface and often hide from predators in mats of floating seaweed.

Like other sea turtles, loggerheads are endangered with extinction, the main reason for which is the scarcity of suitable nesting sites. Mating takes place at sea. Female loggerheads must come ashore to bury their eggs high on gently sloping sandy beaches. These same habitats are also attractive to tourists, who scare the laying turtles away. Along developed coasts today, loggerheads and other sea turtles nest in large numbers at only the few protected sites.

Females lay up to 120 eggs in a deep hole at night. The hatchlings dig themselves out about 50 days later and make a perilous dash for the ocean. Sea birds pick off many of them even before they get wet. The lights from beachside buildings also affect the hatchlings. The young turtles use the moon to orientate themselves so they can find the water. However, after reaching the surface the confused loggerheads can head off up the beach, away from the sea.

**Distribution**: Worldwide including the Atlantic Ocean, Black Sea, Mediterranean Sea and Indian Ocean.
**Habitat**: Warm sea water.
**Food**: Sponges, jellyfish, crabs, clams, fish and squid.
**Size**: 1.25m (4ft); 100–150kg (220–330lb).
**Maturity**: 12 years.
**Breeding**: Clutches of eggs laid every 2–3 years.
**Life span**: 60 years.
**Status**: Endangered.

*Loggerheads are so called because of their large heads and powerful jaws. Unlike larger sea turtles, loggerheads have a hard shell. They are the largest hard-shell turtle in the world – larger even than the giant tortoises of the Galápagos.*

# Leopard tortoise

*Geochelone pardalis*

The leopard tortoise is a very distinctive tortoise, with obvious black and yellowish markings on its shell. The shell patterns are variable; indeed, each pattern is unique, like human fingerprints. Leopard tortoises from Ethiopia are paler than most, while those from South Africa are exceptionally large.

A musk gland near the tail emits a powerful and distinctive smell, which is used by the tortoises to attract partners for mating or to drive away predators. When it becomes hot, the leopard tortoise digs a hole and remains underground to avoid overheating or dehydrating. It stays in the burrow until the temperatures fall and the rains come again. If food becomes hard to find, the tortoises travel long distances to seek more. To continue growing healthy shells and to ensure their bones remain strong, they eat old bones found when they forage.

*The leopard tortoise is straw-coloured, with black blotches evenly spread over the shell. Shell markings are reminiscent of the pelt of a leopard cat, hence the tortoise's name.*

**Distribution**: South and East Africa, south of the Sahara.
**Habitat**: Semi-arid, thorny and dry grassland habitats.
**Food**: Grasses, fruit of the prickly pear, thistles and other plants.
**Size**: 40–65cm (15.75–25.5in); 10–40kg (22–88lb).
**Maturity**: 6–10 years.
**Breeding**: Eggs laid in autumn.
**Life span**: 50–150 years.
**Status**: Vulnerable.

---

**Radiated tortoise** (*Geochelone radiata*): 40cm (15.75in)
The radiated tortoise is a very colourful tortoise with streaks radiating out from each section of its shell. It lives on the island of Madagascar and is less common than it used to be because the Chinese prize it as a purported aphrodisiac. The vegetation where it lives is disappearing, including a type of spiny cactus, which provides important cover for the tortoise. Males and females encounter each other during late afternoon sorties, but they only mate if it is dry.

**Atlantic** or **Kemp's ridley turtle** (*Lepidochelys kempii*): 50–70cm (19.5–27.5in)
The Atlantic ridley turtle is the smallest marine turtle and the most endangered. The turtles live in sheltered areas such as large estuaries, bays and lagoons where they feed on crabs, jellyfish, squid, snails, starfish and a variety of other marine invertebrates, as well as some seaweeds. They have distinctive heart-shaped shells that may be black, grey-brown or olive in colour.

**East African side-necked turtle** (*Pelusios subniger*): 20cm (8in)
The East African side-necked turtle lives in shallow ponds and streams with muddy bottoms. When the pools dry out or it gets too hot or cold, the turtle burrows into the mud and remains protected until the rains come. When threatened, this species pulls its neck to one side rather than bringing it back into the shell like typical tortoises and turtles. They have dark – often black – domed shells with yellow undersides. They are found in East Africa, below the Sahara Desert and throughout Madagascar.

# Pancake tortoise

*Malacochersus tornieri*

The pancake tortoise is very rare and suffered from illegal pet trade in the 1960s and 70s. Its tiny size meant it could be smuggled out of Kenya and Tanzania in very large numbers. The tortoise lives in rocky cliffs, hidden in crevices during the day. Grasses are very important for feeding and breeding. These grassy areas around the cliffs are disappearing through human activity, which prevents the species from increasing its population.

The pancake tortoise has a lightweight shell, which helps it scurry along and escape from predators more quickly. The bony plates that make up the shell are reduced in this species, leaving spaces where the bones would be, making it less heavy and more flexible. The shell is also flattened, which helps the tortoise to rest or escape under very low rocks. The tortoise can wedge itself into crevices by inflating its lungs with air and pushing down with its legs. If the tortoise falls and lands on its back, it can right itself quite easily.

**Distribution**: Kenya and Tanzania.
**Habitat**: Small rocky cliffs called "kopjes", over 1,000m (3,280ft) above sea level.
**Food**: Dry grasses and vegetation.
**Size**: 15cm (6in).
**Maturity**: Not known.
**Breeding**: Single eggs laid 3 or 4 times a year.
**Life span**: 25 years.
**Status**: Endangered.

*The pancake tortoise has a brown shell, marked with pale yellow and black. It has a more pronounced hook to its beak than other species. The males have longer, thicker tails than the females.*

**Spanish terrapin** (*Mauremys leprosa*): 20cm (8in)
The Spanish terrapin is found across southern Spain and Portugal. The species also lives in north-west Africa, between Morocco and Libya. The Spanish terrapin resembles the European pond terrapin but is lighter in colour and often has stripes on the neck. The shell is also slightly more elongated. The terrapin lives in shallow pools and can tolerate high salt contents as the water slowly evaporates away in the heat. If the pools dry out completely, the terrapin burrows into the damp mud until the pool refills.

**Yellow-bellied hinged terrapin** (*Pelusios castanoides*): 23cm (9in)
The yellow-bellied hinged terrapin lives along the eastern coast of Africa from Kenya to Kwazulu in South Africa. It is also found on several offshore islands. The shell is olive-coloured and the plastron (bottom shell) is yellow with black markings. The skin on the legs and neck is also yellow. The terrapin lives in shallow pools and aestivates (becomes dormant in hot weather) in damp mud when the pools dry out.

**Forest hinged terrapin** (*Pelosios gabonensis*): 20cm (8in)
This species is one of the few terrapins to live in the rainforests of Central America. It lives in swamps and pools on the forest floor. It is a favourite food of forest people, despite producing a foul-smelling liquid from its anus when threatened.

# Marginated tortoise

*Testudo marginata*

Marginated tortoises live in the rocky hills of southern Greece. They are also found on many Greek islands. A large population lives in Sardinia after being introduced to the island in Roman times. These tortoises have become rare in the wild because large numbers are collected for the pet trade.

The tortoise's diet consists of thin leaves, such as rocket, radish and clover, as well as grass and fruits. In winter, when food is in short supply in the exposed highland habitat, the tortoises dig long burrows in which to hibernate until spring.

After the tortoises emerge from hibernation, the breeding season begins. During mating the male sticks out his bright red tongue as he produces loud barks. The female buries about 10 eggs in soft soil. They incubate for 100 days before hatching.

**Distribution**: Southern Greece.
**Habitat**: Rocky hillsides.
**Food**: Leaves and shoots.
**Size**: 38cm (15in); 5kg (11lb).
**Maturity**: Several years.
**Breeding**: About 10 eggs laid in spring.
**Life span**: 100 years.
**Status**: Lower risk.

*The marginated tortoise is the largest land tortoise in Europe. As with other European tortoises, the tail of the male is considerably longer than that of the female. The rear of the shell is very distinctive, with thick scales flared outwards with orange markings.*

# Zambezi soft-shelled terrapin

*Cycloderma frenatum*

**Distribution**: Lower watershed of the Zambezi River.
**Habitat**: Lakes, rivers and ponds.
**Food**: Snails and other molluscs.
**Size**: 51cm (20in); 14kg (30.75lb).
**Maturity**: Unknown.
**Breeding**: 20 eggs laid in sand banks.
**Life span**: Unknown.
**Status**: Lower risk.

This species is one of just five soft-shelled terrapins living in Africa. Zambezi soft-shelled terrapins live in the lakes and tributaries that are associated with the Zambezi River system. These terrapins are also known as flap-shell turtles after the flaps of skin at the rear of their shell. The terrapin is more common in the lower areas of the watershed, between Zambia and the delta in Mozambique, where the river flows more slowly. Many lakes, natural and manmade, also feed the river and are good habitats for the terrapin.

The terrapins are hunters, eating mainly shelled molluscs, such as snails and mussels. They use their forelimbs to dig food out of the mud. They then crush their prey's shells with powerful jaws to get at the soft body inside.

The Zambezi soft-shelled terrapin often hides itself by digging into soft sand, so only its snout is visible. The females also dig a hole for their eggs, which are buried in sand banks, often close to a similar nest built by a crocodile.

*This terrapin has a long neck and a pointed snout, which can be poked out of the water to breath like a snorkel. The forelimbs are powerful and used for digging. When the hind legs are pulled into the shell they are covered by flaps of skin.*

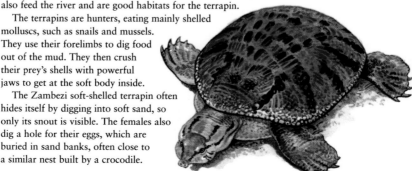

# LIZARDS

*Eighty per cent of all the world's reptiles are lizards and snakes. Lizards are able to move their upper jaws as well as their lower jaws, helping them to tackle large prey and swallow them more easily. Many also possess the ability to lose their tails if attacked by predators; special bones in the tail are pulled apart by muscles and the tail is released from the body. This is called autotomy.*

## Panther chameleon

*Furcifer pardalis*

Throughout the range of the panther chameleon, males and females vary in colour. There are at least 25 different forms, with each one occurring in a different region. Males from north-west Madagascar are bright turquoise and green, with red and gold colours radiating from their eyes and heads. Another type of male from a different region has up to six different body colours with white streaks around its eyes. Breeding females become brighter too, developing black and red-orange colouring. Their black markings vary in pattern. The panther chameleon is able to change colour very quickly when it moves into different vegetation – as camouflage – or when being approached by other chameleons – as communication. They can be very aggressive with one another, and changing colour can warn other individuals to keep away.

*Males have white stripes along their bodies and can display a variety of colours. Females are grey or brown, but turn red-orange when breeding.*

**Distribution**: North and east Madagascar. Introduced to Reunion and Mauritius and neighbouring islands.
**Habitat**: Lowland coastal areas.
**Food**: Small insects.
**Size**: Females 18–23cm (7–9in); males: 30–45cm (12–17.75in).
**Maturity**: Females 5 months; males 12 months.
**Breeding**: 4–6 clutches of 12–30 eggs are laid per year.
**Life span**: Unknown.
**Status**: Vulnerable.

## Mediterranean chameleon

*Chamaeleo chamaeleon*

The Mediterranean chameleon is the only species of these appealing lizards to live wild in Europe. They are restricted to the extreme south of the mainland and are most common on islands such as Malta, Crete and Sicily.

The lizard is found in dry habitats and is generally seen climbing slowly through bushes. As it moves, the chameleon's eyes scan its surroundings; each eye can move independently. If the chameleon spots danger, it inflates its body and turns dark.

As well as looking out for danger, the chameleon is looking for insects. Once it spots a suitable victim it unleashes its long tongue, which is almost as long as the lizard's body and has a sticky tip that clings to prey.

Mediterranean chameleons put a lot of energy into reproduction. The males defend a territory and each female mates with several before climbing to the ground. They dig a trench and lay 30 eggs in it; the eggs might make up half of the female's weight. About a third of females die from exhaustion after their first breeding season.

*This species' leaf-shaped body is flattened laterally. This makes the lizard difficult to see except from side on. However, the chameleon's ability to change colour to match its surroundings, allows the lizard to hide in plain sight.*

**Distribution**: Southern Europe, North Africa and the Middle East.
**Habitat**: Bushes in dry habitats.
**Food**: Insects.
**Size**: 30cm (12in).
**Maturity**: 1 year.
**Breeding**: 30 eggs buried in soil. Hatch after 2–3 months.
**Life span**: 3 years.
**Status**: Common.

**Usambara two-horned chameleon** (*Chameleo fischeri*): 40cm (15.75in)
A large chameleon found only in the forested Usambara Mountains on the border between Kenya and Tanzania. It has two very striking horns pointing straight out of its face. These horns are not present at hatching but develop as the chameleon grows.

**Kenya leaf chameleon** (*Rieppleleon kertseni*): 6cm (2.25in)
This tiny chameleon species lives in the leaf litter of woodlands and thickets in East Africa. It is unusual for its small size but also because it lives on the ground, not in the branches like its cousins. However, this species is well served by its camouflaging ability among the fallen leaves. When not on the move the leaf chameleon rests in termite burrows.

**Giant one-horned chameleon** (*Chamaeleo melleri*): 50cm (19.75in)
The giant one-horned chameleon is the largest chameleon species in Africa. It lives in woodlands and forests that grow beside rivers in southern Tanzania. Its large size is given a boost by a crest of scales running down its back. Males also have a blade-like horn on their noses. This species is found high in the tops of trees, reaching heights of 10m (33ft), where it feeds on large insects. As with other chameleon species, the giant chameleon climbs to the ground only to bury its eggs. This species finds a warm, sunny gap between the trees in which to build its nest. Each female lays 90 eggs in a hole, where they are incubated for several months.

# Slow worm

*Anguis fragilis*

The slow worm has a long, smooth body and lacks legs. Although it is often mistaken for a snake, it is a legless lizard. Unlike snakes, it has movable eyelids so that it can blink. It also has a broader, flatter tongue with a notch at the tip rather than a deep fork.

Slow worms hibernate between October and March. The males appear before the females, and when they come out in the spring, they warm themselves up by resting under rocks and logs. Slow worms are secretive creatures and spend most of their time underground. If they are attacked, they can shed their tails, which continue to wriggle for about 15 minutes. This distracts a predator while the slow worm escapes.

**Distribution**: Europe, South-west Asia and western Siberia.
**Habitat**: Rough grassland, hedgerows, heathland, woodland edges, downs and moorland. Also found in gardens and along railway or motorway embankments.
**Food**: Molluscs and earthworms, and also insects and spiders.
**Size**: 30–50cm (12–19.75in).
**Maturity**: Females 4–5 years; males 3–4 years.
**Breeding**: Mate in summer; eggs incubated inside body.
**Life span**: 10–15 years.
**Status**: Common.

*Females are brown with coppery or reddish-coloured backs. Dark stripes run down each side of the body. Males are brown and lack the dark stripes. Both sexes have whitish or reddish bellies and throats, with copper-red eyes.*

# Savannah monitor

*Varanus albigularis*

*The savannah monitor lizard is a large lizard with a sandy-coloured skin, patterned with lines of small black spots. The amount of black can vary and may be quite extensive. The head is darker on top and the tail has black bands. These lizards inhabit dry savannah or rocky terrain, and feed mostly on invertebrates.*

The savannah monitor lives in very hot, grassy habitats, feeding on small mammals and insects. During the breeding season, males will search for females. In the Namib Desert, they have been known to travel up to 6km (3.75 miles) per day looking for females ready to mate. Their territories may be up to 18sq km (7sq miles) in size. Females ready to breed will climb trees to make themselves more obvious to males, and release a pheromone into the air.

During very hot weather, savannah monitors help to keep themselves cool by sitting with their mouths open and vibrating their throats very quickly. This is known as gular fluttering and allows water to evaporate from the throat, thus cooling the blood passing through this area. They are unable to sweat, and their covering of tough, waterproof scales means they can lose little heat through their skin.

**Distribution**: Eastern and southern Africa.
**Habitat**: Dry grassland or rocky areas.
**Food**: Mainly invertebrates plus reptiles, birds, mammals, eggs and carrion.
**Size**: 1–1.9m (3.25–6.25ft); 6–10kg (13.25–22lb).
**Maturity**: 2 years.
**Breeding**: Up to 50–60 eggs laid in burrows during the spring.
**Life span**: Unknown.
**Status**: Vulnerable.

# Water monitor

*Varanus niloticus*

Water monitors are among the largest lizards in Africa; only the African forest monitor is larger, and that species is classified by some as a subspecies of its more common relative anyway. Water monitors are sometimes called Nile monitors because they have historically been common along the Nile. In the past they were also found in the Middle East. Today, however, the lizards are a purely African species. They live across the continent wherever there is enough flowing water to supply them with food.

Water monitors catch fish and freshwater crabs, but above all they are predators of egg-filled nests. They dig their way into egg mounds left by crocodiles and river turtles. In return, the monitors are frequent victims of crocodiles, who are protecting their nests as well as looking for something to eat.

The lizards themselves sometimes protect their own eggs by burying them in the nests of a termite colony. Water monitors are large enough to be unaffected by the termites' bites and stings, but an attack from termites defending their nest is enough to keep all but the most determined predators away from the monitors' eggs. Otherwise monitors bury eggs beside rotting logs. Eggs hatch after several weeks. Newly hatched monitors are tiny versions of adults. They prey on frogs and insects.

**Distribution**: Africa.
**Habitat**: Rivers.
**Food**: Crabs, fish and eggs.
**Size**: 2.2m (7.25ft).
**Maturity**: At about 1m (3.25ft) in length for males, and half that for females.
**Breeding**: 60 eggs laid in termite nests and under logs.
**Life span**: Unknown.
**Status**: Common.

*Like all monitors, the water monitor has a long body and an elongated head. The thick tail is also longer than the body. The tail is used to support the monitor when it rears up on its hind legs when threatened or fighting over breeding partners.*

# Starred agama

*Laudakia stellio*

A lizard of many names, the starred agama is also known as the hardun, painted dragon and sling-tailed agama. It is the only agama species to live in Europe. All the others live in Africa, Australia and Asia. This species is restricted to warm and dry areas. It is found in southern Greece and on several islands in the eastern Mediterranean, including the Cyclades and Rhodes. It is also a resident of Turkey and other parts of south-west Asia and is also found in north-east Africa.

*The starred agama can change colour, becoming darker when cold and lighter when warm. This makes it less visible at different light levels.*

Starred agamas prefer rocky habitats where there are plenty of places to bask in the sunshine. As a result they are well suited to life in and around human settlement. They are often seen basking on stone walls and roofs. The lizards remain motionless apart from the odd bob of the head. The lizards are quite shy and are ever ready to dive into cracks to hide from potential predators.

Like all reptiles, the agamas must warm themselves before they have the energy to move quickly enough to hunt. The colour of their scales become slightly paler as the lizards warm up. Once warmed enough, starred agamas look for food, often climbing into trees. Like all agamas, the starred agama is an insect-eater. This species also eats smaller lizards and nibbles on fruits and flowers.

Starred agamas breed two or three times a year. Females lay between six and ten eggs in each clutch. The eggs hatch after about 60 days. As they hatch out, the young agamas are about 3.5cm (1.5in) long.

**Distribution**: Greece, Aegean Islands, Malta, Turkey, Middle East and Egypt.
**Habitat**: Rocky areas, roofs and walls.
**Food**: Insects, small lizards and small amounts of plants.
**Size**: 20–30cm (8–12in).
**Maturity**: Unknown.
**Breeding**: 2 clutches of 8 eggs produced each year.
**Life span**: 10–15 years.
**Status**: Common.

## Mozambique agama

*Agama mossambica*

**Distribution**: Southern Tanzania and Mozambique.
**Habitat**: Woodlands.
**Food**: Ants.
**Size**: 20–31cm (8–12.25in).
**Maturity**: Unknown.
**Breeding**: About a dozen eggs laid in decaying leaves in damp locations.
**Life span**: Unknown.
**Status**: Common.

The Mozambique agama lives on the floor of woodlands in southern Tanzania and parts of Mozambique. They forage among leaf litter looking for insects. Although they do eat other insects, this species is something of a specialist and searches out columns of ants on the move through the decaying leaves. The agama is also a good climber and often follows its prey into the branches.

The Mozambique agama is not shy of people and it often searches for food on the outskirts of villages. It feeds on ants and other insects also attracted there by the promise of food waste.

After the males take on their vibrant breeding colours, they defend a territory as they attempt to attract females. Fights between males are frequent and bloody. After mating, females lay up to 14 eggs in a rotting stump or under a log. They choose a location with plenty of damp soil containing a lot of decaying plant matter in which to bury the eggs.

*Mozambique agamas are more slender than other agamas. The females and young are a mottled grey, which helps them blend in to their leaf-litter habitat. The males, on the other hand, take on a vibrant colouring during the breeding season, with a blue head and a pale line on the back.*

---

**Grass lizard** (*Chamaesaura miopropus*): 35–55cm (13.75–21.75in)
This species lives in the marshy savannahs of southern Tanzania and western Zambia. At first glance the lizard looks more like a snake. The forelimbs are tiny and very hard to see, while the hind limbs are longer and have a single toe equipped with a claw. The grass lizard moves over the ground with a curving motion like a snake's. This locomotion allows the grass lizard to chase its insect prey through the grass. This species is viviparous (it does not lay eggs but gives birth to its young instead). Births occur during the rainy season. Most females produce about six offspring each year.

**Long-tailed seps** (*Tetradactylus ellenbergeri*): 20–30cm (8–12in)
Ellenberger's long-tailed seps is a lizard, but it is often mistaken for a snake. It lives in just a few pockets of damp savannah across southern Africa. The forelimbs are absent altogether and the back legs are little more than spikes. From above the seps is a brown-green colour, making it hard to spot among the low-growing plants.

## Tree agama

*Acanthocercus atricollis*

Tree agamas are found across Central and eastern Africa. They occupy woodland habitats, which are increasingly becoming fragmented, as a result of which the tree agama population is split into small pockets. They eat mainly flying insects, plucking them from the air with their large mouths. However, the lizards also eat insects crawling along branches and in some cases they will take small frogs and other lizards.

If threatened, the lizard opens its mouth to display a startling orange lining. Many humans have suffered painful bites from this otherwise harmless agama.

Male agamas are easy to see among the branches with their bright breeding coloration. They display to females by clinging to vertical trunks and nodding their bright blue heads continuously. Once a female has mated and is no longer receptive to the males, she develops orange spots along the spine. When the rainy season arrives, these gravid (egg-carrying) females climb to the ground to lay their dozen eggs in a small hole.

**Distribution**: Eastern and Central Africa.
**Habitat**: Woodlands.
**Food**: Flying insects.
**Size**: 20–35cm (8–13.75in).
**Maturity**: Unknown.
**Breeding**: Eggs laid underground during rainy season.
**Life span**: Unknown.
**Status**: Common.

*As with other agama species, male and female tree agamas look different from each other. Females are grey-green in a pattern that resembles that of the lichens that grow on tree trunks. By contrast the males have bright blue heads and black spots on their shoulders, which earn the lizard the alternative name of black-necked agama.*

## Boulenger's scrub lizard

*Nucrus boulengeri*

Boulenger's scrub lizard lives in broken, rocky habitats in Kenya, Tanzania and Mozambique. As the lizard's name suggests, these dry areas support scrub – a mixture of brush and grass. The tail, which is twice as long as the body, is the lizard's most striking feature. There is also a collar of enlarged scales around the neck.

Boulenger's scrub lizard is a ground-living animal, sheltering in burrows at night and during the hottest parts of the day. This species is also described as a wall lizard because it substitutes rocky areas for stone walls and roofs. The scrub lizard may stay out of sight for long periods and emerges on to the surface only when there are plenty of insects to eat. The lizard is especially active when winged termites emerge from their underground nests in search of new mates and to set up new colonies.

Little is known about the reproductive behaviour of Boulenger's scrub lizards. They lay eggs rather than give birth to their young, although the size of the clutch is unclear. Juvenile lizards have red tails and a pale stripe along the back. These colours fade as the lizard matures.

**Distribution**: Eastern Africa from Kenya to Mozambique.
**Habitat**: Rocks and grasslands. Also seen in walls and roofs.
**Food**: Termites in their winged dispersal form and other insects.
**Size**: 12–18cm (4.75–7in).
**Maturity**: Unknown.
**Breeding**: Lays eggs but clutch size is uncertain.
**Life span**: Unknown.
**Status**: Common.

*Boulenger's scrub lizard lives in and on the ground among rocks, dead leaves and soil. Its brown back has cream and black blotches that break up the outline of its body, making it hard to spot while it forages.*

## Jackson's forest lizard

*Adolfus jacksoni*

Jackson's forest lizards live in forest clearings and edges within East Africa in Kenya, Uganda, Rwanda and the extreme east of the Democratic Republic of Congo. They are most common in the outer regions of the colourfully named Bwindi Impenetrable Forest, the largest area of pristine forest in East Africa. Most of the Impenetrable Forest, which is also known as The Place of Darkness, is located in the southern habitat where it forms a large protected reserve. The forest is home to one of the greatest diversities of wildlife in Africa. A population of mountain gorillas is perhaps its most famous residents.

The forest is a rugged highland region which receives a lot of rain throughout the year. Jackson's forest lizards are often seen on rocks and fallen trunks in sunny places between the trees. They hunt for small insects while clambering over obstacles and over the ground. Members of the species that live outside of the dense forest sometimes forage for food in living trees. However, this behaviour is not seen in forested areas, presumably because other species already exploit that niche.

Little is known about the breeding behaviour of Jackson's forest lizards. The females lay a few eggs (about five) in rocky crevices. Often many females will select the same location in which to lay their eggs, and so a large collection of eggs develops, sometimes numbering in the hundreds. The eggs are of different ages so hatchlings crawl over recently laid eggs to leave the nest. The eggs take about two months to hatch.

**Distribution**: Mainly southern Uganda, but also Kenya, Burundi, Rwanda and eastern fringe of Democratic Republic of Congo.
**Habitat**: Forest edges and clearings.
**Food**: Small insects and other invertebrates.
**Size**: 15–25cm (6–9.75in).
**Maturity**: Unknown.
**Breeding**: Several females lay their eggs in communal nests thoughout the year.
**Life span**: Unknown.
**Status**: Common.

*This small lizard has a large head and long snout. The tail is longer than the body. Dozens of rows of small scales form a speckled pattern on the back and flanks. The belly is yellow.*

# Angolan rough-scaled lizard

*Ichnotropis bivittata*

**Distribution**: Southern Africa.
**Habitat**: Dry savannah.
**Food**: Small insects.
**Size**: 17–20cm (6.75–8in).
**Maturity**: 8 months.
**Breeding**: A dozen eggs laid between April and June.
**Life span**: Unknown, probably less than 3 years.
**Status**: Common.

The Angolan rough-scaled lizard is found across southern Africa from Angola and Namibia in the west to the southern region of Tanzania. It lives in dry grassland areas.

The lizard is active during the day and hunts down small insects among the short grasses. They are fast-moving creatures and rush their prey before they can escape.

Living in such an open and exposed habitat means that life is short for these lizards. They mature within eight months in time for the start of the breeding season in April and May. Many will die soon after that from the stress of competing for mates or producing eggs. Females bury their eggs in soft sand beneath bushes.

Few members of this species will survive beyond two years. Predation is also a major threat, especially for displaying males. Jackals, long-legged secretary birds and airborne birds of prey pick the lizards off as they attempt to attract the attention of females.

*As its name implies, the scales of this lizard are strongly keeled: that is, they have a central ridge. The lizard also has distinctive stripes running down its flanks. The neck is a rich yellow. Juveniles are less brightly coloured.*

---

**Dalmatian algyroides** (*Algyroides nigropunctatus*): 14cm (5.5in)
This small lizard lives on the Dalmatian coast of the Adriatic Sea in south-eastern Europe. Its range runs from Slovenia to northern Greece. The lizards are red-brown and have long, thin tails. The males are longer than the females and also have vibrant blue throats and eyes. The belly of both sexes is orange. The Dalmatian algyroides lives in a range of habitats. It is a good climber and is often found in trees and on walls. It tends to prefer shaded areas.

**Steppe runner** (*Eremias arguta*): 15cm (6in)
A plump lizard with a pointed snout, it lives in dry areas with sparse vegetation. It is a frequent visitor to sand dunes. Its range runs from the Danube Delta area in eastern Romania around the Black Sea to southern Ukraine. The steppe runner is capable of crossing the ground at a high speed, often to get out of sight as quickly as possible. The lizard hides under stones or in the burrows of rodents and also digs its own burrows at the base of small bushes.

**Large psammodromus** (*Psammodromus algirus*): 24cm (9.5in)
This lizard from Portugal, Spain and southern France has a tail that is at least twice as long as its body. It lives in bushy areas and hunts in the leaf litter. This species has pockets on the sides of the neck that fill with mites and other tiny skin parasites. The function of the pockets is believed to be to attract these parasites away from other parts of the lizard's body, where they might do more damage.

# Spiny-footed lizard

*Acanthodactylus erythrurus*

Spiny-footed lizards live in the southern Iberian Peninsula and the Mahgreb region of north-west Africa. Although they are absent from full-blown desert areas, the lizards occupy very dry sandy areas on which there is a thin covering of scrub. The species is often found in large numbers, with 200 individuals crowding together in certain places.

The lizards sometimes come into completely open habitats, such as beaches or rocky areas, which is where people are most likely to come across them. The lizards are not particularly shy, but if one feels threatened it leaves the area with a series of short sprints in a straight line, pausing several times with its tail raised during its retreat. It takes refuge under bushes and may retreat farther into a spiny bush or short burrow. When resting, the spiny-footed lizards raise their forefeet. They also raise their feet in turn while basking in an attempt to reduce the heat their body absorbs from the ground.

**Distribution**: Southern Spain and Portugal and north-western Africa.
**Habitat**: Dry sandy areas.
**Food**: Ants, beetles and bugs.
**Size**: 24cm (9.5in).
**Maturity**: 18 months.
**Breeding**: Single clutch of 8 eggs.
**Life span**: 3 years.
**Status**: Common.

*Adult spiny-footed lizards have pale stripes running along their back. The under parts are white. Juvenile lizards have black and white striped backs and a red tail. The red tail may remain even when the lizard matures. The lizard is named after a comb of spines on its hind legs.*

# Tropical girdled lizard

*Cordylus tropidosternum*

*This little lizard is named after the way its scales are arranged in overlapping rings, or girdles, resembling in some ways the tiles on a roof. The arrangement of the scales makes the lizard very rough to the touch. Most individuals have a wide dark band running from the top of the head and along each side to the groin.*

The tropical girdled lizard lives in dry woodland areas of Central and southern Africa. The most northerly part of its range is the coastal forests of southern Kenya.

The lizards spend most of their time clambering through trees looking for food. Their diet consists of large insects, such as moths, and spiders. They are also partial to the winged termites that swarm through the forests from time to time.

By night, the tropical girdled lizard rests in a tree hollow. It rarely moves too far from this den when feeding during the day. In dry spells, it may stay in the den for days on end. The lizard also becomes dormant during the short winter in southern Africa. The breeding season follows this dormancy.

The females do not lay eggs. Instead, they keep the eggs inside their body, and the young hatch out inside. The young look like miniature versions of adults.

The tropical girdled lizard's armoured and prehistoric appearance makes the species a favourite among reptile enthusiasts. As a result, the wild population is being reduced by people collecting them for sale as pets. Many die before they even arrive at the pet shop.

**Distribution**: Central, eastern and southern Africa. Its most northern occurence is southern Kenya, the most southerly is South Africa.
**Habitat**: Dry woodlands.
**Food**: Spiders and insects.
**Size**: 13–16cm (5–6.25in).
**Maturity**: About 3 years but longer in areas with less food.
**Breeding**: Mating season occurs after winter dormancy. Up to 4 young born in rainy season between 4 and 8 months after mating. Young are born over several days.
**Life span**: Unknown.
**Status**: Vulnerable.

# Rough-scaled plated lizard

*Gerrhosaurus major*

*The rough-scaled plated lizard is also called the tawny plated lizard because of its brown colour, but some members of the species are much greener. The large scales are very rough and arranged in strict rows, giving the back a grid pattern.*

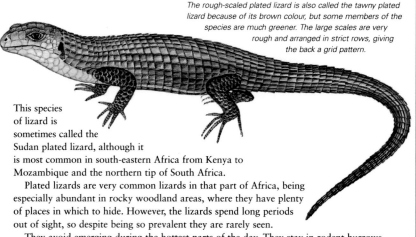

This species of lizard is sometimes called the Sudan plated lizard, although it is most common in south-eastern Africa from Kenya to Mozambique and the northern tip of South Africa.

Plated lizards are very common lizards in that part of Africa, being especially abundant in rocky woodland areas, where they have plenty of places in which to hide. However, the lizards spend long periods out of sight, so despite being so prevalent they are rarely seen.

They avoid emerging during the hottest parts of the day. They stay in rodent burrows, termite mounds or rocky crevices. The lizards are well protected from predators by their rough scales. They rarely bite, but whip attackers with their jagged tails.

These reptiles are omnivorous: they eat both plant and animal foods. They prefer larger insects but also eat worms, smaller lizards and soft fruits. The rough-scaled plated lizard is a popular pet because it is relatively large yet docile and easy to maintain.

**Distribution**: Eastern Africa from eastern Kenya to northern South Africa.
**Habitat**: Rocky hills and areas of semi-desert and scrublands.
**Food**: Insects, worms, fruits and flowers.
**Size**: 30–40cm (12–15.75in).
**Maturity**: Unknown.
**Breeding**: Up to 6 eggs, each 12cm (4.75in) wide, are buried in a shallow hole that is dug underneath a rock or log. Hatchlings are 10cm (4in) long.
**Life span**: Unknown.
**Status**: Common.

# Sand lizard

*Lacerta agilis*

**Distribution**: Central and eastern Europe.
**Habitat**: Meadows, steppe, dunes and hedgerows.
**Food**: Insects.
**Size**: 18–19cm (7–7.5in).
**Maturity**: 2–3 years.
**Breeding**: A dozen eggs buried in a sunny area.
**Life span**: 12 years.
**Status**: Common.

The sand lizard is found throughout much of Europe and central Asia. It is one of the few reptiles to live in Britain. It survives in two tiny pockets, one on the south coast and the other in the north-west. In both places, the lizards live in sandy heathlands. Elsewhere in the lizard's range, which extends from southern Sweden to the Middle East, the lizards are found in similar dry habitats.

During courtship, male sand lizards fight over access to the biggest and most fertile females. Both males and females will mate with several partners during a season, as a result of which the eggs laid by a female will have been fertilized by more than one male. Females lay up to 14 eggs in a nest dug in dry, sandy soil close to vegetation. In the northern parts of the lizard's range these nests are located in sunlit areas to ensure that the eggs do not get too cold. In warmer parts, females may be able to produce two clutches in a single year.

The sand lizard is a colourful species. Males are bright green, while females are generally brown with darker patterning along their bodies. The patterns are very varied across the range. The young resemble the females but are less conspicuously marked.

---

**Giant plated lizard** (*Gerrhosaurus validus*): 69cm (27in)
This huge species of plated lizard lives on the rocky hills in southern Africa and uses the crevices between rocks as places to hide. During midsummer, four or five large, oval eggs are laid between rocks and covered with soil. Giant plated lizards are dark brown or black, with yellow spots and shields on their heads. Their throats are whitish and their bellies are light brown. Males develop a pinkish-purple hue on their throats, chins and the sides of their heads during the breeding season.

**Ocellated lizard** (*Lacerta lepida*): 50cm (19.75in)
This is one of the largest lizards living in Europe. Rare sightings of individuals 80cm (31.5in) long have been recorded. About two-thirds of the lizard's length is made up by its tail. Ocellated lizards live in Portugal, Spain, the south of France and northern Italy. Adults have blue spots on their flanks against a grey-brown background. In the south of their range members of this lizard live in highland habitats. Farther north they are common residents of olive groves and vineyards. They spend most their time on the ground and often climb wall crevices to escape notice.

**Balkan green lizard** (*Lacerta trilineata*): 45cm (17.5in)
This species is very similar to the more widespread green lizard. However, it tends to be slightly larger and is found in drier areas of south-east Europe and Turkey. The two species often occur in the same areas, each one being specialized to either arid or damp habitats.

# Green lizard

*Lacerta bilineata*

The green lizard is found across most of southern Europe as far north as the Channel Islands and east through Austria to southern Ukraine. It also lives on a few of the Mediterranean islands.

The lizard is found in the dense vegetation that grows on the edges of fields and in disturbed areas of woodland. In the southern portion of their range, where the climate is dry, the lizards are confined to damp areas, such as highland meadows.

The green lizard hunts among the branches of low bushes, looking for insects and spiders. It is most active in the cool of early morning and evening. In the middle of hot days and at night the lizards retreat to shadier parts of the bush or into crevices or disused rodent burrows.

Female green lizards lay about 20 eggs. These hatch out after between 7 and 15 weeks, depending on the climate. The eggs take longer to develop in colder areas.

**Distribution**: Southern and eastern Europe.
**Habitat**: Thickets and hedges.
**Food**: Insects.
**Size**: 40cm (15.75in).
**Maturity**: 18 months.
**Breeding**: Two dozen eggs laid.
**Life span**: Unknown.
**Status**: Common.

This large, slender lizard has a tail that is more than twice the length of its body. As the name suggests, the males of this lizard are a bright emerald-green. The females may also be green but less vibrantly so. Other females are brown with a blotchy pattern.

# Viviparous lizard

*Lacerta vivipara*

One of the most common European reptiles, the viviparous lizard is found across northern and central Europe and into northern parts of Asia. It is the only reptile found in Ireland. This indicates that it was the fastest reptile to broaden its range back northwards when temperatures increased following the last Ice Age, reaching Ireland before the Irish Sea rose up and engulfed the land-bridge connecting it with mainland Britain and the rest of Europe.

Viviparous means "live birth" – viviparous lizards don't lay eggs, but give birth to fully formed young. These miniatures of their parents are completely independent from birth, receiving no help from their mothers. However, by keeping the eggs within their bodies until they have hatched, the female viviparous lizards have already given their progeny a head-start, since they don't have to lie prone and defenceless as eggs.

The viviparous lizard is a common sight in the UK, for those that look closely enough. Up close they are striking animals, with delicate patterns of coloured scales. However, from a distance they blend easily into the background, making life difficult for kestrels and other predators.

**Distribution**: Northern and central Europe and northern Asia.
**Habitat**: Wide-ranging habitats including woodland, marshland, heath, sand dunes, hedgerows, bogs and rubbish dumps.
**Food**: Insects, spiders, snails and earthworms.
**Size**: 10–16cm (4–6.5in).
**Maturity**: Not known.
**Breeding**: 3–10 live young born between June and September.
**Life span**: 8 years.
**Status**: Common.

*The skin of the viviparous lizard is patterned with a mosaic of brown, dark green and bronze scales.*

# European glass lizard

*Ophisaurus apodus*

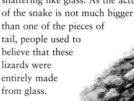

**Distribution**: South-east Europe and south-west Asia.
**Habitat**: Open woodland and fields.
**Food**: Molluscs, insects and small vertebrates.
**Size**: Up to 1.2m (4ft).
**Maturity**: 2–3 years.
**Breeding**: 8–10 eggs.
**Life span**: 60 years.
**Status**: Common.

European glass lizards belong to a family of lizards that have given up the pedestrian way of life, preferring instead to crawl around on their bellies in the manner of snakes. Indeed, having lost their legs almost entirely, glass lizards are often mistaken for snakes. Nevertheless, they can be identified as lizards due to their having ears and eyelids, features which snakes do not possess.

Their body also differs from that of a snake by the length of its tail. The tail of a snake – the portion of the body behind the anus and genitals – usually only makes up a small proportion of its body length, whereas two-thirds of a glass lizard's body is made up of tail. The tail also gives rise to the glass lizard's name. Like other lizards, this species is able to shed its tail when threatened – a process called autotomy. However, unlike those of other lizards, the tail then breaks up into lots of small pieces, as though it were shattering like glass. As the actual body of the snake is not much bigger than one of the pieces of tail, people used to believe that these lizards were entirely made from glass.

*Not a snake but a lizard with no legs, the European glass lizard has a groove down each side of its body. These legless reptiles are fairly common in fields and highly wooded areas, where they hunt hard-shelled snails and insects.*

# African fire skink

*Lygosoma fernandi*

The African fire skink is a medium-sized member of the varied and widespread skink family. It is also one of the most spectacular-looking members of that group. When not in breeding coloration, the male's sides are bright red, merging into the copper colour on its back. This is very impressive in its own right. However, come the breeding season, the red colours extend up on to the back, becoming suffused with the copper and resulting in a brilliant orange. Meanwhile, both pairs of legs darken to near black, with a few light spots, and pearlescent stripes extend from the throat right down the lizard's body. Even juveniles are brightly coloured, having intense light blue tails, which slowly fade as they grow older.

Adult fire skinks are territorial, defending their burrows in the leaf litter on the forest floor from invaders. Their bright colours make them highly visible to predators, so they really need handy bolt holes for when trouble appears.

*The fire skink really lives up to its name, with its shiny scales of many colours – from black and blue to red and gold, including stripes that look like fire on their sides. These fiercely territorial lizards dart among the dead leaves of the forest floor, looking like living flames.*

**Distribution**: West Africa.
**Habitat**: Tropical forest.
**Food**: Invertebrates.
**Size**: 30cm (12in).
**Maturity**: 1 year.
**Breeding**: Female fire skinks lay 6 clutches of 4–9 eggs per year.
**Life span**: 10 years.
**Status**: Threatened.

---

**Four-toed burrowing skink** (*Sepsina tetradactyla*): 10–15cm (4–6in)
This species of skink lives in the decaying leaves that litter the forest floors of Tanzania and Burundi. These habitats are most common in highland areas. The four-toed burrowing skink has an elongated body, even for a skink. The tip of the tail is blunt and round and of similar dimensions to the head. This feature ensures that a predator will be easily confused as to which end to attack first. The limbs are tiny and barely used as the skink writhes through the deep leaves in search of insects.

**Peter's writhing skink** (*Lygosoma afrum*): 16–23cm (6.25–9in)
This long, sausage-shaped skink lives in the savannah regions of East Africa. It has very short forelegs and moves by wriggling its body. It eats termites and other insects living in the rotting wood. The tube-shaped body is an adaptation to burrowing. When weather is inclement or when danger is near, the skink worms its way into sandy soil. Its body is a pale red-brown to match the colour of the ground. Unusually for a skink, this species has movable eyelids.

**Fat-tailed gecko** (*Hemitheconyx caudicinctus*): Females 20cm (8in); males 25cm (9.75in)
Fat-tailed geckos are striking in appearance, with alternating thick bands of colour. They live in dry grassland and woodland in western Africa. If the lizard re-grows its tail following an attack, the tail is much shorter and fatter than before, resembling its head. Again, this is a defence mechanism, designed to fool predators.

# Moorish gecko

*Tarentola mauritanica*

Moorish geckos are Europe's most common geckos. They are also found throughout North Africa. Like many of the world's most successful animals, they have learned to live alongside people and even benefit from their presence. They spend most of their time literally hanging around houses. Geckos are fantastic climbers, even able to climb up panes of glass and hang from ceilings. They are able to do this because of their toes, which have many tiny suction pads on their undersides. The pads actually comprise thousands of micro-hairs, which form a temporary molecular bond with the surface being walked over.

These geckos are usually easy to spot, since they tend to congregate at night around wall lights, waiting for their favourite food – moths – to arrive. As the moths are drawn in by the light, they become easy prey.

These are the only lizards to possess voiceboxes, which allow them to produce the "gecko" calls from which they get their name. They also produce a "tutting" noise, used between rival males.

**Distribution**: Mediterranean regions.
**Habitat**: Dry, rocky areas.
**Food**: Mainly insects.
**Size**: 15cm (6in).
**Maturity**: 2 years.
**Breeding**: Up to 6 clutches of 1–6 eggs per year.
**Life span**: Unknown.
**Status**: Common, but declining due to collection for the pet trade.

*The Moorish gecko is also known as the crocodile gecko because of its rough scales.*

## Armadillo lizard

*Cordylus cataphractus*

The armadillo lizard lives in groups of up to 30 animals. Small groups, with nine lizards or fewer, are usually all females with just one adult male. Larger groups contain more males. They are active during the day, searching for insects in the dry desert areas in which they live. Their sandy colour keeps them hidden from birds and other reptiles, and their spines act as a protective armour.

If they are out in the open, away from cover, and are threatened by a predator, these lizards will roll themselves into balls like armadillos, keeping a tight hold of their tails with their mouths. This exposes their tough, horny skin and spines, making it difficult for a predator to eat the lizard. If the lizard has enough time, or is close to cover, it will squeeze into a small crevice in nearby rocks. Because it has a flattened body, few predators are able to follow it into its hideaway.

*Armadillo lizards have flattened bodies and broad heads. The body is sandy yellow or brown and covered with spiny scales. They have either yellow or violet throats, embellished with brown blotches. When threatened, these lizards roll into a tight ball, creating a spiny ring.*

**Distribution**: Southern tip of Africa.
**Habitat**: Dry, desert areas with plants able to withstand drought and high temperatures.
**Food**: Insects, spiders and other invertebrates.
**Size**: 7.5–16.5cm (3–6.5in); 400–800g (0.9–1.75lb).
**Maturity**: Not known.
**Breeding**: Females give birth to 1 or 2 young lizards towards the end of summer.
**Life span**: Unknown.
**Status**: Uncommon.

## Atlantic lizard

*Gallotia atlantica*

The Atlantic lizard is one of the seven lizard species living on the Canary Islands, which are located off the coast of north-west Africa. This particular species lives on Lanzarote, Fuerteventura and several of the smaller islands. It is found in a range of habitats, from sand dunes and cultivated fields and gardens to the barren malpaís or lava fields that scar the islands.

In vegetated areas, the lizards forage for insects. They also pick over the remains of small birds and other warm-blooded prey that have been discarded by the islands' falcons and other hunting birds. However, in more barren areas, most notably on the lava flows that cover the islands, insects are very rare. Those insects that do live there are very hard to catch. In these places the lizards survive by eating only plant food, mainly fruits and flowers.

Lizards that survive on a diet of insects are smaller than those that eat plants. The reason for this size difference is the quality of the animals' diet. Plants contain a lot less nutrition than insects. As a result the lizards must eat more of them. Being larger allows the plant-eating lizards to consume enough food. The larger reptiles also lose heat more slowly than smaller ones and so they require less food to function efficiently.

Males court females by approaching them slowly, nodding their heads, with their throats inflated. About a month after mating, the females lay two or three clutches of eggs, each containing a few eggs. Babies hatch out between seven and ten weeks later.

**Distribution**: Eastern Canary Islands including Lanzarote, Fuerteventura, Lobos, Graciosa, Alegranza, Monte Clara and Roque del Este.
**Habitat**: Sand dunes and lava flows.
**Food**: Insects, carrion and plants.
**Size**: 22cm (8.75in).
**Maturity**: 1 year.
**Breeding**: 10–15 eggs produced in 2–3 clutches per year.
**Life span**: 5 years.
**Status**: Common.

*The Atlantic lizard is a medium-sized species. The males are larger than the females. Males have blue blobs on their flanks, while the colouring of females and young males is a more muted green and brown. This species and the other Canary Island lizards are most closely related to the psammodromus species of Spain and Portugal.*

# Snake-eyed skink

*Ablepharus kitaibelii*

**Distribution**: South-eastern Europe.
**Habitat**: Oak and chestnut woodlands.
**Food**: Insects.
**Size**: 13cm (5in).
**Maturity**: 2 years.
**Breeding**: Up to 6 eggs buried in soil.
**Life span**: 3 years.
**Status**: Common.

Snake-eyed skinks live in south-eastern Europe. The northern limit of their range is Slovakia. To the south they are found throughout the Balkans as far east as the mouth of the Danube.

In most places, the snake-eyed skink lives in dry woodland habitats, where it hides among fallen leaves and under logs and stones. In southern areas of its range, however, it is also found in grasslands. In these habitats the skink appears to aestivate (become dormant in the high summer). Adult snake-eyed skinks use their forelimbs to pull themselves along, but most of their locomotion is through slithering in a manner similar to snakes.

During mating, a male bites the flanks of his mate. She produces between about four eggs shortly afterwards, which are buried in soil. The eggs double in size over their nine-week development, at which point the young hatch.

*The snake-eyed skink is a tiny lizard. As with all skinks, it has a small head and a thick, rounded body. The legs are very short, and almost useless in larger individuals. The eyes have transparent eyelids, which are always closed, so the skink is unable to blink. This is a feature shared with snakes and other skink species.*

---

**Ibiza wall lizard** (*Podarcis pityusensis*): 20cm (8in)
Native to the Balearic Islands, this is a slim, agile and very hardy lizard, mainly inhabiting barren, sun-baked rocks, often by the seashore. It can also be found combing neglected gardens, rubbish dumps and waste ground for scraps to complement its usual diet of insects and some plant matter. The colouring of this lizard is variable but there seem to be two predominant forms: those from Formentera have green backs with grey-brown sides, while those from Ibiza have brown backs and reddish sides.

**Hierro giant lizard** (*Gallotia simonyi*): 60cm (23.55in)
Once believed to be extinct but rediscovered in 1975, the Hierro giant lizard has at present only a small population of 150 individuals, living on the island of El Hierro in the Canary Islands. It is Europe's most endangered reptile. It feeds almost exclusively on only two types of plant. It is a large, stocky lizard with a broad head and pronounced jowls. The lizard has not coped well with the expansion of tourism in the Canaries.

**Tenerife lizard** (*Gallotia galloti*): 30cm (11.75in)
This species occupies the western Canary Islands. It resembles the Atlantic lizard in colouring and sexual differences, but members of this species are longer and more robust. Like large Atlantic lizards, this species has a mainly plant diet. The lizard forages in a range of habitats but is less common in damper areas such as woodland or heathland.

# Namib web-footed gecko

*Palmatogecko rangei*

As their name suggests, the Namib web-footed geckos have webbed toes on their long, spindly legs. The webbing is not for swimming, not in water anyway: the wide feet stop the lizard from sinking into soft sand. They are also used for digging burrows. The webs are not simply flaps of skin: they contain tiny muscles and can be formed into a scoop for shovelling fine sand. As with other geckos, the toes of this species have intricately folded pads, which are used to grip while climbing over rocks.

Namib web-footed geckos are nocturnal. By day they keep cool in deep burrows in the sand but at night, when the conditions on the surface have cooled, the geckos emerge to hunt. Their diet consists of insects and spiders.

Breeding takes place between April and May. The females lay hard-shelled eggs, which are buried in pairs or singly on occasion, over the next few months. The eggs' hard shell is made from chalky calcium compounds like those in a bird's egg. The shell stops the eggs drying out in the desert heat. A total of about ten eggs is laid. They take eight weeks to hatch.

**Distribution**: Namibia.
**Habitat**: Desert sand dunes.
**Food**: Insects and spiders.
**Size**: 10–15cm (4–6in).
**Maturity**: 1 year.
**Breeding**: About 10 eggs laid in May–August.
**Life span**: 5 years.
**Status**: Common.

*Namib web-footed geckos have almost transparent skin. The only colourful features are the eyes. These are covered in clear and fixed eyelids, which have to be cleaned regularly with the tongue.*

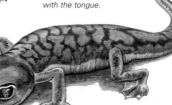

# Mediterranean gecko

*Hemidactylus turcicus*

*This species is typical of Old World geckos (those living in Europe, Asia and Africa): it has eyes with a vertical pupil, no movable eyelids and pads on the tips of its toes. The pads do not extend to the very end of the toes. The vertical pupil is a more efficient system than a circular pupil for controlling the amount of light getting into the eye. Many nocturnal animals have vertical pupils.*

Mediterranean geckos are found all the way around the sea of the same name. They are generally found close to the coast, where the habitats are less arid, although the geckos do follow river valleys a long way inland in certain areas.

The geckos are nocturnal and are often seen in the evening and at night, scurrying up walls and across other rocky surfaces. On cooler days they can also be spotted sunning themselves. They are able to scale vertical surfaces, even glass and other smooth materials, by gripping with the pads on their toes. These pads feel sticky but, contrary to popular belief, they do not exude any adhesive liquids. The grip is due to hundreds of minute folds on the pad's lower surfaces. These increase the pad's surface area hugely and allow the toe to grip on to the slightest deformity.

Mediterranean geckos communicate with each other using a series of calls, and during the breeding season males call females to their territories. The females lay up to six eggs in two or three clutches each year. The eggs are laid under dead leaves or in crevices. They all hatch within three months.

**Distribution**: All parts of the Mediterranean coast and introduced to the Canary Islands and the Americas.
**Habitat**: Rocky areas, walls, roofs and inside houses in coastal areas. Only found inland close to a river.
**Food**: Insects such as moths, cockroaches and beetles.
**Size**: 15cm (6in).
**Maturity**: 6 months.
**Breeding**: 2–3 small clutches of eggs laid under stones.
**Life span**: 3 years.
**Status**: Common.

# European leaf-toed gecko

*Euleptes europaea*

This tiny species of gecko lives mainly on Corsica, Sardinia and a few other islands in the western Mediterranean. The lizards are also found in tiny pockets of mainland along the French and Italian coasts.

Leaf-toed geckos are nocturnal and are rarely seen. They hunt for prey on rocky surfaces but avoid places associated with people. They also avoid cultivated areas. Being an island species, they are at risk from disruption to their habitat, which causes concern for conservationists. Nevertheless, these geckos are present in large numbers in rocky places with plenty of crevices in which to hide.

The gecko stalks its insect prey, at first slowly creeping up on its prey and then making a dash for the kill. The lizard is also capable of making mighty leaps for an animal of its size.

Like other geckos, the leaf-toed gecko calls to attract mates. Males of this species use a "tsi tsi tsi" call to lure females. The females lay small clutches of eggs, numbering just one or two eggs at a time. In warmer parts of their range they may manage three clutches a year, but a single clutch is the norm in highland areas. The eggs take between 8 and 13 weeks to hatch. The hatchlings are about 3cm (1.25in) long. They look like miniature adults.

*This is the smallest species of gecko in Europe. It has relatively short legs compared to the size of its body and tail. Climbing pads are located at the tips of its toes. Females have thicker tails than males.*

**Distribution**: Corsica, Sardinia and smaller Mediterranean islands, including those near the North African coast
**Habitat**: Rocky areas, such as drystone walls. Appears most common in areas with a lot of granite outcrops.
**Food**: Insects.
**Size**: 6cm (2.25in).
**Maturity**: 2–3 years.
**Breeding**: 1–2 eggs laid in rock crevices. Several geckos may use the same site and return to it each year.
**Life span**: 10 years, but double that when in captivity.
**Status**: Lower risk.

# Tropical house gecko

*Hemidactylus mabouia*

**Distribution**: Sub-Saharan Africa; introduced to North and South America.
**Habitat**: Forests and human settlements.
**Food**: Insects.
**Size**: 10cm (4in).
**Maturity**: 1 year.
**Breeding**: Several clutches laid throughout year.
**Life span**: Unknown.
**Status**: Common.

This is one of the most common and widespread species of gecko in Africa. This species is now also common in tropical and subtropical parts of the Americas, having been introduced to the Amazon from Africa by human migrations. In the wilds of Africa these geckos live in forests, where they shelter out of sight under loose flaps of bark. However, as their name suggests, they have also become common in human settlements including even the largest cities.

House geckos are nocturnal hunters. They have wide toe pads, which make the toes sticky so that they can grip on to even very flat surfaces. House geckos often rest on tree trunks and on walls in a head-down position. This allows them to head for the safety of the forest floor (or another hiding place) should danger approach.

By day the geckos sleep on a leaf. Their skin is darker at these times and becomes lighter as they forage. Geckos that are hunting on whitewashed walls have been known to become very pale in response to the white background.

*This common gecko has wide pads on its toes, which help them cling to vertical surfaces such as tree trunks and walls. The body is pale grey with several dark crossbars on the back. These markings begin to fade in bright light so the gecko becomes more difficult to see.*

---

**Gran Canaria gecko** (*Tarentola boettgeri*): 12cm (4.75in)
This gecko species lives on Gran Canaria and El Hierro, two of the Canary Islands. A population also lives on the Selvages (tiny islands uninhabited by people to the north of the Canaries). The individuals on Gran Canaria are yellow, while those living elsewhere tend to be smaller and grey. Like the Tenerife gecko and the two other gecko species on the Canary Islands, this is a coastal animal. It is most often found when people turn over flat stones.

**Eastern Canary gecko** (*Tarentola angustimentalis*): 8cm (3in)
This gecko resembles the Moorish gecko more than the other species living on the other Canary Islands. It is very common on Fuerteventura, Lanzarote, Lobos and the small islands north of Lanzarote.

**Kotschy's gecko** (*Cyrtopodion kotschyi*): 10cm (4in)
Kotschy's gecko ranges from Albania and Greece to the Crimean Peninsula and southern Bulgaria. It lives in dry rocky areas. It is less of a climber than other European geckos and lacks the adhesive pads of other species. Nevertheless, it is very agile and darts over and around rough ground and is often found on walls. Males call females with a "chick" sound. The females lay just two eggs in cracks or under stones. These hatch after three or four months. The baby geckos are a fifth of their adult size, which they reach after two or three years.

# Flat-headed gecko

*Hemidactylus platycephalus*

Flat-headed geckos live in East Africa. This part of the continent is also populated by the more widespread tropical house gecko. The two species are similar and are often found at the same location. Flat-headed geckos are also known as tree geckos (not to be confused with other tree geckos from other continents). The animal's wild habitat is dry forest, where its mottled colouring helps it to blend in with the lichen-covered trees. However, like its close relative the house gecko, the flat-headed species is also a common visitor to houses. It is more aggressive than the house gecko and will eat smaller geckos if provoked.

Males call females with a clicking sound. Females lay their eggs under bark or in tree hollows. They prefer to lay their eggs on baobab trees. Many choose the same places to deposit their eggs, and large communal nests are formed as a result.

**Distribution**: Eastern Africa.
**Habitat**: Woodlands.
**Food**: Moths and other large insects, also other lizards.
**Size**: 12–18cm (4.75–7in).
**Maturity**: 1 year.
**Breeding**: Eggs laid in communal nests.
**Life span**: Unknown.
**Status**: Common.

*This species has body colouring that looks very similar to the tropical house gecko. This poses a problem for observers, since the two live in the same habitats. However, the flat-headed gecko is larger and more robustly built.*

## Yellow-headed dwarf day gecko

*Lygodactylus picturatus*

The yellow-headed dwarf day gecko's common name says it all: the males have a vibrant yellow head and neck. The species is small compared to other geckos; and it is one of the few African species to be active during the day. The species lives in the woodlands and coastal savannahs of East Africa.

Originally a tree-living lizard, the gecko is now a common resident of huts and other rural buildings. It is equipped with toe pads, which help it to grip as it scurries up trunks and walls and through the branches in search of insects. As well as insect food, the yellow-headed dwarf day gecko also laps nectar from flowers.

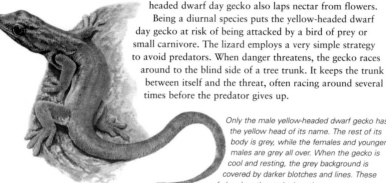

Being a diurnal species puts the yellow-headed dwarf day gecko at risk of being attacked by a bird of prey or small carnivore. The lizard employs a very simple strategy to avoid predators. When danger threatens, the gecko races around to the blind side of a tree trunk. It keeps the trunk between itself and the threat, often racing around several times before the predator gives up.

*Only the male yellow-headed dwarf gecko has the yellow head of its name. The rest of its body is grey, while the females and younger males are grey all over. When the gecko is cool and resting, the grey background is covered by darker blotches and lines. These fade when the gecko is active.*

**Distribution**: Southern Kenya and eastern Tanzania.
**Habitat**: Woodlands, coastal grasslands and villages.
**Food**: Ground- and tree-living insects and nectar from large flowers.
**Size**: 4–9cm (1.5–3.5in).
**Maturity**: Unknown.
**Breeding**: Clutches of two hard-shelled eggs laid at several times throughout the year.
**Life span**: Unknown.
**Status**: Common.

## Common barking gecko

*Ptenopus garrulus*

The common barking gecko is known for the loud calls made by males as they stand at the entrance to their burrows at dusk. The males call as they prepare to set off to forage for food. The function of the call is to advertise the male's presence and so warn off rival males and attract females to the area.

The common barking gecko is a desert species. It lives in the Namib and Kalahari Deserts of Namibia and western Botswana. During the heat of the day the gecko rests in a deep burrow. It uses its long toes and blunt head to dig into the sand. The toes are fringed with flat scales, which make them a more useful shovel.

The wide feet also prevent the lizard from sinking into soft sand as it looks for food during the night. The gecko moves slowly, looking for insects such as beetles, ants and bugs. If it senses danger, the gecko freezes and relies on its camouflaged skin to hide it from a predator. If the threat remains close by the gecko will dash to its burrow or scurry into another nearby hiding place.

Common barking geckos mate at all times of the year. To save water the females lay just one or two eggs a year. These take from two to six months to hatch. The hatchlings are already large and look very similar to the adults.

*This little gecko is a burrowing species and has a large round head to help it push through soft sandy soil. Its upper body is covered by a mottled red-brown pattern, which keeps it camouflaged while moving across sand.*

**Distribution**: Namibia and Botswana.
**Habitat**: Areas of desert with loose sandy soil.
**Food**: Insects and other invertebrates.
**Size**: 6–10cm (2.25–4in).
**Maturity**: Unknown.
**Breeding**: Males bark at dusk to attract female mates. The female lays a single egg after each mating. Most females will mate once or twice a year, generally with different mates each time.
**Life span**: Unknown.
**Status**: Common.

# East African lidded gecko

*Holodactylus africanus*

**Distribution**: Somalia, Kenya and Tanzania.
**Habitat**: Bush and scrub in dry areas.
**Food**: Insects and other invertebrates.
**Size**: 8–11cm (3.25–4.25in).
**Maturity**: 1 year.
**Breeding**: 2 hard-shelled eggs laid in soil.
**Life span**: Unknown.
**Status**: Common.

The East African lidded gecko lives in a few pockets of bush land in Somalia, Kenya and the extreme north of Tanzania. It is most common in the Masai Mara region. The lidded gecko is a burrowing species, using the claws on its large forefeet to dig into the ground. The gecko stays underground during the day to avoid the heat. It has retained movable eyelids as an adaptation to life in soft soil. The eyelids clean soil away from the eyes and can be shut completely if needed. The gecko also has a short and swollen tail, which might also aid its movement underground.

By night the gecko comes to the surface and creeps slowly through the bushes in search of its insect food. It is a ground-living species and does not climb into the bushes. Female East African lidded geckos lay just two hard-shelled eggs during each breeding season. These eggs are buried in sandy soil, protected from drying out by the shell. After laying, the females have no further dealings with their young. The hatchlings emerge after several weeks and look like small versions of the adults.

*The East African lidded gecko is a stout lizard. It is different from most other African and European geckos in that it has movable eyelids, hence its common name. The species is also often referred to as the African clawed gecko due to the long claws on its forefeet.*

---

**Malagasy day gecko** (*Phelsuma madagascariensis*): 22–30cm (8.75–12in)
This robust gecko lives in the forests of northern Madagascar. It is a vivid green with red-orange spots on its back. Males have a swelling at the base of the tail. The geckos cling to tree trunks and branches with large toe pads. They are also common visitors to homes, where they prey on insects. Like many geckos, members of this species stand with their head down when resting on a trunk or wall.

**Elegant sand gecko** (*Stenodactylus sthenodactylus*): 9–10.5cm (3.5–4.25in)
This small, slender gecko lives in the Sahara Desert of North Africa. It has a sand-coloured body speckled with grey. The gecko spends most of its life underground in a burrow, which it digs with its long toes. The gecko emerges on to the ground surface only at night, and during the hottest parts of the year it will stay in the cool of its burrow even at night.

**Forest dwarf day gecko** (*Lygodactylus gutturalis*): 5–9cm (2–3.5in)
Despite its name, this is a medium-sized gecko. It lives in the mountain forests on the western side of the Rift Valley and across Central Africa. It is a diurnal species and lacks the toe pads seen in most African geckos. It forages in leaf litter and on rotting logs. It eats insects especially ants. Breeding takes places at all times of the year, and females may produce several clutches each year. Each clutch contains two eggs with a hard shell.

# Tete thick-toed gecko

*Pachydactylus tetensis*

The Tete thick-toed gecko lives in moist savannahs of southern Tanzania. It is one of several thick-toed geckos living in Africa. These velvety-skinned geckos are named after their extra-large toe pads.

The geckos are nocturnal and are chiefly arboreal lizards, that is they hunt for food in trees. The lizard is closely associated with the giant baobab trees that grow in this region. They shelter during the day in hollow areas inside the massive trunk and branches. In areas where trees are unavailable, the geckos use their large toe pads to scale rocky outcrops. They are often to be found resting in rocky crevices.

Breeding takes place at the start of the rains. Males attract females with calls made at dusk. The females lay several pairs of eggs over the following weeks. They take between two and three months to hatch.

**Distribution**: Southern Tanzania.
**Habitat**: Baobab trees.
**Food**: Insects.
**Size**: 13–18cm (5–7in).
**Maturity**: Unknown.
**Breeding**: Several pairs of eggs laid in wet season.
**Life span**: Unknown.
**Status**: Common.

*As its named suggests, the Tete thick-toed gecko is noted for its large toe pads, or scansors. These are even larger than those of most geckos. The scansors are covered in bristled ridges, which make the toes excellent at gripping on to surfaces.*

# CROCODILES

*The last living members of an ancient group known as the archosaurs, crocodiles are little changed from
the days of the dinosaurs. The 25 surviving species stand as testament to the success of the crocodilian
body design. Thick, scaly skin keeps predators at bay, a special respiratory system allows them to keep
hidden underwater for up to five hours at a time, and powerful jaws make them fearsome predators.*

## Nile crocodile

*Crocodylus niloticus*

The Nile crocodile's powerful
body is covered in greyish plate-
like scales. The powerful tail is
ridged with two keels of scales.

Nile crocodiles were once widespread in eastern
and southern Africa, but are now scarcer.
With powerful jaws, strong tails, a terrifying
turn of speed and stealth belying their
enormous size, these crocodiles are efficient
killing machines. Nile crocodiles have evolved
to be very good at fishing, and during the
times of the year when fish migrate along the
rivers they hunt cooperatively. Forming cordons
across rivers, they herd the fish into shallow
waters, where they can be picked off with ease.
    Nile crocodiles are ecologically important as
predators. They help to keep the environment
in balance by eating catfish, which are predators
themselves. By keeping the catfish numbers
in check, Nile crocodiles allow the smaller fish, which are
eaten by catfish, to thrive, providing food for more than
40 species of bird. In turn, bird droppings fertilize the waters,
keeping them rich enough to support a large diversity of life.

**Distribution**: Africa (not in
the north-west or Sahara
region) and Madagascar.
**Habitat**: Rivers, freshwater
marshes, estuaries and
mangrove swamps.
**Food**: Fish, water birds and
land mammals.
**Size**: 3.5–6m (11.5–19.75ft);
up to 225kg (496lb).
**Maturity**: 10 years.
**Breeding**: 25–100 eggs laid
in nest.
**Life span**: 45 years.
**Status**: Common.

## Dwarf crocodile

*Osteolaemus tetraspis*

**Distribution**: West Africa.
**Habitat**: Freshwater lakes,
swamps and slow-moving
rivers.
**Food**: Fish, birds,
crustaceans and occasionally
small mammals.
**Size**: 1.8m (6ft).
**Maturity**: 6 years.
**Breeding**: Clutches of up
to 20 eggs.
**Life span**: 40 years.
**Status**: Vulnerable.

Like other crocodilians, female dwarf crocodiles make very attentive
mothers. Laying their eggs in mounds of rotting vegetation on the shore,
the females guard them fiercely for the three months it takes for them to
incubate. As hatching time arrives, they dig the eggs out of the nests
to help the hatchlings escape. They may even roll the eggs gently around
in their mouth to break the shells open.
    Once out of their eggs, the young face a
journey fraught with danger down to the
water, but the mothers are there to help
again. With surprising gentleness, they
pick up their babies in their mouths and
flip them into their throat pouches,
before carrying them down to the water.
    Although adapted to life in water, dwarf
crocodiles, like most crocodilians, make
shelters on land. These are underground
dens dug into the banks of rivers and lakes.
They are connected to the outside world by
entrances and exit tunnels, both of which can
be several metres (tens of feet) long.

*Dwarf crocodiles
are also known
as broad-fronted
crocodiles,
because of their
broad, blunt snouts.
People once
thought they were
cannibals as they
carry their young
in their mouths.*

# NON-VENOMOUS SNAKES

*Most snakes do not have a venomous bite and are completely harmless to humans. The largest African snakes – the pythons – are non-venomous. They kill by squeezing their prey until their victims suffocate. Colubrids, typified by the grass snake of Europe, are the largest group of snakes. Most colubrids are non-venomous, although a few use their saliva to stun their prey.*

## Grass snake

*Natrix natrix*

*Grass snakes have dark green bodies with black flecking and whitish-yellow collars around their necks. They inhabit Britain as far as the Scottish border counties.*

The grass snake is the most common snake in Britain. It owes its success to its versatility, being able to hunt both on land and in the water. It prefers to prey on frogs, toads and fish, when it can. To acquire enough heat to be able to function properly, the grass snake has to spend much of its time basking in sunlight. However, this does leave it rather exposed to attack from birds of prey. Foxes, badgers and hedgehogs will also make a meal out of it if they get the chance, but this isn't easy. When threatened, a grass snake has a range of defensive tactics including loud hissing, inflating its body with air, biting, producing a foul-smelling secretion from its anus and playing dead.

Not only is keeping warm a problem for adult grass snakes, it is a problem for the eggs, too. If they are too cold they will take too long to develop, or not hatch at all. Female grass snakes combat this problem by travelling large distances to find suitable places to lay them. Heaps of rotting vegetation, such as compost heaps, are favoured.

**Distribution**: Europe from Scandinavia south to the Mediterranean, North Africa and central Asia east to Lake Baikal, Russia.
**Habitat**: Prefer damp grasslands, ditches and river banks.
**Food**: Amphibians, fish, small mammals and small birds.
**Size**: 0.7–2m (2.25–6.5ft).
**Maturity**: Not known.
**Breeding**: 8–40 eggs laid in June, July or August depending on the latitude, about 8 weeks after mating.
**Life span**: 20 years.
**Status**: Common.

## Western whip snake

*Coluber viridiflavus*

**Distribution**: South-western Europe, Corsica and Sardinia.
**Habitat**: Rocky areas, woodlands and shrubs.
**Food**: Lizards, small mammals, nesting birds and smaller snakes.
**Size**: 1.5m (5ft).
**Maturity**: 3–5 years.
**Breeding**: Up to 15 eggs laid each year.
**Life span**: 20 years.
**Status**: Common.

The western whip snake ranges from the Spanish side of the Pyrenees to Brittany. It is also found in the foothills of the Alps and throughout Italy. The snake is also a resident of Corsica and Sardinia. Northern Croatia is the eastern limit of its range, where it gives way to its close relative, the Balkan whip snake.

The snake is found in thickly vegetated areas and woodlands. It shelters under rocks and in crevices and is often seen among the ruins of buildings. It is a diurnal hunter and is most common in the south of its range. The western whip snake hunts a variety of small animals, most commonly lizards and rodents. The snake hunts by sight and moves in for the kill very quickly. Smaller prey is grabbed in the mouth, while larger prey is constricted.

*Adult western whip snakes have charcoal-grey backs with pale yellow bellies, though a few individuals have striking yellow markings.*

## African house snake

*Lamprophis fuliginosus*

African house snakes exhibit a large number of colour forms in different parts of Africa. In southern Tanzania, for example, the snake is known as the brown house snake, while in the north the snake is chocolate brown with white stripes and in Kenya it is called the sooty house snake.

This species of snake is one of the most successful of all the snakes in Africa. It lives virtually everywhere south and west of the Sahara Desert. However, many naturalists now consider the species to be a complex (a mixture of subspecies and completely separate species). The precise relationship between the continent's house snakes is uncertain, but the snakes appear in so many colour forms that it is likely that in the future they will be recognized as several distinct species.

African house snakes hunt for rodents and go wherever they can find prey. In the wild that takes them to most mild habitats, such as grasslands and woodlands. However, the snakes avoid deserts and dense jungle.

Rodents are common residents of human settlements too, and African house snakes have followed them. They are harmless to humans, and, since they ensure that rats and mice are kept to a minimum, most people are happy to see these snakes in their homes.

**Distribution**: Sub-Saharan Africa.
**Habitat**: Woodland and savannah.
**Food**: Rodents.
**Size**: 60–120cm (23.5–47.25in).
**Maturity**: 6 months.
**Breeding**: About 15 eggs laid in summer.
**Life span**: 8 years.
**Status**: Common.

## Aesculapian snake

*Elaphe longissima*

The Aesculapian snake is reputed to be the species depicted on the rod of Aesculapius, widely recognized as a universal symbol of healing and often depicted on the side of ambulances. The snake itself is rather nondescript: it is long and slender with a small head and a uniformly grey body. The individual seen below has a juvenile colour pattern. Adults are more uniformly coloured.

This snake lives in central and eastern Europe. The western limit of its range is the Atlantic coast of France, although it is absent from the north of that country. To the east, the snake appears in Poland and Ukraine, and it is also found in northern Italy and southern Greece, home to the Greek god Aesculapius after which it is named. Another species, the Italian Aesculapian, lives in pockets of southern Italy. Some people suggest that these populations stem from Aesculapian snakes introduced to these areas by Romans for the snakes' reputed healing powers.

Aesculapian snakes live in shrubs and woodlands and tend to prefer dry and sunny areas. They are hunters and prey on small mammals, lizards and birds. Adults eat every three or four days. The rest of the time they lie hidden under stones and in tree hollows.

Males travel widely in search of mates and often fight other males for access to females. The females lay a dozen pear-shaped eggs in holes at the base of trunks. The eggs are then covered with dead leaves. As these decay they produce heat and keep the eggs warm.

**Distribution**: Northern Spain, southern France, Switzerland, northern Italy, Austria, Czech Republic, Poland and Ukraine. Also found in Turkey and east to northern Iran.
**Habitat**: Dry woodlands, especially in sunny clearings.
**Food**: Mice, voles and squirrels.
**Size**: 2m (6.5ft).
**Maturity**: About 3 years or when they reach 1m (3.25ft).
**Breeding**: Single clutch of elongated 12–18 eggs produced each year. Hatchlings are about 20cm (8in).
**Life span**: 20 years.
**Status**: Common.

**Dice snake** (*Natrix tessellata*): 80–130cm (2.5–4.25ft)
A close relative of the grass snake, the dice snake lives across southern and central Europe. The western limits of its range are Italy in the south and the Czech Republic in the north, and the species is found as far east as Ukraine. The species is also seen across southern Asia. Most dice snakes have several large dark spots on their pale skin. These spots, resembling the dots on dice, are spaced regularly along the back. Dice snakes are an aquatic species and live in lowland rivers. They hunt underwater for fish and amphibians. In several places dice snakes occur in large numbers, with one snake found in every two or three metres of river bank.

**Montpellier snake** (*Malpolon monspessulanus*): 2m (6.5ft)
Very fast and shy, Montpellier snakes will flee at the first sign of a disturbance. They prefer open and dry grassland with stones and slopes exposed to sunlight, where they are active only on warm and sunny days. They feed mainly on lizards, which are hunted by sight.

**False smooth snake** (*Macroprotodon cucullatus*): 60cm (23.5in)
The hooded snake lives in stony parts of Spain, Portugal and North Africa. It preys on lizards, which it attacks while they are sleeping, paralyzing them with a mild venom harmless to people. The hooded snake can move quickly and if surprised it will throw its head back to show its underside before fleeing for shelter.

# Leopard snake

*Elaphe situla*

Lacking any significant amount of venom, leopard snakes are constrictors – they squeeze their prey to death. While the young feed mainly on small lizards, adults prefer to eat rodents. It is this fondness for rats and mice that has made leopard snakes popular pets in some parts of their range. Active by day, leopard snakes are attracted to human settlements by the abundance of rats and mice to be found there. In some parts of Greece, far from being feared, people used to actively introduce these snakes into their homes as a way of controlling pests. They are even considered to be good-luck charms by superstitious people.

The leopard snake's good reputation, and its ability to live alongside humans, has played highly in its favour, and it is still a common sight throughout much of its range in south-eastern Europe.

**Distribution**: South-eastern Europe.
**Habitat**: Dry, rocky slopes.
**Food**: Small mammals and birds.
**Size**: 1m (3.25ft).
**Maturity**: Not known.
**Breeding**: Clutches of 2–5 eggs laid in July or August.
**Life span**: 15 years.
**Status**: Common.

*The magnificent leopard snake is easily identified by the striking red markings after which it is named.*

# Smooth snake

*Coronella austriaca*

**Distribution**: Southern England, France and northern Spain and Portugal.
**Habitat**: Heathland and rocky areas.
**Food**: Small mammals, lizards and nestlings.
**Size**: 70cm (27.5in).
**Maturity**: 3–4 years.
**Breeding**: About 6 babies born in autumn.
**Life span**: 18 years.
**Status**: Common.

Britain's rarest snakes, smooth snakes are restricted to just a handful of sandy heathlands in southern England. Across the Channel, the snakes are found across France and in northern and central parts of the Iberian Peninsula. These snakes are colubrids, sometimes described as typical snakes, largely because they are the most numerous type. Like the great majority of colubrids, they are not venomous at all: they kill their prey by constricting them with their coils. Grass snakes and house snakes are also colubrids.

Smooth snakes hunt during the day. They are secretive reptiles and will slither away into cover if they detect something coming. They are also slow moving. They do not chase prey but stalk it by following its scent and ambushing it as it emerges from a burrow.

These snakes breed in spring. They are the only European species to give birth to their young rather than lay eggs. The young take anywhere between four and five months to develop inside the mother.

*Smooth snakes are so called because, unlike grass snakes, which have keel-shaped scales, they have flat, smooth scales. Female smooth snakes are generally larger than the males. The snakes are smaller in the northern parts of their range.*

## Malagasy leaf-nosed snake

*Langaha madagascariensis*

Also known as twig mimic snakes, the habits of these peculiar looking snakes are not very well known. Lying motionless for hours in the canopy of the tropical forests of Madagascar, leaf-nosed snakes blend into their background incredibly well, becoming extremely difficult to spot. The snake is long and thin like many tree-living snakes, which helps it to spread its weight over a wide area. The slender brown body also creates the illusion that the snake is a twig, and this camouflage is perfected by the remarkable protrusions from the front of their faces. Males possess long, spiky projections, making them look even more like twigs, whereas the females have leaf-like structures instead.

Leaf-nosed snakes are only active for about one hour in every day, normally waiting until midday, the hottest part of the day, before rousing themselves to go hunting. By remaining inactive, the snakes save a lot of energy, which allows them to have long breaks between foraging trips. A decent meal can keep a leaf-nosed snake going for four days or more, before it feels the need to go hunting again. The snakes prey on small tree-living animals, such as frogs, lizards and nestlings.

**Distribution**: Madagascar.
**Habitat**: Tropical rainforests and dry forests.
**Food**: Tree frogs, small birds and reptiles.
**Size**: 1m (3.25ft); 50–80g (0.1–0.2lb).
**Maturity**: Not known.
**Breeding**: Clutches of around 10 eggs laid in November or December.
**Life span**: 10 years.
**Status**: Common.

*The leaf-like snout of the female Malagasy leaf-nosed snake helps to camouflage it among leaves and twigs.*

## Common egg-eating snake

*Dasypeltis scabra*

Very few other snakes share the dietary habits of this fascinating species. Generally most active at night, egg-eating snakes hide out during the day in sheltered areas under rocks or logs. During the night they mainly prey on the eggs of weaverbirds. They are very adept at climbing trees to get to their nests. The snakes test the eggs with their tongues to check whether they have gone off or not. This is important because they cannot spit rotten eggs out once they have swallowed them.

Having found a fresh egg, a snake holds it tightly between its coils and slowly pushes its mouth over and around it. Once the egg is inside the snake's body, it passes farther down the throat until it meets a series of tooth-like structures attached to the vertebrae. These pierce the egg when the snake makes a series of sharp sideways movements of its head. The contents of the egg then drain out of the shell to be digested. Once empty, the egg shell is crushed up and regurgitated from the body. This ability to deal with shells is rare among snakes.

**Distribution**: Southern and central parts of Africa, south of the Sahara Desert.
**Habitat**: Lowland evergreen forest.
**Food**: Birds' eggs.
**Size**: 50–90cm (19.75–35.5in).
**Maturity**: Not known.
**Breeding**: 6–25 eggs laid each year.
**Life span**: 14 years.
**Status**: Common.

*Egg-eating snakes can swallow eggs up to three times the size of their own heads.*

# Mole snake

*Pseudaspis cana*

**Distribution**: East and southern Africa.
**Habitat**: Grasslands.
**Food**: Moles and burrowing rodents.
**Size**: 1–1.80m (3.25–6ft).
**Maturity**: 4 years.
**Breeding**: 90 young born in summer.
**Life span**: 20 years.
**Status**: Common.

A grassland species, mole snakes specialize in hunting for burrowing mammals, such as moles (hence their name), although moles are actually only rarely taken. Most of the snake's prey are burrowing rodents, such as African mole rats.

These snakes have a painful bite but they are not a venomous species. They kill by constricting their prey with their thick, coiled body. Constricting does not crush an animal to death, although bones may be broken by it. Instead the snake steadily tightens its grip and as it does so the victim finds it harder and harder to draw breath. In the end the animal is suffocated to death.

After mating, female mole snakes do not lay eggs. Instead the eggs are retained inside the body of the female for several weeks. The young hatch out while still inside their mother, and are born soon afterwards. Mole snakes have been known to produce huge litters, with over 90 young born at once.

*The mole snake is a large, thick-bodied snake. It has a slightly hook-shaped snout, which is typical of snakes that move through underground burrows. The juveniles are pale brown with cream and black markings. The adults are dark green.*

**Emerald snake** (*Hapsidophrys smaragdina*): 60–110cm (23.5–43.25in)
The emerald tree snake is a forest snake. It lives in the Central African jungles, hunting in the trees for lizards and frogs. However, it is often found hunting in thick vegetation close to the ground, especially along banks of rivers. Like many arboreal snakes, the body is long and thin. The tail makes up 30 per cent of the body. (Although it is hard to differentiate, a snake's tail begins behind the genital opening.) The long body is an adaptation to a climbing lifestyle.

**Splendid tree snake** (*Rhamnophis aetiopissa*): 1–1.5m (3.25–5ft)
The splendid tree snake is a large tree snake living in the lowland rainforests of Central Africa. It has a green body with a brown stripe down the back and black and yellow bands and stripes on either side. It hunts for lizards and frogs by moving slowly up through the branches, using its length to spread its weight over a wide area so that it is supported by several thin branches. It kills with a powerful bite. It is not venomous and is harmless to people. When it is threatened, however, the splendid tree snake inflates its neck to make itself look fiercer than it really is.

# Cape wolf snake

*Lycophidion capense*

The Cape wolf snake lives in the savannahs of Africa. It is distributed mainly through East and southern Africa, from Sudan in the north to Namibia and South Africa. It is a night-time hunter: it has vertical pupils that open very wide and allow its eyes to collect enough light to see by in the gloom of twilight and in the burrows of its prey.

It specializes in eating burrowing animals, especially skinks and sand lizards. While the snake rests in a burrow by day, these lizards forage for food on the surface. As dusk approaches, the snake emerges from hiding and tracks a lizard as it makes its way back to its burrow. The small wolf snake follows its victim into its hiding place. The snake then uses its long curved teeth to make a firm grip on its prey so it can be dragged from the safety of the burrow. The snake generally bites its victims on the back of the neck and, once it has them out in the open, constricts them until dead. Breeding takes place in the wet season. The female lays between three and eight eggs.

**Distribution**: East and southern Africa.
**Habitat**: Savannah.
**Food**: Skinks.
**Size**: 30–50cm (12–19.75in).
**Maturity**: 1 year.
**Breeding**: Up to 8 eggs laid in wet season.
**Life span**: Unknown.
**Status**: Common.

*The Cape wolf snake catches its food underground, so it has a small, flattened head that is easy to fit into the burrows of its prey. The snake is named after its backwards-curved teeth, which are not for delivering venom but for hooking on to struggling prey as they are pulled from their burrows.*

## Schlegel's blindsnake

*Rhinotyphlops schlegelii*

*Schlegel's blindsnake has very small eyes that are barely capable of vision. The snake's tiny head is covered by large protective scales called scutes. These are often referred to collectively as the "beak".*

Schlegel's blindsnake is exceptionally large, being over twice as long as nearly all other blindsnakes. These snakes spend most of their lives underground, earning them their alternative name: worm snakes. The subterranean environment they occupy has meant that blindsnakes' eyes are mere vestiges of those of their above-ground relatives. However, like Schlegel's blindsnake, few are completely blind.

This species is also typical in that it only has teeth in the upper jaw of its small, blunt head. These are all the teeth it needs, because the blindsnake spends most of its time around ant and termite mounds, where it feasts on the soft bodies of the developing insects. The protective beak over the snake's head helps it to tunnel through soft soil without injury. The snake's long, thin body is also covered in smooth, shiny scales that aid in burrowing.

Although they are totally harmless, it is unwise to harass blindsnakes. They have well-developed glands near their anuses, packed full of the most noxious-smelling secretions, which they eject upon attack.

**Distribution**: Southern Africa from Kenya to South Africa.
**Habitat**: Soft, sandy or loamy soils.
**Food**: Pupae, eggs and larvae of ants, termites and other subterranean insects.
**Size**: 1m (3.25ft).
**Maturity**: Not known.
**Breeding**: Lays up to 60 eggs underground, which hatch after 4–6 weeks.
**Life span**: Unknown.
**Status**: Common.

## Zambezi blindsnake

*Rhinotyphlops mucrosa*

The Zambezi blindsnake lives in the soils of eastern Africa. It is most common close to the Zambezi River's watershed in Tanzania, Mozambique and Zambia. This snake is typical of other blindsnakes or worm snakes in that its body is cylindrical, and the head is covered in a scaly beak that helps the snake shovel through the soft soil in search of food. The scales also cover the snake's eyes. The snakes cannot see in the true sense of the word, but their eyes are able to detect whether the animal is in daylight or within the dark of a burrow.

These blindsnakes specialize in eating social insects such as ants and termites. They break into the insects' nest and gorge themselves on the eggs and larvae. Much of this food is stored as fat inside the snake's body. As a result, blindsnakes need to eat just two or three times a year. The rest of the time, the snakes lie dormant underground. The snakes only rarely come to the surface, since their food is all underground. They are most commonly seen after floods. Flash flooding caused by heavy rains waterlogs the soil, so the snakes must come above ground to breathe.

Blindsnakes find it difficult to find mates, so when they do they make the most of it and produce a large number of eggs. Some reports suggest that there can be as many as 60, but half this number is probably more typical. The eggs are laid in an underground chamber and hatch after about six weeks.

**Distribution**: Southern Tanzania and northern Mozambique.
**Habitat**: Soil.
**Food**: Ants and termites.
**Size**: 70cm (27.5in).
**Maturity**: 1–2 years.
**Breeding**: Large clutches of eggs laid each year.
**Life span**: Unknown.
**Status**: Common.

*The Zambezi blindsnake is found in two colour forms. Just after the snake sheds its old skin, its new skin is a blue-grey with black, blotchy markings. Soon, however, the skin darkens to a rich red-brown that matches the colour of the soil more closely.*

# Royal python

*Python regius*

Royal pythons are Africa's smallest pythons. They are generally active at night, when they hunt using eyes that are well adapted to low light levels. They also have special heat-sensing pits around their mouths to detect prey in the dark. Since these pits pick up heat in the form of infrared radiation, they are well equipped to detect the body heat released by their prey.

Pythons are not venomous; they are constrictors. They grab hold of their prey and throw a number of coils around it, holding so tightly that the animal cannot breathe. Constrictors do not crush their prey; they suffocate them.

During the hot dry season, pythons lie inactive (aestivate) in underground burrows. They emerge when the rains arrive in order to mate. However, royal pythons only mate once every three or four years, so that they reproduce at a low rate. This means that their populations are particularly vulnerable to over-hunting. Royal pythons are endangered in the wild because they are collected for the pet trade, as well as being hunted for their flesh and skins.

**Distribution**: Central Africa.
**Habitat**: Grassland.
**Food**: Small mammals, birds, lizards and other species of snakes.
**Size**: 1.2m (4ft).
**Maturity**: 3–5 years.
**Breeding**: 4–10 unusually large eggs.
**Life span**: 25 years.
**Status**: Threatened.

*Royal pythons are also known as ball pythons because when they are threatened they coil up into tight balls with their heads well protected inside.*

---

**Sand boa** (*Eryx jaculus*): 80cm (31.5in)
The sand boa is a European relative of pythons and anacondas. It is a constrictor like these relatives, but is substantially smaller. As its name suggests, it is specialized to a life in dry, sandy habitats. It lives in the southern Balkans and east to the Caspian Sea and central Asia. The snake is also found throughout the Middle East and into North Africa. The snake spends the day in burrows. It might dig its own, but often takes over one dug by a rodent. At night the snake comes to the surface and hunts for prey, which include lizards, insects and small rodents. It generally chases its prey into their burrows and catches them there. However, it also lies buried just below the surface and grabs victims as they walk past.

**Worm snake** (*Typhlops vermicularis*): 40cm (15.75in)
As their name suggests, these snakes look more like large worms than snakes. They are blind and have teeth only on the top jaw. This species is found in the Balkans and east to the Caucasus. They live underground and prefer to make their homes in grassy areas. They eat ants and other underground insects.

# Central African python

*Python sebae*

Central African pythons live across Africa south of the Sahara Desert. They are found in both forested and savannah habitats. Large adults can consume juvenile crocodiles, small antelopes and domestic goats. Most pythons do not survive long enough to grow to that sort of size, and their diet consists of rodents and ground-living birds. The snake hunts in the dark, when most small mammals are on the move. It locates prey using heat-sensitive pits on its snout, which pick up the body heat of prey in the darkness.

Females incubate their eggs to ensure they hatch. The snake wraps its body around several dozen orange-sized eggs. She then shivers her body to generate the heat needed to incubate the eggs.

**Distribution**: Sub-Saharan Africa.
**Habitat**: Forest and savannah.
**Food**: Crocodiles, pigs, goats, birds and antelopes.
**Size**: 3.5–7.5m (11.5–24.5ft).
**Maturity**: 3–5 years.
**Breeding**: 100 eggs incubated by mother.
**Life span**: 30 years.
**Status**: Common.

*The Central African python is the largest snake in Africa. One specimen from the Ivory Coast was nearly 10m (32.75ft) long. However, this was an unusual size, and today pythons over 6.5m (21.25ft) are very rare.*

# VENOMOUS SNAKES

*About 10 per cent of all snakes use modified fangs to inject prey with venom. The main groups of venomous snakes are the vipers, elapids and colubrids. Most of the venomous snakes in Europe are vipers, including the adder, the only venomous species in Britain. One of the largest venomous snakes in the world is the Gaboon viper. However, many African elapids, such as the black mamba, are much more dangerous.*

## Boomslang

*Dispholidus typus*

**Distribution**: Southern Africa.
**Habitat**: Open woodland.
**Food**: Reptiles, mammals and birds.
**Size**: 1.3m–2m (4.25–6.5ft).
**Maturity**: Not known.
**Breeding**: 8–13 eggs laid in early summer.
**Life span**: 18 years.
**Status**: Common.

Weight for weight, the venom produced by the boomslang is more potent than that of either mambas or cobras. However, the boomslang's shy nature has led to it having less of a fearful reputation than its better-known relatives. Boomslangs also lack the large front fangs of mambas and cobras, having small teeth located at the backs of their mouths. To inject a large amount of poison, boomslangs have to deliver more prolonged bites than front-fanged snakes.

The word boomslang means "tree snake" in Afrikaans – the colonial language of South Africa. This name is very apt, since they are very agile snakes that can slide gracefully through the branches of trees, helped by their strong prehensile tails. Nevertheless, while hunting they will come down to the ground on a fairly regular basis in search of prey.

Most of a boomslang's life is spent coiled and immobile among branches. So effective is their camouflage that birds, which make up a substantial part of their diet, have been known to actually perch on them.

*When immobile in trees, boomslangs are very hard to spot. Their green bodies blend perfectly with the foliage. These highly venomous snakes are members of the colubrid snake family, unlike mambas and cobras.*

## Banded water cobra

*Naja annulata*

*The banded water cobra is thought to have at least two subspecies. The first has a yellow-brown body with thick black rings along its length. The less common subspecies, known as the storm water cobra, has just two or three rings near the neck. The rest of the body is more yellow with a blue tinge. The tail is jet black.*

The banded water cobra lives in the waterways of Central Africa. Most are located in the rainforests that grow in the Congo Basin, but the snakes also live around the Great Lakes of East Africa. The banded water cobra spends long periods in water. It is an excellent swimmer and makes long dives to catch prey. It can dive to a depth of 30m (98.5ft) and stay underwater for 10 minutes. Being a cold-blooded reptile, its metabolic rate is low so it can survive perfectly well without a fresh supply of oxygen for this time. The snake hunts for fish underwater. Like all cobras, this species is venomous but as yet biologists are not sure how effective the venom is underwater.

When not hunting for fish, the cobra rests under rocks and in thickets beside the water. It is a frequent visitor to jetties and wrecks close to the shore. However, the cobra is a shy species and will avoid contact with people.

**Distribution**: Congo River Basin and Great Lakes of East Africa.
**Habitat**: Forest lakes, rivers and other bodies of water.
**Food**: Fish.
**Size**: 1.5–2.7m (5–9ft).
**Maturity**: Unknown.
**Breeding**: Unknown number of eggs laid each year.
**Life span**: Unknown.
**Status**: Common.

# Spitting cobra

*Naja pallida*

**Distribution**: Eastern and
Central Africa from southern
Egypt to northern Tanzania.
**Habitat**: Savannah
grasslands.
**Food**: Amphibians, small
mammals, birds, eggs and
other reptiles.
**Size**: 0.7–1.5m (2.25–5ft).
**Maturity**: Not known.
**Breeding**: Clutches of
up to 15 eggs.
**Life span**: 20 years.
**Status**: Common.

As its name indicates, this snake has a
particularly effective method of defence.
When it feels threatened, the spitting cobra rises
up in typical cobra fashion, extending its
hood, which is quite narrow by cobra
standards. Holding its head high off the
ground, it then spits large quantities
of venom over a distance of more
than 2m (6.5ft), aiming for the
attacker's eyes.

The venom is very potent, causing
blindness if it does reach the eyes, and
bites can be fatal to humans. These cobras, however, are very
reluctant to bite, preferring a "spit-and-run" tactic, making off
while their enemy's eyes are stinging. Of course, cobras do not
hold back when they come across prey animals. These are rapidly
killed by the powerful venom injected via the snake's fangs.

Adults are predominantly nocturnal, hiding inside termite hills,
old logs or piles of leaves during the day. Young cobras are active
during the day, and with good cause: adult cobras will eat them.

*The colour of spitting
cobras is very variable.
Individuals may be red,
yellow, pinkish or steely
grey. Cobras (members
of the Naja genus) are a
sizeable group associated
more with Asia.*

---

**Forest cobra** (*Naja melanoleuca*):
1.5–3m (5–10ft)
The forest cobra holds the record, along with
the anaconda, for being the longest-living snake.
It is capable of reaching the impressive age
of 30 years. It is found all over western and
southern Africa, inhabiting many different
habitats. Forest cobras have a reputation for
being ill tempered and dangerous. Their venom
is extremely toxic. They chase attackers off
with mouths agape and ready to bite.

**Rinkhal** (*Hemachatus haemachatus*):
1–1.5m (3.25–5ft)
Rinkhals closely resemble cobras in that they
have hoods, which they spread when feeling
threatened. Found in southern Africa, they differ
from true cobras by having differently shaped
scales, and by giving birth to live young
(whereas cobras lay eggs). In the wild, rinkhals
mainly eat toads, but will make meals of rodents
or any other small animals unfortunate enough
to come too close.

**Green mamba** (*Dendraspis angusticeps*):
1.8–2.3m (6–7.5ft)
The green mamba is a smaller and less-
dangerous cousin of the mighty black mamba.
The green mamba lives high in the trees of
coastal forests of Kenya and Tanzania. There it
preys on small mammals and birds by moving
silently through the branches and setting
ambushes for its victims. Females slither down
to the ground after mating to lay about 10 eggs
in the leaf litter.

# Black mamba

*Dendroaspis polylepis*

The black mamba is probably Africa's most
feared snake, and justifiably so. It is an
aggressive animal, armed with venom
capable of killing humans in four hours.

Raising its head up off the ground to a
height of 1.2m (4ft), black mouth agape,
the mamba charges. It can reach a speed of
16kph (10mph), making it one of the fastest
snakes in the world. Hunting by day using
its excellent eyesight, it usually bites its
prey a couple of times and then lets go.
The stricken animal may make off but in
a short time it is paralyzed by the snake's
toxins, and then swallowed headfirst.

**Distribution**: Southern and
Central Africa.
**Habitat**: Tropical forests
and savannah.
**Food**: Mainly small mammals
and birds.
**Size**: 3.5m (11.5ft).
**Maturity**: Not known.
**Breeding**: Clutches of
14 eggs laid after a long
courtship period.
**Life span**: 26 years.
**Status**: Common.

*Black mambas are
actually grey with
white bellies.
Their name
refers to the
colour of the insides
of their mouths.*

## Cat snake

*Telescopus fallax*

The cat snake lives in the Balkans and Greece. It is found as far north as Bulgaria and the north-east corner of Italy. The snake's range continues east through the Caucasus to western Asia. The snake is considered sacred on some Greek islands.

Although it is more or less harmless to humans, the cat snake does use a weak venom to subdue its prey. It hunts in twilight using its large eyes to see in the gloom. Its vertical pupils allow its eyes to capture as much light as possible.

The snake is small and cannot tackle prey much bigger than a mouse or medium-sized lizard. Its favoured prey are small lizards, which it tracks by scent and sight through rocky habitats. The snake generally follows its victims into their hiding places and kills them with a bite. However, a few victims are also stalked. The prey is paralyzed by the venom, which is delivered along a groove in the snake's two fangs. It is weak and slow acting: the snake must hook a small lizard in its mouth for five minutes as it waits for its victim to die. The snake is relatively harmless to humans because its mouth is too small for its fangs to pump venom into the skin.

**Distribution**: South-east Europe from the Adriatic coast of the Balkans to south-east Bulgaria. It is also found on several Aegean islands including Crete and Rhodes.
**Habitat**: Stony habitats, such as hilly woodlands, ruins, walls and also sandy areas with bushes.
**Food**: Small lizards, slow worms and rodents.
**Size**: 1m (3.25ft).
**Maturity**: 3 years.
**Breeding**: 5–9 eggs laid each year.
**Life span**: Unknown.
**Status**: Common.

*The cat snake earns its name from the pupils in its eyes, which resemble those of a cat. In strong light the pupils close into a vertical slit, not into a ring like human eyes. Pupils like this can be opened more widely than round ones, allowing more light in for night vision.*

## Green water snake

*Philothamnus hoplogaster*

Green water snakes belong to a group of snakes called racers. They have fangs for delivering venom, but these are positioned at the back of the mouth, instead of at the front as in more familiar biting snakes, such as cobras. The venom of green water snakes is very mild. It is thought to be harmless to humans, but may cause paralysis in frogs, the snake's main prey.

The green water snake lives in the swamps and still backwaters of southern and East Africa. It is an active swimmer and patrols the shallow waters for small frogs and any other water animals it comes across.

Like most snakes, the green water snake prefers to keep out of the way of people and as a consequence it is not well understood. When it is encountered, it seems to be a gentle species. It does not inflate its throat like other snakes in an attempt to frighten off attackers and it rarely bites. However, its size and colouring make it hard to distinguish from the green mamba – a deadly snake.

**Distribution**: Southern Kenya to Tanzania, Mozambique and across southern Africa.
**Habitat**: Backwaters, marshes and other areas of shallow water.
**Food**: The main prey are frogs, but any small animal will be eaten if the opportunity arises.
**Size**: 60–93cm (23.5–36.5in).
**Maturity**: Unknown, probably about one year.
**Breeding**: Up to 8 elongated eggs laid at all times of year.
**Life span**: Unknown.
**Status**: Common although rarely seen.

*The green water snake is long and thin. Juveniles have dark crossbars, but most of these fade in adulthood. The adults are either a uniform pale green or more muted grey-blue. Many individuals also have a yellow patch on the throat.*

# Eastern twig snake

*Thelotornis mossambicanus*

**Distribution**: South-east Africa.
**Habitat**: Wooded areas of savannah.
**Food**: Lizards and birds.
**Size**: 90–140cm (35.5–55in).
**Maturity**: 2–3 years.
**Breeding**: Eggs laid in summer.
**Life span**: Unknown.
**Status**: Common.

The eastern twig snake lives in the savannahs of south-eastern Africa as far north as Tanzania. Savannahs are often characterized as grasslands, but they also contain a good number of small wooded areas. It is there that the twig snake makes its home.

The twig snake is named after the wood-like pattern on its body, which helps it to hide among the branches. It hunts for newly hatched birds and small lizards, locating its prey using its sense of smell and vision. Like many tree snakes, this species has horizontal keyhole-shaped pupils. These give the snakes a wide field of view but also allow them to retain forward binocular vision, in which both eyes look at the same object, which is essential for the twig snakes to be able to judge distances. Twig snakes kill with a very potent venom that causes their victims to die from internal bleeding.

*The eastern twig snake is exceptionally long and thin, even for a snake that lives in trees. The elongated body has a red-brown pattern that looks remarkably similar to wood. The snake never leaves the trees, since it would be too conspicuous among the green grass.*

---

**Giant centipede eater** (*Aparallactus modestus*): 35–65cm (13.75–25.5in)
This large burrowing snake lives in the forests of the Congo Basin. It has a small head and short tail which makes it able to burrow through soil. Adults are a dark grey-green, while juveniles can be identified by the pale patch on their heads. The snake digs through the soft forest soil and leaf litter in search of soft-bodied invertebrates. Centipedes certainly make up a part of their diet, but earthworms, slugs and beetle grubs are probably a more common meal. Venom is delivered through fangs at the rear of the mouth. It is harmless to humans.

**Eastern tiger snake** (*Telescopus semiannulatus*): 60–100cm (23.5–39.5in)
This species of eastern African snake is so named after the thick orange and brown bands on its body. The snake hunts on the ground and in trees. Its main prey are birds and lizards, but it also takes roosting bats. The tiger snake is an aggressive species and will bite when provoked. The venom is pumped through fangs at the back of the mouth and a few bites are capable of delivering a harmful dose.

**Dagger tooth snake** (*Xyelodontophis uluguruensis*): 80–130cm (31.5–51in)
This species was first described only in 2002. It lives in the evergreen forests that grow on Uluguru Mountain near the coast of north-eastern Tanzania. When threatened, the snake stiffens its body and inflates its throat. It will readily bite attackers but the potency of its venom is still to be investigated.

# Rufous beaked snake

*Rhamphiosis rostratus*

The rufous beaked snakes live in the sandy grasslands of East Africa, from Somalia and Sudan in the north to Mozambique in the south. They are common in the dry lowland areas on the coastal plains.

The snake has a small head but a powerful body. The head is used to shovel sandy soil out of the way as the snake digs a burrow. It shelters by night in this burrow and emerges to hunt at dawn. The snake kills with a venom that is delivered through fangs located at the back of its mouth. The venom paralyzes the muscles of victims and eventually causes them to stop breathing. However, the venom is weak and prey may be eaten when immobilized but still alive. The venom is harmless to humans.

**Distribution**: Eastern Africa.
**Habitat**: Sandy grasslands.
**Food**: Small mammals, lizards and small snakes.
**Size**: 1.2–1.4m (4–4.5ft).
**Maturity**: Unknown.
**Breeding**: A dozen eggs laid singly of the course of several days.
**Life span**: Unknown.
**Status**: Common.

*The head of the rufous beaked snake is small and has a sloping snout. This is an adaptation to a burrowing lifestyle, making it well suited for pushing through soft soil. However, this species should not be confused with the blindsnakes, another group of burrowing snakes, also with a similar beak-like snout and sometimes called beaked snakes because of it.*

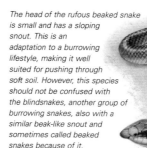

# Egyptian cobra

*Naja haje*

The Egyptian cobra is one of the most deadly snakes in Africa. Its venom is more toxic than most other familiar cobras, such as the Indian cobra, famed for its use in snake charming, and even the king cobra, the world's largest venomous snake. The Egyptian cobra's venom first causes paralysis and soon after death, as the heart and other chest muscles give out. Humans bitten by an Egyptian cobra will die unless an antivenin drug is administered within an hour or two. The death is reputed to be painless. Legend has it that Queen Cleopatra, the Ptolomeic ruler of Egypt during Roman times, chose to use a bite from an Egyptian cobra to commit suicide after hearing of her lover Mark Antony's death.

Egyptian cobras live in any habitat where there is a good supply of food. They sometimes live among humans, attracted by the rodents that also live in human settlements. In the wild young snakes eat toads and birds' eggs, while older individuals eat small mammals. The largest Egyptian cobras eat other snakes. They seem to be particularly fond of puff adders.

Eggs are laid in a termite mound to protect them from predators. The eggs are also kept warm by the heat produced by the insects' nest, and after 60 days of incubation the young hatch.

**Distribution**: Northern and eastern Africa and most of the Middle East as far north as Syria.
**Habitat**: Grasslands, woodlands and deserts.
**Food**: Mammals, eggs and other snakes.
**Size**: 1.3–2.5m (4.25–8.25ft).
**Maturity**: 3 years.
**Breeding**: Up to 20 eggs laid in termite mounds. The eggs hatch after 60 days, and the young are already venomous but have smaller hoods than the adults.
**Life span**: 25 years.
**Status**: Common.

*The Egyptian cobra is the largest cobra in Africa. It is also known as the brown cobra. Like other cobras, this species has a hooded neck; the hood is opened when the snake rears up into a threat posture. The belly below the hood has dark bands before changing to pale brown.*

# Adder

*Vipera berus*

The majority of members of the viper family are venomous, and the adder – or common viper – is no exception. However, it poses little threat to humans. Adders rarely bite humans, and, even when they do, the consequences are usually no more than a painful swelling around the area of the bite. Adders spend most of their day basking in the sunshine, and go out to hunt in the late afternoon. As winter closes in, adders prepare to hibernate, usually burrowing underground to sleep through the cold weather. The duration of hibernation varies with latitude.

The active periods of adders can be divided into three distinct phases. The first phase occurs during spring, when they come out of hibernation and disperse. This is when the males, having shed their skins, go in search of females, and mating occurs. The second phase begins at the onset of summer, when adders migrate along hedgerows and ditches to prime feeding grounds, such as wet meadows. They stay in these areas until summer starts to draw to a close, at which time they head back to drier areas – the third phase. Female adders give birth to their young – they do not lay eggs – which immediately prepare to hibernate, too.

**Distribution**: Throughout Europe and northern and western Asia.
**Habitat**: Open places such as heaths, meadows and woodland edges.
**Food**: Lizards, small mammals, nestlings and insects.
**Size**: 65cm (25.5in).
**Maturity**: Not known.
**Breeding**: 10 young born in late summer.
**Life span**: 15 years.
**Status**: Common.

*The adder's predominantly grey-brown colour, with zigzag markings down the back, is very different from the coloration of the grass snake, yet people often confuse the two.*

# Asp viper

*Vipera aspis*

**Distribution**: Western and central Europe.
**Habitat**: Rocky hillsides and scrublands.
**Food**: Small mammals, frogs, lizards and birds.
**Size**: 60cm (23.5in).
**Maturity**: 3–4 years.
**Breeding**: About 7 young born every 2–3 years.
**Life span**: 18 years.
**Status**: Common.

The asp viper lives in rocky areas of western and central Europe. The viper prefers dry habitats but is also present in damp climates, such as those on the slopes of the Pyrenees and Alps. The northern side of the asp viper's range overlaps with that of the adder. In these areas, the asp viper is restricted to dry and warm locations.

The asp viper is mainly diurnal, although it will hunt at night when the temperature is too high in some parts of its range. Males may hunt over a large home range, while the females tend to stay close to a single den. The snake's diet is mainly composed of mammals, lizards and birds. The venom is relatively weak and victims often manage to run away after being bitten before dying close by. The vipers use their excellent sense of smell to track down their dying victims.

Females breed once every two or three years. They do not lay eggs but give birth to six or seven young three months after mating.

*The asp viper has a broad triangular head that is typical of the vipers, although its body is somewhat more slender than other viper species. Its nose is also only slightly upturned. There are many colour forms across its range.*

---

**Desert horned viper** (*Cerastes cerastes*): 30–60cm (12–23.5in)
The desert horned viper is a resident of the Sahara Desert. Its name also refers to the pointed projections above both its eyes. The powerfully built snake has heavily keeled scales (scales with a marked ridge on them). The keels help the snake to squirm beneath the soft desert sands, where it hides during the heat of the day. The desert horned viper hunts at night and often buries itself in order to ambush its prey. Its victims include rodents and lizards and the occasional bird. When the prey is in range, the snake launches itself out of the sand. When threatened itself, it coils its body and shakes itself to make the keeled scales clatter together and produce a menacing rustling sound.

**Horned adder** (*Bitis caudalis*): 30–50cm (12–19.75in)
The horned adder lives in the deserts and savannahs of south-western Africa. It has a very similar life to the desert horned viper. The southern species also has roughly keeled scales to help it grip loose ground as it side-winds (moves in sideways loops). The scales also help the snake to shuffle under soft sandy soil when resting or forming an ambush. The horned adder always hunts at night. It buries itself just below the surface but leaves the tip of its tail visible. Small mammals see the tail wriggling in the sand and come to investigate, only to be met with the adder's deadly fang. Like its more widespread northern relative, the common adder, this species does not lay eggs, but instead gives birth to live young.

# Nose-horned viper

*Vipera ammodytes*

The nose-horned viper ranges from Austria and Italy in the west, through the Balkans, Greece and Turkey to the Caucasus and then beyond into western Asia. This species is one of the deadliest in Europe. Modern medical intervention has made deaths rare today, but bites to bodily extremities may cause severe swelling and tissue damage. The viper's venom is a neurotoxin (a substance that attacks the nervous system). The nose-horned viper has fangs that are 1cm (0.4in) long. When not in use they fit into a soft sheath at the top of the mouth, a feature common to all vipers and adders. The fangs are hollow and venom is pumped through them deep into a victim's body tissue, where it can act immediately.

Nose-horned vipers are diurnal hunters. They prey on mammals, but in certain parts, such as the Aegean Islands, lizards form their staple diet.

**Distribution**: Central and south-eastern Europe and western Asia.
**Habitat**: Dry habitats.
**Food**: Small mammals, birds and other snakes.
**Size**: 65cm (25.5in).
**Maturity**: 3–4 years.
**Breeding**: A dozen young born in summer.
**Life span**: 15 years.
**Status**: Common.

*The nose-horned viper is named after its upturned snout. It is the only snake in eastern Europe to have such as distinctive "horn." Males tend to be larger than the females. The males are light grey, while the females are a darker grey-brown. Both sexes have the zigzag pattern characteristic of vipers.*

# Puff adder

*Bitis arietans*

*The puff adder is a large snake, despite being relatively short. The body is very bulky and this is made all the more apparent when the snake inflates its body to scare off potential threats. The dark grey chevrons on the sandy background provide the snake with excellent camouflage as it slithers slowly through dry grasses in search of prey.*

Along with the Egyptian cobra, the puff adder is responsible for more deaths than any other African snake. The snake is very aggressive and will bite with only the slightest provocation. The venom is a cytotoxin and begins to break down the body tissue in the region of the bite. That area swells and fills with liquid and becomes excruciatingly painful. A large adult puff adder will inject three times the amount needed to kill an adult human with each bite. The venom is slow acting, however. The destruction of tissue spreads slowly through the body and takes more than 24 hours to cause death, which is often caused by vital body fluids draining from the damaged tissue. If antivenin drugs are not administered quickly, even non-fatal injuries to the body can be permanent.

Male puff adders tend to be smaller and more brightly coloured than the females. The females are large because they produce the largest litters of any live-bearing snake: it is not uncommon for 40 babies to emerge in one go. The maximum recorded is 154 for a single adder.

**Distribution**: Most of sub-Saharan Africa.
**Habitat**: Grasslands. Uncommon in forests.
**Food**: Small mammals.
**Size**: 1m (3.25ft).
**Maturity**: 3–4 years.
**Breeding**: Females release a scent to attract males. The males wrestle each other for access to mates. After mating, 20–40 young are born in a single litter in summer.
**Life span**: Unknown.
**Status**: Common.

# Gaboon viper

*Bitis gabonica*

The Gaboon viper, sometimes known as the Gabon viper, is a forest species. Its pattern of purple and brown diamonds and zigzags provides excellent camouflage among the deep leaf litter of the African rainforest. It is found chiefly in the Congo Basin, but also lives in the forests that grow along the southern coast of West Africa.

This viper hunts at night. It is the heaviest snake in Africa and Europe and so never climbs into trees. Instead, it lies motionless in an ambush for small mammals, lizards and the occasional bird to come within reach. Victims receive a huge dose of venom through the viper's mighty fangs. The venom is weaker than many African vipers, but the size of the dose means that it is likely to be deadly if no medical treatment is received. To service such large fangs, the snake needs to have equally large venom glands. These are located inside the head behind the eyes. This arrangement produces the arrow-shaped heads of vipers and is the reason for the broad triangular-shaped head of the Gaboon viper.

Gaboon vipers mate during the rainy season – for this reason, captive breeders are able to stimulate their pets into action by spraying them with water. The young develop inside their mother for seven months. Up to 60 baby vipers are born in a single litter, although a third of that is normal. The newborn babies are 30cm (12in) long.

**Distribution**: Central and West Africa.
**Habitat**: Forest.
**Food**: Rodents, birds and frogs.
**Size**: 1.20m (4ft).
**Maturity**: 3–4 years.
**Breeding**: About 20 young born every 2–3 years.
**Life span**: Unknown.
**Status**: Common.

*The Gaboon viper is the largest of all viper species. Some other species may grow longer but none achieves the size of the Gaboon viper. The snake has an extremely broad, arrow-shaped head, which contains large venom glands. The viper's fangs are the longest of any snake at 4cm (1.5in) long.*

# Yellow-bellied sea snake

*Pelamis platurus*

**Distribution**: Coast of East Africa and around Madagascar.
**Habitat**: Sea water.
**Food**: Fish.
**Size**: 60–110cm (23.5–43.25in).
**Maturity**: 2–3 years.
**Breeding**: Young born in water.
**Life span**: Unknown.
**Status**: Common.

The yellow-bellied sea snake is the only sea snake to reach Africa. It is found on the coast of East Africa and Madagascar. The same species lives throughout the northern Indian Ocean, around Southeast Asia and into the Pacific. The species is at home on the high seas. However, most snakes prefer inshore water, where small fish are plentiful.

The snakes breathe air at the surface but also extract oxygen from the water through their skin. As a result they can stay underwater for more than three hours. They spend the night resting in deep water, rising to the surface to breathe two or three times at night. During the day they hunt at the surface, using their venom to kill fish. The snake is a good swimmer but is still at the mercy of currents.

The yellow-bellied sea snake never needs to come on to land and is helpless out of water. Mating takes place at sea, as does the birth of the young.

*The yellow-bellied sea snake has a body adapted for swimming. The tail is flattened into a paddle that is waved from side to side to push the snake through the water. The upper body is black and the lower section is a pale yellow. The snake swims at the surface of the ocean, so these colours make it hard to spot from above or below.*

**Lataste's viper** (*Vipera latasti*): 60cm (23.5in)
Lataste's viper lives in most of Spain and Portugal bar the far north and is also found in the Maghreb, between Morocco and Algeria. The viper closely resembles the asp viper, which is found to the east. However, Lataste's viper has a snout that is more upturned into a slight horn. This species of viper lives in rocky areas. It preys on small mammals but also hunts small lizards, slow worms and other snakes. Its venom is harmless to humans. Females of this species breed every two years and produce a litter of about six young. The young eat large invertebrates, such as centipedes and scorpions. They become sexually mature once they reach half their full size.

**Ottoman viper** (*Vipera xanthina*): 1.2m (4ft)
This is the largest venomous snake in Europe. Most of its range covers western Asia, but the viper is found on a few Greek islands and in the north-eastern tip of the Greek mainland. The size alone is enough to differentiate it from other vipers, but this species is also identifiable by the red-brown colouring. The Ottoman viper has cytotoxic venom (a poison that destroys body tissues). Bites are often fatal without medical attention.

# Green night adder

*Causus resimus*

Green night adders live in most of the savannahs of Central Africa. These habitats grow around the edges of forests and typically have a few trees and tall stands of grasses and similar plants. There is an isolated population of these snakes on the coast of Kenya, but most live in damper locations, such as around Africa's Great Lakes.

The green night adder is a largely ground-living species. It hunts for the frogs and toads that frequent the damp grasslands during the dry season. The green night adder is sometimes found in tall overhanging sedges, from where it can pick off prey from the ground. The night adders have short fangs and produce only a weak venom. However, like some other night adders, this species has long venom glands that are located in the body and not just the head, as in most venomous snakes. As a result, they can deliver a large amount of venom in a single bite. A bite from a green night adder can cause painful swelling despite the weakness of the venom.

Green night adders lay eggs rather than giving birth. The females lay about 12 eggs one by one throughout the wet season.

**Distribution**: Central Africa.
**Habitat**: Savannahs.
**Food**: Frogs and toads.
**Size**: 40–75cm (15.75–29.5in).
**Maturity**: 2–3 years.
**Breeding**: 12 eggs laid in wet season.
**Life span**: Unknown.
**Status**: Common.

*The green night adder has a remarkably vibrant body, with bright green scales on top of an electric-blue skin. When the snake inflates itself to ward off predators, the scales are pushed apart and the blue skin is exposed to startle any attackers away.*

# CATS

*The cat family Felidae consists of two groups: big cats and small cats. The former includes lions, cheetahs and leopards, and the latter includes lynxes, caracals and servals. Typically, cats hunt alone by night, using their acute senses of hearing, sight and scent to locate and stalk their prey. Once within pouncing distance, they unsheath their curved claws and deliver neck bites with dagger-shaped teeth.*

## Lion

*Panthera leo*

The social behaviour of lions is unique among wild cats. A typical pride contains about ten related females with their cubs and one or two males. Females do most of the hunting. They may work together to isolate and kill large prey such as zebra or buffalo. Males in a pride help themselves to the females' kills and rarely hunt for themselves. They spend much of the night patrolling, marking territory and driving away rival males. A pride male's reign rarely lasts longer than three years before he is usurped. Once adolescent males are evicted from the prides where they were born and reared, they may stay together in hunting groups, or hunt alone before eventually joining other groups.

*Male lions have thick manes of hair, while the females do not. The manes are symbols of the dominance level in males.*

**Distribution**: Africa, south of the Sahara, and Gir Forest, India.
**Habitat**: Open country.
**Food**: Grazing animals.
**Size**: 2–2.7m (6.5–9ft); 125–180kg (275.5–397lb).
**Maturity**: 3–4 years.
**Breeding**: 1 litter of 2–5 cubs in alternate years.
**Life span**: 16 years.
**Status**: Vulnerable.

## Cheetah

*Acinonyx jubatus*

Cheetahs differ from typical cats in several ways. Instead of stealth, they use speed to run down their prey, assisted by blunt claws that grip the ground. The dew-claws, however, which are used to grasp the prey, are curved and sharp. A cheetah is built like a racing dog, with a small head and long legs and body, but the teeth and jaws are too small and weak to deliver an effective death bite, so the cheetah is forced to suffocate its prey. After the sustained effort of catching and killing a prey animal, a cheetah may need to rest for half an hour before starting to eat.

The cheetah is well known as the fastest animal on land. Sadly, despite captive breeding programmes, it is now an endangered species. A breeding female requires a hunting range of up to 800sq km (300sq miles) and, apart from some national parks and isolated populations, suitable territories are mainly restricted to Namibia and parts of South Africa.

**Distribution**: Most of Africa, Middle East to Turkestan.
**Habitat**: Savannah and open, dry grassland.
**Food**: Gazelles or antelopes.
**Size**: 1.6–2.1m (5.25–7ft); 30–45kg (66–99lb).
**Maturity**: Females 3 years; males 3–4 years.
**Breeding**: 2–6 kittens every 2–3 years.
**Life span**: 15–20 years.
**Status**: Endangered.

*The cheetah's long, flexible spine helps to lengthen the stride of the animal at full sprint. It is the fastest terrestrial animal, capable of sprinting at 110kph (70mph).*

# Eurasian lynx

*Lynx lynx*

*Eurasian lynx have three distinct coat patterns: stripes, spots or plain. These markings can be either faint or clearly visible.*

This golden, delicately marked cat hunts small game by night in cool mountain forests and woodland. A shortened tail helps to conserve body heat, but it hinders communication between cats to a certain degree. As with other short-tailed cats that live in cold climates, the lynx has developed conspicuous ear-tufts to send visual signals instead.

Lack of a tail also impairs a cat's balance when running and climbing; the lynx hunts mainly by the techniques of stealth or ambush.

Its feet are densely furred, even on the pads, giving a good grip as well as warmth on frozen ground.

Most lynxes live in dense forests, but they may also wander into more open country. They build rough beds under rocks and fallen trees, or inside shrubs, resting during the day and hunting at night. While out and about, the lynx climbs trees and fords rivers – swimming if necessary – as it travels far and wide in search of food. It relies on its senses of vision and smell to locate prey, which it then stalks through the trees.

**Distribution**: Eastern Europe, Pyrenees and northern Eurasia, with distinct races in some regions.
**Habitat**: Montane forest and woodland.
**Food**: Rabbits, hares, birds and small deer.
**Size**: 0.8–1.3m (2.5–4.25ft); 18–21kg (39.75–46.25lb).
**Maturity**: 12–15 months.
**Breeding**: 2–4 cubs, weaned at 12 weeks, independent at 12 months.
**Life span**: 10–20 years.
**Status**: Endangered in south-eastern Europe.

---

**Spanish lynx** (*Lynx pardinus*): 65–100cm (25.5–39.5in); 5–13kg (11–28.5lb)
The Spanish, or Iberian, lynx resembles the more common Eurasian lynx in appearance, with tufts on the ears and jaw and a short, bobbed tail. However, on average, members of this species are smaller. As the name suggests, these cats are found on the Iberian Peninsula. The species is highly endangered, with as few as 1,000 individuals now restricted to a few isolated populations in dry woodland areas of Spain and Portugal.

**Jungle cat** (*Felis chaus*): 50–75cm (19.75–29.5in); 4–16kg (9–35.25lb)
The jungle cat is a fierce and robust little predator. It has a sandy grey to reddish coat with tabby stripes along its legs, a dark tail tip and black tufts on its large ears. It has good hearing and is very agile, often leaping almost 2m (6.5ft) into the air to catch birds. This cat ranges from North Africa to South-east Asia. It was sacred to the ancient Egyptians, who trained them to catch birds in an early example of domestic cats.

# Caracal

*Caracal caracal*

The name caracal is Turkish for "black ears". Caracals are also known as desert lynxes because they have short tails and ear-tufts like their northern cousins, an adaptation for cold weather. This has led scientists to conclude that the caracal's ancestors once lived in colder regions.

This adaptation to the cold comes in handy during the night, when caracals generally hunt. It is not unusual for desert temperatures to plunge below 0°C (32°F). Caracals prey on anything they can find and kill, including insects, snakes, lizards, gazelles and even brooding ostriches.

Caracals set up home in the abandoned burrows of porcupines or any other suitable crevices. Like other types of lynx, the caracal hunts at night, stealing up close to its prey before leaping the last few metres in huge bounds. The caracal is the fastest cat of its size. Prey is stalked and then captured after a quick dash or leap. The caracal is easy to tame and has been used as a hunting cat in Iran and India. However, it is also persecuted in this region as a pest.

**Distribution**: Southern Africa to Senegal and India, excluding the Congo and Arabian Desert.
**Habitat**: Dry scrubland, but avoids sand areas.
**Food**: Rodents, hyraxes, hares and small antelopes.
**Size**: 66–76cm (26–30in); 18kg (40lb).
**Maturity**: 6 months to 2 years.
**Breeding**: Litter of 3 young born every year.
**Life span**: 15 years.
**Status**: Lower risk (threatened in Asia).

*Caracals have narrow, pointed ears with long tufts of hair at their tips. These are used to signal to other cats.*

# Leopard

*Panthera pardus*

The leopard is widespread across most of Africa and southern Asia, ranging from open grassland to tropical rainforest and mountain highlands. It is an opportunistic feeder, choosing mainly large hoofed mammals, such as deer and antelope, but will take birds, rabbits and even dung beetles if prey is scarce.

Leopards are well adapted for climbing trees and have been seen hiding the corpses of prey in the branches to eat later. They hunt mostly at night but may switch to the daytime to avoid competition with nocturnal lions and hyenas.

Leopards vary greatly in colour depending on their habitat. On the savannah they are usually a sandy ochre, while the high mountain leopards are very dark gold. They tend to have short legs on long bodies, and their fur is covered in black spots or rosettes. The rosettes help to keep the cats hidden in the dappled light of forests Completely black leopards (black panthers) are usually found only in forests, but they do not represent a different subspecies, merely an infrequent mutation.

*Solitary and nocturnal, the leopard is rarely seen, even though it often lives in close proximity to humans. A melanistic (black, or nearly black) form is found (mainly in Asia), known as the black panther.*

**Distribution**: Atlas Mountains of Morocco, sub-Saharan Africa and southern Asia, from Pakistan to Vietnam and Malaysia. Small groups living in Arabia, the Caucuses and Iran.
**Habitat**: Forest, mountains and grassland.
**Food**: Antelope, deer and rabbits.
**Size**: 1–1.9m (3.25–6.25ft); 20–90kg (44–198.5lb).
**Maturity**: 33 months.
**Breeding**: 2–4 cubs.
**Life span**: 10–15 years in the wild; 25 in captivity.
**Life span**: Endangered.

# Black-footed cat

*Felis nigripes*

The black-footed cat is widespread across the semi-deserts and dry grasslands, or veld, of Botswana, Zimbabwe and Namibia. They are solitary and generally most active at night to avoid the extreme heat of the day.

The hairs on its feet not only provide insulation against the hot ground but also act as sensors that can pick up the movements of small prey animals, such as rodents or insects that are moving on or under the ground nearby. The black-footed cat kills by stalking and pouncing. It delivers a deadly bite with its long canine teeth. During the day the cat rests in a burrow commandeered from a neighbouring animal, such as an aardvark or springhare.

Male black-footed cats control a territory that includes the home ranges of several females. This suggests that each male fathers more than one litter each year. However, the mating season is very short, and males may miss the opportunity to mate. Transient males without territories who travel through an area may be able to mate as successfully as the resident males.

*Black-footed cats are among the smallest of all cat species. The soles of the feet are black and are covered in hairs, which act as protective insulation from the burning-hot ground.*

**Distribution**: South Africa, Namibia, Botswana, Zimbabwe and Zambia.
**Habitat**: Dry steppes and grasslands.
**Food**: Rodents, spiders, birds and insects. The cats also scavenge on carcasses.
**Size**: 33–50cm (13–19.75in); 1.6–2.1kg (3.5–4.5lb).
**Maturity**: 21 months.
**Breeding**: Litter of 2–3 kittens born in November and December. Kittens are raised by mother only.
**Life span**: Unknown; similar species live for 12 years.
**Status**: Common.

## Sand cat

*Felis margarita*

Sand cats are found in three distinct populations. All live in very dry locations. The first is spread across the Sahara Desert from Algeria to Morocco and Niger. The second lives in deserts of the Arabian Peninsula, while the third is found in dry parts of Turkmenistan, Pakistan, Iran and Afghanistan.

As their name suggests, sand cats are one of the few carnivores to survive in dry, sandy areas that can support only the thinnest covering of vegetation. In such places the daytime temperature can exceed 50°C (122°F) but then plummet to below freezing at night.

The sand cat survives in these extremes by hunting at night. Thick fur protects it from the worst of cold night-time conditions. It relies on its sensitive hearing to locate prey in the dark. The species has a larger inner ear compared to other cats. They eat almost anything they can find. By day the cat digs a burrow in the sand to stay cool.

**Distribution**: Sahara Desert, Arabia and Central Asia.
**Habitat**: Deserts.
**Food**: Rodents, snakes, lizards and insects.
**Size**: 45–57cm (17.75–22.5in); 1.4–3.4kg (3–7.5lb).
**Maturity**: 1 year.
**Breeding**: 4–5 kittens born in June and July.
**Life span**: 13 years.
**Status**: Vulnerable.

*Sand cats are similar in size to domestic cats but have tapered outer ears that are larger than those found on pet cats. This cat hunts using its hearing, so large ears are useful.*

# Serval

*Leptailurus serval*

**Distribution**: East and southern African.
**Habitat**: Grassland.
**Food**: Hares, ground-living rodents, frogs and small birds. In spring, the servals also prey on newborn antelopes.
**Size**: 67–100cm (26.5–39.5in); 13.5–18kg (30–40lb).
**Maturity**: 1–2 years.
**Breeding**: Females are pregnant for about 2 months. Litters of 3 cubs born at anytime of year. Male young leave home first.
**Life span**: Unknown.
**Status**: Endangered.

Servals are expert grassland hunters. They specialize in hunting in long grass, where they cannot see, only hear, their prey. They use their huge ears to pinpoint the rustling produced by their intended victims and then pounce with great accuracy. They may not even see their prey until they have trapped it under their paws. Prey are killed by a bite to the neck, which breaks the spine and severs the windpipe.

Servals live alone, staying out of each other's way. The cats are seldom found far from water, where stands of tall grass are more common. They are most active at dawn and dusk, when the changing temperatures and light levels disorientate their prey. At other times, the cats hide out in a den among the tall grass. As well as pouncing on prey (they can leap 3m/ 10ft into the air), servals also catch prey in water. They are known to kill flamingos, for example. Their slender bodies also allow them to reach a long way into burrows to get at prey such as mole rats.

*Servals have the longest ears and legs compared to their body size of any cat. They locate prey by the sounds their victims make and then pounce on them in a single giant bound.*

# HYENAS

*Hyenas are heavily built, long-legged and long-necked carnivores with large, padded feet and short, hairy tails. Their front legs are longer than their back legs and their shaggy coats are either striped or spotted. There are four species, all of which can be found in Africa. The striped hyena, the widest-ranging species, also lives in Turkey, the Middle East and parts of India.*

## Spotted hyena

*Crocuta crocuta*

*Spotted hyenas are dog-like, with sloping backs and long thick necks. They are the only mammal to disgorge indigestible hair, along with grass, hooves, horn and bone.*

Spotted hyenas live in female-dominated groups known as clans. The mothers rear all of the cubs together in a communal breeding den that is only big enough for the cubs to enter. The entrance to the den is guarded by one or two adults, helping to reduce the number of young killed by other carnivores or hyenas.
Spotted hyenas have a complicated greeting ceremony, involving a variety of interactions using scents and physical gestures. These are only used by certain individuals in a clan and are uncommon between females and low-ranking males. They help to reduce stress in the group. Females are very aggressive and, to help them dominate their clans, they have developed false genitals to look like males. They will fight other females to win over and mate with favoured males. Hyenas are very vocal and their wails – howling screams and "laughter" – can inform other clan members of a food source from up to 5km (3 miles) away.

**Distribution**: Most of Africa outside rainforest.
**Habitat**: Woodlands, savannahs, subdeserts, forest edges and mountains.
**Food**: Hunt antelope, buffalo and zebra. Scavenge from the kills of other large carnivores.
**Size**: 1.2–1.8m (4–6ft); 60–80kg (132.25–176.5lb).
**Maturity**: Cubs weaned after 18 months.
**Breeding**: Litter of 1–2 cubs born at any time of the year.
**Life span**: 12 years, and up to 25 years in captivity.
**Status**: Declining in all areas.

## Aardwolf

*Proteles cristatus*

The aardwolf is a specialist feeder and mainly consumes harvester termites. These give off a very toxic spray, and few other predators are able to overcome the chemicals emitted. Aardwolfs find the termites by listening for their movements.

Unlike the spotted hyenas, which have large crushing teeth, aardwolfs only have small peg-like teeth, ideal for crunching small insects. The aardwolf is mainly nocturnal and lives alone, in pairs or in small family groups. Females often live together in the same den to help increase the chances of survival for their pups. Burrows are either taken over from other species or dug by the aardwolfs themselves.

When feeding, adults may travel up to 10km (6 miles) in one night and in this time they may consume 250,000 termites. When threatened, they raise their long manes and erect their tails but, unusually, they keep their mouths closed – the aardwolf has such tiny teeth that it would appear almost harmless if it opened its mouth.

*The aardwolf is slimmer and more agile than the other three species of hyena. When attacked, the aardwolf raises the mane along its back and secretes a foul-smelling odour from its anal glands.*

**Distribution**: Southern Africa and north-east Africa.
**Habitat**: Heavily grazed and trampled grasslands, and sandy plains and plateaux.
**Food**: Termites plus other invertebrates including grasshoppers and maggots.
**Size**: 0.8–1m (2.5–3.25ft); 6–11kg (13.25–24lb).
**Maturity**: Weaned after 16 weeks.
**Breeding**: Litter of 1–4 pups born at any time of the year.
**Life span**: Unknown.
**Status**: Uncommon.

# Brown hyena

*Parahyaena brunnea*

**Distribution**: Southern Africa – most common in Namibia and dry parts of Botswana.
**Habitat**: Semi-desert.
**Food**: Carrion, bone marrow, and small animals.
**Size**: 1.2–1.6m (4–5.25ft); 37–47kg (81.5–103.5lb).
**Maturity**: 30 months.
**Breeding**: 2–3 young born in August to November.
**Life span**: 24 years.
**Status**: Endangered.

*Brown hyenas have long hairs on their necks and backs. Male and female brown hyenas are more or less the same size.*

Brown hyenas are scavengers. They are nocturnal and travel huge distances across the semi-deserts and dry grasslands of southern Africa following the scent of a rotting dead body many miles away. Like other hyenas, this species has short but wide jaws that are capable of producing a bite powerful enough to crack bones. Their large cheek teeth are blunt, making them good for crushing food.

Brown hyenas feed on the carcasses of large antelopes such as wildebeest. Unlike other scavengers, such as jackals or vultures, hyenas can access the meaty bone marrow inside bones. This food is rich in nutrients and allows these large animals to survive in arid habitats. They are especially common in the Kalahari Desert. On the sand-strewn Skeleton Coast of Namibia, the brown hyena is known as the beach wolf because it patrols the coast looking for the stranded bodies of whales, seals and other sea mammals.

Brown hyenas do hunt for small animals when possible and will also eat mushrooms. They live in small clans comprising a breeding pair and their close relatives and offspring. The clan den together but rarely scavenge as a group. Only the highest ranking females and male produce young each year.

# Striped hyena

*Hyaena hyaena*

**Distribution**: North and East Africa. Also lives in smaller numbers across western and southern Asia.
**Habitat**: Dry scrublands and grasslands.
**Food**: Carrion.
**Size**: 1.2–1.4m (4–4.5ft); 26–41kg (57.25–90.5lb).
**Maturity**: 2–3 years.
**Breeding**: Litters of up to 6 cubs born at all times of the year.
**Life span**: 25 years.
**Status**: Lower risk.

The striped hyena is the only hyena species to live outside Africa. However, it is most common on the grasslands of East Africa, which it shares, to apparently no ill effects, with its larger and fiercer relative, the spotted hyena. Beyond this region, the population of striped hyena falls dramatically, but it is still found as far east as India and as far north as the Caucasus.

Unlike its sometime neighbour the spotted hyena, which is a skilled hunter, the striped hyena finds almost all its food by scavenging. Like other hyenas, it has powerful jaws for crushing bones. It specializes in scavenging large and medium-sized animals, such as zebras and impalas. They are largely solitary animals, trotting through the night to find food. They follow their noses to carcasses and will also readily pick through the rubbish produced by humans. In parts of Africa, rubbish is left outside villages so that striped hyenas can dispose of it.

*Striped hyenas have probably kept the same striped pattern as their civet-like ancestors while other species have lost this primitive pattern. Striped hyenas have a mane that is erected when the animal feels threatened.*

# CIVETS AND GENETS

*Civets and genets are small carnivores. Most of them are in the viverrid family, although a few, such as the African palm civet and the species from Madagascar, are more distantly related. Most viverrids live in trees. They have long, slender bodies and many have spotted fur. Biologists think that civets and genets closely resemble the ancestors of today's cats and hyenas.*

## Common genet

*Genetta genetta*

*A row of black erectile hairs is usually present along the middle of the back of the common genet. The tail has black and white rings. A genet's claws can be withdrawn inside the paws, just like a cat's.*

Common genets, also called small-spotted genets, are related to civets. They are common in Africa, and a few are found in western Europe, although biologists think that these are descended from genets introduced to the area many years ago.

Genets live alone or in pairs, resting by day in sheltered spots or abandoned burrows. They feed at night, hunting for small animals in a range of habitats, from dense forest to open grassland. They climb trees to prey on roosting birds or silently stalk victims on the ground.

Genets mainly communicate by sound and smell, but also use their tails to signal. In warmer parts, genets breed during the wet season, with a few females managing to produce two litters each year.

**Distribution**: South-western Europe, including France and Spain, and Africa, excluding tropical rainforests and deserts.
**Habitat**: Forests and grasslands.
**Food**: Rodents, birds, small reptiles and insects.
**Size**: Length 42–58cm (16.5–23in); 1–3kg (2.25–6.5lb).
**Maturity**: 4 years.
**Breeding**: 2 litters of 1–4 kittens every year.
**Life span**: 13 years.
**Status**: Common.

## Fossa

*Cryptoprocta ferox*

The fossa is the largest carnivore in Madagascar. Looking very similar to a cat, it hunts by leaping through the trees to prey on lemurs and other small animals, such as birds and frogs. The fossa lives alone, patrolling its forest territory at dawn and dusk and sheltering in caves or inside disused termite mounds by day.

Fossas sometimes attack domestic animals, such as pigs and poultry, and are often killed as pests by people, who also unnecessarily fear that the fossas may attack them. This persecution, combined with the destruction of their forest habitat, means that fossas have become very rare, like much of Madagascar's native wildlife.

Fossas only spend time with other members of their species during the breeding season, which is between September and October. The females give birth three months later, in the height of summer.

**Distribution**: Madagascar.
**Habitat**: Forests.
**Food**: Rodents, birds, frogs, reptiles and young lemurs.
**Size**: 61–80cm (24–32in); 7–12kg (15.5–26.5lb).
**Maturity**: 4 years.
**Breeding**: Twins born once per year.
**Life span**: 17 years
**Status**: Endangered.

*Fossas walk in a flat-footed manner on their soles, like bears, rather than on their toes, like cat and dogs.*

# Falanouc

*Eupleres goudotii*

**Distribution**: North-western and eastern Madagascar.
**Habitat**: Lowland forests.
**Food**: Earthworms.
**Size**: 45–65cm (17.75–25.5in); 2–4kg (4.5–8.75lb).
**Maturity**: 1 year.
**Breeding**: Litter of 1–2 young born in dens between November and January.
**Life span**: Unknown.
**Status**: Endangered.

Along with many of Madagascar's mammals, falanoucs are in danger of extinction. The boggy lowland forests they occupy are being drained and cut down to make way for farms and other human developments. In addition, the small Indian civet has been introduced to the island, and this species appears to be contributing to the falanouc's downfall.

Falanoucs are nocturnal foragers. By day they sleep inside hollow logs or in rocky crevices. They live alone but might form into groups in areas that have plenty of food. Falanoucs forage by rooting through leaf litter for worms and other buried invertebrates. They have long claws for digging into the soil to find food. The falanouc's cheek teeth are pointed and are used for stabbing prey. The teeth resemble those of moles and shrews more than they do other small carnivores, which have teeth built for slicing.

*This animal is a little larger than a domestic cat. It has a pointed snout for probing through leaf litter and a thick, cylindrical tail.*

---

**Malagasy civet** (*Fossa fossana*): 42cm (16.5in); 1.75kg (3.75lb)
The Malagasy civet is found throughout Madagascar, where it occupies most of the island's types of tropical forest. The local name for this fox-like species is fanaloka. They have a thick coat of short, brown fur, which has four lines of dark spots along the back. This species of civet preys on small rodents and unusual insectivores called tenrecs – another of the island's many unique species. They also feed on small birds, crabs, frogs and reptiles. During periods of drought, the civets survive by metabolizing fats stored in their tails during times of plenty. Malagasy civets mate between August and September and a single young is born three months later.

**Large-spotted genet** (*Genetta tigrina*): 50–60cm (19.75–23.5in)
This species is found mainly in the Cape region of South Africa – another name for it is Cape genet – although its range does extend as far north as southern Sudan. As its name suggests, this species has large grey-brown spots on its back, which are surrounded by paler fur. An alternative common name is blotched genet. This species of genet is found in habitats that contain plenty of good hiding places. They live among tall grasses and dense woodland, and in drier parts of their range are found in the thick vegetation along river banks. Large-spotted genets prey on a variety of small mammals, birds, reptiles and invertebrates. They also supplement their meat diet with fruits.

# Aquatic genet

*Osbornictis piscivora*

The aquatic genet is a very rare cat-like animal that is found in the dense tropical forests of the Congo. Very little is known about the habits of this secretive animal. It is thought that they live alone and spend a lot of time in or near water, feeding on fish. There are also reports that they eat frogs and the roots and tubers of aquatic plants.

Most of what is known is surmised from studying the anatomy of the species. Unlike other genets, aquatic genets do not have hairs on their palms. This difference helps the genets feel for prey in muddy water holes and also grip on to more slippery victims. They also have small olfactory bulbs in their brains, which suggests that they do not have a very good sense of smell – not particularly important for locating prey in water. The aquatic genet's premolars are larger than the molars farther back in the mouth. This is likely to be another adaptation that helps the animal grip on to slippery, struggling prey.

**Distribution**: Central Africa.
**Habitat**: Rainforests.
**Food**: Fish.
**Size**: 45cm (17.75in); 1.5kg (3.25lb).
**Maturity**: 1 year.
**Breeding**: 1 young born each year.
**Life span**: Unknown; other species reach 20 years old.
**Status**: Unknown.

*Unlike other genets, this species does not have spots on its back. It has white spots between the eyes.*

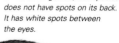

# Angolan genet

*Genetta angolensis*

Angolan genets have dark red fur with large black or brown spots forming a symmetrical pattern on either side of the spine. The longer hairs along the spine stand up into a crest when the genet is threatened. Like in other genets, this species has large eyes for seeing in the dark. Each eye is set facing forwards, so the animals can judge distances accurately.

Angolan genets live across southern African between the latitudes of 5 and 15 degrees south. Their range includes the countries of Angola, Democratic Republic of Congo, Zambia, Malawi and Mozambique. They are most commonly found in forests but will venture out on to savannahs that receive enough rain for tall grasses to grow.

Angolan genets occupy a small territory in which they prey on a range of small animals, including rodents, birds, lizards and reptiles. They hunt mainly in the treetops, using their long agile bodies to weave through the dense branches. They are nocturnal creatures and avoid contact with other genets. They mark the borders of their territories with smelly anal secretions, which are also expelled in larger quantities when the genet is under attack. A male's territory encompasses those of several females, and he will mate with each female once or twice a year. Litters are born 10 weeks after mating.

**Distribution**: Southern Africa, from Zambia and Mozambique to the Congo.
**Habitat**: Rainforest and savannah.
**Food**: Small vertebrates and invertebrates.
**Size**: 40–50cm (15.75–19.75in); 1.5kg (3.25lb).
**Maturity**: Unknown.
**Breeding**: 2 litters of up to 4 young produced each year. The young are hairless and blind and born in a tree hollow.
**Life span**: Unknown, but other genets live for 20 years.
**Status**: Common.

# African linsang

*Poiana richardsonii*

African linsangs are among the smallest viverrids in the world. They differ from Asiatic linsangs in that the Asian species have smaller spots and these never run into bands or stripes on the body, just the head and shoulders.

African linsangs live in the rainforests of equatorial Africa around the Congo Basin. They are nocturnal animals and forage for food among the branches. By day they sleep in nests made from small branches and leaves. They will use this den for a few days before moving to another part of their territory and constructing a new one. This behaviour ensures that they exploit as much of the food supply in their territory as possible.

Little is known about the social behaviour of African linsangs. For much of the year they live alone. They are seen foraging in twos sometimes and it is possible that these are breeding pairs. Some nests have been found containing several linsangs. These might be a family group with adolescent offspring who have stayed with their mother after weaning. It is likely that the young are born at all times of year, and that they are cared for in a den.

**Distribution**: West Africa, from Sierra Leone and Gabon to Cameroon and the Congo. Also found on Bioko Island, in Equatorial Guinea.
**Habitat**: Forests and woodlands.
**Food**: Insects, birds, fruits and nuts.
**Size**: 33–38cm (13–15in); 500–700g (17.5–24.75oz).
**Maturity**: 1 year.
**Breeding**: Litters of 2–3 produced once or twice a year.
**Life span**: 5 years in captivity, probably more in the wild.
**Status**: Unknown

# African civet

*Civettictis civetta*

**Distribution**: Southern and Central Africa, from Senegal to Somalia in the north to the Transvaal of northern South Africa.
**Habitat**: Forest and grasslands.
**Food**: Fruits, carrion, rodents, insects, eggs, reptiles and birds.
**Size**: 68–89cm (26.75–35in); 7–20kg (15.5–44lb).
**Maturity**: 1 year.
**Breeding**: Each female produces 2–3 litters of up to 4 young each year.
**Life span**: 20 years.
**Status**: Common.

The African civet lives all over sub-Saharan Africa, being equally at home in open grassland and dense forest. They are rarely found far from rivers or another permanent source of water. Its coarse hair is black with yellowish spots and stripes. During the day, civets hide in thickets of grass. At night they cross large distances, even swimming across rivers, in search of carrion, small animals, eggs, insects and fruit. They are also sometimes found out and about during cloudy days.

African civets live alone and only settle in one place when nursing young. Breeding takes place at any time throughout the year. The mother can suckle up to six young at a time, but litters of more than four are rare. The young are raised in a den made inside a burrow that has been deserted by another animal. The mother transports her young by clasping the loose skin on the backs of their necks in her mouth.

*Like many other viverrids, the African civet has a mane down its back that can be erected to make the animal appear larger than it really is to attackers. The dark, mask-like pattern across the eyes makes this civet resemble a raccoon, but the two carnivores are not closely related. Unlike genets, in civets the claws are not retractile – they are always sticking out from the paws.*

# African palm civet

*Nandinia binotata*

**Distribution**: Central Africa from Equatorial Guinea, including Bioko, to Sudan, Angola and Mozambique.
**Habitat**: Tropical forests and woodlands.
**Food**: Rodents, carrion, fruits, insects and eggs.
**Size**: 50cm (19.75in); 1.7–2.1kg (3.75–4.5lb).
**Maturity**: 1 year.
**Breeding**: 2 litters of up to 4 young produced in May and October.
**Life span**: Unknown; other similar species live for about 15 years.
**Status**: Common.

African palm civets spend most of the time in the branches of trees. They also forage on the ground and have been known to venture out of the forest into more open habitats in search of food. African palm civets are omnivores – they eat all types of food. When catching live prey, such as rodents or birds, with their forepaws, the civets use their long tails, which are generally the same length as their body, as a balance. The flexible hind feet can also be twisted considerably to get a good grip.

Civets are most active in the hours just after sunset and before dawn. They have scent glands between their toes, which exude a brown sticky substance. Along with other secretions this is used to mark territory. However, the foot glands might also be used to leave a trail of scent that the civet can follow back to its resting place in the dark.

*The mottled coat of an African palm civet helps it to blend in to the background in the dappled light of the forest. Although common animals, they are seldom seen.*

# DOGS

*There are several members of the wild dog family, Canidae, including the African hunting dog, Ethiopian wolf, foxes and jackals. Long legs and muzzles enable these mammals to chase and capture prey. Most have a bushy tail and feet with four toes at the back and five at the front. Small canids are solitary hunters, medium-sized canids hunt alone or in small family groups and large canids hunt in large cooperative groups.*

## African hunting dog

*Lycaon pictus*

Hunting dogs are highly social and live in large packs of around 100 animals. A pack is formed by a group of brothers from one pack meeting with a group of sisters from another. A dominant pair emerges and breeds. Females will fight each other for the top breeding position.

These dogs are truly nomadic carnivores. They are on the move all the time to mark their territories and to avoid conflict with lions. Movement is reduced when there are small pups in the den. Unlike most canids which howl to show their presence, wild dogs use scents that last for months. When packs contain about 20 adults, the older offspring leave to form subgroups and hunt independently.

Individual dogs are capable of killing large prey such as impala antelope, although most hunting is done in packs. Pups typically leave at two to three years of age but sometimes stay to help rear more young. Packs stay together for no more than six years, usually two, when the founder members die. The remaining dogs separate into single-sex groups to find new opposite-sex groups and start all over again.

*The African hunting dog has black, white, brown and yellow-brown blotches. It has large, round ears, a broad, black muzzle and a tufted tail, usually with a white tip. It is also the only carnivore except hyenas to have five toes on all four feet.*

**Distribution**: Non-forested, non-desert areas of Africa.
**Habitat**: Desert plains, open and wooded savannah, and bushed country.
**Food**: Antelope, eland, buffalo and wildebeest.
**Size**: 1–1.5m (3.25–5ft); 17–36kg (37.5–79.5lb).
**Maturity**: Pups follow pack after 3 months and join in hunting at 12–14 months.
**Breeding**: Average of 7–10 pups born in the dry winter months from March to July in the south.
**Life span**: Unknown.
**Status**: Endangered.

## Ethiopian wolf

*Canis simensis*

Ethiopian wolves' main prey are giant mole rats (*Tachyoryctes macrocephalus*), which make up nearly half of their diet when available. During the day, the wolves lie on the mounds made by the giant mole rats. These make good ambush sites to catch their prey. Ethiopian wolves live in packs with two or more adult females, five closely related males and the current offspring of the dominant pair. The females do not always mate with the males in their pack; indeed, three-quarters of matings may be with males from neighbouring packs.

These wolves are extremely vocal, using all types of howls, yelps and screams to mark their territories, which may be 2.4–12sq km (1–4.5sq miles) in size. They forage alone, but the animals will meet in the morning, midday and evening to rest, play, sleep, feed their pups and mark boundaries. This is when they are most vocal.

*Ethiopian wolves have reddish-ginger coats, with white throat patches, inner ears, underparts and lower legs, and dark tails. They have long legs, long muzzles and squared-off noses and upper lips.*

**Distribution**: Restricted to the Ethiopian Highlands of Africa.
**Habitat**: Alpine moorlands.
**Food**: Naked mole rats and other rodents, hares and antelope calves.
**Size**: 1.3m (4.25ft); 11–19kg (24–42lb).
**Maturity**: Unknown.
**Breeding**: 2–6 pups born from August to December.
**Life span**: Unknown.
**Status**: Critically endangered.

# Golden jackal

*Canis aureus*

**Distribution**: Southern Europe, Middle East, northern Africa and southern Asia.
**Habitat**: Open savannah and grassland.
**Food**: Opportunistic feeders.
**Size**: 0.6–1.1m (2–3.5ft); 7–15kg (15.5–33lb).
**Maturity**: Females 11 months; males 2 years.
**Breeding**: 6–9 pups born after 63 days of gestation.
**Life span**: 6–8 years.
**Status**: Common.

The golden jackal is widespread, living across southern Europe, the Middle East and south Asia. It is the only jackal that ranges into North Africa, where it was held sacred to the Egyptian god Anubis in ancient times. It usually sports a golden-brown or yellow coat of short, coarse fur and a black-tipped tail.

Golden jackals mate for life and typically raise pups together. They live in clearly defined scent-marked territories, often in small family groups. Some offspring remain as helpers, taking care of newborn pups and leaving their mothers free to gather food for their families.

The jackals are found mainly in open grassland terrain. They are opportunistic feeders, eating whatever carrion and small mammals they can find, as well as a lot of plant matter. However, golden jackals hunt more than other species, and often compete with hyenas and lions, which will try to steal their prey. The jackals eat very quickly, without chewing their food, and will often bury their kills to hide them from other scavengers.

*Golden jackals can often be seen rummaging around landfill sites near human settlements, looking for tasty refuse.*

---

**Side-striped jackal** (*Canis adustus*): 96–120cm (3.1–4ft); 9.7kg (21.5lb)
This species of jackal lives in Central Africa. They live alongside other jackals on the grasslands and share a similar body form and lifestyle. However, side-striped jackals are also found in moister habitats, such as mountain woodlands. They are easily distinguishable due to a white stripe along their flanks between a rusty saddle-shaped section of fur on the back and dark sides.

**Sand** or **pale fox** (*Vulpes pallida*): 61–74cm (24–29.25in); 2–3.6kg (4.5–8lb)
Found across the Sahel belt in northern Africa, the sand fox lives in family parties comprising an adult pair and their offspring. They dig their own burrows and come out at night or early evening to feed on fruit and berries, which provide them with their daily supplement of water. The sand fox feeds on small mammals and insects.

**Royal** or **hoary fox** (*Vulpes cana*): 40–60cm (15.75–23.5in); 2–3kg (4.5–6.5lb)
A shy, cat-like fox with dense, sandy-coloured fur, the royal fox lives in rock crevices and shelters from Pakistan to northern Egypt. It has excellent hearing to find insects. It will also feed on berries. The tail is long with thick fur, which is thought to help the animal evade predators that may try to catch it. If a predator grasps the tail, the royal fox has a chance to run away even if it means the predator being left with a mouthful of fur or even a piece of the tail itself.

# Raccoon dog

*Nyctereutes procyonoides*

The raccoon dog originated in eastern Asia. In 1927 it was introduced to eastern Europe for fur-farming and is now seen as far west as the French–German border and northern Finland. Unusually for a member of the dog family, the raccoon dog is an agile climber. Adults form pair bonds and have distinct home ranges. However, these are relatively flexible and they will often roam into other raccoon dog territories.

Males and females both help to care for offspring, taking it in turns to guard young while the others hunt for food.

**Distribution**: Siberia and north China; introduced into eastern and central Europe.
**Habitat**: Damp lowland forest.
**Food**: Carrion, fruits, fish, frogs and birds. Scavenges food scraps from near human settlements.
**Size**: 50–60cm (19.75–23.5in); 4–10kg (8.75–22lb).
**Maturity**: 9–11 months.
**Breeding**: 4–9 young born in April–June.
**Life span**: 11 years.
**Status**: Common.

*The raccoon dog looks like a grey and black raccoon, with its characteristic black face mask and bridled greyish body fur.*

# Black-backed jackal

*Canis mesomelas*

**Distribution**: Southern Africa
and East Africa.
**Habitat**: Dry savannahs.
**Food**: Omnivorous diet.
**Size**: 0.7–1.3m (2.25–4.25ft);
6–12kg (13.25–26.5lb).
**Maturity**: Not known.
**Breeding**: Usually 3–4 pups
born July–October in
southern Africa.
**Life span**: Unknown.
**Status**: Common.

*The black-backed jackal is reddish-brown with a white-streaked black band along its back. The thick, hairy tail is also black, particularly at the tip. In parts of South Africa, black-backed jackals used to cause problems by feeding on large numbers of pineapples.*

Black-backed jackals live in closely bonded pairs, sometimes with one or two older offspring staying to help rear the pups. The older offspring increase the survival rate of young pups by providing extra food and guarding the den from predators, such as hyenas. When the parents arrive back from hunting, the pups start begging and this encourages the adults to regurgitate food which they have caught and swallowed earlier.

The jackals communicate with screaming yells followed by three or four short yaps. They make these calls more often during the winter when they start mating. In South Africa, where black-backed jackals are the only species of jackal present, howling is common.

Black-backed jackals have very varied diets, feeding on anything from young antelope, rodents and hares through to birds, reptiles, carrion, invertebrates, wild berries and fruit.

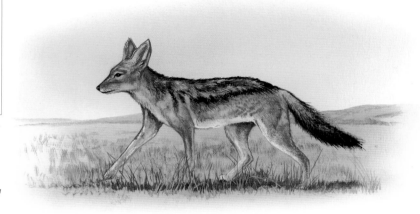

# Red fox

*Vulpes vulpes*

The red fox is a very successful and adaptable species. It is mainly active at night but will forage during the day, particularly when there are hungry cubs to feed. It also enjoys curling up and sunbathing in exposed but private spots, often by railway lines or roadsides.

A pair of foxes shares a home range, often with young from the previous breeding season. Mating takes place from December to February. After a few months, females – also known as vixens – give birth to between 3 and 12 cubs. The availability of food determines whether vixens breed and how many cubs they produce. During the mating season, females and occasionally males give out spine-tingling shrieks.

Red foxes mark their territories with a distinctive scent, which lingers and tells when a fox has been in the area. The scent is left with urine or faeces and is produced by special glands at the base of the tail. There are further scent glands between the pads of foxes' feet and around their lips.

*The red fox is a large fox with a rusty, red-brown coat and a darker bushy tail with a white tip.*

**Distribution**: Europe, Asia
and North Africa. Introduced
to Australia.
**Habitat**: Able to colonize
almost any habitat available.
**Food**: Small vertebrates,
invertebrates, kitchen scraps,
fruit and carrion.
**Size**: 85–95cm (33.5–37.5in);
4–8kg (9–17.5lb).
**Maturity**: 10 months.
**Breeding**: 3–12 pups born
in early spring.
**Life span**: 9 years.
**Status**: Common.

# Fennec fox

*Vulpes zerda*

The fennec fox is the world's smallest fox and lives in the hot deserts of North Africa. The animal gets most of its water from solid food. Its body also ensures that the least amount of water is wasted. Fennec foxes are only active at night, when the temperature is much lower.

The fox's very large ears are used to detect the sounds made by prey, such as grasshoppers and other insects, in or on the sand. The large ears also radiate excess body heat. Cream-coloured fur helps keep fennec foxes well camouflaged against the sand when resting during the day. They are able to dig very quickly to catch any fast-moving prey living in the sand.

Fennec foxes are usually seen in pairs. In the breeding season, females are very protective of their pups and will be very aggressive if anything threatens them.

**Distribution**: Sahara Desert through to the Nubian Desert. Also found in North Arabia.
**Habitat**: Sandy deserts.
**Food**: Various animal and plant foods, particularly insects.
**Size**: 42–72cm (16.5–28.5in); 1–1.5kg (2.25–3.25lb).
**Maturity**: Suckled for 2 months and mature by 6 months of age.
**Breeding**: Mating between January and February. Give birth to 1–5 pups.
**Life span**: Unknown.
**Status**: Common.

*The fennec fox is a small cream-coloured fox with short legs, huge ears, a small pointed muzzle and a black-tipped tail.*

# Bat-eared fox

*Otocyon megalotis*

Bat-eared foxes have very large ears that listen for the movements of harvester termites. Their very thick fur coats protect the foxes from the painful bites of soldier termites that they encounter. They have 46–50 teeth, whereas most mammals have far fewer than this. Their teeth are used to slice up insects that have hard shells and pincers. With the ability to move their lower jaws up and down five times a second, insects are hurriedly chewed and eaten. The bat-eared fox also has very strong claws on its front feet, enabling it to dig very fast.

A pair normally lives together with up to six offspring. They mate for life and have a home range that may be 0.25–3sq km (0.1–1sq miles) in size. Sometimes a second female will join the pair and share the breeding den. Individuals feed by walking long distances over their territories, continually listening for small invertebrates. When they hear something underground, they dig vigorously, catching the prey before it has a chance to get away.

**Distribution**: Southern Africa and East Africa.
**Habitat**: Open country, including short scrub, grassland, steppes, lightly wooded areas and farmland.
**Food**: Harvester termites, beetles and other insects.
**Size**: 75–90cm (30–36in); 3–5kg (6.5–11lb).
**Maturity**: Not known.
**Breeding**: 1–6 pups born from September to November.
**Life span**: Unknown.
**Status**: Common.

*Bat-eared foxes are smaller than most canids. They have huge ears and dark, bushy tails.*

# Cape fox

*Vulpes chama*

*Cape foxes are small, silver-grey foxes with reddish tinges to the head and forelegs. The hind legs have black patches on them. The bushy tail is about half the length of the body.*

The Cape fox is found only in the arid areas of southern Africa. Its range covers Namibia, Botswana and western and central South Africa. This small, slim fox lives in dry grasslands and scrub areas. It avoids forest.

The Cape fox has large pointed ears for detecting faint sounds. Like other dogs, it also has an acute sense of smell. The fox uses these senses to hunt at night. It runs long distances in search of a wide range of food. Most victims are small, such as rodents, lizards and insects, although Cape foxes have been known to attack larger animals, such as young antelopes and livestock.

The foxes always hunt alone, even those within a breeding partnership. Breeding pairs stay together for the breeding season and may pair up again in the following years. They produce pups in late summer and autumn. Several breeding pairs will share a territory and may even den together. The dens are the modified burrows of other mammals, such as aardvarks.

**Distribution**: Southern Africa.
**Habitat**: Grasslands and semi-desert.
**Food**: Rodents, rabbits and insects.
**Size**: 86–97cm (33.75–38.25in); 2.4–4kg (5.25–8.75lb).
**Maturity**: 9 months.
**Breeding**: Females are pregnant for 7 weeks and between 3–5 pups are born from September to November.
**Life span**: Unknown.
**Status**: Common.

# Arctic fox

*Alopex lagopus*

*Arctic foxes have the warmest coat of any mammal – some species have more hair but it is not as warm as the fox's. They exhibit two colour forms. Those that live in exposed tundra regions are more or less white all year around, becoming paler in winter. In warmer places where the snow melts in summer, the white foxes become grey. By contrast, the foxes that live in coastal areas, which are generally less exposed, are a pale brown in summer and tinged pale blue in winter.*

The Arctic fox lives in the far north of Scandinavia and is also found in Greenland, Siberia and the high Arctic of North America. The fox's habitat is barren tundra along the coast of the Arctic Ocean. They also stray into pine forests found in the far north and on high mountain slopes. In winter they move out on to the frozen sea.

The temperatures in these habitats often plunge to far below freezing. Arctic foxes keep out the cold by having a extra thick coat that even grows over the soles of the feet.

There is not very much food among the snow and ice, and Arctic foxes feed on anything they can find. In summer, they feed on small mammals, such as lemmings, but in winter they have to diversify their diet to survive, eating insects, berries, carrion and even the faeces of other animals. When the land is iced over, they rely on sea birds and fish for their meat.

Arctic foxes have difficulty constructing dens because the ground is frozen. As a result, many generations of Arctic foxes den in the same place, often at the foot of cliffs or mounds, sometimes for hundreds of years.

**Distribution**: Scandinavia, Greenland, Canada, Alaska, northern Russia and Siberia.
**Habitat**: Arctic tundra, pine forests and sea ice.
**Food**: Lemmings, fish and carrion of large mammals and birds, plus insects and berries in summer.
**Size**: 50–60cm (19.75–23.5in); 4kg (8.75lb).
**Maturity**: 10 months, although many young stay with parents for second year.
**Breeding**: Mating takes place in spring; litter of 5–8 cubs born two months later.
**Life span**: Unknown, although between 5 and 10 years is normal for other fox species.
**Status**: Common.

# Grey wolf

*Canis lupus*

**Distribution**: Patches of northern and eastern Europe, western and northern Asia, Canada and some locations in the United States.
**Habitat**: Tundra, pine forest, desert and grassland.
**Food**: Moose, elk, musk ox and reindeer. Wolves are also known to prey on domestic animals, such as sheep and cattle.
**Size**: 1–1.6m (3.25–5.25ft); 30–80kg (66–176lb).
**Maturity**: 22 months.
**Breeding**: Once per year; only the alpha pair breed.
**Life span**: 16 years.
**Status**: Vulnerable.

All domestic dogs are descended from grey wolves, which began living alongside humans many thousands of years ago. The wolves were once common in the ancient forests of the Northern Hemisphere. Human hunters have wiped them out in most parts of the world.

Grey wolves are the largest dogs in the wild, and they live in packs of about ten individuals. A wolf pack has a strict hierarchy, with a male and female "alpha pair" in charge. The alpha dogs bond for life and are the only members of the pack to breed. The rest of the pack is largely made up of the alpha pair's close relatives and their offspring.

In summer, pack members hunt alone for small animals such as hares. In winter the pack hunts together for much larger animals, such as deer or wild cattle. Grey wolves are strong runners and can travel 200km (125 miles) in one night. They detect prey by smell and chase them down. The pack harries a victim until it becomes exhausted. The wolves then take turns to take a bite at its face and flanks until the victim collapses.

*Grey wolves howl to communicate with pack members over long distances. Each individual can be identified by its howl.*

# Rueppell's fox

*Vulpes rueppellii*

**Distribution**: North Africa, from Morocco to Egypt, Arabia. Also found in western and south Asia.
**Habitat**: Sand and stone deserts.
**Food**: Insects, small mammals and roots.
**Size**: 34–56cm (13.5–22in); 1.1–2.3kg (2.5–5lb).
**Maturity**: 1 year; many yearlings will stay with their parents for a second year.
**Breeding**: Females are pregnant for 50 days and cubs born in March.
**Life span**: 12 years.
**Status**: Unknown.

Rueppell's fox is a desert animal. It has large ears, which help it to lose excess body heat (their large surface area allows the blood inside to be cooled by the air). The large ears often result in Rueppell's fox being confused with the fennec fox, but this species is generally significantly larger. The fox also has hairs on the soles of its feet to protect the paws from burning on the hot sand.

This species of fox is a nocturnal hunter, being most active before dawn and at dusk. It will eat whatever it can find in the desert. Most of the diet is made up of insects and other arthropods, such as scorpions.

Rueppell's foxes live in small groups, which are probably primarily composed of family members. Like other fox species, Rueppell's fox cubs often stay with their parents for a year or more. This behaviour allows them to learn how to raise their own young – and be better parents when their time comes. It also helps their parents to raise the next litter more successfully. The helper can guard the young while the mother rests or feeds herself. As a result more of the litter survives.

*Rueppell's fox exists in two colour morphs (types). Most have sandy-coloured fur, which helps them blend into their desert habitat. In rocky places, however, the foxes have grey flashes, helping it blend in with the broken landscape. All members of the species have a white tip to their bushy tails.*

# SMALL CARNIVORES

*Some of the small carnivores, the mustelids, are very fast and efficient hunters. They can tackle prey*
*much larger than themselves. Mustelids tend to be solitary animals, defending their territories from*
*all newcomers. Their long, lithe bodies, short legs and sharp claws mean that they are often skilful*
*climbers, capable of reaching the most inaccessible of places and leaving their prey few places to hide.*

## Stoat

*Mustela erminea*

Although rarely seen, stoats are common in the
countryside, where they mainly feed on rodents.
However, the large males will often prey on
rabbits, even though rabbits are considerably
larger. Stoats are famed for mesmerizing their
prey by dancing around them, before nipping
in for the kill. This is not just an old wives'
tale. Stoats have been observed leaping
around near rabbits in a seemingly deranged
fashion. This curious "dance" seems to have
the effect of confusing the rabbits, which just
watch the stoat draw slowly closer and closer, until
it is too late to escape.

As winter approaches, populations of stoats that live in
cooler, northern areas change the colour of their coats. In
summer, they are a chestnut colour but, by the time the first
snows have fallen, the stoats have changed to pure white.
White stoats are known as ermines, and their fur was once
prized for its pure colour and soft feel.

*In mild climates, stoats have
chestnut fur all year round. In
colder areas, they moult into
white fur in winter. Stoats are
distinguished from their smaller
cousins, the weasels, by having
black tips to their tails.*

**Distribution**: Widespread in
northern and central Europe
extending into Asia and
across northern North
America. Introduced to
New Zealand.
**Habitat**: Anywhere with
enough cover.
**Food**: Mammals up to the
size of rabbits.
**Size**: 16–31cm (6.25–12.25in);
140–445g (0.25–1lb).
**Maturity**: 1 year.
**Breeding**: 1 litter per year
of 5–12 young.
**Life span**: 10 years.
**Status**: Common.

## Zorilla

*Ictonyx striatus*

Zorillas have an uncanny resemblance to skunks, although they are more closely related to
ferrets and polecats. Their alternative name is the striped polecat. Not only do they share
black and white markings with their North American relatives, but they also eject a foul-
smelling liquid from glands near their anuses if alarmed. When faced with enemies, zorillas
puff up their fur in an attempt to look bigger, and then squirt their
noxious liquid towards their assailants. If the
liquid gets in a predator's eyes, it causes intense
irritation, as well as smelling very unpleasant.
This strategy is extremely effective, with few
predators prepared to risk the stinking spray.
Zorillas are nocturnal animals, resting
during the day in burrows or rock crevices.
At night they hunt small animals, as
well as eating the eggs of ground-nesting birds,
which are a particular favourite. Zorillas are
predominantly ground-living, but they are also
proficient swimmers and climbers.

*With their bold black and white markings, zorillas
are easily mistaken for skunks.*

**Distribution**: Sudan to
South Africa.
**Habitat**: A wide variety,
including temperate forest,
tropical forest, savannah and
grasslands.
**Food**: Rodents, large insects,
eggs, snakes, birds, frogs
and reptiles.
**Size**: 33–38cm (13–15in);
1kg (2.25lb).
**Maturity**: 1 year.
**Breeding**: 1 litter of 1–3
young born each year.
**Life span**: 13 years.
**Status**: Common.

# Sable

*Martes zibellina*

**Distribution**: Northern Russia and Siberia.
**Habitat**: Mountainous forests.
**Food**: Rodents, birds, fish, nuts and berries.
**Size**: 35–56cm (13.75–22in); 0.7–1.8kg (1.5–4lb).
**Maturity**: 16 months.
**Breeding**: Litter of 3–4 young born in summer.
**Life span**: 15 years.
**Status**: Lower risk.

This carnivore lives in mountainous wooded areas, usually near streams, and an individual may have several dens beneath rocks or large roots. The sable hunts by day or night, roaming across a territory that may be as large as 3,000ha (7,400 acres). Mostly it hunts rodents, but it will also eat small birds, fish, honey and berries.

Sables form individual territories, which are fiercely defended against intruders, but in the mating season the males are more forgiving to passing females. The young are born small and blind during the spring. They open their eyes after around 30 days and are independent by 16 months.

The sable has a luxurious silky coat, usually dark brown or black, and has been hunted for many years. During the 18th century, thousands of animals were trapped for their pelts, and the sable is now raised on farms for the fur industry.

*An elegant relative of the pine marten, the sable was almost hunted to extinction for its sumptuous pelage (fur). The fur is thicker with longer hairs in winter than in summer. Males are slightly larger and heavier than the females.*

---

**European pine marten** (*Martes martes*): 45–58cm (17–23in); 0.5–1.8kg (1–4lb).
This species of mustelid is found across Europe and Asia. It is found as far south as the Mediterranean islands and as far east as the Pacific coast of Siberia. The pine marten was once common in the British Isles, but it is now found only in Ireland and the far north of Great Britain. Despite their name, pine martens live in all types of forest – pine, broad-leaved, or a mixture of both trees. The martens are most at home in ancient forests where the tops of the trees join together. That forms a protective canopy under which the pine martens can hide from their chief prey – eagles. Recently planted forests – or those that are regularly disrupted by people – do not have such a canopy, and martens do not thrive there. In Scotland pine martens often leave forests and hunt on moorlands. Pine martens are nocturnal. They rest in tree hollows, discarded squirrel and bird nests and rocky crevices during the day. The martens eat mainly small rodents, such as voles.

# Beech marten

*Martes foina*

Not found in Britain but common in continental Europe, the beech marten was originally an animal of woodland and hilly habitats. However, it has greatly increased its range by exploiting the habitats humans have created. In some regions of France, Germany and Switzerland, beech martens have become very common in towns, frequently occupying the loft spaces of people's homes.

They can actually be quite a nuisance, chewing electrical wiring and making off with roof insulation to use as bedding. Beech martens have also been reported to have developed a liking for cars. The learned behaviour of sleeping under car bonnets, where it's nice and warm, has spread across central Europe. Every day, up to 40 cars in Switzerland are damaged by beech martens chewing through the wires under their bonnets. This compulsive chewing behaviour is a consequence of the marten's dietary flexibility. Youngsters will test anything and everything to see if it is edible or not.

*Beech martens have a silky dark brown coat with a white throat patch. People tolerate them in towns partly because they help to control rodents. Their main enemies are birds of prey and foxes.*

**Distribution**: Throughout Europe.
**Habitat**: Deciduous woodland, open rocky hillsides and urban habitats.
**Food**: Rodents, fruit and eggs.
**Size**: 42–48cm (16.5–19in); 1.3–2.3kg (2.75–5lb).
**Maturity**: 1–2 years.
**Breeding**: 1 litter of 1–8 kittens per year.
**Life span**: 18 years.
**Status**: Common.

# Least weasel

*Mustela nivalis*

Weasels are common throughout much of the Northern Hemisphere, from Japan and China, across Russia and Europe, including Great Britain but not Ireland, and right across the northern half of North America. They also occur in North Africa.

These animals survive in a wide variety of habitats, though they avoid thick forests, sandy deserts and any overly exposed spaces. For example, they are absent from Arabia and much of the Middle East.

Least weasels have very long bodies, with a long neck and flat head. This allows them to move through broken ground and inside burrows easily. The size of the weasel's body appears to depend on where it is: the largest specimens live in North Africa, and the smallest ones live in North America, where they are called least weasels.

Weasels live alone when not breeding. Males occupy territories that are also home to two or more females. Young are born in summer. They forage at all times of the day or night. They watch and listen for signs of prey before launching an attack, and kill by biting their captured animal in the neck.

**Distribution**: North Africa, northern Europe, northern Asia and North America.
**Habitat**: Forest, moorland, steppe, farmland and semi-desert.
**Food**: Small rodents, such as mice and voles, eggs, nestlings and lizards.
**Size**: 16–20cm (6.25–8in); 30–55g (1–2oz).
**Maturity**: 8 months.
**Breeding**: 2 litters of up to 7 offspring born during spring and late summer. Females are pregnant for a month.
**Life span**: 7 years, although many die in first year.
**Status**: Common.

*Least weasels have large eyes and ears compared to their body size. In summer the brown fur is about 1cm (0.4in) long, while in winter it more than doubles in length. In the far north, the brown coat also turns white in winter. The animal's flat head helps it to wriggle into burrows and other cramped spaces to catch prey.*

# Wolverine

*Gulo gulo*

Wolverines are giant relatives of the weasels and, along with the giant otter, they are the largest mustelids in the world. The name wolverine primarily refers to the North American population. In northern Europe and Siberia, the animals are also known as gluttons due to their liberal feeding habits and voracious appetites.

Wolverines are generally nocturnal but will forage by day if they need to. Their diet varies throughout the year. In summer, they feed on small animals, such as mice and other rodents and ground-living birds, such as pheasants. They also readily feast on summer fruits.

In winter, when most other carnivores are hibernating or sheltering from the cold, wolverines may tackle bigger prey, even something as large as a moose, which is 20 times the size of the predator. The wolverine's wide feet act as snowshoes, allowing them to walk over deep snow, in which hapless deer or wild sheep are easily bogged down, becoming defenceless and unable to make their escape.

Wolverines mate in early summer and young are born in underground dens the following spring. They are weaned at ten weeks and leave their mothers in the autumn.

**Distribution**: Scandinavia, Siberia, Canada and northern United States.
**Habitat**: Tundra and conifer forest.
**Food**: Carrion, eggs, rodents, berries, deer and sheep.
**Size**: 65–105cm (25.5–41.25in); 10–32kg (22–70.5lb).
**Maturity**: 2–3 years.
**Breeding**: Litter of 2–4 born in early spring every 2 years.
**Life span**: 10 years.
**Status**: Vulnerable.

*Wolverines have large heads and heavily built bodies with dense coats of hairs of different lengths to prevent winter snow and ice from getting too close to the skin, causing heat loss.*

# European mink

*Mustela lutreola*

**Distribution**: Europe.
**Habitat**: Beside rivers and lakes.
**Food**: Water rodents, birds, frogs, fishes and insects.
**Size**: 37cm (14.5in); 590g (1.25lb).
**Maturity**: 1 year.
**Breeding**: 4–5 young born in April and May.
**Life span**: 8 years.
**Status**: Vulnerable.

European mink once ranged from northern Spain all the way through mainland Europe to the Ob River Valley, east of the Ural Mountains of Russia. They are now almost extinct across this range and only a few populations survive in the south of France and in Spain. European mink have never lived in the British Isles. The mink species found in Britain is the American mink, which was introduced as a source of fur. The American species has become widespread across Europe and its presence has been one of the factors in the downfall of the indigenous European mink. Other problems have been hunting and habitat destruction.

European mink live along the banks of rivers and lakes, where they hide in dense waterside vegetation. They may dig their own burrows or modify those of water rats and other aquatic mammals. The minks are most active at dawn and dusk. They spot their prey in the water, then pounce.

*Mink have a thick coat of underfur that helps to repel water when the animal is swimming. The undercoat is especially thick in winter to enable the animal to stay warm when wet.*

**Kolinsky** (*Mustela sibrica*): 25–39cm (9.75–15.25in); 650–800g (1.5–1.75lb)
This species, also known as the Siberian weasel, ranges from the European region of Russia to Korea and Japan. It has a dark brown coat that becomes paler during winter, especially in the north of its range. It has a dark "mask" across the eyes.

**European polecat** (*Mustela putorius*): 35–51cm (13.75–20in); 0.7–1.4kg (1.5–3lb)
European polecats are the wild form of ferrets. This form is rare in the British Isles but is found across all forested areas of continental Europe. A large population of feral polecats has also formed in New Zealand. Male polecats are up to twice the size of females. Polecats prey on burrowing animals such as rabbits and rodents. Ferrets were originally bred to flush out or kill rabbits that had gone to ground. Domestic ferrets are inquisitive and affectionate and can be house trained. As a result they make good pets. They sleep for about 18 hours a day, so require less attention than other domestic animals.

**American mink** (*Mustela vison*): 33–43cm (13–17in); 0.7–2.3kg (1.5–5lb)
American mink are small carnivores that live close to water, where they feed on small aquatic animals. They originally came from North America, but were brought to Europe and Asia to be farmed for their fine fur. They have since escaped or been released into the wild and are now a common pest. They are also competition for the similar, and now very rare, European mink species.

# African striped weasel

*Poecilogale albinucha*

The African striped weasel is a skilled burrower. It can dig a tunnel with great speed and spends most of its time underground. When it does emerge to hunt, it does so at night. This behaviour protects it from large birds of prey.

The weasel locates prey by smell and kills or disables it with a bite to the back of the head. Struggling prey are subdued with powerful kicks. The weasel returns to its burrow to feed, taking the meal down to a rounded chamber underground. Food is often stored in this chamber, including injured victims, which are left to die. African striped weasels prey mainly on rodents, and may eat three or four each night.

Most African striped weasels live alone, although small family groups sometimes share a burrow. Courtship between male and female involves the pair growling at each other, while they take it in turns to drag each other around by the scruff of the neck – a practice that mimics the way prey is carried.

**Distribution**: Sub-Saharan Africa.
**Habitat**: Grasslands, marshes, forest edges.
**Food**: Birds, snakes, small rodents and insects.
**Size**: 25–36cm (9.75–14.25in); 230–380g (8–13.5oz).
**Maturity**: 20 months.
**Breeding**: Up to 3 pups born from September to April.
**Life span**: Unknown.
**Status**: Common.

*Even for a mustelid, this species of weasel has very short legs in comparison to its body. The weasel's stripes mean that this species is often confused with the zorilla, an African polecat.*

## Honey badger

*Mellivora capensis*

Honey badgers are secretive hunters and are rarely seen, despite having a wide range that spans most of Africa and southern Asia. The badgers are also known as ratels.

The moniker honey badger might give the impression of sweetness but it belies this hunter's fearsome nature. The name is derived from the animal's love of honey. The badger has evolved a symbiotic relationship with the honey guide bird to locate sources of this food. The honey guide leads the badger to a tree containing a bees' nest. The badger then climbs the tree, knocks the nest down and rips it apart to expose the honeycomb inside. The badger licks at the honey while the honey guide feeds on the beeswax and bee larvae.

Honey badgers generally forage at night. They usually move around alone but sometimes small family groups hunt together. The badgers do not have a den like other species of badger. Instead they roam large distances in search of food, resting in temporary shelters before moving on again. Without a safe place to retreat to, honey badgers will readily fight any threat; in fact they are known for being especially fierce in fights. They will attack an unsuspecting human if cornered and have been known to even bite cars.

**Distribution**: Africa, Middle East, central Asia, India, Nepal and Myanmar.
**Habitat**: Grasslands, rocky areas, semi-deserts, forests and woodlands.
**Food**: Honey, fruits, insects snakes, lizards, rodents, birds, eggs and carrion.
**Size**: 80cm (31.5in); 9–12kg (19.75–26.5lb).
**Maturity**: 14 months.
**Breeding**: Females are pregnant for six months. 1–4 cubs, usually 2, are born in April or May.
**Life span**: Unknown; other badgers live 20 years.
**Status**: Common.

*Although the honey badger does not have stripes on its face like other species of badger, it does have a silver-grey "cape" on its back, which extends from just behind the eyes to the tip of the tail. A few honey badgers do not have a cape at all. The young are rusty brown in colour. Males are only slightly larger than the females.*

## Badger

*Meles meles*

Large members of the mustelid family, badgers have a much more diverse diet than most of the small carnivores. Adept at making a meal out of most situations, badgers will eat anything they find, including berries, fungi and carrion. Worms are a particular favourite, and on warm, damp nights badgers can regularly be observed patrolling through pastureland.

One of the badger's greatest assets is its mouth. The way a badger's skull is structured means that it is physically impossible for the animal to dislocate its jaw, allowing badgers to have one of the most powerful bites in the natural world. This trait makes the badger a fearsome foe for any animal that happens to cross its path.

Unlike most other mustelids, badgers are very social animals. They live in large family groups centred on communal dens, or setts.

*The badger's black and white face makes it instantly recognizable.*

**Distribution**: Throughout Europe (but not north of Arctic Circle) and Asia.
**Habitat**: Favours a mixture of woodland and pastureland, also moving into urban habitats.
**Food**: Omnivorous diet.
**Size**: 65–80cm (25.5–31.5in); 8–12kg (17.5–26.5lb).
**Maturity**: 1–2 years.
**Breeding**: 1 litter of 1–5 young per year.
**Life span**: 15 years.
**Status**: Common.

# European otter

*Lutra lutra*

**Distribution**: Europe, Asia and North Africa.
**Habitat**: Rivers and lakes.
**Food**: Fish, shellfish, frogs, eggs and insects.
**Size**: 57–70cm (22.5–27.5in); 13kg (28.5lb).
**Maturity**: 2 years.
**Breeding**: Pups born mainly in summer.
**Life span**: Unknown.
**Status**: Vulnerable.

This species is perhaps more aptly named the Eurasian otter because it is found as far east as Manchuria. It is also found as far north as the tundra line of Siberia and Scandinavia and as far south as the coastal plain of North Africa.

European otters spend most of their waking hours in water, though they build their nests on land. The nests are often made up of a network of tunnels dug into the river bank or running through roots and thick shrubs. Each otter defends a short stretch of river bank, marking its territory with secretions from a scent gland under the base of the tail.

Within the territory an otter has a designated area for entering the water, basking in the sun and playing. Otters are very playful. They are often seen rolling in grass and sliding down muddy slopes into the water.

Otters can dive for up to two minutes at a time. Once in the water they use sensitive whiskers to detect the currents produced by the movements of their prey. Air bubbles trapped in the fur keep the skin dry.

*The European otter has a brown coat, which is paler in Asian populations. The feet are generously webbed to aid with swimming. Each foot is also equipped with large claws.*

---

**Spotted-necked otter** (*Lutra maculicollis*): 85–105cm (2.8–3.4ft); 4kg (8.75lb)
Spotted-necked otters live in the Great Lakes region of East Africa. They do not swim in cloudy water and are often found foraging beside clear mountain streams. As its name suggests, this species has white spots on its neck and throat against a background of brown fur. They have strongly webbed feet and large claws, which suggests they catch most of their food while swimming in open water. Fish makes up most of their diet, but they also eat frogs, freshwater crabs and insect larvae.

**African clawless otter** (*Aonyx capensis*): 1m (3.25ft); 5kg (11lb)
This species is slightly larger than its close African relative, the Congo clawless otter. It lives in eastern and southern Africa. Like its relative, the African clawless otter has feet with less webbing than most otters and only rounded claws on the hind feet. Members of this species feed on creatures that live on the bottom of rivers and streams, such as crabs and frogs. They locate this prey by touch, using their dexterous, clawless hands.

# Congo clawless otter

*Aonyx congicus*

Congo clawless otters live in the waterways of the mighty Congo Basin, the largest river system in Africa. The otters avoid the main watercourses and are more often found in streams, swamps and ponds in the deep tropical rainforest.

These bodies of water have little or no current and are consequently heavily clouded with sediment. Lacking claws, these nocturnal otters are much better able to feel for slippery prey in this muddy water and overturn stones in search of food than their clawed cousins.

Clawless otters also have shorter whiskers than other species. This suggests that they are not as reliant on whiskers for detecting prey underwater as other otters. This species of otter catches fish and frogs and collects prey, such as shellfish, from the muddy bottom of the river.

The otter's teeth are also more suited to a wide range of food than other otters, which all have teeth adapted for gripping slithering fish. This feature, along with the short whiskers, suggests that Congo clawless otters spend a lot more time foraging on land than other species. Little is known about the breeding habits of this allusive species, but they are probably broadly similar to other species.

**Distribution**: Congo River Basin.
**Habitat**: Swamps and ponds in tropical rainforests.
**Food**: Fish, frogs and shellfish.
**Size**: 78–98cm (30.75–38.5in); 15–25kg (33–55lb).
**Maturity**: 1 year.
**Breeding**: Litters of 2–3 young.
**Life span**: 15 years.
**Status**: Unknown.

*Unusually for otters, this species has no claws or webbing on its forefeet. There is a small amount of webbing on the hind feet and a simple peg-like claw on the three middle toes. Clawless feet help the otters to feel objects under muddy water as they search for prey.*

# MONGOOSES

*Mongooses form a family of carnivores called the Herpestidae. They look similar to most small carnivores, including the mustelids and viverrids, in that they have short legs, long slender bodies and pointed whiskered snouts. This body form is ideal for searching for and tackling prey in tight places. Unlike most small carnivores, which hunt alone, mongooses tend to live in large units, or bands.*

## Banded mongoose

*Mungos mungo*

**Distribution**: Africa south of the Sahara.
**Habitat**: Grassland and dry woodland.
**Food**: Insects and millipedes.
**Size**: 30–45cm (12–18in); 1.5–2.5kg (3.3–5.5lb).
**Maturity**: 9–10 months.
**Breeding**: Litters of 3 or 4, up to 4 times per year.
**Life span**: Up to 12 years.
**Status**: Common.

The banded mongoose is one of the most common mongooses in Africa. It lives in open grassland and areas of dry woodland, and is also found in rocky, broken country. It lives in bands of up to 40 individuals, sharing dens inside old termite mounds or abandoned aardvark holes. The dens have central sleeping chambers, which are reached from several holes.

Dens are used for only a few days at a time, with bands regularly moving on to new foraging sites. Banded mongooses feed during the daytime, returning to their dens before sunset. Their diet consists of invertebrates, such as beetles and millipedes.

Banded mongooses have excellent senses of smell, hearing and vision. Their bands are highly social, with members rarely straying far from each other and communicating by making several distinct sounds. All females in a band breed at the same time. The young are raised together, and are suckled by all the adult females in the band.

*Banded mongooses have brownish-grey fur with dark brown stripes, or bands, across their backs and tails. Each foot possesses five long claws.*

## Meerkat

*Suricata suricatta*

Meerkats are relatives of mongooses, which live in large bands in the arid, semi-desert areas of southern Africa. They are efficient diggers and live in large underground burrows.

Meerkats live in highly organized societies. While feeding, at least one band member keeps a look-out for danger, communicating to the others with an array of sounds. For example, howling warns that a bird of prey is approaching, while double-barking informs the band that a terrestrial predator has been spotted.

A meerkat band has between 10 and 15 individuals, with two or three pairs of males and females which do all the breeding. The young kits stay close to their dens and are looked after by at least one adult while the rest of their band forages for food.

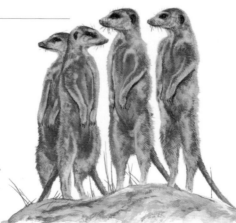

*Meerkats live in dry, open country in southern Africa, especially in the semi-desert regions of Namibia, southern Angola, Botswana and western South Africa.*

**Distribution**: South-western and southern Africa from Angola to South Africa.
**Habitat**: Semi-desert and scrubland.
**Food**: Insects, scorpions, small vertebrates and eggs.
**Size**: 25–35cm (9.75–13.75in); 600–975g (1.25–2.5lb).
**Maturity**: 1 year.
**Breeding**: Litters of 2–5 kits born once per year in November.
**Life span**: 10 years.
**Status**: Common.

# Gambian mongoose

*Mungos gambianus*

**Distribution**: Southern coastal region of West Africa.
**Habitat**: Grassland and woodland.
**Food**: Insects.
**Size**: 30–45cm (12–17.75in); 1–2kg (2.25–4.5lb).
**Maturity**: 10 months.
**Breeding**: Up to 4 litters produced each year.
**Life span**: 10 years.
**Status**: Unknown.

Gambian mongooses are found from Gambia and Senegal to Nigeria. They avoid thickly forested areas and are found instead in grassland and open woodlands.

This species lives in groups of 10–20 individuals. Each group has an equal split of males and females. Some groups swell to up to 40 members, but these tend to split into smaller groups that can exploit sources of food more effectively.

The Gambian mongoose dens as a group in disused burrows, hollow logs and rock crevices. The group moves between dens regularly to avoid depleting food supplies in one area. The Gambian mongoose is diurnal. It hunts as a group, moving in a fixed formation as the animals search for insects. Members of the group communicate with each other by growls and screams. Twittering sounds help the group stay together while feeding, and louder barks warn of approaching danger.

*Gambian mongooses have a uniform grey-brown fur. The only obvious markings are a dark streak on the neck. Males and females are about the same size.*

---

**Long-nosed cusimanse**
(*Crossarchus obscurus*): 30–45cm (12–17.75in); 1.5kg (3.25lb)
Cusimanses are small mongooses that live in patches of swampy forest in West Africa. Their bodies are covered in long brown-grey-yellow hairs. Cusimanses travel in large groups and appear to be most active during the day but are also seen on the move by night. The group takes shelter when convenient in temporary dens. They feed on fruit, seeds, insects and small reptiles, foraging by pushing their long snouts through leaf litter, scratching at soil and overturning stones. Long-nosed cusimanses also crack snail shells and eggs by hurling them between their back legs on to hard stones.

**Pousargues's mongoose** (*Dologale dybowskii*): 25–30cm (9.75–12in); 300–400g (10.5–14oz)
This small species of mongoose lives in the woodlands and grasslands of Central Africa from southern Sudan to the Central African Republic. It is common around the shores of Lake Albert between the Democratic Republic of Congo and Uganda. This mongoose has a bushy tail and a grey face, long claws and simple teeth. This suggests that its diet contains a lot of invertebrates, which the mongoose digs out from underground.

# Black-footed mongoose

*Bdeogale nigripes*

The black-footed mongoose lives in the rainforests of southern Nigeria and those around the mouth of the River Congo in the Democratic Republic of Congo and northern Angola. They are most often found near to rivers. They do most of their foraging on land and rarely climb trees but will move in and out of water as they move around.

Black-footed mongooses are nocturnal. They are most often seen alone, but pairs are also spotted. These may be breeding pairs who are living together for a short period during the mating season or a mother and her juvenile offspring. Breeding takes places in the dry season.

Black-footed mongooses survive by eating mainly insects, most commonly ants, termites and beetles. They also feed on carrion, small mammals and snakes and will take frogs and salamanders from shallow water. While most other species of mongoose have sharp teeth built for killing large prey, the teeth of this species are more adapted for crushing small prey.

**Distribution**: Central Africa.
**Habitat**: Rainforests.
**Food**: Insects.
**Size**: 37–60cm (14.5–23.5in); 0.9–3kg (2–6.5lb).
**Maturity**: 1 year.
**Breeding**: Litter born between November and January.
**Life span**: 15 years.
**Status**: Common.

*This species of mongoose lives near to water and has slightly webbed feet to help it swim strongly. Its coat is also adapted to life in and out of water, with long, thick guard hairs over a softer undercoat.*

## Slender mongoose

*Galerella sanguinea*

The slender mongoose is one of the smaller members of the mongoose family. It is also one of the most widespread of all the African mongooses, with a range that stretches across most of the continent south of the Sahara Desert.

While it avoids the dense tropical rainforests of the Congo Basin, this species is found in a wide array of other habitats, from lush grasslands and savannahs to rock fields and semi-desert. Slender mongooses are also agile climbers and often look for food in the branches of large shrubs and among the trees of open woodlands.

A single male slender mongoose occupies a territory that overlaps those of several females. Females defend their territories from each other, but the male is tolerated by a female when she is ready to mate. Most mating takes place between October and March. At all other times of the year the males forages alone. Mothers and their young sometimes form small groups, but these are short-lived as the offspring leave to find their own territories.

*There are more than 40 recognized subspecies of slender mongoose. These show a range of different colour forms, from yellow and red to brown. Many individuals are spotted.*

**Distribution**: Sub-Saharan Africa.
**Habitat**: Grasslands, scrub and semi-deserts.
**Food**: Insects, lizards and fruit.
**Size**: 27–40cm (10.5–15.5in); 350–900g (12.25–31.75oz).
**Maturity**: 1 or 2 years.
**Breeding**: Single male fathers several litters.
**Life span**: 10 years.
**Status**: Common.

## Egyptian mongoose

*Herpestes ichneumon*

Egyptian mongooses are widespread across Africa but are not found in the rainforests that grow in the Congo Basin and along the coast of the Gulf of Guinea. In addition, the species is not very common in southern Africa. However, they have been introduced to Madagascar – to the detriment of native species – and Italy.

They live around trees that grow beside waterways. This habitat is one of the few to have increased in abundance due to human activity. Today, Egyptian mongooses are equally at home beside a canal or irrigation channel as they are next to a natural river.

These mammals live alone, in pairs or in small groups of up to seven individuals, depending on the availability of food in their area. The species is diurnal and forages for food on the ground, in trees and in the water.

Each mongoose has a sac above the anus that produces a strong-smelling substance. When mongooses travel together at night, the following animal walks with its nose pressed to the anal sac so it can keep in contact with the leader in the dark. The leader is generally a mother being followed by its offspring or a female being courted by a male. Mongooses also mark their territories with these anal secretions.

**Distribution**: Southern Europe, Middle East, North and Central Africa.
**Habitat**: Trees near rivers, lakes, canals and ditches.
**Food**: Fish, insects, snakes and frogs.
**Size**: 54cm (21.5in); 2.85kg (6.25lb).
**Maturity**: 2 years.
**Breeding**: Female's genitals swell and redden when on heat. Gestation is 11 weeks and 2–4 kits are born in summer.
**Life span**: 12 years in the wild but almost twice that in captivity.
**Status**: Common.

*Egyptian mongooses have claws and teeth adapted for their lifestyle. The long claws are used for digging dens, while the teeth are able to slice through meat and grab fish easily.*

# White-tailed mongoose

*Ichneumia albicauda*

**Distribution**: Sub-Saharan Africa.
**Habitat**: Woodland and grassland.
**Food**: Insects.
**Size**: 58cm (22.75in); 4kg (8.75lb).
**Maturity**: 2 years.
**Breeding**: Litters born in rainy season.
**Life span**: 12 years.
**Status**: Common.

Like many other African species of mongoose, the white-tailed mongoose is found across the continent south of the Sahara but is absent from the jungles of Central Africa and the deserts of southern Africa.

White-tailed mongooses are nocturnal. By day they rest inside thickets of vegetation or in burrows abandoned by other animals. When night falls the mongooses forage alone. They are secretive animals and rarely leave the cover of ground vegetation. White-tailed mongooses eat mainly ground-living insects, such as locusts, beetles and mole crickets. They will also eat small vertebrates if given the opportunity. They sometimes steal domestic poultry. This species is also an egg eater: it breaks an egg by throwing it between its hind legs on to a rock. Kits are born in the wet season. They become independent at nine months.

*This large mongoose has a grizzled coat of pale brown underfur with long black guard hairs over it. Only the last half of the large bushy tail is white. The palms are naked and this hairless area extends to the wrists of the forepaws.*

---

**Dwarf mongoose** (*Helogale parvula*): 24cm (9.5in); 320g (11.25oz)
The species shares the title of smallest mongoose with the brown mongoose of Madagascar. The dwarf mongoose lives across Central Africa from Ethiopia to Angola and in parts of eastern South Africa. It occupies savannahs, woodlands and mountain brush. Dwarf mongooses have brown-and-grey speckled coats. They live in a complex social system, where an older, reproductively active female is dominant. Her mate is the group's second-ranking animal. The next most dominant member is the youngest offspring. Other members of the group are ranked according to age, with females always outranking males. Dwarf mongooses eat eggs, small vertebrates and insects, which they find in leaf litter and under rocks.

**Liberian mongoose** (*Liberictis kuhni*): 45cm (17.75in); 2.3kg (5lb)
The Liberian mongoose is the most endangered mongoose species on the African mainland. Only the Madagascan mongooses are similarly endangered. The individuals that do survive live in northern Liberia and Côte d'Ivoire. They are naturally rare and have suffered from overhunting. They are diurnal insect eaters that live in small groups of about five.

# Yellow mongoose

*Cynictis penicillata*

Yellow mongooses are most common in the dry region of southern Africa that spreads from the Transvaal to northern Angola. However, this mongoose does not populate the driest habitats in this region, being found instead in grass and scrublands. It never ventures into forest or very high up in mountains.

These animals are primarily diurnal but they do sometimes forage at night, especially in areas where they are disturbed by people during the day. The yellow mongoose emerges from its den after sunrise and warms itself in the sun for a short while before heading off for a day-long foraging trip. The animals live in social groups made up of a male and female breeding pair and their younger offspring. Older offspring tend to leave the group, but unrelated older individuals may join from other neighbouring groups.

Males roam through the territories of other groups, which means that the relationships between group members might be more complex than a simple family structure.

**Distribution**: Southern Africa.
**Habitat**: Dry grasslands.
**Food**: Insects.
**Size**: 31cm (12.25in); 800g (1.75lb).
**Maturity**: 1 year.
**Breeding**: Young born in August to November.
**Life span**: Unknown.
**Status**: Common.

*There are currently 12 subspecies of yellow mongoose. They differ in the colour and length of their hair and size of tail. Southern yellow mongooses are larger than those in the north, which also have a greyer coat.*

# Ring-tailed mongoose

*Galidia elegans*

Like many Malagasy mammals, the ring-tailed mongoose is in danger of extinction. This threat is largely from the destruction of the African island's tropical forests but is compounded by the fact that this species of mongoose reproduces at a much slower rate than its more fecund relatives – producing only a single kit each year. Madagascan forests are not normal rainforests. They are prone to long periods of drought, which makes food hard to come by. The mongoose's small litter size therefore ensures that mothers will be able to find food for their young each year.

Ring-tailed mongooses are seen alone or in pairs. They are sometimes also found in small groups. Little is known about the social behaviour of this species, but evidence suggests that they form breeding pairs and that groups are family units made up of the parents and two or three offspring. The mongooses are good climbers and will forage for food in trees as well as on the ground. The bushy ringed tail helps individuals keep track of other mongooses while they move through the branches.

*The ring-tailed mongoose should not be mistaken for another resident of Madagascar, the ring-tailed lemur. Like the lemur, ring-tailed mongooses probably use their bushy, striped tails to communicate with each other among thick vegetation.*

**Distribution**: Madagascar, most common in the north, east and west-central regions of the island.
**Habitat**: Subtropical and tropical dry forests.
**Food**: Small mammals, insects, spiders, lizards, fish, eggs and fruits.
**Size**: 32–38cm (12.5–15in); 700–900g (24.5–31.75oz).
**Maturity**: 2 years.
**Breeding**: Gestation period is 3 months. A single kit born in July to February.
**Life span**: 8 years, although 13 years has been recorded in captivity.
**Status**: Vulnerable.

# Broad-striped mongoose

*Galidictis fasciat*

*As its name suggests, the broad-striped mongoose has dark stripes running from the neck to the lower part of the tail. This species is easily mistaken for the small Indian civet, which has been introduced to Madagascar. This introduction has been at great cost to the native species of carnivore, such as this mongoose, and their prey animals alike.*

Broad-striped mongooses live in the forests of Madagascar, where they lead solitary nocturnal lives. Madagascar is divided by a range of mountains that runs north to south. Most sightings of the broad-striped mongooses are made at an altitude of about 800m (2,600ft) on the eastern side of the mountains.

Being a forest dweller, the broad-striped mongoose is a good climber and forages for food in the trees. Its diet is dominated by small vertebrates, such as rodents, lizards and amphibians. It also eats insects and other invertebrates. There are some reports that this species also preys on small lemurs, some of which are little more than the size of a rodent.

Little is known about the breeding habits of the broad-striped mongoose. When compared to its close relatives, it is likely to follow a similar breeding pattern to them, in which adults form temporary pairings to help raise the single offspring.

**Distribution**: Madagascar; most commonly spotted on the eastern slopes of the island's mountains.
**Habitat**: Mountain forest below 1,500m (4,900ft).
**Food**: Insects, small rodents and birds.
**Size**: 57cm (22.5in); 600g (21.25oz).
**Maturity**: 2 years.
**Breeding**: Single young born in July–February. Gestation is between 10 and 12 weeks.
**Life span**: 10 years.
**Status**: Vulnerable.

# Giant-striped mongoose

*Galidictis grandidieri*

**Distribution**: South-western Madagascar.
**Habitat**: Spiny desert, an arid region of cactus-like plants covered in sharp spines.
**Food**: Insects, scorpions and small vertebrates, such as lizards.
**Size**: 40cm (15.75in); 500g (17.5oz).
**Maturity**: 2 years.
**Breeding**: Single offspring born at all times of the year. Gestation period is between 10 and 14 weeks
**Life span**: Unknown, but could be as much as 20 years.
**Status**: Endangered.

This type of mongoose lives in the "spiny desert" of southern Madagascar. The species is very rare, and all individuals are found in an area of 430sq km (165sq miles). The spiny desert is so called because most of the plants that grow there are covered in thorns. This makes it very difficult for large animals, including humans, to travel through the habitat. Consequently, giant-striped mongooses have only rarely been observed in the wild, and many details about their lives remain a mystery.

Giant-striped mongooses are nocturnal. They avoid the heat of the day by resting inside hollows in the limestone outcrops that are common in the region. They form monogamous pairs that stay together all year round. If one is injured, the partner will stay nearby.

These animals eat insects, especially the hissing cockroach, which is now quite familiar as a pet across the world. The mongoose also has long legs and powerful jaws. This suggests that it can also catch and eat larger prey than insects, such as scorpions.

*Despite their name, giant-striped mongooses do not have stripes that are particularly large. They have eight in all, which run down the back from the ears to the base of the tail. Male and female giant-striped mongooses appear to be the same size as each other, although females have a scent pouch near the anus.*

# Narrow-striped mongoose

*Mungotictis decemlineata*

**Distribution**: South and western Madagascar, although not seen in the south for 20 years.
**Habitat**: Savannah.
**Food**: Insects, eggs and small vertebrates.
**Size**: 25–35cm (9.75–13.75in); 600–700g (21.25–24.5oz).
**Maturity**: 2 years.
**Breeding**: Single young born in summer. Mating takes place in early spring
**Life span**: Unknown; other species reach 20.
**Status**: Endangered.

Narrow-tailed mongooses live in the sandy savannahs of southern and western Madagascar. They are active during the day, foraging on the ground and in the small trees that grow sparsely across the region. Like the similar Malagasy mongooses, this species is primarily an insectivore, though they are also known to eat eggs and can tackle small mammals and lizards when given the opportunity. When narrow-tailed mongooses catch prey, they lie on their sides and hold the food with all four feet as they eat it.

These mongooses live in breeding pairs, which are often joined by juvenile offspring. In areas that can support a high population of mongooses, larger social groups form containing up to 20 non-related individuals, though these are becoming very rare as the surviving wild population of narrow-striped mongooses becomes increasingly fragmented. Most foraging is done alone or in pairs. In winter, any larger group breaks up into its constituent pairs.

Mating takes place between December and April, with a peak in March. Kits are born in the summer and weaned within two months.

*Narrow-striped mongooses have between eight and ten thin bands running along the back. The tail is bushy and ringed.*

# RODENTS

*The Rodentia, with over 2,000 species distributed all around the globe, is by far the largest order of mammals. All rodents have two upper and two lower chisel-like incisor teeth. These incisors grow continuously throughout their lives, so, unlike many other animals, they can gnaw everything without their teeth getting worn away.*

## Edible dormouse

*Glis glis*

When awake, all species of dormouse belie their dozy reputation, being incredibly lithe and agile climbers – the edible dormouse being no exception. These dormice spend virtually their entire lives in the treetops, searching for food, and are very reluctant to leave the safety of the branches. If they cannot leap between trees, they will not cross the open areas on the ground. Roads and tracks cut through woodland can therefore inhibit the movement of dormice.

Dormice are champion sleepers, being one of the few types of mammal to enter a true state of hibernation. Come autumn, dormice descend into the bases of hollow trees, wrap themselves into balls and fall into a state of very deep sleep. They allow their body temperature to drop very low, barely more than the temperature of the air around them. Heart rate and breathing also slow right down. By doing this, they are able to conserve enough energy to last them through the winter. When spring arrives, the dormice's metabolism speeds up again, bringing them out of six or seven months of uninterrupted sleep.

*Also known as fat dormice, edible dormice were kept by the Romans in jars, called gliraria, to fatten them for the table.*

**Distribution**: Throughout central and eastern Europe, extending west through northern Spain. Introduced into England.
**Habitat**: The canopy of mature deciduous woodland.
**Food**: Nuts, fruit, fungi, bark, insects and occasionally eggs and nestlings.
**Size**: 13–19cm (5–7.5in), 70–300g (0.15–0.66lb).
**Maturity**: 2 years.
**Breeding**: 1 litter of 2–9 offspring born in summer.
**Life span**: 7 years.
**Status**: Common.

## Water vole

*Arvicola terrestris*

**Distribution**: Widespread across Europe and Asia.
**Habitat**: Banks of slow-flowing rivers and streams.
**Food**: Grasses, rushes and sedges.
**Size**: 14–22cm (5.5–8.5in); 150–300g (0.33–0.66lb).
**Maturity**: 2 months.
**Breeding**: 3 or 4 litters of 5 young born throughout spring and summer.
**Life span**: Up to 3 years.
**Status**: Common.

Water voles are also known – confusingly – as water rats. Ratty, of *The Wind in the Willows* fame, was really a water vole, and, like him, these rodents are found living alongside slow-moving rivers, ditches, dykes and lakes. In areas of central Europe, however, water voles do not live by water, preferring dry habitats instead. In some places they are considered to be a serious agricultural pest.

Water voles excavate extensive burrow systems in the banks of the rivers, with plenty of entrance and exit holes so that they can escape from the various predators they encounter – both in and out of the water. Even so, the average life span of a water vole is a mere five months. Herons, barn owls, brown rats and pike are all known to prey on water voles, but the rodents' most important predators are stoats and mink. Indeed, the introduction of the American mink to Britain has been blamed for the species' recent and rapid decline.

*Water voles are often mistaken for rats, but they differ from rats by having blunter snouts, more rounded bodies, smaller ears and shorter, hairy tails.*

# Siberian lemming

*Lemmus sibericus*

Contrary to popular belief, lemmings do not commit suicide. During favourable years, the lemmings' ability to reproduce very quickly leads to population explosions of amazing proportions. As the population size goes up, space becomes more and more difficult to find, and young are pushed away from the best habitat, down the mountains and into the valleys.

Lemmings are good swimmers when they have to be, but they don't know their limits. During dispersal, youngsters often try to cross large bodies of water, drowning in the process. It is this behaviour which gave rise to the misconception that they kill themselves.

During the summer, lemmings spend much of their time underground in burrows, but, when the ground starts to freeze in autumn, the lemmings cannot dig through the ground and are forced to forage on the surface. The lemmings do not hibernate during the harsh Siberian winter, but construct tunnel systems under the snow in search of food. The tunnels keep them out of sight of hungry predators, such as great grey owls, which are heavily reliant on lemmings as a source of food.

**Distribution**: Siberia and northern North America.
**Habitat**: Tundra grassland.
**Food**: Moss and grass.
**Size**: 13–18cm (5–7in); 23–34g (0.05–0.07lb).
**Maturity**: 5–6 weeks.
**Breeding**: These prolific breeders may produce 8 litters of up to 6 young each throughout the summer.
**Life span**: Less than 2 years.
**Status**: Common.

*Unlike other species of lemming, the Siberian lemming does not change the colour of its coat in winter.*

---

**Alpine marmot** (*Marmota marmota*):
45–60cm (17.75–23.5in); 3–4.5kg (6.5–10lb)
Alpine marmots live in the Alpine and sub-Alpine pastures of the Alps. Like many other marmots, Alpine marmots live in family groups, consisting of a breeding pair and their offspring from previous years. Older male offspring are known to help keep their younger siblings warm during the cold Alpine winters. Litter sizes tend to be small – about two pups. The pups stay with their parents until they are three years old.

**Southern birch mouse** (*Sicista subtilis*):
5–9cm (2–3.5in); 6–14g (0.015–0.03lb)
These tiny mice inhabit the forests, moors, meadows and steppes of eastern Europe and Asia. They excavate shallow burrows, in which they build oval-shaped nests of dry grass and cut plant stems. They travel over the ground in leaps and bounds. They are also great climbers. Strong outer toes grip twigs, and their prehensile tail curls around other branches for additional support.

**Wood lemming** (*Myopus schisticolor*):
10cm (4in); 33g (1.25oz)
The wood lemming lives in the taiga (forests of conifer trees) of Scandinavia and is also found across Siberia as fat east as northern Mongolia. It digs tunnels with its teeth in the thick moss. It eats the moss and make stores of it in autumn to see it through the winter. As with other lemmings, the population of wood lemmings fluctuates wildly. In good years a population explosion results in migrations of large numbers in search of feeding sites.

---

# Eurasian beaver

*Castor fiber*

Eurasian beavers are the largest rodents in Europe and Asia. They live in or beside woodland waterways. Beavers live in family groups of four or five individuals, with each family defending a small area of river and woodland. The family lives inside a den called a lodge, which is a simple tunnel dug up into the bank from below the water line. In places where this construction is not possible, beavers build a castle of mud, stones and branches. To ensure that the entrance to the lodge is underwater, the beavers build a dam across the river to make a deep pool of calm water. On occasion, the lodge is built into the dam.

Beavers dig canals from the river into the woodland. Using their huge teeth, they cut down small trees and cut them into chunks, floating the timber down the canal into the dammed area. The wood is eaten along with water plants, or stored underwater for eating later.

**Distribution**: Northern Europe and Siberia.
**Habitat**: Lakes and rivers.
**Food**: Wood and river plants.
**Size**: 80–110cm (2.5–3.5ft); 17–32kg (37.5–70.5lb).
**Maturity**: 3 years.
**Breeding**: Litters of about 3 born early summer.
**Life span**: 14 years.
**Status**: Near threatened.

*The Eurasian beaver is similar to the American beaver, but is slightly smaller. It is a powerful swimmer, thanks to a flipper-like tail and webbed feet.*

# Hamster

*Cricetus cricetus*

*The common hamster is also named the black-bellied hamster because of the dark stripe that runs from the shoulders along the belly to the base of the tail. Most pet hamsters belong to another species as domestic breeds of the golden hamster – a smaller species living in the Middle East.*

Within Europe, the common hamster is mainly a resident of cultivated fields, where it feeds on the grains of cereal crops, potatoes, beets and other root crops. This diet is mirrored in more wild habitats, such as the great Eurasian steppe. Common hamsters also eat any insect larvae they find in the soil, especially beetle grubs. Despite their relatively small size, these stocky rodents are known to eat small birds, frogs and smaller rodents, such as shrews.

Hamsters stash a lot of their food, making large stockpiles within burrow systems. Food intended for storage is carried back home in the animal's cheek pouches, which gives the hamster's face its characteristic look.

The stored food is consumed over the winter. The hamster sleeps for several days at a stretch during this period but then wakes to eat part of its food cache. In warmer periods, the hamster is active at dawn and dusk, emerging from its intricate network of burrows to forage.

The hamster's breeding season is between April and August. Each female produces two litters each summer. Newborns weigh 7g (0.25oz). They are weaned in three weeks.

**Distribution**: Europe and Siberia.
**Habitat**: Steppe and agricultural land.
**Food**: Seeds, fruits, roots and insect larvae.
**Size**: 20–27cm (8–10.5in); 200–500g (7–17.5oz).
**Maturity**: Females 43 days; males 56 days.
**Breeding**: 2 litters of up to 12 young born in summer. Gestation period is 20 days.
**Life span**: 2 years.
**Status**: Common.

# Crested rat

*Lophiomys imhausi*

The crested, or maned, rat lives across eastern African from Somalia and Sudan in the north to Tanzania in the south. Fossil records show that the rodents also once lived as far north as Israel. They are woodland animals and are common in highland areas that rise up on either side of the region's Great Rift Valley.

Crested rats are nocturnal. By day they rest in rock crevices and hollow tree trunks. They are slow movers and, instead of dashing for cover, they have evolved an elaborate array of defensive behaviours to ward off attackers. At first the rats raise their mane to make them appear larger than they really are. The mane also highlights white stripes that point to anal glands under the tail. If the attacker is undeterred, the crested rat will squirt a foul-smelling liquid from those glands. At the same time, the rat snorts and hisses, snaps its teeth and thrashes its body.

If none of this puts the attacker off, the crested rat has one last line of defence. Its skull has a unique structure (it is strengthened with extra bones and has unusual projections over the eye sockets), and it is presumed that this is a defensive adaptation.

*The crested rat has a bristled mane running from the top of the head and merging with the long bushy tail. The females are generally larger than the males.*

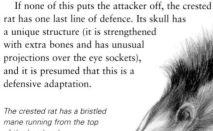

**Distribution**: Eastern Africa including Somalia, Sudan, Ethiopia, Uganda, Kenya and Tanzania.
**Habitat**: Forests and woodlands. Especially common in highland regions.
**Food**: Fruit and roots. The rats hold food in their forepaws.
**Size**: 22–36cm (8.5–14.5in); 750g (26.5oz).
**Maturity**: 1 year.
**Breeding**: 2–3 young in each litter. Probably a single litter produced each year. Newborns are fully haired.
**Life span**: Unknown.
**Status**: Common.

# Gambian pouch rat

*Cricetomys gambianus*

**Distribution:** Sub-Saharan Africa.
**Habitat:** Sheltered areas.
**Food:** Fruits, seeds, leaves and insects.
**Size:** 91cm (35.75in); 4kg (8.75lb).
**Maturity:** 6 months.
**Breeding:** Up to 5 offspring born in summer.
**Life span:** 5 years.
**Status:** Common.

Gambian pouch rats live south of the Sahara Desert, reaching as far south as Zululand in South Africa. They have very little body fat under the skin and so are very susceptible to the cold. They are primarily found in the humid tropical region of Africa where temperatures stay more or less constant all year around. Nevertheless, they are also intolerant of extreme heat, so the rats stay in cool dens tunnelled under the ground during the day.

Although these rats are indeed giant, they are not commonly seen because they do not venture out into the open very much. Instead they search for food under the cover of darkness and populate only those areas that provide plenty of cover. They hoard food in their dens, carrying it back home in cheek pouches.

Gambian pouch rats do not have many natural predators. Adults are rarely preyed upon by anything except humans, who in many parts of Africa traditionally consider the rat to be a delicacy.

*The Gambian pouch rat is the largest rat in the world. Including the tail, it can grow to nearly 1m (3.25ft) long.*

---

**Mouse-like hamster** (*Calomyscus bailwardi*): 10cm (4in); 30g (1oz)
The mouse-like hamster lives in western Asia and south-eastern Europe. Its preferred habitat is highland meadows and it is rarely found below 400m (1,300ft). As its name suggests, the species resembles a mouse in size and body form, but its teeth show that it belongs to a different family. The mouse-like hamster becomes mature at four months and produces one litter of five offspring in summer. Outside of the breeding season, the hamsters are solitary animals. They feed on grains and grasses. In summer they forage for food at night, but in winter, when night temperatures can be very low, they begin to forage in the day.

**Delany's swamp mouse** (*Delanymus brooksi*): 6.5cm (2.5in)
Delany's swamp mouse lives in the eastern half of Central Africa in the marshy forests that grow on mountains. They do not live below 1,700m (5,500ft). They eat seeds and build small nests out of grass that sit in the branches of a shrub. They forage at night. They can climb through the shrubs using flexible feet with opposable toes for gripping and a prehensile tail used as a fifth limb.

# Pouched mouse

*Saccostomus campestris*

The pouched mouse lives in the savannahs and steppes of southern Africa, from Angola and Malawi through to South Africa. It forages on the ground looking for seeds and nuts. It dens under the ground, either by digging its own burrow or by taking over one abandoned by another grassland animal.

Pouched mice are so called because they have cheek pouches, which are used to store food for carrying back to the burrow, where the food is either eaten or stored underground for later consumption. In time of plenty the mice might store nearly three-quarters of everything they find. The stored food is used by nursing mothers, who cannot leave the den until the young are more independent. The stores are also used during droughts when seeds and other plant food are hard to come by. When the food supply is used up and no more food is to be found, the mice enter a torpor, or dormant state similar to hibernation.

Female pouched mice tend to avoid other members of the species, but there is a window of a few hours when females allow males to come near enough to mate. The females then turn violent against the mates. Litters are born 50 days later.

**Distribution:** Southern Africa.
**Habitat:** Grasslands.
**Food:** Seeds.
**Size:** 19cm (7.5in); 85g (3oz).
**Maturity:** Unknown.
**Breeding:** Litters of 5 young born in January–September.
**Life span:** 3 years.
**Status:** Common.

*Pouched mice have bodies built for digging. The legs are short, and the rounded head and small ears make it easier for the mice to move along tunnels.*

## Chestnut climbing mouse

*Dendromus mystacalis*

Chestnut climbing mice live across Africa, south of the Sahara Desert. They are found in grassland areas and shrubs from Somalia to the coast of Nigeria and south to Angola in the west and the northern tip of South Africa in the east. They do not live in desert areas, such as the Kalahari of Namibia and Botswana, and are not found in the dense forests of the Congo Basin.

These mice are closely associated with a short herby weed plant named namirembe. They are also common pests in banana groves and gardens. The mice climb through shrubs and tall grasses in search of food. They spend almost all of their time off the ground, but will cross areas of bare earth if needed.

Chestnut climbing mice build nests from shredded leaves or grasses. The nests are spherical and are suspended from bushes or trees. They have a single entrance and are lined with finely shredded dry leaves.

In equatorial regions most litters of the chestnut climbing mouse are produced between November and January. However, to the north and south, the seasons follow a different pattern and young are produced at other times.

*This species is not always chestnut in colour: the fur can be anything from dark brown to yellow and a few have a pale stripe down the back. The females are slightly smaller than the males.*

**Distribution**: Africa south of the Sahara, from Ethiopia to Nigeria and south to Angola and eastern South Africa. Absent from Namibia.
**Habitat**: Grasslands, farms and scrub. Absent from the tropical rainforests of the Congo.
**Food**: Seeds, grass and insects.
**Size**: 7cm (2.75in); 17g (0.5oz).
**Maturity**: 1 year.
**Breeding**: Litter of 3–4 young born in November–January.
**Life span**: 3 years.
**Status**: Common.

## White-tailed mouse

*Mystromys albicaudatus*

White-tailed mice live in eastern South Africa and Swaziland. Their preferred habitat is dry grassland and semi-desert areas where there are plenty of large cracks in the arid soil. The mice make their burrows in these cracks and hide in them during the day to keep out of the baking heat. At night they emerge to feed.

These mice live in monogamous breeding pairs and produce litters throughout the year. However, they spend much of their time alone, searching for food. Although they forage for seeds and leaves, they will also eat insects when given the opportunity. In laboratory studies they consistently opt for animal food over plant material, but in the wild their diet is likely to consist largely of plant food.

The mice become most active during the short rainy season, when plants are growing at their fastest rate and producing seeds in large numbers. Plants in this habitat have only a short time in which to reproduce and release their seeds, and the white-tailed mouse is used by many as a distributor. The mice digest the seeds' outer coats, and the seeds then pass out in the faeces, ready to germinate.

*The white-tailed mouse has a pale grey upper coat but is white on the belly, and this colour extends on to the whole of the tail. The males are about 25 per cent larger than the females.*

**Distribution**: Eastern South Africa and Swaziland.
**Habitat**: Grassland and semi-desert with dry soils suitable for burrowing.
**Food**: Seeds, leaves and insects. Known to eat dead offspring.
**Size**: 18cm (7in); 87g (3oz).
**Maturity**: 150 days, probably older in the wild.
**Breeding**: Litter of 2–5 young produced every 10 weeks. Breeding pairs are probably monogamous.
**Life span**: 4 years in the wild, double that in captivity.
**Status**: Endangered.

# Malagasy giant rat

*Hypogeomys antimena*

**Distribution**: Western Madagascar.
**Habitat**: Sandy coastal forests.
**Food**: Fallen fruit.
**Size**: 30cm (12in); 1.2kg (2.75lb).
**Maturity**: 1–2 years.
**Breeding**: 1–2 young born in rainy season.
**Life span**: Unknown.
**Status**: Endangered.

Malagasy giant rats live in the deciduous forests that grow along the western coast of Madagascar. These forests are being put under extreme pressure by human activities and have been greatly fragmented. Consequently, the population of giant rats has suffered also and the species is endangered.

Malagasy giant rats dig deep burrows in the sandy forest soil. They have several entrances and reach down 5m (16.5ft) at their deepest point. A burrow is home to a family unit of rats made up of an adult male and female and their offspring from the two previous breeding seasons. Maturing females leave the burrow to set up home nearby, while males migrate further distances to avoid mating with closely related females. Malagasy giant rats mate for life. This strategy ensures that both parents will be present to defend their young against predators. The rats are in considerable danger of being eaten by fossas and boas.

*Both male and female Malagasy giant rats are about the same size. They have long hind feet and sturdy claws, which are used for digging tunnels.*

---

**Grey climbing mouse** (*Dendromus melanotis*): 13cm (5in); 12.5g (0. 5oz)
The grey climbing mouse is a relative of the chestnut climbing mouse. It is found further south than its relative in the drier regions of southern Africa. The grey climbing mouse lives in grasslands and brush from coastal areas to mountainsides. This species has a dark stripe along its back. The tail is long and prehensile and is used when the mouse is climbing through long grass or flimsy branches. The mice move around at night, foraging for insects and seeds. They build their own nests using grasses and leaves but have also been found living in the abandoned nests of weaverbirds and sunbirds.

**Bastard big-footed mouse** (*Macrotarsomys bastardi*): 10cm (4in); 20g (0.75oz)
The bastard big-footed mouse is the smallest Malagasy mouse. It lives in the dry forests of southern and western Madagascar. The species is named after its hind feet, which are more than a third as long as the whole body. The mice live in pairs. They move around by hopping on their large hind feet. By day they lurk in a burrow with the entrance sealed from the inside. At night they forage for plant foods.

# Golden spiny mouse

*Acomys russatus*

Golden spiny mice live in the north-eastern area of the Egyptian desert. Its range spreads into Asia, through the Sinai and across Arabia to Oman and Yemen – a region characterized by its aridity. The spiny golden mouse is most common in areas that receive at least some running water each year. They take up residence in the cracked mud of the banks of dried-up seasonal rivers or in crevices in rock fields. The mice live in greatest numbers in the areas where agriculture is possible. Their population has been boosted in recent years because irrigation has been used to green parts of the desert.

Golden spiny mice eat whatever they can find. They do not need to drink because they can extract moisture from their food. The mice are diurnal, which is unusual for a desert rodent. In many parts of their range, the golden spiny mouse lives alongside a close relative, the Cairo spiny mouse. This second species is nocturnal, and it would appear that this forces the golden spiny mice to forage by day. In places where the Cairo spiny mice do not live, the golden spiny mice become nocturnal.

**Distribution**: Egypt and the Middle East.
**Habitat**: Rocky grassland and deserts.
**Food**: Snails, insects and seeds.
**Size**: 13cm (5in); 45g (1.5oz).
**Maturity**: 3 months.
**Breeding**: Most litters born in wet season.
**Life span**: 3 years.
**Status**: Common.

*This rodent is covered in bristles. These are thickest on the back, where they more resemble spines, but lack a sharp tip. The bristles are tipped with black, making the coat a grizzled brown.*

## Setzer's hairy-footed gerbil

*Gerbillurus setzeri*

This species of hairy-footed gerbil lives in the Namib Desert in Namibia and southern Angola. They dig burrows in the soil of dried river beds, where the top layer is loose gravel washed along by the seasonal flow of water, while deeper layers are damp compacted sand.

The burrows have several entrances and there are numerous branches and chambers off the main tunnel. If the river beds get too crowded, younger gerbils are forced to make less stable homes in sand dunes.

The hairy-footed gerbil avoids the heat of the day by staying underground. If the heat is so intense that even the burrow gets too hot, the rodent spreads saliva over its head and neck to cool itself down. If a predator enters the burrow, a gerbil will thump the ground rapidly with its hind feet to warn others of danger.

The gerbils emerge after sunset to forage for insects and seeds. They move around by jumping. When not feeding, the rodents take sand baths to remove any parasites from their fur.

*This species is one of the largest gerbils. The soles of the feet are covered with hairs to protect the feet against the intense heat of the ground – a feature common among desert creatures.*

**Distribution**: Namib Desert in Namibia from the Kuiseb River as far north as the southern fringe of Angola.
**Habitat**: Areas of desert with gravel soils.
**Food**: Insects, leaves, dried flowers, dried fruits, and seeds.
**Size**: 23cm (9in); 35g (1.25oz).
**Maturity**: Unknown.
**Breeding**: Litters produced all year round.
**Life span**: Unknown.
**Status**: Common.

## Fat-tailed gerbil

*Pachyuromys duprasi*

*Fat-tailed gerbils have shorter tails than other gerbils. The tails, which are club-shaped and lack hairs, act as a storage organ for fat and water, like the hump of a camel.*

Fat-tailed gerbils live in the small desert areas that are scattered across the coastal region of North Africa, west of the Nile to Tunisia and Algeria. They are nocturnal creatures and spend the day in burrows dug up to 1m (3.25ft) into the ground. The gerbils will dig their own burrow if necessary, but often opt to modify a burrow left abandoned by another desert resident. Like other tunnelling creatures, the fat-tailed gerbils play an important ecological role by aerating the upper layers of soil, which makes it easier for plants to put down roots.

A normal burrow contains several individuals. At dusk the fat-tailed gerbils leave their burrows to feed. They generally choose to forage alone. Their diet consists of large amounts of plant material, but they also eat any insects and other invertebrates they find.

During courtship, both sexes are reported to rear up on their hind legs and produce shrieks. This behaviour is often mistaken for fighting.

Fat-tailed gerbils have never been observed giving birth in the wild. Females are pregnant for between two and three weeks. A typical litter comprises between three and nine young. They are hairless and blind when born and raised by the mother in an underground nest. The father plays no part in caring for the young. The young are weaned at the age of three weeks.

**Distribution**: North Africa from Egypt to Libya, Tunisia and Algeria.
**Habitat**: Sandy desert.
**Food**: Insects, such as beetles and crickets, and other invertebrates, such as worms and scorpions.
**Size**: 11cm (4.25in); 37g (1.25oz).
**Maturity**: 3–6 months.
**Breeding**: Litters of up to 9 young born 3 times a year. Captive specimens give birth between April and November.
**Life span**: 5 years, up to 7 years in captivity.
**Status**: Common.

# Libyan jird

*Meriones libycus*

**Distribution**: North Africa and the Middle East.
**Habitat**: Desert depressions.
**Food**: Seeds and grass.
**Size**: 15cm (6in); 85g (3oz).
**Maturity**: Unknown.
**Breeding**: Litters produced several times per year. Gestation is 20 days.
**Life span**: Unknown.
**Status**: Common.

Libyan jirds live across the Middle East, ranging from Iran to Libya in North Africa. They are most common in lowland areas and deep depressions and valleys in the deserts of Egypt and Libya. They make their homes in oasis areas where some vegetation grows.

The jirds are social animals, living in large groups that share communal burrows. Members of the group communicate with each other frequently by stamping their feet and using a series of sounds.

Jirds are largely diurnal and move quickly when out in the open to avoid being targeted by a predator. They are active all year round in warmer parts of the range but may hibernate for a short time in colder regions to the east.

Libyan jirds are very passive and are not easily disturbed when living near to humans. Due to this tolerance, they have become a popular pet. However, many pet owners have found that a peaceful colony of jirds can suddenly turn very violent, with members biting each other, often with fatal results.

*Jirds are relatives of gerbils. This species shares many of the features of a gerbil, except it has a slightly narrower head.*

---

**Sundevall's jird** (*Meriones crassus*): 25cm (9.75in); 70g (2.5oz)
This jird lives in north-west Africa, the Middle East and central Asia. It is a desert creature, living in burrows under sparse vegetation. Like those of other gerbils and jirds, the burrows are a complex network of tunnels connecting several chambers. This jird eats leaves and twigs in winter and seeds in summer, as well as insects and small worms and scorpions. Foraging takes place at night. Food is carried back to the burrow, where most of it is eaten and some is stored for later.

**Angoni vlei rat** (*Otomys angoniensis*): Length unknown; 120g (4.25oz)
The Angoni vlei rat lives in South Africa. It is a medium to large rat and has red-brown fur that is paler at the throat. The rat survives in a range of habitats from dry grasslands and semi-deserts to wet mountain habitats. It is most common in moister areas, where it forages for grasses, roots and bark. The Angoni vlei rat is generally diurnal and spends most of the time alone. Only while breeding will the rat form pairs for a short while. Mature at four months, the Angoni vlei rat can produce up to 15 young in a year in three litters.

# Fat sand rat

*Psammomys obesus*

Fat sand rats live across the Sahara Desert of North Africa, from Mauritania to northern Sudan and Egypt, as well as in parts of the Arabian Peninsula. They are ground-dwelling animals, most commonly found in sandy areas but also occupying rocky deserts, scree and salt marshes. They dig burrows close to food sources.

These animals are active during the day unless it gets too hot at this time, at which point they switch to foraging at night. During colder periods they spend a long time basking in the sun to warm up before feeding. Males have a territory that overlaps those of several other males. Each adult has a complex burrow with several chambers for storing food or waste.

Fat sand rats eat succulent plants that store water in their leaves. This water is often very salty, which would cause problems for most mammals that consumed it, but fat sand rats have very efficient kidneys that can remove all the excess salt.

A male fat sand rat occupies a territory that covers the home range of several females. He mates with all the females, who produce up to seven young between December and April. Most females produce three or four litters per year.

**Distribution**: North Africa and Arabia.
**Habitat**: Deserts.
**Food**: Succulent plants.
**Size**: 19cm (7.5in); 200g (7oz).
**Maturity**: 4 months.
**Breeding**: Up to 4 litters produced in December–April.
**Life span**: 2–3 years.
**Status**: Common.

*Fat sand rats resemble gerbils in some ways, such as having a tufted tail. This rodent also has black skin under its fur to protect the body from the desert sunlight.*

# Wood mouse

*Apodemus sylvaticus*

The wood mouse, also often referred to as the long-tailed field mouse, is the most common wild mouse in Europe. It lives right across the continent except in the far north of Scandinavia. It is found on the British Isles including the smaller, surrounding islands. The wood mouse also ranges across northern Asia except the cold northern regions and is found south of the Himalayas and as far east as the Altai Mountains of northern China. The mice also live in north-western Africa.

With such a wide distribution, it is not surprising that wood mice are able to survive well in several habitats – anywhere with places for the mice to shelter, such as meadows, woodlands, gardens and cultivated fields. They do occupy houses and other buildings on occasion, especially during cold periods, but generally they dig themselves deep burrows and line them with dried leaves. Newborns are raised in the den for the first three weeks.

Long-tailed field mice are excellent swimmers, climbers and jumpers and can forage successfully almost anywhere. They have typical self-sharpening rodent teeth so are able to tackle most foods. They are most active in the twilight of dawn and dusk.

*The wood mouse has large eyes so it can see well at night time and a long nose that is sensitive enough to smell seeds buried underground. The mouse has a long tail but it is not prehensile.*

**Distribution**: British Isles, mainland Europe, North Africa and northern and eastern Asia.
**Habitat**: Meadows and woodlands. Sometimes live in homes or other buildings, especially during winter.
**Food**: Roots, fruits, seeds and insects.
**Size**: 15cm (6in).
**Maturity**: 2 months.
**Breeding**: 4–7 young born in litters produced up to 4 times a year. Gestation period is about 3 years.
**Life span**: 1 year.
**Status**: Common.

# African grass rat

*Arvicanthis niloticus*

African grass rats live in the fertile areas of Egypt and Sudan around the Nile River Valley. They also follow the Blue Nile into Ethiopia and range in the other direction as far west as Mali. The mice's range also continues south to Central Africa, although it does not continue further south than that.

The African grass rat lives in colonial burrows that are dug under well-covered ground, be it by brush, rocks or even a termite mound. These conditions exist in a range of habitats across the rat's range. The burrows run at just 20cm (8in) below the surface and have several entrances, where the residents are often seen associating. They all help to maintain the runways that lead from the burrow's entrances to foraging grounds. These runways are most obvious during the dry season, when grass is trimmed. It is thought that runways serve as high-speed escape routes that lead rats to the burrow when predators appear.

There are equal numbers of males and females in a colony of grass rats. Breeding takes place after the dry season in March. Females are pregnant for three weeks. The newborn females stay in the colony, while the males leave after the age of about three months.

*Male African grass rats are slightly larger than the females. The hind feet are long and used for digging, while the forefeet are smaller with a small opposable thumb that makes them relatively dexterous.*

**Distribution**: Nile River Valley from Egypt to Ethiopia, Sudan and to the Great Lakes region of East Africa. The population extends west to Mali and south to Central Africa.
**Habitat**: Grassland, semi-desert and woodland.
**Food**: Grasses, stems, seeds and bark.
**Size**: 13cm (5in); 120g (4.25oz).
**Maturity**: 4 months.
**Breeding**: About 5 young born in a litter produced after the dry season.
**Life span**: 1 year.
**Status**: Common.

**Black rat** (*Rattus rattus*): 16–22cm (6.25–8.5in); 70–300g (2.5–10.5oz)
Thought to be originally from India, the black rat, also known as the house rat or ship rat, is now one of the most common rodents in the world. It is found wherever humans have settled, including across Europe and Africa. It even survives in Arctic settlements. A few have travelled to Antarctica with human explorers and scientists, but no sustainable population exists on that cold continent. The secret of the black rat's success is its adaptability. Its medium-sized body makes it a good climber, jumper, swimmer and runner; its long teeth allow it to tackle almost any food it comes across, and its high intelligence means that it can investigate areas quickly and remember where suitable food sources can be found. The black rat will forever be remembered for spreading the Black Death – a disease passed to humans by the rat's fleas.

**Brown rat** (*Rattus norvegicus*): 40cm (15.7in); 140–500g (5–17.5oz)
Like the black rat, the brown rat has spread from its native forest habitat in China to become one of the most common rodents in the world. Travelling with human migrants, this species, also known as the Norway rat, is now common on all continents except Antarctica. Considerably larger than the black rat, brown rats still share the characteristics that make its relative such a success. A female brown rat can produce 60 offspring in one year if the conditions are right, which shows just how quickly these rodents can take over a new habitat.

## Eurasian harvest mouse

*Micromys minutus*

The Eurasian harvest mouse is a little rodent that lives across temperate parts of Europe from northern Spain to Russia. Its range extends into Asia, running through Siberia as far east as Korea. The mouse occupies areas of tall grass and consequently is a common resident of fields of cereal crops, including rice paddies.

Eurasian harvest mice each occupy a territory. These overlap, but the mice will avoid coming into contact with each other. When cold weather forces the mice to seek shelter, they congregate in the same place and become more tolerant of each other. Each mouse builds a nest out of grasses, where they sleep for about three hours at a time. Each sleep period is followed by a similar time spent foraging.

**Distribution**: Europe and northern Asia. Northern limit of range is the Arctic Circle.
**Habitat**: Tall grasses.
**Food**: Seeds, fruits and grains.
**Size**: 7cm (2.75in); 11g (0.5oz).
**Maturity**: 35 days.
**Breeding**: Litter of 3–8 young born every 20 days.
**Life span**: 6 months.
**Status**: Common.

*The Eurasian harvest mouse has large ears that allow it to hear the slightest sound. The tail is prehensile and provides extra support while the mouse is climbing.*

## House mouse

*Mus musculus*

**Distribution**: Every continent of the world, including Antarctica.
**Habitat**: Generally near human habitation.
**Food**: Waste food, insects plant matter.
**Size**: 15–19cm (6–7.5in); 17–25g (0.04–0.05lb).
**Maturity**: 5–7 weeks.
**Breeding**: Usually around 5–10 litters of 3–12 offspring during the year.
**Life span**: 12–18 months.
**Status**: Abundant.

The key to the house mouse's phenomenal success as a species is its ability to follow humans around the globe, and the way it is able to make use of whatever food sources people provide. By stowing away on ships and, latterly, aeroplanes, house mice have been able to colonize every continent of the world.

Mice were first domesticated, and in some instances worshipped, by the Romans and ancient Greeks. However, these days house mice are considered to be a major pest. They cause billions of dollars' worth of damage to food stores worldwide every year. They also damage buildings, woodwork, furniture and clothing, and are known to carry various dangerous diseases, including typhus and salmonella.

However, house mice are virtually unrivalled by other mammals in their capacity to adapt to new surroundings. Their generalist habits, rapid breeding rate and talent for slipping into places unnoticed have enabled the house mouse to become possibly the most numerous mammal in the world today.

*A common sight all over the world, the house mouse is capable of making the most of any opportunity.*

## Gundi

*Ctenodactylus gundi*

The North African gundi lives in parts of Morocco, Algeria, Tunisia and Libya. They are found in arid areas that have plenty of rocky outcrops and also survive on the slopes of the region's mountains.

Gundis resemble guinea pigs, but are more closely related to mice and squirrels. They live in large colonies. The size and area occupied by each colony is dependent on the amount of food available. A gundi colony is divided up into territories controlled by a family unit. A family may be made up of an adult male and female and their offspring, though other families are matriarchies, with several adult females and their young.

The families den under rocks, which are a useful heating system: warming up slowly during the day, so that the den stays cool, then cooling more slowly at night than the surrounding land so that the den stays warm. In cold weather gundi huddle together for warmth. To warm up in the morning, they bask on sunny rocks before feeding.

A female gundi is pregnant for about 40 days during the dry season. She produces a litter of two young. Unusually for rodents, the newborns are fully furred with their eyes open.

**Distribution**: North Africa from south-eastern Morocco, northern Algeria, Tunisia and the Libyan Desert.
**Habitat**: Deserts with many rocky outcrops.
**Food**: Leaves, seeds and stems.
**Size**: 16–20cm (6.25–8in); 175–195g (6.25–6.75oz).
**Maturity**: Unknown.
**Breeding**: 2 young born fully furred. Gestation is 40 days, young are weaned in 4 weeks.
**Life span**: 3–4 years.
**Status**: Common.

*Gundis are small diurnal rodents that have very short legs, flat ears, big eyes and long whiskers. Their long but thin fur makes their bodies appear to be almost spherical in windy conditions.*

## Lesser-Egyptian jerboa

*Jaculus jaculus*

The lesser-Egyptian jerboa is distributed from Morocco to central Asia. It lives in desert areas and rocky meadows. Like other jerboas, this little rodent is nocturnal in habit to avoid the intense heat of the day. The jerboas are solitary foragers and live alone in a burrow dug into compacted sand or under rocks. The burrows follow a clockwise spiral and go down to a depth of about 1.2m (4ft). Each burrow has two or three entrances and the nest area is located at the deepest point.

Lesser-Egyptian jerboas stay in the burrow during the hottest and driest periods of the year. Without eating, they enter a dormant state similar to hibernation but called aestivation because it is a response to heat rather than cold.

Being able to jump 1m (3.25ft) in a single bound, the jerboas can forage over a huge area for such a small creature. Some have been found 10km (6 miles) from their burrow.

Males mate with several females but a female jerboa probably mates only once. Breeding takes place twice a year at six monthly intervals.

**Distribution**: North Africa, the Middle East and central Asia.
**Habitat**: Deserts and semi-deserts with areas of sand and stone.
**Food**: Roots, grass, seeds and insects. They do not drink liquid water and get all they need from their food.
**Size**: 10cm (4in); 55g (2oz).
**Maturity**: 8–12 months.
**Breeding**: 2 litters of 3 young produced in late summer and early winter. The gestation period is 25 days.
**Life span**: 2 years.
**Status**: Common.

*The lesser-Egyptian jerboa is the smallest of the desert-living jerboas. It is built like a kangaroo, with long hind feet that are used for hopping. The hind legs may be three-quarters of the length of the body. The long tail helps the rodent balance while jumping.*

**Mzab gundi** (*Massoutiera mzabi*): 24cm (9.5in);
195g (6.75oz)
This species, also known as Sahara gundis, lives
in the heart of the Sahara Desert of Algeria,
northern Chad, Mali and southern Libya. They
are sand-coloured and have plenty of long fur
to protect them against the extreme cold of
the desert night. They are diurnal creatures,
spending the night in crevices between rocks,
and have long whiskers to help them orientate
themselves in the darkness. Mzab gundis
forage for plant food that is on or growing
out of the ground.

**Four-toed jerboa** (*Allactaga tetradactyla*):
26cm (10.25in); 52g (1.75oz)
This large jerboa lives in the deserts of Libya
and Egypt and across the Middle East to central
Asia. They live in coastal salt marshes and semi-
desert areas. By day they lurk in burrows before
foraging for seeds and other plant foods at night.
The jerboas hibernate in cooler parts of their
range, especially in central Asia. They dig deeper
and more complex burrows for the winter.

**Cameroon scaly-tail** (*Zenkerella insignis*):
22cm (8.75in); 220g (7.75oz)
This species of squirrel is related to the gliding
scaly-tailed squirrels: it has the scales on
the tail but lacks the gliding membrane, and
consequently cannot glide from tree to tree.
The scaly-tail lives in Cameroon and Gabon. It
rarely leaves the high canopy of the rainforest,
where it feeds on mainly bark. It is a diurnal
animal, unlike its gliding relatives, which are
all nocturnal foragers.

# Forest dormouse

*Dryomys nitedula*

Forest dormice live across Eurasia from
northern Europe to Japan, where they are
most often seen in thick forests made up of
a mixture of deciduous trees and evergreen
conifers. The species also survives in the
rocky groves of North Africa.

 These animals rarely leave the trees.
They can climb well and are good jumpers,
regularly making leaps of up to 2m (6.5ft).
They are nocturnal and retreat to a nest of
leaves built in the trees. The dormice do not
just sleep in the nest; instead they become
torpid, and enter a more dormant state than
sleep, which saves the animal's energy. This
state is similar to hibernation, although it
lasts only a few hours.

 The forest dormouse does not hibernate
in the normal sense of the word, but it does
have long winter sleeps curled up into
tight balls resting on its hind
feet. In warmer regions, these
sleeps are short or absent, while
in other milder places the
dormouse will wake regularly
for foraging trips.

**Distribution**: Eurasia from
northern Europe to Japan.
**Habitat**: Deciduous forests.
**Food**: Flowers, fruits and
nuts.
**Size**: 13cm (5in); 34g
(1.25oz).
**Maturity**: 1 year.
**Breeding**: Up to 3 litters
each year.
**Life span**: 5 years.
**Status**: Lower risk.

*The forest dormouse has a long, muscular body
that is more similar to a squirrel's than a mouse's.
This helps it to climb more easily through trees. The
tail is bushy but flatter than a squirrel's.*

# Lord Derby's scaly-tailed squirrel

*Anomalurus derbianus*

**Distribution**: West and
Central Africa.
**Habitat**: Rainforests.
**Food**: Bark, fruit, leaves,
flowers and nuts.
**Size**: 40cm (15.75in); 1.1kg
(2.5lb).
**Maturity**: Unknown.
**Breeding**: Up to 3 young
born each year.
**Life span**: Unknown.
**Status**: Common.

The scaly-tailed squirrels are named after rows of scales
on the underside of the tail near the base. This species lives
in the rainforest of Central Africa.

 The squirrels glide (not fly) with their arms, legs and tails
extended, stretching out the membranes. They can travel
up to 250m (820ft) in this way. The scales on their tails
are used as anchors, hooking on to the rough trunks of
trees to prevent them from skidding when they land.
These squirrels are almost helpless on the ground.
They spend their time climbing into the treetops to
feed on a range of plants. They then glide down
to another suitable feeding tree and repeat the process.
Gliding is also a useful escape technique. However,
it also draws attention to the squirrel, so the rodent
will scurry out of sight as soon as it lands.

*Lord Derby's scaly-tailed squirrel is one of several so-called
flying squirrels in Africa. It has a gliding membrane – a fold
of skin that connects the front and back limbs on each side
– which is hairy on top but largely naked underneath.*

## Blesmoles

*Georychus capensis*

*Blesmoles have bodies built for tunnelling: they have short legs and rounded bodies. The large front teeth are used for gnawing through the soil as well as for feeding. Males and females are generally about the same size, although members of both sexes may grow to a giant size with twice the average weight.*

Blesmoles are also called Cape mole rats. They live in areas of the Cape Province in south-western South Africa. They tunnel through hard, compacted soil in search of tubers and similar root storage organs and can be a destructive pest of root crops.

These animals live alone and build their own burrows. They loosen soil with their front teeth and then push it past the body with their feet. They tunnel for food and will also eat any insects that they come across as they dig with their teeth. The mole rats will avoid coming into contact with other moles if they break into an extant burrow. The tunnels will cover up to 10 per cent of the surface area, so it is common for burrows to connect.

The males drum their feet against the floor of the tunnel to advertise their presence. This has the dual effect of keeping rivals away and also attracting females in the breeding season.

After a pregnancy of seven weeks, females produce between three to five naked young. The newborns are weaned after just 17 days.

**Distribution**: South Africa.
**Habitat**: Grasslands areas with hard soils.
**Food**: Underground tubers (plant storage organs).
**Size**: 20cm (8in); 180g (6.25oz).
**Maturity**: 10 months for both sexes.
**Breeding**: 3–5 young born in August to December. The gestation period is 44 days.
**Life span**: 3 years, although probably less in the wild.
**Status**: Common.

## African mole rat

*Cryptomys hottentotus*

African mole rats live on or rather under the plains of the Cape Province of South Africa. The rats spend their whole lives underground, tunnelling beneath grasslands where they eat tubers, bulbs and roots.

These animals live in complex societies, with a dozen or so rats sharing a network of tunnels. Most of the social group are adults, though only one pair of these adults is able to breed. The other adults are non-breeding workers who maintain tunnels, dig for food and fight off predators. In this way the society is similar to those of ants and termites, where all members of the group work to raise the offspring of a single female – a system known as eusociality. The breeding couple suppress the reproductive systems of the rest of the group using a chemical released in their urine.

Each group's members are all related, with the workers being sons and daughters of the breeders. Older mole rats, perhaps the breeders' brothers, sisters and cousins, do not do as much work as the younger ones. They are larger and spend time at the edge of the burrow where they lie ready to defend it. If attacked, the defender may be abandoned as the workers block up the tunnel behind him.

**Distribution**: South-western region of Cape Province in South Africa.
**Habitat**: Soil beneath areas of grasslands.
**Food**: Roots, tubers, bulbs and other underground plant storage organs, herbs and grasses.
**Size**: 16cm (6.25in); 90g (3.25oz).
**Maturity**: Unknown, some individuals will not breed.
**Breeding**: 2 litters of up to 5 pups each year. Gestation is 44 days.
**Life span**: Unknown in the wild but captive mole rats live for about 10 years.
**Status**: Common.

*The body of an African mole rat forms a sturdy cylinder. The limbs are short so that they can move back and forth relatively easily inside narrow tunnels. The rats are blind but their bodies are covered in long, touch-sensitive hairs that work in the same way as whiskers.*

# Naked mole rat

*Heterocephalus glaber*

Naked mole rats live in societies which are more like social insects' colonies than those of other mammals. They live an entirely underground existence, and colonies can occupy 4km (2.5 miles) of tunnels, which are dug out by the rodents' claws and incisors. Some of these tunnels run just beneath the surface of the ground; others descend up to 2m (6.5ft) deep.

Like colonies of bees and ants, naked mole rat colonies are governed by queens, which give birth to the young. The queens are the largest individuals in the colonies, which usually comprise around 70 animals, but can number 300. The other individuals – the workers and drones – are separated into castes depending on their size. The members of each different caste have their own particular jobs, for example foraging, tunnel maintenance, caring for the young or nest defence.

Naked mole rats are the only mammals that have lost the ability to produce their own body heat. Instead, they bask in shallow tunnels warmed by the sun, or huddle together to keep warm.

*As their name suggests, naked mole rats are almost hairless, with the pinkish skin showing through. They use their strong incisors and large claws for digging tunnels. These rodents are virtually blind.*

**Distribution**: Kenya, Ethiopia and Somalia.
**Habitat**: Underground in arid savannah and grassland.
**Food**: Underground parts of plants, particularly the succulent tubers.
**Size**: 6–10cm (2.25–4in); 25–70g (0.05–0.15lb).
**Maturity**: 1 year.
**Breeding**: Usually about 12 young per litter, with 8 litters per year.
**Life span**: Over 20 years.
**Status**: Common.

**East African mole rats** (Tachyoryctinae subfamily): 16–31cm (6.25–12.25in); 160–930g (5.5–32.75oz)
There are 13 species of East African mole rat. They are found in Somalia and Ethiopia and across the Great Lakes region to the eastern part of the Democratic Republic of Congo. They live in woodlands, grassland and cultivated areas. They are mole-like in shape and spend most of their time in tunnels. Their tunnel networks are complex and they are constantly being expanded as the rats dig for food. The rats dig deep bolt-holes to hide in when predators, such as the Ethiopian wolf, attack. Other chambers are used for storing waste food and faeces. In cold weather this material produces heat as it rots and warms the burrow.

**Blind mole rats** (Spalacinae subfamily): 13–35cm (5–13.75in); 100–570g (3.5–20oz)
Another group of tunnelling mole rats, the blind mole rats live under the grasslands and woodlands of south-eastern Europe, the Middle East and north-eastern Africa. Their eyes are covered in skin because they are of no use underground, where the animals eat roots, though the rats do emerge on the surface from time to time to forage for leaves. They rely on their sense of hearing to detect other rats and approaching predators. They communicate with grunts and hisses and butt the ceilings of the tunnels with their heads to attract mates. This head banging produces low-frequency vibrations on the soil, which the rat's ears are highly attuned to detecting.

# Springhare

*Pedetes capensis*

Hopping is a very efficient way to travel, and it allows springhares to bound rapidly around the African savannah at night. Usually they do not move too far from their burrows, but during times of drought they have been known to travel up to 40km (25 miles) in search of water.

Springhares have incredibly keen senses. As well as having fantastic sight, scent and hearing, they use their huge back feet to pick up vibrations from the earth.

Springhares need all their senses to be able to avoid the long list of predators that would happily make meals of them. They are small enough to be manageable for wild cats, jackals, ratels and large owls, but big enough to interest larger predators, such as lions and leopards, should they get close enough to be able to catch them.

*Rather like a small kangaroo, the bizarre springhare is in a family all of its own.*

**Distribution**: Southern and eastern Africa.
**Habitat**: Grasslands with sandy soil.
**Food**: Vegetation, mainly bulbs and grasses.
**Size**: 35–45cm (13.75–17.75in); 4kg (8.75lb).
**Maturity**: 1 year.
**Breeding**: Around 3 or 4 young per litter, with litters born about every 100 days.
**Life span**: 10 years.
**Status**: Common and widespread.

# Red squirrel

*Sciurus vulgaris*

*Red squirrels can be quite variable in colour, with some individuals being jet black, while others are strawberry blonde. The bushy tail helps them to balance in the treetops. These arboreal rodents are very acrobatic.*

The red squirrel has undergone a well-documented decline in Britain due to its not being able to compete with the larger and more robust grey squirrel, which was introduced from North America. The two species actually hardly ever come to blows, and it is thought that the main problem may be that the grey squirrels harbour a viral infection that decimates red squirrels whilst leaving the greys unaffected.

These animals tend to be most active during early mornings and late afternoons. They rest in the middle of the day. As winter sets in, the squirrels rapidly put on weight, and settle down for a long period of inactivity. Squirrels do not truly hibernate. They never let their body temperatures drop, and they regularly wake up to stretch their legs, drink and feed from food caches made in the autumn.

Red squirrels are mainly solitary animals, and apart from when there is a large concentration of food readily available, the only time they get together in any numbers is when the females become ready to breed. Male squirrels fight over them at this time.

**Distribution**: Europe and Asia.
**Habitat**: Primarily coniferous forests.
**Food**: Seeds and nuts when available, and also fungi, eggs, flowers and tree sap.
**Size**: 25–35cm (10–13.75in); up to 350g (0.75lb).
**Maturity**: 9–10 months.
**Breeding**: 2 litters of 5–7 young per year.
**Life span**: 4–6 years.
**Status**: Rare in the UK, common elsewhere.

# Grey squirrel

*Sciurus carolinensis*

Grey squirrels are native to the open woodlands of eastern North America. They have also been introduced into several parts of northern Europe, where they have begun to out-compete the smaller red squirrels for food and breeding sites.

These animals feed primarily on the nuts and buds of many woodland trees. In summer, when they are most active just after dawn and before dusk, grey squirrels also eat insects. In winter, when most animals of their size are hibernating, grey squirrels spend their days eating stores of food that they had buried throughout the previous summer. Grey squirrels may make dens in hollow trees, but are more likely to make nests, or dreys, from twigs and leaves in the boughs of trees.

There are two breeding seasons each year: one beginning in midwinter, the other in midsummer. Males begin to chase a female through the trees a few days before they are receptive to mating. One female may be chased by several males at once. When females are ready, their vulvas become pink and engorged. Litters of three are born six weeks later.

*Grey squirrels have, as their name suggests, greyish fur, although many individuals have reddish patches. Their tails, which have many white hairs, are bushier than those of most other squirrels.*

**Distribution**: South-eastern Canada and eastern United States. The species has been introduced to Britain and northern Europe and is now the most common species in deciduous forests.
**Habitat**: Woodlands, parks and gardens.
**Food**: Nuts, seeds, flowers and buds.
**Size**: 38–52cm (15–20.5in); 300–700g (10.5–24.5oz).
**Maturity**: 10 months.
**Breeding**: 2 litters each year with 2–4 young per litter after a gestation of 3 months. Mating takes place in late summer and winter. Breeding is later in a cold winter.
**Life span**: 12 years.
**Status**: Common.

# Siberian flying squirrel

*Pteromys volans*

**Distribution**: Scandinavia, Russia and northern Asia.
**Habitat**: Forests.
**Food**: Fruit, seeds and leaves.
**Size**: 12–23cm (4.75–9in).
**Maturity**: 1 year.
**Breeding**: 2 litters born in spring and summer.
**Life span**: Unknown.
**Status**: Lower risk.

These animals live across northern Asia. Their range extends from Scandinavia in the west to the Pacific coast of China in the east. The squirrels live in forests of aspen, birch and coniferous trees. This type of forest grows in cold lowland areas and is often referred to as taiga.

Siberian flying squirrels nest in tree hollows. They stay in the nests during the day and leave them by night to look for food, such as young leaves, berries and seeds. In lean winter months, the rodents survive on less nutritious foods, such as nuts and pinecones.

The squirrels rarely touch the ground. They have short legs that are not well suited to walking on all fours, so instead the squirrels climb up tree trunks and then glide on their outstretched membranes across gaps in the forest. Without a rear membrane between the hind legs, the Siberian flying squirrel must adopt a different posture to other flying squirrels when in flight. The forelimbs point out sideways, as is normal, but the hind legs are held backwards. This gives the gliding squirrel an unusual triangular shape.

*Unlike many species of flying squirrel, the Siberian variety does not have a gliding membrane connecting its hind limbs to the base of the tail. Instead, all the gliding is done using membranes between the forelimbs and hind legs.*

---

**African pygmy squirrel**
(*Myosciurus pumilio*): 7.5cm (3in).
The African pygmy squirrel is the smallest squirrel in the world: it is about as large as a person's thumb and the tail is about two-thirds of the length of the body. It lives high up in the forests of West and Central Africa and is also found on the island of Bioko. Pygmy squirrels are omnivores: in addition to plant food they also eat ants and termites.

**Gambian sun squirrel**
(*Heliosciurus gambianus*):
15–21cm (6–8.25in); 250–340g (8.75–12oz)
Gambian sun squirrels live in the woodlands of Central Africa. This habitat is found between the dry savannah south of the Sahara and the rainforests of the Congo Basin. Despite their name, Gambia is the western limit of their range, and the squirrels are found right across Africa to Kenya. Gambian sun squirrels live in the branches of trees. They also make foraging trips into lusher rainforests. There are at least seven subspecies of Gambian sun squirrel, each with its own distinctive colouring.

# Striped ground squirrel

*Xerus erythropus*

The striped ground squirrel is also known as Geoffrey's ground squirrel. It is a common species that lives along the fringes of North Africa's Sahara Desert. It is especially common in the grasslands of the Sahel along the desert's southern fringe.

This animal is a sturdy rodent. It is named after the pale stripes that run from both shoulders along the side of the body to the rump. The squirrel has long claws, which are used for digging burrows.

Striped ground squirrels live in colonies of about ten squirrels. Most of the group are females, the rest are their young. Adult males are allowed to join the group only when the females are ready to mate. Litters are produced at all times of year, but all the females in a group come into season at the same time.

Members of a group communicate with sounds such as chirps and squeaks. They also let each other know how they are feeling using their long and bushy tails. Relaxed squirrels drag the tail along the ground; frightened squirrels hold the tail straight out behind them; while a squirrel that is alert will curl its tail over its back.

**Distribution**: North Africa.
**Habitat**: Dry savannah.
**Food**: Nuts, leaves, fruit, leaves and small animals.
**Size**: 20–46cm (8–18in); 300–945g (10.5–33.25oz).
**Maturity**: 1 year.
**Breeding**: Colony's females produce litters of 3 young all at the same time.
**Life span**: 2 years.
**Status**: Common.

*The colour of the striped ground squirrel's fur often matches that of the surrounding soil. The squirrels may have a mixture of red, yellow and grey hairs. The flattened tail is always darker than the rest of the body.*

# Cape porcupine

*Hystrix africaeaustralis*

The Cape porcupine shares its habitat with a whole array of dangerous predators, but its sharp quills can repel even lions and hyenas. A mane of long, white bristles runs down the neck to the back. The rodent has special hollow quills attached to its tail, which can be rattled together as a warning to any unsuspecting animal that gets too close for comfort. Covering the lower back are 40cm (16in) long quills, equipped with tiny barbs. These quills are only loosely held in the skin and will embed themselves easily into any animal attempting to attack.

Porcupines have keen hearing and an excellent sense of smell, which they use to locate nutritious bulbs underground. The Cape porcupines, like other rodents, also chew bones from carcasses to obtain calcium, phosphorus and other essential minerals. Chewing bones also helps to keep their incisor teeth sharp.

Porcupines will often share burrows, forming clans comprising adult pairs and up to four offspring of varying ages. Members of the clan share common runs, trails and latrines, and also common feeding sites and refuges.

**Distribution**: Widespread in Africa south of the Sahara Desert.
**Habitat**: Grassland.
**Food**: Roots, bark, herbs and fruit.
**Size**: 0.7–1m (2.25–3.25ft); up to 17kg (37.5lb).
**Maturity**: 9 months.
**Breeding**: Mated females produce up to 2 offspring at a time.
**Life span**: Up to 20 years.
**Status**: Endangered in some parts of its range, but common elsewhere.

*The Cape porcupine has the longest quills of any species of porcupine in the world.*

# North African crested porcupine

*Hystrix cristata*

*Like other porcupines, the North African species has thickened hairs on its back that form sharp quills. These quills, which form a crest along the back and neck, are meant as a deterrent to attackers. Thicker quills also stick out from the sides and back.*

The North African crested porcupine is most common along the coast of North Africa and through eastern Africa to the fringes of the Congo's equatorial rainforests. The species is also found in Sicily and Italy, but is very rare in that country.

This animal is able to adapt to a range of habitats, from dense forest to deserts and mountain meadows. It finds shelter in abandoned burrows and caves, but will also dig its own den if required. Adults pair up for life and live in small family groups.

Crested porcupines are nocturnal, although they will stay in when the moon is bright to avoid predators. At other times, they rely on their armoury of quills to protect them. Unlike other Old World porcupines, this species has a rattle of quills on its tail, which is used to warn off predators. The porcupine also raises a crest of quills to make itself look larger. If the predator continues to attack, the porcupine charges at them backwards, stabbing the attacker with a quill.

**Distribution**: Central and North Africa and southern Italy.
**Habitat**: Forests, rocky areas and fields.
**Food**: Roots, bulbs, fruit, bark and grasses. Porcupines also gnaw on bones.
**Size**: 60–93cm (23.5–36.5in); 10–30kg (22–66lb).
**Maturity**: 2 years.
**Breeding**: 1 litter per year.
**Life span**: Up to 20 years but probably less.
**Status**: Common.

# Greater cane rat

*Thryonomys swinderianus*

**Distribution**: Africa south of the Sahara Desert from Gambia and Sudan to Namibia and eastern South Africa. Absent from Cape Province.
**Habitat**: River and marsh banks. Also common in plantations and irrigated fields.
**Food**: Grasses and sugar cane.
**Size**: 48cm (19in); 4.5kg (10lb).
**Maturity**: 1 year.
**Breeding**: 2 litters of 4 young produced in rainy season.
**Life span**: 4 years.
**Status**: Common.

The greater cane rat is found across Africa south of the Sahara Desert. The southern extent of its range is the dry grasslands of Namibia and South Africa. Cane rats are grass eaters. In this context, "cane" is a general term for the tall reed-like grasses that grow on river banks and in shallow water. The rats fell these tall stems using their large incisors.

Like all rodents, the rat's incisors grow continuously. They are worn down by the tough plant food so they never get too long. (The teeth are also self-sharpening: with each bite, the lower teeth cut a chisel-edge on the upper teeth.) The cane rat's teeth make a characteristic chattering sound as they bite through the grasses. As well as grass, greater cane rats eat bark and fallen fruits. They are also well equipped to tackle crops such as sugar cane and corn.

These animals live in small groups made up of a single male, several females and any offspring under one year old. The rodents feed at night and make simple nests among the grass to rest in during the day. The rats escape from danger by jumping into the water. They also warn other rats by stamping their hind feet and grunting.

*Although they are called rats, cane rats are more closely related to porcupines and guinea pigs. They are sometimes called grasscutters. The greater cane rat has brown fur with several flattened bristles growing on the back.*

# Dassie rat

*Petromus typicus*

**Distribution**: Angola, Namibia and western South Africa.
**Habitat**: Rocky hillsides and deserts.
**Food**: Flowers, seeds and leaves.
**Size**: 14–21cm (5.5–8.25in); 170–300g (6–10.5oz).
**Maturity**: 9 months.
**Breeding**: Single litter of up to 3 young born in February or March – the start of the rainy season – after a gestation period of 3 months.
**Life span**: Unknown.
**Status**: Lower risk.

This species of rat is the only member of the Petromuridae family of rodents. This name literally means "rock mouse", but dassie rats are not closely related to mice. Nor is the species a badger, despite the fact that the name dassie means "badger" in Afrikaans. In fact, the dassie rat isn't even a rat, but rather a distant relative of guinea pigs, chinchillas and other rodents that are now found mainly in South America. The rodent's closest African relatives are the cane rats.

Dassie rats live in the rocky semi-deserts of southern Angola, Namibia and western South Africa. They spend the night in small crevices among rocks. They are most active during the early morning and late afternoon, when they forage for plant food. The rats are unique among rodents because they regurgitate their food for a second chew. As with cattle chewing their cud, this helps to break down the tough plant food.

The animals lie flat on rocks and bask in the sun. At the slightest hint of danger, they dart for cover, squeezing into the nearest rock crevice. Females give birth to a small litter and have teats on their sides so that they can suckle their young even when squashed into a narrow space.

*The dassie rat's fur is grey and brown to blend in with the rocks of its habitat. It has short legs, which it often stretches out when jumping. As with a flying squirrel, this helps the rat to travel a little farther with each leap. The soft and silky coat has no insulating underfur, unlike most mammals.*

# RABBITS

*There are 54 species of rabbit and hare, all of which belong to the same family, the Leporidae. They are found in many parts of the world, and some species have been introduced to areas well outside their original range. Strictly speaking, "hare" is the name given to members of the genus* Lepus, *while all other species in the family are referred to as rabbits.*

## Brown hare

*Lepus europaeus*

Unlike rabbits, hares do not live in burrows. They spend most of the time alone, although a few may be seen together at good feeding sites. Hares are mostly active by night. During the day they crouch in small hollows in the grass called forms, sometimes leaving their backs just visible over the vegetation. In Europe, the main breeding season is in spring, and at this time hares can often be seen during the day, with males fighting one another and pursuing females.

A number of predators target hares, and in Europe these include foxes and eagles. If a predator detects a hare, the hare flees, running at speeds of up to 60kph (37mph) and making sharp, evasive turns. Injured or captured hares are known to make high-pitched screams.

In order to reduce the risk of losing all of their young leverets to predators, females hide them in different locations in specially dug forms, and visit them one by one to nurse them. Although brown hares are common, changing farming practices have caused a decline in hare numbers in some countries, such as Britain.

*Brown hares are easily distinguishable from European rabbits by their larger size and longer ears and limbs.*

**Distribution**: Southern Scandinavia, northern Spain and Britain to Siberia and north-western Iran.
**Habitat**: Grasslands and agricultural land.
**Food**: Grass, herbs, crop plants and occasionally twigs and bark.
**Size**: 60–70cm (23.5–27.5in); 3–5kg (6.5–11lb).
**Maturity**: 1 year.
**Breeding**: Litter of 1–8 young; 2 or more litters per year.
**Life span**: 7 years.
**Status**: Common.

## Cape hare

*Lepus capensis*

*Cape hares have red-brown fur and white hair on the inside leg. They are also known as brown hares by African people, although they should not be confused with the Eurasian brown hare.*

The Cape hare is found across areas of Africa that are not covered by forests. The species is also found in the Middle East and as far east as central Asia. The Cape hare survives in a range of habitats from damp, highland meadows and marshes to arid rock fields. There is even a population of Cape hares that lives in the Sahara Desert, cut off from the rest.

Cape hares not only look similar to Eurasian brown hares but also behave in a very similar way. The males box each other when competing for mates. They do this standing on their long hind limbs.

The hind limbs are used to propel the hare along at speeds of 77kph (48mph). The hares can also use them to make leaps of 2.5m (8.25ft).

Unlike rabbits, hares do not dig burrows; instead, they live in shallow dips called forms. (In the cold steppes of Mongolia, Cape hares actually make their homes underground – unique for hares. They take over the burrows of ground squirrels.)

**Distribution**: Africa and western and central Asia.
**Habitat**: Meadows, fields and marshes.
**Food**: Leaves, seeds, berries and mushrooms.
**Size**: 55cm (21.75in); 4.5kg (10lb).
**Maturity**: 8 months.
**Breeding**: Litters of 3–4 young born every 3 months.
**Life span**: 5 years.
**Status**: Common.

## European rabbit

*Oryctolagus cuniculus*

**Distribution**: Originally the Iberian Peninsula and southern France. Introduced to most of Europe, north-west Africa, Australia and many other countries.
**Habitat**: Farmland, grassland and dry shrubland.
**Food**: Grass, herbaceous plants, bark and twigs.
**Size**: 35–45cm (13.75–17.5in); 1.25–2.25kg (2.75–5lb).
**Maturity**: 1 year.
**Breeding**: 1–9 young per litter; up to 7 litters per year.
**Life span**: 9 years.
**Status**: Common.

The rabbit has had a long association with humans, who have prized it for its soft fur and tasty meat. This species was probably introduced to the Mediterranean from its original home in the Iberian Peninsula more than 3,000 years ago. Rabbits often live in large colonies, inhabiting complex labyrinths of burrows, or warrens, that may have hundreds of entrances. Although rabbits live in close proximity to one another, there is a strong dominance hierarchy within a warren. Each male defends a territory, especially during the breeding season.

Rabbits are famed for their rate of reproduction, and a single female has the potential to produce 30 young per year. Rabbits have been introduced to some areas, such as Australia, where there are no predators capable of controlling their numbers. In these places they have created huge problems, crowding out local species and destroying crops. Ironically, rabbit populations in the species' original range in Spain are too small to support their rare predators such as the Iberian lynx and the imperial eagle.

*There are as many as 66 domestic breeds of rabbit, and they vary considerably in size, shape and coloration. In Australia, rabbits occurred in such high numbers that they left little food for local marsupials, and even threatened the sheep industry. Diseases have been successfully introduced to control them.*

**Riverine rabbit** (*Bunolagus monticularis*): 43cm (17in); 1.65kg (3.75lb)
The riverine rabbit inhabits a small part of South Africa. It lives among the scrub that grows along the seasonal rivers of the Karoo Desert in Cape Province. For much of the year the river bed is dry at the surface. If there is any water, it flows through the deep sandy bed. When the rains come, the river is flooded with a rush of water. This flood provides the habitat's plants with most of the water they get all year. The riverine rabbit survives by feeding on the succulent salty plants that grow along the banks. The vegetation is similar to what might grow in a salt marsh close to the sea. The riverine rabbit is one of the rarest mammals in the world. It is endangered by virtue of having such a specialized lifestyle. The species' low numbers are not helped by the fact that females produce only one baby every year, which is highly unusual for a rabbit. This is probably because the harsh environment makes it tough to feed more young.

**Bunyoro rabbit** (*Poelagus marjorita*): 47cm (18.5in); 2.5kg (5.5lb)
Bunyoro rabbits live in several small populations across Africa. Most are found in the Great Lakes region of eastern Africa. The largest population is in southern Uganda, but other populations are found as far north as southern Sudan and west as northern Angola. Despite its name, this species is actually a hare, although its short legs mean that it is often mistaken for a smaller rabbit. Bunyoro rabbits eat grasses and roots and are nocturnal.

## Steppe pika

*Ochotona pusilla*

This species of pika is the only one to live in Europe. Its distribution extends from the Volga River in southern Russia to the Irtysh River in Siberia. The steppe pika eats grass and lives out on the vast Eurasian grassland known as the steppe.

The pika digs a burrow for shelter. While most pika species are diurnal, the steppe pika is found out of its burrow at all times of day or night. Also unusually for pikas, this species does not hibernate. Instead, it remains active in winter, when the steppe may be covered in snow for months on end, which means that the pika has to dig down to the grass below. Their dark bodies stand out against the snow, so pikas restrict their movements to darker days when they are less easy to spot. It is generally too cold at this time of year to feed at night.

Male pikas occupy a home range that overlaps those of many females. It is likely that groups of pikas seen together are families with an adult male and one or more adult females and their offspring.

**Distribution**: South-eastern Europe and Kazakhstan.
**Habitat**: Steppe.
**Food**: Grass.
**Size**: 15cm (6in); 400g (14oz).
**Maturity**: 1 year.
**Breeding**: 3–5 litters born each year.
**Life span**: 5 years.
**Status**: Vulnerable.

*The steppe pika does not have a visible tail. The head and body are covered in long, thin hairs to keep it warm and the soles of the feet are also covered in thick fur.*

# BATS

*With nearly 1,000 species, bats form one of the largest groups among the mammals, living in almost all temperate and tropical parts of the world. They are the only mammals to have truly mastered flight, and more than half of the species use echolocation for navigating and capturing prey at night. Different bats are specialized for eating insects, fruit, flowers, blood, fish and small animals.*

## Greater mastiff bat

*Mops condylurus*

This species is also known as the Angolan free-tailed bat, reflecting the disagreement in its classification. Some scientists place the greater mastiff bat in the same group as the free-tailed bats, while others place it in a separate group.

The greater mastiff bat roosts in caves, mines, hollow trees and can even be found under thatched roofs and in attics. The bats form groups of several hundred individuals. At sundown they fly out of their roosts to hunt insects. A colony of 500 individuals can consume a tonne of insects per year, and ecologists are considering using these bats to control insect pests in Africa, such as mosquitoes that carry malaria. Scientists have designed artificial roosts or bat "hotels" to encourage the bats to feed in areas where insect pests breed. While designing these roosts, researchers discovered that the bats are capable of tolerating up to 45°C (113°F) at midday.

*This bat is characterized by having wrinkly lips and a band of skin joining the ears, over the top of its head.*

**Distribution**: Africa south of the Sahara Desert, including Madagascar.
**Habitat**: Forest, savannah and dry brushland.
**Food**: Insects.
**Size**: 5–6cm (2–2.25in); 7–64g (0.015–0.15lb).
**Maturity**: 3 months.
**Breeding**: 2 breeding seasons per year, with a single young produced per season.
**Life span**: Unknown but most bats live for 5 years.
**Status**: Common.

## Hammer-headed fruit bat

*Hypsignathus monstrosus*

This is the largest bat in Africa, and is remarkable in having the greatest difference between males and females (sexual dimorphism) of any bat species. Males are nearly twice as heavy as females and, unlike females, they have an unusually large square-shaped head, giving the species its name. The male head-shape is one of several adaptations for calling, which include a greatly enlarged voice box, allowing males to produce a continuous and very loud croaking and quacking, probably to attract females.

*The male's head is large and square, and the muzzle is hammer-shaped. The males also have large lips and warty snouts. Females have thinner, fox-like muzzles.*

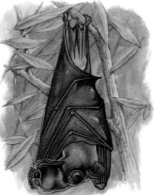

Twice a year, male hammer-headed fruit bats congregate into groups of up to 130 individuals, in order to compete for mates. The males attract attention by croaking as loudly as possible and flapping their wings. The females are very selective, and most opt to mate with just a few of the noisiest males. When the bats are not breeding, they roost quietly during the day in small groups high up in the treetops. At night, hammer-headed bats fly up to 10km (6 miles) from their roost sites to find trees with ripened fruit to eat.

**Distribution**: Central and western Africa.
**Habitat**: Forests, swamps, mangroves and river margins.
**Food**: Fruit, and also reported to have killed and eaten tethered chickens.
**Size**: Up to 90cm (35.5in); up to 0.5kg (1.1lb).
**Maturity**: Females 6 months; males 18 months.
**Breeding**: Give birth to single young, or sometimes twins, once or twice per year.
**Life span**: Unknown.
**Status**: Common.

**Little flying cow** (*Nanonycteris veldkampi*): 5–7.5cm (2–3in); 19–33g (0.04–0.07lb)
This small flower-feeding bat can be found in parts of western and Central Africa. It gets its curious name from the apparently calf-like appearance of its head. This species migrates from forests to savannahs during the rainy season.

**Butterfly bat** (*Glauconycteris variegata*): 3.5–6.5cm (1.5–2.5in); 6–14g (0.01–0.03lb)
This African bat gets its name from its beautifully patterned wings and butterfly-like flight, and can be found roosting in small groups under palm fronds or banana leaves. Butterfly bats feed on small insects, sometimes foraging in broad daylight.

**Lesser noctule** (*Nyctalus leisleri*): 83–113mm (3.25–4.5in); 11–20g (0.4–0.7oz)
This species lives as far west as Ireland and is found across North Africa and the Middle East. It lives in mature woodlands where there are plenty of hollow trees. As its name suggests, this bat is the small relation of the common noctule. It hunts at dawn and dusk and migrates to warmer regions in winter.

# Noctule bat

*Nyctalus noctula*

The noctule bat is one of the largest and most common European bats. In winter, noctules roost in hollow trees or old woodpecker holes, and occasionally in buildings. In some parts of Europe, groups of 1,000 individuals may roost together.

Noctules hunt insects in flight, and are capable of flying at speeds of 50kph (30mph) or more. Usually they forage at dusk, catching insects over woodland or close to water, and sometimes they are seen hunting insects that gather around street lamps in towns.

Although noctules are capable of surviving in cold conditions without food for up to four months, they also migrate to warmer areas where there is more food. Noctules have been known to migrate as far as 2,347km (1,455 miles). In late summer, solitary male noctules set up breeding roosts in tree holes, attracting up to 20 females with mating calls and pheromones. In early summer, pregnant females form groups of related individuals, then they help one another nurse their young.

**Distribution**: Europe to Japan.
**Habitat**: Forests.
**Food**: Insects, especially beetles, and also midges and moths.
**Size**: Wingspan 40cm (15.75in); 15–40g (0.03–0.09lb).
**Maturity**: Females 3 months; males 1 year.
**Breeding**: Single litter of 1, 2 or occasionally 3 young born per year.
**Life span**: 12 years.
**Status**: Declining in some parts of its range.

*The colour of the noctule bat ranges from a golden brown to a dark brown on the back, usually with paler brown coloration on the belly.*

# Pipistrelle bat

*Pipistrellus pipistrellus*

These small bats are common throughout most of Europe, but have declined in some countries due to the loss of natural roosting sites in trees. The reduction is also due to toxic chemicals that have been used to treat wood in the buildings where many pipistrelles roost during winter time. In some parts of Europe, pipistrelles hibernate in winter, either individually or in groups, hidden in crevices in buildings and trees. However, very cold weather may force wintering pipistrelles to move to warmer areas.

Mating usually takes place in autumn, when the bats congregate at traditional breeding roosts. Females give birth to their young in summer, when they come together in large maternity colonies to suckle and care for them.

Pipistrelles leave their roosts early in the evening to feed, chasing after insects in a characteristic fast and jerky pursuit flight, using echolocation. A single pipistrelle can eat as many as 3,000 insects in one night. Usually the high-pitched squeaks that pipistrelles make for echolocation are inaudible to humans, but some people can hear the lower-frequency parts of their calls.

*There are two subspecies of pipistrelle bat, distinguished by the pitch of their calls. One is known as the tenor, while the other is the soprano. The largest colonies may number many thousands.*

**Distribution**: Europe, North Africa, south-western and central Asia, and possibly Korea and Japan.
**Habitat**: Forests, farmland, wetlands and urban habitats, nesting in lofts.
**Food**: Insects.
**Size**: Wingspan 19–25cm (7.5–9.75in); 3–8g (0.006–0.017lb).
**Maturity**: Females 6 months; males 1 year.
**Breeding**: 1 young or occasionally twins produced per year.
**Life span**: 16 years.
**Status**: Common.

# Heart-nosed bat

*Cardioderma cor*

Heart-nosed bats live in the lowland areas of eastern Africa, where they are found in moist grasslands and woodlands from eastern Sudan to northern Tanzania and southern Zambia. By day the bats roost in large numbers in dry caves or in hollows in the immense baobab trees that grow on the open grasslands.

The heart-nosed bat's habitat experiences two rainy seasons. One runs from March to June, the other covers October to December. Most pups are born during these periods, although young are found in small numbers at all times of year.

Like all small bats, this species is nocturnal. They emerge from their roosts just before sunset. The bats hang from a branch and wait for prey to show itself. During the wet seasons, when insects are more common, the heart-nosed bats hunt on the wing, swooping through the air to snatch large flying insects, such as moths or locusts. They also snatch small vertebrates, such as frogs, from leaves and branches. In the dry seasons, the bats grab beetles from the ground. Insects are less common at these times of year, so the bats also target scorpions and centipedes.

*The heart-nosed bat is named after the shape of its nose leaf – a flap of skin that focuses the bat's echolocation calls. The bat has the largest eyes of any small bat in Africa.*

**Distribution**: Eastern Africa from eastern Sudan to northern Tanzania and southern Zambia.
**Habitat**: Dry lowland grasslands often near the coast. The bats are especially common close to caves and baobab trees.
**Food**: Insects.
**Size**: 7.5cm (3in); 28g (1oz).
**Maturity**: 1 year.
**Breeding**: Single pups born in rainy seasons.
**Life span**: Unknown.
**Status**: Lower risk.

# Sucker-footed bat

*Myzopoda aurita*

*Sucker-footed bats have small pads on each ankle and wrist. These pads work as suckers, enabling the bats to cling to flat surfaces such as large leaves. Some American bats have similar suckers but biologists believe that this species evolved separately from them.*

The sucker-footed bat is the only one of its kind in the Old World (Eurasia and Africa). Once relatives of this species lived across East Africa, but today only one species survives. This lives on the Masoala Peninsula of eastern Madagascar, which is the location of the island's largest palm forests. There are similar bat species living in South America, but it is uncertain if they are closely related to the Malagasy bat.

As with many Malagasy species, the sucker-footed bat is facing extinction due to the loss of its habitat. About 90 per cent of the island's unique palm forests have been destroyed during the last century.

Being so rare, little is known about the life of the sucker-footed bat. It is nocturnal and is thought to feed on small flying insects, such as small moths. The bat needs to be an extremely agile flyer to catch such prey, which are themselves very acrobatic. Sucker-footed bats also have an unusual echolocation call that is made up of several elements that are thought to help it detect even the tiniest flying creatures. These two factors also make the bat very hard to catch because it can detect even the finest nets and can easily flit around them.

During the day the bats rest on palm leaves. They use their suckers to cling on in an upright position rather than upside down like many roosting bats.

**Distribution**: Masoala Peninsula in eastern Madagascar.
**Habitat**: Forests of palm trees.
**Food**: Small flying insects, such as moths.
**Size**: 11cm (4.25in); 9g (0.25oz).
**Maturity**: 1 year.
**Breeding**: Unknown.
**Life span**: Unknown.
**Status**: Vulnerable.

# Yellow-winged bat

*Lavia frons*

**Distribution:** Central Africa from Gambia to Angola and Ethiopia.
**Habitat:** Savannahs and woodlands.
**Food:** Insects.
**Size:** 7cm (2.75in); 32g (1oz).
**Maturity:** 1 year.
**Breeding:** Pup born in April.
**Life span:** Unknown.
**Status:** Common.

The yellow-winged bats live in woodlands and savannahs with some tree cover. They are found across Central Africa. They live in monogamous pairs that may stay together for years. The pairs roost in trees and are especially common in umbrella thorn trees. They eat insects, such as ants and grasshoppers, that also live in the tree. Yellow-winged bats do not fly in search of food. Instead they wait for their prey to come to them.

A pair of bats roost about 1m (3.25ft) apart, keeping their distance from other pairs, which are always at least 20m (65.5ft) away. The pair forage independently by flitting from branch to branch and clambering around close to their roosting site. Just before dawn, the pair rendezvous back at the roost. The bats are often out in the open in view of predators, and frequently twist their heads almost completely around as they scan for danger.

*Female yellow-winged bats are slightly larger than the males. Compared to other small bats, this species has large eyes, second only to the heart-nosed bats in their size. The bat uses sight to find prey more than most small bats.*

---

**Woermann's bat** (*Megaloglossus woermanni*): 6–8cm (2.25–3.25in); 14g (0.5oz)
Woermann's bat lives in the rainforest of the western part of Central Africa. It is found from northern Angola and Guinea to the eastern part of the Democratic Republic of Congo. The bat lives on pollen and nectar from banana and sausage tree flowers. It hangs from branches above the flowers and laps up its food using a tongue that is almost half as long as the body, from which it gets its other name of long-tongued fruit bat. This species of bat is an important pollinator for the plants it visits. As it feeds, the bat picks up pollen grains on its body. Some of these are transferred to the next flower that it visits. The pollen fuses with the female part of the flower, which goes on to develop seeds and fruits. Flowers pollinated by day tend to be colourful, but those visited by bats at night are white. Woermann's bats roost under banana fronds, in trees and in houses.

**Soprano pipistrelle** (*Pipistrellus pygmaeus*): 3.5–5cm (1.5–2in); 6g (0.25oz)
It is more or less impossible to tell this species of bat from the common pipistrelle just by looking. Indeed, until recently biologists believed that they all belonged to one species. However, some bats produce more high-pitched calls than others, and these calls include the ones used to attract mates. It was discovered that the bats fall into two groups: high-pitched, or soprano, pipistrelles, which breed only with each other, and lower-pitched, or tenor, pipistrelles, which breed among themselves. Soprano pipistrelles are most common along river banks.

# Egyptian slit-faced bat

*Nycteris thebaica*

Egyptian slit-faced bats live across Africa. They are also found on parts of the Arabian Peninsula, and small populations live in southern Europe, the largest of which is on the Greek island of Corfu. Slit-faced bats are most common on savannahs, but outside Africa they live in dry habitats, such as scrub and olive groves. The bats live in small groups. They roost in any sheltered spots, such as caves, hollow trees and among thick foliage. This species is also often found inside built structures.

Slit-faced bats eat mainly moths, but also catch other insects, such as grasshoppers and beetles. They also eat arachnids, such as spiders and scorpions. The bats catch flying prey on the wing, scooping the prey into their mouths with a membrane of skin around the tail. The bats also hang from trees and listen for the sounds of prey on the ground.

**Distribution:** Africa, Arabia and southern Europe.
**Habitat:** Savannahs and other dry habitats.
**Food:** Insects.
**Size:** 8–16cm (3.25–6.25in); 6.5–16g (0.25–0.5oz).
**Maturity:** 1 year.
**Breeding:** Single pups born at all times of year.
**Life span:** Unknown.
**Status:** Common.

*The Egyptian slit-faced bat is named because its large nose leaf is split in two. The bat's fur varies from brown to grey, with bats living in drier places tending to have paler fur than those living in damper habitats.*

## Straw-coloured fruit bat

*Eidolon helvum*

The straw-coloured fruit bat is the most common and widespread fruit-eating bat in Africa. It is found across the continent south of the Sahara Desert – and there is also a population in Arabia. The bats live wherever there is fruit available and so can survive everywhere from humid rainforests to the most parched savannahs.

The bats roost in large groups in tall trees or in caves during the day. At night they fly off in small groups in search of food. The bats have long but narrow wings, which help them to fly long distances more efficiently. However, the wings do limit the bat's manoeuvrability.

Straw-coloured fruit bats do not eat the flesh of fruits. Instead, they suck out the juice, spitting out any pulp. The bats feed while hanging beside the fruit. Favourite fruits include dates, mangoes, pawpaws, avocados, figs and custard apples.

The colony mates during the dry season, which is generally in early summer. This mating creates embryos, but these do not develop straight away. Their growth is timed so that the pups are born after the rains, when there is plenty of food available.

*Only the neck and back of the straw-coloured fruit bat are actually straw-coloured: the rest of the body is a dull brown-grey. The male bats are slightly larger than the females.*

**Distribution**: Africa south of the Sahara Desert and Arabia.
**Habitat**: Forests, woodlands, and savannahs. These bats do not live in deserts.
**Food**: The juice of fruits such as mangoes, figs, dates and custard apples.
**Size**: 18cm (7in); 290g (10.25oz).
**Maturity**: 1 year.
**Breeding**: Single pup born after rainy season.
**Life span**: 15 years.
**Status**: Common.

## Gambian epauletted fruit bat

*Epomophorus gambianus*

Gambian epauletted fruit bats are found across the non-forested areas of Central Africa, distributed from Senegal and Mali to Ethiopia and also south to eastern South Africa. They roost in small groups in trees and are most common along the edges of woodlands. (The trees are more widely spaced in a woodland than in a forest.)

This species of bat eats figs, mangoes, guavas and bananas. They also suck nectar from some large flowers. Like most other fruit bats, it does not echolocate; instead, it finds food primarily using its sense of smell, following the scent of ripe fruits through the dark. The bat's large eyes allow it to see well in the darkness so it can avoid obstacles while in the air.

Gambian epauletted fruit bats live in mix-sexed groups. Males mate with several females during both the spring and autumn breeding seasons. Pups are nursed by other females in the roosting group, most of which are probably the pup's aunts. In most bat species, mothers must leave their pups in the roost when they go to feed, but the pups of this species come along for the ride, clinging to their mother's chest as she flies.

*Male epauletted fruit bats have pouches of white fur on their shoulders, hence the name. The pale fur is normally hidden, but the males flash their white patches while courting females.*

**Distribution**: Central and southern Africa from Senegal and southern Mali to Tanzania and South Africa.
**Habitat**: Woodland and savannah.
**Food**: Fruits, such as banana, guava, figs and mangoes. Also feeds on nectar.
**Size**: 12–25cm (4.75–19.75in); 40–120g (1.5–4.25oz).
**Maturity**: 1 year.
**Breeding**: 2 litters born each year.
**Life span**: 20 years.
**Status**: Common.

# Peter's dwarf epauletted fruit bat

*Micropteropus pusillus*

**Distribution**: South of the Sahara Desert.
**Habitat**: Woodlands.
**Food**: Fruits and nectar.
**Size**: 6.5–10cm (2.5–4in); 24–34g (0.75–1.25oz).
**Maturity**: 6 months to 1 year.
**Breeding**: Single pups born twice a year.
**Life span**: Unknown.
**Status**: Lower risk.

This small species of epauletted fruit bat lives in woodland areas of western, Central and south-western Africa. From the south, the species is distributed from Angola to Ethiopia and Senegal. The bat does not live deep in the Congo rainforests.

Peter's dwarf epauletted fruit bats roost alone or in pairs, sleeping in the lower branches of trees. When roosting, the wings are wrapped around the body and the bat's eyes are closed, but the ears are constantly scanning the surroundings for signs of danger. Like most fruit bats, this species does not echolocate. Its ears are relatively small compared to those of echolocating bats, and its eyes are large.

This species feeds in the early evening. It lands on large fruit but hovers in front of smaller food, taking a bite on the wing. A mouthful of food is sucked and chewed for about 30 seconds. The juice and soft pulp are swallowed while the tougher fibres are spat out.

*Like other species of epauletted bat, the males of this species have shoulder pouches filled with white hairs. Females have shallow pouches but no white fur.*

---

**Schreibers's long-fingered bat** (*Miniopterus schreibersi*): 5.5cm (2.25in); 9.5g (0.25oz)
This species of bat is one of the most widespread in the world. It lives across southern Europe, Africa and Asia. It is also located in the Philippines and parts of Australia. The bat has very long fingers, which support broad wings. The third finger is so long that it has to be folded back on itself when the wing is not being used. The long-fingered bats are very fast and agile flyers. They seldom fly far from their cave roosts. They are nocturnal and hunt for insects such as small beetles. They hunt at 10–20m (33–66ft) above the ground.

**Whiskered bat** (*Myotis mystacinus*): 6.5–9cm (2.5–3.5in); 4–8g (0.15–0.25oz)
This bat is most common in central Europe, but it is found across northern Asia and North Africa. The species is distinctly furry, with coarse brown hairs on the head and back. Whiskered bats roost in large groups. When the females are nursing young in summer, the males leave the roost and live alone. The bats hunt for small insects such as flies, often hunting over water.

# Rodrigues flying fox

*Pteropus rodricensis*

The Rodrigues flying fox is an extremely large and rare species of bat that lives on the island of Rodrigues, about 1,500km (930 miles) east of Madagascar. Rodrigues is part of the state of Mauritius.

Most bats are nocturnal, but the Rodrigues flying foxes are crepuscular (most active during the twilight of dawn and dusk). They are not able to echolocate like smaller bats. They still use their ears to find prey, but they rely on their eyes to orientate themselves while flying. Their ears are much smaller than most bats, hence this species' resemblance to a fox. Like other fruit bats, their eyes are large to collect more light so the bats can see objects in low light levels.

Most large bats are fruit eaters. The Rodrigues flying fox does eat fruits, but it also hunts for large flying insects, such as moths. The bat catches these insects in mid-air, using its large wings as a net. The size of the Rodrigues flying fox has a detrimental effect on its flying ability and it cannot get aloft in strong winds.

These bats were on the brink of extinction in 1976. As an island species, they are especially at risk of disruption to their habitat. Today the bats are bred in captivity, and other measures have seen the island's wild population reach 3,000 in recent years.

**Distribution**: Rodrigues Island.
**Habitat**: Mangrove and rainforest.
**Food**: Insects.
**Size**: 35cm (13.75in); 285g (10oz).
**Maturity**: 1.5–2 years.
**Breeding**: Single pup born each year.
**Life span**: Unknown.
**Status**: Critically endangered.

*The Rodrigues flying fox has a brightly coloured head. The fur is a mixture of red and yellow fur. This species of bat has a wingspan of 90cm (3ft). It is named a flying fox because of the shape of its snout, which lacks the acoustic adornments of other species.*

## Giant leaf-nosed bat

*Hipposideros commerson*

The giant leaf-nosed bat is found across the equatorial region of Africa and on the island of Madagascar. It is divided into at least five subspecies, including the Malagasy population. Another subspecies occupies the islands of São Tomé and Principe in the Gulf of Guinea to the west of the African mainland. The most common subspecies lives across eastern and southern Africa, from Somalia to Namibia and South Africa.

Giant leaf-nosed bats live in forested areas that have plenty of open spaces for them to fly along. Such flyways are uncommon in the middle of tropical rainforest, so the species is most common along the edge of jungle and woodlands. When not on the move along the flyways, the bats perch to the side. The bat is nocturnal, and the largest roosts are inside caves. Smaller groups of bats will see out the day inside hollow trees. Pups are born in the wet season and the nursery roosts are generally based in caves.

Giant leaf-nosed bats have sharp fangs and powerful jaws, which are used to crush the hard bodies of large beetles. The bat's prey lives on the ground, and it searches for food from a perch or scans the ground as it flies along at a height of 60cm (2ft).

**Distribution**: Sub-Saharan Africa, Madagascar and several surrounding islands.
**Habitat**: Forest edges and clearings.
**Food**: Beetles.
**Size**: 11–15cm (4.25–6in); 130g (4.5oz).
**Maturity**: 1 year.
**Breeding**: Single pups born once a year. Mating takes place between February and June and the pup is born about 4 months later.
**Life span**: Unknown.
**Status**: Common.

*This is one of the largest insect-eating bats, with a wingspan of more than 50cm (19.75in). These bats have elaborate nose leaves used in echolocation. Males have a large crest of bone running down the head.*

## Lesser mouse-tailed bat

*Rhinopoma hardwickei*

The lesser mouse-tailed bat is a widespread desert species. It lives in dry habitats across North Africa, the Middle East and southern Asia. Its distribution stretches as far east as Myanmar (Burma). The bat is well adapted to life in the dusty desert. For example, the wind often whips dust and grit into the air, which could easily cause a problem for a flying bat by blocking its airways. However, lesser mouse-tailed bats are able to continue flying in windy conditions because their nostrils are equipped with a valve inside that closes to keep the dust out.

Most of where the lesser mouse-tailed bats live is treeless, so the bats have only a few places to sleep. They prefer cliffs, caves and walls and other artificial structures. Consequently they crowd into any suitable sites and roost in huge numbers. A large cave will contain many thousands of bats. As is normal with small bats, when the female bats are nursing young, they live in separate roosts to the males.

Mouse-tailed bats are insect eaters. In dry periods, insects are hard to come by, so the bats must stay in their roosts to conserve energy. During this time, the bats become torpid, entering a dormant state, or torpor, similar to hibernation. They survive these periods of inactivity by consuming fat supplies that are stored in the tail.

**Distribution**: North and East Africa, Middle East, and southern Asia.
**Habitat**: Deserts and other dry treeless areas.
**Food**: Insects snatched from the air and gleaned from the ground.
**Size**: 7cm (2.75in); 10g (0.25oz).
**Maturity**: 1 year.
**Breeding**: Single young born in summer, although pups arrive earlier in southern parts of the bat's range.
**Life span**: Unknown.
**Status**: Common.

*This bat and its close relatives are the only species to have such a long tail, which can be longer than the body in some cases. It plays no part in flight, being a food-storage organ.*

# Greater horseshoe bat

*Rhinolophus ferrumequinum*

**Distribution**: Europe, north-west Africa and central and south Asia.
**Habitat**: Woodland and shrublands.
**Food**: Large insects.
**Size**: 6.5cm (2.5in); 25g (0.75oz).
**Maturity**: 3 years.
**Breeding**: Single pup born in summer.
**Life span**: 30 years.
**Status**: Lower risk.

The greater horseshoe bat is the largest horseshoe bat in Europe. It is also found in north-western Africa and across most of Asia as far east as Japan. Horseshoe bats belong to the *Rhinolophus* genus, which means "nose crest".

The greater horseshoe bat is an insect eater. It hunts at night and specializes in catching large insects such as moths and beetles. They fly close to the ground, scanning for prey with pulses of sound, the echoes of which enable them to locate insects. They catch prey mainly in the air. Horseshoe bats prefer to hunt on warm nights, because most insects cannot fly in cold weather. In the northern parts of its range, where winters are colder, members of this species will not leave their roosts for weeks on end.

Greater horseshoe bats roost in caves and smaller holes under rocks. They mate in the autumn, but the females' eggs are not fertilized by the sperm until the following year. Pups are born during the late summer.

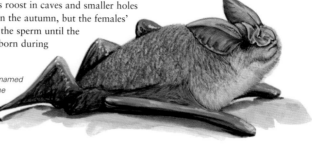

*The greater horseshoe bat is named after the shape of its nose. The upper nose leaf is pointed but the larger flap below the nose forms a horseshoe shape.*

**Egyptian rousette** (*Rousettus egyptiacus*): 15cm (6in); 126g (4.5oz)
This species is also called the Egyptian fruit bat. It is found across most of Africa south of the Sahara Desert and extends up the Nile Valley into the Middle East. From there the bats range into Turkey, Cyprus and east to Pakistan. Unlike all other fruit bats, rousettes use basic echolocation to orientate themselves while flying in the day, although they are more reliant on their eyesight for avoiding obstacles. The bat has a very sensitive nose that can smell even the tiniest morsels of fruit. Egyptian rousettes roost in large groups. They congregate in caves and many of the ancient ruins across their range. As well as fruits, they eat flowers, buds and leaves.

**Livingstone's fruit bat** (*Pteropus livingstonii*): Wingspan: 1.4m (4.5ft); 700g (1.5lb)
The Livingstone's fruit bat, or black flying fox, lives on the Comoro Islands, which are located at the northern end of the deep channel that separates the African mainland from Madagascar. The bat is found on only two of these islands, where dense jungles grow on the sides of steep mountains. It uses its huge wingspan to catch thermals so that it can soar high up the mountainside. The bat is a fruit and flower eater, with much of its diet consisting of figs. The bat locates food by sight and smell and is seen foraging during both day and night. Livingstone's fruit bat is one of the most endangered of all bat, and indeed mammal, species: there are thought to be just 400 left in the wild.

# Mediterranean horseshoe bat

*Rhinolophus euryale*

Like all the horseshoe bats, the Mediterranean horseshoe bat has a semicircular nose leaf below the nostrils. Horseshoe bats emit their echolocation calls through their noses, and the nose leaf is shaped to focus the sound into a beam that can detect a certain size of prey.

Mediterranean horseshoe bats prey on small moths. Many moths are able to hear the high-pitched calls of the bat species and so fly away to safety, but they cannot detect the sounds produced by these bats and so are unable to hear the hunters coming.

The females are slightly larger than the males. Both sexes roost together in caves and other hidden places. The bats prefer places that stay the same temperature all year around. Their wide wings are not long enough to wrap around their bodies as they sleep, so if it gets too cold in the roost the bats become dormant to save energy.

**Distribution**: Southern Europe.
**Habitat**: Mountain forests.
**Food**: Flying insects.
**Size**: 8cm (3.25in); 17g (0.5oz).
**Maturity**: 2 years.
**Breeding**: Single pup born each year.
**Life span**: 27 years.
**Status**: Vulnerable.

*Mediterranean horseshoe bats have broad wings, which are typical of bats that live in forests. They make the bats agile flyers that are able to twist and turn in the air.*

## Lesser woolly bat

*Kerivoula lanosa*

Lesser woolly bats live close to the rivers, lakes and wetlands of south-eastern Africa. Their range extends from the south of the Democratic Republic of Congo through Zambia and Zimbabwe to Mozambique and Botswana. Recently the same species has been found in another population that lives in West Africa.

The bats are associated with water habitats, which are few and far between and often seasonal. As a result, despite having a very wide distribution, the lesser woolly bat is relatively rare, especially in the western part of the range.

Its rarity makes this species difficult to study in the wild and its breeding and other behaviours are not well understood. It is assumed that it lives in a similar way to other small bats. Like other insect eaters, this species hunts at night. They are not fast flyers and tend to flutter in tight circles as they hunt. Many bats hunt over water, where insects are generally more common.

The lesser woolly bat has a long tail membrane supported by a heel bone. The tail membrane extends beyond the toes. The tail might be used for scooping prey off the surface of water or out of the air.

*Like all woolly bats, this species has a thick coat of curly hair. The fur is grizzled, meaning it is darker at the base than at the tips, which gives the fur an overall silvery look. All species have high foreheads, making their heads rounded.*

**Distribution**: Sub-Saharan Africa from the Ivory Coast to the Congo, Zimbabwe and Botswana.
**Habitat**: Rivers, lakes and wetlands. Some specimens have been found in forested regions.
**Food**: Small insects caught on the wing or snatched from leaves and the ground.
**Size**: 8cm (3.25in); 7g (0.25oz).
**Maturity**: 1 year.
**Breeding**: Single pup born after 40 day gestation.
**Life span**: Unknown.
**Status**: Common.

## Western barbastelle

*Barbastella barbastellus*

The western barbastelle lives in hill forests, apart from those in cold regions. For example, in Great Britain it survives only in the milder southern regions. The species is more common in southern Europe and the Mediterranean islands. In summer the bats roost in hollow trees and other relatively open spots, where they often squeeze behind patches of loose bark. In winter the barbastelles retreat to more secluded roosts, such as caves, where they hibernate without becoming completely dormant: they will leave the roost every week or two to hunt.

These bats prey on moths and other soft-bodied insects. They do not seem to eat beetles, which have hardened wingcases and tend to have tougher bodies than most insects. The bats snatch prey in mid-air or grab insects as they perch on leaves and branches. Barbastelles hunt along the edges of forests, where there are more flyways for them and their prey.

Across its entire range, this species is under threat. The main reason for this is the loss of its habitat, in particular a lack of hollow trees in which the bats can roost.

*Western barbastelles have dark hairs with yellow tips. The neck and chin have long hairs that give the impression of a beard. The feature that distinguishes this species from other bats is the ears, which join across the forehead.*

**Distribution**: Great Britain, western and central Europe, Morocco, and the Canary Islands.
**Habitat**: Highland forests in summer but retreat to subterranean caves and mines in winter.
**Food**: Moths and other soft-bodied insects.
**Size**: 6cm (2.25in); 8g (0.25oz).
**Maturity**: 1 year.
**Breeding**: Single pups born in summer. Pups reach full size in about 3 months.
**Life span**: Unknown.
**Status**: Vulnerable.

# Brown big-eared bat

*Plecotus auritus*

**Distribution**: Western
Europe, excluding the British
Isles, and east to South-east
Asia.
**Habitat**: Forest edges.
**Food**: Moths.
**Size**: 5cm (2in); 8g (0.25oz).
**Maturity**: 1 year.
**Breeding**: Mating takes place
in autumn.
**Life span**: 15 years.
**Status**: Common.

The brown big-eared bat is most common in wooded hills.
It has a vast range that extends from Spain to Japan and
India. The bat is most often found flying along the edges of
the forests or in clearings. The species' main food is moths,
but the bats also eat beetles, flies, earwigs and spiders. The
long-eared bats catch prey in three ways: they snatch prey
on the wing, swoop down to the ground to grab it or hover
beside a tree or bush and listen for insects moving on the
leaves and branches. This is where the bat's ears come into
their own. Being so huge, the ears can collect a
lot of sound waves. The bat filters out the
sounds of prey and swoops in for the kill.
All of this takes place in darkness,
although the bat has relatively large
eyes, which might be used in the final
approach to the prey.

The bats roost in hollow trees.
Pups born at the end of summer might be abandoned if
the weather turns too cold for the mother to produce milk.

*This bat has enormous ears that
are almost as long as the rest
of its body. They point forward
during flight to keep the bat
streamlined. When the bat
is resting, the ears are
folded sideways.*

**Grey big-eared bat** (*Plecotus austriacus*):
6cm (2.25in); 10g (0.25oz)
This close relative of the brown big-eared bat
also lives across Europe, Asia and northern
Africa. It prefers warmer climes to its brown-
haired cousin's habitat. It roosts in caves, under
rocks and even hanging from large tropical
flowers. It catches prey using its tail membrane
to scoop victims toward the mouth.

**Daubenton's bat** (*Myotis daubentonii*):
5cm (2in); 10g (0.25oz)
Daubenton's bat ranges from Britain to Japan.
It is a relative of the mouse-eared bats. Most
members of this species live in woodlands
and are always close to a supply of water. In
summer the bats roost under bridges and
in trees. They withdraw into caves and more
sheltered spots in which to hibernate over the
winter. This species hunts for insects that fly
over water. In a single night a bat can eat more
than half its body weight in insects. Thanks to
conservation measures, which protect bat
roosting sites, this species is increasing in
numbers across Europe.

**Long-tailed bat** (*Rhinopoma microphyllum*):
5–9cm (2–3.5in); 6–14g (0.01–0.03lb)
This species, also known as the greater
mouse-tailed bat, has a tail nearly as long as
its body, and lives in dry, treeless regions in
northern and western Africa, parts of the Middle
East and southern India. Long-tailed bats can
often be found roosting in houses, and in Egypt
they are believed to have roosted in the great
pyramids for thousands of years.

# Greater mouse-eared bat

*Myotis myotis*

The greater mouse-eared bat was declared
extinct in Britain in 1990. This is in contrast
to its relative, the Daubenton's bat, which
is one of the few European species that are
increasing in number.

The greater mouse-eared bat is one of the
largest bats in Europe. It is found across
the continent and also in much of southern
and eastern Asia and parts of North Africa.
The species lives in open woodland areas,
roosting in caves and trees. However,
considering its range, this bat is also
a common resident
of churches
and other
quiet, high-
vaulted buildings. A good
roost is one where the
temperature stays more or less
stable for the whole winter.

The greater mouse-eared bat
forages for food over an area about
8km (5 miles) from its roost. It feeds
on a number of insects, including many
flying creatures, but most of its diet
consists of beetles plucked from the
ground. The ideal hunting ground for
this species is thin woodland with grass
covering the ground.

**Distribution**: Europe, Asia
and North Africa.
**Habitat**: Woodlands.
**Food**: Beetles.
**Size**: 9cm (3.5in); 30g (1oz).
**Maturity**: 1 year.
**Breeding**: Pups born in early
summer.
**Life span**: 13 years.
**Status**: Lower risk.

*This species
has rounded
ears, whereas
most bats have
ears with a
convoluted shape
for processing
echolocation calls.
Compared to these, the
greater mouse-eared bat's
ears are relatively simple.*

# AARDVARK AND PANGOLINS

*These two types of mammal specialize in eating ants and termites, but recent scientific work has shown*
*that, although aardvarks and pangolins share some superficial resemblance and behaviour, they do not*
*have common ancestry. Rather, specialist ant-eating mammals evolved independently several times. This*
*is not surprising, given the abundance of ants and termites found in almost all habitats around the world.*

## Aardvark

*Orycteropus afer*

**Distribution**: Sub-Saharan Africa.
**Habitat**: Woodland, savannah, grassland and shrubland.
**Food**: Ants, termites, other insects, small mammals and vegetable material.
**Size**: 1–1.5m (3.25–5ft); 40–70kg (88–154lb).
**Maturity**: 2 years.
**Breeding**: 1 or occasionally 2 young per year.
**Life span**: 20 years.
**Status**: Common.

These animals are often found foraging out in the open at night, systematically covering the ground in search of ants or termites. Aardvarks travel long distances in looking for food, often travelling 10km (6 miles) in a single night. Not surprisingly, given their long tubular ears and snout, they have acute hearing and a good sense of smell with which to detect their prey. They use their powerful front claws to dig open ant and termite nests, and their long sticky tongues to collect the insects. These animals have very thick skin, and seem to be immune to insect bites.

The aardvark's skin is so tough that it also saves it from bites by predators. Aardvarks are very well adapted for digging. When alarmed, they will either run away or start digging a burrow. A single aardvark can dig a hole faster than several people using shovels. Temporary aardvark burrows are less than 3m (10ft) deep, with end chambers large enough for the animals to turn in. More permanent burrows can be 13m (42.75ft) long with several chambers and entrances.

*The word aardvark means "earth-pig" in Afrikaans, reflecting both the burrowing habits and pig-like features of this unusual animal. It has long ears, an elongated snout, a shaggy body and powerful tail. It folds its ears back while making its burrows.*

## Cape pangolin

*Manis temmincki*

There are four species of pangolin, also known as scaly anteaters, living in Africa. Two of them are tree-living animals with long prehensile tails, which they use when climbing. The other two species, which include the endangered Cape pangolin, live in burrows and forage on the ground.

Pangolins feed solely on ants and termites. They have several adaptations, such as having no teeth, which help them in this regard. Like other ant-eating mammals, they have sticky tongues up to 25cm (10in) long for collecting their prey, and strong claws to tear open termite nests. Unlike any other mammals, however, pangolins have scales rather than hairs, giving them a reptilian appearance. When a pangolin is threatened, it rolls up into a tight ball, protecting its soft underparts and presenting a formidable, scaly barrier to predators. The Cape pangolin has declined in numbers because, like its Asian cousins, it is in demand for its scales, which are used in local medicines.

*Pangolins usually walk on their knuckles to save wear and tear on their claws, which they use for opening ant and termite nests. Sometimes they walk on their back legs, using the trailing tail to keep balance.*

**Distribution**: Chad and Sudan to Namibia and South Africa.
**Habitat**: Savannah and shrubland.
**Food**: Ants, termites and occasionally other insects.
**Size**: 40–50cm (15.75–19.75in); 15–18kg (33–39.75lb).
**Maturity**: 2 years.
**Breeding**: 1 or occasionally 2 young.
**Life span**: Unknown.
**Status**: Threatened.

# Giant pangolin

*Manis gigantea*

**Distribution**: Central Africa from Senegal to Uganda and Angola.
**Habitat**: Rainforests and grasslands.
**Food**: Ants and termites. Up to 200,000 ants are eaten in one night.
**Size**: 1.25–1.4m (4–4.5ft); 33kg (72.75lb).
**Maturity**: 2 years.
**Breeding**: Litters born in September and October.
**Life span**: 10 years.
**Status**: Common.

The giant pangolin is the largest of all seven pangolin species (only four of which live in Africa) and lives in the forests of Central Africa. It forages on the ground in the dead of night. A giant pangolin seldom emerges from its burrow before midnight. It digs its own burrow using the long and sturdy claws on its forepaws. The burrows can be immense affairs, reaching 40m (130ft) in length.

When walking through the forest, the giant pangolin puts most of its weight on to its thick back legs. It uses its tail as a counterbalance so that it can free up its forepaws for digging for food. When it does walk on all fours, the forefeet have to be twisted to the side to protect their crucial claws.

Like all pangolins, this species is highly adapted to eating termites and ants. The mighty claws are used for ripping into nests and mounds; then the pangolin uses its long, sticky tongue to lick up the exposed insects.

*As with all pangolins, the only hairs on a giant pangolin are its eyelashes. Instead of hairs, it is covered in thick scales. The claws on the forelegs are long. They are used for ripping open ants' nests.*

---

**Tree pangolin** (*Manis tricuspis*): 35–45cm (13.75–17.75in); 2kg (4.5lb)
This is the smallest of all pangolin species. It lives in the rainforests that skirt the grasslands of East Africa. Like other tree-living pangolins, this species has a long tail that is used to provide support and balance. The tree pangolin also forages on the ground, specializing in cocktail ants and termites. The pangolin sniffs out its prey's nests and licks the insects up with its long tongue. When pulled back into the mouth, the tongue is held in a sheath that extends halfway along the body's length. The pangolin has no teeth and so cannot chew its meal. This function is transferred to the gut lining, which is lined with thin scales that grind the food into a paste as the stomach churns. The pangolin swallows grit and pebbles as it eats, which also help with the grinding process.

# Long-tailed pangolin

*Manis tetradactyla*

**Distribution**: Central Africa.
**Habitat**: Rainforest.
**Food**: Ants and termites.
**Size**: 40cm (15.75in); 3kg (6.5lb).
**Maturity**: 2 years.
**Breeding**: Single young born at all times of year.
**Life span**: 10 years.
**Status**: Common.

The long-tailed pangolin is found in forests across Central Africa in a range that begins in southern Uganda and extends west to Senegal and south to Angola. It is arboreal (built for living in trees), and most of its time is spent in the high canopy of the rainforest; indeed, some individuals may never come down to the ground.

Like its relatives, this species survives on ants. Pangolins have a very long tongue that it is half as long as the body and coated with sticky saliva. The pangolin spends the day licking up ants that are moving along the forest branches. It sleeps in a hollow by night.

The tongue is not the only long body part. This species of pangolin also has a very long, flexible tail. The tip is naked of scales and is highly sensitive to touch. It acts as a feeler and fifth limb and can be wrapped around branches to provide that extra bit of support. When surprised, these pangolins will curl up into a ball and squirt a foul-smelling liquid from anal glands. If the location allows it, the pangolins are known to leap from the branches into the safety of water.

*The most striking feature about this little tree-living pangolin is its hugely long tail, which is roughly twice as long as the body.*

# INSECTIVORES

*The insectivores are a wide-ranging group of small mammals, all with sensitive and highly mobile noses, small eyes and relatively small brains. They are generally solitary, nocturnal animals, the majority of which eat insects, earthworms and other invertebrates. Their teeth are well designed for eating insects, with long incisors for seizing their prey and sharp molars for dealing with their tough bodies.*

## Hedgehog

*Erinaceus europaeus*

Few members of the insectivore family have been able to grow much larger than moles because the food they eat – insects – are so small that they would need to eat a very large quantity. Hedgehogs, however, are more eclectic in their tastes, with a diet that includes earthworms, birds' eggs, frogs, lizards and even snakes. Eating these larger foods has allowed hedgehogs to grow much bigger than is the norm for the group.

Nonetheless, being larger can have its disadvantages, not least being more conspicuous to predators. This is where the hedgehog's most famous asset comes in handy. All over its back the hedgehog has rows of thickened hairs, which narrow at their tips into sharp, prickly points. Using muscles located around the base of the coat, which act like drawstrings, the hedgehog can roll into a ball, becoming an impregnable mass of prickles, which is very effective at deterring the advances of predators.

*The hedgehog's Latin name* Erinaceus *is derived from the word* ericius, *meaning a spiked barrier. Hedgehogs are mostly solitary, but when they do come together they follow a pecking order.*

**Distribution**: Western Europe and Northern Russia.
**Habitat**: Woodland, grassland and gardens.
**Food**: Invertebrates.
**Size**: 22–28cm (8.75–11in); 0.4–1.2kg (1–2.75lb).
**Maturity**: 2–3 years.
**Breeding**: 2–6 young born in summer.
**Life span**: 3–4 years.
**Status**: Common, but declining in the UK.

## Southern African hedgehog

*Atelerix frontalis*

*Like Eurasian hedgehogs, this species is covered in short spines. It stands out from others because it has a thick white band across the forehead.*

The southern African hedgehog lives in two populations. The first is found in south-western Africa, stretching from Angola to northern Namibia, and the second, larger, group lives in Zimbabwe, Botswana and the Cape Province of South Africa. This species' catholic tastes for food mean that it can survive in most places as long as there is plenty of cover.

The southern African hedgehog lives alone. It forages at night and rests by day. This species eats mainly ground-living insects, such as beetles and grasshoppers, but it often scratches around for earthworms and centipedes. The hedgehogs are also known to supplement their diet with mushrooms, lizards and carrion.

Mating takes places throughout the year. The male must court the female by walking around her several times. Litters can contain up to ten young. An older female may have several litters in one year.

**Distribution**: Angola, Namibia, Zimbabwe, Botswana and South Africa.
**Habitat**: Grasslands, rocky areas and gardens.
**Food**: Insects, worms and centipedes.
**Size**: 15–20cm (6–8in); 150–555g (5.25–19.5oz).
**Maturity**: 1 year.
**Breeding**: Litters of between 4 and 10 young born several times a year.
**Life span**: 3 years.
**Status**: Common.

# Russian desman

*Desmana moschata*

**Distribution**: South-western Russia and eastern Europe.
**Habitat**: Slow rivers and oxbow lakes.
**Food**: Aquatic invertebrates, including insects, amphibians, crustaceans and molluscs, and also fish and plant roots.
**Size**: 18–22cm (7–8.75in); 100–220g (0.2–0.5lb).
**Maturity**: 1 year.
**Breeding**: Litters of 1–5 young.
**Life span**: 2–3 years.
**Status**: Vulnerable.

Looking somewhat like a cross between a shrew and a mole, there are only two species of desman alive in the world today. The Pyrenean desman lives in northern Spain and Portugal, and its relative the Russian desman inhabits areas in Russia and eastern Europe.

Desmans have webbed feet and broad tails fringed with stiff hairs. These adaptations help them swim, and it is underwater that desmans do most of their hunting, feeling around with their long whiskers for prey items such as dragonfly larvae and tadpoles.

These animals do not just swim; they also burrow, looking for worms. They tunnel into river banks, making networks of burrows which can extend for many metres. The entrances to the systems of tunnels are always located below the waterline, so that the desmans can come and go as they please, without having to worry about any predators that may be watching from above. There are many predators that will feed on desmans, including hawks, kestrels, foxes and weasels. Several desmans share the tunnel network, although they tend to have their own dens within the burrow.

*Like their close relatives the shrews, desmans must feed almost constantly to keep up their energy reserves.*

---

**Pygmy white-toothed shrew** (*Suncus etruscus*): 3.5–5.2cm (1.5–2in); 1.5–2.5g (0.003–0.005lb)
One of the world's smallest mammals, pygmy white-toothed shrews are found across southern Europe. These shrews have scent glands on their sides, which secrete a pungent odour. The glands are especially well developed in the males during the breeding season, when they are trying to intimidate their rivals and impress females.

**Alpine shrew** (*Sorex alpinus*): 6–7.5cm (2.5–3in); 5.5–11.5g (0.01–0.025lb)
Inhabiting alpine grasslands up to an altitude of 3,400m (11,333ft) above sea level, alpine shrews are often found in rocky habitats. They are especially common on stony banks and beds of fast-flowing mountain streams, seeking out invertebrate prey. Unlike most shrew species, alpine shrews are adept climbers.

**Blind mole** (*Talpa caeca*): 9.5–14cm (3.75–5.5in); 65–120g (0.14–0.25lb)
Unlike the common European mole, the blind mole of southern Europe is physically unable to open its eyes. It has membranous coverings over them, which it cannot pull back. However, the membranes do allow some light through, and it is said that blind moles are not totally insensitive to the visual world, being able to react to changes in light and dark.

# European mole

*Talpa europaea*

The European mole lives across most of Europe, including large parts of Britain, but does not live in southern Europe, which is too dry. However, the species is found across northern Asia as far as China.

Like all moles, this species is a tunneller. It digs using the large claws on its forefeet. Its rounded body and short fur make it easy for the mole to push through loosened soil. The mole needs relatively deep soil to dig in. It pushes the excavated soil out on to the surface, making a molehill.

It is most common in woodlands, where deep soil is held together by tree roots. However, the moles are also found under fields and in gardens. Their tunnels can undermine the structure of the soil, and the molehills ruin lawns.

**Distribution**: Europe and Asia.
**Habitat**: Woodland, fields and meadows.
**Food**: Earthworms.
**Size**: 9–16.5cm (3.5–6.5in); 70–130g (2.5–4.5oz).
**Maturity**: 1 year.
**Breeding**: Single litter of about 3 young born in summer.
**Life span**: 3 years.
**Status**: Common.

*The European mole is adapted for life underground. It has short but sturdy forelegs equipped with wide claws, which are used for digging tunnels and pulling the animal along. The hind legs are much smaller.*

## Golden mole

*Eremitalpa granti*

There are no species of true mole in Africa. Their niche is filled by another group of insectivores called the golden moles. Found mainly in dry sandy areas, golden moles lead entirely subterranean lives, feeding mainly on insects, such as termites. Golden moles also consume small reptiles, such as geckoes and legless lizards, which the moles encounter buried in the sand. Their underground existence means that the moles have little need for vision, and consequently they have lost the power of sight.

Since it is impossible to construct burrows in the dry sands of their desert habitats, golden moles constantly have to plough their way through the sand. Their small but powerful forelimbs are well designed to help them "swim" through sand. They are active at night. By day the golden moles enter a deep sleep, or torpor, which helps them conserve energy. The young are born between October and November. They are suckled for two to three months in a grass-lined nest.

Golden moles may not be able to see, but they do have incredibly acute hearing, being able to pick up the noises made by their insect prey as they move on the surface. Golden moles can pinpoint the precise location of their prey and emerge from below to snatch their meals.

**Distribution**: Cape Province, Namaqualand in South Africa and the Namib Desert.
**Habitat**: Coastal sand dunes.
**Food**: Insects and lizards.
**Size**: 76–87mm (3–3.5in); 120–150g (0.25–0.33lb).
**Maturity**: Unknown.
**Breeding**: 1 litter of 1–2 young born every year.
**Life span**: Unknown.
**Status**: Vulnerable.

*A layer of skin grows over the golden mole's useless eyes, giving them a somewhat bizarre appearance.*

## Tailless tenrec

*Tenrec ecaudatus*

Like other tenrecs, this is an island species. It lives on Madagascar and the Comoro Islands, which lie between Madagascar and the African mainland. The insectivore has also been introduced to several other Indian Ocean islands, including the Seychelles and Mauritius.

The tailless tenrec is a forest animal, but it is highly adaptable and will eat whatever it can find. The species has therefore not suffered from the deforestation that has occurred in Madagascar and elsewhere. Instead it has adapted to life alongside humans and is found everywhere apart from arid habitats.

The insectivores are solitary creatures. They forage at dusk and before dawn among rubbish tips for waste food. In the wild the tenrec survives mainly on insects and other invertebrates but also eats fruits and leaves and hunts for lizards, frogs and small mammals.

Tailless tenrecs give birth in the rainy season after a pregnancy of 9 weeks. Up to 32 young are born in a single litter, but half this number is more usual. The young begin to feed themselves at the age of three weeks.

**Distribution**: Madagascar and Comoro Islands. Introduced to Mauritius, Reunion and Seychelles, all islands in the Indian Ocean.
**Habitat**: Areas with running water where shrubs and bush grow. Most common in the humid forests of eastern Madagascar.
**Food**: Insects, fruits, small vertebrates and rubbish.
**Size**: 39cm (15.25in); 2.4kg (5.25lb).
**Maturity**: 1–2 years.
**Breeding**: 10–20 young born in rainy season. Young are independent at 6 weeks.
**Life span**: 6 years.
**Status**: Common.

*The tailless tenrec is one of the largest insectivores. When young, the tenrecs have a row of white spines along the back. Adult tenrecs shed the spines and grow a mane in its place.*

# Aquatic tenrec

*Limnogale mergulus*

**Distribution**: Madagascar.
**Habitat**: Mountain streams.
**Food**: Insects, frogs and crayfish.
**Size**: 24cm (9.5in); 100g (3.5oz).
**Maturity**: Unknown.
**Breeding**: Litters of 3 young born in March and April.
**Life span**: Unknown.
**Status**: Endangered.

The aquatic tenrec lives in the fast-running streams that flow through the highland region of eastern Madagascar. There are only eight locations where the tenrecs have a sustainable population. Like other aquatic mammals, this species is especially sensitive to water pollution and habitat destruction.

It hunts underwater by night. Its main prey is the larvae of insects such as dragonflies, but it also catches small frogs and crayfish. The tenrecs swim against the rapid current using their large, webbed hind feet. (The species is often also referred to as the web-footed tenrec.) The thick tail is used as a rudder.

Aquatic tenrecs use short whiskers on the their snout to locate prey. The whiskers pick up the tiny eddies created in the water by the movements of small prey. The eyes and ears are small and of less use. By day they rest in bank-side burrows.

*This small tenrec does not have the spiny coat of other species. Instead its sleek fur resembles that of an otter. Unlike other tenrecs, this species has a rounded snout and webbed hind feet.*

**Large-eared tenrec** (*Geogale aurita*): 10cm (4in); 6g (0.25oz)
Large-eared tenrecs are small shrew-like tenrecs that live in the south of Madagascar. They inhabit dry forests and scrub. This sort of habitat is generally hot. This species of tenrec is unusual because its body temperature rises and falls with that of its surroundings, whereas most mammals maintain a constant body temperature, either cooling or warming themselves. These insectivores use their large ears to pick up the sounds of prey. They hunt at night and have poor vision. Large-eared tenrecs consume mainly termites, but also eat other types of insects.

**Lesser hedgehog tenrec** (*Echinops telfairi*): 17.5cm (7in); 200g (7oz)
Tenrecs are generally considered as relatives of the insectivores, such as moles, shrews and hedgehogs. However, recent research suggests that they might be more closely related to aardvarks and elephants. This fact makes the lesser hedgehog tenrec all the more interesting. This small mammal from Madagascar looks very similar to the hedgehogs found throughout Africa, Asia and Europe. It has a coat of spines and short legs for shuffling around undergrowth. Unlike true hedgehogs, however, this species is often seen to climb into trees. The lesser hedgehog tenrec occupies dry habitats in southern and western Madagascar, such as scrubland and dry monsoon forests, that rely on a single deluge of rain for their survival. The tenrecs are night-time foragers. They eat insects, small mammals and plant food.

# Giant otter shrew

*Potamogale velox*

The giant otter shrew is a relative of the Malagasy tenrecs, but it lives on the African mainland. It occupies wetlands and streams that run through the rainforests of Central Africa. In the rainy season, otter shrews cross dry land to hunt in many of the temporary pools that form.

The giant otter shrew swims with its tail, which is flattened to form a vertical flipper. The tail is swung from side to side to power the otter shrew through the water. The legs play no role in swimming. The paws are not webbed and the hind legs are tucked against the body and have a flap of skin along the inside edge that flattens against the body to maintain its streamlined shape.

Otter shrews hunt at night and rely on their sense of touch to find prey. Without webbing, their fingers and toes remain relatively dexterous, but it is their thick whiskers that are their main sense organ. The otter shrews grab prey in their mouths or pin down larger victims with their forepaws.

**Distribution**: Central Africa.
**Habitat**: Forest streams and swamps.
**Food**: Crabs, frogs and fish.
**Size**: 58cm (22.75in); 625g (22oz).
**Maturity**: Unknown.
**Breeding**: Mating takes place in rainy season. Litters usually made up of twins.
**Life span**: Unknown.
**Status**: Endangered.

*The otter shrew has a long, rounded body covered in a sleek brown coat, which consists of long, oily guard hairs over fine underfur. A layer of air trapped between the two layers keeps the animal's skin dry and warm. The nostrils are sealed during swimming.*

## Eurasian water shrew

*Neomys fodiens*

The Eurasian water shrew is found across Europe and Asia. The western limit of its range is Britain. It does not live in Ireland. To the east, the species' range extends all the way to the Pacific coast of Siberia.

Most water shrews live close to fresh water, defending a small area of bank in which their burrow is located. Some members of this species live farther away from flowing water, in damp areas such as hedgerows.

The shrews live alone. They hunt at all times of the day and night, mostly in water. The tail has a keel of hairs on the underside, which helps with swimming. The shrew's fur traps a blanket of air as the animal submerges, which prevents the little mammal from losing body heat too quickly.

These animals eat about half their own body weight each day. They catch prey in their mouths and stun it with mildly venomous saliva. Only a handful of other mammals deploy venom.

Water shrews breed during the summer. Each female is capable of producing several litters in that time. A typical litter contains about five or six young, although twice this number is possible. The young are weaned after 40 days. Females born early enough can breed in their first year.

**Distribution**: Most of Europe, including Great Britain, and Asia from Turkey to Korea.
**Habitat**: Freshwater streams and ponds.
**Food**: Snails, insects and fish.
**Size**: 10cm (4in); 18g (0.75oz).
**Maturity**: 6 months.
**Breeding**: Several litters of between 3 and 12 young produced in summer after a 20-day gestation.
**Life span**: 18 months.
**Status**: Lower risk.

*The Eurasian water shrew is the largest shrew species in Britain. The species is one of the red-toothed shrews. Red-coloured iron compounds coat the tips of its teeth, which makes them more hard-wearing.*

## Eurasian shrew

*Sorex araneus*

The Eurasian shrew, known simply as the common shrew in Britain, lives in damp habitats across Europe. Its range stops at the Pyrenees and the shrew does not live in Spain or Portugal or in much of southern France, where it is too dry for them. The range extends to the east as far as Lake Baikal in western Siberia.

The common shrew lives in meadows, woodlands and in broken habitats covered in rocks. It survives on mountainsides as high up as the snow line.

Common shrews live alone and forage for food at dusk and before dawn. They feed on small invertebrates and must consume 90 per cent of their body weight each day. (Being such tiny mammals, they lose body heat very quickly and therefore must eat huge amounts to stay alive.) Hibernating is not an option because the shrews could not build up enough body fat to survive the winter without feeding.

Common shrews produce large litters of about six young. After a couple of weeks, the young emerge from their burrow for the first time and can be seen following their mother in a "caravan". The shrews form a train, with each one holding the tail of the shrew in front. The young continue to hold on even when the mother is lifted off the ground.

**Distribution**: Europe from Great Britain and the Pyrenees to Lake Baikal in western Siberia.
**Habitat**: Woodlands, grasslands, rock fields and sand dunes.
**Food**: Woodlice, insects, spiders and worms. Also eat plant foods.
**Size**: 6cm (2.25in); 9.5g (0.25oz).
**Maturity**: Between 9 and 10 months.
**Breeding**: 2 litters produced in summer after a gestation of 20 days. The young are weaned after 30 days.
**Life span**: 2 years.
**Status**: Lower risk.

*The Eurasian shrew has a tri-coloured fur coat: the back is reddish brown, the underside is pale grey and the flanks and face are brown. Young shrews have paler fur.*

# ELEPHANT SHREWS

*Elephant shrews, or sengis, are small African mammals. Despite their name, they are not shrews or members of the insectivores. Elephant shrews are known for having flexible snouts – evocative of a trunk – and long legs. They also have a unique form of tail line with thick bristles. No one is sure what the bristles are for, but they may be important for scent marking during fights and courtship.*

## Rock elephant shrew

*Elephantulus myurus*

**Distribution**: South-eastern Africa.
**Habitat**: Savannah grassland.
**Food**: Insects.
**Size**: 10–14cm (4–5.5in); 40–55g (0.09–0.12lb).
**Maturity**: 2 months.
**Breeding**: 1 young per litter.
**Life span**: 1–3 years.
**Status**: Common.

It's not easy being a small diurnal mammal in the African bush. There is a whole host of other animals that are intent on making them their next meal, from hawks and eagles to small cats, mongooses and a multitude of snakes. Rock elephant shrews are well aware of the danger that surrounds them, and they are always on the run from it. They carefully maintain tracks throughout their home ranges, linking feeding areas to bolt holes. These tracks are kept meticulously tidy, and for good reason. The elephant shrews sprint along them at breakneck speed, relying on being simply too fast for their predators to catch them.

Home ranges may be up to 1sq km (0.4sq miles) in size. This is a large area for an animal only 10cm (4in) long to maintain, but, where food is scarce, it needs to search a large area to remain well fed. In places where food is much easier to come by, the home ranges tend to be considerably smaller. Young rock elephant shrews are born very well developed, and after just two days they are able to sprint nimbly around with their mothers.

*Elephant shrews get their name from their elongated, mobile snouts. They are also known as jumping shrews or sengis.*

## Four-toed elephant shrew

*Petrodromus tetradactylus*

**Distribution**: Central and East Africa.
**Habitat**: Forests and rocky areas.
**Food**: Ants and termites.
**Size**: 21cm (8.25in); 200g (7oz).
**Maturity**: 2 months.
**Breeding**: Litters of 1–2 young born all year round.
**Life span**: 4 years.
**Status**: Common.

This is one of 15 elephant shrew species, all of which live in Africa. This one is found across Central and East Africa, where it lives in forest, on rocky ground and in other areas with plenty of thick cover.

Four-toed elephant shrews forage on the ground. They maintain paths, or runways, through the undergrowth, which they scamper along on their long legs, holding their tail up as they run. The shrews use their long snouts to root around among vegetation and into tiny holes to find their prey, which is generally ants or termites.

Elephant shrews do not have nests; instead they sleep outside in thickets. They form monogamous breeding pairs, which work together to maintain a territory. The pair may breed at all times of year.

A single young is the norm, but twins are also seen. Female elephant shrews are pregnant for a long time, up to 65 days, for such a small animal. The young are highly precocious: they can run almost as fast as the adults soon after birth.

*This species of elephant shrew gets its name from having just four toes on its hind foot. All elephant shrews also have a long flexible snout, which resembles an elephant's trunk.*

# APES

*There are three species of great ape in Africa: the chimpanzee, gorilla and bonobo. Within the group of gorillas there are three races, though it is not certain whether they are separate subspecies. The great apes are human beings' closest animal relatives; in fact, humans share 98 per cent of their genetic code with them. Our common ancestor – Kenyapithecus – lived in Africa 15 million years ago.*

## Chimpanzee

*Pan troglodytes*

*Chimpanzees are tool-users, and they are also skilled at communication, which they do with vocalizations and facial expressions.*

These intelligent, social animals are very closely related to human beings, and give us some indication of the kind of animal from which we evolved. Chimps have a number of characteristics that were once thought to be exclusively human. For example, they construct tools – tasks that few other species, except humans and orang-utans, are capable of. One tool used by chimps is a probe, made of a twig stripped of leaves. It is poked into termite nests to extract these insects, which are then eaten.

Chimps live in groups comprising 15–80 animals, which have complex social structures. The dominant males are not necessarily the strongest individuals, but the ones best able to recruit the most allies. Chimps are territorial, and neighbouring groups are aggressive towards one another. Indeed, chimps share an unpleasant characteristic with humans: they go to war, and sometimes individuals of one group will hunt and kill members of rival groups.

**Distribution**: Gambia to Uganda.
**Habitat**: Tropical forest and woody savannah.
**Food**: Fruit, leaves, flowers, bark, insects and animals.
**Size**: 1–1.7m (3.25–5.5ft); 26–70kg (57.25–154.25lb).
**Maturity**: Females 13 years; males 15 years.
**Breeding**: Single young born every 3–6 years.
**Life span**: Around 60 years.
**Status**: Endangered.

## Western-lowland gorilla

*Gorilla gorilla gorilla*

*The armspan of a gorilla is greater than its height – up to a huge 2.75m (9ft). This illustration shows a male silverback.*

Currently, three different races of gorilla are recognized: the western-lowland gorilla, the eastern-lowland gorilla and the mountain gorilla. The western-lowland gorillas are separated from the nearest population of eastern-lowland gorillas by at least 1,000km (620 miles).

Western-lowland gorillas live in relatively small groups of only about six animals. Each group is led by dominant males, or silverbacks – so called because of the grey-white fur only found on the backs of older males.

Although gorillas are large and extremely powerful, they are gentler than chimpanzees. Gorilla groups tend to avoid one another although, on occasion, groups will meet amicably for a short time. Sometimes meetings are not peaceful, and a dominant silverback may respond to intruders by standing up, hooting and beating his chest with cupped hands, followed by a display of strength by breaking branches. This display may lead to an all-out fight between the large males.

**Distribution**: South-eastern Nigeria, west-central and southern Cameroon, south-western Central African Republic, Guinea, Gabon and the Congo.
**Habitat**: Lowland tropical forests.
**Food**: Leaves and shoots.
**Size**: 1.25–1.75m (4–5.5ft); females 70–140kg (154.25–308.75lb); males 135–275kg (297.5–606.25lb).
**Maturity**: Females 7 years; males 15 years.
**Breeding**: Single young, or occasionally twins.
**Life span**: 50 years.
**Status**: Endangered.

# Mountain gorilla

*Gorilla gorilla beringei*

**Distribution**: The Virunga volcanoes lying between Congo, Rwanda and Uganda.
**Habitat**: Montane forest and bamboo forest.
**Food**: Leaves and shoots.
**Size**: 1.5–1.8m (5–6ft); females 110–140kg (240–300lb); males 200–275kg (440–605lb).
**Maturity**: Females 7 years; males 15 years.
**Breeding**: Single young, or occasionally twins, born after 9 months' gestation. Females usually give birth to only 2–3 surviving young in a lifetime.
**Life span**: 50 years.
**Status**: Critically endangered.

Although there is doubt as to whether mountain gorillas constitute a separate subspecies, genetic analysis has shown that they are more closely related to the eastern-lowland gorillas than to the western-lowland gorillas. Mountain gorillas tend to be larger, and have much longer and silkier fur, especially on their arms, than their lowland cousins. They also occupy a very different habitat, and are found almost exclusively in cold mountain rainforests of bamboo, at altitudes over 2,000m (6,560ft).

Scientists George Schaller and Dian Fossey, who spent many years living in close contact with mountain gorillas, studied these enigmatic animals in detail. They found that they live in relatively large groups of up to 30 individuals, and that they communicate with a wide range of calls.

Gorillas travel up to 1km (0.6 miles) in search of food each day, and build crude nests out of leafy branches, usually on the ground, where they sleep at night. Mountain gorillas are only found in the region of the Virunga volcanoes (two of which are active) and Bwindi Forest in Uganda. They number little more than 600 animals in the wild. Mountain gorillas have suffered heavily from poaching and accidental trapping.

*The long, silky fur of the mountain gorilla helps to protect it from the freezing conditions sometimes found in its mountain habitat.*

# Bonobo

*Pan paniscus*

**Distribution**: Central Congo.
**Habitat**: Lowland forests.
**Food**: Mostly fruit, occasionally leaves and seeds, rarely invertebrates and small vertebrates.
**Size**: 70–83cm (27.3–32.75in); 27–61kg (60–135lb).
**Maturity**: 9 years.
**Breeding**: Single young, or occasionally twins, born every 3–6 years after a gestation of 227–232 days.
**Life span**: Probably similar to that of the closely related chimpanzee.
**Status**: Endangered.

Although commonly known as the pygmy chimpanzee, this species is often the same size as its close relative – *Pan troglodytes* – and is also very similar in appearance, though less powerfully built. Unlike chimpanzees, bonobos have never been observed to use tools in the wild, though in captivity they have been seen to use leaves to clean themselves, and sticks to pole-vault over water.

Bonobos are very social animals, and live in groups of 40–120 individuals. These groups move about by day searching for fruiting trees. When a food source is located, individuals make loud calls, probably to alert other members of their group and warn off members of other groups. Like chimps, bonobos construct temporary nests made from leafy branches, to sleep in at night.

Bonobo societies are much less aggressive than groups of chimps. Serious fighting is rare, and they never make deliberate lethal raids on neighbouring groups. Unlike chimp societies, females have equal ranking with males in bonobo groups, and form the cores of bonobo societies. A curious characteristic of bonobo behaviour is the use of sexual contact to settle arguments or to calm down aggressive situations.

*In bonobo groups it is frequently the females that adopt the leadership roles, unlike in chimpanzee societies.*

# MONKEYS

*There are nearly a hundred species of monkey found in the Old World (Africa and Eurasia), all of which belong to the family Cercopithecidae. Most species are well adapted for life in trees and can move with great agility, jumping from branch to branch. Many monkeys live in tropical regions, where leaf and fruit production is year-round, providing these active animals with continuous food.*

## Hamadryas baboon

*Papio hamadryas*

There are five species of baboon living in Africa, although some are known to be able to interbreed, leading some scientists to suggest that they are just different varieties or subspecies. If suitable resting sites are rare, hamadryas baboons can be found congregating in large groups, called troops, consisting of 100 or more individuals.

When baboons start looking for food in the morning, they split up into bands, each consisting of several groups of four or five females and young, led by a dominant male. When a female is ready to mate, the dominant male prevents other males from approaching, striking out when an intruder gets close. Sometimes young male baboons form temporary partnerships to defeat dominant males and get access to females. One of the pair distracts a dominant male by starting a fight with him, while the other mates. At a later time, the individuals in the partnership swap roles, and the one who had to fight last time will have the opportunity to mate.

**Distribution**: North-eastern Africa and western Arabian peninsula.
**Habitat**: Open woodland, savannah and rocky hill country.
**Food**: A wide range of plants and small animals.
**Size**: 61–76cm (24–30in); 14–41kg (30.75–90.5lb).
**Maturity**: Females 5 years; males 7 years.
**Breeding**: Single young.
**Life span**: 30 years.
**Status**: Threatened.

*Male hamadryas baboons have bright red faces and wild silvery hair. Females are smaller, sometimes only half the size of males, and have paler faces with brown hair.*

## Anubis baboon

*Papio anubis*

Anubis baboons are the most widespread of all baboon species. A few small populations live along the southern edge of the Sahara Desert, but most live farther south in Central and West Africa's tropical forests and grasslands. While most monkeys are arboreal, baboons spend most of their time on the ground. They walk on all fours.

Anubis baboons are highly social monkeys, living in well-ordered troops of about 40 animals. Each troop is run by a loose alliance of dominant males. All adult males have a rank. Individual's ranks are frequently challenged and altered by the males of a troop as dominant males age and new males arrive from outside.

The higher-ranking males have access to most of the females. Females also have a hierarchy, which dictates which ones mate with the highest-ranking males. Young male baboons are chased from the troop as they mature. Females stay in the same troop for their whole lives, alongside their sisters and aunts.

**Distribution**: Africa south of the Sahara Desert.
**Habitat**: Grasslands and rainforests.
**Food**: Fruits, leaves, roots, insects, eggs and small vertebrates.
**Size**: 48–76cm (19–30in); 14–25kg (30.75–55lb).
**Maturity**: 8–10 years.
**Breeding**: Single young born at all times of year.
**Life span**: 30 years.
**Status**: Lower risk.

*As with all species of baboon, male anubis baboons are considerably larger than the females. The males also have large canine teeth, which they often display to rivals with a threatening yawn.*

# Mandrill

*Mandrillus sphinx*

This is the largest monkey in the world, with males weighing up to 54kg (120lb). The adult males are particularly colourful, with bright blue and purple nose ridges, scarlet noses and lilac buttock pads. There is a strong hierarchy among male mandrills, and it has been shown that the males with the most prominent facial coloration and the biggest rumps have the most success in attracting females and fathering young.

Mandrills move about in groups of up to ten adult females – with or without infants – around ten juveniles, and single dominant males.

Foraging mandrills cover around 8km (5 miles) per day. Usually the male stays close to the back of the group, but when there is danger he moves to the front to defend the group. Although mandrills are famous for their formidable appearance and ferocity, captive individuals are usually quite gentle.

*A male mandrill's face is very brightly coloured, especially when he becomes excited. Females have duller, blue faces and are less heavily built than males.*

**Distribution**: Southern Cameroon, Equatorial Guinea, Gabon and Congo.
**Habitat**: Dense lowland rainforest.
**Food**: Mostly fruit, nuts and other vegetable material, and also invertebrates and occasionally small mammals.
**Size**: 61–76cm (24–30in); 30–54kg (66–120lb).
**Maturity**: Females 3.5 years; males probably much older.
**Breeding**: Single young born each year.
**Life span**: 45 years.
**Status**: Threatened.

**Drill** (*Mandrillus leucopaeus*): 61–76cm (24–30in); 12–25kg (26.5–55lb)
The drill is a very rare type of forest monkey. It lives in a small area of northern Cameroon and on the island of Bioko, which forms part of Equatorial Guinea. Drills live in lowland rainforests. They prefer pristine forests that have not been changed in any way by human activity, and consequently there are few places left for them to thrive. Drills resemble their close relatives the mandrills in stature, though drills are less brightly coloured. Instead they have a more uniform pale brown coat. The only hint of colour is a male's bright red bottom lip and the bright genital region of the females. This changes from pink to bright blue when the female is on heat. Male drills are twice the size of females and they tend to stay on the ground. Females and the young monkeys are small enough to climb through the lower branches in search of fruits and other plant food.

**Chacma baboon** (*Papio ursinus*): 50–115cm (19.75–45.25in); 15–31kg (33–68.25lb)
Chacma baboons are the largest and heaviest of the five true baboon species. They live in southern Africa, specializing in dry woodland and savannah habitats. As with all baboons, they are highly social and live in troops of 20–80 individuals. Living in dry habitats, the troop must move long distances in search of food, which it does in a defensive formation with dominant males surrounding the females and young. If a threat appears, the males dash forward to attack, while the other troop members flee in the opposite direction.

# Gelada

*Theropithecus gelada*

The gelada baboon is the only species of grazing monkey. It is not closely related to other types of baboon. It is so named because it shares the characteristic of living on the ground with true baboons.

Geladas live in a very specific habitat: the grasslands found high up in the highlands of Ethiopia and Eritrea. The monkeys live in large groups, which are often based near rocky gorges where members can find sleeping sites on the cliffs that are relatively safe from predators. Each troop is broken down into harems, which contain a single dominant male and several females. The members of a harem frequently groom each other to maintain a strong social bond.

Geladas have the most dexterous hands of any African monkey. They are used to pluck just the juiciest grass stems and dig up roots. Geladas have been known to raid cereal crops, which are a manmade grassland. Despite being protected, geladas are often killed by farmers.

**Distribution**: Ethiopian highlands.
**Habitat**: Highland meadows.
**Food**: Grass.
**Size**: 50–72cm (19.75–28.25in); 14–20kg (30.75–44lb).
**Maturity**: 5 years.
**Breeding**: Single young born each year.
**Life span**: 30 years.
**Status**: Vulnerable.

*Geladas have long side whiskers, a mane of hairs on the neck and three bare red patches of skin on the chest and throat. Males have facial hair and a cloak-like mantle of hair.*

## Vervet

*Cercopithecus aethiops*

*Male vervets possess bright blue scrotums, which are used in signals of dominance over other males in a group.*

Like many monkey species, vervets are very social, forming communicative groups of up to 50 individuals. These monkeys have a broad repertoire of calls, and are able to express alarm, excitement, rage and even sadness. Vervets forage in trees and occasionally on the ground. If predators are spotted, particular alarm calls are given, depending on the type of predator approaching. When vervets hear their snake alarm call, they all stand upright, scanning the surrounding grass for pythons. If they hear their leopard alarm call, they run into the trees, keeping their eyes on the leopard, and if they hear their eagle alarm call, they hide deep in the tree canopy.

Female vervets tend to remain in the groups into which they they were born, whereas males are forced to leave when they become sexually mature, moving into new groups.

Vervets have adapted well to living alongside people. They are common in even the suburbs of big cities. Many people welcome their presence, but others treat them as pests because they can damage property and crops.

**Distribution**: Eastern and southern Africa.
**Habitat**: Riverine woodland, wooded savannah, open forests and agricultural land.
**Food**: Fruit and vegetable material, insects, crustaceans, birds' eggs and vertebrates.
**Size**: 35–66cm (13.75–26in); 2.5–9kg (5.5–19.75lb).
**Maturity**: Females 3 years; males 5 years.
**Breeding**: Usually a single young born each year.
**Life span**: 30 years.
**Status**: Common.

## Patas monkey

*Erythrocebus patas*

Patas monkeys are ground-living monkeys. They are found in woodland and savannah areas across the central region of Africa. They do not live south of the Congo rainforest, but are found from Senegal in the west to the huge savannahs of East Africa. This species is one of the few monkeys to be expanding their range. Although deforestation is thinning the African rainforest, patas monkeys stay out of dense jungle and are now found in forest clearings and along the edges of roads cut into the forest.

These monkeys are omnivores. They will eat a range of plant and animals foods and can survive just as well on waste thrown away by people.

Patas monkeys live in groups of 10–40 individuals. One type of group contains the adult females, which are generally closely related to each other, and their offspring of both sexes. The adult males live alone or in small male-only groups. Adult males visit the females in the summer to mate. Rather than actively courting mates, a male will wait for females to choose him. Successful males will build up a harem of mates, which he defends from other males while the females are on heat. In some groups, however, monkeys have a promiscuous mating system in which both males and females breed with several mates. Young are born after a pregnancy of 170 days.

**Distribution**: Western and eastern Africa. Most common in east.
**Habitat**: Savannah and woodland.
**Food**: Fruits, roots, leaves and insects.
**Size**: 70cm (27.5in); 13kg (28.75lb).
**Maturity**: 3–4 years.
**Breeding**: Most births occur in December and January after a gestation of 24 weeks.
**Life span**: 20 years.
**Status**: Common.

*Male patas monkeys are larger than the females, though both sexes have distinctive white beards and moustaches. The monkeys combine a lean body with long legs, which is a good build for running on all fours across the ground. Patas monkeys, however, are also agile climbers and dash into trees or on to other high points if they feel threatened.*

# Talapoin

*Miopithecus talapoin*

**Distribution**: Western central Africa.
**Habitat**: Forests.
**Food**: Insects, leaves, fruits, eggs and small vertebrates.
**Size**: 32cm (12.5in); 1.4kg (3lb).
**Maturity**: 5 years.
**Breeding**: Births occur from November to March.
**Life span**: 25 years.
**Status**: Lower risk.

Talapoins live a range of forest types in the western side of central Africa, including mangroves and rainforests. They are also often spotted in and around human settlements close to the forest. The monkey's distribution runs from Cameroon to northern Angola.

They are highly social monkeys. They live in large groups, or troops, of 70–100 monkeys. Each troop contains adults of both sexes, although there are generally a few more females than males. Dominant males lead the troops, deciding where to forage and when to move on. The males also keep guard over the troop at night. The young and females rest at the centre of the troop, while the males are posed as sentinels at the edges.

Females are ready to breed from May to September. Their perineum swells up as a signal that they are fertile. Females are pregnant for about five months. The young are precocious: they can look after themselves soon after birth, and at just two weeks a young talapoin is able to climb independently of its mother. It is fully independent at three months.

*This species is the smallest monkey in Africa. Both sexes have cheek pouches for storing food, but the females have paler fur than the males.*

---

**Diana monkey** (*Cercopithecus diana*): 55cm (21.75in); 7kg (15.5lb)
The Diana monkey is a resident of the forests of West Africa. They are found only in untouched rainforest, where they eat leaves, fruits and insects. As a consequence of their reliance on this habitat, Diana monkeys are vulnerable to extinction. They are mainly black but also have a white throat ruff and a pointed beard. A white stripe also runs down the thighs. The back of the legs is orange. These patches are visible as flashes of colour as the monkey moves through the dense forest. Diana monkeys are polygynous (the males mate with several females in one season).

**Mona monkey** (*Cercopithecus mona*): 53cm (20.75in); 4kg (8.75lb)
Mona monkeys live in the rainforests of Central Africa. They range from Uganda in the east to Gambia in the west and Angola in the south. This species has also been introduced to the Caribbean island of Grenada. Mona monkeys are very colourful: they have red-brown fur on the back, the rump and front are white, while the face is blue with a pink snout. Mona monkeys live in small groups ruled by a single male. These small harem groups often band together into troops of about 50 monkeys.

# Barbary ape

*Macaca sylvanus*

Barbary apes are a type of monkey called a macaque. Most macaque species live in Asia, where they have adapted well to life alongside humans. The Barbary ape is a North African species, which lives in the dry cedar forests of Morocco, Algeria and Tunisia. The species is most common in the forests that grow on the slopes of the Atlas Mountains, where snow is common in winter. This macaque is the only monkey species to survive in Europe. It was introduced to Gibraltar by the Romans, and a small community still lives there.

The animals forage for food on the ground, in trees and on top of buildings. They feed on a range of plant and animal foods. The European population is highly dependent on humans for its survival.

The social behaviour of the European monkeys is less stable than in the African populations. Natural populations live in mixed sex groups: females in a group are sisters and cousins while the males are drawn from a mixture of neighbouring troops. The males in a troop are organized into a hierarchy, and the top-ranked males mate with most of the females.

*Barbary apes are not apes at all but monkeys. Their common name comes from the fact that they lack a tail, which is one of the characteristic features of true apes, such as gibbons, gorillas and humans.*

**Distribution**: North Africa and Gibraltar.
**Habitat**: Dry forest.
**Food**: Roots, flowers, fruits and insects.
**Size**: 63cm (24.75in); 12.5kg (27.5lb).
**Maturity**: 4 years.
**Breeding**: Single young born once a year.
**Life span**: 30 years.
**Status**: Vulnerable.

## Red-capped mangabey

*Cercocebus torquatus*

Red-capped monkeys are large and very vocal. Their calls can be heard from over 1km (0.6 miles) away. Groups of red-capped mangabeys consist of about 30 individuals, and unlike many species of monkey, their groups may include several adult males, who live peacefully alongside one another and the females. All mangabeys have pale upper eyelids, which they flutter to attract attention and signal sexual intentions and status.

Although mangabeys spend a lot of time in the treetops searching for fruit, they will also forage on the ground, searching the leaf litter for mushrooms and small animal prey.

Mangabeys are territorial when food is relatively scarce in the dry season, and their loud calls help neighbouring groups maintain their distance from one another. At other times of the year, when food is in plentiful supply, mangabey troops come together without conflict.

Mangabeys are threatened by the loss of their forests to logging. However, the red-capped mangabey seems to be quite adaptable to new habitats, hopefully making this species less susceptible to problems in the future. Nevertheless, the monkey is also being hunted to meet the growing demand for bushmeat.

*The fur on the top of this species' head is a dark maroon-red. The white hair on the sides of the head extends around the neck like a collar, giving rise to the other common name of this species: the collared mangabey.*

**Distribution**: Senegal to Congo.
**Habitat**: Mostly tropical rainforest, but also mangroves, degraded forest, swamps and agricultural land.
**Food**: Mostly fruit, but other vegetable matter and insects and small animals are also taken.
**Size**: 38–89cm (15–35in); 7–14kg (15.5–30.75lb).
**Maturity**: Females 4 years; males 5–7 years.
**Breeding**: Single young, or occasionally twins, born at an average 16-month interval.
**Life span**: Probably around 30 years.
**Status**: Endangered.

## Blue monkey

*Cercopithecus mitis*

Most blue monkeys live in the rainforests of the Congo Basin, although they are also found in other habitats farther afield in southern and eastern Africa. Blue monkeys occupy humid places that have plenty of tall trees and a lot of running water available.

Male blue monkeys are generally larger than the females and also have more white facial hair. A single male rules a blue monkey troop, which can contain up to 40 members. The males in an area compete for ranks and only the highest-ranking alpha male mates with the troop's mature females, which come into season at any time throughout the year. The females pout over their shoulder at the male during mating. Alpha males are frequently deposed by younger males moving up the ranks.

Blue monkey troops are very aggressive toward each other. The alpha male leads an attack by the grown males, but the females also join in. Interestingly, blue monkey troops will team up with a group of another species, such as its close relative the black-cheeked white-nosed monkey, to defend an area from other troops and predators. The two species forage for food in different parts of the forest, so they do not compete for resources. Both benefit from working together to keep hold of the territory.

*Only a few blue monkeys are actually blue. Most have dark coloured fur with just a faint bluish tinge to the hairs around the face. Blue monkeys are also called diademed monkeys because of the tiara-shaped triangle of white fur on their heads. There are six subspecies of blue monkey.*

**Distribution**: Central, eastern and southern Africa. Most common in Congo.
**Habitat**: Forest.
**Food**: Fruits and leaves.
**Size**: 65cm (25.5in); 6kg (13.25lb).
**Maturity**: 3 years.
**Breeding**: Each female produces a single young each year. Birth occurs at all times of the year. A single male fathers all the young in a troop.
**Life span**: 20 years.
**Status**: Vulnerable.

# Black-cheeked white-nosed monkey

*Cercopithecus ascanius*

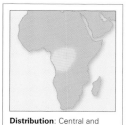

**Distribution**: Central and southern Africa.
**Habitat**: Forests.
**Food**: Fruits, insects and gums.
**Size**: 38–46cm (15–18in); 3–4kg (6.5–8.75lb).
**Maturity**: 4–6 years.
**Breeding**: Mating peaks in November to February.
**Life span**: 30 years.
**Status**: Common.

The black-cheeked white-nosed monkey lives in forests across central and southern Africa. They are most common in Uganda, but populations are further south and west. This species is primarily a rainforest monkey but it can survive in more open habitats as long as there is enough food. The monkeys are fruit eaters but they also consume resins, gums and insects.

Black-cheeked white-nosed monkeys live in groups run by a single male. The group forages and sleeps together. The group travels an average of 1.4km (1 mile) every day. Like many similar monkeys, members of this species often store food inside their cheek pouches. This allows them to carry food to a place where they can eat it safe from attack by predators or from being stolen by other monkeys. Black-cheeked white-nosed monkeys often live alongside leaf-eating monkeys and so do not compete with them for food.

*The black-cheeked white-nosed monkey's name explains this species' most obvious features. Another of its common names is the redtail monkey, which refers to the chestnut-brown colouring on the underside of the tail.*

---

**Grey-cheeked mangabey** (*Lophocebus albigena*): 72cm (28.25in); 11kg (24.25lb)
Grey-cheeked mangabeys are also known as black mangabeys. Most of their body is covered in dark fur, though the facial hairs and shaggy mantle are considerably paler. Males are about 20 per cent larger than the females. Both sexes have very long tails that are slightly prehensile. (This characteristic is unusual for an Old World monkey. It is the American monkeys that are most known for this feature.) Grey-cheeked mangabeys inhabit the lowland rainforests of Central Africa. They live in small groups and each group has just one male. Most of their diet is fruits and nuts.

**Owl-faced monkey** (*Cercopithecus hamlyni*): 40–65cm (15.5–25.5in); 4–10kg (8.75–22lb)
Owl-faced monkeys live in eastern Congo and southern Uganda. This species occupies bamboo forests that grow on the slopes of the Ruwenzori Mountains. The males are twice the weight of the females, but both sexes have similar olive-grey colouring. There is a pale yellow stripe running across the eyebrows and another crossing that one and running down to the upper lip. This T-shaped marking is the species' most obvious feature. The rump and genitals of both sexes are naked, with blue skin. Mature males sport a bright red penis, which stands out against the monkey's muted colouring. Owl-faced monkeys have extremely long fingers, which are used to grip smooth bamboo stems. (Bamboo grows in cold and wet locations, so the stems are also often slippery.) Owl-faced monkeys eat mainly bamboo shoots.

## Allen's swamp monkey

*Allenopithecus nigroviridis*

Allen's swamp monkeys are found only in swamp forest: areas of low-lying tropical forest that are frequently flooded. In the case of Allen's swamp monkey, the swamps are fed by the Congo River. When the river breaks its banks and spills across the forest floor, the monkeys climb into trees for safety. During their time in the trees, the monkeys eat fruits and leaves.

Once the flood has subsided, however, the monkeys descend to the muddy forest floor once again. Their webbed feet help them to walk over the mud as they search for worms, beetles and other invertebrates.

The webbing is also useful during floods. If a monkey is threatened while up a tree, the monkey's first line of defence is to dive into the water, where it can swim away to safety. Allen's swamp monkeys are preyed on by large hawks, snakes and bonobos, which also live in the swampy forests. This species is polyganous, and females develop a sexual swelling when on heat.

**Distribution**: Congo Basin.
**Habitat**: Swamp forest.
**Food**: Fruits, water plants and insects.
**Size**: 60cm (23.5in); 3.5kg (7.75lb).
**Maturity**: 3–5 years.
**Breeding**: Single young born to females at all times of year.
**Life span**: 20 years.
**Status**: Lower risk.

*Allen's swamp monkey has slightly webbed fingers and toes to help it move through shallow swamps. The males are slightly larger than the females.*

## Western red colobus

*Procolobus badius*

The western red colobus is one of the leaf monkeys. Like other colobus monkeys and their relatives the langurs, this species survives by eating leaves or, more specifically in the western red colobus's case, the petiole, or leaf stalk.

Plant food does not contain very many nutrients, so colobus monkeys must eat a lot to sustain them. Plant food is also very hard to digest efficiently; most of a leaf is made up of a tough fibrous substance called cellulose. Although cellulose is made up of chains of sugars molecules, it cannot be digested by a normal monkey. For this reason, the colobus species has a stomach split into four chambers (similar to that of a cow). The different stomach chambers contain bacteria that can break down cellulose fibres into an acidic sugary soup, which the monkeys can then digest themselves. This type of digestion takes a very long time, and so western red colobus monkeys often spend long periods sitting with full stomachs. (The process also produces a lot of gas, so the monkeys often look bloated.)

Having to sit still all the time, western red colobus are easy to hunt. Human hunters have nearly wiped them out in some places, but they are also the favourite prey of another ape – the chimpanzee.

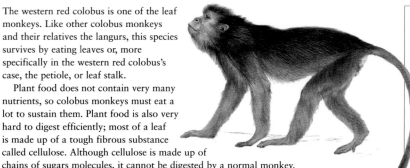

*The western red colobus has a very short, almost useless, thumb and four very long fingers, which it hooks over branches so that it can swing through the trees.*

**Distribution**: West Africa.
**Habitat**: Rainforest, woodlands and savannah.
**Food**: Leaves.
**Size**: 45–67cm (17.75–26.5in); 5–11kg (11–24.25lb).
**Maturity**: Unknown.
**Breeding**: Single young born to each female every 2 years. Females mate with several males when on heat. The exact gestation period is uncertain but is probably about 100 days.
**Life span**: 20 years.
**Status**: Critically endangered.

## Olive colobus

*Procolobus verus*

The olive colobus is found in the coastal rainforests of West Africa, from Sierra Leone to Togo. There is also a small population in eastern Nigeria. The monkey is most commonly seen in the dense undergrowth that grows beneath the high canopy. It moves higher up to sleep in the middle branches when night falls but never climbs to the top of the forest. It is often found close to running water.

Olive colobuses have larger feet than any of the related colobus species and also have very small thumbs. These adaptations allow the monkeys to grip branches as they climb, although reduce their ability to pluck food items.

Olive colobuses live in small groups of adult females, their young and a single adult male. Other males live in separate groups. Groups of olive colobuses are often seen with Diana monkeys. When a Diana monkey gives an alarm call to warn others of an approaching predator, the olive colobus monkeys freeze, their grey-green fur making them hard to spot among the leaves.

Olive colobus monkeys search out the youngest and juiciest leaves. When this food is not available, they will eat the stalks of older leaves, flowers and seeds.

These monkeys have no breeding season. A female reproduces every two years or so. When the female is on heat, her perineum swells. The pregnancy lasts between five and six months.

*The olive colobus is the smallest of the African colobus monkeys. It has a drab coat of olive green. Males are the same size as females but have larger canine teeth. The teeth are used in fights.*

**Distribution**: Coastal region of West Africa from Sierra Leone to Togo, with a small, isolated population living in eastern Nigeria.
**Habitat**: Understory and middle branches of rainforest generally near to water.
**Food**: Young leaves, seeds and shoots.
**Size**: 9–43cm (3.5–17in); 2.2–4.5kg (4.75–10lb).
**Maturity**: 3–4 years.
**Breeding**: Single baby born every 2 years.
**Life span**: 30 years in captivity, probably less in the wild.
**Status**: Lower risk.

**Tana River red colobus** (*Procolobus rufomitratus*):
45–67cm (17.75–26.5in); 5.8kg (12.75lb)
This critically endangered species of colobus
monkey lives in the forests around the Tana
River, which flows from the Kenyan Highlands
to the Indian Ocean. Flooding from the river
supports a tropical forest in a wider region
dominated by savannahs. Nevertheless, the
Tana River forest is considerably drier than the
habitats of other colobus monkeys. This forces
the species to be less reliant on leaves than
other colobus; in fact, less than half the monkey's
diet is made up of leaves. The rest comprises
fruits, seeds, buds and flowers. Living in the
isolation of the Tana River Valley, this red colobus
is not threatened by predators in the same way
as more common colobuses. As a result,
members of this species are less likely
to work together to fend off threats.

**Angolan colobus** (*Colobus angolensis*):
58.5cm (23in); 9kg (19.75lb)
Angolan colobus monkeys are close relatives of
the guereza and king colobus. Like these species,
the Angolan colobus has black and white fur.
It also has white epaulettes and white cheeks,
throat and brow. In addition to inhabiting Angola,
this species ranges as far north as Cameroon
along the western side of Central Africa. It
survives in a range of habitats from bamboo
rainforests to swamps and savannahs. Like other
colobus species, this monkey is primarily a
forest animal. It eats mainly leaves but survives
drought by consuming bark, clay and insects.
The monkeys often climb down beside streams
to eat the herb and water plants that grow there.

# Guereza

*Colobus guereza*

Guerezas are found in a range of habitats,
including the rainforests of the Congo, the
forested hills of Nigeria's Donga Valley and
the wooded grasslands of East Africa. When
in dense jungle, guerezas spend their whole
lives in the trees, but, in
areas where trees are
more widely dispersed,
they often come down to
the ground to feed and
move between trees.

Guerezas eat mainly leaves.
Less than 20 per cent of their
diet is made up of other
items, mainly fruits.
When possible, the
monkeys eat fresh
shoots, but will move
on to tougher, older leaves when necessary.

Guerezas live in small groups made up of
one adult male, four or five adult females
and their offspring. The adult females are
close relatives. The young females stay with
their troop as they mature, while the males
are driven away by the resident male. When
the dominant male is replaced by another,
the new leader will kill the youngest infants.
This brings their mothers into season again
so the new male can breed with them.

**Distribution**: Central and
eastern Africa.
**Habitat**: Forest and
woodland.
**Food**: Leaves.
**Size**: 45–72cm
(17.75–28.25in);
5–14kg (11–30.75lb).
**Maturity**: 4–6 years.
**Breeding**: Breed
once every 2 years.
**Life span**: 20 years.
**Status**: Common.

*The male guerezas are
slightly larger than the
females. The thumb on
each hand is missing
completely, and
the remaining four
fingers are used
for swinging from
branch to branch.*

# King colobus

*Colobus polykomos*

**Distribution**: West Africa.
**Habitat**: Monsoon forests.
**Food**: Leaves, fruits and
flowers.
**Size**: 45–72cm
(17.75–28.25in); 5–14kg
(11–30.75lb).
**Maturity**: 2 years.
**Breeding**: Single baby born
every 2 years.
**Life span**: 20 years.
**Status**: Endangered.

The king colobus lives in tropical forests that have long
periods of dry weather. Such forests are supplied by seasonal
rains or monsoons. West Africa has two monsoons each
year. Unfortunately, much of the land where monsoon forest
grows is also ideal for farming, which is why much of the
king cololubus's forest habitat has been cleared to make way
for fields. As a result, the species is currently endangered.

King colobus monkeys eat leaves during and following
the monsoons, but as drought takes hold of the forest the
monkeys turn to fruits and other plant foods to survive.
King colobus groups contain about twice as many females
as males. The males in the group are organized into a strict
hierarchy and rarely interact with each other. Fights are
rare, occurring only if a subordinate male believes
he can defeat a higher-ranking group member.
The ranking system is tested most frequently
during the breeding season, which coincides with the
rains. Males compete by calling; the dominant male
has the loudest call.

*All members of the Colobus
genus have black and white fur,
but the king colobus is distinctive
because most of its body is jet
black. Only the whiskers, chest
and tail are white.*

# LEMURS

*This is a group of primates that lives exclusively on Madagascar and some of its surrounding islands. The ancestors of lemurs arrived on Madagascar about 40 million years ago, before most modern primates – monkeys and apes – had evolved. The 30 species of lemurs that survive today have evolved from one common ancestor to live in all the varied habitats on the islands.*

## Ruffed lemur

*Varecia variegata*

**Distribution**: Eastern Madagascar.
**Habitat**: Tropical forest.
**Food**: Fruit.
**Size**: 51–56cm (20–22in); 3.2–4.5kg (7–10lb).
**Maturity**: 2–3.5 years.
**Breeding**: 1–6 young, most commonly twins.
**Life span**: 33 years.
**Status**: Endangered.

This is the largest of all the lemurs. Lemurs are prosimians that are found exclusively on Madagascar and some surrounding islands. Ruffed lemurs live in trees, and, although they are good climbers, they are not as agile as some other species of lemur.

Ruffed lemurs are most active at dusk, and at this time it is possible to hear their mournful territorial calls. Sometimes just a pair of ruffed lemurs occupies a territory, but more often groups of about 15 individuals will live together, sharing the same home range.

As well as calls, ruffed lemurs use scent-marking to signal their territorial boundaries. The males mark branches and other objects with a secretion from glands found on their necks. Scent-marking males are seen rubbing their chests, necks and chins on to trees or on the ground. Sadly, like many lemurs, these beautiful animals are in danger of extinction due to the overexploitation of their habitat and also overhunting of the animals themselves for their meat and fur, and for commercial exportation.

*There are two subspecies of ruffed lemur. One has mostly black fur with white markings; the other has mostly red fur with white markings.*

## Ring-tailed lemur

*Lemur catta*

Ring-tailed lemurs are forest animals, but they spend quite long periods of time on the ground, searching for fallen fruit and other plant material. Although fairly common throughout their range in southern Madagascar, these animals are declining in number.

Their habitat is a dry forest, and the animals must endure long periods of drought. During these times they may eat insects, but they are reliant on dry fruits, such as those of the kily tree, a type of tamarind.

Ring-tailed lemurs live in mixed-sex groups, but in most cases only one of the males is sexually active. During the breeding season, which runs from April to June, both sexes fight. The females are battling for resources, while the males are competing for access to mates. During a fight, the lemurs may never touch. Instead they do battle with smell. Each combatant in a stink battle coats its bushy tail with secretions from a gland on the wrists and near the genitals and wafts the strong smell toward its opponent.

From the age of three, a female produces one or two young every year. The newborn clings to its mother's belly, before moving to ride on the back by the age of two weeks. Weaning occurs at 5 months.

**Distribution**: Southern Madagascar.
**Habitat**: Forests and bushes.
**Food**: Plant foods.
**Size**: 38–45cm (15–17.75in); 2.3–3.5kg (5–7.75lb).
**Maturity**: 3 years.
**Breeding**: 1–2 young born in August to October. Young are independent by 6 months.
**Life span**: 30 years.
**Status**: Vulnerable.

*Perhaps the most recognizable of all the lemur species of Madagascar, these animals are named after their striking tail markings.*

# Brown lemur

*Eulemur fulvus*

**Distribution**: Madagascar and the Comoro Islands.
**Habitat**: Forests.
**Food**: Leaves, fruits and bark.
**Size**: 40–50cm (15.75–19.75in); 2–4kg (4.5–8.75lb).
**Maturity**: 2 years.
**Breeding**: Single young born each year.
**Life span**: 25 years.
**Status**: Vulnerable.

Brown lemurs live in the forests in Madagascar and on the Comoro Islands. There are five subspecies, all with a very distinctive colouring. Both sexes of common brown lemurs have dark brown fur and pale beards. Female red-fronted lemurs have red-brown fur, while the males are grey with a crown of red fur. White-fronted lemurs have dark backs and a paler underside; males have pale heads, too. Male collared lemurs are grey-brown, with a darker stripe down the back; the females have redder fur. Both sexes have a red beard. Sanford's lemurs are smaller than the other subspecies. Both males and females are dark brown. Their most distinctive feature is a pale T-shape across the face.

Subspecies are often found mixed together, but each one is most associated with a habitat. The common brown and collared lemurs live in fragments of high forest in north-western Madagascar. The red-fronted lemur lives in monsoon forest along the coasts. White-fronted lemurs are found in rainforests, while the most rare subspecies, Sanford's lemur, lives along forest edges in northern Madagascar.

*There are five subspecies of brown lemur. The common brown lemur is the only subspecies that is actually covered in just brown fur. Others have more distinctive markings that vary between the sexes.*

---

**Fork-marked lemur** (*Phaner furcifer*):
22–28cm (8.5–11in); 300–500g (10.5–17.5oz)
This is one of the few species of lemur that is not classified as vulnerable to or endangered with extinction. It lives in most types of forest on Madagascar. The fork-marked lemur is named after the dark stripe on its forehead that splits in two and continues down either side of the face. Fork-marked lemurs are gum eaters. They have long upper teeth that point forwards to make a dental "comb". This comb is used to collect the sweet liquids that ooze from holes in tree trunks. Fork-marked lemurs live in pairs.

**Crowned lemur** (*Eulemur coronatus*):
34cm (13.5in); 2kg (4.5lb)
Crowned lemurs are named after the patch of orange hair on their heads. Males have brown bodies, while the females are more grey. Crowned lemurs live in northern Madagascar, where they are most common in that region's dry coastal forests. The lemurs are diurnal. They live in small groups and forage for fallen fruits. A typical group of these lemurs contains two adult pairs and a couple of young.

**Bamboo lemur** (*Hapalemur griseus*):
26–45cm (10.25–17.75in); 2.5kg (5.5lb)
This unusual lemur survives almost entirely on bamboo leaves. These are a difficult food because they contain high levels of the poison cyanide and are often covered in grains of hard silica that wear down the teeth. Bamboo lemurs live in small family groups. They forage in the trees and on the ground in the rainforests of eastern Madagascar.

# Mongoose lemur

*Eulemur mongoz*

Most mongoose lemurs live in the dry forests of Madagascar. These forests are filled with deciduous trees that shed their leaves during periods of drought rather than when the weather turns cold. The lemurs also survive on two of the Comoro Islands, where they live in more humid rainforests.

During the dry season, mongoose lemurs are nocturnal. At this time of year the lemurs eat seeds and dry fruits that have fallen from the trees and are lying in wait for the rains. The mongoose lemur is an important disperser of these seeds. As the seeds pass through the lemur's gut, a hard outer coating is digested away, which prepares them for germination when the rains arrive.

In the colder, rainy season, mongoose lemurs are diurnal. At this time they also change their diet to leaves, flowers and pollen.

Mongoose lemurs are monogamous. A pair produces a single litter each year.

**Distribution**: Madagascar and Comoro Islands.
**Habitat**: Dry forest.
**Food**: Flowers, fruits and leaves.
**Size**: 35cm (13.75in); 2–3kg (4.5–6.5lb).
**Maturity**: 2 years.
**Breeding**: 1–2 young born in July–September.
**Life span**: 30 years.
**Status**: Vulnerable.

*Male mongoose lemurs are pale grey with red patches on their flanks and face. The females are darker and have white patches instead of red. Newborns have a white beard.*

# Fat-tailed dwarf lemur

*Cheirogaleus medius*

Fat-tailed dwarf lemurs live in the west and south of Madagascar. They are found in the lower branches of both humid rainforests and drier monsoon forests. In areas that experience a dry season, which is most of Madagascar, these lemurs sit out the dry spells in a dormant state. They build nests in tree hollows and survive on the fat stored in their tails.

At other times of the year, fat-tailed dwarf lemurs are nocturnal foragers. They live alone and survive mainly on fruits, though they also eat petals, pollen and nectar. They also occasionally eat beetles and other insects.

During the wet season (October–March), the lemurs build up a supply of fat in their long tails. The tail triples in size at points by the beginning of the dry season. While lying dormant through the dry season, the lemur loses about 40 per cent of its body weight.

This species breeds in the wet season. They form monogamous pairs. The female is receptive for about 20 days and is pregnant for 62 days. Most litters are made up of twins, although three or four young are not uncommon.

**Distribution**: Mainly in western Madagascar and parts of the south and east.
**Habitat**: Tropical rainforests and drier monsoon forests.
**Food**: Fruits, flowers, pollen and nectar.
**Size**: 20cm (8in); 142–217g (5–7.75oz).
**Maturity**: 1 year.
**Breeding**: Mating takes place in wet season and twins are born in January. Pairs produce litters each year,
**Life span**: 15 years.
**Status**: Endangered.

*These lemurs are about the size of a large rat. They have large eyes to help them see in the dark. Like cats, the lemurs have a reflective surface behind the eyes that makes them glow in the dark.*

# Hairy-eared dwarf lemur

*Allocebus trichotis*

*Both sexes of hairy-eared dwarf lemurs have tufts of long hair on the ears. It is unknown what function this feature might have. The species is nocturnal, so using hairy ears as a visual signal is unlikely.*

The hairy-eared dwarf lemur is one of the rarest primates in the world. Even before the habitats of Madagascar were devastated by human activities in the 20th century, biologists have suggested that this species was rare. Although the species was first described in 1875, it has been observed in the wild only twice for more than a century. In 1989 a small population was discovered living in the Mananara River in the north-east of the island but they still remain largely elusive.

Without being able to watch the lemur behaving naturally, biologists have had to surmise how it survives by looking at dead specimens. The hairy-eared dwarf lemur has long upper teeth that form a toothcomb. This suggests that at least part of the lemur's diet is made up of tree gums (sugary liquids that leak from holes in trunks). The species also has a long tongue compared to other similar lemurs. This tongue is useful for licking gums and also for extracting small food items, such as beetles and pollen.

Hairy-eared dwarf lemurs are monogamous. They live in family groups of one male, one female and their one or two offspring. Breeding occurs during the wet season in November and births occur two months later. Both the male and female help to raise the young.

**Distribution**: North-eastern Madagascar.
**Habitat**: Lowland forest in the Manarana River Valley.
**Food**: Long tongue used to lick up sticky plant gums, nectar. Insects make up about half the lemur's food.
**Size**: 13.5cm (5.25in); 85g (3oz).
**Maturity**: 1 year.
**Breeding**: Mating takes place at the beginning of the wet season in November and December and one or two young born in January and February.
**Life span**: 15 years.
**Status**: Endangered.

# Aye aye

*Daubentonia madagascariensis*

This remarkable species is another prosimian found only in Madagascar. Aye ayes live alone. They are exclusively nocturnal and search for food high up in the trees, moving up to 4km (2.5 miles) a night within a small home range of around 5ha (12 acres). During the day, aye ayes sleep in spherical nests, made from branches and interwoven leaves. The nests are hidden in dense foliage in the forks of trees, and there may be several nests within a single home range.

Aye ayes have a most unusual way of finding food. Using a specially adapted finger, which is very long and thin like a probe, they tap the surface of decaying wood in search of tunnels made by insect larvae or ants and termites. Using a combination of a good sense of touch and a sort of echolocation with their sensitive ears – able to pinpoint a hollow sound from tapping – aye ayes locate the tunnels occupied by their prey. They then use their strong incisor teeth to make small holes in the wood, into which they insert their probe-like finger to extract their insect prey with a hooked claw. Unfortunately, these fascinating creatures are suffering from the loss of Malagasy forest. Local people also persecute them because they are seen as bad omens.

*The aye aye uses its specialized third finger not only for locating and catching insects in decaying wood, but also for determining the milk content of coconuts and extracting coconut pulp.*

**Distribution**: Northern, eastern and west-central Madagascar.
**Habitat**: Tropical forests, but seems adaptable to secondary forest, mangroves and even coconut groves.
**Food**: Fruit, seeds, nectar, other vegetable matter and insect larvae.
**Size**: 36–44cm (14–17in); 2–3kg (4.5–6.5lb).
**Maturity**: 3 years.
**Breeding**: Single young born every 2–3 years.
**Life span**: 20 years.
**Status**: Endangered.

**Grey mouse lemur** (*Microcebus murinus*): 10cm (4in); 60g (2oz)
Grey mouse lemurs are one of the smallest primates in the world. (The smallest is Peter's mouse lemur [*Microcebus myoxinus*] which is only 6.25cm/2.5in long.) The grey mouse lemur lives in the trees of Madagascar's dry forests, where it is a solitary forager. It spends all its life in the trees but is seldom far above the ground. Its diet is mainly insects. The mouse lemur is nocturnal, spending the day asleep in communal nests. Males sleep in pairs, while females gather together in groups of 15 or so.

**Weasel sportive lemur** (*Lepilemur mustelinus*): 24–30cm (9.5–11.75in); 500–900g (1.1–2lb)
This species of sportive lemur lives in deciduous forests in the eastern and western lowlands of Madagascar. As a sportive lemur its hind legs are longer and more powerful than the forelimbs, making the animal an excellent jumper. Weasel sportive lemurs are nocturnal. They eat mainly leaves, but will eat fruits, barks and flowers during dry periods. This species will also eat its own faeces to extract as many nutrients from its food as possible.

**Northern sportive lemur** (*Lepilemur septentrionalis*): 453cm (121in); 800g (1.75lb)
This species is confined to the northern fringes of Madagascar, where it lives in the high branches of dry monsoon forests. It eats leaves and fruits. Males and females only consort with each other during the breeding season from April to August.

# White-footed sportive lemur

*Lepilemur leucopus*

The white-footed sportive lemur is found in two very different habitats in the south of Madagascar. In this dry region there exists both a unique type of spiny forest filled with succulent plants similar to cacti and also gallery forests (forests that grow beside a river), which are denser and more humid. Despite the great differences between these two forests, both habitats are occupied by this sportive lemur. It is found in the lower branches during the night, where it moves from trunk to trunk with bold leaps, and by day the lemur nests in a thicket or tree hollow.

White-footed sportive lemurs are leaf eaters. When leaves are scarce, they move on to fruits and flowers. Some reports suggest that this species extracts more of the nutrients from its food by eating the pellets of half-digested food that pass out of the anus, in the same way as rabbits.

**Distribution**: Madagascar.
**Habitat**: Spiny forest.
**Food**: Leaves.
**Size**: 25cm (9.75in); 500g (1.1lb).
**Maturity**: 18 months.
**Breeding**: Single young born in October to December.
**Life span**: 15 years.
**Status**: Lower risk.

*Like all sportive lemurs, this species has long limbs and especially powerful hind legs, which allow it to make enormous leaps. The hands have large pads for gripping on to vertical tree trunks.*

# INDRI AND SIFAKAS

*As well as the various groups of smaller lemurs, Madagascar is home to three species of larger primates called sifakas, and the largest Malagasy primate, the indri. Like all primates living on Madagascar, the indri and sifakas are vulnerable to extinction. These large primate species are the closest surviving relatives of the giant lemurs that lived on Madagascar a thousand years ago.*

## Indri

*Indri indri*

The indri is the largest of all the living prosimians, and, like the lemurs, it is found only in Madagascar. Indris are arboreal and move about by jumping between tree trunks and stems. Sometimes indris come down to the ground, where they stand upright, moving in series of ungainly leaps.

They are mostly active by day and spend a lot of time feeding on leaves and fruit. Indris live in small family groups of up to five members, and occupy large home ranges. The central part of a home range is defended from others by the adult male, which uses scent markings and calls to signal the limits of the territory.

Sometimes several members of a group will make loud tuneful songs that can be heard up to 2km (1.25 miles) away. These songs are thought to signal occupancy of a territory to other groups, but also to unite groups and broadcast willingness to mate.

*Indris have thick silky fur, which may be useful for living in cold mountain forests, as high as 1800m (6000ft) above sea level. There is considerable variation in fur colour, which ranges from black through browns and greys to white.*

**Distribution**: North-eastern Madagascar.
**Habitat**: Tropical rainforest.
**Food**: Leaves, flowers and fruit.
**Size**: 61–90cm (24–35.5in); 6–10kg (13.25–22lb).
**Maturity**: 7–9 years.
**Breeding**: Single young born every 2–3 years.
**Life span**: Unknown.
**Status**: Endangered.

## Avahi

*Avahi laniger*

*The avahi is also known as the woolly lemur because of its thick and curly fur. The fur is groomed with a toothcomb formed from the lower incisors.*

Avahis live on both sides of Madagascar, and some scientists class the two populations as separate species. In the north-west, they live in the dry monsoon forest that grows on mountain slopes. On the eastern side, they live in lowland rainforests. Avahis cling to vertical trunks and move around by leaping between trees. When on the ground they hop along on their hind feet.

These animals often live in close proximity to indris, their close relative. Both species specialize in eating young leaves, but they avoid competition by foraging at different times: indris are diurnal while avahis feed at night. Avahis eat only the softest parts of a leaf, throwing away the midrib. During droughts, avahis survive by eating flowers and fruits. The avahi's food is low in quality so the primate does not have a lot of energy. As a result it spends long periods resting, waiting for its food to digest.

**Distribution**: Eastern and north-western Madagascar.
**Habitat**: Forest.
**Food**: Leaves.
**Size**: 37cm (14.5in); 950g (2lb).
**Maturity**: 2 years.
**Breeding**: Young born in July–September.
**Life span**: 20 years.
**Status**: Lower risk.

## Verreaux's sifaka

*Propithecus verreauxi*

**Distribution**: South-west
Madagascar.
**Habitat**: Tropical deciduous
and dry evergreen and spiny
forests.
**Food**: Leaves, fruits and
flowers.
**Size**: 45–55cm
(17.75–21.75in); 4–6kg
(8.75–13.25lb).
**Maturity**: 3 years.
**Breeding**: A single young
born in May to July after
5–6 months of gestation.
**Life span**: 23 years in
captivity although probably
less in the wild.
**Status**: Vulnerable.

Verreaux's sifaka lives in the forests of south-western
Madagascar. It occupies two types of habitat – deciduous
and evergreen forest. The trees of deciduous forests
drop their leaves, not because of the cold, but
because of drought. The evergreen forest is also dry,
much of it is spiny forests found only in Madagascar.

This species lives in small groups of up to about 12
individuals. Groups contain more or less equal numbers
of adult males and females. The group defends a small
territory. They use their scent to mark the territory's
boundary. Males have scent glands on their throats, while
females use ones on their genitals. The sifakas mate in
December, at the height of the dry season. A single young is
born five months later and it is weaned after seven months.

Sifakas move through the trees by leaping. The distance
they can jump is increased slightly by small flaps of skin
under the animal's short forearms. These membranes allow
the sifaka to glide slightly. On the ground, the sifakas move
by hopping sideways on both hind feet. The forearms are
held out to the side for balance.

Verreaux's sifakas eat all types of plant material apart
from the roots. In the rainy season they prefer to eat easily
digested soft fruits and flowers, but in the dry season they
rely on wood, bark and leaves.

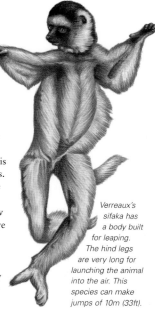

*Verreaux's
sifaka has
a body built
for leaping.
The hind legs
are very long for
launching the animal
into the air. This
species can make
jumps of 10m (33ft).*

## Diademed sifaka

*Propithecus diadema*

**Distribution**: Eastern
Madagascar.
**Habitat**: Mountain and
lowland rainforests.
**Food**: Fruits, flowers, shoots
and leaves. Scientists
suggest that the animal's
athletic nature is due to the
large amounts of caffeine and
other alkaloids in its food.
**Size**: 45–55cm (17.75–21.75in);
6kg (13.25lb).
**Maturity**: 2–3 for females;
4–5 years for males.
**Breeding**: 1–2 young born
in April and May.
**Life span**: 20 years.
**Status**: Endangered.

Diademed sifakas live in the high-altitude forests that grow
above 800m (2,620ft) on the slopes of eastern Madagascar.
This species is almost completely arboreal. They cling to
trunks and make enormous leaps between trees, unlike other
sifaka species, which often hop along the ground. These
animals are diurnal. They live in small groups, which forage
together for young leaves, fruits and other plant foods. The
members of the group communicate to each other with a
series of calls. They warn of a predator approaching on foot
with a "tzisk" noise. Attacking birds illicit a honking call.

A group of sifakas contains several adult males and
females. The males are organized into a mating hierarchy
and only the highest-ranking male mates with the females
in the group. During the summer breeding season (in
December in Madagascar), the top-ranked male is frequently
challenged by other males, which prevents it from mating
with and guarding the females. While the alpha male is
seeing off a threat, lower-ranked males often take the
opportunity to mate with the females. One or two young
are born four or five months later.

*Diademed sifakas are named after the white tiara-like patch on the
head. However, only one subspecies has this colouring: other members
of the species are completely black or completely white.*

# BUSHBABIES

*Monkeys and apes are not the only primates to live in Africa. Primitive primates, such as bushbabies, also live in the continent's forests. These are known as the prosimians, a name that means "before monkey". Biologists think that the ancestors of all the world's monkeys, apes and the lemurs of Madagascar resembled these small tree-living animals.*

## Potto

*Perodicticus potto*

These animals forage high up in the treetops at night, climbing slowly through the branches, using their wide, sensitive eyes to locate fruit in the moonlight, and a good sense of smell to find ants and other insects. Pottos also sleep high up in trees during the day.

Females occupy large ranges, big enough to provide food for themselves and their young. Males occupy larger ranges, which cover as many female ranges as possible. Pottos are fairly solitary creatures, but males and females in overlapping ranges make contact throughout the year, communicating with vocal calls and scent marks.

In the first few days of life, baby pottos cling to their mothers' bellies, but later the mothers leave their young hidden near their nests when out foraging. The young are collected at the end of the night. After a few months, the young pottos begin to follow their mothers around as they search for food. The mothers may carry their young on their backs. Young male pottos leave their maternal territories when they are only six months old, but young females stay with their mothers for much longer.

*When threatened, pottos lower their heads between their forelegs, so that they are protected by their shoulderblades.*

**Distribution:** Guinea to western Kenya and central Congo.
**Habitat:** Tropical forest.
**Food:** Fruit, insects and small vertebrates.
**Size:** 30–90cm (11.75–35.5in); 0.85–1.6kg (1.75–3.5lb).
**Maturity:** 18 months.
**Breeding:** Single young, or occasionally twins.
**Life span:** 25 years.
**Status:** Common.

## Golden potto

*Arctocebus calabarensis*

*This little prosimian has long, thick, woolly fur with a golden sheen. The animal grooms its fur with a long claw on the second toe of each foot.*

The golden potto, alternatively known as the more exotic-sounding Calabar angwantibo, lives among the forests of western equatorial Africa. Its distribution runs from south-eastern Nigeria to southern Congo. The potto prefers areas of forest with dense undergrowth, where it feeds within 5m (16.5ft) of the ground. However, the most pristine rainforests have very little undergrowth because only small amounts of light penetrate the thick canopy of branches. For this reason, golden pottos tend to congregate around gaps in the forest where a tree has fallen, allowing enough light to flood into the gaps for shrubs to grow.

Pottos are solitary animals. They forage for food at night, climbing slowly through the branches. They are cautious climbers: at all times three limbs are in contact with a solid surface. Pottos eat mainly insects. They can catch flying moths and will rub the poisonous hairs off caterpillars before eating them.

**Distribution:** Western Central Africa.
**Habitat:** Forest gaps.
**Food:** Insects.
**Size:** 23–30cm (9–11.75in); 260–460g (9.25–16.25oz).
**Maturity:** 18 months.
**Breeding:** Young born at end of rainy season.
**Life span:** 13 years.
**Status:** Lower risk.

# Bushbaby

*Galago senegalensis*

**Distribution**: All parts of sub-Saharan Africa.
**Habitat**: Woodlands and savannahs.
**Food**: Mainly insects but also eggs, nestlings and fruits.
**Size**: 8–21cm (3.25–8.25in); 95–300g (3.25–10.5oz).
**Maturity**: 1 year.
**Breeding**: A single young, occasionally twins, are produced during both annual rainy seasons. The gestation period is 3–4 months.
**Life span**: 4 years.
**Status**: Common.

The bushbaby, or lesser galago, has the widest distribution of any species of African prosimian. It is found in the trees of open woodland and among the thickets of savannah habitats from Senegal to Tanzania. Bushbabies also live on Zanzibar.

Bushbabies are strictly tree-living animals. They have elongated feet that allow them to hop and leap a little like a kangaroo, but make them far from agile on the ground. The primates live in large crowds, although there is little social interaction. They sleep during the day, several bushbabies often sharing a nest in a thicket of vegetation or tree hollow. When awake in the day the bushbabies are sluggish and cautious, but when night falls the primates transform into agile climbers. They urinate on the hairless palms of their hands and soles of the feet to helps them grip better. The urine also leaves a trail of scent through the branches, which may help the bushbaby to find its way back to the nest in the darkness.

A bushbaby's favourite prey is grasshoppers. They also consume chicks, eggs and fruits. In periods of famine, the animals survive on sap and gum. Bushbabies are polyganous, and males fight for access to mates.

*The bushbaby has wide eyes for seeing in the dark. It also has thickened pads on the tips of its fingers, which give the bushbaby more grip when climbing.*

# Greater galago

*Otolemur crassicaudatus*

**Distribution**: Eastern and southern Africa from Sudan to Angola and South Africa.
**Habitat**: Woodlands and forests.
**Food**: Gums, fruits and insects.
**Size**: 28–37cm (11–14.5in); 1–2kg (2.25–4.5lb).
**Maturity**: 2 years, but males will not breed until later.
**Breeding**: Litters of 2–3 young born once a year, in November in the south but earlier in equatorial regions.
**Life span**: 15 years in the wild but up to 18 years in captivity.
**Status**: Lower risk.

Greater galagos are found in forests from southern Sudan to eastern South Africa and Angola. Like other galago species, the greater galago has thick woolly hair. The animal grooms itself with its tongue, teeth and claws. Also, like its relatives, this species has pads on its fingers and toes to aid with gripping. (These are the same features that have evolved into the loose, wrinkles and folds on the palm of a human's hands.) However, unlike those of the bushbaby, the hind feet of the greater galago are not elongated. Consequently, the greater galago makes smaller leaps and generally moves by climbing from branch to branch.

Greater galagos survive on gums, fruits and insects. The composition of its diet depends on its location: in southern Africa nearly two-thirds of the animal's diet is made up of gum and saps, while in Kenya insects make up half its diet. Termites appear to be the most common insect eaten by greater galagos.

This species is polyganous. Males defend a large home range, which contains the territories of several females. Mating takes place between April and July, depending on geographical location.

*This species is the largest species of galago. Males are larger than the females. The greater galago is also known as the thick-tailed galago on account of its bushy tail.*

# ELEPHANT AND HYRAX

*There is only one living species of elephant in Africa, and it is the largest land animal in the world. Although there is some disagreement among scientists, the closest relatives of the elephants are thought to be sea cows, such as manatees and dugongs, and hyraxes. Neither of these groups bear much physical resemblance to elephants, but similarities in their DNA codes reveal a shared ancestry.*

## African elephant

*Loxodonta africana*

*One of the most distinctive features of an elephant is its trunk. It is a very adaptable tool, and can be used for picking up anything from peanuts to trees. It is used for feeding, drinking, fighting and communication.*

There are two races of African elephants: the savannah elephant, which is the world's largest living land animal, and the smaller forest elephant that lives in the rainforests of Central and western Africa. The savannah elephants are social animals and, like Indian elephants, they form groups consisting of related female elephants and their young.

The leaders of elephant groups are always the eldest and largest females. Male elephants leave their groups at puberty, driven away by older females, to go and join groups of other young males. Males compete to mate, and usually these contests are settled by pushing and aggressive displays, but sometimes fighting leads to fatal injuries.

Forest elephants do not form large groups, but are able to maintain contact with other elephants in the dense jungle by producing deep, rumbling calls.

**Distribution**: Sub-Saharan Africa.
**Habitat**: Forest, savannah, marshland and semi-desert.
**Food**: Grass, leaves, shrubs, bark, twigs, roots and fruit.
**Size**: 6–7.5m (20ft–25ft); up to 7.5 tonnes (16,500lb).
**Maturity**: 10–20 years.
**Breeding**: Single calf born every few years.
**Life span**: 50–70 years.
**Status**: Endangered.

## Rock hyrax

*Procavia capensis*

Close relatives of the elephant, these small rodent-like animals live in groups in rocky areas, where there are plenty of nooks and crannies in which to hide. Hyraxes are surprisingly agile, and can run up even the steepest, smooth rock surfaces with ease, gripping the rocks with the rubber-like soles of their feet. Hyraxes have many enemies, which include leopards, eagles and pythons, so they have to be quick and watchful. In fact, the dominant male of a family group, which typically consists of several females and young, and sometimes a subordinate male as well, usually stands guard while the rest of the group feeds or basks in the sun. If the sentry animal spots danger, he will warn the rest of the group with an alarm call.

Rock hyraxes don't like cold or wet weather, and will stay in their burrows if it is raining. When it is cold, groups of up to 25 animals will huddle together in a shelter to keep warm. On warm days, they come out to feed or bask in the sun. Hyraxes only come out at night if the weather is warm and there is plenty of moonlight, otherwise they stay in their burrows until daytime.

*Rock hyraxes will eat almost any type of vegetation, even plant species poisonous to other mammals.*

**Distribution**: Most of Africa, excluding the north-western regions.
**Habitat**: Rocky scrubland.
**Food**: Grass, leaves and shrubs.
**Size**: 30–58cm (12–23in); 4kg (8.75lb).
**Maturity**: 16–17 months.
**Breeding**: Litter of 1–6 young.
**Life span**: 11 years.
**Status**: Common.

# HOOFED ANIMALS

*Hoofed animals, or ungulates, walk on the tips of their toes. Their hooves are made from the same material as fingernails and claws – keratin. Walking in this way makes their legs very long, and most ungulates are fast runners because of this. Another shared characteristic of hoofed animals is that they are herbivores with highly developed digestive systems, allowing them to feed on tough plant material.*

## Ass

*Equus asinus*

**Distribution:** North Africa and Arabia.
**Habitat:** Hilly desert.
**Food:** Grasses.
**Size:** 2m (6.5ft); 250kg (550lb).
**Maturity:** 2 years.
**Breeding:** Single foal born in rainy season.
**Life span:** 30 years.
**Status:** Common.

The ass is the wild relative of the donkey. Donkeys were probably one of the first beasts of burden. Over the last few thousands years they have spread to all continents, though the natural range of wild asses is from Oman to Morocco.

Wild asses are now very rare, especially in Arabia. They live in small herds made up of a single male and several females. Sometimes larger groups come together, which contain several of these harem-type groups. The group grazes in the morning and evening. This allows it to seek shade and avoid the heat in the middle of the day. Asses are cautious animals and will shy away from the unfamiliar. This is the root of a donkey's stubbornness.

Asses can breed with horses and other members of the *Equus* genus. For instance, mules are a cross between a male donkey (jack) and a mare, a hinny is a cross between a stallion and a female donkey (jenny) and a zebra–donkey cross is called a zonkey.

*The ass looks like a small and sturdy horse. Wild asses tend to be longer but more slender than domestic breeds of donkey.*

## Common zebra

*Equus burchelli*

**Distribution:** Ethiopia to southern Africa.
**Habitat:** Grassland and open woodland.
**Food:** Grass, herbs and leaves.
**Size:** 2.2–2.5m (7.25–8.25ft); 290–340g (640–750lb).
**Maturity:** 3 years.
**Breeding:** Single foal born every 1–2 years.
**Life span:** Up to 40 years.
**Status:** Lower risk.

There are three different species of zebra, all found in Africa and each with its own distinctive pattern of black and white stripes. The stripes make these hoofed mammals blend in to the natural patterns of light and shade in their habitat, making it more difficult for a predator to keep track of its quarry during a chase.

Zebras usually live in small family groups headed by dominant stallions, which lead groups of one to six mares with their young. When young male zebras reach maturity, they leave their family groups and form groups of bachelor males, while females stay behind. Males fight amongst each other for access to females, circling and trying to kick or bite one another. Within a group, zebras can be affectionate, and may spend a lot of time grooming one another.

*The common or Burchell's zebra has the broadest stripes of the three zebra species, and its stripes usually join at the belly.*

## Black rhinoceros

*Diceros bicornis*

The black rhinoceros is the smaller and more abundant of the two species of rhino found in Africa, but it is still critically endangered. These animals form clans that sometimes come together at wallowing sites, where they have mud baths. The baths help to keep the skin healthy and free of parasites. Rhinos within a clan are usually tolerant of each other, though occasionally serious fights may occur between bulls that are courting the same female.

Black rhinoceroses can be quite dangerous. They have very bad eyesight and may charge at anything large enough to be a threat, including vehicles, tents and campfires. However, they usually run away when they detect the scent of humans. Indeed, rhinos have good reason to fear humans. Hunting has destroyed the populations of both of the African species. People have hunted the rhino for sport, for its tough hide, but mostly for its horn. A rhino's horn is made from the same material as hair, and can be carved into ornamental objects or ground into medicinal or aphrodisiac powders. Many countries have banned trade in rhino products, but illegal trading still occurs.

*The black rhino can be distinguished from Africa's second rhino species, the white rhino, by its pointed, prehensile upper lip, as compared to the white rhino's squared, non-prehensile upper lip. Despite the names, there is no colour difference between them.*

**Distribution**: Eastern and southern Africa from southern Chad and Sudan to northern South Africa.
**Habitat**: Scrubland and woody savannah.
**Food**: Twigs, buds and leaves. Also strips bark from woody stems.
**Size**: 3–3.75m (9.75–12.25ft); 800–1,400kg (1,760–3,080lb).
**Maturity**: Females 4–6 years; males 7–9 years.
**Breeding**: Single calf born every 2–5 years.
**Life span**: 30 years in the wild, but can exceed 45 years in captivity.
**Status**: Critically endangered.

## White rhinoceros

*Ceratotherium simum*

The white rhino is among the rarest mammal species in the world. A little more than 150 years ago it was found across Africa from Sudan and Chad to northern South Africa. Today, however, only 400 individuals survive, and all of them live in reserves in eastern and southern Africa.

The reason for the white rhino's demise is hunting. In recent times the rhinos were being hunted for their horn, which could be sold for a high price in China, where it is believed to be an aphrodisiac. The huge black-market price for rhino horn makes poaching an ever-present problem.

White rhinos live in small groups. Each group never strays from a home range of about 8sq km (3sq miles). The groups are made up of females, while the dominant bulls live on their own but remain close to the females. The bull will challenge another male that enters the home range. Such confrontations are generally stand-offs, with combatants making false charges and damaging plants with their horns. Fights are avoided because they involve a large risk of injury.

*White rhinos are huge grazers with two horns on their snouts. The body is covered by a thick and almost hairless hide. The white rhino's characteristic square lip is used for plucking grasses.*

**Distribution**: Eastern and southern Africa from Sudan to South Africa.
**Habitat**: Areas of open woodland and tropical grassland.
**Food**: Grass and other low-growing plants.
**Size**: 3.3–4.2m (10.75–13.75ft); 1.4–3.6 tonnes (3,080–7,920lb).
**Maturity**: 6 years in females; 10 years in males.
**Breeding**: Single calf born every 2 years.
**Life span**: 30 years in the wild but more than 40 when raised in captivity.
**Status**: Critically endangered.

# Giraffe

*Giraffa camelopardalis*

Giraffes are the world's tallest living land mammals, with some exceeding 5m (16.5ft) from top to toe. The giraffe's long neck has the same number of vertebrae as other mammals, but each one is greatly elongated. The giraffe's great height is an adaptation for feeding on young leaves in the upper branches of trees, which other browsing mammals cannot reach.

Giraffes have excellent sight, and because of their height they have the greatest range of vision of any terrestrial animal. If a giraffe spots danger, it will run away at speeds of up to 56kph (34mph). Occasionally, a giraffe will face its attacker, striking out with its front hooves or swinging its head like a club.

In order to reach fresh grass or drinking water, giraffes must splay their front legs apart, so that they can get their heads down to ground level. Giraffes settle on to their withdrawn legs to rest, and lie down when sleeping, resting their heads back on their hindquarters.

In times gone by, giraffes could be found in parts of North Africa, but due to a combination of over-hunting and the effects of climate change on vegetation they are now only thinly distributed south of the Sahara Desert.

**Distribution**: Sub-Saharan Africa.
**Habitat**: Open woodland and savannah.
**Food**: Leaves, grass and grains.
**Size**: 5.9m (19.25ft); 550–1,930kg (1,200–4,200lb).
**Maturity**: Females 3.5 years; males 4.5 years.
**Breeding**: Usually 1 young born every 2 years.
**Life span**: Up to 26 years recorded in the wild, and 36 years recorded in captivity.
**Status**: Threatened.

*Giraffes have prehensile lips and long tongues to help them gather leaves. They also have short horn-like ossicones on their heads – a feature they share with okapis.*

---

**Horse** (*Equus caballus*): 1.8m (6ft) tall; 2 tonnes (4,400lb) Today this species exists only as domestic breeds. These animals live on all continents of the world except Antarctica. In many places feral herds have appeared, such as in the Carmargue wetlands of southern France. The natural range of wild horses is thought to be the Eurasian steppes from Poland to Mongolia. Despite all being descended from domestic breeds, feral horses live in the same harem system as their wild ancestors, with a single male leading a small group of females. There are several breeds of horses, from the miniature Falabella and Shetland ponies to the mighty draft horses bred for hauling carts. Lighter horses were bred for speed. For example, the thoroughbreds used in racing are bred from fast-running Turkish and Arabic military breeds.

# Okapi

*Okapia johnstoni*

The okapi is a close relative of the giraffe. Although okapis are nowhere near as tall as giraffes, they do have relatively long necks and legs. Females are usually larger than males. Okapis have a deep red-brown coloration with distinctive horizontal black and white stripes along their rumps and legs. Despite their large size and unique appearance, they were not known to science until 1900.

Okapis spend most of their time alone, and they are very wary, running into dense cover if they detect danger. Sometimes okapis form small family groups and communicate with vocalizations and mutual grooming.

It is thought that there are between 10,000 and 20,000 okapis in the wild, but their dense forest habitat makes it very difficult for scientists to estimate their true population status.

*Male okapis have small, hair-covered, horn-like ossicones. They also have very long tongues, capable of reaching their eyes.*

**Distribution**: Congo Region.
**Habitat**: Dense tropical forest.
**Food**: Leaves, twigs and fruit.
**Size**: 1.9–2.1m (6.25–7ft); 200–300kg (440–660lb).
**Maturity**: Females reach sexual maturity at 1.5 years; males probably do not have the opportunity to mate until older.
**Breeding**: Single offspring born after a gestation of 421–427 days.
**Life span**: 30 years.
**Status**: Threatened.

# Common hippopotamus

*Hippopotamus amphibius*

These enormous animals spend much of their time in water, where they stay out of the hot sun and take the weight off their legs. Hippopotamuses lie in the water with only their nostrils, eyes and ears above the surface, and they can also submerge for up to 30 minutes, while walking on the bottom of the river or lake.

Hippopotamuses eat only plant food, which does not contain a large amount of nutrients. The water supports some of the weight of the hippos' massive bodies, so resting in water helps the animals conserve their energy and reduces the amount of food they need to eat. After dusk the hippos leave their watery refuge in search of grass, sometimes travelling more than 3km (2 miles) from water.

Large males set up territories along river banks, which they defend against other males. Although neighbouring territory-holders are usually peaceful, confrontations sometimes occur. When this happens, the males challenge each other with displays, including lunging, splashing, scattering dung with their short tails and displaying their tusks with great yawns of their mouths. If neither male backs off, fighting occurs, and sometimes they attack each other with their tusks – which can lead to fatal injuries, or deep gouges at the very least. Older males sport many scars from their past battles.

Males are aggressive towards intruders, including young hippos. Females are aggressive when they have young, and many consider hippos to be among the most dangerous of all African mammals.

**Distribution**: Most of Sub-Saharan Africa, although most common in tropical grassland areas of East Africa
**Habitat**: Deep water near reeds or grassland.
**Food**: Grass and other low-growing plants.
**Size**: 2–5m (6.5–16.5ft); 1–4.5 tonnes (2,200–9,900lb).
**Maturity**: Between 6 and 14 years.
**Breeding**: Successful males breed with several females. Mating takes place in water. Females are pregnant for 240 days. Usually a single young born during rainy season, with 2 or 3 years between births.
**Life span**: Up to 40 years.
**Status**: Common in general, although rarer in western and Central Africa.

*The hippo's tusks – actually its canine teeth – can weigh up to 3kg (6.5lb) each, and are used in fighting. There have been some reports of hippos overturning small boats and biting the occupants to death.*

# Dromedary camel

*Camelus dromedarius*

**Distribution**: North Africa to western India.
**Habitat**: Deserts and scrubland.
**Food**: Vegetation and carrion.
**Size**: 2.2–3.5m (7.25–11.5ft); 300–690kg (660–1500lb).
**Maturity**: 3 years.
**Breeding**: Single young or twins every 2 years.
**Life span**: 50 years.
**Status**: Common.

These tough animals have been domesticated in and around the Arabian peninsula for more than 4,000 years, and are prized for their endurance in hot, dry conditions. The dromedary, or one-humped, camel can carry loads of more than 200kg (440lb) for several days.

Camels can survive for long periods without drinking water. However, when water is available they can drink up to 57 litres (12 gallons) at a time to restore normal levels of body fluids. Camels have almost no sweat glands, so they lose water much more slowly than other mammals. Contrary to popular belief, the camel's hump contains fat, not water, and serves as an energy reserve – although the blubber does hold some water. During the breeding season, dominant males defend groups of up to 30 adult females from other males. Younger males form groups of bachelor males.

*As well as their characteristic hump, camels have other adaptations to the harsh conditions of the desert, including broad feet for walking on loose sand, long eyelashes, hairy ears, and nostrils that can be closed to keep out sand and dust.*

# Warthog

*Phacochoerus africanus*

This species gets its name from the warty protuberances located on the sides of the head and in front of the eyes, found only in the males. These powerful animals have large heads in proportion to the rest of their bodies, and both males and females have sharp tusks.

Unlike most species of wild pig, warthogs are active during the day, except in areas where they are likely to be attacked by humans. There they change to a nocturnal lifestyle in order to avoid human contact. When sleeping or rearing young, warthogs take refuge in holes – often those made by aardvarks.

If attacked by predators such as hyenas or lions, warthogs flee to the nearest available hole, backing into it so that they can face their attackers with their vicious tusks. Warthogs sometimes come together in groups called sounders, usually numbering 4–16 individuals. Although they are fairly abundant throughout their range, people hunt warthogs for their meat and to stop them eating crops. This poses a threat to warthog populations.

**Distribution**: Throughout Africa from Mauritania to Ethiopia, and southward to Namibia and eastern South Africa.
**Habitat**: Savannah and open woodland.
**Food**: Grass, roots, berries, and sometimes carrion.
**Size**: 0.9–1.5m (3–5ft); 50–150kg (110–330lb).
**Maturity**: 18–20 months.
**Breeding**: 1–8 young.
**Life span**: Can exceed 18 years in captivity.
**Status**: Abundant, but the subspecies *P. a. aeliani* is classified as endangered.

*In male warthogs, the upper tusks can exceed 60cm (24in) in length. However, it is the smaller and sharper lower tusks that are the warthog's main weapon. Curiously, warthogs kneel down to feed on grass and roots.*

---

**Pygmy hippopotamus** (*Hexaprotodon liberiensis*): 1.5–1.7m (5–5.5ft); 160–270kg (350–600lb)
This animal is found in hot lowland jungles in parts of West Africa, and, although it looks like a miniature version of the hippopotamus, there are a number of notable differences. These include a more rounded head and eyes on the side, rather than the top of the head.

**Giant forest hog** (*Hylochoerus meinertzhageni*): 1.3–2.1m (4.25–7ft); 130–275kg (285–605lb)
These large wild pigs travel about their tropical forest habitats in groups, or sounders, of up to 20 individuals, led by old males. Males are aggressive, will charge intruding males, and have also been known to charge humans.

**Bush pig** (*Potamochoerus porcus*): 1–1.5m (3.25–5ft); 46–130kg (100–285lb)
These pigs have long pointed ears, long white whiskers, and white crests along their backs. They live in the jungles of West Africa, where they forage for a wide range of food types at night. Their numbers have increased, probably as a result of the reduction of leopard populations.

# Wild boar

*Sus scrofa*

Although domestic pigs usually look quite different from wild boar, they are in fact the same species, and can readily interbreed. Wild boar live in groups called sounders, consisting of females and their young. The males live alone, but join sounders in the mating season, when they compete for access to females.

Male wild boar can be very aggressive. In Doñana National Park in Spain, they have been known to chase adult lynxes away from carrion. Wild boars sometimes construct shelters from cut grass, and female wild boars are the only hoofed animals that give birth and look after their young inside a crude nest.

These animals have an excellent sense of smell, and are able to sniff out nutritious tubers and roots underground, while they snuffle through the leaf litter. Foraging wild boars often leave telltale signs, frequently ploughing up large patches of soil. In some countries, where wild boar have been introduced, they have had a negative impact on local animals and plants, either by feeding on them directly, or by disturbing their habitats.

**Distribution**: Europe, North Africa and Asia.
**Habitat**: Forest and shrublands.
**Food**: Leaves, roots, fungi, small mammals and reptiles, eggs, carrion and manure.
**Size**: 0.9–1.8m (3–6ft); 40–350kg (88–770lb).
**Maturity**: 8–10 months.
**Breeding**: 1 litter of 1–12 young born annually.
**Life span**: 10 years.
**Status**: Common.

*Only male wild boar have tusks, which are extended upper and lower canine teeth. Piglets have striped patterns, which they lose as they get older.*

# DEER

*Deer are a group of hoofed mammals that are found across the Northern Hemisphere. They belong to the Cervidae family of mammals. In form and habit, deer resemble the horned antelopes of Africa, which are actually more closely related to sheep and cattle. However, instead of horns, deer grow antlers. In most species only males have them, and unlike horns which remain for life, antlers are shed annually.*

## Fallow deer

*Dama dama*

Fallow deer are easily distinguishable from other species of European deer by their somewhat flattened antlers and spotted summer coats. In some places fallow deer live alone, while in others they come together to form small herds of up to 30 individuals.

The breeding behaviour of this species is variable, and may depend on the way food is distributed. In some places males come together and attempt to attract females with dance-like rituals and bellowing, a behaviour known as a rut. In other places, males attempt to monopolize a group of females by defending good feeding areas from other males. Fallow deer have been introduced to many new places, but their original populations are falling because of hunting and climate change.

*Only the male fallow deer sport antlers, which can span 80cm (32in) from tip to tip. Adults shed and re-grow their antlers every year.*

**Distribution**: Originally from the Mediterranean and parts of the Middle East, but introduced to Britain, America and New Zealand.
**Habitat**: Open woodland, grassland and shrubland.
**Food**: Grass, leaves and twigs.
**Size**: 1.3–1.7m (4.25–5.5ft); 40–100kg (88–220lb).
**Maturity**: Females at 16 months; males at 17 months.
**Breeding**: A single fawn born annually.
**Life span**: 20 years or more in captivity.
**Status**: Common, but rare in its original range.

## Reindeer

*Rangifer tarandus*

The reindeer, also known as the caribou in North America, is the only deer species in which both males and females possess antlers. Herds are organized into hierarchies based on the size of the deers' bodies and antlers. Most herds make seasonal migrations, moving to where food is available. Northern populations often travel more than 5,000km (3,000 miles). During the migration, reindeer groups congregate into great herds of up to half a million individuals.

Reindeer have been domesticated for 3,000 years, and there are huge numbers in northern Siberia.

*The antlers of males can exceed 1m (3.25ft). Reindeer hooves are broad and flat – an adaptation for walking on soft ground and deep snow.*

**Distribution**: Greenland, Scandinavia, Siberia, Mongolia, north-eastern China, Alaska, Canada, and northern USA.
**Habitat**: Arctic tundra, boreal forests and mountainous habitats.
**Food**: Plant material (especially new growth in spring), leaves, twigs and lichens.
**Size**: 1.2–2.2m (4–7.25ft); 60–318kg (130–700lb).
**Maturity**: 1.5–3.5 years.
**Breeding**: 1 fawn produced annually.
**Life span**: 15 years.
**Status**: Common.

# Elk

*Alces alces*

**Distribution**: Northern Europe, Siberia, Alaska, Canada and northern parts of the United States.
**Habitat**: Marsh and coniferous woodland.
**Food**: Leaves, twigs, moss and water plants.
**Size**: 2.4–3.1m (8–10.25ft); 200–825kg (440–1,820lb).
**Maturity**: 1 year.
**Breeding**: 1–3 young born in spring.
**Life span**: 27 years.
**Status**: Common.

The name elk often causes confusion. In North America elks are known as moose. To compound this confusion, the name elk is also used in the Americas to refer to red deer. Elks are the largest deer in the world. They live in the cold conifer forests that cover northern mountains and lowlands. They are most common in Canada and Alaska but also live across northern Europe and Siberia.

These animals plod through forests and marshes, browsing on leaves, mosses and lichens. They often feed in rivers, nibbling on aquatic vegetation and even dive underwater to uproot water plants. In summer, they are most active at dawn and dusk. In winter, they are active throughout the day. They paw the snow to reveal buried plants and twigs.

Elks may gather to feed, but they spend most of the year alone. In the autumn mating season, the males fight each other for the females.

*Male elks are almost twice the size of females. The males sport huge antlers – nearly 2m (6.5ft) across – and have flaps of skin hanging below their chins, called dewlaps.*

**Roe deer** (*Capreolus capreolus*): 0.9–1.5m (3–5ft); 15–50kg (33–110lb)
This graceful deer is found over large parts of Europe, including Britain, where it lives in forests and on farmland. The smallest type of European deer, the roe deer lives alone or in small groups. Roe deer have been able to adapt well to habitat changes brought about by human activities, and they have actually increased in number. They eat more than 1,000 plant species across their natural range. When grazing out in the open, the deer form large groups of up to 90 members in order to reduce the risks of attack. In forests, where they are more protected from predators, the deer live in smaller groups of less than 15.

**Water chevrotain** (*Hyemoschus aquaticus*): 45–85cm (17.75–33.5in); 7–15kg (15.5–33lb)
The water chevrotain is a small African hoofed animal that lives south of the Sahara, from the coast of Sierra Leone to western Uganda. Chevrotains look like small deer but they actually form a separate group of hoofed animals, most of which live in Asia. Neither sex grows antlers, although males grow tusks. These are long upper canines that stick out of the mouth and extend to below the lower lips. The tusks are a feature shared with the muntjac deer of southern Asia, and may be primitive features now lost by most deer species. Water chevrotains are forest browsers. They are never more than 250m (820ft) away from a river. By day they stay hidden in undergrowth, but under the cover of darkness chevrotains come out into the open and feed in forest clearings and along river banks.

## Red deer

*Cervus elaphus*

Red deer are one of the most widespread of all deer species. As with species that are spread across the world, the common names used can be confusing. In North America the species is known as elk, while populations of red deer living in the far north of Canada are also known as wapiti, though many biologists argue that wapiti are, in fact, a separate species from red deer. Red deer prefer woodlands, while wapiti are more common in open country. Nevertheless, the two groups of deer very closely resemble each other in most other ways.

Only male red deer have antlers, which reach up to 1.7m (5.5ft) across, and a dark shaggy mane. Adult males use their antlers during the rut, which takes place in autumn. The fighting establishes which males will control the harems of females. Antlers fall off in winter and re-grow in time for the next year's conquests.

*Red deer only have red coats in summer. In winter, they grow longer and darker hairs.*

**Distribution**: Northern Africa, Europe, Asia and North America.
**Habitat**: Woodlands.
**Food**: Grass, sedge, forbs, twigs and bark.
**Size**: 1.6–2.6m (5.25–8.5ft); 75–340kg (165–750lb).
**Maturity**: 2 years.
**Breeding**: 1 fawn born in autumn.
**Life span**: 20 years.
**Status**: Common.

# ANTELOPES AND RELATIVES

*Antelopes are a large group of hoofed animals that live mainly in Africa, with a few living in Asia. Antelopes belong to the same group of mammals as cattle, bison, sheep and goats. Gazelles also belong to this same group. Antelopes and their relatives have horns rather than antlers. These are made from bone and are permanent features on the heads.*

## Blue gnu

*Connochaetes taurinus*

The blue gnu, also known as the wildebeest, is one of the most abundant large mammals in Africa. There are thought to be 1.5 million individuals in the Serengeti alone, forming the greatest concentration of wild grazing animals on Earth. Some herds stay in the same place; others are nomadic, constantly searching for sources of food. Migrating gnus travelling in immense herds that number in the thousands are one of the wonders of the natural world.

The males leave their herds when they are over a year old, forming groups of young bachelors. At about three or four years old, males set up small territories, which they defend

**Distribution**: Southern Kenya and southern Angola to northern South Africa.
**Habitat**: Savannah.
**Food**: Grass and succulent plants.
**Size**: 1.5m (5ft); 118–275kg (260–600lb).
**Maturity**: Females 2–3 years; males 3–4 years.
**Breeding**: Usually a single calf born each year.
**Life span**: Up to 21 years in captivity.
**Status**: Abundant, but continuing survival is dependent on conservation efforts.

from other males, and attempt to mate with females entering their areas. Mating activity is seasonal, and is usually timed so that the majority of calves are born close to the beginning of the rainy season, when new grass is plentiful.

Although populations have increased in the Serengeti, numbers have declined in other areas, such as south-west Botswana. There, competition with livestock and destruction of crops has prompted farmers to kill gnus and set up long fences to prevent them from migrating to wetlands when there are seasonal droughts.

*Gnus are named after the calls made by competing males – "genu." There are two species; this one is blue-grey, while the other is dark brown and black.*

## Impala

*Aepyceros melampus*

*Like many other antelopes, impalas have pointed, spiralling horns. Both sexes are similarly coloured, with a white belly, chin and tail, and black-tipped ears.*

Impalas are one of a number of antelopes that live on the African savannah. They are very quick and agile, and are capable of jumping high in the air, often clearing heights of 3m (10ft).

When conditions are harsh in the dry season, impalas come together in mixed herds, which may number in the hundreds, to search for food. During the more plentiful wet season, males and females separate into different groups, with males competing for territories. Successful males mark their areas with urine and faeces and then lure females into them with tongue-flashing displays. This signal has the effect of making the females group together as they pass through the displaying males. Non-resident males run away or flash their own tongues in defiance.

**Distribution**: Kenya and southern Angola to northern South Africa.
**Habitat**: Savannah and open woodland.
**Food**: Grass, and leaves from bushes and trees.
**Size**: 1.1–1.5m (3.5–5ft); females 40–45kg (88–99lb); males 60–65kg (132–143lb).
**Maturity**: 1 year.
**Breeding**: Single fawn born at a time.
**Life span**: 13 years.
**Status**: Common.

# Topi

*Damaliscus lunatus*

**Distribution**: Africa south of the Sahara Desert.
**Habitat**: Moist grasslands.
**Food**: Grass.
**Size**: 1.7m (5.5ft); 130–170kg (286.5–374.75lb).
**Maturity**: 2–3 years.
**Breeding**: Single calf born at end of dry season.
**Life span**: 20 years.
**Status**: Lower risk.

Topis are medium-sized antelopes that live in the savannahs of Africa. They prefer areas that are relatively damp – still too dry for a forest to grow but moist enough for bushes and small trees to grow in places. Topis are found south of the Sahara Desert, from Senegal to Sudan. Their distribution then extends through the plains of East Africa and across southern Africa.

Males defend a territory of grass, which will also be home to a few females and their young. At the centre of the territory is a mound or similar vantage point. The male uses this feature to display to the other topis in the area in order to reinforce his ownership of the territory and to attract more females to his herd. The females also stand on the mound in order to alert other topis of approaching danger.

The male has sole mating rights over the females. Gestation is about eight months, and young are born at the end of the dry season.

*Both male and female topis have horns. Males are slightly larger than females and have darker coats. The coat is a pattern of dark blotches under a fine coat of red-brown hairs. The blotches range from black to dark purple.*

---

**Blue duiker** (*Cephalophus monticola*): 72cm (28.25in); 10kg (22lb)
This small antelope lives across Central Africa. It is the smallest of the duikers, which are all much smaller than the grassland antelopes. The blue duiker is a forest animal. Being small helps it move through undergrowth. Both sexes have horns, although these are little more than short spikes. Blue duikers eat mainly fruits, shoots and buds, but also consume insects, snails and eggs. They live in breeding pairs that stay together for years. Blue duikers live for about 10 years.

**Zebra duiker** (*Cephalophus zebra*): 90cm (35.5in); 20kg (44lb)
This species of duiker, named after the black stripes running across its back, lives in the forests of West Africa. When not raising their young, zebra duikers live alone. They eat fruits and leaves. Most of the best food is located high in the branches and out of reach of the little antelopes. Zebra duikers survive on the leftovers of monkeys and other tree-living foragers who dislodge and drop food on to the ground.

**Common duiker** (*Sylvicapra grimmia*): 100cm (39.25in); 25kg (55lb)
The common duiker, also known as the grey or bush duiker, is the only species of duiker to live in both grasslands and forests. It is found south of the Sahara Desert. Common duikers live anywhere that there is cover for them to hide during the day. They eat a wide range of foods, which vary depending on their location. In forests they eat fruits, flowers and leaves, but in more open areas they dig up roots with their hooves.

# Hartebeest

*Alcelaphus buselaphus*

Hartebeests look a little unusual because their horns grow from a single boney plate on top of the head. This antelope used to be widely distributed. Today, the species' habitat has been turned over to cattle pasture, and the hartebeests now live in several fragmented populations. These are centred on Botswana and Namibia in the south and the East African savannah.

Hartebeest live in large herds. They once gathered into herds of 10,000, but today a group of 300 is more normal. The herd is organized into four types of subgroups. Females and their young form the largest subgroups. The next subgroup contains two-year-old males. They may be sexually mature but are still growing and are rarely sexually active. The other subgroupings are solitary adult males – above the age of three. Younger adult males defend a territory within the herd. Males older than seven have generally been forced from their territories.

**Distribution**: East and south-western Africa.
**Habitat**: Grasslands and woodlands.
**Food**: Grass.
**Size**: 1.5–2.4m (5–8ft); 75–200kg (165.25–441lb).
**Maturity**: 12 months.
**Breeding**: Single calves born at all times of year.
**Life span**: 20 years.
**Status**: Lower risk.

*Hartebeests are large antelopes. There are several subspecies that live in different parts of Africa; they are identified chiefly by the shape of their horns, which grow on both males and females.*

## Arabian oryx

*Oryx leucoryx*

The Arabian oryx is the only oryx found outside Africa. It is adapted to survive in very arid conditions. By the early 1970s the Arabian oryx was thought to be extinct in the wild, due to excessive hunting throughout the early 20th century. At this time, the only herds existed in zoos around the world. However, a captive-breeding programme was started in the 1960s, and oryx have been reintroduced into the wild in Oman, Jordan and Saudi Arabia. Wild populations now number around 500 individuals.

Since dry habitats contain relatively little nourishing plant material, oryx must range over vast areas to obtain enough food. Oryx are surprisingly good at detecting rainfall from a great distance, and will move towards areas where rain is falling so that they can eat fresh plant growth and drink water.

When water is not available, they eat succulent foods, such as melons or bulbs, to get the moisture they need. Oryx live in groups of around ten individuals, consisting of either a dominant male and females, or a group of young males. Although the oryx's exceptionally long and sharp horns are formidable weapons, most contests between males are settled by ritualized sparring.

**Distribution**: Originally in much of the Middle East, now only a few reserves in Oman, Jordan and Saudi Arabia.
**Habitat**: Dry habitats, including arid scrubland and deserts.
**Food**: Grass, shrubs, succulent fruit and bulbs.
**Size**: 1.5–2.3m (5–7.5ft); 100–210kg (220–463lb).
**Maturity**: 1–2 years.
**Breeding**: Single calf born.
**Life span**: 20 years.
**Status**: Endangered.

*Oryx have striking black or brown markings on their heads and lower bodies, and very long, straight horns, up to 1.5m (5ft) in length.*

## Gemsbok

*Oryx gazella*

*Gemsbok are large antelopes with long, slightly curved horns. Females have horns as well as the males, but they tend to be slightly shorter and more slender. Gemsbok living in the northern part of the range are darker than those living in the south.*

Gemsbok are highland antelopes. They live in dry woodlands and more open grassland habitats. Many of the gemsbok's closest relatives are desert animals. High-altitude habitats are also often dry, and this species is also able to survive in areas where food is scarce for long periods. When food is plentiful, the gemsbok consume almost nothing but grass. As this food source reduces during the dry season, they become browsers and select leaves and other food items from bushes and trees. At the driest times, the antelopes use their hooves to dig out roots and other underground storage organs. They have been known to dig up melons and cucumbers, which are full of water and supply the gemsbok with the drink they need before the rains return.

Gemsbok are polygynous, which means that successful males will mate with several females. Small herds tend to contain just one dominant adult male, while in larger herds there are enough females for a few bulls to tolerate each other. There is no breeding season, and males mate with females soon after they give birth.

**Distribution**: Southern and East Africa. Most common in Zambia and Tanzania.
**Habitat**: Highland areas of savannah and grassland.
**Food**: Grasses, roots, leaves and fruits.
**Size**: 1.95m (76.75in); 210kg (463lb).
**Maturity**: 2 years.
**Breeding**: Single calf born every 9 months. Newborn calves hidden in thicket.
**Life span**: 18 years.
**Status**: Lower risk.

# Addax

*Addax nasomaculatus*

**Distribution**: Sahara Desert.
**Habitat**: Desert.
**Food**: Grasses and shrubs.
**Size**: 1.5–1.7m (5–5.5ft);
60–125kg (132.25–275.5lb).
**Maturity**: 2–3 years.
**Breeding**: Single calf born
in spring.
**Life span**: 25 years.
**Status**: Endangered.

The addax antelope is found in the Sahara Desert and is well adapted to some of the driest and hottest conditions on Earth. The antelope rarely drinks liquid water, and can obtain most of the water it needs to survive from the plants it eats. It moves great distances in search of vegetation to eat and often spends long periods out in the open.

This species was once found across North Africa, although the scarcity of food in the desert meant that it was never present in large numbers. However, as one of the few large mammals to live in the deserts of North Africa, the addax has long been a target of hunters, who made use of its meat and hide. As a result of over-hunting in the last century, the addax now lives in a few tiny populations scattered across its original range. It is one of the most endangered of all antelope species. The species has some protection from extinction, however. Large numbers live in zoos.

*During the summer, addaxes are almost white, but their coat darkens in winter. The paler coat helps to reflect the sun's heat during the hottest time of the year.*

**Scimitar-horned oryx** (*Oryx dammah*):
1.7m (5.5ft); 204kg (449.75lb)
This desert antelope, also known as the white oryx, is thought to be extinct in the wild. It was once widespread across the Sahel – the African steppeland that borders the southern edge of the Sahara Desert. (Sahel means "shore" and refers to the "sea" of sand that is the desert.) Hunting was the downfall of this species in the same way as it was for its close relatives the addax and Arabian oryx. In the year 2000, after 35 years of monitoring, it was decided that no scimitar-horned oryxes survived in the wild. It is possible that some still remain in the remoter parts of northern Mali and Chad, but, even if they do, there would more than likely be too few to sustain a wild population in the future. The species survives in zoos. All is not lost, however: the Arabian oryx was saved from extinction by a captive breeding programme in the 1970s, one of the first conservation successes of this kind, so there is still hope for the scimitar-horned oryx.

**Sable antelope** (*Hippotragus niger*):
2.1m (7ft); 230kg (507lb)
The sable antelope, also called mbarapi, is known for the jet-black coat of the adult males. The females and immature antelopes have a red-brown coat. Both sexes have long, curved horns. Sables live in the savannahs of East and southern Africa. They are a favourite on safaris and are common in zoos. Like many grazing antelopes, sables live in small herds populated by several females and their juvenile offspring. The herd has just one adult male, who has sole mating rights over the females in the herd.

# Roan antelope

*Hippotragus equinus*

The roan antelope is also known as the horse antelope. It belongs to a tribe of antelopes called the Hippotragini – the horse-like antelopes. This tribe includes the oryxes, sable and gemsbok, all of which share similarities with horses in the way they look. There is, of course, only a distant relationship with horses.

Roan antelopes live in thickets and areas of shrubs. It lives in two main populations. The first is found in the belt of grassland that grows south of the Sahara Desert and north of the Congo rainforest. Here the roan is found as far west as Gambia and ranges east to Somalia. The second group is centred on Botswana and the surrounding region.

Roan antelopes live in small herds, which rarely contain more than about 20 individuals. Each herd has a single bull and several females. The remaining members are their offspring.

*The roan antelope is one of the largest antelope species. Only the cattle-like elands are appreciably larger. Young roan have pale reddish coats, which darken as the antelope ages. Adults also have a mane of short black hairs.*

**Distribution**: Africa, south of the Sahara Desert.
**Habitat**: Savannah.
**Food**: Grasses and leaves.
**Size**: 1.9–2.4m (6.25–7.75ft); 263kg (579.75lb).
**Maturity**: 2–3 years.
**Breeding**: Single calf born at all times of year.
**Life span**: 17 years.
**Status**: Lower risk.

## Waterbuck

*Kobus ellipsiprymnus*

*Only male waterbucks have horns. There are two races of waterbucks: the northern population has a flash of white on the rump against a background coat of reddish hairs while the southern group has a circle of white on the rump and a grey coat on the rest of the body.*

As their name suggests, waterbucks are seldom found far from water. However, African grasslands are dry places where there is not enough rain for trees to grow, so as a result waterbucks are most often found in valley bottoms, where water drains from higher areas.

There are two populations of waterbuck. The Defassa waterbucks range from the Horn of Africa across the northern fringe of the Congo Basin to the savannahs of West Africa. The southern group, known as the Ellisprymnus waterbucks, lives in parts of south-eastern Africa, such as Zambia, Zimbabwe and South Africa.

Waterbucks live in small herds. The herds are primarily made up of females and their young. Solitary males may adopt a territory that overlaps with those of other herds. These males mate with any females that enter their territory. The females are attracted to the male because he protects them from harassment by younger males. Younger males are non-territorial and have a more opportunistic mating strategy.

**Distribution**: One population in the south-east and another in West and Central Africa.
**Habitat**: Grasslands close to rivers and waterholes.
**Food**: Grass and low-growing herbs.
**Size**: 1.7–2.3m (5.5–7.5ft); 160–300kg (352.75–661.5lb).
**Maturity**: 3–6 years.
**Breeding**: Northern population calves once a year, southern group calves every 10 months.
**Life span**: 20 years.
**Status**: Lower risk.

## Kob

*Kobus kob*

Like their close relative the waterbucks, kobs are closely associated with water. They are found on river banks and beside watering holes on grasslands and along the edge of woodlands. Most feeding takes place in the early morning and evening.

Kobs employ what is known as a "lek" mating system – a system also used by some large deer, bats and birds. The males display in a lek – an array of small territories that are purely symbolic of the male's status because they are too small to hold enough resources to feed the male let alone a mate and young. Females move through the lek and choose which male to mate with. Most matings take place toward the centre of the lek, and territories there are highly contested. The dominant males fight for control of these central areas, and the best territories often change hands.

Only fully mature males can compete in the lek. Younger males stay with the females and young, where they may attempt to mate with females. This unwanted attention drives the females into the lek, where the younger males will not follow.

Outside the mating season, the males live in separate herds to the females and young. The males play no part in raising their young.

**Distribution**: Western and Central Africa south of the Sahara Desert.
**Habitat**: Savannah and woodlands.
**Food**: Grasses and reeds.
**Size**: 1.6–1.8m (5.25–6ft); 105kg (231.5lb).
**Maturity**: Between 1 and 2 years; males are unlikely to mate for several years.
**Breeding**: Dominant males display together in small territories called a lek. Females choose mates and produce a single calf born at end of rainy season.
**Life span**: 20 years.
**Status**: Lower risk.

*Male waterbucks have horns measuring about 44cm (1.5ft) long. Females do not have horns and they are also generally smaller than males.*

# Lechwe

*Kobus leche*

**Distribution**: Southern Africa.
**Habitat**: Floodplains.
**Food**: Grasses.
**Size**: 1.3–1.8m (4.25–6ft); 60–130kg (132.25–286.5lb).
**Maturity**: 2 years; males unlikely to breed until the age of 5.
**Breeding**: Mating takes place before rainy season.
**Life span**: 20 years.
**Status**: Lower risk.

Like other members of the *Kobus* genus, lechwes live close to water. This species is most closely associated with floodplains, where the land is covered by shallow water for some of the year. Lechwes live in the floodplains of the Zambesi River, which runs through Zambia and Mozambique, and the Okavango, which rises in Angola and forms a huge wetland in Botswana.

Lechwes spend long periods wading through water, eating the lush grass that grows there. A grazing animal living in water must face a series of challenges not seen on dry land. For example, the normal fast-running gait of antelopes that allows them to escape from predators is not very efficient in water because the fur on their legs become waterlogged, slowing the antelopes down. The hairs on a lechwe's lower leg, by contrast, are waterproofed with oils to prevent this from happening. Lechwes also run in giant bounds rather than gallops. Overall this method is slower than running on land, but no other antelope can beat a lechwe through water.

*Lechwes often feed while up to their chests in water. To help them walk through mud and across river beds, these antelopes have long hooves that spread the weight and prevent them from sinking into soft ground.*

**Nile lechwe** (*Kobus megaceros*): 1.4–1.7m (4.5–5.5ft); 60–120kg (132.25–264.5lb)
Nile lechwes live in the marshlands of southern Sudan and western Ethiopia. Their wetland habitats are fed by water from the White and Blue Niles. Nile lechwes are smaller than their southern cousins. There is also a more obvious difference between the males and females: as well as lacking horns, the females have pale brown coats, while males are a blackish-brown.

**Puku** (*Kobus vardonii*): 1.5–1.7m (5–5.5ft); 62–74kg (136.75–163lb)
The puku closely resembles the lechwe and kob. Like these antelopes this species lives in rivers and wetlands. It is found in the savannahs south of the Congo rainforest. Pukus are not at high risk of becoming extinct, although they have had problems in the past in some of their range. For example, in the 1930s the entire puku population of Malawi was wiped out by hunting and wetland drainage. Today, pukus have been reintroduced to this area but are reliant on reservations and conservation measures for their survival.

**Mountain reedbuck** (*Redunca fulvorufula*): 1.1–1.4m (3.5–4.5ft); 30kg (66lb)
There are three populations of mountain reedbuck: a southern group lives in the Cape Province of South Africa; another is located in the highlands of East Africa, from Tanzania to Ethiopia; and the third lives in Cameroon. Each population consists of a separate subspecies. Mountain reedbucks are the smallest of all reedbucks, but, like their relatives, they live in alpine meadows or woodlands close to streams.

# Southern reedbuck

*Redunca arundinum*

Southern reedbucks range from the southern fringe of the Congo Basin to northern South Africa. They are found close to water and spend most of their time hidden in thick cover. Reedbucks feed mainly at night. They are grazers and eat mainly grass and sedges.

They are solitary during dry periods, but when the rains come they gather into small family groups. Individuals communicate using whistles to greet and warn other herd members. The whistle is made by sharp exhalations through the reedbuck's nostrils.

The whistling sounds are also used during courtship. At this time the females also perform a dance that involves a series of pronks, or high, floating jumps. The jumps serve to spread the scent of glands located between her hind legs. The scent is released with a pop. After mating, the male defends the female from other males. Once the calf arrives, the male's role comes to an end, although he may return to the family once the calf is several months old.

**Distribution**: Southern Africa.
**Habitat**: Marshy areas and river banks.
**Food**: Grasses.
**Size**: 1.5m (5ft); 58kg (127.75lb).
**Maturity**: 2–3 years.
**Breeding**: Breeding peaks in summer.
**Life span**: 12 years.
**Status**: Lower risk.

*Female southern reedbucks do not have horns and are slightly smaller than the males, though both sexes are slender.*

## Common rhebok

*Pelea capreolus*

Rheboks are relatives of the wetland antelopes, such as the kob, waterbuck and lechwe. However, this species of antelope is unlike its relatives. In fact, with its wild woolly coat and odd-shaped head, it is unlike any other antelope. The rhebok lives in the mountains of South Africa. It occupies rocky alpine meadows and brush-covered areas.

The common rhebok is a browser. Unlike the grazers, which munch on mouthfuls of grass and leaves, this antelope picks the best leaves and buds from bushes and plucks the freshest shoots of grass. The rheboks feed in groups and one individual keeps watch for predators. If danger is near, the lookout animal warns the others in the group with a distinctive coughlike grunt.

Dominant male rheboks defend a harem of females, which typically contains about five females and their young. Most adult males have no harem or territory, however. These individuals are nomadic, and move through the territories of others, keeping watch for an opportunity to depose a dominant bull or sneak a mating with one of his females. During the rut before the autumn mating season, competition between males is fierce. Unusually for antelopes, fights to the death are not uncommon.

**Distribution**: South Africa.
**Habitat**: Rocky mountainsides.
**Food**: Plucks leaves and buds from shrubs and also eats grass.
**Size**: 1.1–1.25m (3.5–4m); 25kg (55lb).
**Maturity**: 18 months.
**Breeding**: Calves born in November.
**Life span**: 8 years in the wild, although unusually these antelopes do not survive that long in captivity.
**Status**: Lower risk.

*Rheboks are often mistaken for mountain goats because they have woolly coats, with hairs that are much longer than any other antelope. Only the males have horns.*

## Springbok

*Antidorcas marsupialis*

Of all the gazelles, this species is perhaps the one most associated with "pronking". These are high and graceful leaps that are inserted at seemingly random intervals as the gazelle runs along. The legs are held straight and stiff during a pronk, with feet together and the head tucked toward the chest. The leaps are thought to be an evasion tactic when the gazelle is being chased by predators. The springbok's chief threats are lions and cheetahs, both of which generally attack from behind and can easily outrun the gazelle over short distances. The leaps make it harder for the predators to judge when to pounce. The antelope's odd posture might add to the hunter's confusion as well as moving the vulnerable hind legs to a less accessible position.

Springboks used to move, or trek, in herds of hundreds of thousands, possibly millions, across the grasslands of southern Africa. Treks of anything approaching this magnitude are almost unheard of now, although larger herds might form in remote parts of Botswana and Angola. Today, most springboks live in nature reserves. Breeding takes place in the dry season. Male-only herds migrate in search of mates.

**Distribution**: South-western Africa from northern Angola to Namibia and Cape Province of South Africa.
**Habitat**: Treeless savannahs often among the tall grass close to dry lake beds.
**Food**: Grass and other low-growing plants.
**Size**: 96–115cm (3.25–3.75ft); 33–46kg (72.75–101.5lb).
**Maturity**: Between 1 and 2 years.
**Breeding**: Females are pregnant for 5 months. A single calf is born at intervals of 2 years.
**Life span**: 7 years.
**Status**: Lower risk.

*Typically of a gazelle, the springbok has long, thin legs and a slender body. Both male and female springboks have horns, which are relatively short and more slender in the female.*

# Dama gazelle

*Gazella dama*

**Distribution**: North-western Africa.
**Habitat**: Semi-desert.
**Food**: Grasses and leaves.
**Size**: 1.4–1.7m (4.5–5.5ft); 85kg (187.5lb).
**Maturity**: 1–2 years.
**Breeding**: Single calf born in September to November.
**Life span**: 10 years.
**Status**: Endangered.

The dama gazelle lives in the dry grasslands around the edge of the Sahara Desert. It is most common in the Sahel region, south of the desert in Mali, Chad and Niger, but it also extends to Mauritania and Sudan. This species is on the brink of extinction because it is a valuable source of meat in a region where food is scarce at the best of times. The gazelle's range has also been reduced by the encroaching desert.

Dama gazelles live in small herds of about 15 individuals comprising a more or less equal mix of the sexes. The gazelles are active during the day. When the rains come and pastures spring up along the edge of the desert, the gazelles migrate north. In the dry season the herds move south in search of food.

Female dama gazelles gestate for more than six months, which is a long time, even for a large gazelle of this kind. The calf is born highly developed, and within a week it is able to run as fast as the adults.

*The dama gazelle is the largest gazelle of all. Even for a gazelle it has exceptionally long legs and a long neck. The S-shaped horns are short and thicker in the males. The red-coloured coat is darkest in western individuals.*

---

**Royal antelope** (*Neotragus pygmaeus*): 50cm (19.75in); 2kg (4.5lb)
This is one of the smallest hoofed animals in the world, and is often found in forest clearings in parts of West Africa. It is well camouflaged, but will make huge bounds if spotted by predators, reportedly achieving leaps of up to 2.8m (9.25ft).

**Thomson's gazelle** (*Gazella thomsoni*): 0.8–1.7m (2.5–5.5ft); 12–85kg (26.5–187.5lb)
These attractive gazelles are found in the dry habitats of Sudan, Kenya and Tanzania. They have brown coats with a dark line running from the foreleg to the rump. This distinctive feature is not seen in other gazelles and may serve as a visual signal to help members of herds stay close together while moving at high speeds. Like several other antelopes, Thomson's gazelles have a behaviour called "stotting". When they spot predators stalking them, they make a series of curious jumps. This behaviour signals to the predators that they have been spotted and should not try to chase the obviously agile gazelles.

**Dwarf antelope** (*Neotragus batesi*): 50–57cm (20–22.5in); 2–3kg (4.5–6.5lb)
Also known as the pygmy antelope, this species lives in lowland tropical forests from southern Nigeria to Uganda. They are also common residents in orchards and plantations. Only male dwarf antelopes have horns. These are short and straight and project backward in line with the face. Dwarf antelopes are nocturnal and live on leaves, buds and fruits. Males defend an area of forest and attract groups of females into it during the mating season at the start of the rains.

# Gerenuk

*Litocranius walleri*

The gerenuk is known for its unusual feeding behaviour. While other browsers are restricted to leaves growing at the bottom of a shrub, which are generally old and tough, the gerenuk can reach the young and tender leaves growing higher up. When the leaves are out of reach of even its long neck, the gazelle rears up on to its hind legs to reach that little bit higher.

Gerenuks are an East African species. They are now dependent on conservation for their survival and few live outside the reserves of Kenya and Tanzania.

Their unusual feeding habits have an impact on the gerenuk's social structure. Males are highly territorial and defend an area containing as many suitable feeding bushes as possible. Females band together and move through the males' territories. When a receptive female meets a male, she initiates courtship. Female calves are weaned for just one year, allowing the mother to give birth again the following year. However, bull calves are suckled for 18 months, presumably to help them grow to a dominant size.

**Distribution**: East Africa
**Habitat**: Grasslands with plenty of shrubs.
**Food**: Leaves.
**Size**: 1.4–1.6m (4.5–5.25ft); 43.5kg (96lb).
**Maturity**: 2 years.
**Breeding**: 1–2 calves born every 1–2 years.
**Life span**: 12 years.
**Status**: Lower risk.

*The gerenuk's most distinctive feature is its exceptionally long neck, which allows it to reach the leaves of tall bushes. Females do not have horns.*

## Kirk's dik-dik

*Madoqua kirkii*

Kirk's dik-dik is a dwarf antelope. It lives in dry brushlands, where there are thick bushes to provide food and cover, seldom venturing out into open country. The species ranges across eastern Africa from southern Somalia to central Tanzania. From there its distribution extends into south-western Africa as far down as northern Namibia. For much of the year, the only moisture dik-diks get is the dew droplets on their plant food.

Dik-diks form breeding pairs that stay together for life. A male defends a large territory, which he shares with a single female. The pair produce young every six months or so. Most calves are born between November and December and then again between April and May. Breeding pairs mark their territory using their faeces. This is done in a ritualized manner, in which the male mixes his droppings and urine into his mate's so that their individual scents form a single odour for the pair.

These antelopes are shy, nocturnal creatures. They are easily spooked and will escape from danger by running in a confusing zigzag path, making a series of leaps as they do so. As it runs the antelope produces a "dik-dik" call, hence its common name.

**Distribution**: From the Horn of Africa across eastern Africa to northern Namibia in south-western Africa.
**Habitat**: Dry areas of brushland.
**Food**: Leaves, herbs and grasses.
**Size**: 52–67cm (20.5–26.5in); 3–6kg (6.5–13.25lb).
**Maturity**: Between 6 and 12 months.
**Breeding**: Single calves born twice a year.
**Life span**: 13 years.
**Status**: Common.

*The most distinguishing feature of these little antelopes is the long, almost pointed, snout. This elongated snout is a mechanism for keeping cool, in that heat is lost through evaporation from the large, damp nasal membrane.*

## Klipspringer

*Oreotragus oreotragus*

Klipspringers are agile little antelopes that live on or around rocky outcrops in dry parts of eastern and southern Africa. They are commonly seen on cliffs and in rocky highland areas. However, the fragmented nature of their habitat means that they live in relatively small populations.

The name klipspringer means "rock jumper" in Afrikaans. The antelopes are well suited to life in steep habitats. Most antelopes have long, extended legs to allow them to run quickly across the open savannah. However, klipspringers' legs are short and robust compared to other antelopes, which makes them more sure-footed and able to withstand jumps on to hard surfaces.

The klipspringer's hair is unique among the antelopes and other bovine animals because it is hollow and only loosely connected to the skin. This makes it much more similar to the hair of deer and the unusual pronghorns of North America.

Klipspringers live in monogamous pairs, which defend a territory together, using their droppings and scent marks from a gland on their faces to advertise their claim to the land. The couple are seldom far from each other. Each year they produce a single calf after a gestation (pregnancy) of about five months. Only half the calves survive their first year.

**Distribution**: Eastern and southern Africa from southern Sudan and Ethiopia to Namibia and most of South Africa.
**Habitat**: Rocky terrain in dry areas.
**Food**: Leaves and fruits.
**Size**: 75–90cm (2.5–3ft); 10–15kg (22–33lb).
**Maturity**: 1 year. The young are forced out of their parent's territory at the age of 7 months.
**Breeding**: A single calf born each year. Twins are produced on rare occasions.
**Life span**: 14 years.
**Status**: Lower risk.

*Male klipspringers have horns, which are short and spike-like. However, the females are slightly larger.*

# Oribi

*Ourebia oureb*

**Distribution**: Central and southern Africa.
**Habitat**: Grassland.
**Food**: Grass and leaves.
**Size**: 92–110cm (3–3.5ft); 12–24kg (26.5–53lb).
**Maturity**: 1 year.
**Breeding**: Most calves born in October or November.
**Life span**: 13 years.
**Status**: Lower risk.

Oribis are widespread antelopes, but despite their large distribution their populations are highly fragmented. The species is found in most parts of Africa south of the Sahara Desert except for the equatorial rainforests. Oribis live in flat areas of grasslands with a few bushes to provide food and cover. Today oribis are unlikely to survive in large numbers outside nature reserves.

The oribi is grouped in the dwarf antelope tribe. Along with its relatives, this species forms monogamous pairs, where a male and a female will mate for life. Occasionally, several individuals, including any young, gather into small herds. Females are smaller than males and achieve adult size as early as 10 months old. Males will take a few months longer to mature. Pairs mark their territories together, but the males have the dominant role. They rub secretions from the prominent preorbital gland on to landmarks such as tree trunks or stands of tall grass.

*Oribis have large preorbital glands (modified tear ducts that produce scented liquids). The black glands form a teardrop-shaped mark below each eye. These antelopes also have tufts of long hair on their knees.*

---

**Salt's dik-dik** (*Madoqua saltiana*): 52–67cm (20.5–26.25in); 4.25kg (9.25lb)
This dik-dik species lives in the dry mountains and stony semi-deserts of the Horn of Africa. They are the smallest of all dik-dik species. Like other dik-diks, this species forms lifelong breeding pairs. Each pair produces young twice a year, generally a single calf each time. As their name suggests, this species is also known for its "dik-dik" alarm call. At times of stress, the hairs on its forehead become erect.

**Dibatag** (*Ammodorcas clarkei*): 1.5–1.7m (5–5.5ft); 22–35kg (48.5–77.25lb)
Dibatags are beautiful antelopes that live in savannah habitats in Ethiopia and Somalia. They have very long, slender necks, which are used to reach the leaves on high branches. The antelopes have a long furry black tail, which is raised when they run. Their name comes from the Somali word for "erect tail". This species is now under threat of extinction due to poaching and war in the region.

**Cape grysbok** (*Raphicerus melanotis*): 61–75cm (2–2.5ft); 8–23kg (17.75–50.75lb)
The Cape grysbok is a rare antelope that lives only in the southern region of South Africa. It is similar in height to steenboks and other dwarf antelopes, but is considerably more stocky in build. Adults have reddish-brown fur, which helps them to blend into their woodland habitat. Grysboks are nocturnal. When they sense danger approaching, they lie down. If this tactic fails, the grysbok flees in the zigzag gallop that is typical of small antelopes.

# Steenbok

*Raphicerus campestris*

Steenboks live in two distinct populations, one in East Africa and the other in the south of the continent. Steenboks are strictly grassland antelopes and never enter woodland areas. Between the great savannahs of East Africa and the velds (another name for grasslands) of southern Africa grows a belt of woodland. This woodland divides the steenbok population in two, and communication between the groups is extremely limited.

Steenboks live alone or in breeding pairs. The antelopes occupy a small territory, which they mark with piles of dung and enforce by chasing away intruders. Unlike most antelopes, the steenbok does not use scented secretions from glands on the face to mark its territory.

Breeding takes place all year round but most calves are born in the summer. They are weaned by 3 months and live independently by the end of their first year.

**Distribution**: South and East Africa.
**Habitat**: Grasslands with cover.
**Food**: Grasses and roots.
**Size**: 70–95cm (2.25–3ft); 7–16kg (15.5–35.25lb).
**Maturity**: 1 year.
**Breeding**: Calves born throughout year.
**Life span**: 12 years.
**Status**: Common.

*Steenboks are small antelopes. Only the males have horns, which protrude directly up from the head. The steenboks have sharp hooves for digging roots and other foods out of the ground.*

## European bison

*Bison bonasus*

These large animals are now very rare, but, like their close relatives the American bison, they used to be very abundant. European bison disappeared from western Europe in the late Middle Ages, and became extinct in eastern Germany in the 18th century. The main reason for this decline was the loss of their habitat and an increase in hunting as human populations rose across northern Europe. By the early 20th century, European bison could only be found in Poland, and by 1925 both populations were extinct. Since then, new populations have been established in these places from captive European bison in zoos.

In former times, European bison formed groups of hundreds of animals during migrations or in good feeding grounds. Nowadays groups are much smaller, consisting of a few related females and their young. During the mating season there is fierce competition over females, and males charge and clash heads.

*European bison have less shaggy manes than those of American bison, but they have more powerfully built hindquarters.*

**Distribution**: Originally found over large parts of Europe including England, but now restricted to eastern Europe.
**Habitat**: Forest and grasslands.
**Food**: Leaves, twigs, bark and grass.
**Size**: 2.1–3.5m (7–11.5ft); 350–1,000kg (770–2,200lb).
**Maturity**: 2–4 years.
**Breeding**: Single calf born every 1–2 years.
**Life span**: Up to around 20 years in the wild, and 40 years in captivity.
**Status**: Endangered.

## African buffalo

*Syncerus caffer*

African buffaloes are formidable animals. They can be very aggressive, and have been known to inflict fatal injuries on lions. Accordingly, lions tend to be reluctant to tackle these large buffalo unless they are very hungry. African buffaloes form herds of between 50 and 500 individuals. These herds are most common in dry habitats, such as grasslands and woodland, and less so in dense rainforests.

Herds contain cows that are closely related to each other. Calves less than two years old stay with their mothers. Young bulls leave the herd after two years and join smaller, single-sexed, bachelor herds. There is a hierarchy of dominance within the bachelor herd, with rigorous competition for the top spots. This competition reaches its peak as the rainy season arrives, when the bulls join the main herd and compete for the cows. Cows take their time to select a mate, waiting to attract as high-ranking an individual as possible. Highly ranked bulls tend to be large and aggressive and will therefore produce large male offspring, which will grow up to become successful breeders themselves. In addition, any female offspring will also prefer to breed with large males.

*African buffaloes are giant animals with huge heads. Both sexes have curved horns that are connected by a thick boss on the forehead. This boss is most developed in the males to protect the head during fights.*

**Distribution**: South of the Sahara Desert. Most common in eastern and southern Africa although they are found as far north as Sudan and west to Guinea.
**Habitat**: Grasslands and woodlands.
**Food**: Grasses and other low-growing plants.
**Size**: 2.1–3.4m (7–11.25ft); 300–900kg (660–1,985lb).
**Maturity**: Females able to produce young at 5 years; males start to breed at 8.
**Breeding**: Single calves born in rainy season after a gestation of about 11 months. Twins are very rare. Females typically produce young every two years.
**Life span**: 15 years.
**Status**: Lower risk.

**Giant eland** (*Taurotragus derbianus*): 2.1–3.4m (7–11.25ft); 330–1,000kg (730–2,200lb)
The giant eland is the largest antelope of all. They are woodland animals, while the slightly smaller common elands are associated with grasslands. They range from Senegal to southern Sudan. As a member of the spiral-horned antelopes this species is more closely related to cattle than the smaller grazing antelopes. Elands resemble cattle in many ways and as a result they are often hunted for their meat. Giant elands are now an endangered species because of this. Young and female giant elands have reddish coats, but this fades to grey in adult males. Both sexes grow horns, but the males' are twice the size of the females'. Giant elands live in small groups of about 25 individuals.

**Mountain nyala** (*Tragelaphus buxtoni*): 2.25m (7.5ft); 225kg (496lb)
Mountain nyalas are an endangered species. They live in the highlands of Ethiopia. During the intense rains that affect the region, the antelopes move to lower altitudes. Mountain nyalas are slightly larger than their lowland cousins. Both sexes have a grey coat, which grows shaggy during the winter.

# Common eland

*Taurotragus oryx*

This is one of two species of eland, both of which occupy similar types of open savannah habitat. The eland is the largest of a number of related species, characterized by spiralling horns and vertical cream-coloured stripes along the flanks and haunches.

Elands occupy large home ranges, using different habitats at different times of the year, and can cover in excess of 220sq km (86sq miles) per year. Approximately 14,000 eland live in the Serengeti National Park in East Africa, where they form small herds, usually consisting of less than 25 animals.

Like many hoofed animals, eland males fight for dominance and the opportunity to mate with females. Competing males shove each other with locked horns, until one gives up and retreats. Elands are easily tamed and, due to their highly nutritious milk, tender meat and good-quality hides, people are trying to domesticate them on farms in Africa and Russia.

**Distribution**: Southern and eastern Africa.
**Habitat**: Savannah and open woodland.
**Food**: Leaves and fruit.
**Size**: 1.8–3.4m (6–11.25ft); 400–1,000kg (880–2,200lb).
**Maturity**: Males 4 years; females 3 years.
**Breeding**: Single calf born.
**Life span**: 23 years.
**Status**: Vulnerable.

*Male elands tend to be larger than females, but both sexes carry characteristic spiralling horns, which may be up to 1m (3.25ft) long.*

# Nyala

*Tragelaphus angasii*

**Distribution**: South-eastern Africa.
**Habitat**: Damp areas of thick grasses.
**Food**: Leaves and grasses.
**Size**: 1.8–2.1m (6–7ft); 55–126kg (121–278lb).
**Maturity**: 2–4 years.
**Breeding**: Breeding peaks in spring and autumn.
**Life span**: 15 years.
**Status**: Lower risk.

Nyalas are seldom far from water in habitats where there are stands of thick grass and other cover. Nyalas are spiral-horned antelopes, and are therefore more closely related to cattle and bison than the grazing antelopes and gazelles.

They are nocturnal browsers, eating fresh leaves and buds. They resort to eating grasses and other low-quality foods only during dry periods. These antelopes live in small herds of about 20 individuals. Females tend to stay in the same herds throughout their lives, while males are more transitory, forming small, temporary, male-only herds that move between groups of females.

Both adult males and females have a crest of hair running along the back. This is often white in the males. During courtship, males raise the crest. This often engenders fighting among the males, and deaths and serious injuries are not uncommon due to the antelope's sharp horns.

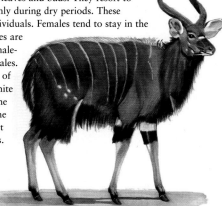

*There is a marked difference between male and female nyalas: females have the same colouring as the young (a red coat with thin stripes down the flanks) while males are larger and have a grey coat. Only males have horns.*

## Greater kudu

*Tragelaphus strepsiceros*

*The greater kudu is not the heaviest but it is one of the tallest antelopes, being up to 1.5m (5ft) at the shoulder. They also have the longest horns, at 1.2m (4ft), of any spiral-horned antelope. The sable and oryxes are the only antelopes to have longer horns.*

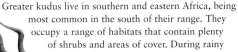

Greater kudus live in southern and eastern Africa, being most common in the south of their range. They occupy a range of habitats that contain plenty of shrubs and areas of cover. During rainy periods the antelopes spend more time in woodlands while in droughts they migrate to river banks.

Members of the southern population of kudus are darker than those in the north. They are blue-grey, while northern kudus are more reddish. In common with their close relatives the nyalas, the males darken as they age.

The sexes are segregated. Adult males live in small herds of about five individuals, while a few adult females form their own herd, which also includes their offspring. The calves stay with their mothers until the age of about three.

The two types of herds occupy neighbouring territories and come together only during the breeding season. This takes place during the second half of the rainy season, which arrives between February and June. Males will mate with as many females as they can. Females give birth about eight months later.

**Distribution**: Southern and eastern Africa. The largest population live in Namibia and the Cape of South Africa. The eastern population is much more fragmented.
**Habitat**: Woodlands and areas of shrubs.
**Food**: Leaves, fruits, herbs and grasses.
**Size**: 1.9–2.5m (6.25–8.25ft); 120–315kg (264–694lb).
**Maturity**: 3 years. Males leave the herd after first year.
**Breeding**: Mating takes place at end of rainy season.
**Life span**: 20 years.
**Status**: Lower risk.

## Bushbuck

*Tragelaphus scriptus*

*Only male bushbucks have horns, which usually spiral once and are otherwise straight and parallel to one another. Females are a paler brown than the males.*

Bushbucks live across Central Africa south of the Sahara Desert to the north of the Kalahari Desert. They are not found in the rainforest of the Congo but live in most other open habitats that have enough cover. They are browsers, picking leaves and fruits from bushes rather than eating grasses. They spend the day hidden among the woodlands and thickets that grow along river banks, but by night they emerge into more open areas to feed.

Bushbucks give birth at all times of year, although in drier areas they tend to wait until the rainy season. In wetter areas, there is enough food available for females to give birth two times each year. Newborn calves cannot outrun predators and so their mothers keep them hidden in the bushes for up to four months. The young calves have no distinctive odour to attract hunters, and their mothers move them to new hiding places regularly.

Unusually for antelopes, bushbucks are solitary creatures. They do not defend a territory and rarely get into disputes. In places with plenty of food, there may be several individuals living close together, though there is little social interaction.

**Distribution**: Central Africa as far south as northern Botswana. Not found in the Congo Basin.
**Habitat**: Woodlands and shrublands.
**Food**: Leaves, twigs and flowers.
**Size**: 1.2–1.5m (4–5ft); 24–75kg (53–165lb).
**Maturity**: 1–3 years.
**Breeding**: Calves born all year round but most commonly during rainy season. The gestation period is about 180 days.
**Life span**: 20 years.
**Status**: Common.

# Bongo

*Tragelaphus eurycerus*

**Distribution**: West Africa, the Congo, northern Kenya and southern Sudan.
**Habitat**: Lowland tropical rainforests.
**Food**: Browses on leaves, fruits and flowers.
**Size**: 1.7–2.5m (5.5–8.25ft); 150–220kg (331–485lb).
**Maturity**: Between 1 and 3 years.
**Breeding**: Single calves born all year round. Twins are seen but only rarely. The gestation period is about 9 months.
**Life span**: 20 years.
**Status**: Lower risk, although at increasing risk of poaching.

Bongos are forest antelopes. They have shorter legs than other antelopes, which is a typical body form of forest herbivores. (Long legs are used for running quickly and this is not possible in dense jungle, whereas shorter legs make the bongos more sure-footed.) Bongos also have distinctive white markings on the legs and above the eyes. These may act as visual signals so that the antelopes can see each other among the dense foliage.

Most bongos live in lowland rainforest, although small populations also live in the highland regions in northern Congo and Kenya. Bongos are both grazers and browsers. They will eat a range of plant foods including leaves, flowers, twigs, thistles and grasses. They have long, flexible tongues, which they use to pluck the freshest leaves. The horns are also used to pull on or break high branches.

Most large forest animals live alone (the lack of space makes it hard for herds to stay together), but bongos do form small herds of around six individuals, containing an equal mix of the sexes.

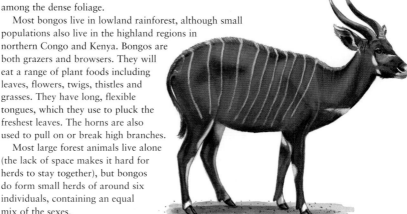

*Along with the elands, the bongos are the only spiral-horned antelopes to have horns on both sexes. The horns of females are straighter than those of the males. Females and young are red but adult males are darker.*

# Sitatunga

*Tragelaphus spekii*

**Distribution**: Central Africa from Namibia and Botswana in the south to Gambia in the west and Ethiopia in the east.
**Habitat**: Swamps and marshes.
**Food**: Water plants.
**Size**: 1.1–1.7m (3.5–5.5ft); 50–125kg (110–275lb).
**Maturity**: Between 1 and 2 years old. Males mature a few months later than the females.
**Breeding**: Young born throughout year after a gestation of 8 months.
**Life span**: 20 years.
**Status**: Lower risk.

The sitatunga lives in swamps and marshy areas of Central Africa. It ranges from the forests of the Gambia to southern Ethiopia and then south to the Okovango Delta in Botswana. It is an excellent swimmer and often moves to deep water to avoid predators. It may submerge completely with just its nostrils emerging above the water, such as when seeking refuge from predators. In shallow water, the antelopes run in bounds, which would be ungainly and slow on land but is the most effective way of moving through, or rather over, water.

Male sitatungas are considerably larger than females. Only the males carry horns. Sitatungas are non-territorial and have only the most basic of social systems. Females form herds, which also contain the young of both sexes. As they approach maturity, males leave their mother's herd and adopt a solitary lifestyle.

Breeding occurs all year around. A male approaches a female and chases her through the water before mating Females produce a single young each year. Young are born in the water and hidden on a dry platform of reeds often surrounded by deep water.

*The sitatunga is a semi-aquatic antelope that spends a great deal of time wading through water. Its hooves are elongated and widely splayed, and, like snowshoes, do not sink into soft wet ground.*

## Chamois

*Rupicapra pyrenaica*

**Distribution**: North-western Spain, Pyrenees and central Italy. *R. rupicapra* is more widespread from Europe to the Middle East.
**Habitat**: Alpine meadows.
**Food**: Herbs, flowers, lichen, moss and pine shoots.
**Size**: 0.9–1.3m (3–4.25ft); 24–50kg (53–110lb).
**Maturity**: 8–9 years.
**Breeding**: 1–3 young born in spring.
**Life span**: 22 years.
**Status**: Endangered.

There are two distinct species of chamois, both found in mountainous areas of Europe. They are both quite similar in appearance and behaviour, but this species – *Rupicapra pyrenaica* – has a more restricted distribution, is rarer than the other, and is now dependent on conservation efforts for its survival.

One of the reasons that chamois are rare is because they were hunted excessively for their meat – considered a delicacy in some regions – and for their hides, which were once made into high-quality leather for polishing glass and cars. Chamois are well adapted to living in mountainous habitats, and are very agile. When they are alarmed, they can bound up steep rocky slopes, and can leap almost 2m (6.5ft) straight up to get to inaccessible rocks.

Chamois live in small herds, usually consisting of females and their young. In autumn, males join the herds to compete for females, fighting each other with their sharp horns. Female herd members will often help one another. If a mother dies, other females will look after the young, and the animals are generally thought to take it in turns to stand guard while the rest of the herd feeds.

*Chamois have long, thick fur to keep them warm in alpine conditions. Both males and females possess the distinctively slender, sharp horns, which are shaped like upside-down "J"s.*

## Barbary sheep

*Ammotragus lervia*

As their name suggests, barbary sheep originally came from the Barbary Coast – the old name for the Magreb region in north-western Africa. The sheep's local name is "aoudad". Today the species is rare in its homeland but has been introduced to Germany and Italy and has also become feral in the south-western United States. This last region shares many similarities with its natural habitats. In the wild, barbary sheep live on the rocky slopes of the Atlas Mountains as high as the snow line.

**Distribution**: North-western Africa as far south as Chad and Sudan; introduced to Europe and North America.
**Habitat**: Deserts, canyons and mountains.
**Food**: Grasses and leaves.
**Size**: 1.5m (5ft); 65–145kg (143.25–319.75lb).
**Maturity**: 18 months to 2 years.
**Breeding**: Breeding season is in autumn with single lambs, or sometimes twins, born at the start of spring.
**Life span**: 10 years in the wild, but more in captivity.
**Status**: Vulnerable in natural range, although doing well in areas where introduced.

Barbary sheep are a desert species. The high mountains may often be cold but they are also very dry, and as a result barbary sheep must be able to survive without drinking for long periods.

Barbary sheep live in flocks with a strict dominance hierarchy. This ranking system runs through both the male and female lines. Even juvenile sheep have a rank, which goes a long way to establishing their future position in adult society. The hierarchy is enforced through frequent violent confrontation, where rivals butt heads and hook horns in twisting wrestling matches.

Most sheep mate between September and November. The gestation period is about 4 months, which means the lambs are born at the start of spring, when their chances of survival are best.

*Barbary sheep are sexually dimorphic (the sexes look different). Males weigh up to twice as much as the females. Both sexes have horns, but those of the females are smaller.*

**Ibex** (*Capra ibex*): 1.1–1.7m (3.5–5.5ft); 35–150kg (77–330.75lb)
A relative of the domestic goat, the ibex lives in alpine regions of Europe, parts of the Middle East, north-eastern Africa and some mountainous regions of Asia. The ibex has massive, curved horns that can be over half the length of the animal's body in males. The coat is grey-brown. Older males have a small beard and a "mane" of longer hairs on the back of the neck. It is threatened with extinction in some parts of its range.

**Walia ibex** (*Capra walie*): 1.5m (5ft); 102kg (225lb)
This species of African goat is often regarded as a subspecies of the more cosmopolitan ibex. It is found only in the mountains of northern Ethiopia, where it lives a precarious existence in the canyons and gorges cut by the torrential rains that fall most years.

**Spanish goat** (*Capra pyrenaica*): 1.2m (4ft); 57.5kg (127lb)
The Spanish goat, also called an ibex, lives in the Pyrenees. It is darker than other ibexes and more closely related to *Capra aegagrus*, a largely Asian species that is the wild ancestor of domestic goats.

# Musk ox

*Ovibos moschatus*

Although musk oxen look like large hairy cattle or bison, they are in fact relatives of goats and sheep. These animals live on the barren, windswept tundra that exists in the far north within the Arctic Circle. This habitat forms in places that are too cold and dry for trees to grow. It might seem odd that this icy land is too dry for trees, but plants need liquid water to grow, and there is only enough water available to sustain grasses and other hardy plants.

Both sexes have large hooked horns that cover most of the forehead. Male musk oxen are larger than females because they must fight other males to win and defend a harem of females. They butt each other with their horns in shows of strength. During the mating season the bulls produce a strong smell, which is what gives the species its name.

**Distribution**: Canadian Arctic and Greenland. Re-introduced to Norway and Russia.
**Habitat**: Tundra.
**Food**: Grass, moss and sedge.
**Size**: 1.9–2.3m (6.25–7.5ft); 200–410kg (440–904lb).
**Maturity**: 2–3 years.
**Breeding**: 1 or 2 young produced every 1–2 years in spring.
**Life span**: 18 years.
**Status**: Common.

*The whole of a musk ox's body is covered in long fur except the area between its lips and nostrils. The hairs keep the animal warm but also defend against the huge numbers of biting insects that swarm across the tundra in the short summer.*

# European mouflon

*Ovis musimon*

**Distribution**: Sardinia and Corsica. Herds also introduced to middle Europe.
**Habitat**: Wooded areas on steep slopes.
**Food**: Grasses.
**Size**: 1–1.3m (3.25–4.25ft); 25–55kg (55–121lb).
**Maturity**: 1 year.
**Breeding**: Lambs born in autumn.
**Life span**: 10 years.
**Status**: Vulnerable.

Sheep were one of the earliest domestic animals. They are now classed as a separate species, *Ovis aries*, although crossbreeding with wild species is still possible. Most of today's domestic sheep are descended from the Asian mouflon, or urial (*Ovis orientalis*), although some breeds have ancestors that were European mouflons. The European mouflon's original wild range was western Asia, but it was introduced to Europe thousands of years ago and now some of the few places where this species lives wild are reserves on the Mediterranean islands of Corsica and Sardinia.

Mouflons live in flocks. In summer the rams stay away from the ewes and young. Fights are rare and flock members seldom wander far from each other. However, this herd instinct may be due to some selective breeding in the past.

*Despite being the smallest wild sheep, European mouflons are sturdy animals, with a thickset neck and strong legs. Males are about 30 per cent larger than females. Adults have paler faces than the young and also grow paler with age.*

# SEALS AND RELATIVES

*The coasts of Europe and Africa are home to pinnipeds – the group of mammals that includes seals, sea lions and walruses. The word pinniped means "fin footed". Unlike other sea mammals, these species are descended from carnivorous, terrestrial ancestors. Like whales and dolphins, pinnipeds have a layer of blubber under their skin, which keeps them warm in cold water.*

## Mediterranean monk seal

*Monachus monachus*

**Distribution**: Less than 20 sites around the Mediterranean and Black Sea and Atlantic coast of Mauritania.
**Habitat**: Subtropical coastline.
**Food**: Fish and cephalopods.
**Size**: 2.3–2.8m (7.5–9.25ft); 250–300kg (550–660lb).
**Maturity**: 3 years.
**Breeding**: 1 pup born every other year.
**Life span**: 24 years.
**Status**: Critically endangered.

The Mediterranean monk seal is possibly Europe's most endangered mammal, with only about 500 animals remaining in small, scattered groups around the Mediterranean and Black Sea. There is also a small isolated population off the Atlantic coast of Mauritania, in West Africa.

Monk seals are very intolerant of disturbance. If a pregnant female is distressed, she will abort her foetus, and mothers may desert their young. The increasing development of the Mediterranean and Black Sea coastlines has meant that there are fewer and fewer secluded spots left for these peaceful animals. They also suffer from hunting pressure and from becoming entangled in fishing nets. Being mammals, all seals have to breathe air; if they get caught in fishing nets and held underwater, they drown before too long.

Females give birth to their young in grottoes and sea caves. Those with underwater entrances are particularly favoured. Youngsters stay with their mothers for about three years, learning how to fish and interact with other seals before seeking their own territories.

*This is the darkest seal of the region, uniformly dark brown except for a white patch on the belly.*

## Harp seal

*Pagophilus groenlandicus*

Harp seals are very social animals, congregating in huge numbers to give birth on ice floes in areas along the Arctic coastline. However, their sociality has led ultimately to their decline. The pups have very soft, thick fur, which is much sought after in some parts of the world. When the pups are gathered in large numbers, they are easy for hunters to find and club to death. Extensive hunting by humans reduced the total harp seal population from around ten million individuals to just two million by the early 1980s. However, once their plight was realized, hunting pressure was reduced and the population is now slowly recovering.

It will take a long time for harp seal numbers to reach their previous levels because the seals have a low rate of reproduction. Producing just one pup a year means that the population does not grow very quickly. When hunting, adult seals may dive to depths of 200m (666ft) in search of herring and cod, which make up the bulk of their diet.

**Distribution**: Arctic Ocean.
**Habitat**: Open sea for most of the year.
**Food**: Pelagic crustaceans and fish.
**Size**: 1.7–1.9m (5.5–6.25ft); 120–130kg (265–285lb).
**Maturity**: 5 years.
**Breeding**: 1 pup born every year.
**Life span**: 16–30 years.
**Status**: Vulnerable.

*The luxuriant fur of the pups keeps them warm on the Arctic icepack.*

**Caspian seal** (*Pusa caspica*): 1.3–1.5m (4.25–5ft); 55kg (121lb)

The Caspian seal lives in the Caspian Sea on the border of Europe and central Asia. It is one of only two seals to live in landlocked waters. Being a relatively small body of water, the Caspian Sea varies in temperature a great deal throughout the year. This variation impacts on the behaviour of the seals. In winter, when the northern part of the Caspian freezes, the seals live in large colonies on the ice. In summer, however, the ice melts and the seals migrate to the deeper water in the south, which remains cooler. Caspian seals eat fish and crabs. Water pollution has killed much of the seals' food supply as well as making many seals infertile. As a result, Caspian seals are vulnerable. Hunting has also been a problem for the seals. For centuries the people have relied on the seals for oils, skins and meat.

# Common seal

*Phoca vitulina*

One of the two seal species found commonly in British waters, the common seal has a dog-like face. Its snout is much more rounded than the Roman-style nose which typifies the grey seal, Britain's other common seal.

It is difficult to get a good estimate of the common seal's population size because it lives in small, widely distributed groups, and is highly mobile.

Common seals have large, sensitive eyes with specialized retinas, which allow them to see well underwater. However, sometimes the water is too murky for seals to be able to hunt by sight. At these times common seals switch to another sense – touch. Their long whiskers are highly sensitive and allow the seals to feel for prey in the gloom.

**Distribution**: North Atlantic, Pacific and Arctic coastlines.
**Habitat**: Sheltered coastal waters.
**Food**: Fish, cephalopods and crustaceans.
**Size**: 1.2–2m (4–6.5ft); 45–130kg (99–285lb).
**Maturity**: Females 2 years; males 5 years.
**Breeding**: Single pup produced every year.
**Life span**: 26–32 years.
**Status**: Common.

*From a distance, a seal's head poking above the waves can closely resemble that of a human. They are sometimes mistaken for swimmers in trouble. The common seal is also known as the harbour seal.*

# South African fur seal

*Arctocephalus pusillus pusillus*

**Distribution**: Coastline of southern Africa and Atlantic and Indian Oceans.
**Habitat**: Breeding colonies form on rocky islands and coastlines.
**Food**: Fish, squid and crabs.
**Size**: 1.8–2.3m (6–7.5ft); 120–360kg (264–794lb).
**Maturity**: 3–6 years.
**Breeding**: Mating season in October. Gestation lasts just under one year.
**Life span**: 20 years.
**Status**: Common.

South African fur seals are a subspecies of the Cape fur seal. Another subspecies, called the Australian fur seal, lives around the coast of southern Australia. The South African fur seal is slightly larger, but the two subgroups are otherwise very similar.

South African fur seals spend most of the year at sea. They rarely venture very far from the land, however, generally staying within 160km (100 miles) of the coast. The fur seals' main foods are free-swimming aquatic animals such as fish and squid. The seals dive to depths of about 40m (130ft) to find food and stay underwater for about 2 minutes. (Their Australian relatives must dive a great deal deeper and for longer to find their food.) South African fur seals also prey on animals living on the bottom of shallow coastal waters, including crabs and other crustaceans.

In spring, the males arrive on rocky islands and coastlines around southern Africa, where they set up territories. A few days later, the pregnant female seals arrive at the shore and choose a place on the beach to give birth. About a week after the calves are born, the males mate with the females in their territory. The products of these matings are born the following year.

*Male South African fur seals are twice the size of the females. They are also grey-black in colour, while the females are browner. Males also have a thick mane that helps their necks to look larger and more powerful and also acts as protection during fights.*

## Grey seal

*Halichoerus grypus*

Grey seals live across the North Atlantic. As well as on the coast of Canada's maritime provinces, the grey seal is found from Iceland to the coast of northern Europe and in the Baltic Sea. A few colonies even exist as far south as northern Spain and Portugal.

Like most pinnipeds (the group of carnivores made up of seals, sea lions and the walrus), male grey seals are larger than the females. Despite the size difference, males reach their full adult size at 11 years old, which is four years earlier than the females.

Grey seals eat a range of fish and also a small amount of aquatic molluscs, such as squid, and crabs and other crustaceans. Grey seals hunt in open water but often return to the shore to rest. Breeding takes place on the coastline. Colonies form in early winter on beaches, rocky shores and in caves. Before breeding, the adults eat a great deal because they will fast while on shore. Females give birth on the beach to the pups conceived the year before, while the males fight for control of the mates. Mating takes place after the calves are weaned.

**Distribution**: Coastlines and islands of northern and western Europe and eastern Canada.
**Habitat**: Rocky coasts.
**Food**: Fish.
**Size**: 1.8–2.2m (6–7.25ft); 150–220kg (330–485lb).
**Maturity**: 3–6 years.
**Breeding**: Breeding season in winter. The males return to sea after mating. Calves are suckled by their mothers for 17 days. The mothers then leave calves on the beach. The calves follow after a few days.
**Life span**: 25 years.
**Status**: Common.

*Both sexes of grey seal are grey, but the males are darker than the females. Females have dark spots on their paler skin, while males have pale spots on their darker bodies.*

## Bearded seal

*Erignathus barbatus*

Bearded seals are solitary animals. They live in the shallow water of the Arctic Ocean. They do come on to gravel beaches on islands and the northern coastlines of Eurasia and North America at times. They have even been seen on the coast of Scotland. However, bearded seals prefer areas covered in broken ice. They haul themselves on to the floes for a rest and then dive between the broken ice to feed. They also ram their heads through thin ice to create breathing holes for use while feeding.

Bearded seals find a lot of their food on the sea bed. Their highly sensitive whiskers detect the tiny water currents produced by the movements of their prey, which include crustaceans such as shrimp and crabs, shellfish such as clams and abalone, and fish.

The seals come together in large numbers only during the breeding season. The males sing a warbling song while underwater to attract the pregnant females to their floes. The calves that were conceived the previous years are then born on the ice. Like all seals, the mothers can only spare a few days to suckle their calves and feed them very fatty milk. After the calves are weaned, the females mate with the male in control of the floe. The resulting embryos lie dormant for several weeks before beginning to develop inside the mothers.

This ensures that they are ready to be born during the next year's breeding season.

**Distribution**: Arctic coastlines and ice floes. A few individuals travel as far south as Scotland and Spain.
**Habitat**: Shallow water covered in thin ice.
**Food**: Shrimps, crabs, clams and fish.
**Size**: 2.4m (7.75ft); 288kg (635lb).
**Maturity**: Females at 3 years; males at 6 years but may take several more years before breeding successfully.
**Breeding**: Breeding season takes place in summer on beaches and ice floes.
**Life span**: 25 years.
**Status**: Common.

*Bearded seals are named after the long white whiskers that grow on the snout. For at least part of the year they have very thick blubber, making the body rounded.*

# Crabeater seal

*Lobodon carcinophagus*

**Distribution**: Antarctica and surrounding landmasses including the southern Cape of Africa on rare occasions.
**Habitat**: Thick pack ice.
**Food**: Krill.
**Size**: 2–2.4m (6.5–7.75ft); 200–300kg (440–660lb).
**Maturity**: 3–4 years but males take many more years to breed successfully.
**Breeding**: A single pup born in spring after a gestation of 11.5 months.
**Life span**: Up to 25 years, although the males tend to die younger than the females.
**Status**: Common.

Crabeater seals are found mainly on the pack ice and barren islands that surround the continental landmass of Antarctica. They are also occasionally found farther north on ocean islands and on the coasts of southern Africa, South America and Australia. Crabeater seals are generally solitary and it is single seals that are spotted along the northern edge of its range. On the Antarctic ice, the seals may gather into large groups during the breeding season.

Despite its name, the crabeater seal never eats crabs. Instead it is a krill eater. It feeds by swimming through a school of krill with its mouth open. It sucks the small animals into its mouth from a distance of about 1m (3.25ft). Crabeater seals also eat small fish, choosing ones that are small enough to swallow whole. They are quite deep divers and get most of their food in the first 30m (100ft) of water.

Crabeater seals are generally solitary creatures but sometimes gather in large herds of more than 1,000 individuals. The largest aggregations occur during the calving and breeding season, which takes place on the pack ice in spring – October in Antarctica. Mating takes place after pups are weaned at the age of three weeks.

*The fur of the crabeater seal changes from dark brown to blonde throughout the year. The winter coat is dark when it grows in autumn but becomes paler from then on. The species is also called the white Antarctic seal because of its pale fur.*

# Walrus

*Odobenus rosmarus*

**Distribution**: Coast of Arctic Ocean.
**Habitat**: Pack ice.
**Food**: Worms, shellfish and fish.
**Size**: 2.25–3.5m (7.5–11.5ft); 400–1,700kg (880–3,750lb).
**Maturity**: Females 6 years; males 10 years.
**Breeding**: Single young born once per year.
**Life span**: 40 years.
**Status**: Vulnerable.

Walruses live among the ice floes of the Arctic Ocean. These huge sea mammals are well known for their long tusks, which they use to stab opponents during fights. Walruses also use their tusks to "haul out", or pull themselves on to floating ice, and sometimes hook themselves to floes so that they can sleep while still in the water.

It was once thought that the tusks were also used to dislodge and dig out prey from the sea bed. However, we now know that walruses use their whiskered snouts to root out prey and blast away sediment with jets of water squirted from the mouth. They tackle shelled prey by holding them in their large lips and sucking out the soft bodies.

Walruses live in large herds, sometimes of many thousands. In winter they feed in areas of thin sea ice, avoiding thick, unbroken ice, which they cannot break through from beneath. In summer, when the ice recedes, they spend more time on land. Mating takes place in the water, and calves are born on the ice 11 months later. The young stay with their mothers for three years.

*Walruses have long tusks growing out of their upper jaws. The males are twice the size of females and also have longer tusks. Their bodies are reddish-brown and sparsely covered in coarse hairs. Males have two air pouches inside their necks, which they use to amplify their mating calls.*

# DOLPHINS AND PORPOISES

*The oceans around Europe and Africa are home to many species of dolphins. Dolphins are small members of the mammal order Cetacea, which also includes the whales. Most dolphins live far out in the ocean, but a few species come close to shore. Porpoises generally live in coastal waters, too. They are similar to dolphins, but tend to be smaller and have rounded snouts, rather than long beaks.*

## Atlantic humpback dolphin

*Sousa teuszii*

Atlantic humpbacks are shy dolphins, making them a difficult species for scientists to observe and study. Political instability in many West African countries along the coasts of which this dolphin lives has also compounded the problems of studying these animals. They inhabit tropical coastal waters, preferring to stay in shallow water. Typical school sizes range from between three and seven individuals, but groups of up to 25 have been observed. As these dolphins get older, they become more and more solitary, and eventually hardly ever associate with other individuals.

The humpback dolphin has a unique way of surfacing: the beak and head break the surface before the body arches tightly, making the dorsal fin more prominent. Orcas are a major threat to this species. They locate the dolphins by listening in to their calls. By staying close to land, the dolphins are able to disrupt their calls and thwart the killers.

**Distribution**: Eastern Atlantic Ocean off West Africa.
**Habitat**: Tropical coastal waters, usually less than 20m (65ft) deep, and tidal zones of rivers.
**Food**: Fish.
**Size**: 1.2–2.5m (4–8.25ft); 75–150kg (165–330lb).
**Maturity**: Between 4 and 8 years.
**Breeding**: Single calf born every 1–2 years.
**Life span**: Unknown.
**Status**: Declining because of habitat loss and entanglement in fishing nets.

*The humpback dolphin gets its name from its distinctive method of surfacing and its slightly bulbous dorsal fin.*

## White-beaked dolphin

*Lagenorhynchus albirostris*

Dolphins are notoriously difficult animals to study because they are small, and also very wide-ranging. Consequently, not much is known about their habits compared to those of most land-living mammals.

Like most cetaceans, white-beaked dolphins live in groups known as schools, which have complex social structures. Schools are usually made up of 2–20 dolphins, but occasionally lots of schools will come together to form large groups containing more than 1,000 individuals.

Dolphins are famed for a behaviour known as breaching, when they leap clear of the water, somersault and splash back down through the waves. Dolphins have also been observed playing games underwater, such as "chase the seaweed". White-beaked dolphins make annual migrations, moving between temperate and subpolar waters, tracking their prey, such as mackerel and herring.

**Distribution**: Ranges widely through the North Atlantic and Arctic Oceans.
**Habitat**: Coastal waters.
**Food**: Medium-sized fish, squid and crustaceans form the bulk of the diet.
**Size**: 2.3–2.8m (7.5–9.25ft); 180kg (396lb).
**Maturity**: Unknown.
**Breeding**: 1 calf born every year.
**Life span**: Unknown.
**Status**: Common.

*The white-beaked dolphin's counter-shaded coloration helps to camouflage it from both above and below.*

# Common dolphin

*Delphinus delphis*

**Distribution**: Mediterranean Sea, Atlantic and Pacific Oceans.
**Habitat**: Ocean waters.
**Food**: Fish, squid and octopus.
**Size**: 1.5–2.4m (5–7.75ft); 100–136kg (220–300lb).
**Maturity**: 12–15 years.
**Breeding**: Single young born every 2–3 years.
**Life span**: 35 years.
**Status**: Common.

This dolphin is also called the short-beaked saddleback dolphin. It is especially common in European waters, including the Mediterranean Sea. The species also swims in the coastal areas of the Atlantic and Pacific Oceans, including along the coasts of the Americas.

Common dolphins are so-called coastal dolphins because they prefer to swim in warmer water near the surface. However, they are still found far out to sea though seldom dive into deep and colder water. They have many small, curved teeth, which are used for snatching small, slippery fish, such as herrings, from the water.

These mammals are one of the smallest dolphins. They live in small family groups called schools. There are reports that many schools sometimes group together, forming clans of up to 100,000 individuals. Most of the time they travel at 8kph (5mph) but can hit speeds of 46kph (29mph).

*The common dolphin is one of the smallest dolphin species. They have a distinctive hourglass pattern of pale skin that connects the dark upper skin to the pale lower surface.*

**Atlantic spotted dolphin** (*Stenella frontalis*): 1.6–2.3m (5.25–7.5ft); 90kg (198lb)
Adult members of this species have a spotted pattern. These spots are not present at birth but appear after weaning. This dolphin is found all around the warmer parts of the Atlantic Ocean. The dolphin rarely moves more than 350km (220 miles) from the coast and spends most of its time in shallow water over sand banks. Spotted dolphins are social animals and live in pods that range in size from a few individuals to groups of several thousand. Within large pods, dolphins of different sexes and stages of maturity are often segregated. The dolphins communicate using high-pitched whistles that are within the range of human hearing. Each individual dolphin has a unique call. Spotted dolphins feed on small fish, such as eels and herrings. They often track shoals, swimming above them just below the surface before diving down to attack as a group.

**Spinner dolphin** (*Stenella longirostris*): 1.8–2.1m (6–7ft); 55–75kg (121–165lb)
Spinner dolphins are oceanic animals. They roam through all the world's oceans, mainly staying in the warmer regions. They seldom come close to land and are only really seen from ships or around remote islands. Spinners track shoals of tuna, swimming at the surface above the fish. Tuna fishermen look out for spinners to lead them to the tuna. As a result, many dolphins get caught and drown in nets meant for the tuna. The spinner dolphins that live nearer to land are slightly different from those found out at sea. Biologists have detected at least four races, which have differently shaped dorsal fins.

# Harbour porpoise

*Phocoena phocoena*

Harbour porpoises are relatively common in European waters and along the coast of North Africa, where they occupy shallow coastal waters. They are also able to withstand fresh water and often travel in the mouths of large rivers.

These porpoises, also known as common porpoises, are social, highly vocal cetaceans. They live in small groups of up to 15 members. They swim more slowly than dolphins and rarely jump out of the water. Instead they rise to the surface to breathe. Some groups migrate long distances, but most occupy a territory.

Harbour porpoises eat fish, such as herrings, sardines and pollack. They also eat squid and shrimp. Like other cetaceans, they use high-pitched clicking sounds to echolocate their prey. Many of the porpoise's prey are also commercially important species, and porpoises are sometimes caught up in fishing nets.

**Distribution**: Mediterranean Sea, Black Sea, North Atlantic and North Pacific.
**Habitat**: Shallow seas and coastal waters. Sometimes venture into estuaries.
**Food**: Fish and squid.
**Size**: 1.3–1.9m (4.25–6.25ft); 35–90kg (77–198lb).
**Maturity**: 5 years.
**Breeding**: Gives birth mainly in summer.
**Life span**: 20 years.
**Status**: Vulnerable.

*Unlike their dolphin relatives, porpoises have blunt snouts without a beak. They also have fewer teeth, which tend to be less pointed and have a chisel-like biting edge. These teeth are suited to holding on to large struggling fish.*

# Risso's dolphin

*Grampus griseus*

Risso's dolphins live in small groups of about ten individuals. The groups move to warm tropical waters in winter and head back toward the poles in summer. The dolphins are often seen leaping out of the water as members of a school play with one another.

Risso's dolphins feed in deep water. They dive down to catch fast-swimming squid and fish. Like other dolphins, they probably use echolocation to locate their prey in the dark depths. They produce clicking noises that bounce off objects in the water. The dolphins can hear each other's clicks and echoes, and groups may work together to track down shoals of fish or squid. In areas where there is plenty of food, dolphin schools congregate, so that thousands of the leaping mammals may be seen together.

Not much is known about the breeding habits of this species. Most births take place in the warmer summer months.

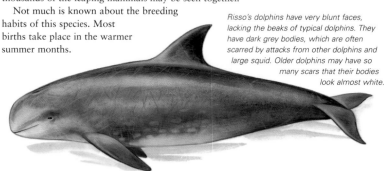

*Risso's dolphins have very blunt faces, lacking the beaks of typical dolphins. They have dark grey bodies, which are often scarred by attacks from other dolphins and large squid. Older dolphins may have so many scars that their bodies look almost white.*

**Distribution**: All tropical and temperate seas. Enters the Mediterranean and Red Seas, but is absent from the Black Sea. This species is not common in the South Atlantic.
**Habitat**: Deep ocean water.
**Food**: Fish and squid and occasionally octopus.
**Size**: 3.6–4m (11.75–13ft); 400–450kg (880–990lb).
**Maturity**: Unknown.
**Breeding**: Single young born once a year.
**Life span**: 30 years.
**Status**: Common.

# Heaviside's dolphin

*Cephalorhynchus heavisidii*

Heaviside's dolphin is a relatively common species that can often be seen from the shore among the waves. However, it is found only off the remote coasts of Angola, Namibia and the Cape Province of South Africa, and therefore is not particularly well understood.

The dolphins swim from just beyond the breakers to about 80km (50 miles) off shore. They prefer water that is less than 180m (590ft) deep. Heaviside's dolphins prey mainly on fish and other animals, such as octopuses and lobsters, that live on or near to the sea floor. The long lower jaw may aid them in scooping prey from the bottom.

They are found mainly in pairs, probably a mother with her calf. Little is known about their reproductive habits, but most births occur in the summer months.

The dolphins often display by tail-flipping. This is a half somersault that ends in a splash with the tail. They are also often seen escorting boats. Heaviside's dolphins are thought to be common in their range, but there are reports that they are increasingly being hunted for their meat and killed by accident by fishing craft.

**Distribution**: South-western Africa.
**Habitat**: Shallow coastal waters. Often seen in the breaker zone.
**Food**: Fish and squid and other swimming animals, as well as octopus and other animals that live on the seabed.
**Size**: 1.7m (5.5ft); 70kg (154lb).
**Maturity**: Unknown.
**Breeding**: Young are born in summer and newborns are large, about half the length of adults.
**Life span**: Unknown.
**Status**: Common, although increasingly at risk.

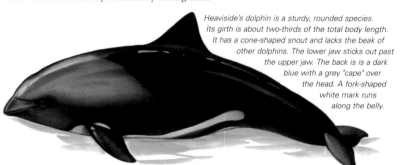

*Heaviside's dolphin is a sturdy, rounded species. Its girth is about two-thirds of the total body length. It has a cone-shaped snout and lacks the beak of other dolphins. The lower jaw sticks out past the upper jaw. The back is is a dark blue with a grey "cape" over the head. A fork-shaped white mark runs along the belly.*

# Atlantic white-sided dolphin

*Lagenorhynchus acutus*

**Distribution**: Along the continental shelf of the British Isles, Norway and other North Atlantic coasts.
**Habitat**: Cold, open water.
**Food**: Shrimps and small fish.
**Size**: 3m (9.75ft); 250kg (550lb).
**Maturity**: 12 years.
**Breeding**: 1 calf born every 2–3 years.
**Life span**: 40 years.
**Status**: Common.

The Atlantic white-sided dolphin is seldom found near shore. It prefers instead to swim far out to sea in the clear water on the edge of the continental shelf, where the sea floor plunges to the great depths of the mid-ocean. It can dive to about 270m (885ft) and generally hunts at about 40m (130ft) below the surface. Down there it uses its long snout and many small teeth to snatch prey from the water. It targets shoaling prey, such as herrings, shrimps and even certain squid. The dolphin plunges into the shoal, snapping up food as it passes through.

Like many oceanic dolphins, this species is social and lives in family groups of about six individuals, although larger clans of more than a thousands dolphins do form. This species is nomadic (it has no distinct migration routes); instead the dolphins travel throughout their range in search of food.

*Female Atlantic white-sided dolphins are considerably smaller than the males, weighing just 180kg (400lb). The dolphin's back is dark grey or black. This becomes paler on the sides and is white or cream on the underside. This coloration makes the animal hard to spot from both above and below.*

**Long-finned pilot whale**
(*Globicephala melas*): 5–6m (16.5–19.75ft); 3,000kg (6,600lb)
Grouped as one of the dolphins, this whale has a black body with a white belly. They do not have a beak but have a rather rounded head instead. This feature earns this species the alternative name of pothead whale. The heads of older males are especially bulbous. Long-finned pilot whales are found in cooler waters around the world. For example, they are common in European waters.

**Cuvier's beaked whale**
(*Ziphius cavirostris*): 6–7m (19.75–23ft); 3,000kg (6,600lb)
This species of whale lives in warmer waters. They stay in areas where the water is more than 10°C (50°F). They also prefer deep water and eat squid and fish. However, they are sometimes seen on African coasts. Males are smaller than females. The whales usually travel in small groups.

# Bottlenosed dolphin

*Tursiops truncatus*

This is one of the most common and familiar dolphin species. It is found worldwide including along the Atlantic coasts of Africa and Europe.

Bottlenosed dolphins live in shallow water close to land and they are generally spotted breaking clear of the water in large bays. They often enter lagoons and the mouths of large rivers. They do not appear to migrate; instead they make a lifelong journey that may take them to all parts of the world. Since they prefer warmer waters, they tend to move between the Atlantic and Pacific Oceans around the Cape of Good Hope and via the Indian Ocean.

Bottlenosed dolphins travel at about 20kmh (12mph) and are rarely seen travelling alone. They hunt as a team, corralling shoals of fish and shrimp by circling around them and taking it in turns to dive through the shoal, snatching mouthfuls of food. They often follow fishing boats, snapping up the by-catch discarded over the side.

**Distribution**: Tropical and temperate coastal waters worldwide.
**Habitat**: Warm shallow water.
**Food**: Fish.
**Size**: 1.75–4m (5.75–13ft); 150–200 kg (330–440lb).
**Maturity**: 5–12 years.
**Breeding**: Single calf born every 2–3 years.
**Life span**: 40 years.
**Status**: Unknown.

*This is the largest of the beaked dolphins, so called because of their short snouts, which are common in oceanic dolphins. River dolphins tend to have longer, slender snouts, while pilot whales and porpoises have no snout at all.*

# TOOTHED WHALES

*Within the Cetacea order (which includes whales, dolphins and porpoises), there are 23 species of toothed whale. These cetaceans are hunting whales, and they include the world's largest predator, the sperm whale. Toothed whales live in family groups called pods. They hunt for food using echolocation – a sonar system that is focused through a fatty mass called the melon, which is located at the front of the head.*

## Narwhal

*Monodon monoceros*

**Distribution**: Parts of the Arctic Ocean near Greenland and the Barents Sea. Their range is patchy.
**Habitat**: Coastal Arctic waters.
**Food**: Cuttlefish, fish, crustaceans and squid.
**Size**: 4–5.5m (13–18ft); 800–1,600kg (1,760–3,520lb).
**Maturity**: Females 5–8 years; males 11–13 years.
**Breeding**: Single calf born every 2–3 years.
**Life span**: 50 years.
**Status**: Common.

Some people believe that the bizarre appearance of the narwhal first gave rise to the legend of the unicorn. The function of the male's long tusk is not properly known, but it may function as a hunting implement, or as a tool to break up ice and allow access to the air, so that the animals can breathe. However, the most favoured explanation is that the males joust with each other, fighting over access to females during the breeding season.

The narwhal's swollen forehead is known as its melon, a feature shared with other toothed whales, such as dolphins. The melon serves to focus the ultrasonic clicks that narwhals use, like other small cetaceans, to navigate and find their food. As in a sophisticated sonar system, narwhals listen as the high-frequency sounds they make rebound off objects nearby. So sensitive is this method of orientation that narwhals are able to tell not only what is food and what is not, but also how big, how distant and how quickly a potential prey item is moving.

*The male narwhal's tusk is in fact an elongated front tooth that spirals as it grows from a hole in its lips. Females may possess a short tusk, too. Their name means "corpse whale" in Old Norse, perhaps referring to their bluish-grey skin with white blotches.*

## Beluga

*Delphinapterus leucas*

Beluga means "white" in Russian, so these whales are sometimes called white whales. However, they should not be confused with white sturgeon – large fish that produce beluga caviar. Belugas also have a nickname of sea canaries because they call to each other with high-pitched trills.

Belugas live in the far north, where days are very short for much of the year. Some beluga pods spend all their time in one area of ocean while others are always on the move. The pods are ruled by large males, and all pods spend their winters away from areas of thick ice, which may mean being farther or nearer to land depending on where they are. In summer, they enter river estuaries and shallow bays, navigating with the sonar system. Calves are born in late summer, and their mothers will mate again in early summer a year or two later.

**Distribution**: Arctic Ocean, Scandinavia and Siberia.
**Habitat**: Deep coastal waters and mouths of large rivers.
**Food**: Fish, squid, octopuses, crabs and snails.
**Size**: 3.4–4.6m (11.25–15ft); 1.3–1.5 tonnes (2,850–3,300lb).
**Maturity**: Females 5 years; males 8 years.
**Breeding**: Single calf born every 2–3 years.
**Life span**: 25 years.
**Status**: Vulnerable.

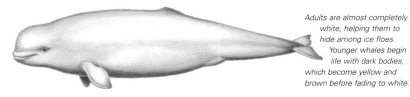

*Adults are almost completely white, helping them to hide among ice floes. Younger whales begin life with dark bodies, which become yellow and brown before fading to white.*

# Orca

*Orcinus orca*

**Distribution**: Throughout the world's oceans.
**Habitat**: Most common in coastal waters.
**Food**: Seals, other dolphins, fish, squid, penguins and crustaceans.
**Size**: 8.5–9.8m (28–32.25ft); 5.5–9 tonnes (12,000–20,000lb).
**Maturity**: Females 6 years; males 12 years.
**Breeding**: Single young born generally in autumn every 3–4 years.
**Life span**: 60–90 years.
**Status**: Lower risk.

Orcas are also known as killer whales. They are expert hunters, being armed with up to 50 large, pointed teeth, and they catch prey in all areas of the ocean. Although orcas have been detected 1km (0.6 miles) below the surface, they prefer to hunt in shallow coastal waters and often swim into bays and mouths of rivers to snatch food near the shore.

Orcas typically live in pods of five or six individuals. Generally each pod is run by a large male, although larger groups have several adult males. Females and their young may split off into subgroups. Like other toothed whales and dolphins, orcas produce click sounds that are used for echolocation. The whales also communicate with each other using high-pitched screams and whistles. Orcas have several hunting techniques. They break pack ice from beneath, knocking their prey into the water, or they may rush into shallow water to grab prey from the shore. It is reported that they may crash on to the shore to drive prey into the surf, where other members of the pod pick them off. Orcas breed throughout the year, although most mate in the early summer and give birth in the autumn of the following year. Each pod has a single male, which mates with all the adult females.

*Orcas have black upper bodies and white undersides. They also have grey patches behind their dorsal fins and white patches along their sides and above the eyes. These "whales" are really one of the largest members of the dolphin family.*

**False killer whale**
(*Pseudorca crassidens*):
3.7–5.5m (12.25–18ft);
1.2–2 tonnes (2,650–4,400lb)
Like its namesake the killer whale, the false killer whale is actually a member of the dolphin family. This is a wide-ranging species, which travels throughout the world's oceans. The false killer whale is able to reach speeds of up to 30 knots (30 nautical mph or 55kph) and is often encountered racing ships. It preys on smaller dolphins.

**Southern bottlenose whale**
(*Hyperoodon planifrons*):
6.5–7.5m (21.25–24.5ft);
5.4–7.25 tonnes
(12,000–16,000lb)
This large-toothed whale is found in the Antarctic Ocean and can be seen in the waters off South Africa. (A northern species is seen in the Arctic.) They move in small groups and feed on squid and fish. The whales dive to 1km (3,300ft). They locate food in the dark water by echolocation and also communicate with sound.

# Sperm whale

*Physeter catodon*

The sperm whale is supremely well adapted to life in the deep oceans. These are the largest hunting predators in the world, with teeth up to 20cm (8in) long and the largest brain of any animal, weighing over 9kg (20lb). They prefer areas of ocean with cold upwellings at least 1km (3,300ft) deep where squid – their favourite food – are most abundant.

Sperm whales can dive to incredible depths to hunt, occasionally up to 2.5km (1.5 miles). They are social animals and live in groups of 20–40 females, juveniles and young. Sperm whales have been hunted for their oil since the mid-18th century, and, after serious population declines between the 1950s and 1980s, this species is now protected. In the north, sperm whales mate between January and August. In the south, they mate between July and March.

**Distribution**: Ranges throughout oceans and seas worldwide.
**Habitat**: Deep oceans.
**Food**: Mostly squid, including giant deep-sea squid, but also several species of fish and shark.
**Size**: 12–20m (39.5–65.5ft); 12–50 tonnes (26,500–110,000lb).
**Maturity**: Females 7–13 years; males 25 years.
**Breeding**: 1 calf born every 5–7 years.
**Life span**: 77 years.
**Status**: Vulnerable.

*The box-like head of the sperm whale contains the spermaceti organ, which is filled with the fine oil that is so valued by whalers. The purpose of this organ is unclear but it may be to do with focusing sounds produced by the whale.*

# OTHER WHALES

*The largest members of the Cetacea order are called baleen whales. There are about a dozen species of
baleen whale and many of them pass the coasts of Africa and Europe as they make long migrations
between the world's warm and cold waters each year. Instead of teeth, these whales have baleen plates –
a thick curtain which hangs down from the upper jaw. This curtain sieves food items from the water.*

## Humpback whale

*Megaptera novaeangliae*

*Humpback whales are so
called because of their dorsal
fins, which may be swelled
into humps by deposits of fat.
Humpbacks have the longest
pectoral (arm) fins of any
whale – about a third as long
as their bodies. These baleen
whales have throat grooves,
which expand to enlarge the
throat size as the feeding
whale gulps water.*

Humpbacks spend their
summers feeding far from shore, in
the cold waters near the poles. They feed by taking
in huge mouthfuls of sea water, from which their
baleen plates then strain out any fish or krill.
Pairs of humpbacks also corral fish by blowing
curtains of bubbles around them. The fish will
not swim through the bubbles and they crowd together as the
whales rush up from beneath with their mouths wide open.

In winter, the whales stop feeding and head to warmer,
shallow waters near coasts to concentrate on reproduction.
The males sing for days on end to attract receptive females
that are not caring for calves that year, and also help rival
males to keep away from each other. Pregnant females stay
feeding for longer than the other whales, and arrive in the
wintering grounds just in time to give birth.

**Distribution**: All oceans.
**Habitat**: Deep ocean water.
They come closer to land to
mate and calf.
**Food**: Small fish, shrimps
and krill.
**Size**: 12.5–15m (41–49.25ft);
30 tonnes (66,000lb).
**Maturity**: 4–5 years.
**Breeding**: Single young born
every 2–3 years. Mating
takes place in winter.
Gestation is 11 months.
**Life span**: 70 years.
**Status**: Vulnerable.

## Bowhead whale

*Balaena mysticetus*

*Bowhead whales, also known
as Greenland right whales or
Arctic whales, are among the
largest animals in the world.
They are named after the
U-shape of the lower jaw,
which is white. The rest
of the body is black. The
bowhead whale's mouth is
the largest of any animal
on Earth: it is large enough
to swallow a van.*

Bowhead whales live in the Arctic Ocean, where they live
among ice floes. One of the many amazing things about this
giant animal is its immense life span. Ivory and stone harpoon
heads from the 19th century have been found in living
specimens. Analysis of the whale's eye suggests that this species
can live for 200 years, which makes it the longest-living
mammal on Earth. However, hunting has made the bowhead
one of the most endangered sea mammals. Biologists estimate
that the population along the northern European coast
is numbered in just the hundreds. Bowheads feed on tiny
floating crustaceans, such as krill and copepods. They can eat
1.8 tonnes (4,000lb) in one day.

**Distribution**: Northern
waters.
**Habitat**: Cold water.
**Food**: Plankton and krill.
**Size**: 11–20m (36–65.5ft);
50–60 tonnes
(110,000–132,000lb).
**Maturity**: 20 years.
**Breeding**: Calves born
in spring.
**Life span**: 200 years.
**Status**: Critically endangered.

# SEA COWS

*The sea cows are a small group of sea mammals that are not related to whales or seals. Instead, their closest relatives are elephants and hyraxes. Sea cows are thought to be the source of mermaid myths. Both remaining species of sea cows, the manatees and dugong, are tropical mammals. Steller's sea cow once lived in the Arctic but was hunted to extinction in the 18th century.*

## Dugong

*Dugong dugon*

**Distribution**: Coasts of eastern Africa, and southern Asia.
**Habitat**: Shallow water.
**Food**: Sea grass.
**Size**: 2.4–2.7m (7.75–8.75ft); 230–908kg (500–2,000lb).
**Maturity**: 9–15 years.
**Breeding**: 1–2 young born every 3–7 years.
**Life span**: 70 years.
**Status**: Vulnerable.

The dugong is a distant relative of the elephant, and is placed in the order Sirenia along with the manatees. Dugongs live in shallow coastal regions where the sea grass on which they feed is abundant. They rarely make long-distance migrations, though in some places they make daily movements from feeding areas to resting sites in deeper water.

Dugongs have unusually shaped mouths, with overhanging upper lips that are used for cropping sea grasses. They can swim at up to 20kph (12.5mph) if pursued.

The young are born underwater after one year's gestation. At first they ride on their mothers' backs, breathing when the females come to the surface. Sharks attack dugongs, but groups of dugongs will gang up on them and ram them with their heads. Orcas (killer whales) have also been known to attack dugongs, but by far their greatest enemy is human beings, who have hunted them extensively for their meat, hides and ivory.

*Dugongs have thick, smooth hides, usually dull grey-brown in colour. Unlike the closely related manatees, which have rounded, paddle-shaped tails, dugongs have fluked tails like those of whales and dolphins.*

## African manatee

*Trichechus senegalensis*

**Distribution**: Western Africa.
**Habitat**: Coastal waters and freshwater river mouths.
**Food**: Water plants.
**Size**: 3.7–4.6m (12–15ft); 1.6 tonnes (3,500lb).
**Maturity**: 3 years.
**Breeding**: Calves born in late spring and summer.
**Life span**: 28 years.
**Status**: Vulnerable.

The African manatee is a plant-eating aquatic mammal. It lives between the mouths of the Senegal River (the border between Mauritania and Senegal) in the north and the Cuanza River in Angola. It occupies shallow coastal water and often swims in the mouths of rivers and swamps.

Manatees are plant eaters and consequently have long guts. Bacteria in the gut break down the tough plant food. Plant food also gradually wears down the teeth. To counter this, the manatees use the same system as their relatives, the elephants. As worn teeth become useless, they are pushed out at the front. New teeth are exposed at the back of the mouth, and gradually move to the front, pushed along by more teeth behind. The supply of teeth is not endless, but it is enough to last for a normal lifetime.

*This species is very similar to the West Indian manatee, which lives in the Caribbean and Florida. It has large, flexible lips and thick bristles. Their tails are more rounded than those of the dugongs.*

# ANIMALS OF ASIA, AUSTRALIA AND NEW ZEALAND

Asia is the world's largest continent, stretching halfway around the globe, while Australia, an island between the Indian Ocean and the Pacific, is the smallest continent. Being an island, Australia's wildlife has been isolated for many millions of years and today the animals that live there are very different from those found in Asia and beyond. While Asia is home to mammals such as elephants, orang-utans, wild horses and camels, Australia is populated by kangaroos, wombats and possums. Most of Australia's mammals carry their young in pouches, and a few even lay eggs like reptiles. The reptiles and amphibians of Australia are more similar to those found in Asia, but they are by no means ordinary. Perhaps the most unusual reptile of all, the tuatara, lives in New Zealand, a group of islands in the South Pacific. These ancient reptiles have no living relatives anywhere else in the world.

*Above from left: Carpet python, pretty face wallaby, koala.*

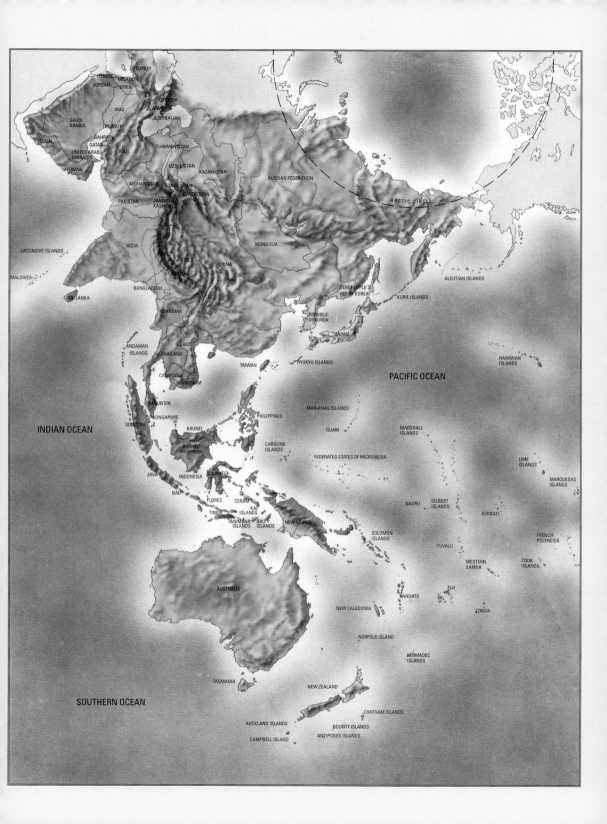

# SALAMANDERS AND RELATIVES

*Salamanders can be found in both aquatic and terrestrial habitats, although they need water for survival during the early stages of their lives. Young salamanders breathe through external gills. Once they reach adulthood, salamanders develop lungs and start to breathe air, but they can also absorb oxygen through their skins, which allows them to spend long periods underwater.*

## Ceylon caecilian

*Ichthyophis glutinosus*

*With eyes covered by skin and bone, caecilians are totally blind. Their slender body shape makes them perfectly adapted for a subterranean, burrowing lifestyle. The family holds over 90 species in all.*

Caecilians look like snakes or worms, but they are neither. In fact they are amphibians, being closely related to frogs, toads and salamanders. Unlike most amphibians, which have few or no teeth, caecilians have two sets of backward-pointing teeth on their upper and lower jaws.

While being relatively common in their forest habitats, Ceylon caecilians are difficult animals to find. This is because they spend virtually their entire lives under the thick leaf litter of tropical forests, away from the sharp eyes of the many birds, mammals and reptiles that would eat them. Being blind, caecilians find food and mates using smell. They have small tentacle-like appendages that protrude from just behind their nostrils. These tentacles smell the environment immediately around them, detecting their prey – insects and earthworms – and mates. Females produce strong odours when they are fertile.

**Distribution**: Sri Lanka.
**Habitat**: Underground in damp forest soils.
**Food**: Insect larvae, termites and earthworms.
**Size**: 30–50cm (12–20in).
**Maturity**: Not known.
**Breeding**: 7–20 live young born after gestation of 9–11 months.
**Life span**: 6–7 years.
**Status**: Common.

## Japanese giant salamander

*Andrias japonicus*

*This huge salamander is dark brown with black spots. It has characteristically warty skin on its head. Its pepper-like smell is caused by mucus from glands in the skin.*

This salamander is one of Japan's most impressive inhabitants, and one of the world's largest salamanders. It belongs to a small group of salamanders called *Cryptobranchidae*, to which American hellbenders also belong. Weighing over 20kg (44lb) and reaching sizes well in excess of 1m (3.25ft), the Japan giant salamander is found only in cold, fast-flowing mountain streams. It spends the daytime hiding under rocks and branches, coming out at night to feed on its prey, which it catches using a sticky tongue and powerful jaws.

This creature actually has three names in Japanese; they are "Osanshouuo", "Hanzaki", and "Hajikamiio". These names are derived from the fact that the salamanders secrete mucus from their skins that smells like the Japanese peppers called "sansho" and "hajikami". Until recently the Japanese giant salamander was a highly prized source of food for people living in the mountainous regions of Japan. However, the pressures of over-hunting and water pollution have caused the population to drop very sharply, and now the giant salamander is strictly protected by law.

**Distribution**: Japan.
**Habitat**: Cold, fast-flowing mountain streams with rocky bottoms.
**Food**: Mainly worms and insects, and also crabs, fish, frogs, snakes and mice.
**Size**: 40–70cm (16–28in), up to 140cm (56in); over 20kg (44lb).
**Maturity**: 5–10 years.
**Breeding**: 500–600 eggs laid in autumn, hatching after 40–50 days.
**Life span**: 70 years.
**Status**: Vulnerable.

## Western Chinese mountain salamander

*Batrachuperus pinchonii*

**Distribution**: Sichuan Province, China.
**Habitat**: Fast-flowing mountain streams.
**Food**: Mainly insects.
**Size**: 15–20cm (6–8in).
**Maturity**: Not known.
**Breeding**: 7–12 eggs laid per year.
**Life span**: Not known.
**Status**: Locally common.

This sturdy salamander inhabits the fast-flowing streams of the mountainous Sichuan province of China. These streams are too cold for a lot of animals, especially fish, which tend to be a major predator of salamander larvae. Therefore, the young salamanders grow up in relatively predator-free environments; they just have to contend with the cold.

This species' tail is relatively short for a salamander, and is flattened from side to side – laterally – into a paddle. This helps the salamander swim against the fast currents. Eggs are laid under stones so that they do not get washed away. In the very cold conditions, the salamanders have low metabolic rates and do not move very quickly, appearing a bit slow and ponderous. They take many years to reach maturity in their chilly habitat.

*The Western Chinese mountain salamander is a robust amphibian with a mainly glossy, brown or green skin, generally with spots.*

**Paddletail newt** (*Pachytriton labiatus*): 12–15cm (4.8–6in)
Found only in southern China, the paddletail newt is aptly named. It has a very broad, flat tail, which helps it to swim rapidly through the slow-flowing rivers in which it lives. It has very smooth, shiny skin which is dark brown along its back, but bright red with black patterning on its belly. It is a very secretive animal, spending most of its time hiding away under rocks and in crevices, only coming out at night to feed.

**Afghan salamander** (*Batrachuperus mustersi*): 12–17cm (4.8–6.8in)
Found only in the Paghman Mountains of Afghanistan, this salamander inhabits cool highland streams fed by glaciers. Indeed, it seems that it cannot survive in streams that are warmer than 14°C (57°F). The Afghan salamander is entirely aquatic and has a dark olive-brown coloration, with little in the way of markings. The restricted range of this animal means that it is highly endangered, and it is feared that it may have been badly affected by the recent conflicts in Afghanistan.

**Chinese fire belly newt** (*Cynops orientalis*): 10cm (4in)
Found throughout most of China, fire belly newts are striking little animals. Although they are dark grey or brown on top, when they are turned over it is easy to see how they got their name. Their bellies are coloured bright red, with small black spots. Chinese fire belly newts spend most of their time in water, but come on to land occasionally in search of the small invertebrates that make up their diet. In the breeding season, females lay single eggs on the leaves of water weeds and then fold the leaves over to hide the eggs.

## Crocodile newt

*Tylototriton verrucosus*

The crocodile newt is named after the raised spots that line its back, reminiscent of the raised scutes of crocodiles. However, the newt's bumps are bright orange as a warning to predators that they secrete foul-tasting toxins. Crocodile newts leave the water at the onset of winter, when they bury themselves into soft soils to hibernate. During their active period – in spring, summer and autumn – the newts only come on land when water has become too scarce.

Like most newts, crocodile newts have a very acute sense of smell, being able to find food even in total darkness. They are mainly nocturnal and often forage in muddy pools. These newts can locate prey by smell alone when the density of mud makes their sense of sight useless. They also use smell to attract their mates. The males release a sex-smell which attracts the females to them. Males then perform courtship dances to induce the females into picking up their packages of sperm, known as spermatophores, which they deposit as they dance in circular patterns.

**Distribution**: Mountains of south-east and southern Asia.
**Habitat**: Aquatic habitats, mainly shallow temporary pools.
**Food**: Worms and insects.
**Size**: 12–22cm (4.8–8.8in).
**Maturity**: 1 year.
**Breeding**: 30–150 eggs laid, which take about 2 weeks to hatch.
**Life span**: 12 years.
**Status**: Endangered.

*The crocodile newt has black skin, an orange head and limbs, and raised orange spots down its spine and back.*

# FROGS AND TOADS

*Frogs and toads, collectively known as anurans, are by far the best known of the three groups of amphibian. Adult anurans are characterized by their lack of a tail, which is lost in the metamorphosis from tadpole to adult. Tadpoles tend to feed mainly on algae and plant matter, whereas adults tend to eat insects and other animals. Adult frogs are also characterized by their strong rear legs, used for jumping.*

## Oriental fire-bellied toad

*Bombina orientalis*

Despite the remarkably vivid colouring of its underbelly, the fire-bellied toad merges perfectly with its surroundings; its dull brown to bright green back renders it almost invisible against the muddy margins of the pools and ponds where it lives. The back is also usually dotted with glossy black spots, which further help to camouflage it. Its skin gives off a milky secretion which irritates the mouth and eyes of would-be pedators.

When the fire-bellied toad feels threatened, it has a surprising trick, known as the unkenreflex. The toad flips over on to its back and arches its body, revealing the bright warning colours on its belly. These colours warn potential predators that the toad can secrete poisonous chemicals in its skin. When a predator has tasted these secretions once it will rarely try to attack a fire-bellied toad again. However, some snakes and birds do appear to be able to eat the toads with no ill-effects.

*Oriental fire-bellied toads have green backs with black blotches. Their bellies are orange-red with black mottling – colours that warn predators.*

**Distribution**: Korea.
**Habitat**: Warm, humid forest areas, usually near water.
**Food**: Invertebrates, including worms, molluscs and insects.
**Size**: 4–5cm (1.6–2in).
**Maturity**: 2 years.
**Breeding**: 40–250 eggs laid in batches of 3–50 eggs throughout the summer. Hatch in June–July.
**Life span**: 30 years.
**Status**: Common.

## Asian horned frog

*Megophrys montana*

*The points of skin above the eyes constitute the "horns" of the Asian horned frog. These and its leaf-like coloration help it to camouflage itself among fallen leaves on the forest floor.*

The Asian horned frog inhabits the dense rainforests of South-east Asia. It is a master of disguise, and might easily be mistaken for a leaf. A long snout, large eyelids and skin the colour of dried leaves all help the animal to stay hidden on the forest floor. By doing this it can remain motionless, in relative safety from predators, while waiting for its next meal to walk past.

The tadpole of the Asian horned frog has evolved a curious specialization that concerns its mouth. The tadpole gets most of its food from the surface of the pool or stream that it is living in. Most tadpoles have downward-pointing mouths, but this would make it difficult for this particular species to reach food, so it has evolved a mouth that points upwards instead. The tadpole is therefore able to cruise just beneath the surface of the water and pick off the tiny plants on the surface.

**Distribution**: Thailand, Malaysia, Indonesia and the Philippines.
**Habitat**: Rainforest.
**Food**: Insects.
**Size**: 10–13cm (4–5.2in).
**Maturity**: Unknown.
**Breeding**: Unknown.
**Life span**: Unknown.
**Status**: Common, but declining due to habitat loss.

# Southern gastric brooding frog

*Rheobatrachus silus*

**Distribution**: Queensland, Australia.
**Habitat**: Rocky creek beds and rainforest rock pools.
**Food**: Small insects.
**Size**: 3–5.5cm (1.2–2.2in).
**Maturity**: 1 year.
**Breeding**: 18–30 eggs are brooded for 6–7 weeks within the stomach of the adult female.
**Life span**: 3 years.
**Status**: Extinct in the wild, but survives in captivity.

There are two species of gastric brooding frog, both now feared to be extinct in the wild. They are the only species in the world to share a particularly bizarre method of looking after their young. Immediately after laying her eggs, the adult female frog, somewhat surprisingly, swallows them. However, she has the extraordinary ability to switch off the production of digestive juices, and she turns her belly into a nursery for six or seven weeks, during which time she is unable to eat. The eggs hatch, and the tadpoles develop to near-maturity within the safety of their mother's stomach, before being "born again" through her mouth.

Southern gastric brooding frogs were only discovered in 1973, at which time they were thought to be relatively common. However, during the following few decades a combination of habitat destruction, increased pollution levels and over-collection for the pet trade have seen this incredible species driven into extinction in the wild.

*This small, dull-coloured frog with large bulging eyes has a special method for looking after its young. The tadpoles develop within the mother's stomach before emerging out of her mouth.*

---

**Stonemason toadlet** (*Uperoleia lithomoda*): 1.5–3cm (0.6–1.2in)
This tiny frog is found only in the northernmost areas of Australia. Emerging from its underground burrow only when the infrequent rains arrive, the stonemason toadlet has to find a mate rapidly and produce young before conditions again become too dry. The male produces a strange click-like courtship call which sounds like two stones being knocked together. It is this call which gave the stonemason toadlet its name.

**Asian painted frog** (*Kaloula pulchra*): 5–7cm (2–2.8in)
After a heavy bout of rain, the deep, booming bellows of this frog can be heard from most drains, culverts, lakes and ponds throughout much of South-east Asia. This chubby little frog lives up to its name, being coloured with browns, blacks and beige. When threatened, it puffs itself up with air, and contorts its face as a warning to any would-be predator.

**Brown-striped frog** (*Limnodynastes peronii*): 3–6.5cm (1.2–2.5in)
Also known as the Australian grass frog, this long-limbed amphibian with dark stripes running down its body lives in and around swamps in eastern Australia. This amphibian is nocturnal in its habits, feeding at night on insects and other invertebrates. During the winter and dry periods, it buries itself underground. During mating, pairs make floating foam nests into which 700–1,000 eggs are laid. The eggs hatch quickly and the tadpoles develop very rapidly, too.

# Giant tree frog

*Litoria infrafrenata*

Found in forests and gardens, the giant tree frog is Australia's largest native species of frog, and one of the largest tree frogs in the world. As its name suggests, this frog spends most of its life in the branches of tall trees, feeding on insects at night. During the day, when it is more visible to predators such as birds of prey, it stays well out of sight in foliage. Its green coloration helps to camouflage it as it hides away.

Following spring storms, males gather in trees around swamps, lakes and ponds and produce bizarre calls in an attempt to attract females to mate. The mating calls resemble the deep-throated barks of large dogs, but it isn't just dogs that the frogs can sound like. When distressed, giant tree frogs may make loud meowing sounds, just like the distress calls of cats.

Once the eggs have been laid they develop quickly, hatching within 28 hours. Hatching so quickly means that the young only spend a short period of time lying motionless and prone to predation.

**Distribution**: Northern Australia to Indonesia.
**Habitat**: Occurs in a variety of habitats, ranging from tropical forest to cultivated areas.
**Food**: Insects.
**Size**: 14cm (5.6in).
**Maturity**: Unknown.
**Breeding**: Between 200 and 300 eggs laid in spring and summer.
**Life span**: Unknown.
**Status**: Common.

*Usually an olive or emerald-green shade, the giant tree frog has the ability to change colour depending on temperature and the surrounding vegetation.*

# Cane toad

*Bufo marinus*

*The large, brown cane toad has become a common sight in eastern Australia in recent years. The amphibian has a large, wide head with bony ridges on the top and sides, large protruding eyes, and a stout, powerful body. The glands on its shoulder blades produce a venom that is capable of killing goannas, crocodiles, snakes, dingoes, quolls, cats, dogs and humans within the space of 15 minutes. Cane toads eat almost anything, including pet food, carrion and household scraps, as well as their main diet of insects and small vertebrates.*

The cane toad, or marine toad, is now most famous for being a serious pest. Originally native to the Amazon Basin, it was deliberately released into Australia in the 1930s in the hope that it would control the grey-backed beetle, a pest of sugar cane. Unfortunately the cane toad preyed on almost everything except the grey-backed beetle, which stayed out of reach high up the stems of cane crops. Now a number of Australian species, including other frogs and toads, are in danger of dying out after being extensively preyed upon by these toads.

The cane toad's success in both its native habitat and in new areas where it has spread is helped by the fact that it has two glands just above its shoulder blades, which produce large quantities of highly toxic venom. This venom is so potent that snakes, which have tried to eat the toads, have been found dead with the toads still lodged in their mouths. Snakes are not the only animals affected. Native marsupial predators such as quolls, along with introduced cats and dogs, are all at risk if they try to eat the toads. Cane toads also push native tree frogs out of the best breeding grounds, further establishing their reputation as a serious problem for Australia's native wildlife.

**Distribution**: Originally from the Amazon Basin, now introduced into Australia, the United States, the West Indies, Puerto Rico, Taiwan, Hawaii, the Philippines and many other islands.
**Habitat**: Wide-ranging and adaptable to many different habitats.
**Food**: Insects and small vertebrates.
**Size**: 24 cm (10in); 1.8kg (4lb).
**Maturity**: 1 year.
**Breeding**: 2 clutches of between 8,000 and 35,000 eggs produced each year. Eggs hatch into free-swimming tadpoles that become adult in 45–55 days.
**Life span**: 40 years.
**Status**: Common.

# Holy cross frog

*Notaden bennetti*

*The holy cross frog is also known as the catholic frog or crucifix frog. A native of Australia, it is a yellow or greenish amphibian, and its name is derived from the dark cross-like pattern on its back. It is a desert-dwelling frog, surviving the heat by burrowing underground.*

Summer in the Australian desert is not a hospitable season. The sun bakes the ground with great ferocity and there is virtually no water to be found anywhere. However, despite these harsh conditions, the holy cross frog is able to survive. It is active for only a few weeks every year, just after the rains, when it emerges from its burrow and busily sets about the business of finding a mate, reproducing and preparing to sit out another summer.

When it rains, holy cross frogs are able to absorb water through glands in their skins. They can absorb as much as half of their body weight, and become as round as balls. Then, when the rains stop, they burrow 30cm (12in) under the desert floor, where they stay until the next rainfall. During this time they virtually shut down completely, with their vital processes running at the lowest possible level to make sure they do not use any more water than they need to. This survival mechanism is called aestivation.

**Distribution**: Australia.
**Habitat**: Widespread throughout arid regions.
**Food**: Small black ants form the main element of the diet.
**Size**: 4cm (1.6in).
**Maturity**: 1 year.
**Breeding**: Occurs after heavy rains in summer.
**Life span**: Unknown.
**Status**: Common.

# Hochstetter's frog

*Leiopelma hochstetteri*

**Distribution**: North Island, New Zealand.
**Habitat**: Under stones or vegetation alongside creeks.
**Food**: Insects, spiders, worms and slugs.
**Size**: 5cm (2in).
**Maturity**: 1 year.
**Breeding**: Egg clusters laid in damp, shady places.
**Life span**: Unknown.
**Status**: Threatened.

The Hochstetter's frog is believed to be one of the world's most primitive frogs. It is one of the few species of frog that shares some specific physical characteristics with fish, which are relatives of the amphibians. For example, it has no external ear openings, and no vocal sac. Also, the frog does not croak, and can only manage a quiet squeak at the best of times. Additionally, it has two tail-wagging muscles, but no tail.

Hochstetter's frog lives mainly under rocks and boulders near mountain streams and other wet places in New Zealand. In fact, it is one of only three species of frog native to this region. It is still relatively common in some localized areas of the North Island, whereas the other two species are exceedingly rare, confined to just a few offshore islands.

The tadpoles of this species are unusual in that they don't feed until they change into adult frogs. When a female lays her eggs, she does so into a large, water-filled capsule. After hatching, the tadpoles stay within this capsule until they mature.

*This small brown frog is believed to be one of the most primitive of all frog species.*

---

**Solomon Islands horned frog** (*Ceratobatrachus guentheri*): 5–8cm (2–3.2in)
Unusually for a frog, this species has tooth-like projections growing from its lower jaw. It uses these to keep hold of its prey, such as worms and insects. The projections may also play some role in competition between males for mates, because they are larger in the males than they are in females. After mating, the females lay batches of eggs which develop directly into miniature adult frogs, with the tadpole stage occurring within the eggs.

**Fijian ground frog** (*Platymantis vitiensis*): 3.5–5cm (1.4–2in)
Confined to the forests of Fiji, little is known about the habits of this small orange-brown frog. It has very prominent eyes and large eardrums, as well as large pads on its toes, which help it to climb around. The female lays a small number of large eggs directly on to the ground. The young develop directly into young adults, the tadpole stage being completed within the eggs. Fijian ground frogs are highly endangered due to their limited original habitats being deforested.

**Ornate narrow-mouthed frog** (*Microhyla ornata*): 2–3cm (0.8–1.2in)
The ornate narrow-mouthed frog inhabits the rainforests and paddy fields of South-east Asia, where it feeds on insects and other invertebrates. This small frog has a plump, smooth-skinned body, with short front legs, and long back legs. It is mainly coloured yellow, with dark stripes along the back and a darker marbled pattern on its back.

# Corroboree frog

*Pseudophryne corroboree*

The strikingly beautiful corroboree frog is thought to be Australia's – and possibly one of the world's – most endangered species of frog. Less than 200 individuals are still alive, isolated from each other in small groups numbering no more than 25. It is believed that corroboree populations have been decimated by a disease known as chytrid (pronounced kit-rid).

The frogs are particularly at risk due to their slightly peculiar lifestyle. Corroboree frogs have much slower breeding cycles than other frogs. While tadpoles are fully formed just four weeks after the female has laid her eggs, they don't actually hatch out of the eggs for another six months. Having finally broken out of their eggs, the tadpoles then take a long time to reach maturity and become adult frogs.

This slow lifestyle means that it takes corroboree frog numbers longer to recover from a population crash than it would other frogs. The population is at a very low ebb today, and is in danger of dying out.

**Distribution**: Kosciuszko National Park in New South Wales, Australia.
**Habitat**: Bogs and surrounding woodland.
**Food**: Insects.
**Size**: 2.5–3cm (1–1.2in).
**Maturity**: 2 years.
**Breeding**: 16–38 eggs laid in summer, hatching 7 months later.
**Life span**: Unknown.
**Status**: Critically endangered.

*The corroboree frog is a spectacularly colourful species, with well-defined black and yellow markings.*

## Asian blue-web flying frog

*Rhacophorus reinwardtii*

*Well camouflaged by their green skins amongst the leaves, the blue webbing between the flying frog's toes provides a startling contrast when they jump.*

Flying frogs don't fly as such – they glide downwards from tree to tree using the webbing between their toes. When feeling threatened, these frogs will leap from their current branch into the air. They spread their toes, expanding the flaps of blue skin between them, and use these as parachutes. This technique allows the frogs to glide more than 12m (40ft) between trees, giving them a useful technique for escaping predators.

This species of flying frog has an interesting breeding method. The females create foam nests in which they lay their eggs. These nests are positioned above pools of water that collect in leaves high up in the forest canopy. The foam prevents the eggs from drying out while the tadpoles are developing within. Once sufficiently mature, the tadpoles then break out of their foam nests and drop into the water below, where they complete their development into adult frogs. The generally green coloration provides camouflage in the forest canopy.

**Distribution**: Indonesia, Malaysia and South-east Asia.
**Habitat**: Rainforest.
**Food**: Insects.
**Size**: 4–7cm (1.6–2.8in).
**Maturity**: Not known.
**Breeding**: Clutches of up to 800 eggs in a foam nest placed above a pool of water.
**Life span**: 5 years.
**Status**: Common.

## White's tree frog

*Litoria caerulea*

It may look as though the blue-green skin of White's tree frog is ill-fitting, but it is this skin which is the frog's key to success. During very wet conditions, the amphibian is able to absorb large amounts of water and store it under the loose folds of skin. The water can then be used in times of drought. However, water-storing is not the only talent possessed by this frog's skin. It also produces various anti-bacterial compounds, and a chemical which has been shown to be useful for treating high blood pressure in humans.

During the mating season, males often cling to the backs of females for days on end, waiting for them to lay eggs, which are then laid in an unusual fashion. Instead of carefully placing their eggs into water, like many frogs, female White's tree frogs squirt their eggs underwater with such great force that they may travel for more than 2m (6ft) before coming to a stop. White's tree frogs are able to produce some very loud sounds. When alarmed, the frogs will emit ear-piercingly loud screams – enough to put off many predators.

**Distribution**: Australia and southern New Guinea.
**Habitat**: Moist, forested environments are preferred, but can live in drier areas.
**Food**: Moths, locusts, cockroaches and other insects.
**Size**: 7–11.5cm (2.8–4.6in).
**Maturity**: 2 years.
**Breeding**: 1,500–3,000 eggs hatch within 2 or 3 days of being laid.
**Life span**: 21 years.
**Status**: Common.

*The White's tree frog has a waxy, blue-green colour and rolling skin folds of fatty material that have earned it the nickname of "dumpy tree frog".*

**Indonesian floating frog** (*Occidozyga lima*): 10–12cm (4–4.8in)
The Indonesian floating frog spends most of its time simply bobbing about in the ponds and lakes in which it lives. It holds on to a piece of weed with one or more feet, looking like a fallen leaf resting on the surface of the water. When insect prey come close enough, they are gobbled up with quick lunges.

**Black-spined toad** (*Bufo melanostictus*): 10cm (4in)
One of Asia's most successful amphibians, the range of the black-spined toad stretches from India in the west to Hong Kong in the east and Indonesia in the south. It has been able to colonize cultivated and urban areas, making use of drainage ditches, ponds and paddy fields. These toads have numerous warts on their backs, and it is these that have given them their name. Black-spined toads produce venomous secretions from their warts, which also have the effect of staining their skin black.

**Crab-eating frog** (*Ratia cancrivora*): 8–10cm (3.2–4in)
The crab-eating frog is one of the few species of amphibian that can tolerate living in salty, brackish water. Inhabiting brackish waters brings the frog into contact with prey that frogs would not usually encounter, crabs being a good example. As their name suggests, crab-eating frogs will often feast on crabs when they get the chance, but they are not fussy, and will eat pretty much any prey that is small enough for them to swallow.

## Giant frog

*Cyclorana australis*

**Distribution**: Northern Australia.
**Habitat**: Grassland and open woodland. Can survive in more arid areas than most species.
**Food**: Insects.
**Size**: 7–11cm (2.8–4.4in).
**Maturity**: 2 years.
**Breeding**: Occurs after the summer rainy season. 7,000 eggs laid in temporary ponds. Tadpoles mature quickly before pools dry up.
**Life span**: Unknown.
**Status**: Common.

The giant frog is a species of frog that is able to live in much drier areas than most frogs. It survives the long, dry days of an Australian winter by cocooning itself in a mixture of shed skin, mucus and damp earth. It can also retain large amounts of water beneath its skin and in its bladder and body cavity – an adaptation which helps it to sit out long dry spells in the safety of its cocoon.

The ability to hold large amounts of water has made the giant frog, and its relative the water-holding frog, a valuable animal for Aboriginal people, who dig them up and squeeze the pure water out of the frogs to gain a drink. The frogs are released lacking water supplies but otherwise unharmed.

Once the summer rains arrive, the frogs leap into action, feasting on the large numbers of insects and preparing to mate. The males gather around the edges of temporary pools and call to females, which come down and lay up to 7,000 eggs. The young have to hatch and develop into adult frogs within the space of a few short weeks, before their pools of water dry up in the hot sun.

*The giant frog's large eyes give it excellent vision, which it uses to spot insects such as beetles, grasshoppers and termites. It is a nocturnal, burrowing frog, and is usually only seen above ground after rain. These amphibians of dry terrain in Australia are much prized by the local Aboriginal people, who use them to gain moisture when water is scarce.*

## Asian tree toad

*Pedostibes hosii*

The Asian tree toad, also known as the brown tree toad, is a large and stocky toad that lives in lowland tropical forest below 660m (2,165ft) above sea level. It is distributed throughout Borneo and is also known in Sumatra, Peninsular Malaysia and southern Thailand. The tadpoles develop in quiet pools of water and at the bottoms of streams, amongst dead leaves. When they become adults, the toads develop arboreal skills and spend some of their time in trees, hence their name.

This toad is unusual among toads in its extraordinary ability to climb. While most toads lead purely terrestrial lives, the Asian tree toad has sucker-like pads on its toes, which enable it to climb with ease. It spends its days hidden away in crevices in trees and in foliage, only becoming active when the sun sets.

Throughout the night, the tree toad comes down to the forest floor along rivers and streams and feeds mainly on ants, which it picks up with its long, sticky tongue. The animal calls to other toads by making a grating, slurred squawk that rises slightly in pitch from beginning to end.

The female lays her eggs in strings in rivers. These rivers need to be fairly fast-flowing because the eggs need to be kept in conditions where the concentration of oxygen in the water is relatively high. Once they hatch, however, the tadpoles have to battle against the fast water currents to prevent themselves from being washed away. They have large sucker-like mouths with which they cling to rocks, anchoring themselves against the flow.

**Distribution**: South-east Asia.
**Habitat**: Lowland tropical forest.
**Food**: Insects, mainly ants.
**Size**: 5–11cm (2–4.4in).
**Maturity**: 2 years.
**Breeding**: Many small eggs laid in a string in rivers.
**Life span**: 16 years.
**Status**: Common.

*The Asian tree toad varies in colour from greenish-brown to black, with a dense pattern of yellow spots. Some females are dark purple. Unlike most toads, this South-east Asian species is a skilled climber, shinning up trees with the aid of the sticky pads on its toes.*

# TURTLES

*Among the oldest surviving groups of reptiles, turtles first evolved about 200 million years ago. They have changed very little since then, a fact that bears testament to their successful body design and lifestyle. Turtles live both on land and in water, with the land-living species being more commonly referred to as tortoises. All species of turtle lay their eggs on land.*

## Common snake-necked turtle

*Chelodina longicollis*

*The neck of the common snake-necked turtle is very long. When extended, the neck is longer than half the length of the shell.*

With their long, flexible neck, good eyesight and strong jaws, snake-necked turtles are formidable predators in their aquatic habitats. They are cosmopolitan animals, feeding on any creatures they can catch, including frogs, tadpoles and fish.

Breeding occurs in September and October – the spring months in Australia – and in November the females lay clutches of eggs in holes in the banks of swamps or ponds. They then cover the holes over and leave the eggs to develop on their own. After three to five months the young turtles hatch and dig themselves out of the holes, scurrying down to the comparative safety of the water.

Most snake-necked turtles live close to streams, rivers, swamps and lagoons in eastern Australia. From time to time, they migrate over land in groups to search out new habitats. It is not unusual for these turtles to colonize artificial ponds.

**Distribution**: South-eastern and eastern Australia.
**Habitat**: Swamps, lakes, slow-moving waterways, creeks and billabongs.
**Food**: Frogs, tadpoles, small fish and crustaceans.
**Size**: 30cm (12in); 1.2kg (2.6lb).
**Maturity**: 4–5 years.
**Breeding**: Clutches of 8–24 eggs hatch after 3–5 months.
**Life span**: 50 years.
**Status**: Common.

## Chinese soft-shelled turtle

*Pelodiscus sinensis*

**Distribution**: China, Korea and Japan.
**Habitat**: Rivers, lakes, ponds and reservoirs.
**Food**: Snails, molluscs, crabs, fish, shrimp, insects, frogs and earthworms.
**Size**: 20–35cm (8–14in).
**Maturity**: Not known.
**Breeding**: Eggs hatch 28 days after laying.
**Life span**: Unknown.
**Status**: Endangered.

The Chinese soft-shelled turtle inhabits slow-flowing rivers and ponds with sandy or muddy bottoms. Occasionally it can be found out of water, basking on stones, but it is quick to disappear underwater when it feels threatened. The Chinese soft-shelled turtle is a predominantly nocturnal animal, foraging on the riverbed at night for prey. This turtle is extremely cosmopolitan in its tastes, eating most animals that it can get its powerful jaws around. Crayfish, snails, insects, fish and amphibians are all on the menu during a night's foraging.

The soft-shelled turtle's jaws are also useful for defence. Unlike most types of turtles, this species cannot fully retract its head under its shell. It also lacks the hardened, bony plates on the shell which protect other turtles. Instead it has a vicious bite, enough to protect it from most would-be predators. The turtle's long snout acts as a snorkel, allowing it to stay completely submerged in shallow water and yet still breathe.

*The Chinese soft-shelled turtle has a flat, soft and rubbery shell and a long snout which acts as a snorkel.*

**Indian starred tortoise** (*Geochelone elegans*): 24–27cm (9.6–10.8in)
One of the world's most distinctive species of tortoise, the Indian starred tortoise is found only on the Indian subcontinent. It has a bizarrely shaped and beautifully marked shell. Each section of the shell, known as a scute, rises to a domed point. These tortoises are mainly active in the monsoon season, when there is plenty of moisture around. During the driest season, they are active only in the mornings and evenings.

**Pig-nosed river turtle** (*Carettochelys insculpta*): 70–75cm (28–30in)
Found only in the far north of Australia, the pig-nosed river turtle is unlike most freshwater turtles in that it has broad flipper-like limbs, more reminiscent of sea-living turtles. Its name refers to its pig-like snout, which is used for breathing while the rest of the body remains underwater.

**Chinese box turtle** (*Cuora flavomarginata*): 10–12cm (4–4.8in)
The Chinese box turtle has a hinged line along its plastron (the underside of its shell). This allows it to close up entirely when it feels in danger. Found only in a small area of eastern Asia, this endangered species spends most of its time in paddy fields feeding on fish, crustaceans, worms and fruit.

## Asian leaf turtle

*Cyclemys dentata*

The early part of an Asian leaf turtle's life is spent almost entirely in water. The young are virtually exclusively aquatic. However, as they grow older the turtles spend increasing amounts of time on land. This species of turtle is omnivorous in habits, feeding on both plant and animal matter. It will quite happily switch from eating leaves to picking off passing snails or crickets.

The lower half of a turtle's shell is called the plastron, and in most turtles this features a series of radiating lines. In the Asian leaf turtle the plastron is hinged along the length of the animal in such a way that, when threatened, the turtle can pull its head and legs fully into its shell, and then pull the lower part of the shell up to close off the holes. This forms a near-impenetrable barrier, behind which the turtle can take cover.

*The Asian leaf turtle has a flatter shell than most turtles. It is usually dark brown in colour, but can be lighter.*

**Distribution**: South-east Asia.
**Habitat**: Streams.
**Food**: Invertebrates, tadpoles and some plant material.
**Size**: 15–24cm (6–9.6in).
**Maturity**: Not known.
**Breeding**: 5 clutches of 2–4 eggs laid each year.
**Life span**: Unknown.
**Status**: Unknown.

# TUATARA

*While looking like a typical lizard, the tuatara is actually a member of a completely separate group of reptiles known as the* Rhynchocephalia, *of which it is the sole remaining example.*

## Tuatara

*Sphenodon punctatus*

*Tuataras are often described as living fossils. They are the only surviving members of a group of reptiles that otherwise died out long ago.*

**Distribution**: Coastal islands of New Zealand.
**Habitat**: Underground burrows.
**Food**: Insects, small lizards and birds' eggs and chicks.
**Size**: 50–60cm (20–24in); 0.5kg (1.1lb).
**Maturity**: 20 years.
**Breeding**: 6–10 eggs once every 2–5 years.
**Life span**: 100 years.
**Status**: Lower risk.

The *Rhynchocephalia* flourished about 200 million years ago, living alongside the dinosaurs. However, most of the species suffered the same fate as the dinosaurs: extinction. The only members to survive were the tuataras. There are only two species still living, both found in New Zealand. Unlike lizards, tuataras have a third eye. This is a light-sensitive organ lying just under the skin on the top of the head. When they are young, the third eye absorbs ultraviolet rays, helping the youngsters produce vitamin D – essential for bone growth. Nearly everything about the lifestyles of tuataras is slow. Eggs develop within the female's body for about ten months before they are laid. It then takes another year for the baby tuataras to hatch. They do not become sexually mature until the age of 20 years. Tuataras have very slow metabolic rates, and breathe on average only once every seven seconds. However, they can hold their breath for over an hour.

# LIZARDS

*The most diverse and widespread group of reptiles is made up of the 3,000 species of lizards. They vary in size from just a few centimetres to almost 3m (10ft) long, and exhibit huge variation in shape, coloration and feeding habits. From legless burrowers to forest dwellers that "fly" from tree to tree, lizards manage to carve themselves a niche almost everywhere on earth.*

## Frilled lizard

*Chlamydosaurus kingii*

In normal circumstances, the frilled lizard looks somewhat similar to other large lizards. It is drab-coloured, being able to blend into its background and remain hidden from its predators. However, should this hiding tactic not work, then the lizard's amazing, brightly coloured frill is brought into action. When the lizard opens its mouth, rods of cartilage attached to the jaw cause the frill to open out like an umbrella. At the same time the lizard makes a loud hissing noise. The combination of the loud hiss and opening frill is enough to frighten most predators into believing that this mostly harmless lizard is a fearsome creature not to be messed with.

Frilled lizards forage mainly on the ground but are also very good climbers, being able to chase their insect prey up trees. When on the ground, the frilled lizard has an enviable turn of speed, being able to outrun most humans.

*Possibly one of the most spectacular lizards in the world, this animal uses its incredible frill to frighten would-be predators into believing that it is dangerous.*

**Distribution**: Northern Australia and southern New Guinea.
**Habitat**: Woodland.
**Food**: Predominantly insects, but also small lizards and mammals.
**Size**: 55–70cm (22–28in).
**Maturity**: 2–3 years.
**Breeding**: 2 clutches of 10–20 eggs produced every year.
**Life span**: 20 years.
**Status**: Common.

## Thorny devil

*Moloch horridus*

*The incredibly spiny appearance of the thorny devil helps to protect and camouflage it, as well as collect water in its harsh desert habitat.*

Australia plays host to many strange animals, and the thorny devil most definitely ranks among the most bizarre. Its entire body is covered by a barrage of spines, which are buff or grey in colour. These spines help to break up the lizard's outline, so it is difficult for birds of prey to spot it from above. However, the main benefit of the spines is less obvious – they are a source of water. Thorny devils live in extremely hot and arid areas, where water is at a premium. During the night, condensation collects on the lizard's skin; the spines help to channel this water down into grooves that run along the body to its mouth. This method of collecting water means that the thorny devil never needs to drink directly from a puddle or pond.

Thorny devils eat only ants, which they pick off one by one using their sticky tongues. They are very efficient at this process, being able to eat 50 ants per minute. A single meal may contain 3,000 ants.

**Distribution**: Western and central Australia.
**Habitat**: Desert.
**Food**: Ants.
**Size**: 15–18cm (6–7.2in); 90g (0.2lb).
**Maturity**: 3 years.
**Breeding**: 4–10 eggs laid in summer.
**Life span**: 20 years.
**Status**: Lower risk.

## Water dragon

*Physignathus cocincinus*

**Distribution**: South-east Asia: Thailand, Vietnam and Cambodia.
**Habitat**: Tropical rainforest, near water.
**Food**: Invertebrates, small mammals, birds, lizards, frogs and fruit.
**Size**: 80–100cm (32–40in).
**Maturity**: 1 year.
**Breeding**: 5 clutches of 10–15 eggs laid each year, hatching after 2–3 months.
**Life span**: 15 years.
**Status**: Common.

With a prominent crest running from the back of the head down the spine, the water dragon is a large, impressive lizard. During the breeding season, males are bright green in colour, but become duller at other times of the year.

The water dragon is equally at home in water, on land and even in the trees. However, it will always head very swiftly for the comparative safety of water when it feels threatened.

Having mated, females scrape out shallow hollows in which to lay their clutches of 10–15 eggs. They then cover the eggs with soil and leaves, and leave them to develop on their own. After two to three months the young hatch out of the eggs, measuring a mere 15cm (6in). However, they grow quickly and become sexually mature at just one year of age.

*The bright green coloration of the male water dragon only lasts during the breeding season, at other times of the year he is duller, resembling the female.*

---

**Sailfin lizard** (*Hydrosaurus pustulatus*): 80–100cm (32–40in)
Hailing from the Philippines, sailfin lizards are grey-green in colour. Adults have crests running down their backs and larger crests running down their tails. The tail crests can be up to 8cm (3.2in) high, and help the lizards to swim. Whilst they spend most of their time in trees, they run to water if threatened. The sail-like fin means that they can swim at high speed.

**Crocodile lizard** (*Shinisaurus crocodilurus*): 40cm (16in)
The only member of its family, the crocodile lizard is found solely in the Guilin and Guangxi regions of China. It gets its name from rows of large olive-green bony scales on its back and tail, which are reminiscent of a crocodile's skin. Local people call this species "the lizard of great sleepiness" because it can remain motionless, in a metabolic pause for hours or days on end.

**Bearded lizard** (*Pogona vitticeps*): 30–45cm (12–18in)
Inhabiting the dry, arid interior of Australia, bearded lizards are great survivors. They forage for their diet of small insects and vegetation in dry forest and scrubland. These lizards are territorial, defending their home patches from intruders. Within their territories they tend to have regular areas, where they rest and bask in the sun during the early mornings. When confronted with potential predators, bearded lizards puff out their black throat patches and open their mouths wide in the hope of intimidating their foe.

## Flying lizard

*Draco volans*

Also known as flying dragons, flying lizards have sets of wing-like membranes, which are actually skin stretched over elongated ribs. The lizards do not really fly, but glide through the forest from tree to tree. A single glide can be up to 10m (33ft) long. When not gliding, the "wings" are folded away down the sides of the body. Flying lizards have a third flap of skin under their chins, which can be extended at will. These chin flaps are larger and coloured yellow in the males, being used in courtship dances.

These small lizards spend virtually their entire lives in trees. The females only come down to the ground for short amounts of time to bury their eggs in soil. Having laid their eggs and covered over the holes, the females will fiercely defend the eggs for approximately 24 hours, before returning to the trees and leaving the young to develop independently. Having hatched, the young climb the nearest trees; the males will probably never set foot on the ground again.

*The skin stretched over its elongated ribs gives the flying lizard a pair of wing-like membranes, which it uses to glide from tree to tree.*

**Distribution**: South-east Asia, Indonesia, the Philippines and Borneo.
**Habitat**: Forest and woodland.
**Food**: Ants and other small insects.
**Size**: 15–22cm (6–8.8in).
**Maturity**: 1 year.
**Breeding**: Clutches of 5 eggs laid in holes in the ground.
**Life span**: 8 years.
**Status**: Common.

## Tokay gecko

*Gekko gecko*

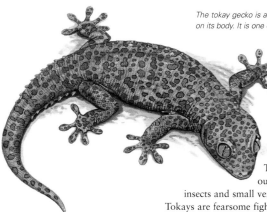

*The tokay gecko is a grey-blue lizard with orange spots on its body. It is one of the world's largest geckos, and is able to cling to smooth surfaces when upside down.*

The tokay gecko is among the largest species of gecko in the world, reaching lengths of almost 40cm (16in). It gets its name from its most common call, an explosive noise sounding like "to-kay, to-kay, to-kay". The gecko is nocturnal, coming out at dusk to forage for the insects and small vertebrates that make up its diet. Tokays are fearsome fighters, with powerful bites which are enough to cause considerable discomfort to any predators attempting to make a meal of them. Male tokays are highly territorial and will attack any other males wandering into the wrong area after failing to heed the warnings given by the residents. Tokay fights are fast, furious and generally deadly to their enemies.

Like the majority of gecko species, tokay geckos have specialized pads on the ends of their toes that allow them to grip smooth surfaces with ease – they are adept at climbing vertically and even upside down. In houses where they are welcomed as a sign of good luck, they climb up windows and across ceilings in search of food. Sometimes they can be found near lights, hoping to catch the moths that are attracted to them at night.

**Distribution**: South-east Asia.
**Habitat**: Bushes, trees and on or around rocks. Also commonly found in or near houses, where it is tolerated because it is believed to bring good luck.
**Food**: Insects, hatchling birds, and also small mammals and reptiles.
**Size**: 20–37cm (8–15in).
**Maturity**: 1–2 years.
**Breeding**: Females lay 1–2 eggs, usually in crevices in rocks or walls.
**Life span**: 10 years.
**Status**: Common.

## Flying gecko

*Ptychozoon kuhli*

The flying gecko is another species of reptile, along with the flying snake and flying lizard, that has taken to gliding around the forests of South-east Asia by using flaps of skin as airfoils. However, unlike the other "flying" reptiles, the flying gecko doesn't use flaps of skin stretched over elongated ribs, but instead it has flaps which grow between its long toes, in the same manner as flying frogs. These flaps of skin give the gecko a very fat-handed appearance, and this has given rise to its alternative name, the thick-fingered gecko.

Flying geckos are exceptionally well camouflaged. They closely resemble the bark patterns on the trees upon which they rest motionless, with their heads facing downward for hours on end, waiting for their insect prey to come close enough to grab. They even have lighter patches on their skins, which look like the patches of lichen growing on the tree trunks.

*Unlike the flying lizard, the flying gecko uses webbing between its toes as parachutes to glide from tree to tree.*

**Distribution**: South-east Asia.
**Habitat**: Tropical forests.
**Food**: Insects.
**Size**: 18–20cm (7–8in).
**Maturity**: 6 months.
**Breeding**: 5–6 clutches of 2 or 3 eggs laid throughout the summer.
**Life span**: 3 years.
**Status**: Common.

# Blue-tongued skink

*Tiliqua scincoides*

One of Australia's most familiar reptiles, the cosmopolitan habits of the blue-tongued skink mean that it is been able to make the best of most situations. It has a varied diet, including insects, snails, fruit and flowers, as well as carrion and the contents of rubbish bins.

As its name suggests, the blue-tongued skink does indeed have a blue tongue. This is very large, almost the same size as the lizard's head, and when the lizard feels threatened, it will stick its bright tongue out at the attacker, presenting the predator with a warning signal. Combined with a fierce hiss, this display is often enough to discourage all but the most persistent predators.

During the breeding season, males set up territories from which they exclude other males. When females enter their territories, the males chase them around briefly, and then pin them down by the backs of their necks until they have finished mating.

*The blue-tongued skink is a stocky reptile with a wide head, thick-set body and short limbs. The blue tongue discourages predators.*

**Distribution**: Eastern Australia.
**Habitat**: Wide-ranging, including forest and parkland.
**Food**: Very varied, including insects, molluscs, carrion, fruit, flowers and food scraps from human settlements.
**Size**: 45–50cm (18–20in).
**Maturity**: 3 years.
**Breeding**: Up to 25 young born live.
**Life span**: 25 years.
**Status**: Common.

---

**Knob-headed giant gecko** (*Rhacodactylus auriculatus*): 20cm (8in)
On the Pacific islands of New Caledonia there is a group of bizarre geckos that have evolved in isolation for many thousands of years. The knob-headed giant gecko is one of them, and is so-called because it has a series of raised crests on its skull that give it a knobbed or horned appearance. It is highly variable in colour, from being mottled to having striking broad bands of brown and white running down its body. Unlike most geckos, which are predominantly insectivorous, adult knob-headed giant geckos eat mainly fruit.

**Leach's giant gecko** (*Rhacodactylus leachianus*): 30cm (12in)
This gecko is among the world's largest and is reputedly the only gecko in the world that growls. This strange nocturnal call may be one of the reasons why some locals consider this and other giant geckos to be "devils in the trees".

**Long-tailed skink** (*Mabuya longicauda*): 30–35cm (12–14in)
Living in open habitats such as gardens and parks, often near water, the long-tailed skink is aptly named. Its tail may be twice as long as the rest of its body and head combined. The long-tailed skink lives in South-east Asia, where it is a common sight rooting around leaf litter in search of insects and spiders. Female long-tailed skinks do not lay eggs, but give birth to live young. The young are miniatures of their parents, and receive no parental care after they are born.

# Emerald tree skink

*Lamprolepis smaragdina*

Few reptiles can claim to be as brightly coloured as the emerald tree skink, which inhabits the tropical forests of South-east Asia and New Guinea. It is an adept climber, spending the majority of its time hiding among the dense foliage on tree trunks and branches, rarely venturing down to the ground. The emerald tree skink actively forages for its insect prey, which it catches with rapid, darting movements.

Like a lot of lizards, this species has the ability to shed its tail if grabbed – a phenomenon known as autotomy. This is a very useful tactic when attacked by predators. Once shed, the tail carries on moving and will often distract the predator, usually a bird of prey or snake, long enough for the rest of the lizard to make its escape.

**Distribution**: South-east Asia and New Guinea.
**Habitat**: Tropical forest.
**Food**: Insects.
**Size**: 18–25cm (7.2–10in).
**Maturity**: 6 months.
**Breeding**: Clutches of 9–14 eggs laid in summer.
**Life span**: 4 years.
**Status**: Common.

*The bright green coloration of the emerald tree skink camouflages it very effectively among the foliage of its tropical forest habitats in South-east Asia and New Guinea.*

## Sand monitor

*Varanus flavirufus*

The sand monitor, or goanna, is one of the largest Australian lizards. It is also sometimes known as the racehorse monitor because it is capable of extreme speeds, often running only on its two back legs, using its long tail for balance.

Sand monitors are found throughout most of Australia, and have managed to be very successful by turning most situations into opportunities. They will eat virtually anything, searching for morsels of food with their long forked tongues, which are used for tasting the air. They will even dig up the nests of crocodiles when the mother's back is turned, and feast on the eggs within.

These lizards are not overtly aggressive, preferring to stay out of trouble whenever possible, but they can put up a serious fight if need be. They use their long whip-like tails, powerful jaws and long slashing claws to defend themselves from predators. Their claws also allow them to climb trees, usually in search of birds' nests.

**Distribution**: Australia.
**Habitat**: Woodland, shrubland and grassland.
**Food**: Lizards, insects, spiders, scorpions, centipedes and even small mammals and carrion.
**Size**: Up to 1.6m (5.5ft).
**Maturity**: Unknown.
**Breeding**: 10 eggs laid into a deep burrow.
**Life span**: Unknown.
**Status**: Common.

*Sand monitors have flattened bodies, long powerful tails, stout limbs, long fingers and very sharp claws. Their well-developed hind legs help them achieve high speeds.*

**Lace monitor** (*Varanus varius*): 1.5–2m (5–6.5ft)
Found in eastern Australia, the lace monitor is dark grey in appearance, with whitish markings, a long neck and tail and long, sharp claws, which it uses to climb trees. The long tail helps the monitor to balance while it is climbing, and it also can become a useful weapon when faced with a predator.

**Borneo earless lizard** (*Lanthanotus borneensis*): 40–45cm (16–18in)
This lizard is nocturnal and highly secretive, and therefore its elongated red-brown form is rarely seen in its native range of north-west Borneo. The earless lizard belongs to a family of its own, but is most closely related to the monitor lizard. It is a good swimmer and a proficient burrower, having a long muscular tail, short stocky legs and a blunt snout. It is able to close its nostrils when diving underwater. Other than this, little is known about the lifestyle of this intriguing species.

## Green tree monitor

*Varanus prasinus*

The green tree monitor blends wonderfully well into the foliage of the trees where it spends most of its days. It also has other adaptations that help it live an arboreal life, such as thick, rough scales on the soles of its feet, which help it to grip branches. Most importantly, it has a highly dextrous tail, which acts like a fifth limb while climbing. Many species of monitor will use their tails as a whip during defence. However, the tail is such an important organ to the green tree monitor that it actively defends it from predators.

Not much is known about the lifestyle of this lizard, due to its secretive nature and the inaccessibility of its habitat. However, it is known that it forages in the forest canopy, mainly for large insects. Some of these insects, such as some katydids, are very well protected with long spiny legs. Before attempting to eat these prickly morsels, green tree monitors therefore tend to strip the legs off and discard them, eating only the nutritious and less spiky body parts.

**Distribution**: New Guinea.
**Habitat**: Rainforests, palm forests, mangroves and cocoa plantations.
**Food**: Large insects and the occasional small mammal.
**Size**: Up to 1m (3.25ft).
**Maturity**: 2 years.
**Breeding**: 2 or 3 clutches of up to 5 eggs produced per year.
**Life span**: Unknown.
**Status**: Common.

*A long, graceful lizard with a pointed head and a whip-like tail, the green tree monitor can be many shades of green, from pale to very dark, depending on where it lives.*

# Komodo dragon

*Varanus komodoensis*

The Komodo dragon is probably the world's most infamous lizard. Not only is it the largest and most aggressive living lizard, but it is also one of the most endangered. It belongs to the same family as the monitor lizards, but has evolved separately for millions of years, becoming incredibly large in the process.

The Komodo dragon is just one of many giant species of animals that have evolved on islands around the world. It is also thought that Komodo dragons originally became so big that they were able to prey on a species of pygmy elephant that inhabited Indonesia thousands of years ago. These pygmy elephants have since become extinct, and the dragons now prey on other mammals, all of which have been introduced into their islands by human populations. The dragons lie hidden for hours upon end, waiting for prey animals to wander past, and then spring from their ambush positions with incredible bursts of speed.

Usually the prey is overpowered within seconds. However, should it escape, the problems for the victim are not yet over. Komodo dragons have a wealth of poisonous bacteria living in their mouths. When they bite prey animals, these bacteria are introduced to the wound, and often cause it to go septic and fester. This results in a slow, painful death.

Female Komodo dragons lay an average of about 20–25 soft, leathery eggs in September. About twice the size of chicken's eggs, they incubate for 8–9 months during the wet season. The young hatch out and immediately start to look for insect prey. However, they have to be careful, because they could well end up on the menus of larger dragons.

**Distribution**: Indonesian islands of Komodo, Rintja, Gillimontang, Padar and the western tip of Flores.
**Habitat**: Dry savannah and woodland.
**Food**: As adults, the bulk of the diet is made up of large mammals: goats, deer, pigs, horses and water buffalo. Birds and reptiles will also be taken.
**Size**: 3m (10ft); 150kg (330lb).
**Maturity**: 5 years.
**Breeding**: 20–25 eggs laid, incubation 8–9 months.
**Life span**: 30 years.
**Status**: Endangered.

*This is the world's largest lizard. The huge form of the Komodo dragon belies the speed with which it can move.*

# Burton's snake lizard

*Lialis burtonis*

**Distribution**: Australia and southern New Guinea.
**Habitat**: Wide-ranging, from forests to desert.
**Food**: Lizards, mainly skinks.
**Size**: Up to 60cm (24in).
**Maturity**: Unknown.
**Breeding**: 1 clutch of 2 eggs laid per year.
**Life span**: Unknown.
**Status**: Common.

While it may look like a snake, this species is actually a legless lizard. Furthermore, it is a lizard that feeds on other lizards, which it catches in a cunning way. Having located a likely victim, the Burton's snake lizard keeps its body very still, but raises the tip of its tail slightly, and wiggles it. The skinks, upon which it feeds, are curious animals and are lured over to investigate. While the skink is preoccupied with the wiggling tail, it fails to notice the head watching it intently from a few centimetres away. Once in range, the snake lizard strikes, holding its prey tightly in its mouth until it suffocates to death. Burton's snake lizard likes to be hot; if the outside temperature drops down to about 21°C (70°F), it will enter an inactive (dormant) state in order to save energy.

*Very variable in colour and markings, Burton's snake lizard is legless and has a broad, blunt snout used for burrowing.*

# CROCODILIANS

*Little-changed since the time of the dinosaurs, crocodiles are notorious for their stealth and ferocity while on the hunt. Despite their bloodthirsty reputation, female crocodiles are caring mothers. They guard their nest sites, help the young hatch from their eggs and carry them to the water. Even though they spend much of their time in water, crocodiles are also effective on the land, and can outrun humans.*

## Saltwater crocodile

*Crocodylus porosus*

*The saltwater crocodile is probably the most fearsome reptile in the world. Better education is encouraging people to stay away from these giant animals.*

This dark grey reptile is the largest of the crocodile species and the heaviest reptile in the world. A full-grown adult can weigh over 1,000kg (2,200lb) and be as much as 7m (23ft) long. It has a large head and powerful jaws, designed for holding and crushing. The crocodile eats pebbles, which are thought to aid digestion by grinding food, and they also act as a ballast for maintaining buoyancy.

The female "saltie" builds a nest from earth and grasses, which keeps the eggs safe from flooding. She guards the eggs from predators and carries the new hatchlings to the water.

Juvenile crocodiles eat crustaceans, fish and reptiles, but as they grow larger, they often take creatures as big as a buffalo or domestic livestock. Humans are occasionally killed or injured.

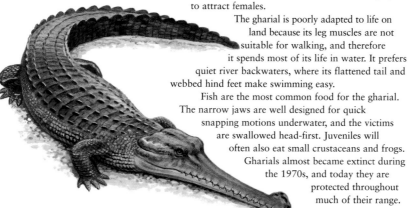

**Distribution**: South-east Asia and Northern Australia.
**Habitat**: River mouths and swamps.
**Food**: Mammals, birds and fish.
**Size**: 5–7m (16–23ft); 500–1,000kg (1,100–2,200lb).
**Maturity**: 10–12 years.
**Breeding**: 40–60 eggs laid in summer.
**Life span**: 70 years.
**Status**: Common.

## Gharial

*Gavialis gangeticus*

The gharial is easily recognized by its long, slender snout, which is filled with interlocking razor-sharp teeth. The male has a bulbous growth on the tip of the nose, used for making vocalizations and producing air bubbles when underwater. It uses bubble displays to attract females.

The gharial is poorly adapted to life on land because its leg muscles are not suitable for walking, and therefore it spends most of its life in water. It prefers quiet river backwaters, where its flattened tail and webbed hind feet make swimming easy.

Fish are the most common food for the gharial. The narrow jaws are well designed for quick snapping motions underwater, and the victims are swallowed head-first. Juveniles will often also eat small crustaceans and frogs. Gharials almost became extinct during the 1970s, and today they are protected throughout much of their range.

**Distribution**: Northern India, Bangladesh and Pakistan.
**Habitat**: Wide, calm rivers.
**Food**: Fish.
**Size**: 4–7m (13–23ft).
**Maturity**: 10 years.
**Breeding**: 30–50 eggs laid from March–May.
**Life span**: Unknown.
**Status**: Endangered.

*The bizarre-looking slender snout of the gharial helps it to grip its slippery fish prey. The reptile rarely comes on land except to nest.*

# Mugger

*Crocodylus palustris*

*As its name suggests, the mugger crocodile rarely passes up an opportunity to grab a meal. Adults capture prey as large as buffalo.*

This medium-sized crocodile is named from a Hindu word meaning "water-monster", and true to its name, the reptile poses quite a threat to any prey that catches its eye. The young crocodiles will take mostly small crustaceans and fish, but the adults will also prey on snakes, turtles and even deer and buffalo. They prefer slow-moving fresh water, not more than around 5m (16ft) deep, and will travel long distances over land in search of water during the dry season.

Mugger crocodiles look very similar to alligators, with broad snouts and flattened heads. However, their sharp teeth are perfectly aligned, and this is what distinguishes them from the alligators in appearance. They have flattened tails and are strong swimmers, but do not use their feet to swim, despite their being webbed.

Like all "crocs", muggers are social animals. The adults and juveniles often call to each other and, during the mating season, males establish territories and dominance by raising their snouts high above the ground and thrashing their tails.

**Distribution**: India, Pakistan and Sri Lanka.
**Habitat**: Shallow, slow-moving fresh water.
**Food**: Juveniles feed on fish, frogs and crustaceans; adults take a wide range of prey, including reptiles and mammals such as deer and buffalo.
**Size**: 2–5m (6.5–16ft).
**Maturity**: Females 6 years; males 10 years.
**Breeding**: Up to 28 eggs laid between February and April.
**Life span**: 40 years.
**Status**: Threatened.

# Chinese alligator

*Alligator sinensis*

This small and secretive alligator is found only in one small part of China, along the banks of the Yangtze River. There are believed to be less than 200 Chinese alligators alive in the wild. Protection is in place, but to many farmers these alligators are nothing more than a nuisance, prone to attacking their wildfowl. Consequently, many are killed on sight. The loss of suitable habitat is also a major problem, and many captive breeding programmes have been postponed because there is not the space for the new specimens to be reintroduced to the wild.

Chinese alligators grow to around 2m (6.5ft) long and weigh up to 40kg (88lb). They are usually dark green or black in colour. Juveniles have bright yellow cross-banding. In common with the more familiar American species, *Alligator mississippiensis*, Chinese alligators have long, upturned snouts and bony ridges along their bodies and tails.

The teeth of Chinese alligators are well adapted for crushing, as they feed extensively on crustaceans and molluscs. They hunt mostly at night and during the summer months. They are opportunistic feeders, not averse to catching ducks or rats if they find them. They will rarely attack larger mammals.

**Distribution**: Yangtze River in China.
**Habitat**: Slow-moving fresh water.
**Food**: Aquatic invertebrates and fish.
**Size**: 2m (6.5ft); 40kg (88lb).
**Maturity**: 4–5 years.
**Breeding**: 10–50 eggs laid from July–August.
**Life span**: Unknown.
**Status**: Critically endangered.

*Young Chinese alligators have bold markings of yellow and black, but these fade as the alligators mature, becoming more and more grey as time passes.*

# SNAKES

*The highly evolved snakes make fearsome and deadly predators of animals of all sizes, from insects to antelope. Snakes cannot chew their food, but can disassociate the two halves of their jaws and swallow their prey whole. Some species of snake produce the most potent natural toxins in the world, however they are in the minority, and only a small fraction of these reptiles pose any threat to humans.*

## Banded sea krait

*Laticauda colubrina*

**Distribution**: Pacific and Indian Oceans from Japan to Australia and Africa.
**Habitat**: Shallow coastal waters.
**Food**: Eels and fish.
**Size**: Typically 1–1.5m (3.3–5ft), up to 3.6m (12ft).
**Maturity**: 18–24 months.
**Breeding**: Clutches of 8–20 eggs laid on land.
**Life span**: Unknown.
**Status**: Common.

The banded sea krait is a tropical marine snake, well adapted to life underwater and on land. It is a venomous but docile snake with distinctive black and yellow bands along its body and a creamy underbelly. It spends much of the time in water, but returns to the land to breed and shed its skin. On land, well-developed stomach scales known as scutes give the snake considerable terrestrial agility and tree-climbing ability, but once egg-laying is over, it returns to the sea.

Sea kraits stay mainly in shallow, tropical waters around South-east Asia and Australia, where they eat eels and small fish. They have flattened paddle-shaped tails for swimming, nostril flaps to keep out the water and specialized glands under their tongues for excreting salt from sea water. Average males, at 0.7cm (2.5ft) long, are dwarfed by females, which can easily reach 1.25m (4ft). As a result, females often venture into deeper waters in search of larger eels, avoiding competition for food.

*Silver and black stripes cover the entire body of the banded sea krait, from the neck area to the tip of the tail.*

## Taipan

*Oxyuranus scutellatus*

The taipan of Australia is one of the most venomous snakes in the world, with a bite that can kill a mouse in three seconds and an adult human in 30 minutes. It is highly aggressive and employs a snap-and-release attack strategy, whereby a thrust and sudden bite is followed by withdrawal to avoid being crushed by the possible death throes of the victim.

Taipans thrive on the northern coasts of Australia, possibly because they only eat mammals. When the highly toxic cane toad was introduced to the area, it caused the numbers of frog-eating snakes to decline, leaving plenty of prey and vacant habitat for the taipan. Its lethal bite and athletic lunging have earned it the nickname the "poison pogo-stick".

The female taipan becomes sexually mature at a smaller size than the male, and will often lay two clutches of 10–20 eggs during the breeding season. The hatchlings are around 45cm (18in) long. They are usually a light olive colour, with creamy underbellies and reddish eyes.

*Taipans are very variable in colour, ranging from sandy and light russet through to jet black.*

**Distribution**: North Australian coast.
**Habitat**: Open grassland and woodland.
**Food**: Small mammals.
**Size**: 1.5m (5ft).
**Maturity**: 6–12 months.
**Breeding**: Females lay 1 or 2 clutches of 10–20 eggs per year.
**Life span**: Unknown.
**Status**: Common.

# Malayan pit viper

*Calloselasma rhodostoma*

The Malayan pit viper probably bites more humans each year than any other species of snake in Asia, and there is a good reason why this is so. It is a nocturnal hunter and spends the day curled up in leaf litter on the forest floor, well camouflaged by its red-brown triangular markings. Unfortunately this behavioural trait means that the snake will not move out of the way or give any kind of warning if a human is walking towards it; it will bite.

Like all vipers, the Malayan pit viper has long, hinged fangs, which lie pointing backwards when the snake has its mouth closed, and snap forward into position when the snake opens its mouth and rears up to strike. It has heat-sensing pits located between its eyes and nostrils, which are so sensitive they can detect the warmth given off by the bodies of their prey. This allows the snake to hunt in darkness.

*A well-camouflaged and deadly beauty, the Malayan pit viper is one of Asia's most dangerous snakes.*

**Distribution**: South-east Asia.
**Habitat**: Rubber plantations and rainforests.
**Food**: Small mammals.
**Size**: 0.7–1m (2.3–3.3ft).
**Maturity**: 1 year.
**Breeding**: 2 clutches of 13–25 eggs laid per year.
**Life span**: Unknown.
**Status**: Common.

---

**Red-tailed pipe snake** (*Cylindrophis rufus*): 0.7–1m (2.3–3.3ft)
This harmless pipe snake is usually found underground but sometimes takes to water, actively hunting small eels and other snakes. When attacked, it raises its tail, showing the red underside, thus mimicking a cobra raising its head. Not only does this make the snake appear more dangerous than it actually is, but it also confuses predators as to which end is the head and which is the tail.

**Sunbeam snake** (*Xenopeltis unicolor*): 1–1.3m (3.3–4.3ft)
Under dull light this snake appears dark brown to black, but under sunlight it displays an iridescence of red, blue, green and yellow. The highly polished, glimmering scales give the sunbeam snake its name. It spends most of its time underground, coming out at night to feed on frogs, lizards and small mammals. It is found throughout southern China and South-east Asia.

**Pacific ground boa** (*Candoia carinata*): 0.7–1m (2.3–3.3ft)
Highly variable in colour and patterning, the Pacific ground boa – from Papua New Guinea and the Solomon Islands – can be striped, blotched or banded. However, most individuals have a flowery, blotched pattern and range in colour from yellow, grey and beige to black or even orange and red. The ground boas living in the Solomon Islands never leave the ground, while those found in New Guinea will climb trees and bushes quite readily in search of the small animals upon which they feed.

# King cobra

*Ophiophagus hannah*

The king cobra is one of the largest snakes in the world, sometimes reaching 5.5m (18ft). It can rear up as tall as a human. It has flaps of loose skin around the head that can be flattened out to form a narrow hood. The king cobra is not strictly a true cobra and, as such, has an unmarked hood.

Depending on its habitat, the king cobra may vary its colour, and it is often darker when in forest than when in open savannah. It has good eyesight and will chase down fleeing prey over long distances. Unusually, king cobras eat only reptiles – mostly other snakes.

The intelligent king cobra is the only snake known to build a nest, which is fiercely guarded by the female. Once hatched, the young are just as deadly as the adults, ready to hunt from only ten days old. The smaller young are vulnerable to mongooses and giant centipedes, but the only threat to the adults tends to come from humans, who kill them for use in medicinal drugs.

*The open hood of a king cobra is a sure sign of trouble. Being able to lift its head over 1.5m (5ft) from the ground, the snake is a fearsome predator. Its scientific name means "eater of snakes".*

**Distribution**: Northern India to Hong Kong and Indonesia.
**Habitat**: Tropical rainforest and savannah.
**Food**: Reptiles, especially snakes.
**Size**: 4–5.5m (13–18ft).
**Maturity**: 5 years.
**Breeding**: 20–40 eggs laid between January and April.
**Life span**: 20 years.
**Status**: Threatened.

# Green tree python

*Morelia viridis*

**Distribution**: Papua and Iran Jaya in New Guinea and the Cape York Peninsula of Australia.
**Habitat**: Tropical forest.
**Food**: Birds are the main prey item.
**Size**: 1.8–2.4m (6–8ft).
**Maturity**: Over 12 years.
**Breeding**: Females lay clutches of 6–30 eggs in hollow tree trunks.
**Life span**: Unknown.
**Status**: Common.

*Masters of disguise: green tree pythons are virtually impossible to spot among the foliage when they are coiled motionless in a tree.*

This beautiful bright green snake spends almost its entire life in the treetops. Most functions – from eating and drinking to mating and egg laying – are performed off the ground. The green coloration gives good camouflage against the leaves, and the prehensile tail lets the snake cling firmly to branches. It will often wait, coiled around a branch and with its head hanging downwards, ready to pounce on passing birds. Vertical pupils make its eyes very sensitive to movement, and the scales around its mouth have heat-sensitive pits which pick up the body heat of animals to aid prey detection.

This species displays the body shape characteristic of pythons: a thick body with a small head, covered with many small scales. Eggs are usually laid in clutches of anywhere from 6–30, in holes in tree trunks. The green coloration of mature snakes is not present in the young, which tend to be bright yellow or occasionally red. They are hunted by birds of prey.

# Reticulated python

*Python reticulatus*

The reticulated python is easily recognized by its unmarked head and sheer size. It is the longest snake in the world. It is a strict carnivore, and kills most effectively by waiting in trees to ambush unsuspecting victims. It tends not to hunt actively, preferring to conserve its energy. It will usually eat birds and small mammals, as well as deer and pigs. Like all reptiles, it has a low metabolic rate and can go for long periods without eating. A captive reticulated python once refused food for 23 months, and then resumed normal feeding.

The reticulated python has a striking net-like pattern of markings, made up of darker triangular shapes along its sides, and patterns of yellow or cream running down its back. The head is largely unmarked, apart from a thin black stripe running across the top.

Reticulated pythons are strong swimmers, although they prefer to spend most of their time on land, hiding in trees. They are nocturnal, and usually breed during the winter months. Large eggs are laid in hollow trees or burrows, then the female coils around them and shivers to keep the eggs warm. Once the baby snakes are hatched, however, they are left to fend for themselves.

**Distribution**: South-east Asia.
**Habitat**: Tropical rainforest.
**Food**: Mainly mammals.
**Size**: 6–10m (20–33ft); up to 200kg (440lb).
**Maturity**: 2–4 years.
**Breeding**: 25–80 eggs.
**Life span**: 30 years.
**Status**: Common.

*The beauty of the world's longest snake is matched by its strength and power. The reticulated python gets its name from its distinctive skin markings.*

# Mangrove snake

*Boiga dendrophila*

**Distribution**: South-east Asia.
**Habitat**: Forest near coasts
and rivers.
**Food**: Lizards, birds and frogs.
**Size**: 2–2.5m (6.5–8.5ft).
**Maturity**: 1–2 years.
**Breeding**: Clutches of
4–15 eggs.
**Life span**: Unknown.
**Status**: Common.

The brightly coloured mangrove snake is easily recognized – it is mainly black, but with bright yellow bands along the length of its body. These bands do not form complete circles around the body, but are interrupted by a pronounced ridge running down the length of the back. It also has yellow lips and throat.

Mangrove snakes are nocturnal hunters, and usually take small vertebrates such as frogs and lizards. They are mildly venomous, and keep their fangs pointing towards the backs of their mouths. As their name suggests, mangrove snakes tend to live in or around mangrove swamps, choosing trees either in coastal waters or near rivers farther inland. They spend most of their time coiled in tree branches and are often fairly docile during the day. The females lay their eggs in piles of rotting leaf litter or old hollow tree stumps.

*The bright yellow markings on its jet-black body make the mangrove snake one of the world's most striking reptiles.*

---

**Golden tree snake** (*Chrysopelea ornata*):
1–1.2m (3.3–4ft)
Also known as the ornate flying snake, this dramatic snake can spread its ribs to form a concave wing shape, allowing it to glide over long distances. When threatened, it will leap from its perch and glide safely to the ground, leaving its hungry predator at the top of the tree. The golden tree snake has only a very mild poison, preferring to kill its mainly lizard prey by crushing it in its powerful jaws.

**Tentacled snake** (*Erpeton tentaculatum*):
0.7–1m (2.3–3.3ft)
This sluggish, nocturnal snake has two short soft tentacles on its snout. It lives in water and hunts by ambush – lying still and hidden by weeds and waiting for its prey to swim past. When fish or amphibians come within range, the tentacled snake rapidly strikes with a sideways motion, clinging tightly on to its prey before it has a chance to escape.

**Blue coral snake** (*Maticora bivirgata*): 1.2–1.4m
(4–4.5ft)
The highly venomous nature of the blue coral snake is advertised by the bright orange markings on its head and tail. The rest of its body is black, with two beautiful light blue stripes running down each flank. Despite its venom, this species of snake is relatively docile and rarely bites humans, preferring to use its toxins to overpower the other species of snake upon which it feeds. Whilst being primarily nocturnal, it can occasionally be found lying stretched out on forest trails in the early morning, basking in the sunshine.

# Red-tailed racer

*Gonyosoma oxycephala*

The red-tailed racer has a somewhat misleading name. It has a plain green body, fading into a tail which varies in colour from brown to orange or grey, but it is never truly red. It is an arboreal snake, active during the daylight hours. It spends most of its time foraging and hunting for birds, small mammals and bats, searching with its large eyes for any animal sizeable enough to form a good meal.

Its green coloration gives it excellent camouflage while moving through the tropical rainforests where it lives. It rarely comes down from the trees, and even mating takes place in the branches. Despite its relatively small size, the racer is an aggressive snake, always ready to defend itself. When it is threatened by birds or larger mammals, it will inflate its throat to look bigger, and lift itself into an S-shaped attacking posture, ready to strike.

**Distribution**: South-east Asia.
**Habitat**: Tropical forest.
**Food**: Birds and rodents.
**Size**: 1.6–2.4m (5.3–8ft).
**Maturity**: Not known.
**Breeding**: Clutch of 40 eggs.
**Life span**: Unknown.
**Status**: Common.

*Despite its name, none of the red-tailed racer's long, thin body is actually red.*

# CATS

*Different species of cat can be found in many different habitats across the globe. The big cats are distinguished from the small cats by several visible characteristics, although size is not necessarily one of them. Also, the small cats cannot roar. However, cats around the world share the same lithe, sinuous grace and agility, combined with killer instincts and razor-sharp claws.*

## Tiger

*Panthera tigris*

*The largest and most powerful of the cat family, the tiger's orange and black striped coat helps it to blend into dense undergrowth.*

Tigers lack the speed of other big cats, but their large and strong hind legs allow them to make surprisingly long leaps of up to 10m (33ft) in length. They have retractable claws, which means that the claws stay sharp, not getting worn down in day-to-day life. Their foreshortened jaws give them immense crushing power in their bite.

Predominantly solitary, tiger groups usually consist of mothers and their young, which stay with them for two years. Clearly marked home ranges keep accidental meetings and disputes to a minimum, but high levels of social tolerance have been observed, often at kill sites.

Tigers are now critically endangered due to poaching, logging and deforestation.

**Distribution**: India, Myanmar, Thailand, China and Indonesia.
**Habitat**: Tropical rainforest, coniferous forest and mangrove swamps.
**Food**: Hoofed mammals, including pigs, deer and cattle.
**Size**: 1.9–3.3m (6.25–11ft); 65–300kg (143–660lb).
**Maturity**: 3–4 years.
**Breeding**: 3–4 cubs.
**Life span**: 15 years.
**Status**: Critically endangered.

## Leopard

*Panthera pardus*

**Distribution**: Sub-Saharan Africa and southern Asia.
**Habitat**: Forest, mountains and grassland.
**Food**: Antelope, deer and rabbits.
**Size**: 1–1.9m (3.25–6.25ft); 20–90kg (44–200lb).
**Maturity**: 33 months.
**Breeding**: 2–4 cubs.
**Life span**: 10–15 years.
**Status**: Common.

The leopard is widespread across most of Africa and southern Asia, ranging from open grassland to tropical rainforest and mountain highlands. It is an opportunistic feeder, choosing mainly large hoofed mammals, such as deer and antelope, but will take birds, rabbits and even dung beetles if prey is scarce.

Leopards are well adapted for climbing trees and have been seen hiding the corpses of prey high in the branches to eat later. They hunt mostly during the day to avoid competition with nocturnal lions and hyenas.

Leopards vary greatly in colour depending on their habitat. On the savannah they are usually a sandy ochre, while the high mountain leopards are very dark gold. They tend to have short legs on long bodies, and their fur is covered in black spots or rosettes. Completely black leopards – black panthers – are usually found only in forests, but they do not represent a different subspecies, merely an infrequent mutation.

*Solitary and nocturnal, the beautiful form of the leopard is rarely seen, even though it often lives in close proximity to humans.*

# Clouded leopard

*Neofelis nebulosa*

The clouded leopard is not a close relation of the true leopard, and is believed to be an evolutionary link between the small cats and big cats. This shy and retiring creature has short legs, but a long tail and teeth. It has distinctive cloud-shaped markings on its pelt, which tends to be pale yellow to grey. It also has two large black bars on the back of its neck.

Not much study has been done on clouded leopards due to their shyness of humans. They have been observed running head-first down tree trunks and hanging underneath branches, and will often retire to the trees to digest their meals. They are carnivorous, eating mainly deer, cattle and monkeys. It is thought that most of their hunting is done on the ground.

Like most of the big cats, clouded leopards have no real predators, and their biggest threat comes from human activities. Loss of habitat and pressure of hunting for their beautiful pelts is driving them deeper into the forest. It takes around 25 animals to make a single fur coat. Their bones are also used in traditional medicine.

**Distribution**: South-east Asia.
**Habitat**: Deep tropical forest and jungle.
**Food**: Mainly deer, cattle and monkeys.
**Size**: 75–90cm (30–36in); 20–30kg (44–66lb).
**Maturity**: 9 months.
**Breeding**: 1–5 kittens born in summer.
**Life span**: 17 years.
**Status**: Vulnerable.

*Elusive and agile, these handsome cats are little known and highly endangered.*

---

**Fishing cat** (*Felis viverrinus*): 75–85cm (30–34in); 8–14kg (17–31lb)
The fishing cat lives mostly near the mangrove swamps, lakes and marshes of South-east Asia. Unlike a lot of cats, it actually likes water and is able to swim well, in addition to being able to scoop fish from the water with its paws. It is even capable of diving underwater and surfacing below unsuspecting waterfowl.

**Flat-headed cat** (*Felis planiceps*): 50–65cm (20–26in); 1.5–2kg (3.3–4.4lb)
The flat-headed cat of Indonesia has unusually small and flattened ears and partially webbed toes. It is a naturally good swimmer and hunts mainly for fish and other aquatic animals in mangrove swamps and lakes. In the wild, these cats are predominantly solitary, coming together only to breed. They have short, stumpy legs and, unlike the majority of cat species, cannot fully retract their claws.

**Snow leopard** (*Panthera uncia*): 1–1.3m (3.25–4.25ft); 25–75kg (55–165lb)
The snow leopard is found on upland steppe and forest in central Asia. It can take prey as large as a yak, but tends to feed on smaller creatures, such as sheep, goats, hares and birds. It is very secretive, hiding away in caves and crevices for much of the day. The snow leopard's luxuriantly thick coat keeps it warm and enables it to live at very high altitudes without suffering from the cold. However, this coat now carries a price: snow leopards are often hunted for their skins, which can be sold for very high prices in Asian countries.

# Jungle cat

*Felis chaus*

Often found living around farms and other human settlements, the jungle cat is a fierce and robust little predator. It has a sandy grey to reddish coat with tabby stripes along its legs, a dark tail tip and black tufts on its large ears. It has good hearing and is very agile, often leaping almost 2m (6.5ft) into the air to catch birds as they fly past.

There is no distinct breeding season, so litters may be born throughout the year. Kittens are generally darker than the adults, with more pronounced stripes. Male jungle cats are often more protective of their young than females, and family groups are common.

This species, along with the African wildcat, was sacred to the ancient Egyptians, who trained them to catch birds – possibly the start of the domestication of cats.

While the jungle cat is common, it shows greater density in natural wetlands than near human habitations, and may be suffering from loss of habitat.

**Distribution**: Middle East, India and south-east China.
**Habitat**: Jungles and swamps.
**Food**: Small mammals, lizards and frogs.
**Size**: 50–75cm (20–30in); 4–16kg (9–35lb).
**Maturity**: 18 months.
**Breeding**: 3–5 young.
**Life span**: 15 years.
**Status**: Common.

*Jungle cats were worshipped as guardians of the underworld by the ancient Egyptians. Their mummified remains have been found in tombs throughout ancient Egypt.*

# DOGS

*Tough and adaptable, larger species of dog tend to be highly gregarious creatures, living in large and complex social groups called packs. Bonding behaviour in packs is common and important for the stability of relationships between animals of the group. These behaviours include licking, whining and tail-wagging – all traits still readily seen in domesticated dogs.*

## Asian red dog

*Cuon alpinus*

*The Asian red dog's coat is cinnamon with white patches on the throat and face. The ears are lined with white fur.*

The Asian red dog, or dhole, ranges from the alpine forests of Russia to the rainforests as far south as Java, but never lives in open habitats. A highly social animal, it is often seen in packs of around ten animals, sometimes as many as 25. In these packs it hunts large deer and sheep up to ten times as big as itself, and has been seen killing tigers and bears. Larger victims are often partially devoured while still alive. An adult Asian red dog can eat 4kg (8.8lb) of meat in one hour. The animal has a powerful square jaw, enabling it to disembowel its prey easily.

Whether hunting or resting, the Asian red dog leads a well-organized life. The existence of strict hierarchies in packs means that fighting is rare. Females are very sociable and will share their dens with other mothers while giving birth. The males of a pack will help out by hunting and regurgitating food for hungry pups and mothers to eat.

**Distribution**: Throughout Asia, from India to China.
**Habitat**: Tropical rainforest and forest steppes.
**Food**: Small to sizeable mammals, including deer and sheep, occasionally berries and reptiles.
**Size**: 90cm (36in); 17–21kg (37–46lb).
**Maturity**: Not known.
**Breeding**: 8 pups.
**Life span**: 12 years.
**Status**: Threatened.

## Dingo

*Canis dingo*

**Distribution**: Mainland Australia, Burma, Philippines, Indonesia and New Guinea.
**Habitat**: Forests, woodlands and open arid grasslands.
**Food**: Rabbits, rodents and marsupials.
**Size**: 0.7–1.1m (2.25–3.5ft); 8.6–21.5kg (18–47lb).
**Maturity**: 1 year.
**Breeding**: 5–6 pups born from June–July.
**Life span**: 12 years.
**Status**: Common.

Thought to have arrived in Australia around 4,000 years ago, dingoes are believed to be the ancestors of various true dog breeds. They can be distinguished from dogs that have been descended from wolves by the shape of the skull and through genetic analysis. They usually have ginger coats with white markings.

In Australia, dingoes are widespread and classed as vermin in many states, due to their taste for livestock. When sheep are not available, they will hunt large marsupials, rabbits and lizards. In Asia they tend to exist on rice and other scavenged food, but will also catch small rodents. The Australian dingo is slightly larger than the Asian variety, and their main enemy in both cases are humans. In Australia, bounties are paid for skins and scalps, and in the Asian islands dingoes often make substantial meals for hungry people.

*Dingoes were introduced into Australia so long ago that they have evolved into an entirely separate species from domesticated dogs.*

# Raccoon dog

*Nyctereutes procyonoides*

The raccoon dog originated in eastern Asia, across northern China and Japan, as well as Siberia and Manchuria. In 1927 it was introduced to eastern Europe for fur-farming and is now seen as far west as the French–German border and northern Finland.

Unusually for a member of the dog family, the raccoon dog is an agile climber, and even the cubs can regularly be seen playing amongst the branches of trees.

Adults form pair bonds and have distinct home ranges. However, these are relatively flexible and they will often roam into other raccoon dog territories. Males and females both help to care for offspring, taking it in turns to guard young while the others hunt for food. They eat whatever they can find, varying with the seasons. Their diet includes fish, amphibians, small mammals, birds, fruit and carrion. They are the only species of dog to "winter sleep". This behaviour resembles hibernation, but doesn't involve a lowering of body temperature.

*The raccoon dog looks like a grey and black raccoon, with its characteristic black face mask and brindled greyish body fur.*

**Distribution**: Siberia and north China. Introduced into eastern and central Europe.
**Habitat**: Damp lowland forest.
**Food**: Carrion, fruit, fish, frogs and birds. Scavenges food scraps from near human settlements.
**Size**: 50–60cm (20–24in); 4–10kg (8.8–22lb).
**Maturity**: 9–11 months.
**Breeding**: 4–9 young born from April–June.
**Life span**: 11 years.
**Status**: Common.

# Golden jackal

*Canis aureus*

The golden jackal is widespread, living across southern Europe, the Middle East and south Asia. It is the only jackal that ranges into North Africa, where it was held sacred to the Egyptian god Anubis in ancient times. It usually sports a golden-brown or yellow coat of short, coarse fur and a black-tipped tail.

Golden jackals mate for life and typically raise pups together for about eight years. They live in clearly defined scent-marked territories, often in small family groups. Some offspring remain as helpers, taking care of new-born pups and leaving their mothers free to gather food for their families.

These jackals are found mainly in open grassland terrain. Dominance fights are common, and golden jackals spend more time away from their groups than other social canids. The dominant cubs tend to be the ones that leave their groups, but in unfavourable conditions they will drive the weaker ones from their packs.

Jackals are opportunistic feeders, eating whatever carrion and small mammals they can find, as well as a lot of plant matter. However, golden jackals hunt more than other jackal species, and often come into competition with hyenas and lions, which will try to steal their prey. The jackals eat very quickly, without chewing their food, and will often bury their kills to hide them from other scavengers.

**Distribution**: Southern Europe, Middle East, northern Africa and southern Asia.
**Habitat**: Open savannah and grassland.
**Food**: Opportunistic feeders.
**Size**: 0.6–1.1m (2–3.5ft); 7–15kg (15–33lb).
**Maturity**: Females 11 months; males 2 years.
**Breeding**: 6–9 pups born after 63 days of gestation.
**Life span**: 6–8 years.
**Status**: Common.

*Golden jackals can often be seen rummaging around landfill sites near human settlements, looking for tasty refuse.*

# BEARS

*Bears are the largest carnivores on land. However, many bears consume high proportions of vegetation in their diets – as much as 95 per cent in some species. Bears have small eyes and ears and large snouts. Their sense of smell is extremely well developed, and this serves them well while foraging and hunting. Bears tend to be exceedingly strong, and a single blow can break a human skull.*

## Sun bear

*Helarctos malayanus*

The world's smallest bear rarely stands taller than 1.5m (5ft) and has a short, glossy, black coat with an orange U-shaped marking on its chest. Very little is known about its behaviour and habitat in the wild or, indeed, about just how endangered it might be.

The sun bear is a stocky creature, with large, curved claws for climbing trees and an elongated tongue for eating insects which it finds in the canopy. It will also eat rodents, lizards, honey and the soft insides of palm trees. In more urban areas, it has been seen eating banana crops and refuse. In common with most bears, it is hunted for its medicinal value according to local beliefs, and a combination of hunting and habitat destruction has led to a serious decline in populations of sun bears, with possibly only a few thousand left in the wild.

*Barely reaching 1.5m (5ft) in height, the sun bear is the smallest of the bear family.*

**Distribution**: South-east Asia.
**Habitat**: Lowland tropical rainforest.
**Food**: Honey, insects and rainforest vegetation.
**Size**: 1.2–1.5m (4–5ft); 30–60kg (66–132lb).
**Maturity**: Not known.
**Breeding**: 2 cubs born after 3.5 months of gestation.
**Life span**: 25 years.
**Status**: Endangered.

## Sloth bear

*Melursus ursinus*

The sloth bear is something of an anomaly. In terms of diet, this medium-size bear has more in common with anteaters than other bears. It was named for its ungainly appearance and long, curved claws, but in fact can run faster than a human and is very active and noisy at night. Its preferred food is termites, and to this end it has developed a gap in the front teeth through which it sucks up the insects. It can open and close its nostrils at will, and a hairless patch on the front of the snout protects it against the termites' defensive secretions. A sloth bear at work on a termite nest can be heard a long distance away through the forest. The bear usually lies alone at night. If surprised by humans in the undergrowth, it rears up on its hind legs and brandishes its heavy claws. Sloth bears have been known to injure humans, but they usually run away when disturbed.

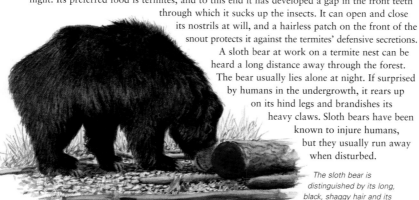

*The sloth bear is distinguished by its long, black, shaggy hair and its highly dextrous nose.*

**Distribution**: India, Sri Lanka and Bangladesh.
**Habitat**: Low-altitude dry forest and grassland.
**Food**: Termites.
**Size**: 1.5–1.9m (5–6.25ft); 80–140kg (176–308lb).
**Maturity**: Not known.
**Breeding**: 2 cubs born each year.
**Life span**: 40 years.
**Status**: Vulnerable.

# Giant panda

*Ailuropoda melanoleuca*

One of the most famous and easily recognized animals in the world, the giant panda is also one of the most endangered. Scarcely 1,000 individuals are believed to survive in the wild – in central and south-western China – with another 140 animals in zoos across the world. Habitat loss and poaching are the major dangers, and because the panda has a very slow reproductive cycle, it takes a long time for populations to recover. Females usually give birth to two cubs, one of which survives and stays with the mother for up to three years. In a lifetime, a female may raise only 5–8 cubs.

A panda's diet is almost exclusively bamboo, occasionally supplemented by other grasses and small rodents. Its digestive system is ill-equipped to digest the fibrous bamboo efficiently, so it has to spend most of its days foraging and eating. An elongated wrist bone with a fleshy pad of skin forms a functional but awkward thumb which is used to grasp the stems, and strong teeth then crush them into a more digestible pulp.

Pandas were once thought to be solitary creatures. However, new evidence suggests that small social groups may form outside the breeding season. These well-loved animals are the focus of much detailed research, always aimed at preserving the species. Recent research into in-vitro fertilization of pandas may help in the battle to prevent extinction.

**Distribution**: Mountain ranges in central China.
**Habitat**: High-elevation broadleaf forests with bamboo understorey.
**Food**: Bamboo.
**Size**: 1.2–1.8m (4–6ft); 110kg (242lb).
**Maturity**: 4–8 years.
**Breeding**: 1 cub born every 3–4 years.
**Life span**: 35 years.
**Status**: Critically endangered.

*Black with white spectacle-like markings around its eyes, the giant panda is instantly recognizable to animal-lovers across the globe.*

# Asiatic black bear

*Ursus thibetanus*

The Asiatic black bear has the dubious accolade of being the bear most prized by poachers. Its organs are believed locally to be of particular medicinal potency. Formerly it roamed across most of Asia, from Afghanistan to Japan, but thanks to hunting pressure it is now restricted to small, isolated pockets of high-altitude woodland. It looks similar to the American bears, with black-brown hair and a cream-coloured V-shape across its chest. However, it has larger ears than most other bears.

In the wild, Asiatic black bears are omnivorous, eating small mammals and birds as well as invading bee nests and termite mounds. They are good tree-climbers, despite their short claws, and will spend most of their days aloft. In cooler regions they hibernate, sleeping from November until early April. Females lose nearly half of their body weight during hibernation, so they have to eat well beforehand. In warmer climes the bears often migrate to the lowlands to avoid a winter sleep.

*The Asiatic black bear's whitish chest patch gives it the nickname "moon bear".*

**Distribution**: Southern Asia, Russia, Korea and Japan.
**Habitat**: Deciduous tropical forest and brushland.
**Food**: Small mammals, insects, honey and fruit.
**Size**: 1.2–1.9m (4–6.25ft); 90–115kg (198–253lb).
**Maturity**: 4 years.
**Breeding**: 1–4 cubs born 6–8 months after mating.
**Life span**: 25 years.
**Status**: Endangered.

# SMALL CARNIVORES

*Small carnivores tend to have long, lithe, sinuous bodies, and are extremely efficient predators, often crucial in the control of rodent populations. Being very adaptable animals, they have been able to carve niches in a wide variety of habitats – from the otters of lakes and seas to the raccoons and martens, some of which now live alongside humans in cities.*

## Red panda

*Ailurus fulgens*

*The beautiful and elusive red panda is known locally as the "fire fox" in its native country of Nepal.*

The red panda is a smaller relative of the more familiar giant panda, although modern biologists are unsure exactly how closely related they are. The red panda is slightly bigger than a large housecat, with a very cat-like face, rusty coloured fur and a long, striped tail. It has partially retractable claws and very tough jaws for chewing the bamboo shoots that are an essential part of its diet. These shoots offer very little nutrition and, like other carnivores, the red panda's digestive system is very short, so it is unable to get the most out of its food. Because of this, the red panda has a low metabolic rate, and chews every mouthful thoroughly. In the wild, red pandas are usually solitary creatures, with clearly defined scent-marked territories. They roam through the forests on the slopes of the Himalayas, which are deciduous hardwoods and rhododendrons with a bamboo understorey. Unfortunately, this fragile ecology and their particular diet means that these beautiful creatures are no longer as widespread as they once were.

**Distribution**: Himalayas.
**Habitat**: Highland bamboo forests.
**Food**: Bamboo leaves, berries, mushrooms and occasionally eggs or young birds.
**Size**: 510–635mm (20–25in); 3–6kg (6.5–13lb).
**Maturity**: 18 months.
**Breeding**: 1–4 cubs per year.
**Life span**: 14 years.
**Status**: Lower risk.

## Sable

*Martes zibellina*

**Distribution**: Siberia and northern Europe.
**Habitat**: Mountainous forests.
**Food**: Rodents, birds, fish, nuts and berries.
**Size**: 35–56cm (14–22in); 0.7–1.8kg (1.5–4lb).
**Maturity**: 16 months.
**Breeding**: Litter of 3–4 young born in summer.
**Life span**: 15 years.
**Status**: Lower risk.

This carnivore lives in mountainous wooded areas, usually near streams, and an individual may have several dens beneath rocks or large roots. The sable hunts by day or night, roaming across a territory that may be as large as 3,000ha (7,400 acres). Mostly it hunts rodents, but it will also eat small birds, fish, honey and berries.

Sables form individual territories, which are fiercely defended against intruders, but in the mating season the males are more forgiving to passing females. The young are born small and blind during the spring. They open their eyes after around 30 days and are independent by 16 months.

The sable has a luxurious silky coat, usually dark brown or black, and has been hunted for many years. During the 18th century, thousands of animals were trapped for their pelts, and the sable is now raised on farms for the fur industry.

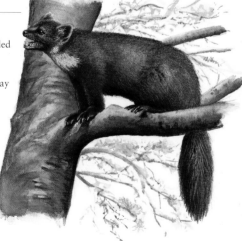

*An elegant relative of the pine marten, the sable was almost hunted to extinction for its sumptuous pelage (fur).*

# Short-clawed otter

*Aonyx cinerea*

The short-clawed otter is one of the smallest otters in the world and, as its name suggests, has very small claws. These claws are in fact tiny blunt spikes that barely protrude beyond the tips of its paws. Unusually, the feet are webbed only to the last knuckles – not to the ends of the toes, as in other otters. These adaptations mean that it has considerable manual dexterity and sensitivity of touch compared to other otters.

Short-clawed otters tend to catch food using their nimble paws rather than their teeth. They favour mostly crabs and molluscs, and have developed large, broad teeth for cracking the shells. Other food includes frogs and small aquatic mammals. They rarely eat fish, and so there is little competition for food when they live alongside other species of otter.

This Asian otter is highly social, and breeding pairs often stay together for life. Small social groups of up to 12 animals are common, and 12 distinct calls have been recorded. These otters also make rewarding pets, and some have even been trained to catch fish by Malay fishermen.

*The short-clawed otter's finger-like front toes make this the most dextrous of the otters. Its front paws are more hand-like than any other otter, allowing it to feel for food in shallow water. It also has a strong tail, making it an excellent swimmer. The short-clawed otter has short dark brown fur with pale markings on its face and chest.*

**Distribution**: South-east Asia, Indonesia and the Philippines.
**Habitat**: Freshwater wetlands and mangrove swamps.
**Food**: Crabs, molluscs and frogs.
**Size**: 450–610mm (18–24in); 1–5kg (2.2–11lb).
**Maturity**: 2 years.
**Breeding**: 1–6 young born yearly.
**Life span**: 20 years.
　　**Status**: Threatened.

---

**Burmese ferret badger** (*Melogale personata*): 33–43cm (13–17in); 1–3kg (2.2–6.6lb)
This small, flexible badger has a long bushy tail and white or yellow markings on its cheeks and between its eyes. The ferret badger spends most of its days asleep in burrows, only stirring as night sets in, when it then forages. It eats insects, birds and small mammals and will often climb trees looking for insects, snails and fruit. The Lepcha and Bhotia peoples of northeast India keep Burmese ferret badgers in their homes to control cockroaches and other insect and rodent pests.

**Palawan stink badger** (*Mydaus marchei*): 32–46cm (12–18in); 3kg (6.6lb)
Found only on the islands of Palawan and Busuanga in the Philippines, the Palawan stink badger lives up to its name, squirting a noxious fluid from its anal glands when it feels threatened. Active by both day and night, it is a slow-moving creature with a stocky body and a long, flexible snout for sniffing out small grubs and worms. Due to its restricted range and secretive habits, little is known about the ecology of this species.

# Hog-badger

*Artonyx collaris*

The hog-badger, or "bear-pig", roams across much of South-east Asia, living mainly in forested areas. It gets its name from its pink, hairless snout and its pig-like feeding behaviour. Rooting in the ground, using its canines and incisor teeth as pick and shovel, it finds small invertebrates and roots, as well as taking fruits and any small mammals that might wander past. Some local peoples have reported it to be a keen fisherman, taking crabs from rivers and streams.

The cubs of this nocturnal animal are playful creatures, but in maturity there is little social interaction. The hog-badger sleeps in deep burrows or caverns under large rocks, and can dig fast enough to escape from some predators – usually leopards or tigers. With strong jaws and sharp claws, it is not an easy meal to catch. In common with other badgers, it also employs a pungent defence mechanism, secreting noxious fumes from its anal glands when in danger.

**Distribution**: South-east Asia.
**Habitat**: Jungle and wooded highlands.
**Food**: Omnivorous: worms, fruit, roots and tubers.
**Size**: 55–70cm (22–28in); up to 14kg (30lb).
**Maturity**: 8 months.
**Breeding**: 2–4 young born in early spring.
**Life span**: 13 years in captivity.
　　**Status**: Lower risk.

*The hog-badger is much like the Eurasian badger in colour and appearance, but with much longer foreclaws and tail. These animals scavenge when food is scarce.*

**Palm civet** (*Paradoxurus hermaphroditus*): 54cm (21in); 3.5kg (7.7lb)
Also known as the toddy cat, this carnivore is found throughout most of South-east Asia, from Timor to India. The palm civet has distinctive markings, with black stripes down its back and small spots on its face. Civets divide their time between the ground and branches, where they feed on fruits, nuts and bulbs. They pick their fruit carefully, leaving less ripe fruit for eating at a later date.

**Indian grey mongoose** (*Herpestes edwardsi*): 43cm (17in); 1.5kg (3.3lb)
This mongoose ranges from Arabia to Sri Lanka, living in areas of bush and tall grass. It has a grey-brown coat speckled with flecks of black. The Indian grey mongoose is solitary by nature. A diurnal (day-active) species, it forages on grassland and in open woodland. Its diet is varied, including insects, eggs and small snakes, and it also eats some fruit.

# Spotted linsang

*Prionodon pardicolor*

There are two species of linsang living in Asia, and they are the smallest of the viverrids, the family that includes the cat-like civets and genets. Unlike many other viverrids, they do not produce pungent scents used in defense.

Surprisingly little is known about these carnivores because they are very difficult to observe, especially in their natural forest habitats. They are nocturnal and spend a lot of time in the trees, where they move with sinuous agility through the branches, using their retractable claws to grip on to bark and their long tails for balance. They also forage for food on the ground. During the day, they shelter in nests constructed from sticks and leaves – either in tree hollows or in burrows. Nothing is known about their social behaviour; they are probably territorial like most other small carnivores.

**Distribution**: Eastern Nepal, southern China and northern Indochina.
**Habitat**: Forests.
**Food**: Small mammals, reptiles, birds' eggs and insects.
**Size**: 30–41cm (12–16in); 598–798g (1.3–1.75lb).
**Maturity**: 2–3 years.
**Breeding**: Up to 2 litters of 2–3 young per year.
**Life span**: 10 years.
**Status**: Endangered.

*Spotted linsangs are sleek, with thick, velvety fur. Their black spots are arranged in rows along their flanks over an orange-buff or pale brown background. Their long tails have dark rings.*

# Binturong

*Arctictis binturong*

The binturong is the largest member of the civet family in Asia. Binturongs are nocturnal animals, and spend most of their time up in the trees. Although they are good climbers, they move slowly and carefully through the branches, and have never been observed to make leaps. They are the only carnivores, along with the kinkajou of South America, to have prehensile tails, which they use when climbing.

Binturongs are also capable swimmers, and sometimes dive and hunt for fish. They are easy to domesticate and make affectionate pets. However, surprisingly little is known about these animals in the wild. They can be active both night and day, and although they are usually solitary, one or two adults are sometimes seen together with young. Captive animals make a wide variety of calls. Like so many species, binturongs are declining because of habitat destruction.

*The binturong has very long, black, coarse fur, often tipped with grey or buff colours. It has conspicuous tufts of long, straight fur on the backs of its ears, which project well beyond the tips.*

**Distribution**: Sikkim, Indochina, Malaysia, Sumatra, Java and Borneo.
**Habitat**: Thick forests.
**Food**: Fish, birds, carrion, fruit, leaves and shoots.
**Size**: 61–96 cm (24–38in); 9–14 kg (19–30lb).
**Maturity**: 2.5 years.
**Breeding**: 2 litters of 1–6 young per year.
**Life span**: 25 years.
**Status**: Vulnerable.

# RODENTS

*The rodents are the largest group of mammals in the world, with over 2,000 species living in a variety of habitats. With the unintentional help of humans, many rodents have greatly expanded their ranges. All rodents have very distinctive incisor teeth, which are used for gnawing. These teeth keep growing throughout the animals' lifetimes to make up for wear and tear from cutting hard materials.*

## Australian water rat

*Hydromys chrysogaster*

The Australian water rat, also known as the beaver rat, is one of the few Australian mammals adapted to living in water. It can be found in freshwater rivers, brackish estuaries and saltwater coastal habitats. These rodents are excellent swimmers and hunt for their prey underwater, usually moving along the bottom in search of fish and large aquatic insect larvae. Australian water rats will tackle relatively large prey, including fish up to 30cm (12in) long. They usually carry their prey to feeding sites on logs or rocks.

Unlike many other Australian rodents, the water rat is not strictly nocturnal, and often hunts during the day, though it is most active in the evenings at sunset. This species is very common, and populations may have increased as a result of irrigation projects that have created more suitable watery habitats. However, four closely related species of water rat, which live only in New Guinea or on surrounding islands, are classified as vulnerable.

*The Australian water rat has partially webbed hind feet used for paddling, and thick, sleek, seal-like fur.*

**Distribution**: Australia, New Guinea and many surrounding islands.
**Habitat**: Rivers, streams, swamps and estuaries.
**Food**: Fish, amphibians and aquatic invertebrates.
**Size**: 12–35cm (5–14in); 0.3–1.3kg (0.6–2.8lb).
**Maturity**: 4 months.
**Breeding**: 1–7 young per litter; 2–3 litters per year.
**Life span**: 6 years.
**Status**: Common.

## Golden hamster

*Mesocricetus auratus*

A number of species of small rodent are commonly referred to as hamsters, all of which belong to the same subfamily, the *Cricetinae*. Although wild populations of golden hamsters live in only a small area of Syria, people have introduced them into many other parts of the world. Golden hamsters are easy to keep, and have become very popular pets.

In the wild, this species lives in burrows in dry, rocky habitats. Burrows can be quite large and often comprise a number of chambers and entrances. Hamsters live alone in their burrows and are usually very aggressive towards one another. Indeed, captive hamsters must be kept apart in order to prevent them from killing one another.

Golden hamsters have huge cheek pouches for carrying food back to their burrows. If their young are threatened, female hamsters have been known to place as many as 12 baby hamsters in their cheek pouches. Although golden hamsters are common household pets and the third most common laboratory animal after rats and mice, the wild population inhabits such a small area that the species is listed as endangered.

*Wild specimens have rich golden-brown fur on the upper side, but selective breeding in captive populations has produced a wide range of colours and fur types.*

**Distribution**: Wild population restricted to Syria in the region of Aleppo.
**Habitat**: Semi-desert, rocky hills and scrubland.
**Food**: Wide variety of plant material, including leaves, seeds and fruit. Also known to eat meat.
**Size**: 15–20cm (6–8in); 97–200g (0.2–0.4lb).
**Maturity**: 2 months.
**Breeding**: 2–5 litters of 2–16 young produced annually.
**Life span**: 3 years.
**Status**: Endangered.

# Flying squirrel

*Petaurista elegans*

**Distribution**: Nepal, Burma, South-east Asia, southern China, Sumatra, Java, Borneo and some surrounding islands.
**Habitat**: Mountain and hill forests.
**Food**: Fruit, nuts, leaves, shoots and maybe also insects and their larvae.
**Size**: 30.5–58.5cm (12–23in); 1–2.5kg (2.2–11lb).
**Maturity**: 1 year.
**Breeding**: 1 young.
**Life span**: 15 years.
**Status**: Common.

This animal, also known as the spotted giant flying squirrel, is one of the largest of over 40 species of flying squirrel found in the world. There are ten species of giant flying squirrel, all of which live in high-altitude forests in eastern Asia, at elevations usually exceeding 900m (3,000ft). In the Himalayas, the spotted giant flying squirrel lives as high up as 4,000m (13,000ft).

During the day, these animals hide in hollow tree trunks or in the thick foliage of high branches. At dusk, they start moving about in search of food. Usually, they move through the treetops in the same way as common tree squirrels, jumping from branch to branch. However, when they come to gaps in the trees too wide to cross by jumping, they leap from high branches and glide across the gaps on the broad webs of skin stretched between their limbs and tail. They have been known to make leaps as long as 450m (1,500ft). Although these animals don't actually fly, they are quite skilful in the air, making several banking turns in one leap and even riding rising air currents.

*Giant flying squirrels have very long bushy "bottlebrush" tails, which are not flattened like those of some other species of flying squirrel. The tail acts as a rudder, both when the squirrel is leaping and when gliding through the air.*

# Giant squirrel

*Ratufa indica*

**Distribution**: Peninsular India.
**Habitat**: Forests.
**Food**: Fruit, nuts, bark, insects and birds' eggs.
**Size**: 25–46cm (10–18in); 1.5–3kg (3.3–6.6lb).
**Maturity**: 2 years.
**Breeding**: 1–5 young.
**Life span**: 20 years.
**Status**: Vulnerable.

*The giant squirrel has dark brown fur on its upper side and buff-coloured underparts. It has particularly broad hands and long claws to help it grasp branches and climb.*

This is the world's largest species of tree squirrel, with a head to tail length of up to 90cm (36in) and a weight of nearly 3kg (6.6lb). Giant squirrels spend most of their time in the treetops and are very agile, moving rapidly through the forest canopy. These squirrels are active during the day, and shelter in holes in trees at night.

During the breeding season, they construct large spherical nests from sticks and leaves, where the females give birth and care for their young. Giant squirrels live alone or in pairs, and are thought to have relatively small home ranges, centred on their nest sites. The squirrels make low "churring" calls when content, and loud chattering calls when alarmed. They are very wary and will dash into thick forest at the least indication of danger. As a result, they are very difficult to study, and relatively little is known about the species. They are now endangered due to the destruction of their habitats.

**Beautiful squirrel**
(*Callosciurus erythraeus*): 13–28cm (5–11in); 150–500g (0.3–1.1lb)
This is one of 15 species of so-called beautiful squirrels, found in the forests of India and eastern Asia. The squirrels are among the most brightly coloured of all mammal species, and often have a distinctive three-colour pattern. This species has an olive-coloured upper side and a rich red-brown underside.

**Long-eared jerboa**
(*Euchoreutes naso*): 7–9cm (2.8–3.6in); 30–50g (0.06–0.1lb)
This curious rodent from Mongolia and northern China has exceptionally large ears – longer than its head. Like other jerboas, it hops around on long back legs, like a miniature kangaroo, keeping its balance with the aid of a long, tufted tail. This little-known jerboa is now thought to have become endangered due to the loss of its habitat.

# BATS

*Bats are the second largest group of mammals – with 977 species – and the only mammals capable of true flight. Bats live in all temperate and tropical regions around the world and, because of their ability to fly, they have even colonized remote oceanic islands. Bat species are not evenly distributed around the world. For example, there are over 100 species of fruit bat living around Indonesia and New Guinea.*

## Flying fox

*Pteropus edulis*

*Flying foxes are fruit bats with fox-like muzzles and ears, and large eyes.*

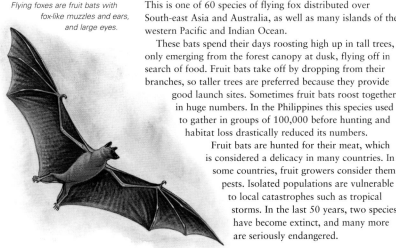

This is one of 60 species of flying fox distributed over South-east Asia and Australia, as well as many islands of the western Pacific and Indian Ocean.

These bats spend their days roosting high up in tall trees, only emerging from the forest canopy at dusk, flying off in search of food. Fruit bats take off by dropping from their branches, so taller trees are preferred because they provide good launch sites. Sometimes fruit bats roost together in huge numbers. In the Philippines this species used to gather in groups of 100,000 before hunting and habitat loss drastically reduced its numbers.

Fruit bats are hunted for their meat, which is considered a delicacy in many countries. In some countries, fruit growers consider them pests. Isolated populations are vulnerable to local catastrophes such as tropical storms. In the last 50 years, two species have become extinct, and many more are seriously endangered.

**Distribution**: South-east Asia, Indonesia, the Philippines and the Nicobar and Andaman Islands.
**Habitat**: Lowland tropical forest and surrounding agricultural land with trees.
**Food**: Fruit, flowers, nectar and pollen.
**Size**: 1–1.8m (3.25–6ft); 0.6–1.6kg (1.3–3.5lb).
**Maturity**: 2 years.
**Breeding**: Single pup born annually.
**Life span**: 30 years in captivity.
**Status**: Common.

## Schneider's leaf-nosed bat

*Hipposideros speoris*

There are 69 species of leaf-nosed bat which live in tropical and subtropical parts of Africa, Asia and Australia. These bats have strangely shaped noses which help them to focus their ultrasonic vocalizations – calls emitted from the nostrils and used in echolocation. These bats can locate flying insect prey and determine how fast they are moving, as well as detecting obstacles, such as branches, from the type of echoes returning from their calls.

Different echolocating bats make different types of call, depending on the kind of habitat in which they live. Schneider's leaf-nosed bats hunt insects in a particularly wide range of habitat types, including inside forests and the edges of more open areas. Although they can hunt and navigate in pitch darkness, these leaf-nosed bats often hunt around dusk and dawn when many species of swarming insects are most active. However, during these times they are more vulnerable to predators such as birds of prey. Although Schneider's leaf-nosed bats are fairly common throughout their range, 13 other species from the same genus are either declining in number or in danger of extinction.

*The muzzles of these bats have strange leaf-like growths of skin, consisting of frontal horseshoe-shaped parts and leaf-like structures running across their centres. These structures focus the ultrasonic calls that help them catch insect prey.*

**Distribution**: Southern India and Sri Lanka.
**Habitat**: Roost in hollow trees, caves and buildings.
**Food**: Insects taken in flight.
**Size**: 4–9cm (1.6–3.6in); 20–50g (0.04–0.11lb).
**Maturity**: 18–19 months.
**Breeding**: Single young born annually.
**Life span**: 12 years.
**Status**: Unknown.

**Short-tailed bat** (*Mystacina tuberculata*): 60–68mm (2.4–2.7in); 12–15g (0.02–0.03lb)
This is one of two species of bat found in New Zealand – the only native mammals to live there. Like many forest bats, this species roosts in tree hollows but, unusually among bats, it is a ground forager and can move with great agility along the forest floor, where it preys on large invertebrates.

**Bulmer's fruit bat** (*Aproteles bulmerae*): 24cm (9.5in); 600g (1.3lb)
This rare fruit bat was first known from fossil remains in central Papua New Guinea, and living specimens were later discovered in the 1970s. Unlike most species of fruit bat, it roosts in caves rather than in trees. This species was thought to have gone extinct until some individuals were rediscovered in the early 1990s.

**Pygmy fruit bat** (*Aethalops alecto*): 65–73mm (2.5–2.9in); 19g (0.04lb)
This is the smallest of the fruit bats of Asia, and lives in high-altitude forests on the mountains of Malaysia and Indonesia. This nocturnal bat feeds on fruit and pollen, and during the day it roosts alone or in twos or threes. The species is threatened by the deforestation of its habitat.

# Common blossom bat

*Syconycteris australis*

These small fruit bats are members of a group of similar bats, all of which have long, slender tongues with brush-like projections for picking up pollen and nectar from flowers. Although blossom bats usually roost alone, they may form "camps" like those of flying foxes, roosting together in groups at certain times of the year.

Some blossom bats stay in the same areas, apparently trying to defend their flowers from other bats, while others move freely between different foraging areas. Like many fruit bats, this species has large eyes, well adapted for seeing in low light.

At night, blossom bats congregate in areas with many flowers, and large numbers can be seen flying around some species of tree when they are in bloom. Perhaps surprisingly, relatively few blossom bats attempt to defend rich nectar sources because of the increased disturbance from the large number of bats attracted to such sites.

**Distribution**: North-eastern Australia, New Guinea and several island groups of Indonesia and the western Pacific.
**Habitat**: Wide range of forest types.
**Food**: Nectar, pollen and occasionally fruit.
**Size**: 5–7.5cm (2–3in); 11.5–25g (0.02–0.05lb).
**Maturity**: Unknown; probably around 1 year.
**Breeding**: 1 young or very occasionally twins born.
**Life span**: Unknown.
**Status**: Common.

*Common blossom bats are one of the smallest fruit bats in the world. They have red-brown or grey-brown fur on top, and pale undersides. Like some species of fruit bat, they are important pollinators. There is concern that their numbers are declining in Australia.*

# Colugo

*Cynocephalus variegatus*

The colugo is also known as the flying lemur, but this name is somewhat misleading because these animals are not lemurs, and although they can glide almost horizontally for 100m (330ft) or more, they are not capable of true flight either.

Colugos have very well developed gliding membranes which, unlike those of other gliding mammals, stretch all the way to the tips of their fingers, toes and tails. As their wide eyes suggest, these animals are largely nocturnal, sleeping in holes or hollows high up in trees during the daytime. At dusk they leave their shelters, climbing up to find good take-off positions, and then glide away in search of food.

In the branches they hang upside down, moving hand over hand, with their tails tucked under their bodies. Little is known about the social behaviour of these animals, except that they usually live alone, but occasionally come together in small groups. A second species of colugo only lives on certain islands of the Philippines, and is now threatened by the loss of its habitat.

*Colugos have dark fur with white spots on their upper side that makes them difficult to see against the bark of trees. The colugo's head is surprisingly similar to that of the flying fox.*

**Distribution**: South-east Asia and the East Indies.
**Habitat**: Primary and secondary forest, coconut and rubber plantations.
**Food**: Young leaves and perhaps also fruit, flowers and buds.
**Size**: 32–42cm (12–17in); 1–1.75kg (2.2–3.8lb).
**Maturity**: Not certain, but probably around 3 years.
**Breeding**: 1 or 2 young are reared annually.
**Life span**: 15 years.
**Status**: Unknown.

# ELEPHANT AND DUGONG

*The first ancestors of the elephants originated in Africa around 40 million years ago. From this prehistoric family, two different groups evolved: the mastodons and the modern elephant family. The relatives of the Asian elephant appeared in Africa, and then spread into Asia and Europe. Elephants have few relatives. They are thought to share ancestry with hyraxes and sea cows – dugongs and manatees.*

## Asian elephant

*Elephas maximas*

**Distribution**: Originally found in the Middle East, India, southern China, South-east Asia, Java, Sumatra, Borneo and Sri Lanka.
**Habitat**: Tropical forest, open woodland and grassland.
**Food**: Grass, leaves, roots, stems, fruit and other crops.
**Size**: 5.5–6.4m (18–21ft); 2,720–6,700kg (6,000–14,750lb).
**Maturity**: 9 years.
**Breeding**: 1 calf born every 2–8 years.
**Life span**: 80 years.
**Status**: Endangered.

The Asian elephant is one of the world's largest land animals, second only to its close relative, the African elephant. Asian elephants live in small groups of 15–40 individuals, consisting of related females and their young, led by old matriarchs – head females.

Asian elephants are intelligent animals, and they have been reported to be able to use tools. For example, they sometimes use sticks held in their trunk to scratch themselves or to swat insects. They have been domesticated for many thousands of years and have been used as draught and war animals up to modern times. However, the Asian elephant can be an agricultural pest, eating up to 150kg (330lb) of crops per day.

*Asian elephants can be distinguished from their African cousins by their smaller ears, sloping backs and by having only one rather than two projections on their trunks.*

## Dugong

*Dugong dugon*

The dugong is a very distant relative of the elephant, and is placed in its own order – the *Sirenia* – along with the manatees. Dugongs live in shallow coastal regions where the sea grass on which they feed is abundant. They rarely make long-distance migrations, though in some places they make daily movements from feeding areas to resting sites in deeper water.

Dugongs have unusually shaped mouths, with overhanging upper lips that are specially designed for cropping sea grasses. They can dive for up to three minutes before coming up to breathe, and will swim at up to 20kph (12mph) if pursued.

**Distribution**: Coasts of tropical East Africa, tropical Asia and Oceania.
**Habitat**: Shallow coastal waters.
**Food**: Sea grass and occasionally algae and crustaceans.
**Size**: 2.4–2.7m (8–9ft); 230–908kg (500–2,000lb).
**Maturity**: 9–15 years.
**Breeding**: 1 or 2 young born after about 1 year's gestation, every 3–7 years.
**Life span**: 70 years.
**Status**: Vulnerable.

The young are born underwater, after which they ride on their mothers' backs, breathing when the females come to the surface.

Sharks attack dugongs, but groups of dugongs will gang up on them and ram them with their heads. Orcas (killer whales) have also been known to attack dugongs, but by far their greatest enemy is human beings, who have hunted them extensively for their meat, hides and ivory.

*Dugongs have thick, smooth hides, usually dull grey-brown in colour. Unlike the closely related manatees, which have rounded paddle-shaped tails, dugongs have fluked tails like those of whales and dolphins.*

# HOOFED ANIMALS

*Hoofed animals are separated into two main groups by the shape of their hooves. The* Perissodactyla, *which includes the horses, zebras, tapirs and rhinos, have hooves with an odd number of toes, with most of the animal's weight supported on the middle toe. The* Artiodactyla, *in contrast, have an even number of toes, and include animals such as deer, cattle, antelope, pigs, camels, giraffes and hippopotamuses.*

## Muntjac

*Muntiacus reevesi*

Only the males of these dainty deer carry antlers, and these rarely exceed 15cm (6in) in length. However, the male muntjac's main weapons are its long upper canine teeth, which curve outwards from its lips like tusks. The teeth are usually used in fights to settle territorial disputes with other males, but can also inflict savage injuries on dogs and other attacking animals.

Male muntjacs defend territories of around 20ha (50 acres) in size, usually close to water, and try to encompass as many of the smaller female territories as possible. When they are nervous, muntjacs make a call that sounds like a dog barking, giving muntjacs their other common name, "barking deer". These calls are probably aimed at predators that use ambush tactics to catch their prey. By calling, the muntjacs let the predators know that they have been spotted, and therefore are unlikely to succeed in their ambushes. Muntjacs were introduced into Britain in 1901, and feral populations have established themselves well.

*As well as the protruding canine teeth that are also found in a few other species of deer, the lower portions of a male muntjac's antlers are covered in fur. Instead of antlers, females have small bony knobs with a coating of fur.*

**Distribution**: Southern China and Taiwan. Introduced to Britain.
**Habitat**: Forest and farmland surrounded by vegetation.
**Food**: Grass, tender leaves and shoots.
**Size**: 0.6–1.4m (2–4.75ft); 14–33kg (30–73lb).
**Maturity**: Females 1 year; probably older for males.
**Breeding**: Single fawn born each year.
**Life span**: 15 years.
**Status**: Common.

## Sambar

*Cervus unicolor*

*This large Asian deer has particularly stout six-pointed antlers that can measure as much as 1m (3.25ft) along the outside curve. Sambars are very cunning and can live close to human habitation.*

The sambar is one of ten closely related species of deer, all in the genus *Cervus*, which includes the European and American red deer and the oriental sika deer. Like red deer, male sambars fight during the mating season. Victorious males set up small territories marked with scent, and mate with any females that pass through. In some nature reserves in India, sambars are important prey animals for dholes (Asian red dogs), Asiatic lions and tigers. Although they are an important prey for some rare predators, sambars can also be troublesome to nature reserve managers because they sometimes kill large trees by stripping their bark, leading to considerable habitat destruction. In some countries where sambars have been introduced, such as New Zealand, they are hunted for sport.

**Distribution**: India to south-eastern China, Malay peninsula, Sri Lanka, Taiwan, Hainan, Sumatra, Borneo and surrounding islands. Introduced into Australia, New Zealand, California, Texas and Florida.
**Habitat**: Forests.
**Food**: Leaves, buds, berries, twigs, grass and fallen fruit.
**Size**: 1.6–2.5m (5.25–8.25ft); 109–260kg (240–570lb).
**Maturity**: Females 2 years; first mating older in males.
**Breeding**: Single fawn.
**Life span**: 25 years.
**Status**: Abundant.

# Przewalski's horse

*Equus przewalskii*

**Distribution**: Altai Mountains of Mongolia.
**Habitat**: Grassy plains and deserts.
**Food**: Grass, leaves, twigs, buds and fruit.
**Size**: 2.2–2.8m (7.25–9.25ft); 200–300kg (440–660lb).
**Maturity**: Females 4 years; males 5 years.
**Breeding**: Single foal born every 3 years.
**Life span**: 38 years.
**Status**: Extinct in the wild.

Some scientists consider this horse as simply a subspecies of the domestic horse – *Equus caballus* – rather than a separate species. Most certainly, Przewalski's horse represents a unique animal, either as the last remaining truly wild variety of domestic horse, or as a unique species. In fact, Przewalski's horse, named after the Russian explorer who discovered it in 1879, has very similar habits to feral populations of domestic horses.

It lives in groups of around ten individuals, consisting of females with their young and a single dominant male or stallion. The stallion may lead his harem of females and young for many years, taking great care to protect them from rival males and other dangers such as predators.

These horses spend their days in dry areas, and in the evenings move to wetter areas with better grazing and drinking water. In some parts they make seasonal migrations to track the rainfall and the richest grazing sites. The horses have not been seen in the wild since 1968, and it is feared that they are now extinct in their former range. However, the species survives in zoos.

*Przewalski's horses are slightly smaller than domestic horses, with light reddish-brown-coloured upper parts, pale flanks and white undersides. Plans have been made to reintroduce these horses to their former range.*

---

**Sika deer** (*Cervus nippon*): 0.9–1.4m (3–4.75ft); 80kg (176lb)
This species of deer lives in eastern Asia, including most of China and Japan. Like red deer, male sika deer fight during the rutting season in order to control harems of up to 14 females. Sika deer are very vocal, and can produce at least ten different sounds, ranging from soft whistles to loud screams.

**Giant muntjac** (*Megamuntiacus vuquangensis*): 96cm (38in); 34–50kg (75–110lb)
This animal was unknown to science until 1994, when descriptions of a few individuals found in Vietnam were first published. Like other species of muntjac deer, the males have sharp elongated canines used in fighting. Giant muntjacs are hunted for their meat, and may also be suffering from habitat loss.

**Four-horned antelope** or **chousingha** (*Tetracerus quadricornis*): 0.8–1m (3–3.25ft); 17–21kg (15–46lb)
This small antelope lives in Nepal and India in open forests, usually close to water. The males are unique among the *Bovidae* – the family including antelope, cattle and goats – in that they have four horns. These horns are smooth and cone-shaped, and have made this species sought after by trophy hunters.

# Babirusa

*Babyrousa babyrussa*

There are probably little more than 4,000 of these wild pigs roaming the Indonesian forests of Sulawesi and its surrounding islands.

Babirusas are most active during daylight hours. Males usually live alone, while females and young go about in groups of about a dozen. The tusks are not well designed for combat, and although males are aggressive when they meet, they rarely use their tusks in fighting. Females do not usually fight among themselves, but they sometimes attack by trying to bite the front legs of their opponents. Babirusas are fast runners and good swimmers. They sometimes swim out to sea to reach small islands.

**Distribution**: Sulawesi, Indonesia, and some nearby islands.
**Habitat**: Damp, tropical forests.
**Food**: Leaves and fallen fruit.
**Size**: 0.9–1.1m (3ft); up to 100kg (220lb).
**Maturity**: 1 year.
**Breeding**: 2 litters of 1 or 2 young produced annually.
**Life span**: 24 years.
**Status**: Vulnerable.

*Unlike any other species of wild pig, whose tusks grow from the sides of the jaw, the upper tusks of the babirusa grow upwards through the muzzle. These pigs often visit salt licks, where scientists observe their behaviour.*

# Bactrian camel

*Camelus bactrianus*

Archaeological evidence has revealed that bactrian, or two-humped, camels were first domesticated around 2500 BC. It used to be believed that the one-humped, or dromedary, camel evolved from domesticated bactrian camels. However, 3,000-year-old rock drawings in the Arabian peninsula show horsemen hunting dromedaries, and 7,000-year-old dromedary remains suggest that one-humped camels had wild-living ancestors.

Bactrian camels and dromedaries can interbreed, and their young have either a long single hump with a slight indentation, or a large hump and a small hump. Camel humps contain fat deposits that provide the animal with energy when there is no available food.

Over the last hundred years there has been a great reduction in wild bactrian camel numbers. Although there are around a million domesticated animals, only 1,000 or so wild ones remain, and these are affected by hunting and herders who prevent them from reaching water holes. Camels have many adaptations to cold and heat, and can survive for long periods without water. They have very few sweat glands, so lose little liquid through their skins. They are able to drink brackish water, which would make other animals sick.

**Distribution**: Wild populations now only found in Mongolia and north-western China, but domestic animals found in many parts of central Asia and beyond.
**Habitat**: Dry steppes and semi-deserts.
**Food**: Unpalatable plants and carrion.
**Size**: 2.2–3.4m (7.25–11.25ft); 300–690kg (660–1,500lb).
**Maturity**: Reach maturity after more than 3 years.
**Breeding**: Single calf produced every 2 years. Occasionally twins are born.
**Life span**: Probably around 20 years in the wild.
**Status**: Endangered.

*Wild bactrian camels are quite different in appearance from domestic ones, and have much lighter coats, shorter fur, leaner bodies and smaller humps.*

# Indian rhinoceros

*Rhinoceros unicornis*

This is the largest of three different species of rhinoceros living in Asia. Apart from mothers with their calves, these rhinos live alone, though occasionally several come together at muddy wallows or good grazing areas. They live in home ranges of 2–8sq km (0.75–3sq miles), which overlap with those of other rhinos. Meetings between neighbouring rhinos are often aggressive affairs. Although Indian rhinoceroses usually flee when disturbed, they sometimes charge at humans. Females with calves are particularly dangerous, and several fatal attacks are recorded every year in Nepal and India.

This species used to be common in north-western India and Pakistan until around 1600, when large areas of lush lowland grasslands were turned into farmland. As well as losing much of their prime habitat, rhinos came into conflict with farmers and sportsmen. By the early 1900s the species was close to extinction. International law now protects these rhinos, and their numbers have increased. There are now around 2,000 individuals in the wild.

**Distribution**: Originally found in northern Pakistan, Nepal, northern India, northern Bangladesh and Assam.
**Habitat**: Grasslands, swamps, forests and farmland.
**Food**: Grass, leaves, fruit, twigs and crops.
**Size**: 3.1–3.8m (10–12.5ft); 1,600–2,200kg (3,500–4,800lb).
**Maturity**: 7–10 years.
**Breeding**: Single calf born every 3–5 years.
**Life span**: 40 years.
**Status**: Endangered.

*Both males and females have horns that can grow up to 53cm (21in). The skin is greatly folded, and is covered in rivet-like knobs that make it look like armour.*

# Yak

*Bos grunniens*

Yaks are closely related to cattle, and have been domesticated since around 1000 BC. There are nearly 13 million domestic yaks around the high plateaux of Central Asia, where they are used as draught animals and for milk, meat and wool production.

Yaks are well suited to cold, high-altitude conditions, being powerful but docile. There are probably only a few thousand wild yaks, ranging from eastern Kashmir along the Tibetan–Chinese border into the Qinghai province of China. Yaks spend the short summers feeding in sparse alpine meadows, and in winter they descend into the valleys. Females usually live together in large herds that used to be thousands strong when wild yaks were more abundant. Males live alone or in small groups of less than 12 animals until the breeding season, when they join the herds to fight over females.

**Distribution**: Originally found in highlands of Siberia, Nepal, Tibet, western China and adjacent areas around the Himalayas.
**Habitat**: Highland and mountainous steppes.
**Food**: Grass, herbs and lichens.
**Size**: 3.3m (11ft); 400–1,000kg (880–2,200lb).
**Maturity**: 6–8 years.
**Breeding**: Single calf every 2 years.
**Life span**: 25 years.
**Status**: Endangered.

*Yaks have stocky bodies and very long black-brown woolly fur that almost reaches to the ground, to help keep them warm. Wild yaks are larger and have stronger horns than domestic yaks.*

**Gaur** (*Bos gaurus*): 2.5–3.3m (8–11ft); 650–1,000kg (1,400–2,200lb)
The gaur is closely related to domestic cattle, and is characterized by its short red-brown or black-brown fur, with white lower legs. This species lives from Nepal and India to South-east Asia, including the Malay peninsula, inhabiting forested hills. In some places the gaur is diurnal, in others it is nocturnal, depending on the level of persecution by humans.

**Mountain anoa** (*Bubalus quarlesi*): 1.6–1.7m (5–5.5ft); 150–300kg (330–660lb)
There are thought to be two species of anoa, both restricted to the island of Sulawesi. Mountain anoas live in dense forests and are very secretive. Usually anoas will flee when disturbed, but occasionally they have been known to charge. These animals have a very restricted range and have suffered from excessive hunting and habitat loss.

**Axis deer** or **chital** (*Axis axis*): 1–1.7m (3.25–5.5ft); 27–110kg (60–240lb)
Found in India, Nepal and Sri Lanka, these deer are characterized by their slender body shape. At certain times of the year they have white spots on their fawn-coloured fur. They live mostly in open habitats, presumably so that they can see approaching predators. Indeed, axis deer are the favourite prey of tigers in many parts of India.

# Nilgai

*Boselaphus tragocamelus*

Nilgai used to be widespread across the Middle East but in recent years they have disappeared from Bangladesh, though they continue to survive in India, Pakistan and Nepal, and have been introduced into Texas.

During the mating season, males compete for territories, usually by aggressive displays or ritualized fighting, involving pushing each other with their necks. Occasionally, proper fighting occurs, and they drop to their knees, lunging at each other with their short stabbing horns. The winners have the opportunity to gather harems of up to ten females.

**Distribution**: Eastern Pakistan, India, and Nepal. Introduced into Texas.
**Habitat**: Forests, jungles and occasionally open grasslands.
**Food**: Grass, leaves, twigs, and will also eat fruit and sugar cane.
**Size**: 1.8–2.1m (6–7ft); up to 300kg (660lb).
**Maturity**: Females 2 years; males 5 years.
**Breeding**: Occasionally 3 calves born at a time; twins very frequent.
**Life span**: 10 years.
**Status**: Threatened.

*Only the male nilgai have horns, but both sexes possess manes on their necks. The wiry coat is reddish-brown in males and a paler colour in females.*

**Serow** (*Capricornis sumatraensis*): 1.4–1.8m (4.75–6ft); 50–140kg (110–308lb)
This is the most widespread of three species of serow living in large parts of China, the Himalayan region, South-east Asia and parts of Indonesia. The other two species are restricted to the islands of Taiwan and the Japanese archipelago. Serows are related to goats, and similarly live on rocky slopes. Both males and females possess sharp horns rarely more than 25cm (10in) long, which can inflict deadly injuries to hunting dogs.

**Sao la** (*Pseudoryx nghetinhensis*): 1.5–2m (5–6.5ft); 100kg (220lb)
Despite its large size and striking colours, the sao la, with its long, straight, smooth horns and striped facial pattern, was unknown to science until 1992. This animal was first identified from several sets of horns obtained from hunters in a nature reserve on the Laos-Vietnam border. Unfortunately, shortly after its discovery it was classified as endangered, and is threatened by poaching and habitat loss.

**Tibetan antelope** or **chiru** (*Pantholops hodgsoni*): 1.3–1.4m (4.25–4.5ft); 25–55kg (55–120lb)
This animal is actually more closely related to goats than to true antelopes, and lives on the high plateau of Tibet, Kashmir and north-central China. The males have slender, ridged horns up to 70cm (28in) long, rising straight upwards. They use these sabre-like horns when fighting for control of females during the rutting season, sometimes inflicting fatal injuries.

## Himalayan tahr

*Hemitragus jemlahicus*

Himalayan tahrs are closely related to goats. There are two other species of tahr: the Arabian tahr, which is only found in Oman, and the Niligri tahr, which lives around the Niligri Hills in southern India.

Both male and female Himalayan tahrs have luxuriant manes over their necks and shoulders, presumably as a defence against the cold mountain air. Tahrs are very wary, and at the least alarm they will scamper off over rocks and through forest, moving easily over the steep terrain.

Tahrs live in herds usually consisting of around ten individuals. During the mating season, males lock horns and wrestle one another in order to win the right to mate with females.

Competition with domestic goats and hunting has begun to reduce all three species of tahr. Arabian and Niligri tahrs are now officially classified as endangered by the IUCN.

**Distribution**: The Himalayas, from Kashmir to western Bhutan. Introduced into New Zealand.
**Habitat**: Forested hills and mountains.
**Food**: Mostly grass.
**Size**: 0.9–1.4m (3–4.75ft); 50–100kg (110–220lb).
**Maturity**: Females around 1.5 years; probably older for males.
**Breeding**: 1 or 2 young at a time.
**Life span**: 21 years.
**Status**: Vulnerable.

*Himalayan tahrs resemble goats, but unlike goats, males do not sport goatee beards and do not have twisted horns.*

## Saiga

*Saiga tatarica*

Saigas are related to goats and sheep, and around two million years ago, in the Pleistocene epoch, these animals were very abundant, ranging right across Europe and Asia from Britain to Alaska. Nowadays, saigas are not so common. They have been exterminated from some parts of their range, such as Crimea, by over-hunting and habitat loss.

Saigas are nomadic, constantly moving about in search of food. In autumn, many saiga populations migrate south to warmer climes and better feeding grounds, returning north in the following spring. Saigas move rapidly, covering 80–120km (50–75 miles) per day during their migrations.

Adult saigas can run at up to 80kph (50mph), and even two-day-old saiga kids can outrun humans. In winter, after the migration is over, males try to herd females into their territories, and successful males gather between 5–15 females. Competition is intense, and fights between saiga males are sometimes fatal.

*The saiga has an unusually shaped nose with large, downward-pointing nostrils. The strange internal structure of this nose is only found in one other type of mammal – whales. It is thought to warm inhaled air in cold winters, and to help cool the saiga during hot summers.*

**Distribution**: Western Ukraine to western Mongolia.
**Habitat**: Steppes and dry grassy plains.
**Food**: Grass, herbs and shrubs.
**Size**: 1–1.4m (3.25–4.75ft); 26–69kg (57–150lb).
**Maturity**: 12–20 months.
**Breeding**: 1–2 calves.
**Life span**: 10–12 years in the wild.
**Status**: Vulnerable.

# Water buffalo

*Bubalus bubalis*

**Distribution**: Nepal, India, Sri Lanka, South-east Asia, Malay peninsula, Borneo, Java and Sumatra. Introduced into many other areas, including South America, Europe, Australia and Hawaii.
**Habitat**: Wet grasslands, swamps and lush river valleys.
**Food**: Green grass and water vegetation.
**Size**: 2.4–3m (8–10ft); 700–1,200kg (1,540–2,640lb).
**Maturity**: 18 months.
**Breeding**: Single calf every 2 years.
**Life span**: 25 years.
**Status**: Endangered in the wild; domestic population is common.

These large animals were domesticated as long ago as 5000 BC in southern China, 3000 BC in the Indus valley and 2000 BC in other parts of the Middle East. There are now estimated to be around 150 million domestic water buffalo around the world. So useful are these beasts that they have been introduced into many new areas, including Australia, South America, southern Europe and Hawaii.

Domestic water buffalo are very docile, produce excellent milk and meat, and are strong and easily managed work animals. In some areas, they form an important part of agricultural economies and ecosystems by providing a reliable and easily maintained source of power and by conserving wallowing sites that harbour a wide diversity of animal and plant life.

Wild water buffalo from original undomesticated stock are very rare, and very few populations remain. These wild buffalo live in herds of up to 30 individuals, consisting of females and their young, led by elder females. During the dry season males live in bachelor groups away from the females, and in the wet season the dominant males enter herds to mate. The female herd leaders remain in charge of their groups even when bulls are present, and after mating the males are driven away.

*Wild water buffalo have the longest spread of horns of any cattle – up to 2m (6.5ft), measured along the outside edge.*

# Markhor

*Capra falconeri*

The markhor is one of seven species of wild goat, all of which live in mountainous regions of Europe and Asia. This species lives in certain mountain ranges of Central Asia. As a protection against the cold continental winters, markhors have thick white and grey coats and long shaggy manes covering their necks and shoulders. In summer, markhors lose their winter coats, which are replaced by shorter red-grey coats, and they move higher up the mountains to feed on the rich spring growth.

*Male markhors are characterized by their long corkscrew-shaped horns that can reach up to 1.6m (5.25ft) in length. Females also have horns, but they rarely grow longer than 25cm (10in).*

**Distribution**: Mountainous areas of central Asian countries, including Turkmenistan, Uzbekistan, Tajikistan, Afghanistan, Pakistan and Kashmir.
**Habitat**: Mountainous areas close to the treeline, rocky areas, dry country and steep meadows.
**Food**: Grass, leaves and twigs.
**Size**: 1.4–1.8m (4.75–6ft); 32–110kg (70–240lb).
**Maturity**: 2.5 years.
**Breeding**: 1 or 2 young born at a time.
**Life span**: 12 years.
**Status**: Endangered.

Females live in small herds, usually comprising about nine individuals, but occasionally up to 100. Males are solitary, only joining the female herds in the mating season. During this time, they fight one another for females, lunging at one another and locking horns. Markhors are sought by trophy hunters and are also killed for their meat and hides. There are three subspecies, the rarest of which numbers only around 700 individuals. The political instability that has plagued some of the countries in the markhor's range has made it difficult to control illegal poaching.

# TREE SHREWS

*Tree shrews are not closely related to other shrews and are placed in an entirely different group, or order, called the* Scandentia. *Tree shrews are an important group of mammals because it is from their ancestors that the primates evolved. Unlike other shrews, they have large eyes and good vision, and look more like squirrels with long snouts. There are now only 16 species, all living in forested areas of eastern Asia.*

## Lesser tree shrew

*Tupaia minor*

**Distribution**: Malaysia, Sumatra and Borneo.
**Habitat**: Forests.
**Food**: Insects, small vertebrates, fruit, seeds and leaves.
**Size**: 14–23cm (5.5–9in); 100–300g (0.2–0.6lb).
**Maturity**: 3 months.
**Breeding**: 1–3 young.
**Life span**: 12 years.
**Status**: Unknown.

This is the smallest of 11 species of tree shrew from the genus *Tupaia*, named after the Malay word for squirrel, *tupai*. These tree shrews do indeed resemble squirrels, with their long, bushy tails. Unlike most other species of small mammal, they are active throughout the day, though they also have short rests at regular intervals.

Their main predators are eagles, other birds of prey and snakes. Tree shrews are inquisitive, and are constantly searching in holes and crevices for food. Like squirrels, they hold their food in their front paws and eat while sitting on their haunches. Although they are called tree shrews and are capable climbers, they spend a lot of time on the ground or in the branches of bushes.

Tree shrews are highly territorial, with males defending an area of just over 1ha (2.5 acres), which covers the ranges of one or more females. They repel intruders of the same sex by chasing them and making loud squeals of aggression. Tree shrews also make other calls, which include chattering in response to disturbance, and clucking and whistling during courtship and mating.

*Lesser tree shrews' fur colour ranges from a rusty-red colour through dark browns to grey. They have squirrel-like bushy tails and sharp claws for climbing trees.*

## Indian tree shrew

*Anathana ellioti*

Walter Elliot, an English civil servant based in Madras during the mid-19th century, was the first person to describe this species, hence its Latin name. However, very little has been learned about it since then, even though it seems to occur over much of southern India.

Unlike other species of tree shrew, this species is rarely found in close proximity to human dwellings. It has been seen in the dry deciduous forests on India's Deccan Plateau, and presumably has very similar habits to other tree shrews. It has also been found living in rocky upland habitats, without trees, at altitudes of 1,400m (4,600ft).

The Indian tree shrew spends a large part of the day searching for food and then returns to a hole among rocks before nightfall, where it shelters until dawn. These shrews appear to be solitary animals, almost always foraging alone and rarely, if ever, sharing shelters. However, occasionally small groups of three or four individuals have been observed playing together for short periods.

*The Indian tree shrew, also sometimes called the Madras tree shrew, can be distinguished from other species of tree shrew living in India by its larger and more thickly haired ears.*

**Distribution**: India, south of the Ganges River.
**Habitat**: Forests.
**Food**: Insects, earthworms and fruit.
**Size**: 17–20cm (7–8in); 160g (0.3lb).
**Maturity**: 3 months.
**Breeding**: 1–3 young born in related species.
**Life span**: Unknown.
**Status**: Threatened.

# PRIMITIVE PRIMATES

*Although these primates have simpler social structures and smaller brains than the monkeys and apes, in other ways they are well adapted for their particular habitats. There are 57 species of primitive primate, the majority living in Madagascar, with some living in tropical Asia. They are all nocturnal tree-dwellers, and are characterized by their large, round eyes.*

## Tarsier

*Tarsius bancanus*

These little primates are nocturnal hunters, living in forests with thick ground-level vegetation. During the day, they sleep clinging to vertical branches, and slowly wake up as it gets dark. They move about through the branches like tree frogs, making leaps between branches. They have round pads on their fingertips and toes that help them grip on to surfaces.

*As well as their round eyes and long naked tails, tarsiers have very powerful back legs with extremely long anklebones – or tarsals – which give them their name.*

When hunting at night, they scan for prey with their huge eyes, which measure 16mm (0.6in) across. Thanks to special vertebrae, they can turn their heads almost 180 degrees in either direction. When they spot prey, which may be an insect, a small bat or even a poisonous snake, they jump, catch their prey in their hands and kill it with a bite to the back of its neck.

Usually tarsiers live alone, but sometimes adult males and females live together. Tarsiers make a whole range of calls that serve to attract mates and warn off competitors. Females carry their babies in their mouths, or sometimes the babies ride on their mother's back. Baby tarsiers become independent very quickly, and after only 26 days they are able to hunt by themselves.

**Distribution**: Southern Sumatra, Borneo and possibly Java.
**Habitat**: Forests, mangroves and scrub.
**Food**: Insects and small vertebrates.
**Size**: 9–16cm (3.6–6.4in); 80–165g (0.17–0.36lb).
**Maturity**: Unknown.
**Breeding**: 1 young per year.
**Life span**: 13 years.
**Status**: Common but decreasing, partly due to habitat loss.

## Slender loris

*Loris tardigradus*

The slender loris and its cousins the slow lorises are closely related to the bushbabies of Africa. Unlike the bushbabies, which have long fluffy tails, lorises lack tails. Like the tarsiers and other primitive primates, the slender loris is a tree-dwelling animal, mostly active at night. But unlike the tarsiers, the slender loris moves through the branches very slowly and deliberately, always supported by at least three of its limbs. The slender loris has opposable thumbs and big toes which it uses to grasp branches while climbing. When it spots prey, it cautiously stalks and, once it gets within range, grabs it with both hands.

Lorises usually live alone and, if forced to share space with others in captivity, they will fight one another. These animals make a variety of calls, including squeals and growls that indicate distress and disturbance, and whistles that are often heard when familiar males and females meet. The slender loris is threatened in India because its forest habitat is becoming increasingly fragmented, and because it is hunted for use in traditional medicines.

*The slender loris differs from the slow loris in having a much more slender body and limbs. All lorises have thick woolly fur.*

**Distribution**: Southern India and Sri Lanka.
**Habitat**: Mountain and lowland forests.
**Food**: Insects, young leaves, shoots, fruit, birds' eggs and small vertebrates.
**Size**: 18–26cm (7–10.5in); 85–348g (0.19–0.75lb).
**Maturity**: Females 10 months; males 18 months.
**Breeding**: 1–2 young born every 10 months.
**Life span**: 15 years or more in captivity.
**Status**: Vulnerable.

# APES

*There is only one species of great ape living outside of Africa – the orang-utan of Sumatra and Borneo. In contrast, all 11 species of lesser ape, or gibbon, live in tropical China, South-east Asia and the East Indies. Like the great apes, the gibbons are tailless and move in the treetops by swinging from branch to branch (brachiating), though with considerably more agility than their heavier, more terrestrial relatives.*

## Orang-utan

*Pongo pygmaeus*

The orang-utan is unique among large primates because it is relatively solitary and lives in trees, whereas other large primates, such as humans, chimps, gorillas and baboons, live in social groups and spend most of their time on the ground. The name orang-utan means "forest people" in the Malay language.

Female orang-utans sometimes accompany each other while travelling and will eat together. Males, on the other hand, usually avoid one another. Orang-utans travel less than 1km (0.6 miles) per day through their home ranges, moving from branch to branch at a leisurely pace. These apes sleep in nests high in trees, made from leafy branches. Like the other great apes, orang-utans are intelligent animals, and have often been observed using tools. For example, they use large leaves as umbrellas to keep the rain off, and smaller leaves as pads to protect their hands and feet when moving through thorny vegetation.

*Old adult male orang-utans can sometimes get very fat, and these have very round faces because of deposits of fat under their skin.*

**Distribution**: Sumatra and Borneo.
**Habitat**: Primary rainforests.
**Food**: Mostly fruit, but also other vegetable matter, insects, small vertebrates and birds' eggs.
**Size**: 1.25–1.5m (4–5ft); 30–90kg (66–200lb).
**Maturity**: 12–15 years.
**Breeding**: Single young born every 3–4 years.
**Life span**: 60 years.
**Status**: Vulnerable, due to habitat loss.

## Siamang

*Hylobates syndactylus*

**Distribution**: Peninsular Malaysia and Sumatra.
**Habitat**: Rainforests up to 1,800m (6,000ft) altitude.
**Food**: Leaves, fruit, flowers, buds and insects.
**Size**: 75–90cm (30–36in); 8–13kg (17–29lb).
**Maturity**: 8–9 years.
**Breeding**: Single young born every 2–3 years.
**Life span**: 40 years.
**Status**: Threatened.

Siamangs are the largest of the lesser apes or gibbons. All species of gibbon live in trees, and are among the most agile animals in the world. The distance across the outstretched arms of a siamang can be up to 1.5m (5ft) – far greater than its standing height.

Gibbons use their long arms to swing, or brachiate, through the trees, and can move 3m (10ft) in a single swing. They do not tolerate other gibbons in their territories, and use loud calls which can be heard from several kilometres away to warn away intruders. Both male and female siamangs possess naked throat sacks that inflate with breath and resonate their calls. Sometimes male and female siamangs sing together in duets, the male making booms and loud screams and the female barking and booming at the same time.

Females usually give birth to a single offspring, which they nurse for several months. Males take an active part in caring for the young, carrying the infants around with them.

*To help grasp wide branches, gibbons have long thumbs, which attach at the wrist rather than the palm – like those of great apes and humans.*

# Lar gibbon

*Hylobates lar*

Lar gibbons live in small social groups consisting of an adult male and female, and up to four immature offspring. Like the siamangs, adult lar gibbons defend their territories from intruders by calling, often in duets with males and females alternating their calls. However, lar gibbons spend much more time calling than siamangs, making calls nearly every day.

Female lar gibbons are much less social than female siamangs and, although the males spend a lot of time showing apparent signs of affection such as embraces and grooming behaviour, the females rarely reciprocate. Males are probably more likely to lose their partners to competitors than siamangs, hence the greater amount of calling.

Lar gibbons sleep in the highest trees in the forest, usually those giants that emerge from the forest canopy. They almost never sleep in the same place from night to night, and this is thought to be a strategy to prevent predators, such as pythons and birds of prey, from learning their position.

*All lar gibbons have white hands and feet, giving them their alternative name, the white-handed gibbon.*

**Distribution**: Southern China, eastern and southern Burma, Thailand, Malaysian peninsula and northern Sumatra.
**Habitat**: Lowland tropical forest.
**Food**: Fruit, leaves and insects.
**Size**: 45–65cm (18–26in); 5–8kg (11–18lb).
**Maturity**: 8–9 years.
**Breeding**: 1 young born every 2–2.5 years.
**Life span**: 25 years.
**Status**: Endangered.

---

**Kloss's gibbon** (*Hylobates klossi*): 45–65cm (18–26in); 6kg (13lb)
This species is found only on a few islands in the Mentawai group, near western Sumatra. Due to its restricted range and low numbers, it is classified as vulnerable by the IUCN. Like other gibbons, this species defends territories in the forest, the males advertising their presence and strength to rivals by singing just before dawn.

**Javan gibbon** (*Hylobates moloch*): 45–65cm (18–26in); 4–9kg (9–20lb)
Javan gibbons are found only on Java, where they have lost over 95 per cent of their original forest habitat in recent decades. As a result, it is estimated that only 250 adults remain, making this the world's rarest gibbon.

**White-browed gibbon** (*Hylobates hoolock*): 45–65cm (18–26in); 4–9kg (9–20lb)
This gibbon has the most westerly distribution of all the gibbons, living as far west as Bangladesh. The white-browed gibbon is the only species of gibbon that can swim, while all other species avoid water. Although gibbons can walk upright, they almost never cross open ground on foot. This means that features such as rivers and open spaces will act as barriers to the spread of gibbon populations.

# Crested gibbon

*Hylobates concolor*

This species used to be much more widespread than it is today; at one time it lived in much of southern China, and was found as far north as the Yellow River in eastern China. It has suffered considerably from the loss of its forest habitat to logging and agriculture. It has also been hunted for its meat, which is considered a delicacy by some Chinese people, and for its bones, which are prepared as a local medicine to treat rheumatism.

Wars in South-east Asia have helped throw this species into decline, so that it now numbers less than 2,500.

Like other gibbons, the crested variety moves around the treetops searching for fruit and tender leaves during the day. However, unlike any other species, crested gibbons sometimes live in polygamous groups, with one adult male sharing a territory with up to four adult females.

**Distribution**: South-eastern China, Hainan, north-western Laos and Vietnam.
**Habitat**: Tropical forest.
**Food**: Fruit, leaves and insects.
**Size**: 45–65cm (18–26in); 5–9kg (11–20lb).
**Maturity**: 8–9 years.
**Breeding**: Single young born every 2–3 years.
**Life span**: 25 years.
**Status**: Endangered.

*Male crested gibbons are black, while females are golden or grey-brown in colour. Females are born almost white, and only attain their adult colour at between 2 and 4 years of age.*

# MONKEYS

*Around half of the 96 species of Old World monkey live in south-central Asia, South-east Asia, Japan and Indonesia, where they are commonly known as langurs and macaques. Most Old World monkeys live in hot, tropical climates, but a few species, such as the Japanese macaque, can be found in very cold habitats at northerly latitudes.*

## Proboscis monkey

*Nasalis larvatus*

Scientists are not sure why proboscis monkeys, particularly older males, have evolved such strange noses, but they may be involved in attracting females or even used to radiate excess heat. Proboscis monkeys are very social and sometimes feed together in bands of up to 60 or more animals. Usually they live in smaller groups of 2–27 animals, consisting of a single dominant male, a harem of 1–9 females and their young.

Young females stay with the group, while young males move away to join bands of bachelor males. Proboscis monkeys rarely move more than 1–2km (0.6–1.2 miles) away from fresh water. They sleep close to rivers or in mangrove trees in coastal areas. These monkeys are among the best swimmers of all primates. They even have partially webbed feet, which help them to paddle or walk across soft mud.

*Proboscis monkeys have peculiar protruding noses that become particularly long and bulbous in old males. The infants have blue faces.*

**Distribution**: Borneo.
**Habitat**: Lowland rainforest and mangroves.
**Food**: Leaves, fruit, flowers and seeds.
**Size**: Females 53–61cm (21–24in), 7–11kg (15–24lb); males 66–76cm (26–30in), 16–22kg (35–48lb).
**Maturity**: Not known.
**Breeding**: Usually single young born at a time after a gestation of about 166 days.
**Life span**: 23 years.
**Status**: Vulnerable.

## Crab-eating macaque

*Macaca fascicularis*

The crab-eating macaque is one of the most widespread of the 20 species of macaque, most of which live in parts of the Indian subcontinent, southern China, South-east Asia and Indonesia. Crab-eating macaques live in groups of around 30 individuals, which consist of adult males and females and their young. Crab-eating macaques live in ordered societies based on dominance hierarchies. Dominant individuals often force lower-ranking animals away from the best feeding and resting sites and give them few opportunities to mate. Indeed, low-ranking females take longer to reach sexual maturity than high-ranking females because they eat less food.

Although crab-eating macaques prefer mangroves and forests around rivers, they have adapted to a range of habitats and sometimes live among people in towns. These monkeys sometimes raid crops and orchards, and they can be aggressive to humans.

*Crab-eating macaques have tails that are longer than their bodies, giving them their alternative name, the long-tailed macaque.*

**Distribution**: Malaysia, Indonesia and the Philippines.
**Habitat**: Forests, coastal mangroves and urban areas.
**Food**: Leaves, fruit, flowers, crustaceans, molluscs, insects, birds' eggs and small vertebrates.
**Size**: 40–47cm (16–19in); 3–7kg (6.6–15lb).
**Maturity**: Females 4 years; males 6 years.
**Breeding**: 1 young born every 2 years.
**Life span**: 35 years.
**Status**: Near threatened.

## Hanuman langur

*Semnopithecus entellus*

These monkeys live in a wide variety of habitats, from hot tropical forests to cold mountain habitats, up to 4,000m (13,000ft) above sea level. Although they are principally tree-living animals, langurs are happy to live on the ground in habitats with few trees.

In areas with lots of food, hanuman langurs live in groups that may include a number of adult males as well as females and young, but in areas with less food, such as certain mountain habitats, there is only one adult male per group.

Like the crab-eating macaque, both sexes show a dominance hierarchy, though it is less pronounced in female hanumans than in female macaques. Males sometimes form groups of up to 30 individuals. Occasionally all-male groups attack male–female groups, and if they succeed in overthrowing the alpha male or males, the newcomers kill all the infants in the group. This makes the females come into oestrus quicker, so the new leaders can start to father their own offspring.

**Distribution**: Tibet, Nepal, Sikkim, northern Pakistan, Kashmir, India, Bangladesh and Sri Lanka.
**Habitat**: Tropical and temperate forests, savannah, farmland, alpine scrub and desert edges.
**Food**: Leaves, fruit and flowers.
**Size**: 41–78cm (16–31in); 5.5–23.5kg (12–52lb).
**Maturity**: Females 3–4 years; males 6–7 years.
**Breeding**: 1 or 2 young born every 2 years.
**Life span**: 25 years.
**Status**: Near threatened.

*Hanuman langurs have dark faces and prominent brow ridges. They usually have grey, brown or buff-coloured upper-parts, and orange-white or yellow-white heads and chests. Their tails are longer than their bodies.*

**Pig-tailed langur** (*Simias concolor*):
45–52cm (18–20in); 6.5–8kg (14–18lb)
This rare monkey is only found on a few islands in the Mentawai group off the south-west coast of Sumatra, and gets its name from its short naked tail with a tuft of fur on the tip. It lives in thick forest in hilly country. It is not as social as many other langur species and usually lives in pairs with 1–3 young.

**Douc langur** (*Pygathrix nemaeus*): 56–76cm (22–30in); 10kg (22lb)
This brightly coloured monkey is found in Cambodia, Vietnam and Laos. Like most monkeys it is very social, living in groups of 4–15 individuals consisting of mostly females, but including one or more adult males. This is one of the most brightly coloured species of monkey, with some varieties sporting bright yellow faces surrounded by pure white whiskers, and rich red-chestnut coloured legs.

**Banded leaf monkey** (*Presbytis femoralis*):
42–61cm (16–24in); 5–8kg (11–18lb)
This is the most widespread of eight species of leaf monkey from the same genus. It is found throughout the Malay peninsula, parts of Sumatra and Borneo and surrounding islands. Despite its broad range, this monkey is becoming rare. These leaf monkeys are characterized by crests of hair on the top of their heads. Sometimes they are forced out of their feeding areas by the smaller but more aggressive crab-eating macaque.

## Snub-nosed monkey

*Rhinopithecus roxellana*

This is one of the few species of primate living exclusively outside the tropics, inhabiting the cold mountain forests on south-eastern slopes of the Tibetan plateau in China.

These monkeys are mostly tree-living, but will come to the ground occasionally to search for wild onions and to eat grass. In summer, when food is relatively abundant, up to 600 snub-nosed monkeys may live together, but as winter falls and food becomes more scarce, these large gatherings split up into smaller groups of 60–70 animals.

Snub-nosed monkeys have many vocalizations, the most common being a loud "ga-ga" call made when food is found.

There are probably fewer than 15,000 left in the wild because they have been hunted for their beautiful fur and for other parts that are used in medicines.

**Distribution**: Mountainous areas of the Tibetan plateau in south-western China.
**Habitat**: Mountain broadleaf and conifer forests.
**Food**: Leaves, buds, bark, grass and lichens.
**Size**: 57–76cm (22–30in); 12–21kg (26–46lb).
**Maturity**: Females 4–5 years; males 7 years.
**Breeding**: 1 or occasionally 2 young.
**Life span**: Unknown.
**Status**: Vulnerable.

*Although these monkeys have dull, grey-black fur on the top of their head, shoulders, back and tail, other parts of the body are covered in a rich, golden fur, giving them their other name, the golden monkey.*

# MONOTREMES

*Some scientists do not consider the monotremes to be true mammals, but intermediate forms between mammals and reptiles. Indeed, their anatomy, digestion, reproductive organs and excretory systems have many similarities to those of reptiles, for example they lay eggs. However, monotremes also show mammalian characteristics: they have fur, they nourish their young with milk and they are warm-blooded.*

## Short-nosed echidna

*Tachyglossus aculeatus*

The short-nosed echidna is one of two species of echidna. It is found throughout Australia and parts of New Guinea. The other rarer species, the long-nosed echidna, lives only in the highlands of New Guinea. The short-nosed species regularly feasts on ants or termites, thus earning its common nickname, the spiny anteater.

Short-nosed echidnas live alone, foraging during both the day and the night. They locate their food by smell, and it is also thought that they may be able to pick up electric signals from prey animals using sensors in the tip of their snout. They are powerful diggers, using their clawed front paws to dig out prey or create burrows for shelter.

The short-nosed echidna lays a single egg with a leathery shell into a pouch on its abdomen, and the young hatches soon afterwards. The baby is incubated in the pouch for 10–11 days, and finally leaves the pouch after around 55 days. The mother will continue to suckle her young even after it has left the pouch.

**Distribution**: Widespread throughout Australia, including Tasmania.
**Habitat**: Most habitats, from semi-desert to highlands.
**Food**: Ants, termites and earthworms.
**Size**: 30–45cm (12–18in); 2.5–7kg (5.5–15.5lb).
**Maturity**: Not known.
**Breeding**: Single young at a time, incubated in a pouch on the mother's abdomen.
**Life span**: 50 years.
**Status**: Low risk.

*The short-nosed echidna has a long, hairless snout. The protective spines are enlarged hairs. They cover its back and sides, and are much thicker than those of the long-nosed echidna.*

## Platypus

*Ornithorhynchus anatinus*

Platypuses live in burrows in stream banks, which they excavate with their powerful front legs. There are two kinds of burrow: one for shelter and one for incubation. The incubation burrows can be up to 18m (60ft) long and rise 1–7m (3–23ft) above the waterline. As part of the courtship ritual, females carry bundles of wet leaves to their incubation chamber, at the ends of the burrow. Females then plug the tunnel with soil and lay 1–3 eggs in the incubation chamber. The eggs hatch after ten days and the young stay in the burrow, where the mothers keep them warm and suckle them. They finally emerge after four months.

Males possess spurs on their hind feet that are attached to venom glands, which produce poison strong enough to kill dogs. These are thought to be used in fighting.

*This is surely one of the strangest living mammals, with a snout resembling a duck's bill, a tail like a beaver's, and clawed, webbed feet. The bill is thought to contain an organ for detecting the electric pulses produced by prey.*

**Distribution**: Eastern and south-eastern Australia and Tasmania.
**Habitat**: Freshwater streams and lakes.
**Food**: Freshwater crustaceans, insect larvae, snails, tadpoles and small fish.
**Size**: 30–45cm (12–18in); 0.5–2kg (1.1–4.4lb).
**Maturity**: 2–3 years.
**Breeding**: 1–3 eggs laid at a time.
**Life span**: 13 years in the wild; up to 21 years in captivity.
**Status**: Fairly common, though may be declining.

# MARSUPIALS

*The marsupials are a group of mammals with a peculiar reproductive method. The young are very small and underdeveloped when born, and after making their way to their mother's nipples, they grow and develop in safety inside a pouch. Nearly 75 per cent of all marsupial species are found in and around Australia and New Guinea, with the rest being found in the Americas.*

## Squirrel glider

*Petaurus norfolcensis*

This is one of five closely related species of gliding possums, including the sugar glider, that live in Australia and New Guinea. These animals resemble flying squirrels, they are mostly nocturnal and have large eyes to help them see in low light. They are arboreal, and during the day they sleep in nests made from leaves in the hollows of trees.

Squirrel gliders have membranes of skin that stretch from their wrists to their ankles, which form gliding surfaces (aerofoils) when their legs and arms are spread out. The closely related but smaller sugar gliders can glide for distances of up to 45m (150ft), and the larger fluffy glider of the same genus can glide up to 114m (375ft).

Squirrel gliders live in social groups, usually consisting of one adult male, several adult females and their young. These animals communicate with a variety of calls, including chatters, nasal grunts and repetitive short grunts, which seem to serve as alarm calls and warnings to squirrel gliders from other groups. During the breeding season, females develop pouches in which the young stay for around six months. After this time, the pouches wither away.

*Squirrel gliders have beautiful long tails, grey fur on top and pale fur underneath. They have attractive dark stripes from their noses all the way to their rumps, and stripes across their eyes.*

**Distribution**: Eastern and south-eastern Australia.
**Habitat**: Open forests.
**Food**: Nectar, pollen, sap, insects and other invertebrates and small vertebrates.
**Size**: 12–30cm (5–12in); 200–260g (0.4–0.6lb).
**Maturity**: Females end of first year; males beginning of second year.
**Breeding**: 1 young, or occasionally twins, annually.
**Life span**: 12 years.
**Status**: Threatened.

## Long-clawed marsupial mouse

*Neophascogale lorentzii*

This is one of over 50 species of marsupial mice, all of which live in Australia and New Guinea. All are carnivorous, taking any prey small enough to be overpowered. Very little is known about this species, probably because it lives in the remote and inaccessible wet forest habitat of the interior of New Guinea, at elevations of up to 3,000m (10,000ft). However, the long-clawed marsupial mouse is quite similar in appearance and habits to the better-known species living in Australia, such as the brush-tailed marsupial mouse.

Like the Australian species, the long-clawed marsupial mouse is nocturnal and arboreal, though it is also sometimes active during the day. It is highly territorial, with females occupying huge territories – about double the size of male territories. Females are very aggressive with one another and can usually dominate males. Daughters sometimes inherit parts of their mothers' territories when they become independent, but sons are always driven away to seek their own territories.

*The long-clawed marsupial mouse resembles a tree shrew, with its long, thin muzzle and large, bushy tail. As its name suggests, it has particularly long claws on all four feet.*

**Distribution**: Western and central mountains of New Guinea.
**Habitat**: Upland wet moss forests.
**Food**: Insects and perhaps other small animals.
**Size**: 17–23cm (7–9in); 110–230g (0.25–0.5lb).
**Maturity**: 8 months.
**Breeding**: 8 young.
**Life span**: 1–2 years.
**Status**: Unknown.

# Koala

*Phascolarctos cinereus*

**Distribution**: South-eastern Australia.
**Habitat**: A range of habitats, from coastal islands and tall eucalyptus forests to low woodlands inland.
**Food**: Eucalyptus leaves.
**Size**: 60–85cm (24–34in); 4–15kg (8.8–33lb).
**Maturity**: Sexual maturity at 2 years in females and males, but first breeding probably not until 5 years old in males.
**Breeding**: 1 young, or occasionally twins, born annually.
**Life span**: 20 years.
**Status**: Near threatened.

Koalas are placed in their own family, which shows how different they are from other marsupials. These animals live practically their whole lives in stands of eucalyptus trees that form the core of their territories. Eucalyptus leaves are by far the most important food for koalas. The animals even smell of eucalyptus oil. A problem with eucalyptus leaves is that they are very fibrous and difficult to digest, so koalas have cheek pouches and long intestines, and occasionally eat soil or gravel. All these traits are adaptations to help them break down the tough eucalyptus leaves.

Koalas are very solitary animals and, although the territories of males and females overlap, males will not tolerate intruders of the same sex. Resident koalas usually attack intruders savagely. Males mark out their territories with strong-smelling scent, and make loud calls to warn off other males.

During the breeding season, males try to guard as many female territories as they can. The single young or joey stays in its mother's pouch for seven months, then rides on its mother's back until the next season's joey matures. Koalas used to be very common in south-eastern Australia, but a mixture of hunting for fur in the early 20th century, habitat loss and severe forest fires have reduced their numbers.

*Koalas have dense grey fur, which is paler on their undersides. They have two opposable thumbs and three fingers on each of their hands, which helps them to grip strongly on to branches.*

# Common wombat

*Vombatus ursinus*

This is the most common of three species of wombat, all of which live in Australia. Wombats resemble small bears and have large heads, short, stocky bodies and short, powerful legs. The common wombat can be distinguished from the other two species by its hairless nose and rounded ears. Unlike bears, wombats are not predators, and tend to be shy and timid animals. In fact, they make good pets, being playful and affectionate.

In the wild, wombats dig out large burrows that may be up to 30m (100ft) long. Although there is only one entrance, a burrow may branch off into different chambers. The wombat makes a nest out of leaves or bark in one of the chambers.

Wombats are usually nocturnal, but sometimes they sunbathe in specially prepared spots, close to the entrances of their burrows. Common wombats live in large home ranges and, although they tend to be solitary, neighbouring territories overlap considerably. Although wombats are sometimes aggressive towards each other in captivity, some observations in the wild suggest that wombats sometimes make visits to one another's burrows.

*Wombats resemble small, chubby bears, having compact bodies covered with a dense coat of grey-brown hair. Evidence from fossils suggests that there were once hippo-sized wombats.*

**Distribution**: Originally found throughout south-eastern Australia and Tasmania.
**Habitat**: Hilly or mountainous coastal country, creeks and gullies.
**Food**: Grass, roots of shrubs and trees, and fungi.
**Size**: 0.7–1.2m (28–48in); 15–35kg (11–77lb).
**Maturity**: 2 years.
**Breeding**: 1 or occasionally 2 young born in late autumn after 20 days' gestation.
**Life span**: 25 years.
**Status**: Common.

# Brush-tailed possum

*Trichosurus vulpecula*

Large numbers of Australasian marsupials are commonly referred to as possums, which belong to several families. These are not to be confused with opossums, which are marsupials from an entirely separate group, living in the Americas.

This possum is the most common of three possum species, all known as brush-tailed possums due to their long, furry prehensile tails. It is closely related to the cuscuses of Sulawesi, New Guinea and surrounding islands.

The brushed-tailed possum is nocturnal and arboreal. It is a very adaptable animal, and can live in semi-desert areas in the Australian interior by sheltering in eucalyptus trees and along rivers. It even lives in large numbers in most Australian cities, hiding under the roofs of houses.

Possums generally live alone and defend well-defined territories marked with scent. Encounters often result in fights. When these animals are disturbed, they rear up to their full height on their back legs, spread their forelimbs and make piercing screams. They are fierce fighters.

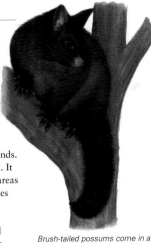

*Brush-tailed possums come in a variety of colours, including grey, brown, black, white and cream. Males tend to have red-brown coloration on their shoulders.*

**Distribution**: Most of Australia, including Tasmania. Introduced into New Zealand.
**Habitat**: Forests, rocky areas, semi-deserts with scattered eucalyptus trees and suburban habitats.
**Food**: Shoots, leaves, flowers, fruit, seeds, insects and occasionally young birds.
**Size**: 32–58cm (12–23in); 1.3–5kg (2.8–11lb).
**Maturity**: Females 9–12 months; males 24 months.
**Life span**: 13 years.
**Status**: Common.

---

**Numbat** (*Myrmecobius fasciatus*): 17–27cm (7–11in); 300–600g (0.6–1.3lb)
This marsupial from southern parts of Australia is also known as the banded anteater and, as the name suggests, it specializes in eating ants and termites. Like other anteaters, it has a long snout, a sticky tongue, which can extend at least 10cm (4in), and powerful claws for ripping open rotting logs to expose termite nests.

**Marsupial mole** (*Notoryctes typhlops*): 9–18cm (3.5–7in); 40–70g (0.08–0.15lb)
This unusual species is not related to other moles, and is only distantly related to other marsupials. It is white or cream in colour, but otherwise resembles a placental mole. It spends a lot of time underground and has long, spade-like claws on its forelimbs for digging, and tiny eyes hidden under its skin. This is a good example of "convergent evolution" between marsupial mammals and placental mammals – having evolved similar adaptations for the same lifestyle.

**Native cat** or **quoll** (*Dasyurus geoffroi*): 29–65cm (11–26in); 500g (1.1lb)
This is one of six species, all from the same genus, that are called native cats or quolls. They are not related to the true cats, but get their name from their somewhat cat-like appearance and their predatory behaviour. All species of native cat have coats with white spots. They are unpopular with farmers because they occasionally raid chicken coops. As a result of habitat loss, persecution and possibly competition and predation by introduced red foxes, all species of native cat are declining.

# Tasmanian devil

*Sarcophilus harrisii*

The Tasmanian devil comes from a family of carnivorous marsupials that includes marsupial mice and native cats, or quolls, which used to live all over Australia. They are now restricted to the island of Tasmania, which was never colonized by dingoes.

The Tasmanian devil is nocturnal and spends a lot of its time snuffling over the ground trying to pick up the scent of food. It is a very efficient scavenger, and uses its powerful jaws to crush bones and chew up tough skin.

During the day, Tasmanian devils take refuge in nests of bark, grass or leaves inside hollow logs, old wombat burrows or other sheltered spots. The ferocity of Tasmanian devils has been greatly exaggerated, and although they will sometimes fight savagely amongst themselves when feeding, they are apparently docile and safe to handle.

**Distribution**: Originally found over much of Australia, but now only occurs in Tasmania.
**Habitat**: Coastal heath and forest.
**Food**: Carrion, small invertebrates and vertebrates.
**Size**: 52–80cm (20–32in); females 4.1–8.1kg (9–17lb); males 5.5–12.8kg (12–28lb).
**Maturity**: 2 years.
**Breeding**: Litter of 1–4 young.
**Life span**: 8 years.
**Status**: Common.

*These stocky little carnivores look like tiny bears, but have long tails. They usually have black or dark brown fur, with white markings on their throat, rump and sides.*

# Musky rat kangaroo

*Hypsiprymnodon moschatus*

*Musky rat kangaroos have dense rich brown or rusty grey fur that is lighter on their undersides. Compared to other rat kangaroos, their back legs are less well developed. These animals carry seeds away from the area where the fruit falls and bury them for eating later when food is scarce. Some seeds germinate, and produce trees for future seed supplies.*

This is the smallest of ten species of rat kangaroo, all of which live in Australia. Most rat kangaroos have short fur on their long tails, but some have tails that are hairless and scaly. Like kangaroos, these animals have large feet and well-developed hind legs. However, unlike other species in the family, this rat kangaroo usually moves about on all fours rather than hopping kangaroo-fashion.

Both the males and females emit musky scents, probably to attract mates. Although they usually live alone, they do not seem to defend territories. Unlike all other rat kangaroos, they are most active during the day, when they forage on the forest floor, looking for insects and worms by turning over forest debris and rummaging in the leaf litter with their forepaws. Sometimes they take a break from foraging and stretch out to sunbathe in bright spots in the forest. At night, musky rat kangaroos sleep in nests between the buttress roots of trees or in tangles of vines. The range of these animals is contracting because of forest clearance for agriculture.

**Distribution**: North-eastern Queensland, Australia.
**Habitat**: Dense vegetation in tropical rainforest.
**Food**: Insects, worms, roots, seeds, palm fruit, fungi, flowers, twigs, leaves, lichen and bark.
**Size**: 21–34cm (8–14in); 337–680g (0.75–1.5lb).
**Maturity**: Between 18 and 21 months.
**Breeding**: Usually 2 young born at a time.
**Life span**: Unknown.

# Red kangaroo

*Macropus rufus*

**Distribution**: Most of Australia.
**Habitat**: Grassland and savannah with some cover.
**Food**: Grass.
**Size**: 0.8–1.6m (32–64in); 20–90kg (44–180lb).
**Maturity**: 2 years.
**Breeding**: 1 or 2 born when conditions are favourable.
**Life span**: 27 years.
**Status**: Common.

*Like other members of the family, red kangaroos have large bodies with a relatively small head, large ears, well-developed hind legs, huge feet and a long muscular tail. Males are usually a rich red-brown colour, while females are blue-grey.*

The red kangaroo is the largest of the 61 species comprising the kangaroo and wallaby family, and stands up to 1.8m (6ft) tall on its hind legs. This marsupial mammal has a unique way of travelling. When grazing, it moves around slowly by supporting its body on its forelegs and tail and swinging its back legs forwards. When moving fast however, it hops on its powerful back legs and can make single leaps of more than 9m (30ft).

This is a very efficient way of moving across rough terrain, and kangaroos bounce along at speeds of up to 48kph (30mph) on their springy back legs, using much less effort than a running placental mammal of similar size.

Kangaroos live in dry conditions and can live for long periods without water. They are able to survive on low-quality vegetation found in dry habitats, thanks to a digestion process that uses gut bacteria to help break down tough plant material. However, unlike other large species of kangaroos, reds usually move in search of better feeding conditions during droughts, sometimes travelling more than 200km (125 miles). Red kangaroos are not territorial, but males will fight one another by boxing with their arms and kicking with their back legs, to win control of groups of females during the breeding season.

# Doria's tree kangaroo

*Dendrolagus dorianus*

**Distribution**: Western, central and south-eastern New Guinea.
**Habitat**: Mountainous rainforests.
**Food**: Mostly leaves and fruit.
**Size**: 52–81cm (20–32in); up to 20kg (40lb).
**Maturity**: Not known.
**Breeding**: 1 young born at a time.
**Life span**: 20 years.
**Status**: Vulnerable.

There are ten species of closely related tree kangaroo, all of which live in New Guinea and on a few surrounding islands, or in tropical northern Queensland in Australia. This species is the largest of the tree kangaroos and, like others in the group, it has a thick tail that can be longer than the body. Unlike most ground-living kangaroos, which have well developed back legs, the front and back limbs of tree kangaroos are almost the same size.

As their name asserts, tree kangaroos live in trees, but they frequently come to the ground to search for food and to move to new trees. Indeed, this species actually spends most of its time on the ground, while smaller species may spend as much as 98 per cent of their time in the branches of trees.

Tree kangaroos are very agile, and can jump between trees, dropping as much as 9m (30ft) from one branch to another. They are able to jump to the ground from as high up as 18m (60ft). Most species of tree kangaroo live alone, but related females of this species sometimes gang together to drive away unfamiliar males. Most species of tree kangaroo are declining because of increased hunting and habitat loss.

*This species of tree kangaroo has fur in various shades of brown, but other species are among the most colourful of all marsupials, with bright yellow markings and different shades of red.*

**Large Celebes cuscus** (*Ailurops ursinus*): 0.5–0.6m (20–24in); 7–10kg (15–22lb)
This animal only lives on the Indonesian island of Sulawesi (Celebes) and belongs to the same family as the Australian possums. It has a stocky body with thick, dark-coloured fur above and pale fur below. Unlike the other two species of cuscus living on Sulawesi, this species lives in trees and has a long prehensile tail to help it climb.

**Rock wallaby** (*Petrogale lateralis*): 50–80cm (20–32in); 3–9kg (6.6–18lb)
There are 14 species of rock wallaby, all from Australia and all characterized by long, powerful hind legs, long tails and large ears. These animals live in dry rocky habitats, close to cover. They are incredibly agile on cliffs and rocky outcrops. They can make leaps of 4m (13ft) and easily bound up the steepest slopes.

**Mountain pygmy possum** (*Burramys parvus*): 10–13cm (4–5.2in); 30–60g (0.06–0.13lb)
This species was only known from fossils until 1966, when a live specimen was caught in a ski hut on Mount Hotham in south-western Australia. It is now known that around 1,000 individuals survive high up in the mountains, and pass the cold winters in hibernation. In spring and summer, the animals forage for seeds, fruit, insects and worms at night, sometimes climbing into bushes with the help of their prehensile tails.

# Bilby

*Macrotis lagotis*

Bilbies, or rabbit-eared bandicoots, belong to a distinct group of marsupials with 22 species, all of which live in Australia, Tasmania, New Guinea and on some of the surrounding islands. They are characterized by their long, pointed muzzles, and have hind legs that are larger and more well developed than their front legs, though not to the same degree as the kangaroos.

There used to be two species of bilby, but the smaller of the two has not been seen since 1931 and is probably extinct. Unlike other species of bandicoot, bilbies are powerful diggers and excavate spiral-shaped burrows.

Bilbies are nocturnal, sleeping in their burrows during the day. They live alone or in small colonies, usually with one adult male, several females and a number of young. Bilbies have the shortest gestation of any mammal – 14 days. Once born, the babies spend around 80 days in their mother's pouch, followed by a further two weeks in the burrow.

**Distribution**: Originally found over most of temperate and arid Australia; now restricted to pockets in Western Australia, Northern Territory and south-western Queensland.
**Habitat**: Dry habitats, including dry woodland, scrub, savannah and semi-desert.
**Food**: Insects, small vertebrates and some vegetable material.
**Size**: 29–55cm (11–22in); 0.6–2.5kg (1.3–5.5lb).
**Maturity**: Females 5 months; males 12 months.
**Breeding**: 1 or 2 young.
**Life span**: 7 years.
**Status**: Endangered.

*Males are usually bigger than females, but both have very long finely furred ears. Bilbies have long grey, black and white tails with a crest of long hair on the end.*

# INSECTIVORES

*Insectivores are perhaps the oldest mammal group, dating back 135 million years. Today, the group includes the smallest mammals in the world. All insectivores have five digits on each limb and they usually have small eyes, long snouts and primitive teeth. As their collective name suggests, insectivores commonly feed on insects and other small invertebrates.*

## Moonrat

*Echinosorex gymnura*

Moonrats are related to hedgehogs and are one of the largest insectivores. Females tend to be larger than males, but both sexes are otherwise similar in appearance, with narrow bodies, long snouts and coarse black fur with white markings on their heads. Their exceptionally narrow bodies allow the creatures to search for prey in tight spaces. Moonrats are nocturnal, and during the day they sleep in protected spots, such as hollow logs, under tree roots or in holes. At night they search through the leaf litter for small prey.

Moonrats usually live close to water and sometimes swim in streams in search of fish, frogs, crustaceans and other aquatic prey.

*Moonrats have long, hairless and scaly tails up to 30cm (12in) long.*

They sometimes carry parts of their prey to their resting sites, to be eaten later. Moonrats are solitary animals and except during mating, they do not tolerate each other's presence. They mark out their territories with strong-smelling scents to warn off intruders. Moonrats often respond to encounters by making hissing noises and low roars.

**Distribution**: South-east Asia.
**Habitat**: Lowland forests, plantations, mangroves and agricultural land.
**Food**: Worms and other leaf litter invertebrates, fish, amphibians and aquatic invertebrates.
**Size**: 26–46cm (13–23in); 0.5–2kg (1.1–4.4lb).
**Maturity**: 1 year.
**Breeding**: 2 litters of twins born every year.
**Life span**: 4 years.
**Status**: Common.

## Indian hedgehog

*Paraechinus micropus*

The Indian or desert hedgehog is similar in appearance to the common European hedgehog, except that it tends to be smaller in size. Indian hedgehogs come in different colours; some have banded spines of dark brown, with black and white or with yellow, and there is also an unusually large proportion of black and white individuals.

As their alternative name suggests, these animals are well adapted to living in dry desert conditions. They escape the heat of the day by lying up in burrows about 1–2m (3–6ft) deep, which they dig themselves. When the temperatures drop at night, they come out and search the desert floor for prey. If they are alarmed or are chasing frogs, these hedgehogs can move surprisingly fast considering their short legs, reaching speeds exceeding 2kph (1.25mph).

They often bring food back to their burrows for later use. When water or food is scarce, Indian hedgehogs may stay sleeping in their burrows for long periods to conserve energy and water. These hedgehogs stay in the same places all year round and live alone.

*Some Indian hedgehogs have a banded appearance with a brown muzzle and a white forehead and sides. Unlike European hedgehogs, which have smooth spines, they have rough spines.*

**Distribution**: Pakistan and India.
**Habitat**: Deserts and other dry habitats.
**Food**: Insects, small vertebrates and birds' eggs.
**Size**: 14–27cm (5.6–13.5in); up to 435g (1lb).
**Maturity**: 1 year.
**Breeding**: 1–6 young born per litter.
**Life span**: 7 years.
**Status**: Lower risk.

# Tibetan water shrew

*Nectogale elegans*

There are several species of shrew that are at home in water. All of these have silky fur that repels water, long tails and fringes of stiff hairs along the edges of their feet, toes, fingers and tails that help them swim. In smaller species, these hairs allow the shrews to run across the surface of the water for short distances, supported by the surface tension.

The Tibetan water shrew is the only species of shrew to have webbed feet. It also has disc-like pads that may help it keep its footing on slippery wet stones. This shrew lives in a burrow dug in a stream bank.

Most aquatic shrews forage by making repeated dives in the same spot, each dive lasting usually less than 20 seconds. After each dive, they shake their fur dry. If no prey is found, they move along the stream 1m (3ft) or so and dive in a new position. The Tibetan water shrew has sharp teeth that seem to be specialized for catching fish, which are its main prey.

*The Tibetan water shrew has a long dark coloured tail with several fringes of short, stiff white hairs that shine with rainbow iridescence when wet.*

**Distribution**: Tibet, south-central China, Nepal and northern Burma.
**Habitat**: Mountain forest streams.
**Food**: Small fish and aquatic invertebrates.
**Size**: 9–13cm (3.5–5in); 25–45g (0.05–0.09lb).
**Maturity**: 6 months.
**Breeding**: Unknown.
**Life span**: Unknown.
**Status**: Common.

**Asian musk shrew** (*Suncus murinus*): 7.5–12cm (3–4.8in); 10–32g (0.02–0.07lb)
This species lives in large numbers in and around human settlements, and is very common in houses throughout its range. It originated in India, but has been spread by people, right the way down the coast of East Africa and all the way east across Asia to Indonesia and a number of oceanic islands, including Mauritius and Guam, where it threatens small native reptiles.

**Mole shrew** (*Anourosorex squamipes*): 8.5–11cm (3.4–4.5in); 14–25g (0.03–0.05lb)
This strange shrew lives in large parts of China and South-east Asia and, although it is in the shrew family, it looks and behaves much more like a mole. It lives in mountain forests up to 3,100m (10,000ft) above sea level, and spends its time underground, burrowing among the roots of plants, searching for insects and earthworms that form its diet.

# Asian mole

*Euroscaptor micrura*

There are six species of mole living in South-east Asia, southern China and Japan. Like the more familiar European moles, they spend much of their time underground and their bodies have a number of special adaptations to suit their subterranean lifestyle.

Members of the mole family, the *Talpidae*, generally dig tunnels in soil where earthworms are in abundance, along with other prey, and where they are safe from marauding predators. They possess large, powerful front paws on short, stocky forelimbs, which enable them to dig rapidly through even hard ground while using their shovel-like snouts to push loose soil aside.

The Asian moles have the largest front paws in relation to body size of all the moles. In the darkness of their tunnels they have no need of sight and so their eyes are tiny, and probably only able to detect light and dark. However, like many other moles they are very sensitive to ground vibrations, and can use them to find moving prey.

Two species of Asian mole have become rare due to habitat destruction, and one of these species, from a small region of Vietnam, is considered to be critically endangered.

*Like other moles, Asian moles have short, velvety hair that will lie in the direction in which it is brushed. This makes it easy for moles to move both forward and backwards through tight tunnels.*

**Distribution**: Nepal, Sikkim, Assam, northern Burma and southern China.
**Habitat**: Forests with deep soils in mountainous regions.
**Food**: Insects, earthworms and other soil invertebrates.
**Size**: 10–16cm (4–6.5in); 29g (0.06lb).
**Maturity**: Not known.
**Breeding**: Litters of 2–5 young.
**Life span**: Not known.
**Status**: Lower risk.

# SEA MAMMALS

*There are two main groups of sea mammals: the cetaceans (whales and dolphins) and the pinnipeds (seals, sea lions and walruses). The cetaceans evolved from a primitive group of hoofed mammals and became the masters of the oceans. The pinnipeds evolved from a carnivore ancestor and, although they can stay submerged for over an hour, they still have to come on to land to give birth.*

## Ganges river dolphin

*Platanista gangetica*

*This species has a long, slender snout and a very low, ridge-like dorsal fin. The side, or pectoral, fins of this species have very square back edges.*

The large majority of dolphins live in saltwater marine habitats. However, there are at least seven species of dolphin that regularly visit or permanently live in the freshwater habitats of large rivers, including the Ganges in India, the Yangtze in China and the Amazon in South America.

Because rivers often carry a lot of cloudy sediment, especially during times of heavy rain, visibility can be very poor. Indeed, these dolphins have very small deep-set eyes that lack lenses and are probably only useful for detecting light and dark. Ganges river dolphins emit clicks frequently and rely strongly on echolocation to find their way around. These dolphins also hunt for prey using echolocation and by probing in the mud on the river bottom using their sensitive snouts.

These dolphins may inhabit fast-flowing rivers, where the flow can be violent, especially during times of flood. This means that they have to be able to be swim 24 hours a day to avoid being washed away and injured.

**Distribution**: Ganges, Brahmaputra, Meghna Rivers and Karnaphuli River of India, Nepal and Bangladesh.
**Habitat**: River habitats, from the foothills of the Himalayas to tidal limits.
**Food**: Fish, shrimp and other bottom-dwelling invertebrates.
**Size**: 2–3m (6.5–10ft); 51–89kg (1122–195lb).
**Maturity**: 10 years.
**Breeding**: Single young born at a time.
**Life span**: 30 years.
**Status**: Endangered.

## Hector's dolphin

*Cephalorhynchus hectori*

Hector's dolphins are among the rarest species of marine dolphin, with probably less than 5,000 individuals remaining. These dolphins only live in shallow areas around the coast of New Zealand.

Hector's dolphins live in groups of 2–8 individuals, though they may occasionally come together in aggregations of as many as 50 individuals. They hunt for fish and squid from the surface to the sea floor, and sometimes they follow the nets of trawlers in search of stray fish.

The critically endangered population around New Zealand's North Island has only 100 adults, but is unlikely to be helped by individuals from populations around the South Island because of very low migration rates. The northern population is almost certainly doomed to extinction.

**Distribution**: New Zealand.
**Habitat**: Muddy waters.
**Food**: Fish, crustaceans, squid and invertebrates.
**Size**: 1.1–1.8m (3.5–6ft); 26–86kg (57–190lb).
**Maturity**: 6–9 years.
**Breeding**: Every 2–3 years.
**Life span**: 20 years.
**Status**: Vulnerable.

*Like other species in the same genus, Hector's dolphins are characterized by distinctive black and white markings. Their heads, pectoral and dorsal fins and tails are black and their flanks are grey, but their undersides are white. There are also two characteristic fingers of white going from their bellies and along their sides towards their tails – a pattern unique to this species.*

# Sperm whale

*Physeter catodon*

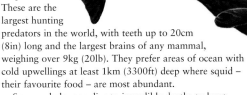

The sperm whale is supremely well adapted to life in the deep oceans. These are the largest hunting predators in the world, with teeth up to 20cm (8in) long and the largest brains of any mammal, weighing over 9kg (20lb). They prefer areas of ocean with cold upwellings at least 1km (3300ft) deep where squid – their favourite food – are most abundant.

Sperm whales can dive to incredible depths to hunt, occasionally up to 2.5km (1.5 miles). They are social animals, and they live in groups of between 20 and 40 females, juveniles and young. Sperm whales have been hunted for their oil since the mid-18th century, and after serious population declines between the 1950s and 80s, this species is now protected.

*The box-like head of the sperm whale contains the spermaceti organ, which is filled with the fine oil so valued by whalers. However, the purpose of this specialized organ is unclear.*

**Distribution**: Ranges throughout oceans and seas worldwide.
**Habitat**: Deep oceans.
**Food**: Mostly squid, including giant deep-sea squid, but also several species of fish and shark.
**Size**: 12–20m (40–65ft); 12,000–50,000kg (12–50 tonnes).
**Maturity**: Females 7–13 years; males 25 years.
**Breeding**: 1 calf born every 5–7 years.
**Life span**: 77 years.
**Status**: Vulnerable.

---

**Leopard seal** (*Hydrurga leptonyx*): 2.4–3.4m (8–11.25ft); 200–591kg (440–1,300lb)
These predatory seals live all around the Antarctic and occasionally they can be found in temperate waters around New Zealand, southern Australia and Argentina. They have large, sleek bodies, almost reptile-like heads and long canine teeth. Leopard seals eat krill, which they filter from the water using their cheek teeth. They are fearsome predators too, and also eat other seals and penguins.

**Australian sea lion** (*Neophoca cinerea*): 2–2.5m (6.5–8.25ft); up to 300kg (660lb)
This species lives around the coast of southern Australia, from Shark Bay in Western Australia to the south-eastern edge of Australia. The Australian sea lion eats fish, squid and crustaceans. It forms breeding colonies of around 100 individuals on small offshore islands, where dominant males defend small territories centred on females. As well as being strong swimmers, these sea lions are surprisingly adept on land, and can even climb steep cliffs.

**Chinese river dolphin** (*Lipotes vexillifer*): 1.4–2.5m (4.75–8.25ft); 42–167kg (92–334lb)
This freshwater dolphin lives in the Yangtze River in China from its estuary to around 1,900km (1,200 miles) upriver. Like the Ganges river dolphin, it has small eyes, a long, thin snout and a reduced dorsal fin. This species has suffered extensively from boat traffic strikes, hunting and the decline of its prey brought about by the construction of dams and pollution. It is probably the most endangered of all the dolphins.

# Baikal seal

*Phoca sibirica*

This is the only one of 33 species of seal and sea lion that lives exclusively in fresh water. It has one of the most restricted distributions of all the pinnipeds, only being found in Lake Baikal in south-central Siberia.

In winter the lake is entirely covered in a thick layer of ice. During this period, the seals spend most of their time under the ice, coming up to breathe through access holes which they keep open by scratching with the claws on their front flippers and by abrading the edges with their teeth and heads.

Baikal seals dive for about 25 minutes when foraging for fish, but can remain submerged for an hour if frightened. During the breeding season in May, successful males gain access to harems of several females. Mating occurs underwater, and the pups are born in late winter or early spring. Females construct a chamber in the snow, where they give birth to and suckle their young.

**Distribution**: Lake Baikal.
**Habitat**: Fresh water.
**Food**: Fish and aquatic invertebrates.
**Size**: 1.1–1.4m (3.5–4.75ft); 50–130kg (110–260lb).
**Maturity**: 6–7 years.
**Breeding**: Usually 1 pup, but occasionally twins.
**Life span**: 55 years.
**Status**: Near threatened.

*The long whiskers are very sensitive to touch and are probably very important for locating prey in the dark conditions under the winter ice.*

# GLOSSARY

**Aestivation** A period of dormancy during hot and dry weather.

**Amphibian** One of a group of backboned animals that spend part of their lives on land, part in water, and are dependent on water to breed. Amphibians include frogs, toads, newts, salamanders and caecilians.

**Anatomy** The study of how bodies are constructed.

**Animal** A complex organism that collects food from its surroundings.

**Arthropod** A member of the large group of invertebrate animals, including insects, spiders, crustaceans and centipedes.

**Bacterium** A microscopic, usually single-celled organism. Many are parasitic and cause disease.

**Baleen** The horny plates found inside the mouths of some whales, which are used to strain the animal's food.

**Biome** A large area with a distinctive climate and community of wildlife.

**Blubber** A layer of fat found under the skin of many aquatic animals that live in cold environments. It provides insulation, helping the animal to retain body heat.

**Caecilian** A worm-like amphibian.

**Camouflage** The colour and patterns on an animal's skin that help it to blend in with its surroundings and so hide from predators or prey.

**Canine** A member of the dog family; or a long, pointed tooth.

**Carnivore** An animal that eats mainly meat, or a member of the group of mammals of the order *Carnivora*, most of which are carnivorous.

**Cartilage** A tough, gristly substance found in the skeletons of vertebrates. In fish such as sharks, almost the whole skeleton is composed of cartilage, not bone.

**Cell** One of the tiny units from which living things are made. Some living things consist of just one cell; others consist of millions of cells.

**Circadian** A lifestyle with a daily rhythm.

**Colony** A group of animals that live together and cooperate to find food and rear their young.

**Continent** A large landmass.

**Crepuscular** Active at dawn or dusk, or both.

**Diurnal** Active during the daytime.

**DNA** A molecule found inside the cells of living organisms, which contains instructions to form the bodies of offspring when the organism reproduces. The instructions take the form of coded sequences called genes. DNA is short for deoxyribonucleic acid.

**Drey** A squirrel's nest.

**Echolocation** A technique that allows animals such as bats and dolphins to orientate themselves in darkness or murky water, and locate their prey. The animal emits a stream of high-pitched sounds and listens out for the echoes that bounce back off solid objects.

**Egg** The female reproductive cell; or the earliest stage of development for reptiles, amphibians and many other animals.

**Embryo** Any developing young animal in an egg or womb. In mammals, this is the stage before the unborn animal becomes a foetus.

**Evolution** The process by which living things gradually adapt in order to become better suited to their environment.

**Extinction** When all the individuals in a species die out, so that none is left.

**Foetus** A baby mammal developing in the womb, which is older than an embryo.

**Fossil** The remains or imprint of a once-living organism that has been preserved in stone.

**Fungi** A group of organisms that includes mushrooms, toadstools and yeasts.

**Gene** A section of DNA that carries the coded instructions for a particular trait in a living thing.

**Genetics** The study of heredity and variation.

**Genus** The second smallest division in taxonomy.

**Gestation** The period between mating and birth, during which young mammals develop inside their mother.

**Gland** A structure on the inside or outside of the body that secretes a chemical substance.

**Habitat** The external environment in which animals and other organisms live. Deserts and rainforests are examples of habitats.

**Herbivore** An animal that eats mainly plant matter.

**Hibernation** A period of dormancy that enables animals such as dormice to survive cold weather. During true hibernation the animal's body temperature, heart rate and breathing slow right down, so that it appears to be dead.

**Incisor** One of the sharp chisel-shaped teeth found at the front of some mammals' jaws, which are used to gnaw or nibble food.

**Invertebrate** An animal without a backbone. Invertebrates make up about 95 per cent of the animal kingdom. This huge supergroup includes insects, crustaceans, molluscs, worms, jellyfish, sponges and starfish.

**Kingdom** In taxonomy, the initial and largest grouping into which living things are divided. All life on Earth is grouped within five kingdoms: animals, plants, fungi, protists and monerans, which include bacteria.

**Larva** An immature stage in an animal's lifecycle, e.g. in amphibians the larvae are tadpoles, which occur after hatching and before they become adults. The larvae differ greatly from the adult form.

**Mammal** A vertebrate animal with hair on its body, which feeds its young on milk.

**Marsupial** One of a group of mammals whose young are born early and complete their development in their mother's pouch.

**Migration** A regular seasonal journey undertaken by an animal or group of animals to avoid adverse weather, to find food or a mate, or to reach a favourable site for raising offspring.

**Monotreme** One of a small group of unusual mammals that lay eggs instead of giving birth to live young.

**Mutation** A variation in the genetic code. Mutations occur naturally and may be harmful, beneficial or have no effect.

**Natural selection** The process by which unsuited organisms are weeded out, leaving only the strongest or most suitable to breed, thereby passing on their genes. Over time, natural selection helps to bring about evolution, resulting in organisms that are best adapted to the environment.

**Nocturnal** Active at night.

**Organ** A part of an animal's body with a distinct function, such as the heart, kidney or eye.

**Organism** A living thing, such as a plant, animal or fungus.

**Pampas** A grassland in South America.

**Parasite** An animal that lives on or inside another animal, and feeds on its flesh or its food.

**Permafrost** The permanently frozen ground that lies beneath the topsoil in cold biomes.

**Photosynthesis** The process by which plants turn carbon dioxide and water into glucose, using the energy in sunlight.

**Phylum** The second largest taxonomic division after kingdom.

**Placenta** A blood-rich organ that develops within the womb of a pregnant female mammal to nourish the unborn young.

**Plankton** Microscopic plants and animals that float near the surface of oceans and lakes, and provide food for many larger animals. Microscopic plants are known collectively as phytoplankton; microscopic animals are known as zooplankton.

**Plant** A complex organism that photosynthesizes.

**Population** The total number of individuals in a species, or the number in a group that is geographically separated from other groups of the same species.

**Prairie** A grassland in North America.

**Predator** Any animal that catches other animals – its prey – for food.

**Protein** A complex chemical made up of chains of smaller units and used to construct the bodies of organisms.

**Protist** A single-celled organism.

**Reflex** A fast, involuntary muscular movement made in response to an external stimulus such as pain, involving nerve signals but not normally routed through an animal's brain.

**Reptile** One of a group of scaly-skinned vertebrate animals most of which breed by laying eggs. Reptiles include lizards, snakes, crocodiles, turtles and tuataras.

**Retina** The light-sensitive layer at the back of the eye.

**Rodent** One of a group of mammals with long front teeth called incisors. The group of rodents includes rats and mice.

**Salinity** Salt content.

**Savannah** A grassland or open woodland in Africa or Australia.

**Scavenger** An animal that feeds on decaying organic matter.

**Social** Living with others of the same kind in a cooperative group.

**Solitary** Living alone.

**Species** A particular kind of organism. Members of a species can interbreed to produce more of the same kind.

**Spinal cord** The main nerve in the body of vertebrates that runs down inside the backbone to link the brain with smaller nerves throughout the body.

**Steppe** A grassland in eastern Europe and Asia.

**Symbiosis** A relationship between two different types of living things, from which both organisms benefit.

**Taxonomy** The scientific discipline of categorizing organisms.

**Territory** An area which an animal uses for feeding or breeding, and defends against others of its species.

**Timberline** The zone on a mountain beyond which the climate is too cold for trees to grow.

**Toxin** A chemical which is poisonous.

**Tundra** The barren, treeless lowlands of the far north.

**Veldt** A grassland in southern Africa.

**Venom** A cocktail of poisons made by a variety of animals to defend themselves.

**Vertebrate** An animal with a backbone.

# INDEX

# PICTURE ACKNOWLEDGEMENTS

The copyright holder would like to thank the following illustrators for creating the artworks for this book.

**Peter Barrett:** 429b, 431b, 434b, 435t, 436t.

**Jim Channell:** 166–7, 174–9, 213–17, 228–9, 240–3, 245b, 246–7, 252t, 373t, 427b, 428, 429t, 430b, 431t, 432–3, 436b, 437.

**Julius Csotonyi:** 248–50.

**Rob Dyke:** 257–8, 260–3, 310b, 315–17, 378b, 379b, 380b, 381–2.

**John Francis:** 108t, 109b, 122b, 123, 126–7, 131b, 137t, 165t, 218, 219t, 220–1, 226t, 303t, 306, 308t, 309t, 310t, 311, 314b, 318b, 347t, 410t, 458–9, 460t, 461, 463b, 471t, 472, 476b, 486b, 496b.

**Rob Highton:** 320–1, 323, 325–7, 329, 332–3, 349–51, 413b, 415, 416t, 417t, 418, 419b, 421b, 422b, 423.

**Stuart Jackson-Carter:** 46–65 (all habitats), 72–5, 84–7, 90–1, 96–7, 106–7, 108b, 109t, 114–17, 122t, 142–3, 146–7, 150–5, 160–1, 164, 165b, 180–1, 208, 212, 230t, 231t, 232b, 233b, 234–5, 238–9, 244, 245t, 251, 252b, 253, 319, 322, 324, 330–1, 334, 335b, 338b, 340, 346, 359, 362t, 364t, 365t, 402b, 403b, 405, 406b, 407–8, 410b, 412t, 420t, 421t, 424t, 426, 427t, 430t, 434t, 462b, 463t, 471b, 475b, 476t, 477, 478t, 479–81, 482, 486t, 487–8, 496t, 497b.

**Paul Jones:** 88–9, 92–5, 110–13, 118–19, 156–7, 162–3, 168–9, 172–3, 204–5, 230b, 231b, 232t, 233t, 388b, 389t, 391, 392b, 395–6, 397b, 399.

**Martin Knowelden:** 100–5, 120–1, 124–5, 128, 129t, 130, 131t, 132–3, 138t, 144–5.

**Stephen Lings:** 98–9, 186–201, 206–7, 209–11, 282t, 283t, 284, 302, 366–7, 386t, 387t, 388t, 390t, 448–9, 456t, 457t, 473, 474, 485.

**The Magic Group:** 279b, 280t, 285t, 286b, 288, 292b, 293t, 314t, 336t, 337, 338t, 339t, 343b, 344t, 347b, 348, 354, 355t, 356, 357t, 360b, 361, 363b, 377, 386b, 387b, 389b, 390b, 392t, 393, 394b, 398b.

**Shane Marsh:** 286t, 287, 294–5, 296t, 328, 453–5, 464–7, 468b, 469b, 470, 494–5.

**Robert Morton:** 256, 259, 264–277, 282b, 283b, 285b, 289, 292t, 296b, 297–9, 305t, 368–72, 373b, 374–5, 435b, 440–1, 450–1, 452, 456b, 457b, 460b, 462t, 475t, 478b, 484, 497t.

**Richard Orr:** 148–9, 158–9, 182–5, 219b, 222–5, 236–7.

**Fiona Osbaldstone:** 293b, 318t, 352–3, 355b, 357b, 358, 362b, 363t, 364b, 365b, 379t, 380t, 384–5, 400b, 401, 402t, 403b, 404, 406t, 409, 411, 412b, 413t, 414, 416b, 417b, 419t, 420b, 422t, 424b, 425.

**Mike Saunders:** 129b, 134–5, 137b, 138b, 139–41, 278, 279t, 280b, 281, 290–1, 300–1, 303b, 304, 305b, 307, 308b, 309b, 312–13, 335t, 336b, 339b, 341–2, 343t, 344b, 345, 383b, 442–7.

**Sarah Smith:** 170–1, 202–3, 360t, 376, 378t, 383t, 394t, 397t, 398t, 400t, 468t, 469t, 483, 489–93.

**Ildikó Szegszárdy:** 226b, 227.

The publisher would also like to thank the following for granting permission to use their photographs in this book. Key: l=left, r=right, t=top, m=middle, b=bottom.

**NHPA:** 14bl, 22tr, 22b, 26t, 26b, 27t, 29t, 29br, 32br, 34t, 36t, 36b, 37tl, 38bl, 39b, 40t, 42t, 43t, 43b.

**Tim Ellerby:** 32t, 32bl, 41b, 43m, 438r.